THE CONSERVATIVE EFFECT, 2010–2024

After fourteen years of Conservative government, we rightly ask what changed for the better or worse during this prolonged period of power? The country experienced significant challenges including austerity, Brexit and Covid: did they militate against the government's making more lasting impact? Bringing together some of the leading authorities in the field, this book examines the impact of Conservative rule on a wide range of economic, social, foreign and governmental areas. Anthony Seldon, Tom Egerton and their team uncover the ultimate 'Conservative effect' on the United Kingdom. With powerful insights and fresh perspectives, this is an intriguing study for anyone seeking to understand the full scope of the Conservative government's influence on our nation. Drawing the immediate lessons from the last fourteen years will be pivotal if the country is to rejuvenate and flourish in the future.

Sir Anthony Seldon is the country's top political historian and acknowledged national authority on all matters to do with the government and Number 10. His book *Churchill's Indian Summer: The Conservative Government, 1951–55* (1981) was published forty years ago, and since then he has written or edited many books, including *The Blair Effect, 2001–5* (with Dennis Kavanagh, Cambridge, 2005), *The Coalition Effect, 2010–2015* (with Mike Finn, Cambridge, 2015) and *The Impossible Office?* (Cambridge, 2021). He has been the honorary historian at Number 10 Downing Street and chair of the National Archives Trust, and has interviewed virtually all senior figures who have worked in Number 10 in the last fifty years.

Tom Egerton has worked with Anthony Seldon on various publications, including the *Sunday Times* bestseller *Johnson at 10* and *The Impossible Office*. He is the editor and founder of *The Political Inquiry* and was educated in history and politics at the University of Warwick.

'In the wake of five Conservative prime ministers in fourteen years, if ever an independent audit was needed on a period of government, it is now!

Sir Anthony Seldon and Tom Egerton engage the expertise of more than a dozen top professionals in their fields to provide this vital and much-anticipated appraisal.

With insightful analysis on how we got here and invaluable pointers on where we might be heading, this is an essential read for anyone seeking to understand the political landscape of our time.'

Adam Boulton
Political journalist and presenter of *Times Radio*

'The turmoil of the last fourteen years needs a book like this: a stable of excellent authors, offering accessible and thoughtful judgement on the broad trends rather than the trivia.'

Philip Cowley
Co-editor of *Sex, Lies and Politics: The Secret Influences that Drive Our Political Choices*

'A peerless appraisal of a period in British political history which could have been so different and arguably so much better. Terrific: what a cast.'

Julia Hobsbawm, OBE
Award-winning business writer
and commentator for *Bloomberg*

'This is a comprehensive reference book for a blighted political era, full of facts and written by some of Britain's finest researchers. I will be consulting it whenever I need to remember what happened since 2010 – and to grasp the depth of the problems Labour is set to inherit.'

Harry Lambert
Staff writer and editor at the *New Statesman*

'This sweeping account is rooted in the most deceptively simple questions of politics: why do governments with energetic plans for national revival deliver less than they might – and how should we distinguish failures and miscalculations from "stuff happens" circumstances beyond their control?

From the long tail of the austerity years after the global financial crisis to the multiple impacts of Brexit and the pandemic and across a wealth of key policy areas, Seldon and Egerton have convened an expert cast of analysts to dissect the Conservatives' lengthy recent stint in power.

For some of the contributors, it is a study in "breaking all the wrong records". For others, a curate's egg. The result is an invaluable account of a wild ride in Britain's political history, rich in examples and warnings to successors, whatever their political hue.'

Anne McElvoy
Executive Editor, *POLITICO*

'A wonderful book – lively, sane, imaginative and considered. If only we all looked at government in such a balanced, detailed and objective way!'

Rory Stewart
Former UK Secretary of State for International Development and co-presenter of the *The Rest is Politics* podcast

THE CONSERVATIVE EFFECT, 2010–2024

14 Wasted Years?

Edited by

Anthony Seldon
Tom Egerton

CAMBRIDGE
UNIVERSITY PRESS

Shaftesbury Road, Cambridge CB2 8EA, United Kingdom

One Liberty Plaza, 20th Floor, New York, NY 10006, USA

477 Williamstown Road, Port Melbourne, VIC 3207, Australia

314–321, 3rd Floor, Plot 3, Splendor Forum, Jasola District Centre,
New Delhi – 110025, India

103 Penang Road, #05–06/07, Visioncrest Commercial, Singapore 238467

Cambridge University Press is part of Cambridge University Press & Assessment,
a department of the University of Cambridge.

We share the University's mission to contribute to society through the pursuit of
education, learning and research at the highest international levels of excellence.

www.cambridge.org
Information on this title: www.cambridge.org/9781009473088

DOI: 10.1017/9781009473101

© Cambridge University Press & Assessment 2024

When citing this work, please include a reference to the DOI 10.1017/
9781009473101

First published 2024

A catalogue record for this publication is available from the British Library

A Cataloging-in-Publication data record for this book is available from the Library of Congress

ISBN 978-1-009-47308-8 Paperback

Contents

CONTENTS

Contributors

Jon Agar is Professor and Co-Head of the Department of Science and Technology Studies at University College London. He is a historian of modern science and technology, and author of books including *The Government Machine* (2003), *Constant Touch: A Global History of the Mobile Phone* (2nd ed., 2012), *Science in the Twentieth Century and Beyond* (2012) and *Science Policy under Thatcher* (2019). He is working on a book on science policy from Major to Blair.

Tim Bale teaches politics at Queen Mary University of London, focusing mainly on political parties and voters in the UK and abroad. As well as various edited works and more specialised journal articles, he has written several approachable books on British and European politics, the latest of which is *The Conservative Party after Brexit: Turmoil and Transformation* (2023). Tim has written for almost every UK newspaper and appears now and then on various radio and television programmes to talk about politics. He posts on Twitter/X as @ProfTimBale and his media writing is collected at proftimbale.com

Clare Bambra (PhD) is Professor of Public Health, Newcastle University. She is an elected Fellow of the Academy of Social Sciences (FAcSS) and a Senior Investigator in the National Institute for Health and Care Research (NIHR) Academy. Her research focuses on understanding and reducing health inequalities. She has extensively analysed

Covid-19 and health inequalities and, together with Professor Sir Michael Marmot, she was an expert independent witness to the UK Covid-19 Public Inquiry. She has published widely including several award-winning books and her research is regularly covered by the media.

Michael Clarke is the former Director General of the Royal United Services Institute and a visiting professor in Defence Studies at King's College London. His most recent books include *The Challenge of Defending Britain* (2019), (with Helen Ramscar) *Tipping Point: Britain, Brexit and Security in the 2020s* (2019) and (also with Helen Ramscar) *Britain's Persuaders: Soft Power in a Hard World* (2021). His latest book is *Great British Commanders: Leadership, Strategy and Luck* (2024).

John Curtice is Professor of Politics at Strathclyde University in Glasgow, Scotland, and Senior Research Fellow at the National Centre for Social Research and the ESRC's 'The UK in a Changing Europe' initiative. He has written extensively about voting behaviour in elections and referendums in the UK, as well as on British political and social attitudes more generally. A former co-director of the British Election Study, he has been a co-editor of NatCen's annual British Social Attitudes reports series for thirty years, and is a regular contributor to British and international media coverage of politics in the UK.

Tom Egerton has worked with Anthony Seldon on various publications, including the *Sunday Times* bestseller *Johnson at 10* (2023) and *The Impossible Office?* (2021). He is the editor and founder of *The Political Inquiry* and was educated in history and politics at the University of Warwick.

Carl Emmerson is Deputy Director of the Institute for Fiscal Studies (IFS), an editor of the annual *IFS Green Budget* and a Director of the Pensions Review. His research includes issues around the UK's public finances, and household retirement saving decisions. He is also a member of the Social Security Advisory Committee, the advisory panel of the Office for Budget Responsibility, and the UK Statistics Authority's Methodological Assurance Review Panel. He previously served as a specialist adviser to the House of Commons Work and Pensions Select Committee.

Dieter Helm is Professor of Economic Policy at the University of Oxford and Fellow in Economics at New College, Oxford. From 2012 to 2020, he was Independent Chair of the Natural Capital Committee, providing advice to the government on the sustainable use of natural capital. In 2017, he also produced the *Cost of Energy Review,* an independent report for the government. Dieter has written many books on energy, regulation and the environment. In his latest, *Legacy: How to Build the Sustainable Economy* (Cambridge, 2023), he addresses the question: what would the sustainable economy look like and what would it take to live within our environmental means? Dieter is a Vice President of the Exmoor Society, a Vice President of Berkshire, Buckinghamshire and Oxfordshire Wildlife Trust, and Honorary Fellow, Brasenose College, Oxford.

Paul Johnson has been Director of the Institute for Fiscal Studies since 2011. He is a columnist for *The Times,* and is a regular contributor to other broadcast and print media. He is a visiting professor at the University College London Policy Lab and Department of Economics. He was for ten years a member of the UK Climate Change Committee, and has served on the council of the ESRC and of the Royal Economic Society. Paul led reviews of pension auto-enrolment and of inflation measurement for the UK government, and of fiscal devolution for the Northern Ireland executive. Previous roles have included time as chief economist at the Department for Education and as director of public spending at HM

Treasury, where he also served as deputy head of the government economic service. Paul published the *Sunday Times* bestseller *Follow the Money* in 2023. He was appointed CBE in the 2018 birthday honours.

John Kampfner is an award-winning author and commentator. He began his career reporting from East Berlin and Moscow for the *Telegraph*. After covering British politics for the *Financial Times* and BBC, he edited the *New Statesman*. He is the author of seven books, including the bestselling *Blair's Wars* (2004), *Why the Germans Do It Better* (2021) and recently *In Search of Berlin* (2023). He has been a major figure in UK culture, establishing and chairing the Creative Industries Federation. He was founder chair of the highly successful Turner Contemporary gallery in Margate and is currently chair of the soon-to-launch Quentin Blake Centre for Illustration.

Peter Kellner is a journalist and pollster. At different times since 1969 he has been a regular contributor to the *Sunday Times, New Statesman, Independent, Observer, Evening Standard* and *Prospect*. He was political editor of BBC *Newsnight* from 1990 to 1997, and an election night analyst for BBC Television between 1992 and 2017. He was YouGov's Chairman (2001–7) and the President (2007–16), winning the Chairman of the Year award from the Quoted Companies Alliance in 2006. He received a Special Recognition Award from the Political Studies Association in 2011, and a CBE for services to charity in 2023. He is currently a visiting scholar with Carnegie Europe.

Michael Marmot has been Professor of Epidemiology at University College London since 1985, and is Director of the UCL Institute of Health Equity. He is the author of *The Health Gap: The Challenge of an Unequal World* (2015) and *Status Syndrome* (2004). He has led research groups on health inequalities for nearly fifty years. He chaired the World Health Organization (WHO) Commission on

Social Determinants of Health, several WHO Regional Commissions, and reviews on tackling health inequality for governments in the UK. He served as President of the British Medical Association (BMA) in 2010–11, and as President of the World Medical Association in 2015. In 2000 he was knighted by Her Majesty The Queen, for services to epidemiology and the understanding of health inequalities. He was appointed a Companion of Honour for services to public health in the King's 2023 New Year Honours.

Brendan O'Leary is Honorary Professor of Political Science at Queen's University Belfast. An Irish, European, and US citizen he is an honorary member of the Royal Irish Academy. Among his thirty books, *A Treatise on Northern Ireland* (three volumes 2020) won the James S. Donnelly Sr. History and Social Science Prize of the American Conference on Irish Studies, while *Making Sense of a United Ireland* (2022) won the Brian Farrell Prize of the Political Studies Association of Ireland. O'Leary is the inaugural winner of the Juan Linz Prize of the International Political Science Association for lifetime contributions to the study of federalism and multinational democracies. He chairs the public opinion committee of ARINS (Analyzing Ireland North and South), a joint initiative of the University of Notre Dame and the Royal Irish Academy. He is the current chair of the Political Science department at the University of Pennsylvania and was previously chair of the Government Department at the London School of Economics & Political Science. He is a member of the Governing Authority of University College Cork.

Nick Ridpath is an economist at the Institute for Fiscal Studies and a doctoral student in Economics at the University of Oxford. His research focuses on questions around post-16 education, early years care and household decision-making.

Meg Russell is Professor of British and Comparative Politics and Director of research centre the Constitution Unit at University College London (UCL). She is the author of five books, most recently *The Parliamentary Battle over Brexit* (2023), alongside numerous reports and papers on different aspects of the UK constitution. She is a particular specialist on parliament, and has served as adviser to parliamentary committees and to the Leader of the House of Commons. She currently leads a project on 'Constitutional Principles and the Health of Democracy' at the Constitution Unit, which seeks to strengthen such values following the divisions of the Brexit years.

Sir Anthony Seldon is the country's top political historian and acknowledged national authority on all matters to do with the government and Number 10. His book *Churchill's Indian Summer: The Conservative Government, 1951–1955* (1981) was published forty years ago, and since then he has written or edited many books, including *The Blair Effect, 2001–5* (with Dennis Kavanagh, Cambridge, 2005), *The Coalition Effect, 2010–2015* (with Mike Finn, Cambridge, 2015) and *The Impossible Office?* (Cambridge, 2021). He has been the honorary historian at Number 10 Downing Street and chair of the National Archives Trust, and has interviewed virtually all senior figures who have worked in Number 10 in the last fifty years.

Professor Alan Smithers BSc, PhD, MSc, PhD, MEd, CPsychol is Director of the Centre for Education and Employment Research at the University of Buckingham. He has held chairs in education since 1977, successively, at the University of Manchester, Brunel University, the University of Liverpool and the University of Buckingham. He was seconded to BP in 1991–2. Originally a cell biologist, he switched to researching education in 1967 intrigued by the difficulty the University of London, where he was a lecturer, was having in modularising its degrees. He was Standing

Adviser to the Commons Education Select Committee from 1997 to 2015.

Rachel Sylvester is a journalist at *The Times* and chair of The Times Health Commission and Times Education Commission. She was a political reporter on the *Daily Telegraph* and political editor of the *Independent on Sunday* before joining *The Times* as a columnist and interviewer in 2008. She also presents the Times Radio podcast *What I Wish I'd Known.*

Paul Webb is Professor of Politics at the University of Sussex and a Fellow of the Academy of Social Sciences. He has authored or edited numerous articles and books on party and electoral politics, the most recent of which is *An Advanced Introduction to Party Systems* (2024). He is editor of the journal *Party Politics.*

Introduction: What Difference Do Governments Make?

Anthony Seldon

THIS IS THE MOST IMPORTANT OF THE seven books I have edited in this series, which began with *The Thatcher Effect* (with Dennis Kavanagh), published on the tenth anniversary of her coming to power in May 1989, and continuing with *The Major Effect* (with Dennis Kavanagh, 1994), *The Blair Effect 1997–2001* (2001), *The Blair Effect 2001–5* (with Dennis Kavanagh, 2005), *Blair's Britain* (2007) and *The Coalition Effect* (with Mike Finn, 2015). These volumes were preceded by *Ruling Performance: British Governments from Attlee to Thatcher* (with Peter Hennessy, 1989).

The formula has remained the same. The spotlight has always been on the difference, behind all the distortions of party politics, that the government has made. The guiding questions have remained consistent:

- What changed between the government(s) coming to power and its ending?
- What and who was responsible for those changes, and how far did they take place at the instigation of the prime minister(s)?
- How far were changes driven by other factors, including ministers, think tanks, party pressures and external factors?
- How successful have the changes been, when judged obviously at this particular point in history?

The impact of the series has rested on its drawing on acknowledged authorities on each of the subjects chosen, all addressing the common questions, and giving each volume a weight that might not be achieved by any individual author lacking the same detailed grasp of each and every area covered.

This book, edited with Tom Egerton, is unusual because it examines not one but five premierships – the first in the series to cover a multi-prime-ministerial time period, which in itself illustrates a new volatility in British politics. The work has been published in the run-up to a general election when the need for objective and scholarly analysis of the impact of governments is all the greater due to the highly politicised and tribal dialogue that has affected discourse, further inflamed by Brexit and culture wars. Politics and contemporary history are more divisive than at any point since this series started examining government impact in 1979, and indeed long before.

British history since 1951 has seen five phases, in each of which a single party was dominant: the Conservatives from 1951 to 1964, Labour from 1964 to 1979 (with an interlude of the Conservatives from 1970 to 1974), the Conservatives from 1979 to 1997, Labour from 1997 to 2010 and, finally, the Conservatives from 2010 to 2024 (in government with the Liberal Democrats for the first five years).

The book opens with a chapter by Peter Kellner examining the so-called 'thirteen wasted years' under the Conservatives from 1951 to 1964, a narrative which became poignant in the run-up to the 1964 election and influenced the immediate historiography of the period. By most measures, the fourteen years since 2010 compare unfavourably with it. But what of our period, can it really be labelled 'fourteen wasted years'? Authors were asked to compare their own areas of study, not just to earlier periods of one-party domination, but also, where they could, to look at what governments abroad were doing over the same years as well as acknowledging global trends or crises.

The chapters that follow tell their own story of policy and reversal in the various areas. In the Conclusion, we assess the extent of the achievement over the fourteen years, and ask, if less has been achieved than expected or the needs of the hour demanded, how might one explain the disappointing net effect? All history is contemporary. We cannot but judge the past through the prism of the present. This book will have value not just in 2024 and the immediate years that follow it, but in 2049 and 2074 too for those who want to learn how contemporary scholars saw these years. What we cannot know now is whether future observers will look back at these fourteen years as a time of comparative calm before the storm, or regard them with even greater alarm as a time of wasted opportunity.

1

Thirteen Wasted Years (1951–1964)?

Peter Kellner

H ERE IS A THOUGHT EXPERIMENT. Imagine it is the year 2084, and we are looking back at the 2010–24 era of Conservative rule. With the benefits of hindsight, how would we judge its record? The experiences of the people who lived through it would, of course, loom large in any verdict: living standards, productivity, public services, social harmony, government finances, crime, welfare and so on. But would we not also examine how it tackled Britain's longer-term challenges and prepared the ground for the decades ahead? Did it address the fundamental forces that affected the country for good or ill? Did it pursue short-term objectives at the expense of longer-term goals?

Any attempt to peer sixty years into the future is bound to get many, perhaps most, things wrong. But we can at least attempt to answer those questions about the thirteen years of Conservative rule, from 1951 to 1964. We are now in the same position in looking back at that era as someone in 2084 inspecting the Cameron/May/Johnson/Truss/Sunak years.

Of course, we know things about the past sixty years that nobody from that time could possibly foresee. It would have taken a genius to predict when and how the Cold War would end, the revolution in information technology, the economic trajectory of China, and the emergence of climate change as an existential threat to humanity. Like all governments, those from Winston Churchill to Alec Douglas-Home had to feel their way forward through the fog of long-term uncertainty.

On the other hand, not everything is shrouded in fog. Underlying forces that shape Britain are often visible. One way to judge a government's success is to look at how it attends to these. This provides a useful prism for assessing Conservative performance from 1951 to 1964, as Britain recovered from the austerity of the immediate post-war years. Did the governments of the day get the big calls right and lay solid foundations for their successors?

Any such exercise is bound to be tentative, and different people will draw different conclusions. Its purpose here is not to propose some definitive truth, but to suggest that the thought experiment could help us to examine the past fourteen years, by prompting similar questions about the governments led by the last five prime ministers from David Cameron to Rishi Sunak.

Let us start by recalling how the 1951–64 government was viewed as it came to a close. Here are extracts from the 1964 manifestos of the two main parties, setting out their rival verdicts:

Conservative:

Our policy of peace through strength has brought Britain safely through years of tension and danger. It contributes to the security of the free world . . . . We remain convinced that the political and economic problems of the West can best be solved by an Atlantic partnership between America and a united Europe . . . . Entry into the European Economic Community is not open to us in existing circumstances . . . . We shall work . . . for the closest possible relations with the Six consistent with our Commonwealth ties . . . .

In 13 years of Conservative government the living standards of the British people have improved more than in the whole of the previous half-century . . . . Rising incomes and lower taxes have made possible a spectacular increase in spending on the essentials, the comforts and what were once regarded as the luxuries of life . . . . We have set up the National Economic Development Council, bringing together Government, management and unions in a co-operative venture to improve our economic performance . . . . Record progress is being made in modernising industry. Today capital investment in new factories, construction, plant and equipment is twice as high as when the Socialists left office . . . .

The past thirteen years have seen improvements in the nation's health greater than in any comparable period. ... One family in every four is living in a new home built under the Conservatives. ... Since 1951 homes have been built at an average rate of 300,000 a year ... . Education is the most rapidly developing feature of our social outlay. Its share of the expanded national wealth has risen since 1951 from 3 per cent. to 5 per cent., and will go on rising.[1]

Labour:

The scientific revolution is now making it physically possible for the first time in human history to provide the whole people with high living standards .... Since 1951, however, these opportunities have been disastrously wasted largely because of the Conservative determination since they took office to end the purposive planning of the post-war Labour Government and replace it with an economic free-for-all .... Our record is now among the worst in the western world. If we had only kept up with the rest of Western Europe since 1951, our national income in 1964 would be one-third more than it is.

Only 18 months ago a Tory Government, driven by economic failure, lost its nerve and prepared to accept humiliating terms for entry into the European Common Market in the vain hope that closer contact with a dynamic Europe would give a new boost to our wilting economy.

In social security, we still have austerity, National Insurance benefits that impose poverty standards on the retired, the sick and the unemployed .... In education we are faced today with a chronic shortage of teachers, with oversize classes, with far too many scandalously out-dated school buildings. ... The National Health Service ... has been starved of resources and has failed to adapt sufficiently to modern needs ... [Tory policies] have condemned yet another generation to squalid and over-crowded housing.[2]

[1] F. W. S. Craig, *British General Election Manifestos 1900–1974* (Basingstoke: Macmillan, 1975), pp. 240–3.

[2] Ibid., pp. 256–7.

There are plainly specific differences between 1964 and 2024. The Conservatives no longer seek 'a united Europe'; Labour does not talk of 'purposive planning'. But the similarities of tone and agenda are considerable. Living standards, public services and Britain's place in Europe were at the core of the argument then, as they are now. The Conservatives listed a wide range of achievements, while Labour marshalled evidence of 'thirteen wasted years' – a term coined by Harold Wilson, Labour's leader, in the run-up to the 1964 election.

The facts offered by both parties were essentially true. Living standards did improve sharply – in 1957, Harold Macmillan was right to say 'most of our people have never had it so good' – but other economies in the western world did grow faster. Spending on health and education did grow substantially – but long hospital waiting lists persisted and schools suffered from a shortage of teachers. More than 300,000 new homes were built each year, but 'squalid and over-crowded housing' continued to blight the lives of many families. On these broad issues, the arguments concerned the same controversies as they do today.

Yet step back and what is striking is not just that Labour and Conservative then offered much the same agenda in their battle for votes as they do today, but also that, six decades later, that agenda looks incomplete. Three of the big challenges of that time were either misjudged or ignored by one or both parties. Let us take each in turn.

WINDS OF CHANGE: THE UK'S ROLE IN THE WORLD

In 1951 the UK was still a global power, although its imperial status was in the process of being unwound. Under the 1945–51 Labour government, India had become independent and the UK had withdrawn from Palestine. Between 1951 and 1964 almost all of Britain's remaining colonies gained their independence; most of them becoming members of the Commonwealth, an association of (in theory) equal countries.

As the UK's imperial status declined, its other international roles became more relevant: its position as one of the five permanent members of the United Nations Security Council (formed in

1945) and as a founder member of NATO (in 1949). The 1951 government also inherited advanced plans for Britain to become the third country to develop nuclear weapons, after the United States and Soviet Union; the first test took place in 1952.

The event that had the most decisive effect on the UK's international role in 1951–64 era was the 1956 Suez crisis. Egypt had only recently achieved full independence from Britain. In July 1956, its president, Gamel Abdel Nasser, nationalised the Suez Canal, which had been owned by the Anglo-French Suez Canal Company. Anthony Eden, the UK prime minister who had succeeded Winston Churchill the previous year, regarded Nasser's 'aggression' to be on a par with Hitler's in Europe before World War II. Eden was determined not to repeat the UK's appeasement strategy of the 1930s. The UK conspired in secret with France and Israel to invade Egypt and seize the canal.

The invasion was a disaster. Egypt managed to sink forty ships in the canal, and so prevent its use, before the invading troops could take control. America's President Eisenhower, who had warned against the invasion, forced the UK and France to withdraw. That was not all. The pound came under pressure in the currency markets. The government did not want to devalue the pound; it was determined to defend its value of $2.80 (this was a time of fixed exchange rates, when devaluation was politically damaging). This meant that the Bank of England had to spend much of its US dollar currency reserves to support the pound's value. In the end, it applied to the International Monetary Fund for a loan – a loan which the United States promptly vetoed. In time the currency markets stabilised. The humiliation, both military and financial, to the UK and its global status was immediate and obvious. The limits to the UK's 'special relationship' with the US were clear. Britain could never again send troops on a major military action overseas without, at the very least, US acquiescence.

Eden, who had been ill throughout the crisis, resigned soon afterwards. His successor, Harold Macmillan, spent much of the next seven years seeking to redefine the UK's world role. For the first three of those years he sought to maintain the UK's position not just as a nuclear power, but a completely independent one, at least in the formal sense of owning its own technology and delivery systems. At the heart of this was the Blue Streak inter-mediate-range ballistic missile. It was wholly British and, as became gradually clear, ruinously expensive. In April 1960 the project was cancelled. British hopes then rested on Skybolt, an Anglo-American missile programme. The Americans cancelled this in December 1962. From then on, Britain's nuclear weapons relied on Polaris missiles, bought from the US. Six years after the Suez crisis, Britain was even more emphatically the junior part-ner in its 'special' relationship with the US.

Did the UK have an alternative focus for its international role? In 1946, while in opposition, Churchill had proposed a 'United States of Europe'. This paved the way for the Council of Europe and the European Court of Human rights, both established in 1949 to assert the importance of democracy and liberal values in a continent ravaged by war and tyranny. Britain played a full part in both. However, Britain's politicians were more wary of economic integration. When the European Coal and Steel Community was formed in 1950, Britain's Labour government decided to stay out.

In office, though the Conservatives' 1951 manifesto said 'we should all continue to labour for a United Europe',[3] Churchill did not seek to join the Coal and Steel Community; so when this was transformed by the Treaty of Rome in 1957 into the Common Market, Britain was not a member. By the end of the fifties, Macmillan considered this a mistake. In August 1961 he announced that the UK would apply to join it. In January 1963, France's General de Gaulle vetoed the application, an early example of France deciding that its interests were best served by keeping Britain at bay. By now the UK was not just militarily junior to the US, it lacked the clout it hoped for in Europe – thwarted by France, its co-conspirator at Suez just over six years earlier.

Macmillan, though, felt he had a third option: the Commonwealth. He believed the empire had bequeathed to

[3] Ibid., p. 171.

the now-independent countries around the world links of language, culture, commerce, legal systems and sport (notably cricket and athletics) that could benefit Britain and amplify its influence. In early 1958 he undertook a six-week tour of the Commonwealth. A second, five-week tour, this time of African Commonwealth countries, followed in 1960. These absences from Britain were of a length unimaginable in any prime minister these days. They testified to the importance that Macmillan placed on the Commonwealth.

The issue – unresolved today, as it was then – is whether Macmillan (or other prime ministers in the decades following the end of empire) got the balance right in his attempts to negotiate Britain's relationships with the US, Europe and the Commonwealth. He could, however, reasonably claim to make the right judgement calls in two respects: Britain's need to play a fuller role in Europe, and the need to respect racial equality and national pride in Britain's former colonies. He stressed this in his second Commonwealth tour. This is remembered for his speech in Cape Town at the end of the tour in which he said, to the consternation of his South African hosts, that 'the wind of change' was blowing through Africa. This was rightly taken to be a rebuke to South Africa's apartheid system of racial oppression.

In fact, this tells only part of the story. Macmillan had first used the phrase a month earlier in Ghana. In his main speech in Accra, he said: 'It is our duty to see that the great changes taking place in Africa are carried through in such a way as to ensure a peaceful and prosperous future for all its inhabitants ... these constitutional advances are not confined to the countries with which we in Britain have a particular association. The wind of change is blowing right through Africa.'[4] In Cape Town, Macmillan was more explicit: 'As a fellow member of the Commonwealth it is our earnest desire to give South Africa our support and encouragement, but I hope you won't mind my saying frankly that there are some aspects of your policies which make it impossible for us to do

---

[4] National Archives, 'The Prime Minister's African Tour' (1960), p. 25.

this without being false to our own deep convictions about the political destinies of free men to which in our own territories we are trying to give effect.'[5] He was indeed warning his apartheid hosts that they were on the wrong side of history. It was, moreover, a message that distanced him from the self-styled 'empire loyalists' on the right of the Conservative Party.

Missing from Macmillan's tour and his speeches was any commitment to impose his 'deep convictions' on Southern Rhodesia (now Zimbabwe), where a white minority (200,000 people out of a total population of 4 million) was clinging to power. In 1963, his successor, Douglas-Home, said the self-governing colony would not be granted independence without action to end racial discrimination and move towards majority rule. However, Britain took no action, beyond denial of independence, to make change happen. A year after the Conservatives left office, Rhodesia's government declared independence unilaterally to preserve white rule. This sparked a decade and a half of intermittent civil war, with more than 20,000 deaths. The regime finally gave way to majority rule in 1979. In retrospect, could Macmillan and Douglas-Home have done more to bring white minority rule to an earlier, less violent, end?

The principles of 'the wind of change' were also ignored far closer to home. Six counties of Ulster remained part of the United Kingdom when the rest of Ireland seceded in 1922. Northern Ireland's own elected parliament had considerable powers, which were used to entrench the dominant role of the province's Protestant majority. Not only did Catholic and Protestant communities lead separate lives – they lived mainly in different housing estates and sent their children to different schools – but Catholics were largely frozen out of senior positions in Northern Ireland's public services. Protestant families were favoured when new council housing was allocated; the Royal Ulster Constabulary was an almost entirely Protestant police force that was, as we would say nowadays, institutionally biased against the Catholic minority.

Yet nothing significant was done to change this state of affairs. In a way, this was understandable. For all the discrimination it

<hr>

[5] Ibid., p. 157.

suffered, the Catholic community seemed quiescent. Living standards in the province rose substantially as industries such as shipbuilding and linen prospered – while the still overwhelmingly rural Irish Republic struggled economically. Despite the discrimination they suffered, few of the province's Catholics hankered after reunification.

From the late fifties, the mood of quiet acceptance started to change. The post-war expansion of education, especially higher education, produced a growing group of Catholics with university degrees and skills that qualified them for professional, administrative and well-paid skilled jobs. Demands for civic, social and economic equality started to grow – and were ignored not just by Stormont, the province's parliament, but by London. Eamonn McCann, a civil rights activist who later became a prominent advocate of reunification, has said: 'In the late 1950s and early 1960s there was a widespread realisation and acceptance, in the nationalist community, that there was not to be a united Ireland in the short term, and therefore the thrust for social equality in Northern Ireland became the main focus for Catholic nationalists in the North.'[6]

Looking back at the horrors of 'The Troubles' from the late 1960s to late 1990s, we can see that much of what happened flowed from the earlier failure to recognise the long-term dangers of sustained and systematic discrimination. This was a clear example of the way the urgent so often trumps the important. Until the late sixties, the gathering storm in Northern Ireland was never urgent. This is, perhaps, obvious only with the benefit of hindsight and our knowledge of what happened well after the Conservatives lost power in 1964. Whether or not it is fair, six decades later, to say that ministers between 1951 and 1964 should have been more aware of the problems and done more to confront them, the fact remains that matters were allowed to drift, and with terrible long-term consequences.

---

[6] Lorenzo Bosi, 'Explaining the emergence of the civil rights protest in Northern Ireland', *Journal of Historical Sociology*, 21:2–3 (2008), 242–71, p. 251.

'NEVER HAD IT SO GOOD': HOW BRITAIN'S ECONOMY FARED

Offered the chance, today's politicians would surely be tempted to privatise their grandmother in order to repeat the economic record of 1951–64. An average growth rate of more than 3 per cent; low inflation after the first year; unemployment averaging just half a million; more than 4 million new homes built. In 1951, few families had a car, television, telephone, fridge or washing machine. By 1964 all were commonplace. Following the grim years of post-war austerity came the choices and freedoms of a consumer society. Drab clothes gave way to Mary Quant, stale songs to the Beatles, weeks in rainy Blackpool to fortnights in sunny Spain. The government banished rationing, conscription and smog[7] – and introduced motorways, parking meters and premium bonds. All in all, the lives of millions of citizens changed between the early fifties and the mid sixties in myriad ways, some small, some huge.

One should add that economic fluctuations, which provoked sharp headlines and occasional political turbulence, were tame by more recent standards. The most dramatic came in 1958 when the Treasury team resigned *en masse* over Macmillan's demand to increase public spending. In the same year, a flu epidemic caused many factories to close briefly. The economy contracted by 2.4 per cent, but quickly bounced back. Compared with Covid in 2020–1, the impact was tiny, although described as a crisis at the time. Likewise with an increase in the bank rate from 5 to 7 per cent in September 1957: another 'crisis' at the time that led to allegations of 'stop–go' policies that threatened to plunge the economy into recession. In fact, with the benefit of hindsight, these episodes can be seen as little more than minor ripples on

---

[7] Smog was the lethal combination of smoke and fog that caused or exacerbated lung disease. The 1956 Clean Air Act led to smokeless fuels replacing coal as the means for heating homes. A particularly thick smog in London in December 1952 was estimated to kill around 12,000 people, and led to calls for legislation. The Clean Air Act was the result and (unlike previous laws going back 100 years) achieved its goal.

the surface of a remarkable steady record. The economy grew year-on-year throughout the 1951–64 government. In 1951 Churchill's government inherited an inflation rate of 11.9 per cent. Once they got it down to 3.1 per cent in January 1953, it never exceeded 6 per cent. Later governments that grappled with recession and/or double-digit inflation would have been delighted to match that record of financial stability.

This was, moreover, a time of consensus, at least as far as economic management was concerned. Churchill's chancellor was Rab Butler; Labour's shadow chancellor was Hugh Gaitskell. So similar were their policies (despite outward signs of partisan conflict) that *The Economist* introduced a new word to the English language: Butskellism. It was defined by the *Oxford English Dictionary* as the economic policy of Butler that was 'largely indistinguishable' from that of his rival.

However, this happy picture of harmony and rising prosperity is not the whole story. Growth was strong in most industrial countries as the world economy recovered from World War II. Compared with its European rivals, Britain's performance was nothing to boast about. Per capita income in other countries first caught up with Britain's, then overtook it.

All this was known at the time. Indeed, two popular movies satirised the post-war world, one with more justice than the other. Both were released in 1959 and both starred Peter Sellers, one of the era's most popular stars. In *I'm All Right Jack*, he played a Communist trade union official, Fred Kite, who called his members out on strike in defence of restrictive practices that enabled them to be paid for doing little or no work. The film's depiction of company bosses as corrupt and complacent was equally fierce. Like all satires it exaggerated reality; but like good satires its depiction of British industry was too close for comfort.

The other film, *The Mouse That Roared*, was rooted in the widespread view that Britain suffered from having been on the winning side in the war. A fictional country, Grand Fenwick, declared war on the United States. Peter Sellers played three roles: Grand Fenwick's military, political and royal leaders. Their aim was not to win the war but to lose it, in order to benefit from the kind of largesse that America had bestowed on the wrecked economies of continental Europe. In fact, the United Kingdom was the biggest recipient of Marshall Aid – the remarkable American plan to put Europe's economies back on their feet; *The Mouse That Roared* fed the comfortable illusion that Britain's relative decline was not really its fault.

A more accurate and brutal depiction of the challenges facing Britain's post-war economy was given by John Maynard Keynes early in 1945. In a memorandum to the War Cabinet he deployed his familiar technique of enlivening detailed analysis with flashes of vivid prose. He wrote:

> If by some sad geographical slip, the American Air Force (it is too late now to hope for much from the enemy) were to destroy every factory on the North-East coast and in Lancashire (at an hour when the directors were sitting there and no-one else), we should have nothing to fear. How else we are to regain the exuberant inexperience which is necessary, it seems, for success, I cannot surmise.[8]

Keynes's fears were borne out by what happened in the years that followed. Britain underwent a social but not industrial revolution. Clement Attlee's Labour government created a welfare state with the new National Health Service at its heart. These reforms were popular, if expensive: the Conservatives, having opposed them at the time, knew when they returned to office in 1951 that they could not be undone. Unfortunately, Attlee's government did less to modernise Britain's economy than expand social welfare. Its main industrial policies were to nationalise the coal, gas, electricity, transport and iron and steel industries, as well as the Bank of England. However, it gave little thought to how it would transform these sectors or invest in their future. Public ownership was the objective, rather than a means to achieve a more productive future.

---

[8] Vernon Bogdanor, 'Britain in the 20th century: the attempt to construct a socialist commonwealth, 1945–1951', lecture published by Gresham College (2011), p. 5.

The 1951–64 government had the opportunity to succeed where Labour had failed. As we have seen, its overall management of the UK's finances did secure reasonably steady growth, low inflation and full employment. After 1951, however, the new Conservative government did no better than its predecessor to modernise British industry. It made the same mistake from the opposite ideological direction. Churchill had set the tone in a radio broadcast in 1948 with his call to 'set the people free'. His 1951 manifesto railed against socialism and promised 'the freest competition'. It proclaimed the benefits of 'hard work, good management [and] thrift', while warning against 'restrictive practices on both sides of industry'[9] and companies that made excess profits from Britain's post-war rearmament programme. What it did not do was set out specific plans to overhaul Britain's industry, infrastructure and education. Freedom was to be both the goal and the method.

The use of Marshall Aid funds provides a telling contrast between the UK and the European mainland. Germany, France and Italy used much of their Marshall Aid money to rebuild their factories and electrify their railway systems, Britain preferred to employ its funds to protect its gold and currency reserves and its main financial legacy of empire: the Sterling Area. As a result, successive governments failed to tackle the malaise identified by Keynes and confirmed in 2005 by the historian Tony Judt in *Postwar*, his magisterial account of Europe since 1945:

> British factory managers preferred to operate in a cycle of under-investment, limited research and development, low wages and a shrinking pool of clients, rather than risk a fresh start with new products in new markets.[10]

An instructive example is the car industry. Post-war German governments (like, it must be said, the Nazis in the 1930s) backed its 'national champions' – Volkswagen, BMW and Mercedes-Benz, which competed in home and, increasingly, overseas

---

[9] Craig, *British General Election Manifestos*, p. 171.

[10] Tony Judt, *Postwar* (London: Heinemann, 2005), p. 358.

markets by selling reliable, well-engineered cars. Britain chose a different path: high output rather than high quality. At first it did well, with exports earning valuable foreign currency: demand outstripped supply across Europe and the empire for some years. But as Germany, and other European countries, rebuilt their industrial base with state support, invested in the latest machines, managed more effectively and trained their workforce to become more skilled, they overtook the British car industry in world markets. And, as Judt points out, while governments across the Channel ensured the consolidation of car manufacture into fewer, larger and more efficient factories, Britain's laissez faire approach left 'British automobile firms hopelessly atomized: in 1968 British Leyland consisted of sixty different plants'.[11]

Britain's industrial failings then, and in other decades before and since, are all the more striking, given the country's advantages: world-class universities and outstanding original research, reflected in Britain's tally of Nobel prizes. To take just one example, Britons were responsible for two of the ground-breaking advances that led to the now familiar worlds of computers and information technology. The 'Universal Turing Machines' – the world's first programmable computers – were named after Alan Turing, best remembered for his role in cracking Germany's Enigma code during the war. The other breakthrough came from Geoffrey Dummer, a pioneering engineer with the Telecommunications Research Establishment in Malvern. At a symposium in May 1952, he unveiled the concept of the integrated circuit: 'it now seems possible to envisage electronic equipment in a solid block with no connecting wires'.[12] The result was the microchip, the heart of all modern technology. (We might note that Dummer's words were delivered at a symposium not in Britain but in Washington, DC, on 'Progress in Quality Electronic Components'; and the first working example

---

[11] Ibid., p. 356.

[12] Linda Hall Library blog, *Scientist of the Day*, 25 February 2020, citing paper presented at the US Electronic Components Symposium in Washington, DC, 7 May 1952.

of an integrated circuit was produced by an American company, Texas Instruments.)

Plainly, the government of the day was not the only, or even main, culprit in Britain's failure to convert Turing's and Dummer's theoretical breakthroughs into industrial riches for the domestic economy. Missed opportunities are inevitable failings of all governments. But the story of how Britain lost its initial lead in the development of computers and modern technology is just one example of how other countries reaped the benefits of British fundamental research of astonishing quality. This was itself one chapter in a larger story of relative decline, that the governments of 1951–64 (along with others) did too little to avert.

The economic record of that time is not unremittingly bleak. As we have seen, 'never had it so good' was not an empty boast. Indeed, in one respect, British free-market policies proved superior to continental statism and provided consumers with long-term benefits. One of the final decisions of the 1951–64 government was to outlaw price fixing by manufacturers. Until 1964 they could force retailers to sell their products only if they agreed to charge a minimum price for each item. This effectively prevented retailers competing with each other on price. The Retail Prices Act allowed retailers to charge what they wanted: manufacturers could no longer withhold supplies to any shop that wanted to cut its prices. As a result, competition caused retail companies to become more innovative, invest in new retail technology and keep prices low. Six decades later, the benefits continue; Britain has one of the world's most advanced and competitive retail sectors.

A more fundamental defence of the Conservatives' record is that Britain suffered at the time from something no government could avoid: what one leading economist called the country's 'premature maturity'.[13] The phrase, coined by Nicholas Kaldor, referred to the fact that Britain was the first country to undergo

---

[13] Anthony Philip Thirlwall, 'Nicholas Kaldor's life and insights into the applied economics of growth', *Acta Oeconomica*, 67 (S) (2017), 11–30, p. 18.

an industrial revolution. This entailed a significant shift in employment from the land to the factory through the nineteenth century. As making things with machines was generally more productive than growing food, in the value of output per worker, this shift accelerated Britain's economic growth in the Victorian age. By 1951, agriculture, fisheries and forestry employed just 1.2 million workers. The number continued to fall, but only slowly. The transfer of workers into the higher-productivity manufacturing sector could no longer contribute significantly to Britain's economic expansion.

In contrast, most European economies entered the post-war world with, proportionately, far larger farming sectors. Their greater transfer of workers in the 1950s and 1960s from agriculture to manufacturing helped them to sustain higher overall economic growth rates. The extent to which Britain's 'premature maturity' held the UK back has been the subject of debate among economists. However, two observations are hard to dispute: first, that the structure of the labour force in 1951 did reduce Britain's ability to grow; second, that this made it even more imperative for government policies that would improve the skills of British workers and encourage the manufacturing sector to innovate, invest and modernise as fast as possible. Britain's 'premature maturity' was indeed a problem, but it was one that the Conservative government of the time (like, it must be said, the Labour governments that preceded and followed it) did too little to solve.

One innovation designed to remedy matters was the creation of NEDC – the National Economic Development Council – in 1962. Straying from Churchill's 'let the people free' agenda, this brought together government, business leaders and trade unions to discuss tripartite policies for different sectors of industry. It was intended to emulate France's Economic and Social Council, which had been set up a few years earlier to advise the government in Paris on industrial laws and policies. While NEDC generated reports and recommendations, it lacked the power and authority to make a significant difference. (The French council turned out to have the same weakness.) NEDC was downgraded by Margaret Thatcher in the 1980s and finally abolished by John Major in 1992.

SOCIAL CHANGE

The first Cabinet of the 1951–64 government contained seven Old Etonians and no women. Thirteen years later, its final Cabinet contained eight Old Etonians and no women. It is not quite true to say that there were no female Cabinet ministers in those years. In 1951 Florence Horsbrugh was appointed Minister for Education outside the Cabinet. Her position was promoted to the Cabinet status in September 1953; she resigned thirteen months later. The Cabinets of Churchill, Eden, Macmillan and Douglas-Home contained no other women.

Across a range of social issues, progress ranged from modest to non-existent. This was a national, not just governmental, problem. Women were as rare in the top echelons of businesses and town halls as in politics. Horsbrugh was one of only 17 MPs (out of 625) elected in 1951. By 1959, the Conservatives' final election victory before losing office, the number had crept up to 25 (out of 630). The first female Permanent Secretary, Dame Evelyn Sharp, was appointed in 1955. Chief constables, ambassadors and High Court judges were all men throughout this era.

Almost twice as many men as women worked during these thirteen years. In fact the number of working women fell slightly as demobbed servicemen returned to civilian life following the sharp rise in female employment during World War II. Overall, men continued to earn twice as much as women throughout the 1950s and 1960s – a mixture of men dominating higher-paid jobs and the absence of laws requiring equal pay for equal work.

One notable reform was the introduction of women peers. Until 1958, the House of Lords comprised hereditary peers together with a handful of bishops and judges – in other words, all men. The Life Peerages Act in 1958 created a new category of peers, appointed by the monarch on the advice of the government, and allowed women to join the upper house. The reform had its critics. During passage of the Bill, one Conservative peer, Earl Ferrers, opposed it strenuously:

> Frankly, I find women in politics highly distasteful. In general, they are organising, they are pushing and they are commanding. Some of them do not even know where their

loyalty to their country lies. . . . I believe that there are certain duties and certain responsibilities which nature and custom have decreed men are more fitted to take on; and some responsibilities which nature and custom have decreed women should take on. It is generally accepted that the man should bear the major responsibility for life. It is generally accepted, for better or worse, that a man's judgment is generally more logical and less tempestuous than that of a woman. Why then should we encourage women to eat their way, like acid into metal, into positions of trust and responsibility which previously men have held?[14]

The point here is not that Ferrers prevailed – he didn't – but that the climate of the times made it possible for such a speech to be delivered and heard as if it were a reasonable contribution to public debate.

Social class was another broad issue that divided opinion. Around 70 per cent of all adults were working class throughout this era: that is, people whose head of household had a 'blue-collar', manual job, rather than the 30 per cent who had a 'white-collar', non-manual job or profession. (The equivalent figures today are: 'blue-collar' 43 per cent, 'white-collar' 57 per cent.) The great majority of 'white-collar' voters backed the Conservatives, while most 'blue-collar' voters backed Labour. However, the Conservatives consistently attracted around one-third of working-class votes; added to their middle-class support, this enabled them to win three general elections in a row.

Britain had entered the post-war era with an educational plan intended not so much to build a classless society as to make sure every child attended a school designed to develop their talents. Under the 1944 Education Act, pupils from the age of 11 would attend a grammar school if they were academically minded, a technical school if they had the talent to become skilled manual workers, or a secondary modern school if they belonged to neither of those groups.

---

[14] Earl Ferrers, House of Lords Hansard, 3 December 1957, col. 707.

In the event, technical schools never really took off. Only a handful were established and not all of these survived. This meant that, in practice, secondary education reflected the wider class divide. Although grammar schools were presented as a route for working-class children to better and higher-paid jobs than their parents, the amount of social mobility that took place was limited. In as far as there was some mobility, this was a result of economic more than educational changes – in particular the growth of non-manual jobs for women, from the 1960s on.[15] Moreover, one of the objectives of the 1944 Act, that pupils should be able to transfer easily from one type of school to another, was never achieved. Transfers were rare.

All this caused resentment to grow towards of the eleven-plus exam, which was deemed to divide children into grammar school sheep and secondary modern goats. From the mid 1950s Labour promised to abolish the exam and expand the system of comprehensive schools, a few of which had been established on an experimental basis in the early post-war years. Right to the end, the Conservatives resisted this policy. During the 1964 election campaign, Quintin Hogg, the education secretary, described plans to abolish grammar schools as 'an educational crime'.[16]

From the late 1950s, the watchword of much debate about education and class was meritocracy – and has remained so ever since. The word was invented by Michael Young, a free-thinking sociologist and social entrepreneur, whose fertile mind subsequent generations should thank for the creation of the Open University and the Consumers' Association (publishers of *Which?*). His book, *The Rise of the Meritocracy* was published in 1958. He created the word from a combination of Latin (*mereo*, or merit) and ancient Greek (*kratos*, or strength). However, few people then and since have appreciated that his goal was not equality of opportunity. His book was in fact a satire that warned

[15] Lindsay Richards, 'Can we ever return to the Golden Age of social mobility?', British Academy blog, 15 March 2016.

[16] David Butler and Anthony King, *The British General Election of 1964* (Basingstoke: Macmillan, 1965), p. 141.

against the dangers of removing bright working-class children from their roots. He predicted that this would lead to a more divided, heartless society in which too many people would be left behind and condemned as deserving their fate. In 1994 he wrote a new introduction to his book, in which he advocated a more fundamental idea of equality:

> Even if it could be demonstrated that ordinary people had less native ability than those selected for high position, that would not mean that they deserved to get less. Being a member of the 'lucky sperm club' confers no moral right to advantage.[17]

For almost seven decades, Britain has achieved neither a meritocratic society nor Young's preferred alternative. We have yet to test Young's warning that a truly meritocratic society might actually be rather grim.

In one feature of public life, however, the 1950s and early 1960s saw a significant change – in part as a result of Conservative support for private enterprise. In 1955, independent television, funded by advertising, took on the licence fee-funded BBC which had previously enjoyed a monopoly. In its quest to reach the maximum audience at a time when 70 per cent of adults were working class, ITV actively created programmes which spoke to the culture and lives of its viewers – whose spending power in the new consumer age made them valuable targets for advertisers. So whereas the BBC had offered a daily radio 'soap', *Mrs Dale's Diary*, which revolved round a family doctor's wife in a prosperous London suburb, ITV created *Coronation Street*, a gritty drama set amid the back-to-back homes of Weatherfield, a fictional suburb of Manchester. ITV also provided a showcase of young working-class performers in talent shows. The most significant was *Opportunity Knocks*, which, among other innovations, was judged by viewers voting by post rather than experts in the studio. Alumni of the show include Su Pollard, Paul Daniels, Little and Large and Pam Ayres.

---

[17] Michael Young, *The Rise of the Meritocracy* (Piscataway, NJ: Transaction Publishers, 1994), p. xvi.

ITV's arrival spurred the BBC to expand its own cultural range, especially in pop music, which had previously been dominated by middle-class performers. Programmes such as *Juke Box Jury* and *Six Five Special* helped to establish a new generation of performers such as Tommy Steele and the Beatles, while ITV's *Oh Boy!* introduced viewers to talented teenagers, including the Shadows, who had originally appeared on the show as the Drifters. All in all, the arrival of ITV demonstrated the power of the Law of Unintended Consequences (assuming, that is, the loosening of the middle-class grip on popular culture was unintended: there is no sign that this transformation was planned or predicted in advance, however inevitable it might look in retrospect).

Alongside the changes in television came a broadening of theatre's agenda, with the so-called 'kitchen sink' dramas in which young playwrights explored the grimmer realities of post-war life, especially for those who were struggling. They included *Look Back in Anger* by John Osborne (about the tensions between a young working-class man and his upper-middle-class wife), *A Taste of Honey* by Shelagh Delaney (about a northern working-class teenager who becomes pregnant) and *Chips with Everything* by Arnold Wesker (about conscripts from different class backgrounds coming together in the Air Force).

Such plays questioned the culture of the post-war world – as did the eruption of satire in the early 1960s, though from a different social direction. The creators of the magazine *Private Eye*, the theatre revue *Beyond the Fringe* and the TV show *That Was the Week That Was* were mainly Oxbridge graduates from comfortable families. They mocked the people in power – people largely of their own social class. Their work contributed to a growing sense that that the Conservatives had grown out of touch with the lives and attitudes of the electorate. On one occasion the middle-class satirists collided with the middle-class arbiters of decency and good taste. At the time, theatre censorship was still in practice. All scripts had to be submitted in advance to the Lord Chamberlain. This led to a bizarre exchange regarding one of *Beyond the Fringe*'s stage directions. The original version said: 'Enter two outrageous old queens.' With homosexuality still outlawed, the Lord Chamberlain insisted this be changed to: 'Enter two aesthetic young men.' It made no difference to what the audience saw. The absurdity of this contributed to calls for theatre censorship to be abolished, which it was in 1968.[18]

The century-old law prohibiting obscene books was amended almost a decade earlier. The 1959 Obscene Publications Act was intended to produce only limited reform, by allowing the defence of publication in the public good. This was tested the following year, when Penguin published an unexpurgated version of *Lady Chatterley's Lover*. D. H. Lawrence had written the book more than thirty years earlier, but it had never been published in full in Britain. Penguin Books was prosecuted under the new Act. The trial turned on the prosecution's argument that the book would corrupt and deprave the reader, versus the defence's contention that the book's graphic depiction of a sexual affair had literary merit and was in the public good. The jury's unanimous acquittal of Penguin had the effect of raising the bar for prosecuting publishers for obscenity far higher than ministers had intended. As a result, the Act has been variously blamed and credited for helping to open up an era of permissiveness that became a hallmark of 1960s Britain.

In other areas, social reform was more limited. Debates about capital punishment had started in the late 1940s. In 1949, Clement Attlee set up a Royal Commission to recommend 'whether the liability to suffer capital punishment should be limited or modified'.[19] It reported four years later to a Conservative government and essentially recommended the status quo. However, as campaigns against the death penalty grew – mainly, but not only, among Labour MPs – parliament passed the Homicide Act, which restricted the death penalty to the most serious 'capital' murders, such as killing a police officer, using a gun or in the course of theft. Hangings continued, albeit less often, until 13 August 1964, nine weeks before Labour returned to power. In 1965, on a free vote, the new House of

---

[18] Steve Nicholson, *The Censorship of British Drama 1900–1968*, vol. 4: *The Sixties* (Exeter: Exeter University Press, 2015).

[19] Clement Attlee, House of Commons Hansard, 20 January 1949, col. 329.

Commons voted by more than two-to-one to abolish the death penalty. The House of Lords offered the sight of two reforms coming together. The abolition bill was sponsored by Baroness Wootton of Abinger – the first woman to enter the Lords under the Life Peerages Act.

Reforms of the laws on homosexuality and abortion followed a similar trajectory: campaigns in the 1950s were resisted by ministers of the time, but successful on free votes during the Labour governments of 1964–70. In 1954 the government set up a commission chaired by Sir John Wolfenden to consider changes to the law on prostitution and homosexuality. Its recommendation that gay sex should be legalised was both clear and trenchant:

> We have had no reasons shown to us which would lead us to believe that homosexual behaviour between males inflicts any greater damage on family life than adultery, fornication or lesbian behaviour . . . . Unless a deliberate attempt is made by society, acting through the agency of the law, to equate the sphere of crime with that of sin, there must remain a realm of private morality and immorality which is, in brief and crude terms, not the law's business . . . . We accordingly recommend that homosexual behaviour between consenting adults in private should no longer be a criminal offence.[20]

The establishment was divided. *The Times*, *Spectator* and Archbishop of Canterbury backed Wolfenden, but the government didn't. One Conservative MP who backed the status quo cited history ancient and modern: 'One only has to look back to find that it was the condoning of this sort of offence which led to the downfall of the Roman Empire. I feel that it was the condoning of these offences which led to the fall of Nazi Germany.'[21] A free vote legalised gay sex in 1967 for men over 21.

One might add that, unlike some social problems, this was not really a case of an elite protecting its own. The diaries of Henry 'Chips' Channon, diarist extraordinaire and Conservative

---

[20] Lord Wolfenden, *Report of the Committee on Homosexual Offence and Prostitution* (London: HMSO, 1957), paras. 55, 61, 62.

[21] James Dance, House of Commons Hansard, 26 November 1958, col. 437.

MP from 1935 to 1958, described a rampant, illegal gay culture within his well-connected Tory circles. To take just one example, here is his diary entry following the death of his friend Philip Sassoon in 1939:

> He was a homosexual but there was never an open scandal, although much amused speculation on the subject. His favourites were usually young pilots in the Force. He was Under-Secretary of State for eleven years, and was an adequate if uninspired administrator.[22]

Nor was it the case that only the lower orders were ever prosecuted. One prominent peer, Lord Montagu, was jailed in 1954. Admittedly many other well-known politicians escaped prosecution. One was Robert Boothby, a bisexual Conservative MP who had a long affair with Harold Macmillan's wife, Dorothy, as well as being provided with young men by East End gangsters. Then as now, the publicly declared values of sections of society sat uneasily with the private practices of some of their members.

The same is probably true of abortion, although its incidence in high society was, not surprisingly, less well documented than that of homosexuality. In the 1930s a government committee recommended that the law should be clarified to allow doctors to perform an abortion to save a woman's life; but reform was put into abeyance during World War II. In the 1950s, campaigns for change were mounted alongside calls for women's rights more generally. Right to the end, the government consistently blocked proposals to amend the law – and not only from its political opponents. In June 1964 Commander John Kerans, a Conservative MP, asked Henry Brooke, the Home Secretary, to revisit the issue, as the ban led to illegal abortions 'in many cases in appalling circumstances, and this causes hardship to many young girls and a lot of misery in their homes'.[23] Brooke turned him down flat. The law was finally changed three years later. David Steel, a Liberal MP, introduced

---

[22] Henry Channon, *Henry 'Chips' Channon: The Diaries* (London: Penguin, 2021), p. 134.

[23] John Kerans, House of Commons Hansard, 4 June 1964, col. 1219.

a private members bill with the support of Labour's reform-minded home secretary, Roy Jenkins.

There is, then, a pattern to the record of the 1951–64 governments on social change. Their consistent stance was, in the full sense of the word, conservative. It was reluctant to disturb the status quo on gender, education, the death penalty, homosexuality and abortion. Progress was not entirely absent, but when it happened it was painfully slow. Yet ministers were not alone in resisting change. For example, the Tories cannot be held responsible for men continuing to dominate the higher reaches of trade unions or business. And while there were more Labour than Conservative women MPs throughout the period, the difference was marginal.

Public attitudes to social reform were mixed. As early as 1954, Gallup found a majority of more than two-to-one in favour of equal pay for women.[24] (The available data is not broken down by sex; but, at the very least, a substantial minority of men must have supported the principle of equal pay.) In 1960, the public backed publication of *Lady Chatterley's Lover* by a margin of more than two-to-one.[25]

On the other hand, in 1957, Gallup found that voters disagreed with the Wolfenden proposal to legalise gay sex by 47–38 per cent.[26] And large majorities – almost four-to-one in 1964 – rejected the abolition of capital punishment throughout the thirteen years.[27] What little evidence we have from that era on abortion suggests that for many people circumstances mattered more than principle, with trauma (such as rape) more acceptable than social choice as a reason for a legal termination. Few voters took the same, absolutist stance as the government against abortion.

Any attempt to assess any government's record on social change confronts two questions whose answers depend on the view of the observer. First, how far, if at all, can one apply the values of a later age to an earlier era? Second, should a government's basic

---

[24] George Gallup, *The Gallup International Public Opinion Polls, Great Britain 1937–75* (London: Random House, 1975), p. 321.

[25] Ibid., p. 571.   [26] Ibid., p. 427.   [27] Ibid., p. 774.

stance on such matters be one of (a) protecting traditional values, (b) abiding by the broad sentiments of public opinion, or (c) challenging public attitudes by promoting reforms that it believes would promote liberty and justice? Between 1951 and 1964 the government generally chose (a) while most Labour MPs chose (c). (Labour's official stance was generally to leave such decisions in parliament to free votes rather than whipped party policy.) Which was more appropriate to the time? Many people had strong opinions then, as they do now. Objectivity here is even more elusive than in other policy areas.

Much the same applies to the perennially vexed issue of immigration, on which the record of 1951–64 is more complex. Recent controversies around the fate of the 'Windrush' generation may have left the impression that the 1950s was a decade of significant net immigration. In fact, more people left the UK than arrived. The issue was one more of race and culture than numbers. White families emigrating to Australia, Canada, New Zealand and the United States outnumbered non-white people arriving in Britain, especially from the Caribbean. Workers coming to Britain helped to ease big labour shortages, notably in transport and the National Health Service. In the NHS the problem was exacerbated by the emigration of a high proportion of British-trained doctors. In 1963, the health minister launched a campaign to recruit qualified doctors from abroad. He was Enoch Powell, who just a few years later was to complain vociferously about the numbers of non-white immigrants settling in Britain.

For most of the thirteen years of Conservative rule, entry to Britain was easy for those coming from Commonwealth countries. Their right to come was enshrined in the 1948 Nationality Act. In 1962, as controversies over immigration intensified, the Commonwealth Immigrants Act limited that right, which was restricted further by future Labour as well as Conservative governments.

Could the governments of 1951–64 have done better? Unless a way could be found to reduce emigration *from* Britain, cutting immigration *to* Britain would have been economically damaging, perhaps even disastrous – not least because, as we have seen, the UK did not have a surplus of agricultural workers to draw on to fill vacancies elsewhere in the economy. The luxury of hindsight suggests that a better approach would have been to design and implement effective plans for housing and for social integration. Housing was far from solely a race problem. Despite the impressive figures for house-building, white as well as non-white families continued to suffer from racketeering landlords and festering slums. But the price of feeding a hungry labour market with workers, many of them on low wages, was to make a bad problem worse. Oswald Mosley tried to resurrect his pre-war British Union of Fascists with a new, anti-immigrant 'Union Movement' in the 1950s. As in the 1930s, he failed miserably when he stood for election; nevertheless, he articulated the resentment of many white voters, especially in areas with a high concentration of non-white immigrants.

Perhaps the clearest lesson from the story of immigration between 1951 and 1964 is one that applies to many challenges, then and since. Immediate policies, however necessary, can lead to later headaches if ministers consider only today's needs, and not the future consequences of meeting them. A broader question (and it is a question, not a statement) is whether governments are more likely to do better if their senior ministerial ranks broadly reflect the diversity of the wider population. From 1951 to 1964, they were exclusively white, almost exclusively male, over 50 and educated at public schools, and largely Oxbridge graduates.[28]

CONCLUSION

A ministerial time traveller from the 1951–64 government landing in Britain in 2024 would surely insist that sixty years of hindsight gives an unfair advantage to anyone seeking to judge his performance (and the time traveller would almost certainly be a man). All anyone can do is make the best of the challenges that are known to them. However, some of the problems were

---

[28] Full disclosure: the author of this analysis is also a white, male Oxbridge graduate over 50.

known but not properly tackled. Perhaps we should give extra credit to those judgements that have stood the test of time, such as Macmillan's attempt, albeit thwarted, to reposition Britain's place in the world following both World War II and the decline of empire, alongside the disaster of Suez. Edward Heath finally took the UK 'into Europe' in 1973.

The Suez crisis was the one moment when Britain's political direction changed. No such discontinuity occurred when Churchill gave way to Eden in 1955, or Macmillan to Douglas-Home in 1963. For example, Rab Butler remained Chancellor of the Exchequer when Eden became Prime Minister, likewise Reginald Maudling when Douglas-Home entered Downing Street. Domestically, the thirteen years can be seen as a time of caution and continuity. Churchill set the tone, by promising to 'set the people free'; however, his policies to expand market freedoms were accompanied by decisions to keep the National Health Service (whose creation his party had fiercely opposed) and to include trade unions in discussions on economic policy. By appointing Walter Monckton, a centrist who opposed tougher union laws, as Minister of Labour, Churchill clearly favoured conciliation over confrontation.

Reviewing the record from 1951 to 1955, Robert Blake, the pre-eminent chronicler of Conservative history, concluded that Churchill was 'an anachronism. It was as if time had been warped in some strange way, and an eighteenth-century Whig was leading a twentieth-century Tory party.'[29] However one assesses Churchill's outlook, the point is that his domestic legacy was not overturned by his successors (in part because he largely withdrew from the day-to-day fray during his peace-time spell as Prime Minister, following his severe stroke in June 1953). The general outlook of the governments from 1951 to 64, whether labelled Whig or otherwise, was one of a pragmatism that moderated a centre-right ideology that was anyway milder than its rhetoric implied. It broadly adopted the outlook of one-nation pre-war

---

[29] Robert Blake, *The Conservative Party from Peel to Thatcher* (London: Fontana, 1985), p. 272.

leaders such as Stanley Baldwin. Later Tory prime ministers – Heath briefly, Thatcher more fully – embraced ideology and provoked more fundamental arguments which have persisted ever since. Thatcher would have regarded Monckton as soaking wet.

How far a government should be guided by pragmatism and how far by ideology depends on the viewpoint of the observer, the circumstances of the time and the issues at stake. Sixty years later, it is still possible to debate whether less cautious, more ideologically committed and, perhaps, more socially progressive policies would have been more successful. More recent governments offer examples on both sides of that debate. Whatever the merits and failings of the Thatcher and Blair administrations, both introduced major changes that outlasted their time in office: Thatcher having embraced the ideology of the free market; Blair, in contrast, having repudiated the ideology of traditional socialism and determined to do 'what works'. Of course, one thing that Thatcher and Blair shared was a full decade in office, something that none of the four prime ministers managed between 1951 and 1964, or the five since 2010. But how far was the longevity of Thatcher and Blair in power a cause of their prowess, and how far a consequence of it? All in all, it is hard to offer a single template with which to judge any sustained period of government. Elements of one administration can illuminate elements of another: which can help, sometimes a lot, but isn't everything.

One of the few general truths is that all governments have successes and failures. Should we judge them purely by what they set out to do, or by wider criteria? Time and again the social conservatism of 1951–64 governments triumphed against campaigns for social change: does that record count as a success (mission accomplished) or failure (mission mistaken)? Today the notion that abortion and gay sex should be criminal offences would be dismissed as cruel and outrageous. Six decades ago public opinion was more divided. Likewise, there are bound to be some of today's controversies that will be settled in years to come, provoking judgements that might seem harsh to politicians grappling with the values and attitudes of our time.

It is also an unhappy fact of political life that results often fall short of intentions. That is not always true: the abolition of resale price maintenance did what it said on the tin; it worked. So did the 1956 Clean Air Act. The NHS was preserved, more homes were built, and living standards improved. And sometimes results exceed intentions: the transformation of popular culture owes much to the creation of ITV, whose genesis was ideological rather than egalitarian. Given the propensity of the noblest plans to go wrong, it is churlish to deny credit to governments that preside over accidental triumphs.

On the other hand, in standing firm in their opposition to much social change, the Conservatives lost the opportunity to burnish their image as a party for the modern world. A range of reforms resisted by the Conservatives were enacted during Wilson's premiership and never reversed. No leading Tory of that era set out to rebrand their party in the way that David Cameron did half a century later, on climate change and gay marriage.

There is, however, a wider point. In as far as the governments of Churchill, Eden, Macmillan and Douglas-Home stand in the dock of history for their shortcomings, they are not alone. The analysis of Britain's long-term problems was just as defective in the media and other political parties. It was not so much that the Conservative leadership remained the prisoner of nostalgia, refusing to grasp the challenges of the future, but that it operated in a climate in which those who made what most people today would regard as the right calls were generally in a minority.

Moreover, Labour made mistakes that were different from the Tories but just as big. Two fundamental errors stand out. The first was its devotion to a version of socialism that had comprehensively failed. In his party conference speech in Scarborough in 1963, Harold Wilson, the party's new leader, famously said Labour was 're-defining and we are restating our Socialism in terms of the scientific revolution' and planning a new Britain forged in 'the white heat of this revolution'. Less well remembered is the country that inspired his analysis. Britain, he said, must rise to 'the formidable Soviet challenge in the education of scientists and technologists, and above all, in the ruthless application of scientific techniques in Soviet industry'.[30] Wilson's solution was 'democratic planning'. He said nothing about the role of markets or private sector innovation, let alone the fact that the Soviet economy was in fact a basket case in which political tyranny and bureaucratic incompetence snuffed out enterprise and initiative.

Second, Labour in the early 1960s set its face against economic association with the rest of Europe. In 1961, when Macmillan was seeking to negotiate Britain's entry into the Common Market, Labour's then leader, Hugh Gaitskell, warned that entry would mean 'the end of a thousand years of history'.[31] Following de Gaulle's veto of British entry, Labour's 1964 manifesto argued that Britain had been saved from a deal that would have forced the relegation of Commonwealth countries to the status of 'third-class nations. Though we shall seek to achieve close links with our European neighbours, the Labour Party is convinced that the first responsibility of a British Government is still to the Commonwealth.' (Labour, like the Conservatives, was divided on Europe then, as it was for the decades that followed. Majorities in both parties fluctuated between pro-European and Eurosceptic stances down the years. The early 1960s was one of the times when the Conservative leader happened to be substantially keener than Labour's leader on close ties with countries across the Channel.)

Failures of opposition cannot absolve any government of blame for its own mistakes. At most, they might assist a plea of mitigation. Above all, how far should the 1951–64 governments be criticised for their failures to heed the warnings of Keynes and others, and for presiding over the UK's relative decline? Did caution prevent the boldness that the times demanded?

We might add a related question, to which different people now, as then, give very different answers. Did Britain benefit or suffer in the long run from emerging from the Second World War with its democratic arrangements intact? On mainland

---

[30] Harold Wilson, *Report of the Sixty-Second Annual Conference of the Labour Party* (London: Labour Party, 1963), p. 140.

[31] Hugh Gaitskell, *Text of Speeches by Hugh Gaitskell and George Brown* (London: Labour Party, 1962), p. 10.

Europe, Germany, France and Italy all had to reshape their shattered societies as well as repair their crippled economies. Marshall Aid accompanied the creation of new political structures and a pressing need to run countries differently. Victorious Britain saw less need to clear away the past and make way for the new. It was not so much the mouse that roared as the cat that purred and went back to sleep. Were the political stability and economic drift of the 1950s two sides of the same coin?

As for Britain's place in the world, the status quo was abruptly undermined by the Suez crisis. This was unquestionably a catastrophe – a military disaster and a political scandal of conspiracy and deceit. It forced an overdue transformation of Britain's international role. This was led by Macmillan, who replaced Eden as prime minister less than three months after the humiliation of Suez. Macmillan identified the need for new relationships with Europe, the United States and Britain's former colonies. On all three, he had to combat resistance from large sections of his own party. His actions required political courage. Moreover, his judgements have stood the test of time.

However, as we have seen, the immediate consequences of Macmillan's foresight were failure not success: de Gaulle's veto, the cancellation of Blue Streak and Skybolt, Rhodesia's racist rebellion. Six decades later, we might consider that the challenges of the new world order should have been identified earlier. Should we blame the ministers of the time, especially in the early 1950s, for addressing them too late and maintaining an excessive faith in the power of the Commonwealth – or single out Macmillan for at least trying to place Britain on the right side of history? Maybe the answer is both.

To ask these questions about both domestic and foreign policy is not just to acknowledge the hazards of reaching an overall verdict on the thirteen years of post-war Conservative rule, but to suggest that similar difficulties face any dispassionate attempt to assess any sustained period of government. There is a perfectly reasonable case for saying that the principal task for any peacetime government is simply to keep the show on the road: to preserve the peace, protect democracy, maintain social stability and secure steadily rising prosperity. By those yardsticks, the governments of Churchill, Eden, Macmillan and Douglas-Home did pretty well.

But is it enough to run a country as if it is a well-tuned engine that just needs to be kept ticking over? Should a government also *lead* the country, identifying the underlying forces bearing down on a nation, and taking effective steps to prepare for the future? And if it should lead, how far is it proper, and even democratic, to go beyond the views and values of the wider public, especially in the realm of social reform? These are vital questions that need to be asked about governments of any era. Six decades of hindsight offer big advantages in attempting to answer them – but even then, doubts and disagreements are bound to remain. To those who attempt the thought experiment suggested at the beginning of this chapter – how will the Conservative governments since 2010 look in 2084? – the best of luck.

2

External Shocks

Tom Egerton

B EFORE DISSECTING THE RECORD of the Conservative governments of 2010–24 any fair analysis must account for the exogenous shocks which have dramatically shaped the government's hand. However, crises can also obscure contemporary historical judgement, portraying false dichotomies of rise or fall, success or failure. Besides their use in legacy-shaping they are also live political arguments deployed by governments to avert responsibility and depoliticise. For this reason, caution is needed. Any exploration into external shocks may be seen by some as an attempt to create 'get out of jail free cards' for governments. Others may view it as an intriguing, but ultimately worthless, historical thought process. It is not. Instead, analysing an entire government's record with an eye to crises, particularly the constraints and opportunities created by them, is the only fair way to reach a conclusion and learn lessons for the future.

So, how do the external crises of 2010–24 compare to what previous governments faced?

Many post-war governments have grappled with external shocks, whether through sharp events or slow-burning external problems. The 1945–51 Labour government led by Clement Attlee inherited a Britain damaged by the largest shock the country has ever faced: the destruction of war. Reconstruction against the backdrop of this shock, and in the face of Britain as a declining power in the world, evident in Britain's painful acceptance of the American loan and Bretton Woods order, was a difficult political challenge to overcome. By 1949 the pressure became too much, with a forced Sterling devaluation. Attlee's government also experienced several external shocks in foreign policy, whether in the declining empire over the loss of India and the Palestine conflict or in the initiation of the Cold War, with the Greek civil war and the Korean War. The period 1945–51 was anything but stable considering these significant external pressures, yet a high-achieving premiership was still forged out of it.

As Peter Kellner examined in the 1951–64 period of Conservative government, several external factors played a pivotal role in Britain's economic and political outlook. The Suez crisis is the notable shock, a stark representation of how Britain's power had continued to dissipate in the world. Other shocks followed, from the Blue Strike debacle, which revealed the insecurity of the special relationship and Britain's supposed 'sovereign' foreign policy, to the new threat of the European economic rejuvenation leading to Britain's relative economic 'slowdown' and, tangentially, President De Gaulle's striking rejection of British EEC entry in 1963. After the supposed lost thirteen years, Harold Wilson faced several external shocks, Labour's forced devaluation in 1967 due, in part, to the inequalities of the Bretton Woods structure and market pressure, for example. Wilson also battled with the continued relative global market decline of British industry, and the escalation of violence in Northern Ireland – an internal conflict which was consistently treated as anything but by both major parties.

Crises and shocks were ever-present in what many consider as the 'managing decline' premierships of 1945–70, or, in other words, the premierships which could enjoy the fruits of an increasingly affluent, plateauing Britain. Whatever the failures of them all, there are reforms and achievements these governments could point to. It's consistently forgotten that the period of this so-called post-war consensus (1950–75), in which narratives of decline and external crisis dominate, actually experienced higher economic growth and lower income inequality than the later, neoliberal period

(1975–2000).[1] The lesson here is that even when facing a series of external crises – both long and short term – governments still retain agency to act and achieve success.

The disintegration of the so-called post-war consensus was a period of crisis on its own, one almost impossible to attribute to a single government and thus an ongoing constraint from 1970 until 1979. It is not the topic for this chapter. However, if one conclusion is to be taken it is that, when crises do combine – externally and internally – Britain can seem almost ungovernable. This was not the case for 2010–24. The 1970s external shocks cannot be compared with the external shocks faced by the twenty-first-century Conservatives *because* they intertwined with a settlement of nationalised industries and trade union collective bargaining. The dominance of capital and the offshoring of industry in the 2010–24 period changes how superficially 'similar' external shocks are experienced, the inflation or geopolitical instability resulting from the 1973 Yom Kippur War a prime example – differing greatly from Ukraine's impact in 2022.

The argument that governments retain agency in times of crisis is perhaps best exemplified by the 1979–97 Conservative governments. Margaret Thatcher's strident reforms moved the nation out of the 1970s: the trade unions were targeted and eventually crushed by an increasingly forceful state, while simultaneously the benefits of a revitalised free market economy were realised, especially in the City and through growth of the services industry in the 1980s and 1990s. But it's important to note that the government faced mostly internal shocks, and if anything created a Britain more exposed to future external market shocks with the transition to a service-based economy. There were external shocks, such as inflation, sterling pressures between 1979 and 1982 partly due to North Sea oil, the post-1979 Iranian Revolution oil price surge, the 1982 Falklands War, the 1987 global recession and the European Exchange Rate Mechanism (ERM) crash in 1992, but these were spread evenly over almost eighteen years, with some, such as the Falklands and North

---

[1] David Edgerton, *The Rise and Fall of the British Nation: A Twentieth Century History* (London: Penguin, 2019), pp. 283, 407.

Sea oil, creating opportunities as much as challenges. The Thatcher–Major period enjoyed more benign external conditions with the West entering a more peaceful settlement as the Cold War ended. It's also worth noting that Britain's diminished position in the world required less responsibility for the state and posed less overall danger compared to the period of Empire. The government utilised this respite by forcefully tackling Britain's internal political crisis with success.

The new settlement which resulted, loosely labelled as neo-liberalism, was broadly maintained by Tony Blair's New Labour from 1997. Under Blair, and continuing with Gordon Brown until 2008, capital was consistently globalised, without much focus on national industry. In short, Blair prioritised economic stability rather than innovation, especially after the events of the ERM crash had fatally damaged Major's government. Britain, for a time, reaped the rewards of continued market globalisation. In fact, of all post-war governments the 1997–2008 period experienced a significantly decreased period of external crisis as the global economy boomed. The agreement of peace in Northern Ireland in 1998 ended the ongoing troubles, while most wars fought by Labour, ending in the notorious Iraq conflict, had little direct short-term impact on national political and economic circumstances, and were largely self-imposed. With that said, however, the rise of terrorism after 9/11 was a key shock Labour had to manage. On a domestic level, Labour used this time to introduce a series of meaningful governmental and constitutional alterations, in addition to significant spending increases, and reforms, in the public sector – of which the positive impact goes far beyond budget spreadsheets. But given the lack of external shocks, and the traditional desires of the Labour Party, this period can be seen as a missed opportunity. New Labour, unlike Thatcher's Conservatives, did not take the opportunity to reshape the country in their image.

This opportunity ended abruptly in 2008. Most of the developed western world had ignored the trade-offs of global integration in search of growth. The last fourteen years have demonstrated that under any system of politics, external shocks significantly impact the government. Indeed, for the neoliberal consensus, it is this very acceptance of risk through the state's absence in certain structurally sensitive areas to allow for market freedom – or, as some have quoted from Ulrich Beck, the 'organised irresponsibilities' in society.[2] It was through these risks – spanning health, finance, national inequality, democratic/elite legitimacy and geopolitical danger – that a decade of external crisis has been felt.[3] Despite this, as demonstrated by previous premierships, governments can still succeed during periods of instability.

It is important to note that not every shock is purely external. The shocks analysed in this chapter have primarily external origins, but as later touched on in this chapter and particularly around Brexit, domestic politics plays a key role. A further investigation into this interplay is needed, but exceeds the limits of debate in this chapter. So, beginning with the financial crash and moving through each major crisis up to the most recent of inflation, this chapter examines the pain incurred by compounding external shocks in Britain, how they impacted the government, what opportunities arose and whether they should place a meaningful asterisk on the record of the 2010–24 Conservative governments.

THE GREAT FINANCIAL CRASH (GFC)

The 2010–24 period of Conservative government, in reality, began in the aftermath of 2008. The 2000s were an era of ever-increasing technological change and debt-fuelled global consumerism. The Cold War was over, and the world had settled into a more stable state. The markets, underpinned by low interest rates and low inflation, were content with steady growth, led by independent central banks fixated on keeping the 1970s spectre of stagflation and trade union power consigned to the past. This was the peak of free-market economics, promoted to its twenty-first-century neoliberal form by Ronald Reagan and Margaret Thatcher. Mervyn King, in a speech in 2003 as Bank of England (BoE) governor, labelled this period as 'NICE' – 'Non-

---

[2] Ulrich Beck quoted in Adam Tooze, *Shutdown: How Covid Shook the World's Economy* (London: Penguin, 2023), pp. 10–11.

[3] Ibid., p. xx.

Inflationary Consistently Expansionary'.[4] For the UK in the 2000s, the market and government were in harmony, with wages rising and sustained GDP growth. Economic meltdown was not a thought which entertained much space in New Labour's mind. Brown's infamous mantra said it all: 'there will be no return to boom and bust'.[5] This hubris would inevitably be followed by nemesis, though the causes of the financial crash are not directly attributable to one man.

To understand the impacts of the Global Financial Crisis (GFC), it's best to start with the City of London. The City had formed a hypnotising lock on successive UK governments. First asserting its modern dominance through its position as home of the 'Sterling zone', then transforming its place in financial markets as a source of 'Eurodollars' before maintaining its desirability through loose regulation and 'passporting', giving it access to the Eurozone markets through equivalence.[6] It was for these reasons London grew to be a cornerstone of globalised capitalism by 2007, leading the world in interest rate derivatives (43% compared to Wall St's 24%) and foreign exchange (35% of global turnover, over $1 trillion a day).[7] Over decades, numerous UK governments chased higher growth in the City and the corresponding higher tax receipts, allowing for easier budget and spending decisions.

What made the GFC a significant problem for Britain was the City's interconnected position in the global finance system – bridging banks in Europe and the US, a financial pseudo-geographical and regulatory undercutting role between the continents. When

---

4   Mervyn King, governor of the Bank of England, East Midlands Development Agency/Bank of England Dinner, Leicester, 14 October 2003 (accessed at www.bankofengland.co.uk/speech/2003/east-midlands-development-agency-dinner, 6 August 2023).

5   Deborah Summers, 'No return to boom and bust: what Brown said when he was chancellor', *Guardian*, 11 September 2008.

6   Stephen Jones, 'The impact of Brexit on the future of the UK's financial services', in Sophie Loussouran (ed.), *Brexit and Its Aftermath* (London: Bloomsbury, 2022), pp. 76–86.

7   Adam Tooze, *Crashed: How a Decade of Financial Crisis Changed the World* (London: Penguin, 2019), p. 81.

the contagion of US bank funding reached Britain and its inter-connected European partners, the pain was substantial – acutely felt by the specialised mortgage lender Northern Rock, which eventually had to be nationalised. Brown's response of bank reca-pitalisations (partial nationalisations) for RBS and Lloyds TSB-HBOS, and extra support funds for those such as Barclays, was successful, even influencing the US Federal Reserve's early policy response to the crisis. However, saving the City proved expensive, the upfront fiscal cost, in 2008, of Brown's policy to the taxpayer totalled £289 billion, with a final cost of around £550 billion (with some estimating exposure as high as £1.1 trillion).[8] But Brown's finest final hour was his role in the G20, where he coordinated a global response innovatively incorporating emerging economies with new voting rights and securing over $1 trillion extra resources for the International Monetary Fund (IMF). For the economic historian Adam Tooze it 'proved that he was perfectly suited as Treasury Secretary to the world'.[9] Regardless of the swift policy response, the consequences were catastrophic for the British econ-omy. To save the nation's head, it had to sacrifice an arm.

Between Q2 2008 and Q2 2009 the UK saw five consecutive quarters of economic contraction, leading to an overall GDP loss of over 6 per cent.[10] Excluding the post-Second World War reces-sion 2009 experienced the largest calendar year loss in GDP since 1931, and also the longest recession in the G7 (but not the deepest).[11] Peak unemployment reached 2.7 million (8.4 per cent) by 2011, the highest quarterly rate since 1995.[12] Household wealth losses in 2008–9 were estimated at $1.5 trillion –

---

[8] CRESC and University of Manchester, 'An alternative report on UK bank-ing reform', 28 September 2009, p. 33.

[9] Tooze, *Crashed*, p. 272.

[10] ONS, 'The 2008 recession 10 years on', 30 April 2018 (accessed at www.ons.gov.uk/economy/grossdomesticproductgdp/articles/the2008recession10years on/2018-04-30, 18 September 2023).

[11] 'Key issues for the New Parliament 2010', House of Commons Library, p. 28 (accessed at www.parliament.uk/business/publications/research/key-issu es-for-the-new-parliament/).

[12] ONS, 'The 2008 recession 10 years on'.

50 per cent of GDP in just a year.[13] The shock also triggered a sharp period of wage and productivity stagnation lasting into the 2020s – although this is entangled with later Conservative economic policy, the effects of which are explored in Chapters 3 and 9. The economic downturn seamlessly translated into politics: it ended New Labour's claim to economic competency – which directly contributed to their defeat in the 2010 general election. This was evident in the 2010 British Election Study, with economic factors dictating three-fifths of voting intention.[14] Other studies of the election directly found that in parts of the country which experienced higher economic downturn, measured through unemployment claimants, the Labour vote decreased by 8.2 per cent, in comparison to 4.4 per cent in the lesser affected areas.[15] Undeniably, then, Labour had lived and died by the sword of the neoliberal settlement and its resulting economic external shocks.

What David Cameron inherited in 2010 was a crisis of market and political confidence – not purely deficit or budget. While structural deficits were present, they were, in hindsight, minimal.[16] The UK's debt as a proportion of GDP in 2010 was 65 per cent with the deficit peaking at 10 per cent.[17] However, debt levels were reasonably safe and, by historical standards, low, facilitated by the low interest rates created by the monetary innovation of Quantitative Easing (QE), first deployed by the Fed in 2008. The method, which entailed central banks buying government-issued bonds (which lowers yields and thus borrowing rates), ensured that

---

[13] Petya Koeva Brooks, 'Households hit hard by wealth losses', *IMF Research Department*, 24 June 2009.

[14] Face-To-Face Survey, British Election Study, 2010.

[15] Stephen Fisher, John Curtice and Robert Ford, 'The British general election of 2010: the results analysed', *American Political Science Association 2010 Annual Meeting*, p. 6.

[16] Paul Johnson and Daniel Chandler, 'The coalition and the economy', in Anthony Seldon and Mike Finn (eds.), *The Coalition Effect: 2010–15* (Cambridge: Cambridge University Press, 2015), p. 165.

[17] Carl Emmerson, 'Two parliaments of pain: the UK public finances 2010 to 2017', Institute for Fiscal Studies, 2 May 2017, p. 4 (https://ifs.org.uk/pu blications/two-parliaments-pain-uk-public-finances-2010-2017).

the large stimulus responses, as seen in the US, could be funded cheaply. By January 2009, the BoE had cut interest rates to 1.5 per cent – the lowest they had been in its 315-year history – later cutting them to a mere 0.5 per cent. By May, King had marked the end of the 'NICE' era, the pain of economic bust was back.[18] The BoE was forced to implement a UK version of QE, originally totalling £150 billion before rising to £200 billion to stabilise the market, and later increasing again to over £400 billion.[19] Ultra-low interest rates and QE were deployed in an attempt to return confidence and accessible liquidity to a world financial system paralysed for fear of further bank capitulations and funding scares. There were both opportunities and dangers in these monetary policy shifts for future governments to explore. King himself, however, believes the long-term factors of QE, born of the financial crisis, were highly inflationary.[20]

Radical monetary policy, mixed with Brown's recapitalisations and mergers, proved effective stabilisers as liquidity propped up the UK financial system. The response has been historically criticised as depoliticised top-down economics that simply increased inequality.[21] Without it, however, the multiple critical bank and business failures may have been terminal for the economy, even if the rows over bankers' bonuses were an embarrassing display of greed at a time of harsh recession.[22] Britain stayed afloat, but its economy and key industry, the City, was notably weakened, as was the political and economic

---

[18] Mervyn King, *Quarterly Bank of England Inflation Report*, Bank of England, 14 May 2008.

[19] Andrew Rawnsley, *The End of the Party: The Rise and Fall of New Labour* (London: Penguin Viking, 2004), p. 616; see also later QE rises in Duncan Weldon, *Two Hundred Years of Muddling Through* (London: Little Brown, 2021), p. 290.

[20] Mervyn King, *The End of Alchemy: Money, Banking, and the Future of the Global Economy* (New York: W. W. Norton, 2016).

[21] Stefan Eich, *The Currency of Politics: The Political Theory of Money from Aristotle to Keynes* (Princeton, NJ: Princeton University Press, 2022), pp. 206–20.

[22] Rawnsley, *End of the Party*, pp. 607–9.

future of the country. Cameron inherited a fraught position, but one that had been significantly stabilised by Brown, at the expense of his party. It wasn't Cameron who had to think about nationalisations or stimulus, something which would have proved difficult to square with Conservative MPs, or have his economic competency damaged by an external shock. If Cameron had won the uncalled 2007 general election he may have. Instead, Cameron entered Downing Street in 2010 with a vulnerable world economy more prone to external shocks and a British economy in need of rejuvenation and consolidation. The task was difficult, but not impossible. The effects of the 2008 crisis, and Cameron's reaction to it, run through almost every analysis of policy area and topic you will read in this book, and are mentioned by most contributors. The GFC laid the foundations of further crises in global capitalism and national politics, even if, thanks mostly to central bank policy, the worst possible fiscal and monetary impacts were subdued. The next shock was a prime example of how 2008 continued to influence the next fourteen years with the Eurozone crisis originating in the most over-leveraged banks and overwhelmed countries after 2008.

THE EUROZONE CRISIS

In 2010, on a wave of discontent at thirteen years of New Labour and the post-GFC economic downturn, David Cameron led his modernised Conservative Party into coalition with Nick Clegg's Liberal Democrats, beginning fourteen years of continuous Conservative rule. The political fallout of the GFC had been compounded in 2010 by the ongoing Eurozone crisis – particularly Greece's looming default. Many Eurozone countries had become dangerously unstable with over-leveraged banks. The prime example was Ireland, which had become notorious for its low-regulation regime, enticing global capital. When the financial crash hit, later turning into the Eurozone crisis, Ireland found its banks were leveraged to an equivalent 700 per cent of the entire country's GDP.[23] Without the short-term funding markets that provided vital liquidity, several banks

[23] Tooze, *Crashed*, pp. 185–6.

faced imminent failure, posing catastrophic risks to the country, which relied on major banks as critical infrastructure from bond buying to mortgages and retail bank accounts. The contagion spread to several Eurozone countries, triggering a crisis of funding. The financial and the national realms were set to face a reckoning: the halls of Brussels were the battleground as the European Central Bank (ECB) attempted to accommodate the divide between the south and the north.

Enter Greece, a country indebted from spending in the 1980s–90s, but with a deficit that actually fell between 2001 and 2006. However, by 2010 it required a hefty bailout to stabilise its deficit, spiralling due to the now fracturing private market and collapsed funding mechanisms. Debt simply became harder and harder to pay. But Greece's pain, unlike that of Ireland, Portugal or Italy, was prolonged as it transformed into a proxy for the Euro debate over economic structures and actions: namely, between fiscally conservative hawks and those in favour of bailouts and/or debt restructuring. The 'Troika' of the ECB, European Commission (EC) and IMF were catastrophically divided. The Troika's delayed and painful bailout was a clear 'statement of the "bait and switch" situation, by which a problem of excessive bank lending was turned into a crisis of public borrowing'.[24] George Osborne, with Cameron, had captured this exact narrative of fear – managing to attribute the source of the GFC and now Eurozone crisis to structural deficit rather than a more nuanced debate around its origin in over-leveraged private finance and banking. It was a lesson in how an external crisis can present both opportunities and dangers. Greece, for the Conservatives, proved the prime example of the debt-default fears. It was an impressive political manoeuvre, and one which created the political opportunities for economic change in their first five years of government.

The breaking news of the Eurozone crisis during the 2010 coalition negotiations frightened the Liberal Democrats.

---

[24] Ibid., p. 344.

Financial instability in the markets dominated the very real governing scenario the party found themselves in for the first time in almost a century. The Cabinet secretary Gus O'Donnell even took the step of continually messaging the negotiating parties urging them to reach a hasty agreement, sacrificing political positioning for time.[25] Clegg and his party were keen not to be blamed for keeping the Treasury in limbo during economic crisis and capitulated in several areas on economic policy, as Nick Clegg's biographer Chris Bowers put it:

> The Lib Dems were even willing to concede some ground on their campaigning themes: the idea that action to cut the budget deficit should not start too quickly for fear of endangering the economic recovery. The Greek crisis, coupled with the sense of urgency communicated by the Bank of England, had led to a change in emphasis in the Lib Dem position.[26]

Sceptics could argue that the Lib Dems were continuously moving right on the economy between 2005 and 2010 (see the notorious *Orange Book*), possibly in anticipation of a Lib–Con coalition after naturally being in opposition to Labour for thirteen years. The Eurozone crisis, mixed with the aftermath of the GFC, simply offered the Lib Dems an easier political opportunity to conform to Osborne's austere 2010 emergency budget. There was, however, nothing inevitable about the economic choices agreed in the coalition. It was a mark of Cameron and Clegg's converging politics and personal relationship, mixed with a desire to urgently form a government in the face of financial instability, which heavily influenced the next five years of government.[27] As a senior Lib Dem put it, 'stability was the watchword'.[28] Thought for future consequences, not so much.

---

[25] Ben Riley-Smith, *Right to Rule: Thirteen Years, Five Prime Ministers and the Implosion of the Tories* (London: John Murray, 2023), p. 23.

[26] Chris Bowers, *Nick Clegg: The Biography* (London: Biteback, 2012), p. 228.

[27] Finn, *The Coalition Effect*, pp. 31–58.   [28] Private interview with author.

It is significant to reiterate the tough governing position Cameron and Clegg were in – the need to keep the coalition together in a time of market instability was fundamental, and constrained certain political actions. However, it was Osborne and Cameron's successful framing that ensured fiscal consolidation became a necessary political position to take in 2010, appearing in all three main parties' manifestos.[29] The degree of austerity, timing and methods were the primary points of party contest. The specific politicised areas of budget cuts, notably the cuts in capital expenditure and areas such as local government, became a poison the Conservative Party would feel the harsh political consequences of in later elections. There were several knock-on economic effects of austerity, and the GFC in general, namely, rising inequality, a weakened pound, reduced trust in elites, sluggish GDP growth and stagnating wages. Cameron's stabilisation became too ideological. Far from the institutions being the risks which could turn Britain into Greece, the unfolding QE delivered by the BoE spurred the small economic growth Cameron enjoyed – without it fiscal austerity may have been politically undeliverable.[30]

The other factor to consider with the Eurozone crisis is the response from the ECB, which moved to centralise monetary policy and create new structures in order to better respond to economic crisis, even initiating its own version of QE by 2015. The further divergence in economic structures and push for political supranationalism only ignited the question of Britain's position in the EU, particularly with regard to the City of London's position. Overall, the GFC, and the subsidiary Eurozone crisis, created destabilising and long-lasting constraining implications for the government. There was, however, nothing inexorable about the policy response which created further pain for future Conservative governments, as well as repercussions for society as whole (see Michael Marmot and Clare Bambra in Chapter 9).

[29] Finn, *The Coalition Effect*, p. 45.   [30] Tooze, *Crashed*, p. 534.

EXTERNAL INFLUENCES ON BREXIT AND ITS AFTERMATH

It's impossible to attribute the Leave vote in the 2016 Referendum purely to external shocks and factors. Academics such as John Curtice have rightly identified British voters' lack of association with European identity.[31] The Leave vote, however, was not just a question of identity or history. There were several significant external factors which contributed to the result, namely the two aforementioned crises, immigration and the general constraints globalisation imposed on national sovereignty.

One important factor in Brexit was undoubtedly immigration. The issue had been building since Blair's decision in 2004 to allow unrestricted immigration from eight newly accepted central and eastern European countries: the Czech Republic, Estonia, Hungary, Latvia, Lithuania, Poland, Slovakia and Slovenia. In addition, the ongoing Syrian civil war and disruption in the Middle East had increased immigration pressures from 2014 onwards. Immigration, dominating the headlines, had a discernible influence on the Leave vote, feeding into core campaign messages of a 'lack of control'.[32] It's unsurprising that Brexit chronicler Tim Shipman contends 'If we had to pinpoint a day when [vote] leave gained the upper hand [in the referendum] it is undoubtedly 26 May, the day the latest immigration figures were published. For Cameron they were disastrous ... net migration had reached 330,000.'[33] The external shock electrified the campaign, exacerbating Remain's weakness and Leave's strength. What's also notable is how the anti-EU immigration appeal mixed with a wider backlash against globalisation and the state of the British nation, which had begun eight years earlier during the GFC.

---

[31] John Curtice, 'Why Leave won the UK's EU referendum', *Journal of Common Market Studies*, 55:51, (2017), 19–37.

[32] Martin Moore and Gordon Ramsay, *UK Media Coverage of the 2016 EU Referendum Campaign* (London: Policy Institute at King's, 2017).

[33] Tim Shipman, *All Out War: The Full Story of Brexit* (London: William Collins, 2017), p. 286.

A second external cause of Brexit was the undermining of, and subsequent wider backlash against, elites. The GFC generated a broad-based anger amongst voters at the greed and incompetence of elites in the City who had helped generate a once-in-a-generation financial crisis. Politicians were also blamed for the handling of the crisis, and later implicated in their own greed through the 2009 expenses scandal. The crisis likely contributed to the degradation of trust in politicians, which had fallen to just 18 per cent by 2009, down from 38 per cent in 1986.[34] But what ultimately fuelled the fire of resentment was the simple fact that the UK bailouts were, in essence, the funnelling of taxpayers' money directly to those financial institutions which caused the crash. When banks that had been partly nationalised announced six- or seven-figure bonuses to those senior traders and staffers partly responsible for the financial meltdown, the subsequent backlash was predictable, especially during an austere recovery. The undermining of elites benefited the Brexit campaign, particularly in reaction to Cameron's leadership (with only 37 per cent of Conservatives following their leader's call for Remain) and his post-GFC economic policies.[35]

A third external influence on Brexit rested in the Eurozone. If the economic argument for Remain was based partly on the idea of EU competency, the political-economic difficulties of the Eurozone crisis and its bailouts were stark evidence against. The Eurozone had entered the crisis without the necessary monetary structures to respond to a multinational banking crisis, and only just managed to accommodate the countervailing interests of hawkish states such as Germany and those in southern Europe. Countries such as Greece had paid the price. Naturally the 'better together' argument was weakened, with voters uncomfortable, feeling they were 'paying' for a currency union and its growing

---

[34] Alison Park, Caroline Bryson, Elizabeth Clery, John Curtice and Miranda Phillips (eds.), *British Social Attitudes: The 30th Report* (London: NatCen Social Research, 2013), p. xiv.

[35] Curtice, 'Why Leave won the UK's EU referendum', p. 32; see also Jonathan Hopkin, *Anti-System Politics: The Crisis of Market Liberalism in Rich Democracies* (Oxford: Oxford University Press, 2020), pp. 71–6.

institutions which the UK had no direct part in. The Eurozone crisis also caused what Helen Thompson described as a 'clear divergence between British and Eurozone economies' when the BoE and ECB enacted dramatically different monetary responses in reaction to the 2011 inflation spike.[36] The result ensured that Britain 'with Germany, effectively became the employer of last resort for the Eurozone',[37] triggering increased economic immigration and ending the hopes that Cameron could meet his pledge to reduce immigration to the 'tens of thousands'. When the exogenous factors of heightened immigration, post-GFC distrusted elites and the Eurozone failures combined it proved a potent political argument. Vote Leave knew this, and consequently centred the campaign on the results of these shocks.

To oversimplify, this was a general backlash against globalised external forces, manifesting in a desire for greater national control and sovereignty. The effects were evident in the Brexit vote, the result of a perceived lack of democratic validation mixed with years of economic pressures resulting from the GFC/austerity and a Remain campaign led by an elite deemed out of touch.[38] There was, in other words, a political *and* economic deficit, which nullified the Remain campaign. The nation, for many who voted Leave, was still the last economic lifeline. For David Goodhart's 'somewheres', it was the vehicle for security from these global shocks.[39] But the desire of 'place and people' only contrasted with the lack of control the nation had against the globalised crisis which transcended traditional borders, only made worse by the EU institutions' tendency to do the same. Any cultural causes for Brexit were exacerbated, and likely enabled, therefore, by global shocks and the state's perceived inability to withstand them.

---

[36] Helen Thompson, *Disorder: Hard Times in the 21st Century* (Oxford: Oxford University Press, 2022), p. 156.

[37] Ibid.

[38] Thiemo Fetzer, 'Did austerity cause Bexit?', *American Economic Review*, 101:9 (2019), 3849–86.

[39] David Goodhart, *The Road to Somewhere: The New Tribes Shaping British Politics* (London: Penguin, 2017), pp. 19–48.

However, as Robert Saunders has argued, any analysis of Brexit and its impacts must take into account high politics.[40] Cameron failed to realise how globalised shocks would deeply affect a generational decision – as they always will. By contrast, the Vote Leave campaign, led by Dominic Cummings, utilised the 'big forces' of the time.[41] This was contingent on their defeat of rival campaign 'Leave.EU' to produce a professional campaign by Cummings, demonstrating the importance of individual agency.[42] Neither can one forget the importance of the figureheads of Michael Gove and Boris Johnson taking advantage of the political opportunity and joining Leave – adding political clout and skill to the campaign.[43] Shipman astutely remarked after Gove and Johnson's rebellion that 'it was not inevitable that Brexit would happen, but the pieces were in place that meant it could'.[44] However, it was also in Remain's failures, not just to counter Leave's campaigning but to actively play into their anti-establishment, anti-globalisation message – whether Cameron's leadership or the sometimes economic tone-deaf message to many left hurting since the 2008 financial crisis and austerity. Missing too in the Remain campaign was the leader of the Labour Party, Jeremy Corbyn, probably the one figure who could have united more left-leaning voters, many of them in Labour's electoral heartlands. Overall, compounding external crises combined with significant internal politics to produce a result which shocked the UK system to its core.

[40] Robert Saunders, 'How do we write the history of Brexit?', *Political Quarterly*, 94:2 (2023), 230–6.

[41] Dominic Cummings, Startup Party #1: Reflections on the last 20 years, 3 June 2023 (accessed at https://dominiccummings.substack.com/p/the-startup-party-reflections-on, 17 August 2023).

[42] Shipman, *All Out War*, pp. 588–90.

[43] Ibid. and Anthony Seldon and Raymond Newell, *Johnson at 10: The Inside Story* (London: Atlantic, 2023), pp. 21–35.

[44] Shipman, *All Out War*, p. 184.

Thus, the causes of Brexit were only partially external, but the shock it created within the British political system was undeniable, igniting four fraught years of deadlock and division. Our politics was torn apart, and the unwritten constitution tested at every stage. The reckoning of a powerful decision by direct democracy against an opposed, or more accurately confused, representative body was destined to be messy. May's 2016–19 government became completely destabilised by the shock, with Cabinet rebellions after Chequers 2018, Letters and Votes of No Confidence led by the ERG Brexiteers and three devastating Commons defeats in early 2019. Government bandwidth since has only just recovered. Brexit infected parliament so deeply that the government–opposition convention partially broke, aided by a controversial speaker and a disintegrating party system. The party system was so vulnerable that by May 2019 there was a four-way battle between Labour, the Brexit Party, the Lib Dems and the Conservatives.[45] Many politicians, advisers, civil servants and experts were caught in the crossfire of the Brexit wars – with simple affiliations crashing entire careers without much regard for consequences, Johnson's purging of twenty-one MPs the most egregious. The political culture, by Remainers and Leavers, was toxified in parliament and country – a debate which created political tropes of dubious factuality and enabled disingenuous political and academic players to spin real electoral desires for national identity or new economic settlements into pseudo-wars over postcodes and xenophobia.

Though the political fallout is obvious, the economic impact of Brexit is harder to evaluate. As soon as Britain reconciled its *actual* exit with Johnson's Withdrawal Agreement, leaving on 31 January 2020, Covid hit. What is undeniable is that the short-term economic impact has been harsh; Paul Johnson's central view is roughly a 5 per cent drop in GDP due to Brexit (see Chapter 3). The City has been left rejected and confused in the 2021 Trade and Cooperation Agreement, not unconnected to

---

[45] Robert Ford, Tim Bale, Will Jennings and Paula Surridge, *The British General Election of 2019* (London: Palgrave Macmillan, 2021), pp. 171–2, 283.

the politics of the financial crash interacting with, and partly creating, the politics of the 'f**k business' Johnson. Inflation pressures increased due to the increased import and labour costs (as well as diminished trade). The economy is feeling a Brexit hangover, but whether the hangover transforms into something more serious or merely wears off is unknown. The supposed opportunities created by Brexit are not yet clear – there is no obvious 'Brexit dividend', though there are increased global opportunities for the government to take, whether in tax setting, regulation changes or trade deals (though of lesser value so far). In the long term, Brexit could become an opportunity which began as a crisis. But for the time-frame relevant to our analysis, it has only hindered the country, and thus government. As a self-imposed issue by Cameron to partly assuage internal Tory splits, not much nuance needs to be sought for the effect on his government: namely, a sorry end. But, for the post-Brexit governments, it is only fair to judge while taking into account the crisis they inherited, destabilising Whitehall and occupying governing bandwidth. However, the flawed implementation of the policy and its continued use as a tool to divide and conquer ensures responsibility for its failure must be partly shared by all of those that followed Cameron. While some of the motives for the Brexit vote were well founded, the party knew (or should have known) that they were playing with fire. It has subsequently burnt every post-2016 premiership.

COVID-19

Out of all the external shocks considered in this chapter Covid proved the most existential – the GFC the only other comparable in scale. In 2008 the US Federal Reserve ensured that the financial crash quickly turned from a global catastrophe into a question of regional and national recovery through QE and its international swap lines (an underrated global phenomenon). With a pandemic, however, dollars were simply not enough. The threat was biological – almost alien to western populations which had lived under the myth they had conquered the spectre of contagious disease with high life expectancies and relatively well-equipped health systems. This was proven dramatically wrong. The decisions made during the pandemic by Johnson's government are considered in Chapter 5. Here the analysis focuses on Covid's creation of large constraints and partial opportunities.

Covid's contested arenas became twofold, much like war, encompassing the national economy and the health of the population. But unlike the world wars, 'the problem was not how to mobilise the armies. The challenge was to demobilise the economy and keep people at home.'[46] The economy, still damaged by the previous financial crisis and adjusting to Brexit, was in a vulnerable position – it needed stability. But, in the face of an expanding disease from Wuhan, the world market, moving first, began to crash in February 2020 as the FTSE All-World stock markets closed 13 per cent down, losing a staggering $6 trillion of value.[47] By March the Fed engaged in what Thompson termed 'QE Infinity' to stabilise the US bond market and ensure liquidity remained in the global financial system.[48] At the height of the programme the Fed was buying $1 million bonds a second, ending with 5 per cent of the entire market (around $20 trillion).[49]

Where the Fed led in policy, so the other major central banks followed. The Bank of England initiated another £450 billion of QE in 2020–1, raising the total balance sheet to £895 billion. In Number 10, Johnson and now chief adviser Cummings engaged in a series of high-stakes meetings between 12 and 23 March, leading to a UK lockdown.[50] By 30 March Chancellor Rishi Sunak and the Treasury had introduced the largest peace-time welfare stimulus labelled 'furlough' for 11.7 million jobs, costing £70 billion.[51] Furlough ensured that while the economy crashed, with GDP falling

---

[46] Tooze, *Shutdown*, p. 135.

[47] Robin Wigglesworth, 'How the coronavirus shattered market complacency', *Financial Times*, 28 February 2020.

[48] Thompson, *Disorder*, p. 142.   [49] Tooze, *Shutdown*, p.129.

[50] Seldon and Newell, *Johnson at 10*, pp. 191–206.

[51] Francis-Devine, Andy Powell and Harriet Clark, 'Coronavirus Job Retention Scheme: statistics', House of Commons Library, 23 December

9.9 per cent in 2020, the population's health could be prioritised by not breaching NHS capacity.[52] The government, in an alliance with the market, was also pivotal in the vaccine production, procurement and rollout – led by Kate Bingham and deployed by Emily Lawson from the NHS, delivering over 52 million first doses, 49 million second doses and over 38 million booster doses.[53] Pandemic policy became, as Peter Hennessy stated, Keynesian economics 'on steroids'.[54]

While Johnson declared victory over Covid in July 2021 with all lockdown restrictions permanently lifted, the pandemic was to remain high in Britain's consciousness for the remainder of the year, notably around the Omicron scare in December 2021, which caused dynamic Cabinet divisions.[55] However, the market–government alliance of the vaccine, national lockdowns and the NHS had finally conquered the realm of health once again with booster programmes proving highly effective blocks on hospitalisations and deaths. With the pandemic over, the UK population stepped back to assess the catastrophic impact: over 230,000 deaths involving Covid-19 between 2020 and 2024.[56] However, death or GDP metrics will not capture the social, mental and emotional costs that the pandemic, and lockdown, had on many. Neither will the knock-on effects of so-called long

2021 (accessed at https://commonslibrary.parliament.uk/research-brief ings/cbp-9152/, 27 September 2023).

[52] ONS, GDP monthly estimate UK: December 2020, 12 February 2021 (accessed at www.ons.gov.uk/releases/gdpmonthlyestimateukdecem ber2020, 27 September 2023).

[53] 'Covid vaccine: How many people are vaccinated in the UK?', BBC, 4 March 2022 (accessed at www.bbc.co.uk/news/health-55274833, 29 September 2023).

[54] Peter Hennessy, *Duty of Care: Britain Before and After Covid* (London: Penguin, 2023) p. 124.

[55] Seldon and Newell, *Johnson at 10*, pp. 367–72.

[56] 'Deaths with COVID-19 on the death certificate', UK Government (accessed at https://coronavirus.data.gov.uk/details/deaths, 25 August 2023).

Covid (estimated at 2 million) or Covid-caused health weakness.[57] Nor the fact that the best part of a year of policy and politics was almost entirely devoted to the pandemic – Johnson's government lost vast amounts of time, and political capital in his party, in dealing with the pandemic. Cabinet was cleaved down the middle between doves, more concerned with the impact of Covid the on population's health, and hawks who were more worried about how to pay for the estimated £400 billion cost of pandemic policy without a functioning economy.[58] Johnson himself almost died from Covid, entering the ICU on 6 April 2020 with a 50/50 chance of survival. The destabilisation at the heart of government should not be under-stated. But mistakes were made, most notably on lockdown tim-ings, opening up the economy early or in specific areas such as care home protection or PPE.

During, and directly after, Covid there was a momentary politics of unity which formed – a unity notably absent from the previous four years of Brexit anguish. Hennessy contended that this unity was found in a shared experience, and how 'above all, Covid Britain will rank in popular memory alongside the intense shared histories of the two world wars – where were you and what did you do in 2020–1?'[59] For some it proved a moment to reevaluate national democracy and search for a new political settlement, for others a reason to pursue the government's 'levelling up' further. It seemed an opportunity for a new Britain to emerge from Covid – an undeniable political opening. For a time, this began, with a new fiscal strategy, subtly forgetting structural deficit as a target and instead switching to a debt interest focus. Post-2021 politics had been undeniably altered. Large-scale intervention, both fiscal and monetary, had been deployed by the US and mirrored in Britain. Industrial strategy on PPE supply chains and Covid production/procurement proved necessary for a national economy in a dangerous global

---

[57] ONS, 'Prevalence of ongoing symptoms following coronavirus (COVID-19) infection in the UK', 2 February 2023.

[58] Seldon and Newell, *Johnson at 10*, p. 533.

[59] Hennessy, *Duty of Care*, p. 121.

system where zoonotic disease was one of many external dangers. Perhaps a new politics could have developed, designed to better protect the country from the numerous external shocks of the last decade.

But for all the hype of change, British politics shifted back to its 'normal' script, and Johnson's final year of his premiership – from the lifting of Covid restrictions in July 2021 until his downfall in July 2022 – marked a focus on foreign policy rather than his newly constrained domestic desires. A factor in Johnson's domestic inertia was the insurgent chancellor Rishi Sunak, who, backed by powerful Treasury orthodoxy, was intent on reducing Covid debt, which had peaked at just over 100 per cent of GDP.[60] There was no 'build back better', nor was it clear what Johnson would have actually done if the fiscal room had been allowed. On balance, however, the pandemic proved the worst external shock Britain had faced since 2010. The performance by Johnson's government, as Rachel Sylvester notes in Chapter 5 and the Covid Inquiry has investigated, could have been far better, and thus the costs and pain of the pandemic less severe. There were also opportunities missed in the recovery from Covid. But if there is one external shock that warrants an asterisk on the performance and stability of government in the 2010–24 period, Covid was it – a novel, highly complex disease that would have deep effects on Britain's economic and political outlook even if the handling had been improved. Its legacy, particularly with inflation, was brutal and will continue to be felt for years to come.

THE RUSSO-UKRAINIAN WAR

No prime minister since Winston Churchill had to grapple with a large-scale war on the European continent. In 1999 Blair had led an intervention in Kosovo based on his 'doctrine of

---

[60] Institute for Fiscal Studies, 'How did COVID affect government revenues, spending, borrowing and debt?' (accessed at https://ifs.org.uk/taxlab/ta xlab-key-questions/how-did-covid-affect-government-revenues-spending-b orrowing-and-debt, 4 November 2023).

international community' later laid out in his Chicago speech, but his foreign policy of interventionism, as with the size and scale of the war, proved ephemeral.[61] The Russo-Ukrainian War came at a time of global weakness and overshadowed any European conflict since 1945. Twelve months earlier the UK had still been in lockdown, US democracy was reeling in the aftermath of the Capitol Hill riot of 6 January 2021, EU vaccine supplies were still catastrophically low and China was experiencing the pain of an early housing crisis and the effects of a 'zero Covid' policy. By spring 2021, American and British intelligence were detecting whispers of a possible Russian invasion of Ukraine. By October these whispers had become definitive shouts of increasing Russian mobilisation on the Ukrainian border – war was coming. The UK felt so sure of an imminent conflict that, led by Defence secretary Ben Wallace, anti-tank aid was sent in haste in late 2021.[62]

The war, analysed in Chapter 4 by Michael Clarke, began on 24 February 2022. The Ukrainians, expected to collapse like the other Western-funded army in Afghanistan had eight months earlier, survived. The Battle of Kyiv was determined mostly around the Hostomol and Vesyhiv airports and the Russian battle columns arriving from the north in Chernihiv and east to Sumy. The Ukrainian army effectively held, before pushing back the primary Russian advances in the south, and stabilising the eastern front. The vital port of Odesa was saved, as was regional capital Kharkiv – which had been heavily bombed. But Ukraine, in a strategic decision to prioritise Kyiv, had lost key cities, including Kherson (without a fight due to alleged sabotage and ill-organisation), and eventually the industrial stronghold of Mariupol, where over 21,000 had died, as well as most of the Donetsk and Luhansk regions.[63]

---

[61] Christopher Hill, 'Foreign policy', in Anthony Seldon (ed.), *The Blair Effect: 1997–2001* (London: Little Brown, 2001), pp. 340–3.

[62] Seldon and Newell, *Johnson at 10*, pp. 425–6.

[63] Serhii Plokhy, *The Russo-Ukrainian War* (London: Allen Lane, 2023), pp. 183–8.

But the initial Ukrainian defence proved resilient in a way many Westerners had never imagined possible for a borderlands nation struggling to establish its national sovereignty in the face of a powerful neighbour. Zelenskyy's skilful political leadership and the Ukrainian army's staunch defence, regardless of how disorganised Russia was, catalysed a change in global politics. Sanctions, led by a coalition of Johnson and President Biden, were imposed on Russia. Europe rapidly transitioned to the more expensive liquid natural gas (LNG) as Russia progressively limited oil and gas supply to Europe. Ironically, China and India's switch to Russian gas actually reduced the demand for LNG, making it more affordable.[64] However, the war added significant inflationary pressures to the global system, which created large constraints on the Conservative government, as analysed in the next section. As Clarke notes in Chapter 4, the conflict also ensured further military and financial pressures in an attempt to defend Ukraine, leading to increased defence spending in order to refill stockpiles.

But, if the Russo-Ukrainian War is truly analysed from a British perspective it's debatable if, beyond obvious economic impacts, there were any substantial political or governing negatives for the prime minister. Arguably the war momentarily helped Johnson who, mired by scandal and struggling for a cohesive vision, used the crisis, as Ukrainian historian Serhii Plokhy stated, 'to very decisively reassert [Britain] within European politics' and his own position as PM.[65] Wars are always a significant risk for PMs, especially when they intertwine the conflict's success with their own premiership. This has produced dramatic successes as seen with Thatcher in the 1982 Falklands War or John Major in 1990 Gulf War, but also caused unmitigated damage to premierships, notoriously with Blair's Iraq in 2003 or Anthony Eden's Suez in 1956. The Russo-Ukrainian War, however, was not a war with British armed forces actively engaged – instead it was the army's lethal aid through its

---

[64] Ibid., p. 291. [65] Ibid., p. 253.

stockpiles and arms industry, along with its intelligence services, which were the active forces helping Ukraine.

The crisis was a chance for the UK to engage with its updated defence policy enabling the government to exercise point three of its 2021 Integrated Review (IR) as a leading defender of the liberal democratic community.[66] The Russo-Ukrainian War posed the question of whether Britain could readjust its (and more importantly Europe's) economic integration with Russia in order to align economic policy with geopolitical strategy. This was a test, with heavy economic consequences, but it was a test many in Britain were willing to take – one which offered important geopolitical opportunities but also stored up challenges for the future. It was not, however, a major *political* constraint.

INFLATION AND ECONOMIC STAGNATION

The 2022–3 inflation crisis had a myriad of causes, some stronger than others. A possible primary cause for the crisis was Covid – with the world economy still in a very vulnerable state. As a result, supply chains were still inefficient and constrained, while the labour market remained tight with many vacancies from those who had not returned to the workforce after Covid. There had also been the beginnings of a slight paradigm shift, with supply chains becoming more regionalised and strategic, as economist Ed Conway put it at the time: 'the idea that you should simply buy technology from wherever is cheapest – which is, mostly, to say China – is fast losing credibility'.[67] This move away from hyper-globalisation, influenced partly by 2008 and the resultant politics of populism, was later continued in President Biden's impactful Inflation Reduction Act (IRA) and

---

[66] *Global Britain in a Competitive Age, the Integrated Review of Security, Defence, Development and Foreign Policy*, 16 March 2021 (www.gov.uk/government/c ollections/the-integrated-review-2021).

[67] Ed Conway, 'Broke Britannia', *New Statesman*, 5 July 2023.

CHIPS Act, as well as Europe's response with large green subsidies.[68] This nascent shift towards regional and national production has reshaped supply chains and undoubtedly added to the factor of inflation. The other desire of Biden's two Acts, in conjunction with his previous Stimulus, was to run the US economy 'hot' to fuel recovery after Covid. The Fed gladly acquiesced, less concerned about the prospect of a 'wage–price spiral' due to the inherent weakness of the trade unions after the 1980s changes.[69] This detail is significant as some economists argue that, regardless of the Bank of England's or Treasury's actions, if the Fed was set on pumping the global economy (through Covid QE) it would inevitably mean the UK would feel the inflationary effect too.[70]

If the Covid recovery laid the foundations for inflationary pressures, the Ukrainian War catalysed those fears. Putin's invasion in February 2022 began a period of significant inflation increases, with Russia and the West entering a war of sanctions and trade – particularly on energy. Without ease of access to Russian oil and gas, and the disruption of Ukraine's food production, large inflationary pressures were mounted on European economies. In the UK, between January 2022 and January 2024, food inflation rose 24.8 per cent, which accounted for thirteen previous years of increases in just two years.[71] According to the Energy & Climate Intelligence Unit, gas price increases (February 2022 – February 2023) alone cost an extra £50 billion – 60 billion, a sixfold increase on normal consumption costs.[72] Brexit also contributed to higher inflation with importing goods, especially

---

[68] Adam Tooze, *Chartbook #221: IRA and the Fed,* 17 June 2023 (accessed at https://adamtooze.substack.com/p/chartbook-221-the-ira-and-the-fed, 30 August 2023) and Javier Espinoza and Sam Fleming, 'EU opens subsidy race with US to fight exodus of green projects', *Financial Times,* 9 March 2023.

[69] Tooze, *Crashed,* pp. 289–90.   [70] Conway, 'Broke Britannia'.

[71] Brigid Francis-Devine et al., 'Rising cost of living in the UK', House of Commons Library, 8 March 2024.

[72] 'The cost of gas since the Russian invasion of Ukraine', Energy & Climate Intelligence Unit, 21 February 2023 (accessed at https://eciu.net/ana

food types, taking longer and requiring more paperwork. Labour flows have decreased from the EU, with economic immigration from the continent reducing in percentage. Overall, it's slightly harder for businesses that need easy access to goods and high-skilled labour to find it – leading to increased costs.

The short-term impact of inflation requires further attention. As inflation peaked in October 2022, at a remarkable 11.1 per cent, the cost of living crisis surged. Liz Truss introduced an emergency energy price cap, later tapered (but continued) by chancellor Jeremy Hunt and prime minister Rishi Sunak. Truss's downfall was seemingly intertwined with rising inflation: the markets lost faith in her government and the Bank of England's ability to control rising costs (leading to higher interest rates and government debt repayments). However, the trigger of her exit was not the external shock of inflation but Truss's own mini-budget – listing £45 billion of unfunded tax cuts without assured market, OBR, Treasury or BoE support.[73] The political effect of the crash in market confidence was an enforced shift of government – from economic expansion to fiscal conservatism. But it was the economic pain that lingered, mostly through higher debt costs when interest rates continued to rise until July 2023, reaching 5.25 per cent. The economy paid the price. One area that felt acute pain was mortgages, with average two-year fixed deals reaching 6.86 per cent in late July, and five-year fixed peaking in early August at 6.37 per cent.[74] For a housing market which had experienced rates of just 2.35 per cent a mere eighteen months earlier, it was a big shock – and one which deeply hurt household income.[75] According to the OBR, 2022–3 confirmed the largest

lysis/reports/2023/the-cost-of-gas-since-the-russian-invasion-of-ukraine, 30 August 2023).

[73] Josh Kirby and Georgie Frost, 'MoneyFacts data', *The Times Money Mentor* (accessed at www.thetimes.co.uk/money-mentor/article/mortgage-rates-uk-news-will-they-go-down/, 30 August 2023).

[74] Anthony Seldon and Jonathan Meakin, *Truss at 10* (London: Atlantic, 2024).

[75] Ibid.

year-on-year living standards drop since records began with a 2.2% decrease of household disposable income.[76] In May 2023 the Office for National Statistics (ONS) found that 66 per cent of adults were still reporting an increase in the cost of living, while 92 per cent believed it was the key issue facing the UK.[77] Inflation cannot be used as an explanation for Johnson or Truss's political downfalls – though both were partially constrained by it. In reality, Johnson's last year of economic policy was deadlocked because he could not work with his chancellor nor govern effectively. Truss is purely responsible for her own downfall. These were primarily internal political crises, and self-inflicted ones at that, not purely external problems. One should also note previous Conservative and Labour governments' inability to better insulate the economy from volatile inflationary pressures – especially in the energy industry, where more secure supply, or better use of excessive energy profits, evident in countries such as France, helped to limit inflation to just under 6 per cent during the 2022–3 crisis.

In partnership with high inflation, the UK has suffered a period of low growth. The increase in interest rates, due to inflation, has played a role in the UK's slow growth, as has its weak capital and business investment for years (and a post-2020 Brexit effect) – hence Hunt's business investment allowance policy in March 2023. However, the OBR continues to forecast negligible growth. Hunt's tax cuts in the Autumn statement (2023) and March budget (2024) have failed to fundamentally alter the economic outlook.[78] Higher growth would have allowed for easier spending decisions when external shocks hit. The constraints on Sunak's government have thus been significant: higher borrowing costs – both due to interest rates and the Truss scare in the

---

[76] OBR, 'Economic and fiscal outlook', March 2024 (accessed at https://obr .uk/efo/economic-and-fiscal-outlook-march-2024/).

[77] ONS, 'Public opinions and social trends', 2 June 2023 (accessed at www .ons.gov.uk/peoplepopulationandcommunity/wellbeing/bulletins/publi copinionsandsocialtrendsgreatbritain/17to29may2023).

[78] Andy Haldane, 'Britain's hunt for growth goes on', *Financial Times*, 9 March 2024 (accessed at www.ft.com/content/86d4729b-343a-47e2-8118-3ad83f26ed34).

bond markets. The basic electoral conservative coalition has also been harmed by the ending of low interest rates.[79] One slight positive is the increasing tax receipts from inflation (and the ability to deploy the silent but significant policy of fiscal drag in the freezing of tax thresholds). But seeing as inflation was caused by many factors outside Sunak's control, it is an area which must rest heavy in our minds when evaluating his governing period – it is, arguably, one of the ultimate constraints in a market-based economy once embedded. The asterisk is harder to extend to previous premierships, specifically the self-inflicted downfalls of Johnson and Truss. If Keir Starmer becomes prime minister in 2024, the next book in the *Effect* series will have to place caveats on the underlying inflation and high interest rates he may inherit – an obvious limiting factor on what a government can feasibly do and something he and Labour will have to overcome if he wins office.

CONCLUSION

It is easy to get lost in the complexity of events and crises covered in this chapter. Put simply: a lot has happened. Not every exogenous factor deserves the classic 'caveat' status when judging the 2010–24 period of Conservative government. What has made this period highly abnormal is the rate at which international crises have filtered into the British political system. However, while many of these external shocks have produced difficult policy choices, none have terminally intertwined with the British political system as happened in the 1970s: the shocks have also occurred, apart from the Ukrainian war inflation crisis, during a period of favourable monetary conditions and stable energy supply.

The prelude of the 2008 GFC was a difficult start for any government to inherit, placing the very global market system in doubt and forcing the government to prioritise stability as every structurally significant UK bank shuddered with fear. It is easy to forget the degree of danger which faced a UK economy heavily

---

[79]   Stephen Bush, 'End of cheap money era manifests itself in voter "realignment"', *Financial Times*, 15 August 2023 (accessed at www.ft.com/content/26180d8e-9ef3-4e73-843b-6f636c665618).

reliant on the globalised capitalism of the City. The crash caused a large loss of GDP and capital, and contributed to a period of wage and productivity stagnation. However, the monetary innovation of QE, and the doggedly low interest rates guaranteed by central banks which persisted, were opportunities for Cameron's government – enabling cheap borrowing (and spending) and thus a less constraining economic recovery. When the GFC combined with the Eurozone crisis, further emphasis was placed on economic stability in the face of national defaults. This spectre of European debt disintegration had significant impacts on the governing period – namely the fast and fruitful Lib Dem-Conservative coalition negotiations in a country under acute market pressure and averse to cross-party negotiations. Largely ignored, however, is how the Eurozone crisis created the opportunity for Osborne and Cameron to strategically craft the national-debt default narrative which enabled austerity measures. Those measures have aged badly, and in part contributed to the UK's weakened state heading into further crisis – such as low growth, health vulnerability (see Chapter 9) and energy infrastructure.

Whatever underlying feelings of democratic deficit felt by the UK population before 2008, the following eight years exponentially increased it. The GFC, with its UK taxpayer-funded bailouts, helped to sow the seeds of popular resentment against the establishment – hardly helped by other timely stories of expenses scandals and bankers' bonuses – that is without mentioning the inequalities fuelled by QE or austerity. The Eurozone crisis damaged the aura around the superiority arguments for EU mechanisms, while also fuelling a degree of economic immigration making Cameron's pledge impossible. On immigration, the 2014–16 crisis only increased the salience of borders and sovereignty: summarised in a Vote Leave campaign centred on control. The high politics of Cameron's failed renegotiation, the timing of the vote, Johnson and Gove's gamble, Remain's strategic mistakes and Vote Leave's overall impact all have their significant place in the Brexit vote, but all would have been mostly ineffective without the impact of underlying global shocks on our democracy. The aftermath of the vote is another pain point for the 2010–24 government, seeing four different prime ministers grapple with the negotiations and impositions of Brexit. The party, and country, became divided and politics, as such, stopped working. The economy has, in the short term, been seriously damaged. Theresa May's government, for all her strategic failings, must get the largest benefit of the doubt. However, seeing as the main trigger for the vote, and the external shock's role in the result, lies with Cameron and the party, there cannot be much absolution for the government as a whole. The 2010–24 Conservative government's record will always be complicit with Brexit's repercussions – good and bad.

Brexit's delivery in 2020 coincided with one of the hardest shocks the country has had to face: Covid. With a weakened political system, and loss of the UK's largest trading partner, Britain was not best placed to deal with a dangerous pandemic. The nation faced deaths, economic downturn and countless difficult choices as the government battled against an unknown global pandemic – though it must be said leadership and policy undeniably failed at times. Finances were heavily hit and governing time for anything else practically vanished for a year. The recovery from Covid, however, did offer opportunities for the government after the revitalising possibilities of industrial strategy between a market–government initiative of the vaccine. The after-effects of Covid were not escaped quickly – and it's questionable if they could have been. Of all the external shocks, this was the harshest. It would have warranted the largest caveat on any of the government's records even if it had conducted its action and vision in a professional and clear manner. Johnson's actions (especially post-2021) have ensured that any asterisk is harder to attribute, though easier for the lasting impacts of Covid in health and finances which Sunak has faced.

The last two shocks again potently combined, with the Russo-Ukrainian War creating geopolitical instability with its physical nature comparable to that of World War II mass-European warfare. The inflation crisis, silently brewing, was catalysed by the war, with food and energy prices skyrocketing. The government's hand was indisputably weakened – with borrowing costs increasing and the country in desperate need of expensive policies such as price freezes in a cost of living crisis. But Ukraine also offered an opportunity for the Johnson government to place the UK at the heart of European politics once again, constraining a key enemy in Russia, while also evaluating the Integrated Review strategy against the very real threats it predicted in 2021. To simply explain the shocks of inflation and economic downturns as simple external factors is perhaps being too kind. For Sunak the policy opportunities were minimised, but for Cameron, May and Johnson there were many opportunities, especially considering the favourable monetary and energy conditions. However, by the early 2020s missed opportunities of the early 2010s had begun to hurt the Conservative Party and constrain the government's options – none more so than in times of inflation. The low growth is certainly not explicable just through external shocks, nor the absolute impact of inflation, especially when compared to European inflation rates. The 2010s governments must share part of the responsibility for the position the country had found itself in by the inflation crisis.

In evaluating all six shocks in full against the last fourteen years of Conservative government, one must note the context around paths taken and policies made within the constrained positions each of the five prime ministers found themselves in. When placing the premierships against the compounding crises it must be said that the earlier premierships in the 2010–24 period had more space, agency, fiscal headroom and better geopolitical conditions to make their political decisions and enact policy. Their failures would increasingly strain later governments. However, a crisis can never be simply viewed as a total negative. The best governments and the top prime ministers have utilised shocks to their advantage and remade the state, and sometimes the world, in their image. Some would argue that as Britain slipped to the sixth largest economy, with heavily reduced global power and no longer part of a meaningful economic bloc it is almost impossible for governments to escape the negatives of global shocks or have an impact on the world stage. To a degree this is correct. But in previous periods of crisis-bred economic and geopolitical readjustment, whether between 1945 and 1951 or 1979 and 1997, the most impressive prime ministers have successfully taken the opportunities provided by external shocks. Others, in the 1970s, or late 2000s, were consumed by them. Yet even those that were brought down by external crisis have a legacy they can defend before resorting to the external shock as a caveat to explain what they couldn't do.

No one should view any conclusions drawn in any of the forthcoming chapters on the 2010–24 governments without considering the political and economic crisis on which these prime ministers acted. However, external shocks should not be used as a complete exoneration from possible failure. The era of global shocks did not produce a world of complete political losers – though, at times, even the best have struggled. But it is in times of global struggle when the best are proven. It is for the rest of the contributors and readers to decide whether the 2010–24 governments succeeded or failed.

3

The Economy

Paul Johnson, Carl Emmerson and Nick Ridpath

INTRODUCTION

From the moment the Coalition government was formed follow-ing the general election in May 2010, the new prime minister, David Cameron, stated that its first priority was to 'reduce the deficit and restore economic growth'.[1]

The parliament from 2010 to 2015 was certainly dominated by the fiscal consolidation, more widely known as austerity. The Global Financial Crisis (GFC) had opened up a budget deficit – that is the difference between total government spending and total government revenues – that was at a record high for the UK since 1946–7 and the focus on getting it down involved cuts to public spending on a scale that had not been delivered in recent decades. Despite the shock of the Brexit referendum result, by 2019, the current budget – that is the gap between total govern-ment revenues and non-investment spending – had, just about, been returned to surplus.

The twin shocks of Covid-19 and the subsequent 'cost of living crisis' saw the deficit grow again, reaching a new record high in 2020–1. As we approach another general election the fiscal situ-ation continues to dominate economic debate as the combined effects of these three shocks on borrowing has been to leave government debt at above 90 per cent of national income, more than twice its pre-financial crisis level (of around 35 per cent), and not falling. In contrast to the period between 2010 and 2019, the

---

[1] Queen's Speech 2010, Lords Hansard, 25 May 2010, col. 5.

parliament that began in December 2019 has seen big increases in both spending and tax.

While the deficit did fall from 2010 to 2018 it was more painful and more protracted than originally planned. It was blown off course by events. The record on restoring growth has been even worse. The UK's economy grew slowly throughout the 2010s, and has struggled to weather the shocks of the 2020s. Productivity and national income per capita have been virtually stagnant, with serious implications for wages and living standards.

These two key themes of the last fourteen years have intertwined. Poor growth has driven the increase in the size of the national debt relative to national income.

The 2010s were remarkable not only for poor economic performance and the scale of public spending retrenchment, but also for the loosest monetary policy in history. The Bank of England Bank Rate never rose above 0.75 per cent between March 2009 and May 2022. It had never been that low before in the more than 300-year history of the Bank of England. That pushed up asset prices, including house prices, and combined with tight fiscal policy and terrible earnings growth to entrench an advantage for an older, wealthier generation. Higher inflation and sharply increased interest rates present new challenges at the tail end of this period.

We start this chapter with an overview of the performance of the economy since 2010, where we discuss growth, productivity and wages. We then discuss the possible causes of the poor performance, and what policymakers did, or didn't do, that might have contributed to it. Next, we turn to an overview of the two distinct eras of fiscal policy since 2010: the austerity and then policy stagnation of 2010 to 2019, followed by fiscal responses to the series of shocks the UK weathered from 2019 to 2024. Finally, we touch on the monetary policy of the Bank of England, and how it interacted with government policy throughout the period.

THE STATE OF THE ECONOMY

Relative to the decades leading up to the Global Financial Crisis, the performance of the economy has been very poor. Figure 3.1 highlights this. The solid line shows actual GDP per capita, the dashed line what it would have been had growth continued on its pre-financial crisis path. If this had happened, GDP would have reached £50,200 per person by 2023, a 35 per cent increase since 2008. Instead, it was £39,400, an increase of just 6 per cent over a fifteen-year period. Economic growth this slow over this long a period has no precedent in the UK since at least the end of World War II.

The international comparison in Figure 3.2 demonstrates that the UK is not unique. Other major European economies like Germany (which had done much better through the Global Financial Crisis) and France have also experienced historically slow growth over this period. The United States has done somewhat better, especially since 2019, reflecting in part both different effects of economic shocks and quite different policy responses. While differences are not huge over the period as a whole, the UK has performed poorly since 2019, relative both

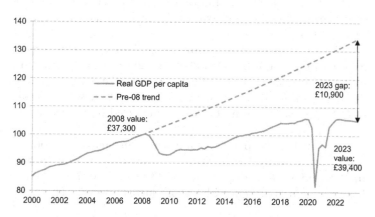

Figure 3.1 GDP per capita compared to pre-recession trend. Indexed, 2008 values equal to 100

Source: Office for National Statistics series IHXW (Gross domestic product (Average) per head, CVM market prices: SA). Pre-recession trends based on authors' calculations of growth rate from 2000 to 2008.

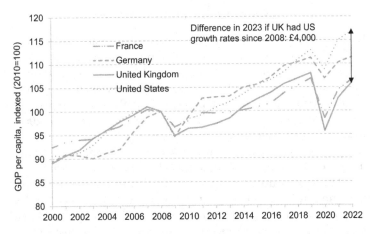

Figure 3.2 GDP per capita compared to the US and the EU. Indexed, 2008 values equal to 100
Source: IMF World Economic Outlook Database. Difference comparisons based on authors' calculations.

to past performance and to some other countries. This has taken the form both of a bigger hit to the economy than other countries during the Covid-19 pandemic, and a relatively sluggish recovery from it.

The EU27 as a whole has done rather better. GDP per capita grew by 14 per cent between 2008 and 2023, in part reflecting catch-up by some of the former communist countries like Slovenia and the Czech Republic, which now have similar levels of GDP per capita to the UK when measured on a Purchasing Power Parity basis.

For much of the period what became known as the 'productivity puzzle' lay at the forefront of the debate about poor growth in the UK and across Europe.[2] Figure 3.3 shows how the economy has continued to struggle with low productivity growth. There was

[2] See Alina Barnett, Sandra Batten, Adrian Chiu, Jeremy Franklin and María Sebastiá-Barriel, 'The UK productivity puzzle', *Bank of England Quarterly Bulletin,* Q2 (2014); Alex Bryson and John Forth, 'The UK's productivity puzzle', IZA Discussion Paper no. 9097 (2015).

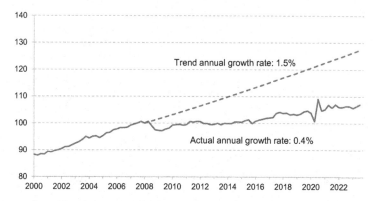

Figure 3.3 Labour productivity compared to pre-recession trend. Indexed, 2008 values equal to 100

Note: Pre-recession trends based on authors' calculations of growth rate from 2000 to 2008.

Source: Office for National Statistics series LZVB (UK Whole Economy: Output per hour worked SA).

strong growth in labour productivity in the run-up to the Global Financial Crisis. Since then labour productivity has almost entirely stalled: it is only 7 per cent higher than it was in 2008. The UK's labour productivity has lagged behind other countries much more than its GDP and GDP per capita have: output per hour worked has since 2008 grown more slowly in the UK than in every G7 country besides Italy. Big increases in the employment rate have boosted UK output, but it will not be possible for the employment rate to grow forever. For GDP per capita to continue to keep pace with even the poor economic performance seen in Western Europe, let alone return to pre-Great Recession growth rates, productivity will need to improve.

The minimal productivity growth since 2010 has also had meaningful negative consequences for living standards. Poor growth in output per hour worked has passed through to a stagnation in the wages workers receive. Figure 3.4 shows how nominal and real wages have changed since the Conservatives took office. The top line shows that in nominal terms, the average earnings of UK employees have increased

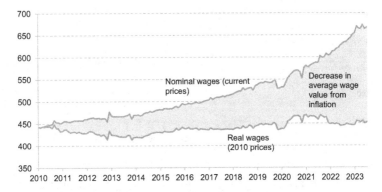

Figure 3.4 Nominal and real wages since 2010 (measured in average weekly earnings, £)
Source: Office for National Statistics Series KAB9 (AWE: Whole Economy Level (£): Seasonally Adjusted Total Pay Excluding Arrears) and Series D7BT (CPI INDEX 00: ALL ITEMS 2015=100)

from £450 to £650 per week. However, when accounting for inflation, there has been no increase in real wages in that time: £650 was worth as much in 2023 as £450 was in 2010.[3] Unusually for the aftermath of economic downturns, there was no recovery in real wages following the Great Recession, with real wages continuing to drop until 2014, since which they have very slowly recovered to 2010 levels. This lack of growth in real wages is unprecedented in the last two hundred years of British economic history: there has been no longer period without growth in real wages since the Napoleonic Wars.[4]

---

[3] It is worth noting that small growth in productivity and stagnation in real wages does not imply an additional puzzle in real wages. This can be explained by the fact that wages are adjusted by CPI (a measure of household inflation), which has grown by more than the GDP deflator (a measure of economy-wide domestic inflation), by which productivity is deflated.

[4] Nicholas Crafts and Terence C. Mills, 'Trends in real wages in Britain, 1750–1913', *Explorations in Economic History*, 31 (1994), 176-94; Charles H. Feinstein, 'New estimates of average earnings in the United Kingdom', *Economic History Review*, 43 (1990), 595–632; and ONS: Series Code LNMQ.

This has, naturally, created a significant drag on working-age household incomes, which have also grown much more slowly than before the Great Recession. Without wage increases, only increased levels of employment have pushed up incomes among working-age households. (Benefits and tax credits have been cut, and taxes overall have risen.) Meanwhile, household incomes for those over 65 have increased, as a result of increased income from pensions, leading to a dramatic increase in the proportion of pensioners at the top 15 per cent of the income distribution, and a decrease in the proportion in the bottom 15 per cent of the income distribution, while the trend for working-age households has gone the other way, held back by lagging wages.[5]

Meanwhile, there has been little change in income inequality, at least across the bulk of the distribution. Wages at the bottom of the distribution have been boosted by significant increases in the living wage/minimum wage and earnings by increased levels of employment, but this has been offset by cuts to benefits and tax credits. At the top end, at least as far as the 95th percentile, wages have been stagnant and, for some of the highest earners, taxes have risen quite sharply.[6]

THE PRODUCTIVITY PUZZLE REVISITED

The UK's struggling productivity can be broken down into two periods. The first is the period until 2019, under the premierships of David Cameron and Theresa May, where growth was poor, but not uniquely so compared to other advanced economies. The second is that covered by the parliament of 2019 to 2024, under the premierships of Boris Johnson, Liz Truss and Rishi Sunak, where the UK emerged from a turbulent time for the global economy having fallen behind its neighbours.

[5] Pascale Bourquin, Mike Brewer and Thomas Wernham, *Trends in Income and Wealth Inequalities*, IFS Deaton Review of Inequalities (London: Institute of Fiscal Studies, 2022).

[6] Jonathan Cribb, Giulia Giupponi, Robert Joyce et al., *The Impact of the National Living Wage on Wages, Employment and Household Incomes* (London: Institute of Fiscal Studies, 2021).

One of the problems in determining the cause of the productivity slowdown is that many of the candidate explanations have been much longer standing than the slowdown itself. For example, investment (public and private) as a share of GDP fell sharply after the Great Recession, and has remained below the rest of the G7. However, as Figure 3.5 shows, the UK had a relatively low level of investment since long before the Conservatives came to office. Some of this can most likely be put down to the heavier focus of the UK economy on services, which are less capital intensive, but it is hard not to suspect that the UK may be suffering from chronic underinvestment, with little progress since 2010.

Public investment levels fell sharply in 2010 as capital spending was cut as part of the response to the record deficit. Low public investment over most of the 2010s is perhaps particularly noteworthy given the historically low interest rates at which the government could borrow during the period. Indeed, then permanent secretary to the Treasury Nick, now Lord, Macpherson said in 2023 'With hindsight we probably should have taken advantage [of low interest rates] and borrowed more when

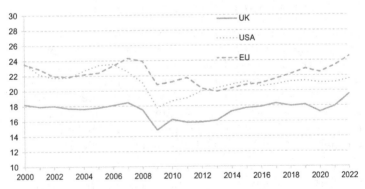

Figure 3.5 Investment levels compared to the US and EU. Gross fixed capital formation as a percentage of GDP
Source: IMF World Economic Outlook Database.

times were more stable . . . and invested more.'[7] Capital spending was ramped up later in the period, reaching its highest level in decades by the early 2020s. But by 2023 the forward plans were to cut the real level of capital spending over the subsequent five years. Here, as elsewhere, the lack of consistency in economic policy over the period from 2010 to 2023 has been quite striking – sharp cuts, followed by an increasingly serious increase, followed by further planned cuts.

The inconsistency of public investment is perhaps best exemplified by High Speed 2, aimed at increasing rail speed and capacity between London, Birmingham, Manchester and Leeds. Announced by the then chancellor George Osborne, it was subject to frequent discussions about whether it should be cancelled by successive chancellors long after construction had already begun, before the Leeds connection was dropped by Boris Johnson and the Manchester connection dropped by Rishi Sunak. This inconsistency only serves to add risk for firms looking to make long-term investment decisions.

The path of the corporation tax rate has demonstrated this lack of consistency even more powerfully. Between 2010 and 2018 George Osborne and then Philip Hammond gradually brought down the main rate from 28 to 19 per cent, in an effort to spur private sector investment. By 2023 the headline rate had returned to 25 per cent though even that reversal was not without its own convoluted path – the new higher rate having been announced by Mr Sunak while he was chancellor, reversed during the 38-day chancellorship of Kwasi Kwarteng and then reinstated by Jeremy Hunt on the day he replaced Mr Kwarteng. Aside from the merits of lower corporation tax for encouraging investment, the uncertainty created around policies intended to encourage businesses to invest in the UK has most likely served only to discourage such investment.

One major macroeconomic success may provide another part of the answer to the productivity puzzle: employment has boomed, and unemployment has remained remarkably low. The

---

[7] BBC Radio 4, *Analysis* (www.bbc.co.uk/programmes/m001r7rj).

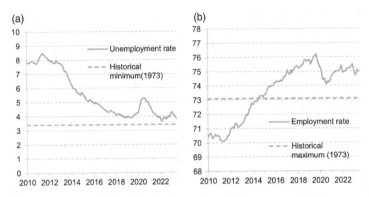

Figure 3.6 Unemployment and employment rates since 2010. All figures shown as a percentage

Source for employment rate: Office for National Statistics Series LF24 (employment rate, aged 16 to 64, seasonally adjusted). Historical data from records since 1970. *Source for unemployment rate:* Office for National Statistics Series MGSX (Unemployment rate, aged 16 to 64, seasonally adjusted).

left chart on Figure 3.6 shows the course of the unemployment rate over the Conservatives' time in power. While it was high after the Great Recession, it fell to near historic lows over the premierships of Mr Cameron and Mrs May, and has stayed there in spite of stormy global macroeconomic conditions. This cannot simply be explained by workers leaving the labour force, either: the right chart on Figure 3.6 shows that the employment rate has gone far past historic highs, as more and more people have entered the labour force with particularly strong growth in the employment rate among women. The paradigm shift to low unemployment and high employment has been a welcome development, and has helped keep household income rising in spite of stagnant wages, and has helped to boost GDP per capita. However, it may have also contributed to lower productivity: at lower levels of unemployment, less productive workers have entered the labour force. This is clearly not the main explanation for poor productivity, but to the extent that it plays a role, it is less of a problem.

The capacity of the economy to produce jobs is understated even by these figures. Rising activity rates, increases in the state pension age, and substantial net immigration have between them led to an increase of around 4 million in the number of people in employment between 2010 and 2023 – an increase from 29 million to 33 million.[8]

The 2016 referendum vote to leave the European Union and eventual exit in January 2020 has also had harmful impacts, though their precise scale is hard to disentangle from the impacts of Covid-19. Several academic analyses have attempted to estimate how UK exports have been affected. The decision for the UK – apart from Northern Ireland – to leave the single market led to new non-tariff barriers to trade for British exporters. The evidence suggests that this significantly damaged exports of goods, particularly where firms form part of global manufacturing supply chains.[9]

Figure 3.7 shows business investment since 2010. There is a sharp fall relative to the post-2010 trend from around the date of the June 2016 referendum: the uncertainty created by the Brexit vote, and associated political turmoil, appears to have led to a substantial decrease in business investment relative to what we might otherwise have expected. Indeed, by the start of 2023 business investment in the UK was no higher than it was in June 2016 – a phenomenon not replicated in other advanced economies. This gap between the pre-Brexit trend and the outturn amounts to approximately £4,200 per worker per year by 2023 and a shortfall of this magnitude can be expected to have negative consequences for growth. Frequent shifts in possibility of different outcomes of the Brexit negotiations, from an anticipation of remaining in the single market in pre-referendum

---

[8] Table 2, series MGRZ, www.ons.gov.uk/employmentandlabourmarket/people inwork/employmentandemployeetypes/datasets/summaryoflabourmarket statistics

[9] See, for example, Jun Du, Beyza Satoglu and Oleksandr Shepotylo, 'How did Brexit affect UK trade?', *Contemporary Social Science*, 18:2 (2023), 266–83; Jonathan Portes, 'The impact of Brexit on the UK economy: reviewing the evidence', VoxEU Column, 7 July 2023.

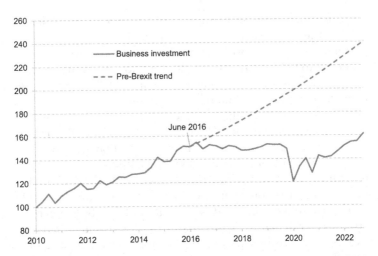

Figure 3.7 Business investment compared to pre-Brexit trend. Indexed, 2010 values equal to 100

Note and source: Office for National Statistics, Series NPEL (Gross Fixed Capital Formation: Business Investment: CVM SA). Deflated according to GFCF Deflator. Pre-Brexit vote trend based on authors' calculations.

rhetoric to frequent high-profile threats of a 'No Deal' Brexit with tariffs on trade, most likely damaged investment in Britain more than a less chaotic strategy that led to the same post-Brexit arrangements with the EU would have done.

One expected consequence of Brexit that has not materialised is a sharp decline in overall immigration. A decline in immigration from the EU has occurred, but it has been more than made up for by an increase in immigration from outside the EU, though the skill mix and location of workers has been affected by this shift.

In total, quantitative estimates based on comparisons to similar countries estimate the negative effect of Brexit on economic activity to be equivalent to approximately 5 per cent of GDP.[10] The Office for Budget Responsibility (OBR) judges that post-Brexit trading arrangements will reduce UK productivity

---

[10] John Springford, 'The cost of Brexit to June 2022', Centre for European Reform, November 2022.

by 4 per cent relative to remaining in the EU.[11] However, it is worth noting that it is incredibly hard – to say the least – to disentangle the impact of Brexit from other growth issues the UK has faced since 2016, particularly those that did not affect comparable countries.[12] In the years since 2019, the global economy was hit by shock after shock, which the UK will have different exposures to and may have dealt with comparatively worse.

The first of these is the Covid-19 pandemic. In all countries, this created a major downturn in output, as economic activity stalled – first because of precautions even in sectors such as manufacturing and construction and then for a much longer time after that in public-facing sectors, with demand completely eliminated in many service sectors. At the time of writing it appears that the UK economy has recovered less well than many others from the effects of Covid – though it is worth saying that problems with measurement and the interpretation of economic data through this period make even this judgement subject to some uncertainty.

The UK's response to the pandemic was, fiscally, bigger than that in most other countries. The Coronavirus Job Retention Scheme (CJRS) announced by the then chancellor Rishi Sunak, widely known as furlough, subsidised the wages of many private-sector employees who did not work during the pandemic, in an attempt to preserve the links between employees and employers. Many European governments implemented similar policies, in an attempt to ensure that employees could return to their jobs quickly. However, the United States took a different approach, and rebounded much quicker from the pandemic. Instead of preserving worker-firm links, they implemented generous unemployment insurance, which meant that workers searched for new jobs as the economy reopened. Given

---

[11] Office for Budget Responsibility, *Brexit Analysis* (https://obr.uk/forecasts-in-depth/the-economy-forecast/brexit-analysis/#assumptions).

[12] Graham Gudgin and Saite Lu, 'The CER doppelganger index does not provide a credible measure of the impact of Brexit', UK in a Changing Europe Working Paper 5 (2023).

that the post-pandemic economy looked rather different from the pre-pandemic economy, this freedom to seek out other work may well have helped productivity in the US. In contrast, the Conservatives maintained the furlough scheme, which kept employees attached to their pre-Covid jobs, until the autumn of 2021, when all restrictions on movement and gatherings had been lifted. The gross cost of the CJRS scheme over the nineteen months it was in place came to £70 billion, with a further £28 billion spent on support for the self-employed. The untargeted scheme looks to have been maintained for too long, slowing the reallocation of workers to new sectors. It may well have harmed productivity in the aftermath of the pandemic, as workers remained at jobs that did not realise their full potential.

As the significance of Covid-19 waned, another major shock hit western economies. The Russian invasion of Ukraine caused a major upwards shock to global oil and gas prices. This created fewer problems for countries with greater energy independence, either because they had their own sources of fossil fuels, like the US, or because they mostly used nuclear power, like France. Since the UK's energy supply mostly comes from gas, the UK economy may well have suffered more, with inflation persisting for longer potentially necessitating greater and more damaging action to bring it down.

THE PUBLIC FINANCES

When the Conservatives came to office in 2010, they pledged that their first priority was to 'reduce the deficit and create growth'. The Great Recession resulted in very big increases in borrowing across Europe, and the UK's total deficit amounted to 10 per cent of GDP, or £160 billion, an unprecedented level in modern times. This was seen as unsustainable both by the outgoing Labour government, and by both members of the incoming coalition government. While the coalition government planned to cut the deficit more quickly than promised by Labour, there was in truth considerable cross-party agreement on the need to focus on repairing the public finances albeit with some differences over the speed and mix of the fiscal medicine that should be administered. Debt rose from 35 per cent of GDP to 65 per cent of GDP between 2007 and 2009, and was forecast to still be increasing in 2016.

As Figure 3.8 shows, the road to bringing the national debt under control has been a rocky one. The deficit fell under the coalition government, though considerably less quickly than planned, in large part because economic growth was lower than expected. By 2015 debt had stabilised as a percentage of GDP. It wasn't until the eve of the pandemic that current budget balance (borrowing only for investment) was reached, this having been the key fiscal target for most of the period. In 2015 George Osborne even legislated a supposed commitment to get to overall budget balance from the financial year 2019–20, an economically unwise move, and something rarely achieved over the last century. This target was appropriately swiftly binned in the aftermath of the Brexit referendum.

By 2019 the deficit was at normal levels of around 2 per cent of GDP and the debt stable. Since then national debt has risen again mostly as a result of the huge levels of borrowing required to cover the costs of the Covid-19 pandemic, and then big additional spending to protect households and businesses from the

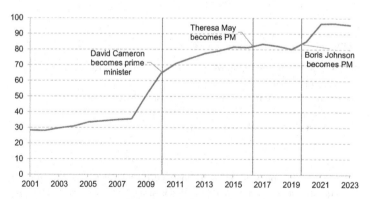

Figure 3.8 Total national debt as a percentage of GDP
Source: Office for Budget Responsibility.

worst effects of the rise in energy prices.[13] Even as these costs have dissipated, public spending has risen over the 2019 parliament and, despite a swiftly growing tax burden, the national debt has risen further and is now stuck rather than decisively falling.

Future governments will have to reckon with this. Getting the national debt back on a falling path will require some combination of tight spending, yet more tax increases, and a much more impressive growth performance.

Figure 3.9 plots in more detail the course of the current budget deficit since 2010. It shows how Mr Cameron and Mr Osborne leant on spending cuts, rather than tax rises, to bring down the deficit – in a ratio initially designed to be about 80 per cent spending cuts to 20 per cent tax rises, which by 2015 turned out to be more heavily towards spending cuts.[14]

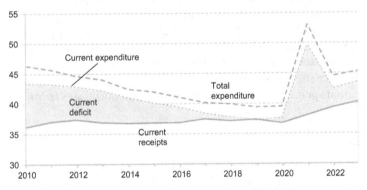

Figure 3.9 Public expenditure and receipts since 2010. Each shown as a percentage of GDP
Note: Current expenditure is equal to current spending plus depreciation. Total expenditure is equal to current expenditure plus net public investment.
Source: Office for Budget Responsibility.

[13] Much of the uptick in 2020 is driven by a drop in GDP, though the ratio not coming back down as GDP rebounded indicates the role increased borrowing played.
[14] Carl Emmerson and Gemma Tetlow, 'UK Public finances: from crisis to recovery', *Fiscal Studies*, 36 (2015), 555–77.

Non-investment spending dropped from 43 to 38 per cent of GDP over the course of Mr Cameron's premiership. This meant a real-terms cut to spending, unprecedented in modern history – more details below – though expenditure never dropped below where it was on the eve of the Global Financial Crisis. The project of eliminating the current deficit was completed under Mrs May and Mr Hammond, until the government ran a small current budget surplus in 2019. Covid and the 2022 cost of living crisis resulted in temporary surges in spending. But the 2019–24 parliament has also seen substantial permanent spending increases. This was partly a change in political direction, partly a response to the ongoing ageing of the population (with the large cohort born just after World War II now placing increasing demands on the NHS and social care systems), and partly a consequence of cuts in the previous decade being reversed to a small degree. In response, the 2019–24 parliament has seen the biggest increase in the tax-to-GDP ratio of any parliament since at least World War II, taking it to its highest level over that period.

In the rest of this section we will look at two periods separately. The first of these, 2010–19, could perhaps be split further: Mr Cameron and Mr Osborne's time in office was focused heavily on deficit reduction and austerity. The period 2016–19 was overshadowed by uncertainties around Brexit, but fiscal policy did not change dramatically. The second period, 2019–24, saw a string of major adverse economic shocks and big increases in both spending and taxation. For each era, we will break down the key fiscal decisions that defined it.

THE COALITION AND AUSTERITY (2010–2019)

The coalition government assumed office in extraordinary and difficult circumstances. The Global Financial Crisis of 2008 had led to an economic downturn and a large fiscal deficit. Net borrowing represented almost 10 per cent of GDP, a then post-war record high, as tax receipts fell and spending continued to increase. The scale of the problem was a focus of the 2010 election campaign, with the three major UK parties emphasising the reduction of the deficit as a key priority. In the run-up to the election, all three pledged to implement fiscal tightening worth almost 5 per cent of national income by 2017, though the Conservatives aimed to get there a year quicker.

Larger differences lay in the planned composition of fiscal tightening – the Conservatives' aim was focused more heavily on spending cuts than either of the other two main parties, and this showed in their approach in government. There were some big tax increases, although also some big tax cuts, so the net tax rise was dwarfed in size by the spending cuts, which represented 5 per cent of GDP over the course of the coalition government, one of the biggest reductions as a proportion of GDP of any British government in the post-war period. More remarkably, this meant that the government cut spending in real terms, and did so on the biggest scale of the post-war era.

Of course, it was not only the UK which faced large deficits in the aftermath of the Global Financial Crisis. Much of Europe was struggling, with Spain, Greece, Ireland and others plunged into much larger fiscal crises. In terms of the scale of fiscal restraint, the UK was also not an outlier. Mostly, the level of deficit reduction a country pursued was a function of how the Great Recession affected the deficit: Ireland and Spain pursued much stronger austerity measures, Germany much weaker. Compared to other large economies with similar increases in borrowing after the crash, like France and Italy, Britain's fiscal tightening was similar in size. Rather, what was unique about the approach taken by the Conservatives, compared even to their ideological bedfellows, was that this was mostly done through spending cuts. The centre-right governments of Italy and France at the time, on the other hand, raised taxes by more than they cut spending.[15]

These spending cuts were felt very differently by different parts of the state. Mr Cameron and Mr Osborne specifically ring-fenced the NHS, schools and foreign aid from cuts to their day-to-day

---

[15] Carl Emmerson and Gemma Tetlow, 'Fiscal responses of six European countries to the Great Recession: a crisis wasted?' [Comment] Institute for Fiscal Studies (2015) (accessed at https://ifs.org.uk/articles/fiscal-respons es-six-european-countries-great-recession-crisis-wasted, 31 August 2023).

budgets. Figure 3.10 shows this variation, both in total size of change and in percentage change of non-capital spending. The Department of Health and the Foreign, Commonwealth and Development Office can be seen as the only two departments protected by budget increases. Growing pressures on the NHS meant that health resource spending actually increased by 15 per cent in real terms – though that still represented a much slower rate of growth than it had enjoyed historically, and was barely enough just to keep up with the growing size and age of the population. Despite the ring-fencing of day-to-day school budgets, other areas of education were heavily cut. The tripling of tuition fees represented a significant cut in spending for the Department for Education, though significantly increased university budgets. Further education also faced significant cuts, while flagship New Labour education policies, Sure Start and the Education Maintenance Allowance, had their funding heavily cut or were scrapped. Overall this resulted in a smaller education budget.

Areas that were not ring fenced had their budgets cut by much larger percentages. Current spending by the Ministry of Justice dropped by a quarter, with prisons, courts and legal aid all suffering cuts. Funding to local authorities from central government was cut in half over the course of the Cameron years. Those authorities most dependent on central funding – largely poorer and metropolitan areas – suffered most. Social care services, a large proportion of local budgets, were prioritised, though still faced cuts. This left other services like libraries, planning and local subsidies for public transport facing cuts often in excess of 30 per cent.[16] Other central government departments, including Defence, Transport and the Home Office, also faced large cuts.

In the early period capital budgets were cut much more drastically than resource spending, and spread more evenly across departments. This meant, for example, significant reductions in spending on the maintenance and construction of new

---

[16] Tom Harris, Louis Hodge and David Phillips, *English Local Government Funding: Trends and Challenges in 2019 and Beyond* (London: Institute for Fiscal Studies, 2019; available at https://ifs.org.uk/publications/english-l ocal-government-funding-trends-and-challenges-2019-and-beyond-0).

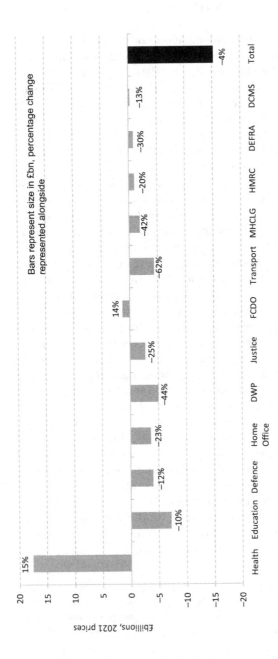

Figure 3.10 Spending changes by department, 2010–19

Note: Size of bar represents change in £billions, figure on chart represents percentage change. X-axis ordered according to department budgets in 2010. Baseline taken as 2011 for Home Office and Ministry of Housing, Communities and Local Government, due to the transfer of police grants between them in 2010.

Source: Office for Budget Responsibility.

schools, hospitals and local government buildings. Capital spending on prisons and courts, while smaller proportions of the capital budget, also faced large cuts. These costs did not have a major effect during the period of austerity, but mean that it is likely that future governments will need increased capital spending to account for these major cuts. The health service is suffering already from poor building maintenance and lack of machinery. The problem with Reinforced Autoclaved Aerated Concrete (RAC) in schools, which came to light in 2023, cannot be put down entirely to cuts over the 2010s but will have been exacerbated by them.

The above all relates to public-service spending. Meanwhile spending on pensioner benefits was protected, and indeed increased, while working-age benefits were made less generous. The Coalition introduced the triple-lock principle for the State Pension, which guaranteed that it increased each year by the maximum of 2.5 per cent, inflation and growth in average earnings, meaning that over time it would increase relative to both prices and earnings.

Reforms to working-age benefits took a very different trajectory. Significant cuts were made to the generosity of means-tested benefits and tax credits and hence to the new Universal Credit (UC) that is still being rolled out fourteen years after it was announced.[17] Delays and cuts apart, the introduction of UC, which rolled six different working-age benefits into one and which has simplified and automated the benefit system, may in the end be seen as one of the lasting achievements of the Conservative years.

Other smaller cuts proved particularly controversial, including a cut to housing benefit for working-age individuals in social housing deemed to have a spare bedroom – dubbed by its opponents as the 'bedroom tax'. The Conservatives went into the 2015 election pledging further big – but largely unspecified – cuts to working-age welfare to be implemented within two years.

---

[17] Nicholas Timmins, *Universal Credit: From Disaster to Recovery* (London: Institute for Government, 2016; available at www.instituteforgovernment.org.uk/publication/report/universal-credit-disaster-recovery).

Following the general election, cuts were delivered on a slower timescale, with the biggest being a four-year cash freeze to most benefits. The 'two-child limit', which limits means-tested support (in most cases) to only the first two children, was introduced from 2017. Its effect will grow over time as it only applies to children born after its introduction, but it has already been shown to be increasing rates of child poverty.

The taxation picture under Mr Cameron and Mr Osborne was more mixed than that of spending. Taxes rose overall. The biggest increase was an increase in the main rate of VAT from 17½ to 20 per cent, raising £13 billion. Other tax increases came from National Insurance, the rate of which the government increased from 11 to 12 per cent in 2011, raising £9 billion. Further increases to National Insurance came from an end to the practice of contracting out of paying some National Insurance in 2016, raising another £4 billion. Substantial cuts to the generosity of caps on the amount that can be contributed to a pension each year represented a further tax increase.

At the same time, and remarkably in the context of austerity, the income tax personal allowance was increased by a third in real terms, removing 2 per cent of adults from the tax base and reducing the level of income tax for all but the highest earners, at a cost of £5 billion per year. Meanwhile, the main rate of corporation tax was cut from 28 to 19 per cent between 2010 and 2018. This was partially offset by a broadening of the tax base from increased anti-avoidance measures, but the policies in combination still reduced receipts by £13 billion. The additional rate of tax, paid by those on the highest incomes, was also cut from 50 to 45 per cent. The effect of this was weakened by the threshold for paying it being frozen at £150,000, and then eventually being cut to £125,000 in 2022, meaning that the number of people paying the higher rate of tax increased fourfold over the period. Finally, the real rate of fuel duties was cut consistently over the decade. Each year, planned increases to rates of fuel duties have been either delayed or cancelled, a practice that continued beyond 2019. As a result, they have been frozen by successive governments since 2011.

A NEW ERA OF TAX AND SPEND (2019–2024)

The 2019 election was fought on a very different manifesto to that in 2015. Rather than promising cuts the Conservatives were focused on areas demanding increased spending or investment, including plans to 'level up' less prosperous parts of the country, and major plans to increase investment, including large capital investment in hospitals.

The sprouts of increased overall spending could be seen earlier, however. In 2018, Mrs May pledged to return NHS spending to historical growth levels and as chancellor Mr Hammond set out a rising trajectory for capital spending. Plans for real-terms spending increases were announced by Mr Sunak in the new government's first budget in early March 2020, just before it started to become clear how severe the Covid-19 pandemic would be.

These plans would be blown out of the water by the pandemic, as spending increased massively, and borrowing rose to 17 per cent of GDP, a level never before seen in the UK in peacetime. Most of this growth in borrowing came from £310 billion of discretionary spending to support households, businesses and public services in the pandemic. Almost half of this came in the form of direct support to households, most notably through the furlough scheme.[18] The rest came from a combination of relief to firms and increased health spending, with £37 billion spent on the 'test and trace' system and £12 billion on personal protective equipment. The furlough scheme and the £20 per week uplift to Universal Credit remained in place beyond 2020, both expiring in September 2021. Meanwhile, pressures on health spending continued into the second year of the pandemic, with additional costs from high hospitalisation numbers and the vaccine rollout.

---

[18] Pascale Bourquin and Tom Waters, 'The temporary benefit increases beyond 2020–21', in *IFS Green Budget 2020* (London: Institute for Fiscal Studies, 2020), pp. 372–415.

As a fraction of GDP, this increase in discretionary spending ranked towards the top of all advanced economies, with only the US spending significantly more.[19]

Public spending has remained well above its pre-pandemic level, as shown in Figure 3.9, with increases quite broad based. Health spending has continued to grow as a share of the total, and demographic change will continue to push up spending on health, pensions and social care.

The second crisis of the parliament arrived with the war in Ukraine and the subsequent surge in energy costs. The government stepped in with the Energy Price Guarantee, which subsidised household energy bills, limiting the energy price cap to £2,500 per year for the average household. This was estimated to cost the government £37 billion, or 1.5 per cent of GDP.[20] This enormous, and entirely untargeted, intervention was in fact announced during the short-lived Liz Truss premiership. By contrast with the £45 billion package of tax cuts this policy remained almost completely intact, though Jeremy Hunt raised the cap to £3,000 for the winter of 2023.

Meanwhile, inflation increased to levels not seen in decades, driven in part by the energy price rises, but also by other supply constraints that emerged in the aftermath of the pandemic. The magnitude and duration of both the fiscal and monetary response to Covid also played a role. Subsequent increases in interest rates not only raised costs for mortgagors (now only 30 per cent of households, well down from a peak of 40 per cent in the mid 1990s) but also hit government finances as the cost of servicing debt grew from around 1 per cent of national income to over 4.4 per cent at its peak in 2022–3, a figure that had not been exceeded since 1948–9. While these costs will fall somewhat as inflation eases, debt interest spending is set to remain much higher than historically, and will continue to constrain fiscal policy for years to come. This is the

[19] International Monetary Fund, www.imf.org/en/Topics/imf-and-covid19/Fiscal-Policies-Database-in-Response-to-COVID-19

[20] Autumn Statement, 2022, www.gov.uk/government/publications/autumn-statement-2022-documents/autumn-statement-2022-html

consequence of much-elevated levels of debt due to the three crises since 2008 (the Global Financial Crisis, Covid-19 pandemic and the cost of living crisis) and interest rates at higher levels than we had during the 2010s.

As the UK weathered a series of global macroeconomic shocks, the Conservatives provided a macroeconomic shock of their own. The election of Liz Truss as Conservative Party leader and prime minister led to a tumultuous forty-nine days. In a 'mini-budget' on 23 September 2022, her first chancellor Kwasi Kwarteng introduced a series of major tax cuts. In his time as chancellor, Rishi Sunak had promised to introduce a new health and social care levy – 1.25 per cent tax on earnings paid by employees, employers and the self-employed – supposedly hypothecated to fund increased health and social care costs, as well as the first increase in the main rate of corporation tax since 1973, from 19 to 25 per cent, each to take place in April 2023. Mr Kwarteng immediately scrapped both of these, and then added some additional tax cuts of his own, including the abolition of the 45 per cent additional rate of tax, paid by those with an income over £150,000. In total, this was estimated to represent a £45 billion tax cut, equivalent to 2 per cent of GDP, one of the largest tax-cutting budgets in history. No tax rises or spending cuts were announced to offset the cost of these cuts, and no forecast of the effects was presented, either by the chancellor – who on his arrival at the Treasury had immediately dismissed its permanent secretary – or the Office for Budget Responsibility. And the chancellor promised there would be more to come.

The markets responded swiftly and negatively. The pound fell to its lowest-ever level against the dollar. Gilt rates, the interest rate on government debt, rose by over a percentage point within a week, a greater change than gilt markets normally see over the course of a year. The Bank of England intervened in bond markets to protect Defined Benefit pension schemes. Mr Kwarteng, and then Ms Truss, were ejected from Downing Street. Their replacements, first Jeremy Hunt as chancellor and then Rishi Sunak as prime minister, swiftly reversed most of the tax cuts, though the health and social care levy was not reintroduced. Gilt rates dropped back down to near their level before the mini-budget upon their replacement, before increasing broadly in line with interest rate rises by the Bank of England.

The biggest tax rise of the 2019–24 parliament, though, came about through the freezing of income tax and National Insurance thresholds, initially for four years (announced by Mr Sunak as chancellor in 2021) and extended to six by Mr Hunt. In an era of high inflation this now looks set to be a £40 billion a year tax rise. It will undo two-thirds of the increase in the income tax personal allowance which was such a centrepiece of the coalition's tax policy between 2010 and 2015, and will result in a near doubling of the number of higher-rate taxpayers. In a final twist in November 2023, Mr Hunt announced a cut in National Insurance from 12 to 10 per cent, more than reversing the increase put in place by Mr Osborne in 2011. Despite costing £10 billion, this tax cut is far smaller than the amount raised by freezing personal tax thresholds through fiscal drag.

The overall effect of these policies will be to take tax as a fraction of national income to its highest-ever level. The 2019–24 parliament will see taxes rising by more than any other parliament since at least 1950. Elevated debt – and with it debt interest spending – slow growth and pressure to spend more on health, pensions, defence and many other areas of public provision, suggest to us that this high level of tax is here to stay.

MONETARY POLICY

While the Bank of England has operational independence, it is impossible to understand the course of the economy over the last fourteen years without considering the role monetary policy has played. The period between 2010 and 2021 was marked by an unprecedented period of low interest rates and use of unconventional monetary policy (quantitative easing, QE). The shift to higher interest rates since 2022 has been sharp and sudden, with significant implications for both households and government debt. Figure 3.11 shows the course of monetary policy since the

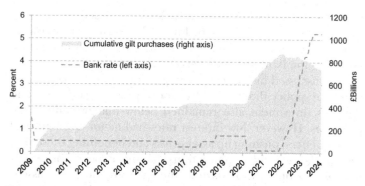

Figure 3.11 Bank rate and quantitative easing
Source: Bank rate data from Bank of England. Quantitative easing data from Office for National Statistics Series FZIU (BoE: Asset Purchase Facility: Total gilt purchases)

Global Financial Crisis, when the Bank of England began its programme of quantitative easing.

The dotted line shows that the bank rate stayed below 1 per cent from March 2009 all the way until May 2022. As the Bank's traditional main tool for monetary policy, it was kept low in response to sluggish economic growth and fears that any tightening would risk deflation, and edged down further in response to expected negative shocks, including the Brexit vote and the pandemic. The Bank also made use of QE, in attempts to stimulate the economy. There have been a series of QE interventions following an initial injection of cash in 2009. In 2011, the Bank purchased £175 billion worth of gilts over the course of a year in an attempt to provide some additional stimulus. Another smaller programme of £60 billion immediately followed the Brexit vote. The Bank responded to the Covid-19 pandemic by reducing interest rates from 0.75 to 0.1 per cent and also by the largest QE programme of all, with over £400 billion of assets purchased over the course of less than two years, taking the total amount of money injected into the economy to over £800 billion. Given the supply constraints created by the pandemic, which are likely to have been almost as severe as the hit to demand, the scale of QE from 2020 has been described by many as excessive – former Bank of England governor Mervyn King called it 'a terrible mistake', and said that printing money was the last thing the Bank should have done.[21]

As discussed in the section on growth, twelve years of loose monetary policy did not lead to more public investment, and business investment also remained below that of comparable countries. However, low interest rates had major distributional consequences, pushing up asset prices and benefiting those with wealth (largely older generations) at the expense of largely younger people who started the period with few assets. Younger generations have experienced much lower levels of homeownership than did older generations at the same age. Middle-income people in their early thirties are now still largely renting privately, rather like their low-income peers. Twenty-five years ago they were, like their better-off peers, largely home-owners. By contrast, homeownership rates among older generations are around 80 per cent. They benefited not only from rising asset and house prices driven in large part by loose monetary policy, but also by fiscal policy which has generally benefited those over state pension age more than the young. At the same time, as we have seen, wages have been stagnant. The combined impact of increases in asset prices and stagnant wages means it is harder for someone reliant on wages to save their way up the wealth distribution. This generational redistribution will be an important legacy of the 2010s. It also means that for younger generations inheritances are becoming increasingly important, further reducing scope for social mobility.[22]

Assuming interest rates stabilise at levels nearer 2 or 3 per cent than the less than 1 per cent that was prevalent for so long, some of these effects may unwind a little as asset prices

[21] Mervyn King, 'The Bank of England made a terrible mistake', *New Statesman*, 12 October 2022.

[22] Sonya Krutikova, Lindsey Macmillan, David Sturrock and Laura van der Erve, *Intergenerational Mobility in the UK* (London: Institute for Fiscal Studies, 2023; available at https://ifs.org.uk/publications/intergenera tional-mobility-uk).

partly fall back – though the immediate pain will be felt by a relatively small group of the population: those largely in their thirties with big outstanding mortgages relative to their earnings. By 2023 we had already seen a fall in household wealth fall by around one-third of national income.

As we saw above, the combination of higher interest rates and weak growth is also having a major effect on the public finances. It means that for the next few years at least we will need to run primary surpluses – that is raise more in revenue than we spend on everything other than servicing the national debt – just to stop the national debt being on an ever-increasing trajectory. That is not something that has been achieved since 2001–2.

CONCLUSION

The period between 2010 and 2024 has been extraordinary from an economic point of view. For most of the period, interest rates were at their lowest level in history. Earnings grew at probably their slowest rate in more than 200 years. The period from 2010 to 2019 saw the biggest and most sustained cuts in public spending since World War II. These changes accelerated a trend which saw older generations and those with substantial assets doing far better than younger generations.

Brexit led to a complete reappraisal of our trading links with the European Union, and created huge economic uncertainty. The response to the Covid pandemic involved unprecedented levels of public support for the economy, and borrowing on a scale even greater than that seen during the financial crisis which set the context for the period as a whole. Taxes rose by more during the 2019–24 parliament than in any parliament since at least 1945.

The period of low interest rates came to an abrupt end from 2022 when a combination of international and domestic pressures forced up inflation. Real earnings and real incomes fell. The legacy for the next government will be a difficult one. Expected economic growth is slow. The fiscal policy responses to the three shocks of the financial crisis, Covid-19 and the cost of living crisis mean that public sector debt is high, and a combination of high interest rates and low growth means that even running a primary surplus will not be enough to get it on a downward trajectory. That primary surplus appears to be achievable only with a combination of further tax rises – from a record high base – and extremely tight spending settlements. As of autumn 2023 spending plans for the period after the election imply cuts for many departments, which we might suspect will not be delivered.

High debt, low growth, and high interest payments have arrived at a particularly difficult time. Demographic pressures are starting to tell. It is hard to see how health spending – the biggest part of public spending – will do anything other than rise quite swiftly over the coming years. The share of adults over the state pension age will also increase, and pressures on social care are intense. International pressures and commitments mean that defence spending, a traditional source of savings to spend elsewhere, is more likely to have to rise than be available for cuts. Most other areas of public spending suffered cuts through the 2010s which look hard to repeat.

Through all this the Coalition and Conservative governments made some big choices. The first was to focus on deficit reduction achieved largely through spending cuts in the first half of the 2010s. This included big cuts in investment spending, which are likely to have created longer-term problems not only for economic growth but for the performance of public services. Many other countries chose a more even balance between tax rises and spending cuts. Like previous governments they, relatively, prioritised health spending over spending on other public services. They chose to increase the level of state pensions while cutting working-age benefits – thereby exacerbating the distributional consequence of loose monetary policy. The introduction of Universal Credit is likely to be seen as a lasting, if vastly delayed, achievement. Overseas aid spending rose swiftly to 0.7 per cent of national income, though has since been pared back to 0.5 per cent. Local government, the justice system, prisons, have faced among the biggest spending cuts, and have struggled to cope.

In most respects tax policy has been notable only for its inconsistency. Quite contrary to initial intentions the legacy will be an income tax system in which far more people are paying higher rates of tax, and with more taxpayers than ever. The corporation tax, initially cut sharply, will be raising more as a fraction of national income than it has before in the UK on a sustainable basis, and more than in most OECD countries. VAT was raised straightaway and remains at 20 per cent, but it also remains unreformed and applicable to, by international standards, an unusually small fraction of spending. The one consistent change is the one that was denied in every Budget – each and every year chancellors promised that rates of fuel duties would rise in line with inflation in the following year, and each and every year they failed to do so. A much lower real rate of fuel duties and no plan to move to any form of taxation for driving electric vehicles is another unwanted legacy which the next government will need to deal with.

The growth and productivity slowdown from which the British economy suffered was far from unique among developed country economies. But on most forecasts the future looks harder. Inflation is higher in 2023 than in either the US or the Eurozone. Private investment and trade intensity fell relative to our competitors after the Brexit vote and implementation. Productivity per hour worked is 13 per cent less than in Germany and 8 per cent less than in France. On purchasing power parity metrics median household income is 22 per cent below Germany.

There are opportunities. A return to stable government with reasonably consistent economic policy should be enough to make some progress. There are evident opportunities to improve growth through shifting policy on investment, education, planning, tax, trade and elsewhere. But an incoming government will need to pursue any such policies from the starting point of a most precarious fiscal situation. In a now infamous note the last chief secretary to the Treasury in the last Labour government told his successor 'there is no money'. That remains true today.

4

Foreign and Defence Policy

Michael Clarke

C OMING TO POWER IN 2010 in the teeth of the global
economic crisis, the Conservative-led Coalition government put a brave face on Britain's foreign and defence policy.
There would be continuity and, notwithstanding extreme pressures on the national economy, Britain would play to its
strengths in external relations – as it had always tried to do. Of
course, one of the most ubiquitous elements of continuity was
what the historian Peter Hennessy named as the 'management
of decline', the underlying structural challenge to Britain's foreign and defence policies that went back to the 1940s.[1] All British
governments since the 1960s had accepted the absolute decline
in Britain's role in the world, but they generally interpreted it in
relative terms as a series of hard-headed transformations.

The Coalition government would do the same. So Britain
would continue its fifty-year trajectory of transition from being
one of the western 'pillars' of the international order to
a significant western 'player' in it; from having a 'special' relationship with the United States to having a 'significant' relationship; from being a 'global' economic power to a country good at
harnessing 'globalisation'; from fielding 'traditional' military
forces to 'transitional' military forces – something that still
packs a punch when bigger powers are again building up fearsome military establishments that Britain cannot afford. In this
vision, Britain can be a respected member of the international
community, pursuing its national interests and its own prosperity.

---

[1] Peter Hennessy, *Winds of Change: Britain in the Early Sixties* (London: Allen
Lane, 2019), pp. 217–19.

In a disorderly world it can aim to be recognised, as it was in the pre-imperial eighteenth century, fundamentally as a nation of 'polite and commercial people'.[2]

In this vein, Prime Minister David Cameron's premiership began from the proposition that he was a 'liberal conservative, not a neo-conservative' in foreign policy, and Foreign Secretary William Hague asserted that there would be 'no strategic shrinkage' in the country's global diplomatic profile, despite the economic circumstances. Foreign policy would be pursued on the basis of enlightened self-interest and involve a more explicit 'prosperity agenda'.[3] In that respect, the Coalition government was distinguishing itself from Labour's 'ethical dimension' in foreign policy and Tony Blair's enthusiastic embrace of the invasion of Iraq in 2003 and the re-engagement in Afghanistan after 2006. This Conservative-led government was getting itself out of those entanglements. And though its Liberal Democratic coalition partners put the country's foreign aid commitments into domestic law and demanded a fresh review of the nuclear deterrent, the traditional conservatism of the government's approach was clear enough. If the government could weather the immediate economic storm, it was hoped, there would be scope by the end of a first term in 2015 to be more expansive. As if to justify the cautious optimism of the early years, the London Olympics and Paralympics of 2012 were a resounding soft power success that boosted Britain's image all over the world. At least on the surface, an approach of restrained, Conservative-led continuity seemed to be alive and well.

The reality, however, was that the relatively stable power structures and institutions of the international world that for fifty years had provided the bedrock of British continuity in global affairs were changing very fast during this decade. The

---

[2] Paul Langford, *A Polite and Commercial People: England 1727–1783* (Oxford: Oxford University Press, 1989), pp. 1–7.

[3] David Cameron, *For the Record* (London: William Collins, 2019), pp. 145–6; Foreign and Commonwealth Office, 'Britain's foreign policy in a networked world', 1 July 2010 (www.gov.uk/government/speeches/britain-s-foreign-p olicy-in-a-networked-world–2).

international world underwent more structural change after 2010 than any time since the end of World War II, little of it conducive to British interests. And in the midst of this decade and a half – for a number of different reasons – Britain took itself off the international front line in a political nervous breakdown from which it is still trying to recover.

Far from continuing the generational transition to become a significant, savvy player in the globalised world, the Britain that emerges in the mid 2020s appears to its international partners to have been doing little more than succumbing to absolute and relative decline with little ability to 'manage' it one way or another. There are mitigating considerations, of course, and there may be some redemption for Britain in the later 2020s. But the 2008 global economic crisis, which Conservative-led governments inherited, steadily exposed underlying weaknesses in British foreign and defence policy that left the country a much-diminished presence in global politics and less able to defend its own national interests during turbulent years.

The Cameron approach to these growing foreign and defence policy challenges was essentially reactive. He believed that economic recovery was fundamental to Britain's ability to operate globally; William Hague was an experienced politician with a steady hand at the Foreign and Commonwealth Office (FCO); Andrew Mitchell and then Justine Greening were able development ministers; and defence spending, first under Liam Fox and then Philip Hammond, would have to be brought under tighter control. This team looked solid enough for 'liberal conservative' continuity during the early years. But it was being overtaken by events by the end of the government's first term and consistent political leadership was simply lacking. David Cameron was famously impatient with 'strategic thinking' of any sort, but particularly in foreign affairs, and he was increasingly distracted, first by economic and then by constitutional issues. After its early years, the government fell into a leadership merry-go-round in external relations. There were five prime ministers during this whole period, four of them after 2016. Cameron could have chosen to take more interest in foreign and security affairs while he was prime minister, but his successors after 2016 were simply consumed in the toxic politics of Brexit. Between 2010 and 2024 there were eight foreign secretaries, six of them after 2016; seven defence secretaries, five of them from 2016; nine ministers for foreign aid, seven of them since 2016. Only three ministers – Hague at the Foreign Office, Greening at the Department for International Development DFID (both before 2016) and latterly Ben Wallace at Defence – did four years in post. A couple of others did three years; all the others did less and in many cases their stewardship was measured in months during the hiatus between three prime ministers in quick succession. Little wonder that foreign, aid and defence policies were running largely on auto-pilot through most of this period, pending some stability and consistent thinking within Westminster and Whitehall.

THE MANAGEMENT OF CRISES: INTERNATIONAL CHAOS

To begin with, the 'no strategic shrinkage' slogan meant that all 196 of Britain's foreign missions would be maintained and the FCO was pressed to do more to contribute to the 'prosperity agenda'.[4] The prime minister's 'enlightened self-interest' would not go looking for crises to alleviate – still less with any Blairite crusading zeal – but would react to whatever came along with a hard-nosed pragmatism. And when the inevitable spending cuts and the beginnings of the Conservative-led 'austerity policies' were introduced in October 2010, it was evident that the foreign, defence and security establishments were reduced less than the departments of environment, business, or the Home Office, and considerably less than local government. The 2010 *Strategic Defence and Security Review* (SDSR) was criticised for its lack of vision, but in truth, the vision was to maintain the country's triple-A international credit rating without sacrificing too much of Britain's global profile. Spending cuts in October 2010

---

[4] See Foreign and Commonwealth Office, 'Britain's foreign policy in a networked world'.

in the order of 15 per cent had been widely anticipated, but, against Treasury advice, defence was only cut by 8.6 per cent in real terms. The FCO was cut by 24 per cent, but most of this was loaded onto the BBC World Service; only some 10 per cent was cut from the FCO's core budget in real terms. Indeed, the overseas aid budget, now fixed in law by the Coalition Agreement as 0.7 per cent of Britain's GDP, actually required an increase of 37 per cent.[5] The country's intelligence agencies, funded mainly through the Single Intelligence Account, were also known to have got off lightly. By 2015, it was generally assumed, the public finances would be back on track, so some of the pressure might be taken off austerity budgeting to let Whitehall departments breathe more easily.

Ministry of Defence budgeting was anyway ready for tighter scrutiny after 2010 as a series of military commitments wound down. The bulk of British troops had left Iraq in 2009 and were due to withdraw from any combat role in Afghanistan, when the Americans did, by 2014. There was time for the Royal Navy and the Royal Air Force to recapitalise their key military equipment programmes, and there would be time soon for the Army to refocus itself, and its future equipment, after the draining expeditionary operations in Iraq and Afghanistan. Meanwhile, counter-terrorist policies within Britain itself were proving effective – there had been no successful terror attacks on home soil since 2005.

Cameron and Clegg were also keen to replace the Cabinet committee for foreign and security affairs with a fully fledged National Security Council (NSC), and the creation of a specifically designated National Security Adviser. Accordingly, a new central machinery was brought into existence to deepen and streamline the inputs from across Whitehall to create a more powerful instrument serving the prime minister and Cabinet in making strategic decisions.

---

[5] Though it was actually expressed in terms of a percentage of Gross National Income (GNI). See also HM Treasury, *Spending Review 2010* (Cm 7942, October 2010), p. 20; Foreign Affairs Committee, *FCO Performance and Finances* (HC 1618, 2012), para. 19.

Sensible enough as it was, the drawback of this general approach was that Britain's international environment was not following the same lines of historical continuity. As crises and challenges emerged, the stakes became ever higher and potentially more serious for Britain. The problem was not that the NSC or the wider foreign and security bureaucracy could not see what was happening; indeed, there was a high degree of analytical clarity in the work that flowed into the NSC in these early years. The problem was rather that Britain felt it lacked sufficient means during austerity budgeting to rise effectively to the challenges, and the prime minister's own reactive mindset set the government's overall tone in such matters.

The emerging truth of Britain's international environment was based on what every serious analyst could see was a reversion to the dominance of great power competition in global affairs. The 'big four' – the US, China, Russia and India – were big in different ways and for different reasons, but they were the powers that, after an interregnum of more than a generation, were now creating the political weather for everyone else. The US–China relationship became increasingly competitive as Xi Jinping, undisputed Chinese leader from 2012, asserted his country's 'historical right' to a dominant and non-western role in the politics and globalised economies of the world. Russia's President Putin became steadily more assertive after the global economic crisis of 2008 and his invasion of Georgia that same year. And in 2014 Narendra Modi led his Hindu nationalist BJP party to power in India, finding a willing domestic audience for a more assertive foreign policy, particularly in relation to the strategic challenges it perceived Beijing to be posing to it with every passing year.

By the mid 2010s, it was evident that the second-rank and smaller powers of Europe would have to pursue their interests in the space between the geopolitical wheels of the big four that were again turning remorselessly. It was also apparent by 2015 that two of the big four – China and Russia – were now explicitly revisionist powers, each set on a major realignment of global politics and each prepared to manipulate and undermine the western-based rules of the international system. Meanwhile, the

United States was actively reorientating itself away from European and Atlantic concerns to Asian and Pacific matters. President Obama, taking office in 2009, was unimpressed by European politics and felt the Europeans should be far less dependent on US support in all matters. So too, in the Middle East. With indigenous US energy production at its strongest in over a century, Obama didn't want to be drawn into regional politics across the Levant and the Gulf. He wanted a nuclear deal with Iran that would restrain nuclear proliferation and have the effect of pressing a 'reset' button on traditional US commitments all across the region, not least to Israel. Though in the event, the US was not able to achieve much of a reorientation away from the Middle East and Europe, Obama's 'Pivot to Asia' was a serious US attempt to reassess its long-term strategic priorities and reflected nothing less than the reality – and inevitability – of open-ended US–China competition in Asia.[6]

Such underlying structural changes became all too evident as the government batted away successive international crises as they arose. The 'Arab Uprising' that gathered pace in 2011 began a process of revolution and counter-revolution, which threw the Middle East into rapid and violent geopolitical change that it had not seen since the Franco-British Sykes–Picot Agreement of 1916. The government was keen to take an assertive attitude towards Colonel Gaddafi in 2011 to prevent him massacring his own rebellious civilians. A British, French, United States-driven initiative to create a UN-mandated NATO operation to stop him seemed like a good exercise in muscular diplomacy. But the operation that began swiftly in March was militarily open-ended, and in April the US took a back seat, leaving Britain and France uncomfortably in the lead and a NATO alliance that was not militarily united – some refused to be involved, others agreed only with severe limitations. NATO's eight-month air campaign in Libya and its operational success actually left the alliance politically weaker rather than

---

[6]   Michael J. Green, 'The legacy of Obama's "pivot to Asia"', *Foreign Policy*, 3 September 2016.

stronger. The collapse of the Gaddafi regime also created the conditions for a second Libyan civil war, which began in earnest in 2014 alongside the progressive destabilisation of neighbouring Mali to the south, and thence in the Sahel more generally.[7] After the agonies of Iraq and Afghanistan, there was no appetite, and certainly no resource, to try another national reconstruction effort in Libya's case, or even some serious containment of the wider effects on the region.

The 'Arab Uprising' also provoked a full-scale and vicious civil war in Syria in 2012. This exposed more structural change in global politics, in two particular respects. One was in the toleration of the widespread use of chemical weapons during the conflict. The Assad regime had incontrovertibly broken the international taboo on chemical warfare by using the nerve agent sarin against several thousand civilians in the Damascus suburb of Ghouta. President Obama declared that a critical red line had been crossed and was prepared to take 'coercive' action, short of being drawn into the war itself. Cameron was on board and within eight days of the event, British aircraft and all the associated services were in Cyprus, ready for a joint strike against a range of Syrian targets. But with the shadow of 2003 hanging over it, the government recalled parliament and put it to a vote. It was a fiasco. The government contrived to make the issue seem eerily like a rerun of 2003. And it had no answers to the sensible strategic question of what the next move would be if a brief bombing campaign failed. The Commons motion was, by then, one that would simply delay a decision on strong action, though the government could have supported an alternative Labour motion that would have kept all options alive. In the event, the government lost its motion by thirteen – the first time since 1782 that a motion concerning war had been voted down. Instantly, the prime minister was on his feet in the Commons saying that parliament had spoken and nothing more could be done. Within seventy-two hours Obama had backed off any immediate

---

[7] Compare Cameron, *For the Record*, pp. 275–7, 286, with Borzou Daragahi, 'The years ago Libyans staged a revolution: Here's why it has failed', Atlantic Council briefing paper, 17 February 2021.

attacks, since Congress had then become doubtful. America's clear 'red lines' on chemical weapons, which Britain had backed so strongly, had been crossed with impunity by Assad. President Putin stepped in with a sham agreement from Assad that got the international community off the immediate hook.[8] Nevertheless, well over two hundred recorded chemical attacks on Syrian civilians followed.[9] It seems ironic that British policy, for once, had so much influence on Washington. But the damage was done, and in the years since, that irresolution of 2013 has been seen as pivotal to the decline of western influence across the region.[10]

The other respect in which Syria had real structural significance was in the way that Russia, emboldened by western hesitancy in 2013, stepped in directly to save the Assad regime from imminent defeat less than two years later. In 2015 Putin used both Russian regular elite forces and his favoured 'Wagner' mercenary group, along with the Russian air force, to win Assad's war for him. More chemical use followed, alongside systematic attacks on civilians that began with the targeted destruction of hospitals and medical facilities. By 2022, with Russian help in return for military bases at Tartus and Latakia, Assad was back in control of Syria and being rehabilitated into the Arab League. While the western powers had been pursuing a military counter-terrorist campaign against the barbaric 'caliphate' of the Islamic State terrorist movement between

[8] In April 2018, in the years of President Trump and Prime Minister Theresa May, there was a US, British and French air strike on Syrian chemical weapons after Assad's chemical assault on Douma. A handful of targets were hit, but beyond the rhetoric of enforcement, it had no discernible effect on the way Assad and his Russian backers conducted their civil war.

[9] The Syrian Network for Human Rights recorded 222 chemical attacks in the region between December 2012 and August 2023; 98 per cent by the Syrian regime, 2 per cent by Islamic State. See also Kenneth D. Ward, 'Syria, Russia and the global chemical weapons crisis', *Arms Control Today*, September 2001.

[10] Jordi Quero and Andrea Dessi, 'Unpredictability in US foreign policy and regional order in the Middle East', *British Journal of Middle Eastern Studies*, 48:2 (2021), 311–30.

2014 and 2019, Russian support for a regional power dictatorship in Damascus had been seen to work. It was a lesson not lost on other brutal dictators, and would-be dictators, across the Middle East and Africa.

It was evident that the policy establishment in Britain was prepared to address the crises of these years with some useful, limited, military resources in conjunction with the United States and insofar as they could make a difference, but there was little or no willingness for the country to take any leading diplomatic roles, either independently or, still less, at the head of any European diplomatic initiatives.

Most telling, and closer to home, the 2014 'Maidan revolution' in Ukraine against its pro-Moscow leadership began a cumulative crisis in Eastern Europe that affected energy, resilience and much besides. Facing the 'Maidan revolution', Putin orchestrated a counter-revolution in 2014 that immediately established Russian control in Crimea and, a few months later, manipulated unrest in the Donbas region to create self-declared republics in Luhansk and Donetsk. For him, as he subsequently boasted in a televised interview,[11] this was designed to bring Russian peoples left outside the Federation in 1991 back into the motherland; it was a new version of Catherine the Great's 'Novorossiya'.[12] The western world condemned it all, of course, but President Obama thought it was Europe's problem and he was anyway more preoccupied with Syria at the time.

Such Russian action not only fundamentally challenged international law but also the long-held behavioural norms of European international relations. Along with the US and Russia, Britain had been one of the signatories to the 1994 Budapest Memorandum, acting as a joint guarantor of Ukraine's security in return for Kyiv's agreement to surrender the nuclear weapons it had inherited when the Soviet Union collapsed. No other European state had been so confident in 1994 to involve itself

---

[11] On 1 March 2015. BBC, 'Putin reveals secrets of Russia's Crimea takeover plot', *BBC News Website*, 9 March 2015.

[12] Adrian A. Basora and Aleksandr Fisher, 'Putin's "Greater Novorossiya" – the dismemberment of Ukraine', *Foreign Policy Research Institute*, 2 May 2014.

in the negotiations, still less to offer a security guarantee to underwrite them.[13] But it was all quietly forgotten by London twenty years later in February 2014. Russia had egregiously breached its obligations under the agreement, so the whole thing was anyway invalidated. But the FCO and Downing Street failed even to acknowledge the wreck of Budapest to which Britain had put its signature. More than that, the government was frankly uninterested in getting involved in any diplomatic front to address the conflict. France, Germany and the EU External Relations Service took the lead in concluding the Minsk II process and the 'Normandy Format' that year to outline a way forward.[14]

For Britain, these crises added up to more than the 'events dear boy, events' characterisation of statesmanship's challenges famously attributed to Harold Macmillan.[15] These 'events' illuminated a depth of structural change between the major countries and corresponding power shifts in the regions most important to Britain. They also posed a more acute problem for Britain than for most of its European partners. Britain invested rather more of its political capital – and a great deal more of its defence and security capital – in relations with the United States. The relationship between Tony Blair and US President Bill Clinton had been very good. But Blair's, and then Gordon Brown's, relationship with George W. Bush was much more edgy. Bush was sentimentally warm towards Britain, but his administration was aggressive and divisive among the allies – and not only over the 2003 Iraq War. The Coalition

---

[13] See FCO, 'Joint statement by foreign ministers of UK, US and Ukraine on Budapest Memorandum', *Gov.UK*, 5 March 2014, which regretted that Russia absented itself, but remained determined to fulfil the intentions of the arrangement. France, by contrast, only agreed a diluted form of security guarantee in a separate, associated, document.

[14] Steven Pifer, 'Minsk II at two years', *Brookings Commentary*, 15 February 2017.

[15] Though it may be a famous misquotation used by Adam Raphael in a 1984 *Observer* article. Macmillan was never known to have said it, though he did once say 'the opposition of events' in answer to a similar question; but that was a phrase originally used by Winston Churchill in 1919.

government inherited the Obama administration that was much cooler on Britain. Washington spoke the language of 'liberal internationalism' but Britain had less to offer in that common cause during the decade, and the Obama administration was no less transactional in its approach to Britain than its Republican predecessor. And in reality, much of Obama's liberal internationalism was stymied by both the polarisation of US domestic politics and a relative decline in US influence abroad. It was not the superpower it had once been.[16] The NATO communiqué after the 2014 Summit in Wales pulled few punches and, unusually, named names as it committed the alliance to a series of specific actions in response to the 'threat' of Russia and the 'systemic challenge' of China to the western world order.[17] But the reality of western reactions to this approach were slipping steadily in the opposite direction to the rhetoric, certainly in Britain where the effects of the economic crisis were worryingly persistent.

If the international system was undergoing rapid structural, and largely malign, change, it was natural enough that leaders and officials might resist so stark a conclusion.[18] They thought – hoped – that Moscow and Beijing could be habituated into a managed evolution of the existing world order without fracturing the essential framework. Russia was seen as a constant problem for Europe, perpetually aggrieved and intermittently aggressive, but not a fundamental strategic threat unless it was somehow mishandled. Putin was the playground bully, but nevertheless a carefully calculating one. The collapse of this belief with the Russian invasion of Ukraine in 2022 can hardly be blamed on the policy elite; it was not an unreasonable position to take at the time and it was an assumption widely shared across the western world.

---

[16] Jeffrey Goldberg, 'The Obama Doctrine', *The Atlantic*, April 2016.

[17] North Atlantic Treaty Organization, *Wales Summit Declaration*, 5 September 2014 (www.nato.int/cps/en/natohq/official_texts_112964 .htm).

[18] See Peter Ricketts, *Hard Choices: What Britain Does Next* (London: Atlantic Books, 2021), chapter 5.

More at odds with the growing evidence was the 'systemic challenge' that China's new outlook posed for Europe. The Coalition government felt it could both mitigate this and exploit China's economic interest in Europe by creating a special economic relationship between London and Beijing. George Osborne, chancellor of the exchequer from 2010 to 2016, was a key driver behind an initiative that saw a state visit for Xi Jinping and a series of investment initiatives that were hailed as the fruits of a 'golden era' of collaboration between Britain and China now they had put the handover of Hong Kong behind them. But if this seemed to be going with the grain of China's natural influence in the globalised economy, it was going increasingly against the political grain of China's relations with western countries. The approach quickly foundered on the row over Huawei technology in Britain's 5G network, Chinese espionage networks, its industrial plundering of British innovation and increasing abuses against the Muslim Uighur population in China's Xinjiang province. The final nail in the coffin of the bilateral 'golden era' was Beijing's reaction to the Hong Kong protest movement in 2019.[19] The 1997 British handover agreement for Hong Kong had guaranteed the territory's special status within China until 2047. As its terms were progressively violated by Beijing, London's protests were simply waved away and accompanied by escalating threats. The 'golden era' was dead and could offer no economic leverage over Beijing's policy; Britain was powerless to influence events one way or the other.

The harsh fact was that no mitigation the western powers were prepared to offer could keep Moscow and Beijing sufficiently consensual to make them meaningful 'partners' in global politics.[20] Notwithstanding an awareness that environmental and climate change put all major producing countries in

---

[19] Jonathan Ford and Laura Hughes, 'UK–China relations: from "golden era" to the deep freeze', *Financial Times,* 14 July 2020.

[20] See, for example, Thomas Wright, 'China and Russia vs America: great power revisionism is back', *The National Interest,* 27 April 2014.

essentially the same boat, Russia and China had simply become adversarial powers for Britain at a time when it struggled to defend its own national interests effectively.

THE CRISES OF MANAGEMENT: DOMESTIC CHAOS

The years between 2012 and 2015 turned out to be extraordinarily important for the future direction of the external environment in which Britain would operate. If the government's policy had begun adequately in 2010 it was nevertheless being distracted by domestic challenges by 2014 and moving towards mere autopilot settings, which would not be relinquished until 2021 when a new path was mapped out in the Integrated Review. There were many mutually reinforcing drivers of this autopilot phenomenon.

Conservative governments didn't make it easy for themselves. It was not that the parliamentary party was riven with different views about foreign and defence policy. Unlike the Labour Party, Conservatives have always enjoyed a high level of consensus on external affairs – some disagreements, to be sure, over Israel and the Palestinians, or tactical differences over handling China – but Cameron's pragmatic liberal conservatism spoke for the vast majority. Unlike Tony Blair, whom he rather admired, Cameron certainly didn't like blueprints or road maps and after the Libya crisis became more sceptical in taking military advice. The government was happy enough to play its due role with the Obama administration in moving towards the 2015 nuclear deal with Iran, though there was always persistent concern about what the president's 'pivot to Asia' might really mean. Cameron took his NSC seriously, chairing almost all its weekly meetings. The NSC shifted the locus of influence partly away from the Cabinet's Joint Intelligence Committee, and the NSC began to suffer from the natural bureaucratic drag of Whitehall. But Cameron's government nevertheless made the body into a powerful instrument that could drive both the formulation and implementation of policy. It would serve any leader well as long as the prime minister had a clear vision of what he or she wanted to achieve.

But reactive pragmatism was a questionable approach to the turbulent times that 2014 presaged. The government was reduced to impotence when Israeli forces moved into the Gaza Strip and Palestinian casualty numbers provoked international outrage. The Coalition was split internally over whether to announce a – purely cosmetic – suspension of arms export licenses to Israel. Baroness Warsi resigned from the government on the grounds that its silence was 'morally indefensible' – a British prime minister not even prepared to say as much as the UN secretary general. When a shaky truce was in place, the government delivered a few platitudes. One Downing Street insider, having opined that the prime minister had been intellectually lazy over Syria in 2013 – because he wouldn't think issues through far enough – now thought this latest issue 'the lowest point' he could recall since the Coalition came to power.[21]

Government irresolution came full circle in the summer of 2014. Islamic State's (IS) conquests in Syria and then across Iraq created a manifest crisis in the Levant. In June, the US began a limited air campaign against IS targets in Iraq, as protection for its own forces. Britain merely offered some 'non-lethal' support for it – a euphemism for its extant intelligence cooperation – and made some humanitarian airdrops to the beleaguered Yazidi peoples encircled by IS. It was the first time since the Cold War that Britain was not in with the US on 'day one' of a joint military operation. But in September Obama announced that the allies would go after IS directly – extending the campaign into Syria. For Downing Street, this occurred in the fraught week of the Scottish independence referendum. And parliament again must be consulted. In principle, it was a rerun of the Syria vote of the previous year. The government seemed tentative, all the parties were split, and some prominent Labour figures – Hilary Benn among them – offered influential calls to action. Two weeks after the US announcement, parliament then agreed by a significant

---

[21] Personal information. See also Michael Clarke, 'The Coalition and foreign affairs', in Anthony Seldon and Mike Finn (eds.), *The Coalition Effect, 2010– 2015* (Cambridge: Cambridge University Press, 2015), p. 364.

majority that Britain would participate in this latest US-led coalition. It joined as a minor player (six Tornado aircraft) in a working coalition among US, French, Australian forces and those of five Arab monarchies. Britain was the ninth to join. 'Operation Shader' technically began in August 2014 and is still ongoing.

Meanwhile, the first Russian war on Ukraine had begun earlier that year. Russia was not a foreign terror group; it was undermining by force part of the stability of Britain's own neighbourhood. But again, the government was preoccupied with its austerity programme, the Scottish referendum, and a growing crisis of migrants crossing the Channel in trucks and trains. And it then felt it had enough on its hands with the Islamic State threat in the Levant. The deeper strategic importance of the 2014 Ukrainian War seemed to elude governmental thinking. Even if the NSC saw the issue for what it was, the government lacked the political will, and the policy bandwidth, to do more than let other European partners deal with it.

In one respect, the government fully acknowledged the challenges. The new SDSR of 2015 was folded into the National Security Strategy to provide a holistic view of how external policy would be approached. It presented a vision of Britain's future in world politics, acknowledging that, 'The world is changing rapidly and fundamentally. We are seeing long-term shifts in the balance of global economic and military power.'[22] But it was relentlessly upbeat about the various strengths the country could deploy in response. The three overriding national objectives were to 'protect our people', to 'project our global influence' and to 'promote our prosperity'.[23] But the ongoing imperatives of austerity still meant that resources would be tightly constrained. It boasted that the Ministry of Defence's (MoD) persistent budget 'black hole' – unfunded future commitments; £38 billion it

---

[22] HM Government, *National Security Strategy and Strategic Defence and Security Review 2015: A Secure and Prosperous United Kingdom*, Cm 9161, November 2015, para. 3.1, p. 15.

[23] Ibid., paras 110–15, pp. 11–12.

was claimed by Conservative defence ministers – had finally been eliminated. But both the black hole and its elimination were illusions of balance sheet manipulation.[24] The real financial pressure on the MoD was that after 2010 the government had switched most of the capital costs – not the operating costs – of replacing the nuclear deterrent from the Treasury's central budget to that of the MoD directly. Within two years of the 'balanced budget' review of 2015 the MoD was running up another deficit of some £2 billion a year – roughly the annualised size of the extra deterrent costs it had been made to bear.

The 2015 review was, however, strategically literate. It articulated more clearly than the 2010 review the 'ends, ways and means' of Britain's external policy. That added up to a strategy. But while it was fairly realistic on the 'ways' of policy, it didn't seem that political leaders willed the 'ends' sufficiently strongly, and the Treasury was far too stingy about the 'means'. In any case, most of the damage had been done by the end of 2014. *The Economist* described the government's whole foreign policy as 'feeble'. *The Spectator* said it was 'dismal'. Anand Menon, a British academic, wrote for an American audience, 'factors including fatigue following the wars in Afghanistan and Iraq, a recession; and a prime minister with little apparent interest in foreign affairs have conspired to render Britain increasingly

---

[24] In 2009 the National Audit Office (NAO) assessed the extent of the defence deficit for the coming decade. The NAO said, 'If the defence budget remained constant in real terms, and using the Department's forecast for defence inflation of 2.7 per cent, the gap would now be £6 billion over the ten years. If, as is possible given the general economic position, there was no increase in the defence budget in cash terms over the same ten-year period, the gap would rise to £36 billion' (www.nao.org.uk/publications/0910/mod_major_projects_report_2009.aspx). In other words, if the Treasury chose to hold the MoD to a 'flat cash' regime so that real-terms defence spending fell, and the MoD did nothing in response to such real-term cuts, then, of course, a £6 billion deficit could increase over the decade to £36 billion. Not quite what ministers said in public.

insular.'[25] Even Britain's attractive 'values' in the international world, in which the prime minister set great store, seemed to have declined in potency.[26]

If British foreign and defence policy had lacked drive and ambition before 2016, it was completely stymied for the next four years by the shock of Brexit and the introspection and party-political chaos it sparked. David Cameron had gambled, and won, a tricky Scottish independence referendum in 2014. Then he had won, against expectations, a narrow but working majority in the 2015 general election. Now he gambled again in 2016 that he could settle the Eurosceptics in his own party, and in the country, with another risky referendum.[27]

The ever-divisive Brexit issue should not have affected foreign and defence policy directly; these sectors remained national prerogatives and lay outside European Union competence, notwithstanding anything said in the Lisbon Treaty. But in reality, Brexit had a huge effect on Britain's foreign and defence policy. It represented the greatest shift in the country's external relations for half a century; a massive call on the direction of Britain's future strategy. And neither the FCO nor the MoD had anything to say about it. As a supremely political decision, Brexit was – democratically and appropriately – a matter for noisy public debate. But Whitehall was under strict instructions to sit it out, in Cameron's belief that any contingency planning would concede too much to the Brexiteers before the

---

[25] 'Running out of gas', *The Economist*, 21 June 2014; Alex Massie, 'Britain abandons foreign policy. And abandons debate about it too', *The Spectator*, 19 August 2014; Anand Menon, 'Little England, the United Kingdom's retreat from global leadership', *Foreign Affairs*, 94:6 (2015), 93–100.

[26] Oliver Daddow, 'Constructing a "great" role for Britain in an age of austerity: interpreting coalition foreign policy, 2010–2015', *International Relations*, 29:3 (2015), 303–18.

[27] Angela Merkel offered to help him by letting him beat up the Germans and win important concessions from them as long as he didn't make it an 'in/out' referendum. Cameron demurred, so she sat on her hands while the 'remain' argument slipped away.

referendum.[28] It was hardly surprising, then, that the Brexit verdict in June 2016 hit Whitehall like a thunderbolt and left it facing a knotty future, replete with unintended consequences, with nothing more than a blank sheet of paper.

The political hiatus of Brexit has already been exhaustively documented. Its disruptive effects on foreign and defence policy took two mutually reinforcing forms. Firstly, it bent the policy machine out of shape – or at least into a different shape. In 2016 the Department for Exiting the European Union (DExEU) – the 'Brexit Department' – of 650 people was created to handle all negotiations, and hence all future trade negotiations with the EU. The FCO, the Department for Business Innovation and Skills (BIS) and Cabinet Office had some of their functions transferred to it. A new Department of Trade was created to deal with non-EU trade matters. The BIS was subsequently repurposed as Business, Energy and Industrial Strategy (BEIS), giving it a less international focus. The FCO was effectively excluded from the Brexit process altogether, dealing instead with wider international interests. All this represented a concentration of power around Number 10 and the Brexit Department which might have been helpful if the politics of Brexit were not so toxic. But in the event, Theresa May's Downing Street became beleaguered and characterised as the 'death star' from which nothing emerged, and the Brexit Department was a poisoned chalice – even for its civil servants. David Davis was given the first ministerial responsibility for it and when he resigned, Dominic Raab took it on until he resigned. Steve Barclay saw it through the final fourteen months before it was dissolved. It was ironic, but certainly not unthinking, that Prime Minister Theresa May made Boris Johnson – the greatest architect of Brexit – foreign secretary in this rearrangement, thereby sidelining him from any substantive role in the process. Johnson himself thought he was 'nothing more than a translator' for the PM in this role. He was

---

[28] This is not the case in general elections where Whitehall always does some contingency planning – whatever an opposition might be intending. A similar instruction had been issued over the Scottish independence referendum.

unfocused – 'the worst foreign secretary in living memory' – it was apparently said around Whitehall, so preoccupied was he with the party's agonies over Brexit and his own shot at the premiership.[29] And when he became prime minister in July 2019, Johnson continued the tight centralisation around Number 10 and the Brexit Department, transferring the talented and pugnacious David Frost from the FCO to become 'chief negotiator' for the whole process. This was not the sort of machinery that allowed any foreign matters to breathe adequately within government.

The second consequence followed from the first. Foreign and defence policy, running now completely on autopilot, showed little genuine ambition, and no discernable strategy, until the whole withdrawal process could be completed. The Brexit campaign had promoted the idea of 'global Britain' emerging from the referendum result. But in the first two years after the referendum, no single government document appeared to explain the slogan. In 2018 parliament's Foreign Affairs Committee failed to get 'a definitive explanation' from a number of different ministers, still less from the FCO itself.[30] The best the FCO managed was a webpage and the repurposing of some existing staff and bits of its policy programme budget.[31] It was never clear whether 'global Britain' meant doing more of the same but with extra enthusiasm, or something distinctly new. Certainly, there was no evidence of any transfer of significant resources to new tasks, or of short-term policy trade-offs that might indicate different priorities. Meanwhile, under Theresa May's premiership, a mini-defence review followed in 2018 which now divorced what was termed the 'National Security Capabilities Review' from the 'national security strategy' – no

---

[29] Matthew Parris, 'Johnson premiership will fall apart in a year', *The Times*, 8 June 2019; Brian Appleyard, 'Danger ahead: UK diplomacy is racing towards a cliff edge of its own making', *Sunday Times*, 3 March 2019.

[30] House of Commons Foreign Affairs Committee, *Global Britain*, HC 780, 12 March 2018, pp. 3, 7, 11.

[31] House of Commons Library, 'Brexit reading list: global Britain', Briefing Paper 8338, 22 August 2018, p. 3.

one could explain why.[32] The MoD resisted the associated spending cuts on the grounds that it was now conducting its own review.[33] That turned out to be essentially vacuous but it fended off more cuts. The result was that two reviews appeared in 2018, a 'capabilities' one from the Cabinet Office, and a 'modernising defence' review from the MoD; though neither indicated more than further management of defence contraction.

Despite having been foreign secretary for two years, Johnson had no ideas whatsoever about the foreign policy he wanted his government to pursue when he became prime minister. And like Theresa May, he had the misfortune to have part of his premiership coincide with the presidency of Donald Trump, who moved into the White House in January 2017. Having two explicitly revisionist powers among the four big was challenging enough for a naturally Atlanticist, status quo country like Britain. But under President Trump the prospect grew that the United States itself had to be regarded as effectively revisionist – and he personally thought of Brexit as exactly the sort of disruptive change the international system needed. Trump's behaviour in foreign and defence policy was, at best, quixotic. He reneged on Obama's nuclear deal with Iran, pulled the US out of the Paris Climate Accords, increased protectionist trade barriers, went some way to rehabilitate the North Korean leadership, backed off any criticism of President Putin's actions and Russia's (since acknowledged) interference in US and European elections, and threatened – apparently quite genuinely – to pull the US out of NATO and see the organisation collapse. He wrecked G7 summits and looked as if he might kill the group off, too. To US analysts, this approach could be characterised as 'Jacksonian nationalism'.[34] But to most in Britain and the rest of Europe it was simply vainglorious chaos, and just as dangerous to

---

[32] HM Government, *National Security Capabilities Review* (unnumbered), March 2018.

[33] Ministry of Defence, *Mobilising, Modernising and Transforming Defence* (undated, unnumbered), 2018.

[34] Walter Russell Mead, 'The Jacksonian revolt: American populism and the liberal order', *Foreign Affairs*, 96:2 (2017).

international order as anything coming from Moscow or Beijing. The prospect of Britain continuing to hitch its wagon to so disruptive a power as Trump's America attacked the foundations of the most fundamental strategic assumptions British governments had made since the 1940s. All Britain could do was try to hang on for better times in Washington, but it contributed greatly to the foreign policy sclerosis. Downing Street, no less than Whitehall, was profoundly grateful that Donald Trump was defeated after a first term. Staying on the right side of the Trump administration, whilst simultaneously avoiding the appearance of being enslaved by a destructive Washington, was an act of political schizophrenia that could not have been maintained very long into a second presidential term.

Johnson made the first attempt to break out of this torpor when the EU Withdrawal Agreement was finally concluded and his government had won the December 2019 election. An 'Integrated Review' of all aspects of Britain's external relations was launched, then suspended during the Covid pandemic, and finally published in March 2021.[35] Five years after the Brexit referendum, the government was finally trying to give substance to a historic strategic reset of the country's external relations. By then, the National Security Council had become moribund. The Covid pandemic provided a singular example. The possibility of a pandemic of some sort had long been listed as one of the NSC's 'tier one' threats among its responsibilities and for which it would plan and coordinate. But when Covid-19 hit the country, the NSC was ignored and the government scrambled into a series of ad hoc coordination arrangements that were, by all assessments, suboptimal.

Still, by common consent, the Integrated Review was a welcome and long-overdue exercise. It was coherent and strategically literate in conception. But by the time it appeared, the government's autopilot setting had already mortgaged a number of significant policy choices that had their own global impacts.

---

[35] HM Government, *Global Britain in a Competitive Age: The Integrated Review of Security, Defence, Development and Foreign Policy*, CP 403, March 2021.

The FCO and the Department for International Development were merged, so that overseas aid reverted to its pre-1997 status as the responsibility of the Foreign Office. It was a hasty merger that created significant dysfunctionality both in the foreign policy and in the overseas aid machinery.[36] More than that, the foreign aid budget was reduced by 29 per cent.[37] The effects were felt in immediate ad hoc funding cuts wherever they could most easily be made – chiefly in discretionary, as opposed to international organisational, funding. The Conflict Stability and Security Fund, for example, cut its funding to various activities in South Asia by 88 per cent, and more than 50 per cent in the Middle East and North Africa, particularly affecting youth education programmes (which the Integrated Review had particularly boasted about), schemes for combatting international crime and government corruption, and conflict reduction schemes.[38] Meanwhile, defence had been given a sudden and relatively generous four-year settlement that put £7 billion of genuinely new money into the system by 2024–5 – though the government claimed a (misleading) £16.5 billion. Nevertheless, it helped defence get back on track – at least until rising inflation took its toll on spending, but it squeezed related external policy spending elsewhere.

When it then appeared, the Integrated Review foreshadowed a 'tilt to the Indo-Pacific' in British policy, but the Defence Command Paper that accompanied it played that down in favour of more traditional Atlanticist priorities. Any reference to the importance of the EU in Britain's future external relations was tellingly – some said insultingly – omitted. Science and technology (S&T) were given pride of place as the great enablers

---

[36] See Independent Commission for Aid Impact, *Annual Report 2022–2023*, pp. 8–9; Jim Dunton, '"Dysfunctunal" FCDO systems left aid watchdog unable to recruit staff and pay contractors', *Civil Service World*, 25 May 2023.

[37] Reducing it from 0.7 to 0.5 per cent of GNI on the legal technicality that it could be so reduced in an emergency. A permanent reduction would require new legislation.

[38] Joint Committee on the National Security Strategy, *The Conflict, Stability and Security Fund*, HC 1389, HL 253, 20 September 2023, para. 8.

of Britain's new competitive edge, but the funding commitments to S&T were still considerably below the OECD average.[39] The review claimed in an extended essay that Britain was a 'soft power super power', but very little followed from that particular idea.[40] The document had been in the works for sixteen months and the Integrated Review's decision on what to do about the moribund NSC was – to review it again. By 2022, regardless of its conceptual clarity and vision, there was scant evidence the Integrated Review was any sort of policy driver, still less a hinge that was swinging Britain towards a new sort of 'globalism'. It represented, as usual, a shopping list of boxes, some of which were beginning to be ticked, while others were effectively postponed or ignored, in view of economic constraints and faint political leadership. In light of the Russian invasion of Ukraine, there was a review 'refresh' exercise in 2023 – the eighth review in twenty-five years – but it changed nothing.[41]

Overall, Britain presented a lamentable picture in its external policies in the years spanning the premierships of David Cameron, Theresa May and Boris Johnson. Cameron had little interest in foreign matters and no feel for strategy. Theresa May was shackled by the Brexit hospital pass Cameron let fly when he resigned. Johnson used the chaos to become prime minister with no preparation, and little instinct for top-level policy. Britain increasingly succumbed to the pressures of its external circumstances. None of these prime ministers showed the leadership or statecraft that might have allowed the country to rise above such pressures. And they were followed by the premierships of Liz Truss – an aberration as prime minister in all respects that matter in foreign relations – and Rishi Sunak, who could be no more than a caretaker in Downing Street; at best, intelligently reactive in overseas matters.

---

[39] Government policy was to achieve, by 2027, the OECD average spend on S&T as a percentage of GDP.

[40] HM Government, *Global Britain in a Competitive Age*, pp. 49–50.

[41] HM Government, *Integrated Review Refresh 2023: Responding to a more contested and volatile world*, CP 811, March 2023.

SHOOTING AT REDEMPTION IN UKRAINE

There were, however, a couple of fortuitous brighter spots amid the chaotic Johnson premiership. The 'AUKUS' deal to develop new submarines between the US, Australia and Britain rather fell into London's lap when Canberra performed a volte-face on its extant deal with France to buy new vessels. This was excellent industrial news for Britain and strategically significant, though Johnson diminished its early political benefits when he mocked the understandable anger of Paris when the news came out – and Britain had kept one of its closest European allies quite in the dark as the alternative deal was being finalised.[42] On another tack, Britain was already scheduled to host the 2021 G7 meeting and then the COP 26 climate summit that autumn. Both were helpful opportunities for British diplomacy and they were well-chaired and successful enough at the time; though neither achieved the status of landmark meetings. Under the Sunak premiership, Britain appeared to back away from some of its COP 26 commitments; it certainly didn't present a subsequent image of relentless drive towards the 2021 goals.

The true redemption, both for some of the country's reputation and for Prime Minster Johnson himself, was in the Russian invasion of Ukraine in February 2022. Though Britain's reactions to the Russian attack on Ukraine in 2014 had been flimsy, the Ministry of Defence then showed some creative initiative in establishing a training programme for Ukrainian armed forces under the rubric of 'Operation Orbital'. In 2016 there was a bilateral defence cooperation agreement that formalised the initiative, and later on, a Memorandum of Understanding to help Ukraine develop its naval forces.[43] The MoD would have done rather more for Kyiv – defence minister Michael Fallon pushed hard – but the FCO (during Johnson's tenure as foreign secretary) and Downing Street (under Prime Minister May), were

---

[42] David Camroux, 'AUKUS: Why Britain was the big winner', *The Diplomat*, 2 December 2021.

[43] House of Commons Library, *Military Assistance to Ukraine 2014–2021*, Research Briefing, 4 March 2022.

cautious in case such assistance needlessly provoked Moscow. But then as prime minister, Johnson took a more assertive view. His earlier, unfocused, attempts in the FCO to create a reset with Russia had been rebuffed and the Salisbury poisonings of 2018 had altered his view of Putin. During 2020 he had established a good rapport with the new president of Ukraine, Volodymyr Zelenskiy. In 2021, under Johnson's uncharacteristically strong direction, British policy hardened towards Russia. By October 2021, US and British intelligence services thought they knew in some detail how Russian policy would play out. They went public with their interpretation, were widely disbelieved across Europe and ridiculed inside Russia, but they were overwhelmingly right.

Britain suddenly seemed to click back into the old routine. Johnson was fully focused on the Russian invasion, which was duly launched on 24 February. He was emotionally invested in the conflict as a defence of democracy. Policy was driven very firmly from Number 10; and he had a tough-minded and effective team inside the building – John Bew, Stephen Lovegrove, Jamie Norman and Simon Gass. They had anticipated the challenge and now helped him shape policy and drive it through those parts of Whitehall that were more cautious.[44]

The effects were politically dramatic and militarily effective. Britain was in lock-step with Washington in opposing Russia's aggression and some way ahead of the EU in mobilising for action. Johnson pushed immediately for tough sanctions, wanting to have Russia thrown out of the SWIFT payments system – something earlier regarded as an economic 'nuclear option', but a threshold that was quite quickly crossed. Russian individuals and organisations were swiftly sanctioned by Britain in a series of national packages that set the trend for the more powerful multinational sanctions packages the EU was able to assemble. And Britain joined the US in leading the way with military support, giving Kyiv the weapons it most urgently needed to fend off

[44] John Bew, special adviser on foreign policy; Stephen Lovegrove, national security adviser; Jamie Norman, civil service military adviser; Simon Gass, chair of Joint Intelligence Committee.

Russian attacks and the sort of critical intelligence only Washington and London could provide. In April, though the EU's Ursula Von der Leyen beat Johnson to it by twenty-four hours – to his intense annoyance – the British prime minister was the first G7 leader to walk the streets of Kyiv with President Zelenskiy in a show of courage and support. The Kremlin dubbed Johnson 'the most active anti-Russian leader' – exactly the sort of compliment Johnson and the British defence establishment cherished.[45]

Quite suddenly, the western alliance seemed to have resumed textbook form. The US was leading the allies strongly. Trump had threatened to administer a shot to NATO's head; now Putin gave it a strong shot in the arm. NATO was organising a tough military response to the Russian invasion, strengthening itself and helping Ukraine. The EU was coordinating unprecedented levels of economic sanctions against Russia to render it an economic pariah. In a single speech, Germany's Olaf Scholz reversed two decades of appeasing German engagement with Moscow.[46] And Boris Johnson's 'Brexit Britain' could now be seen playing again a classic Atlanticist role – working with the US, exhorting its European allies, deepening partnerships with non-NATO and non-EU countries in northern Europe, setting an example – and being courageous in calling out Moscow's intentions, even at the cost of some goodwill among international partners. Suddenly, Johnson was full of ideas and strategies that placed him ahead of conventional Washington thinking. This was international leadership, dangerous and intoxicating.

Some have argued that what happened next was classic political tragedy.[47] In April 2022, just as all this was swinging into action, the Metropolitan Police sent the prime minister a fixed penalty notice over his breaking Covid lock-down rules,

---

[45] Andrew Gimson, *Boris Johnson: The Rise and Fall of a Troublemaker at Number 10* (London: Simon and Schuster, 2023), p. 390.

[46] German Federal Government, 'Policy statement by Olaf Scholz, 27 February 2022 in Berlin'.

[47] Sebastian Payne, *The Fall of Boris Johnson: The Full Story* (London: Pan Books, 2023), pp. 95–6.

and the draining saga of Johnson's personal integrity and management incompetence was back on the agenda, until it finally brought him down. Johnson's Ukraine policy, it was often thought, was a tantalising glimpse of what might have been.

But perhaps not. The centralised system that had planned the politico/military strategy so well had no obvious grasp over the domestic effects of the war on Britain itself – a new energy crisis, inflation, the advance of global recession, another squeeze on public expenditure, and the economic downsides of imposing sanctions. Then too, Britain could take a lead in coordinating military aid to Ukraine. It led the 'tank-coalition' and then the 'fighter coalition' to persuade allies to cross those thresholds in supplying key categories of equipment to Kyiv. It put £4.6 billion into Ukrainian aid in 2022–4 – the second greatest single contributor behind the $113 billion of the US. But in truth, Britain's stocks of the sort of military equipment Ukraine really needed were exhausted by the end of 2022. German military aid was slowly but steadily ramping up, as were its financial contributions. As popular as Boris Johnson was in Ukraine, by the end of 2023 Kyiv's most important interlocuters were Joe Biden, Olaf Scholz and Ursula Von der Leyen in the EU Commission.

Nevertheless, though Britain's Ukraine policy probably overstated the country's ability to determine collective strategies within its European neighbourhood, it was at least one example of 'setting the tone for the UK's international engagement in the decade ahead' as Johnson had written in the Integrated Review.[48]

In that sense, it was a glimpse of what might still be. But Johnson's successors in Downing Street blew hot and cold on Ukraine. Liz Truss was recklessly hawkish but no one took much notice. Rishi Sunak inherited Johnson's Churchillian mantle over the war but didn't wear it comfortably. Unlike almost all its European partners, Britain would not increase its defence expenditure by an amount that made any difference. Prime Minister Sunak maintained Britain's rhetorical stance on the war, but felt too economically constrained to move off the

---

[48] HM Government, *Global Britain in a Competitive Age*, p. 5.

plateau he had inherited from Johnson, both in Ukraine and British defence policy priorities.

During the Gaza War of 2023–4, Sunak's government was drawn into some military muscularity in helping the United States defend freedom of navigation in the Red Sea, as the regional effects of the war became more destabilising. But though the action was presented as a mark of confidence, it also demonstrated fairly clearly that British forces were operating near the limits of their sustainability. It showed, again, that Britain could certainly 'contribute' something in defence and humanitarian terms, but could not make much strategic difference in ways the Integrated Review had envisaged. For all the renewed vigour that Lord Cameron, having become foreign secretary, brought to Britain's diplomatic role, this upheaval showed Britain had little real influence in the Middle East, though the Middle East had a big influence on Britain's own security and prosperity.

The 'Conservative effect' in foreign and defence policy after 2010 was certainly more depressing than uplifting. The country did not rise above the economic constraints created by the 2008 global financial crisis. None of its prime ministers grasped foreign and defence policy as a particular personal commitment. They were, in any case, preoccupied in 2014 – which turned out to be a critical year in global politics – by the dire prospect of a breakup of the Union, and then from 2015 by the Conservative psychodrama around Brexit. Events over the last decade in Asia, the Middle East and in Eastern Europe demonstrated how profoundly global politics have changed. And these transformations are not mere strategic abstractions for Britain; they are challenges the country has had real difficulty in meeting. As the 2022 war in Ukraine demonstrated, if British policymakers had not already noticed, the 'holiday from history' that Francis Fukuyama and Henry Kissinger detected in the immediate post-Cold War years was clearly over.[49]

---

[49] See the final paragraph of Francis Fukuyama, 'The end of history?', *The National Interest*, 16 (1989), 18; Henry Kissinger, *World Order: Reflections on the Character of Nations and the Course of History* (New York: Penguin, 2014), pp. 327–9.

5

Health

Rachel Sylvester

David Cameron's face was plastered across billboards in the weeks leading up to the 2010 election. There was a vigorous debate at the time about whether the fresh-faced leader of the opposition's image had been airbrushed in the much-mocked Conservative Party campaign ads. Privately, strategists joked that the truth was 'much worse' and 'he really does look like that'.[1] The words that accompanied the picture on the Tory election posters had a much more significant political message, however. 'We can't go on like this,' the quote from Cameron declared. 'I'll cut the deficit, not the NHS.' It was a surprising decision for the Conservatives to put health – an issue on which they had traditionally been behind Labour in the polls – at the heart of the election campaign. But it was a deliberate and carefully calibrated choice. Internal Tory Party polling had shown that, when voters were asked 'what is the biggest risk of having David Cameron as prime minister and the Conservatives in government?', one of their greatest fears was that a Cameron-led government would slash public spending too deeply and undermine the NHS.

In fact Cameron himself felt a deeply personal attachment to the health service. He had spent many nights sleeping on a hospital floor next to the bed of his severely disabled son Ivan, who suffered from a rare condition called Ohtahara syndrome, which caused sudden and terrifying seizures. Ivan had died at St Mary's hospital in Paddington in 2009 at the age of 6. Cameron remained profoundly grateful for the care that he

---

[1] Private conversation.

received and passionately committed to the principles of a universal NHS, free at the point of use. Just a few months after being elected party leader in 2006 he had used health policy as an example of 'how the Conservative Party is changing' in a speech to the King's Fund, a health think tank. 'I want us to leave no one in any doubt whatsoever about how we feel about the NHS today,' Cameron told his audience of policy wonks and MPs. 'We believe in it. We want to improve it. We want to improve it for everyone in this country.'[2] The health service had become central to the Tory modernisers' attempt to reposition their party.

The billboard ads were part of a concerted attempt to change negative public perceptions – linking a leader who had credibility on the NHS to a political promise of support. The commitment to the health service, once described by Nigel Lawson as 'the closest thing the English people have to a national religion',[3] was an integral part of the so-called 'decontamination' of the Conservative brand and the strategy was starting to work. By the 2010 election Labour's lead over the Tories on the question of who voters trusted to run the health service was narrower than ever before. That did not last. Fourteen years, five Conservative prime ministers and seven Tory health secretaries later, the NHS is going through its worst crisis in history and has once again turned into a political liability.

When Cameron arrived at Number 10, the NHS was going in the right direction on most key metrics. Waiting lists for non-urgent procedures had fallen dramatically. Around 2.5 million people were waiting for hospital treatment in England,[4] but the number waiting for more than three months had been slashed from 700,000 to 7,000. Virtually no one had to wait for more than six months.[5] The Labour government had significantly

---

[2] King's Fund speech, 4 January 2006.

[3] Nigel Lawson, *The View From No. 11* (London: Bantam Press, 1992).

[4] 'NHS Pressures in England', House of Commons Library, 17 December 2019.

[5] Anthony Seldon and Mike Finn (eds.), *The Coalition Effect, 2010–2015* (Cambridge University Press, 2015), p. 290.

increased spending on the health service. Health inequalities had begun to narrow. A ban on smoking in public places had started to nudge people towards a healthier lifestyle. As a result, the NHS was enjoying unprecedented public support. The British Social Attitudes Survey showed overall satisfaction with the NHS stood at 74 per cent in 2010, compared to only 39 per cent in 2001. When Danny Boyle set out to showcase the best of Britain in the opening ceremony for the 2012 London Olympics he put the health service at the heart of the show, with children jumping on hospital beds surrounded by dancing nurses.

By 2023 the NHS was breaking all the wrong kinds of records. The waiting list for elective surgery reached a record high of 7.8 million, almost tripling over a decade, and the Health Foundation think tank predicted that it could peak at over 8 million by the end of 2024.[6] More than a million patients were waiting at least four weeks to see their GP.[7] Accident and emergency departments were overwhelmed. There were queues of ambulances outside hospitals and patients on trolleys in corridors. In December 2022, over 54,000 people had to wait more than twelve hours for a bed at A&E and about 800,000 waited more than four hours to be seen. In one case, a patient had to wait ninety-nine hours for a bed. Staff vacancies in the NHS had rocketed, with many doctors and nurses complaining of burnout and some looking for less stressful jobs abroad. Around 10 per cent of hospital beds were filled with people who were medically fit to be discharged but could not go home, often because of a lack of social care. The obesity crisis was deepening. There was an epidemic of mental illness and health inequalities were widening again.

Industrial action compounded the problems left by the pandemic. In December 2022, nurses in England went on strike for the first time in their history. The following September junior

---

[6] Health Foundation, 'The NHS waiting list: when will it peak?', 27 October 2023.

[7] Eleanor Hayward, 'GP wait times: 1.3 million patients a month wait four weeks to see doctor', *The Times*, 18 July 2023.

doctors and hospital consultants staged an unprecedented joint walk out. The annual winter crisis in the NHS morphed into an apparently permanent state of emergency. One A&E consultant compared it to Narnia in *The Lion, the Witch and the Wardrobe* – explaining that 'it's always winter but never Christmas'.[8] As the NHS celebrated its seventy-fifth anniversary, public satisfaction with the health service was at an all-time low. A YouGov poll for The Times Health Commission, published in January 2023, found that more than two-thirds of people thought that NHS services were 'bad', 80 per cent thought the health service had got worse and 39 per cent were not confident that it would be there for them in an emergency.[9]

The question is – how much were the Conservative-led governments since 2010 to blame? The Covid-19 pandemic, which reached the UK in early 2020, was a once-in-a-generation disaster that would have put unprecedented pressure on any health care system. George Osborne, who was chancellor between 2010 and 2016, acknowledges that 'the NHS is facing a very challenging situation'. But he insists that there are global trends at play. 'Most healthcare systems in the Western world are facing these pressures. You have ageing populations, you have rising medical costs through new treatments, you have a shortage of healthcare workers in every advanced economy. And so what looks like a very UK-specific debate . . . needs to be put in a wider context.' He rejects the idea that austerity is to blame. 'After a big crash, the country is less rich and has less money to spend.'[10]

There is no doubt, however, that decisions taken by Conservative ministers over the previous decade made the NHS, the social care system and the wider population less resilient when the virus hit. Chris Ham, co-chair of the NHS Assembly and former chief executive of the King's Fund think tank, believes political failure created the crisis in the NHS and social care because short-term fixes were prioritised over long-term solutions:

[8]   Interview with the author.
[9]   'Alarm bells are all ringing', *The Times*, 15 January 2023.
[10]   Evidence to The Times Health Commission, 2 May 2023.

Since 2010 there's been a steady decline in the performance of the NHS – affecting patients as well as staff – because the funding hasn't kept pace with growing and ageing populations. This is a failure of the political system because the warning signs have been clear. I've been involved in the NHS for all of my career – almost 50 years – I can never remember a time when politicians haven't acted in response to evidence of that kind and done something. The challenges for the NHS have been made even greater by the fact we have a creaking social care system that is on its knees and there hasn't been the priority for prevention and public health policies. For the first time, we're seeing long-term reductions in life expectancy going into reverse and inequalities in health becoming even more severe.[11]

A REFORM SO BIG YOU COULD SEE IT FROM SPACE

The first big mistake came in 2010 when the Conservative-led coalition embarked on a massive reform of the NHS that nobody around the Cabinet table could explain and few understood. The Conservative manifesto in 2010 had promised that a future Tory government would 'increase health spending in real terms every year'. It would 'strengthen the powers of GPs as patients' expert guides through the healthcare system . . . putting them in charge of commissioning local services'. It would 'scrap politically motivated targets' and 'create an independent NHS board'. Cameron told the Royal College of Nursing Congress that if he became prime minister 'there will be no more of those pointless reorganisations which aim for change but instead bring chaos'.[12] Yet within months of coming into power his government had launched a reform of the NHS that in the memorable phrase of David Nicholson, the chief executive of the health service at the time, was 'so big you could see it from space'.[13]

Jeremy Heywood, the widely respected late Cabinet secretary who worked for Tony Blair and Gordon Brown as well as

---

[11] Chris Ham, evidence to The Times Health Commission, 23 May 2023.
[12] May 2009, RCN Congress, Harrogate.
[13] David Nicholson, NHS Alliance Conference Speech, 18 November 2020.

Cameron and Theresa May, used to tell his civil service colleagues that politicians all want to get their hands on what he called 'the biggest train set on Whitehall',[14] the NHS. None was more enthusiastic about playing with his engines and tracks than Andrew Lansley, who was the Conservative Party's shadow health spokesman from 2004 to 2010 and health secretary between May 2010 and September 2012. Like Cameron, Lansley had strong views about the NHS, driven by personal experience. His father had been a biochemist, who had worked on hospital-acquired infections and his then wife was a doctor. Lansley himself had suffered a stroke at the age of 36, having had a blood clot on his brain misdiagnosed as an ear infection. He had also been Cameron's boss as head of the Conservative Research Department, and some in Number 10 detected that he retained a sense of authority over the youthful prime minister.

Lansley's aim was to liberate the health service from direct ministerial control by transferring responsibility to an independent body, NHS England. This would oversee new local clinical commissioning groups, which would allow GPs to decide on the commissioning of certain services from 'any qualified provider'. Competition would be placed at the heart of the health service's legal framework. Lansley was determined that his legislation would be so far-reaching, detailed and fundamental that it would be 'irreversible for a political generation'. No future secretary of state would be able to simply tear the changes up.[15] It was bound to be controversial but – despite the political sensitivity – when Lansley unveiled his radical blueprint nobody in government seriously challenged his ideas. According to one Whitehall source, civil servants who suggested holding a consultation before rushing ahead with the 'interesting' proposals were told by the new secretary of state: 'No I have a mandate.'[16]

[14] Isabel Hardman, *Fighting for Life* (London: Penguin, 2023), p. 225.

[15] Nick Timmins, *Never Again? The Story of the Health and Social Care Act 2012* (London: The King's Fund and Institute for Government, 2012), pp. 38, 60, 63.

[16] Private conversation.

Cameron's pollster Andrew Cooper, who was brought in as director of strategy at Number 10 in early 2011, says:

> Lansley refused to listen, right from day one. There were working sessions in Number 10 where Cameron and Jeremy Heywood and the senior officials, the policy unit advisers and Oliver Letwin [the Cabinet Office minister], who was basically in charge of ticking off all the policy stuff, had these presentations from the different ministers. They had to decide 'What are we going to go for? What are we not?' Jeremy Heywood said to me, 'nobody could make any sense at all of what Andrew Lansley was saying'. There was then a discussion about, do we just park this one or do we go with it? They had another session just with Lansley, and it was just as impenetrable. Everyone looked to Oliver Letwin and said, 'Oliver, does this make any sense?' Oliver said, 'Yes, I think we should go for it.' It was basically – do we stick or twist? George [Osborne] said to me later that he bitterly regretted not saying 'no, we don't really understand this. We don't get the politics of it. We shouldn't be doing it.'[17]

Cooper himself was baffled. 'No one ever convincingly explained to me what the benefit of this was supposed to be. Andrew Lansley, is a decent, well-meaning guy, but in the context where the strategic imperative is not frightening people about the NHS and we had said there will be no top-down reforms of the NHS it was mad,' he says.[18]

Yet the plans were signed off and in July 2010 the government published its White Paper 'Equity and Excellence: Liberating the NHS'. The following January, a 550-page Health and Social Care Bill was tabled in parliament. The bill passed its second reading in the House of Commons by 321 votes to 235, with all Tory and Lib Dem MPs voting in favour. Then somebody read it. Clare Gerada, the newly appointed head of the Royal College of GPs, described the proposals as 'the end of the NHS as we currently know it'.[19] Alarm bells started to ring in different

---

[17] Interview with the author. [18] Interview with the author.

[19] Denis Campbell, 'Doctors warned to expect unrest over NHS', *Guardian*, 19 November 2010.

parts of the health service. Nicholson had a series of increasingly tense discussions with Lansley about what he wanted to do. In one meeting, the head of the NHS accused the health secretary of turning the health service on its head for no obvious benefit. Lansley retorted: 'If you think I'm mad, you should meet Michael Gove.'[20]

Political as well as medical opposition grew. In March 2011, the Conservatives' coalition partners the Liberal Democrats voted for important changes to the bill at their spring conference. Baroness [Shirley] Williams, a national treasure as well as a Lib Dem party favourite, spearheaded the rebellion in the House of Lords. Nick Clegg, the Lib Dem leader and deputy prime minister, saw his party haemorrhaging members and insisted that changes would have to be made. The Conservative side of the coalition also started to realise that the situation was not sustainable. Downing Street became increasingly exasperated with Lansley. One aide suggested privately at the time that the health secretary 'should be taken out and shot' for his handling of the flagship reforms.[21]

In the spring of 2011, the three most senior political advisers – Cooper, Craig Oliver, who was then director of communications, and Stephen Gilbert, the political secretary – decided that things could not go on. They wrote a paper for the prime minister insisting that there was a serious political problem brewing and the toxic Lansley bill should be halted. Cooper recalls:

> There was an excruciatingly embarrassing meeting in Downing Street, in Cameron's office where Lansley was told this is being paused. Cameron said it and [Lansley] went sort of purple and was furious and started saying that people weren't backing him up and everyone had agreed to this. Nick Clegg said to him, 'Andrew, this is entirely your fault, because you put the legislative cart before the political horse.' ... Lansley had got himself to a place where he was doing something really

[20] Sue Cameron, 'David Nicholson – the man who believed in being ruthless with the NHS', *Daily Telegraph*, 26 March 2014.
[21] Private conversation.

complicated that nobody understood either the need for or the detail of. And he had made an enemy of every single stakeholder who could have been trusted to help explain this and validate it and say it was OK, or needed, even. It was obviously a fiasco. It wasn't explainable or defensible.[22]

On 4 April a humiliated Lansley told the Commons that there would be a 'pause' in the legislative process to reconsider the plans. After a two-month break, during which civil servants conducted a 'listening exercise', there were some modest changes made to the bill. NHS services would be able to be run by 'any qualified provider' rather than 'any willing provider'. The regulator Monitor would promote integrated care and would no longer be tasked with 'promoting competition', instead being responsible for 'tackling anti-competitive behaviour'. Hospital doctors and nurses would also be added to clinical commissioning groups so that GPs did not dominate. Clegg declared it a victory but his party members and peers disagreed. There were more rebellions in the Lords. Although the legislation limped through and eventually became law, the verdict of Nick Timmins, the veteran social policy expert, was: 'Fifty days of debate in Parliament had produced a piece of legislation even longer, more complex and in some areas ... appreciably less clear than the original huge edifice.'[23]

Few people – either inside or outside the government – thought the Lansley reforms were a success. In reality they became largely irrelevant because the NHS found ways to work around them. Lansley says: 'Although there was a large debate about my legislation ... the NHS completely ignored it and did what they wanted to do and they didn't do what the legislation said.'[24] In 2014 the health service's 'Five Year Forward View' put the emphasis on integration rather than competition. This was eventually formalised with the Health and Care Act 2022, which effectively dismantled the Lansley reforms, replacing the clinical commissioning groups with integrated care boards. But

---

[22] Interview with the author.   [23] Timmins, *Never Again?*, p. 121.
[24] Evidence to The Times Health Commission, 11 July 2023.

many experienced NHS leaders lost their jobs or had to reapply for positions in the new organisations that had been set up. According to Chris Ham, 'Time that could have been spent improving NHS efficiency was directed to restructuring which was widely perceived as both damaging and distracting.'[25]

Political capital had also been sacrificed. In a note to Cameron in September 2011, Cooper warned: 'Many voters already think that we are largely fulfilling their pre-election fears about what a Cameron-led government would do. Our response should be to reassert modern, compassionate credentials and reassure on our values, not to strengthen the feeling that you were never a modern, compassionate Conservative in the first place.'[26] A longer memo in March 2012, after the NHS and Social Care Act had reached the statute book, set out what Cooper described as a 'frank review' of the political fallout.

> The NHS is – as we all recognise – an issue of existential political importance for the government. Through more than 18 months of legislative wrangling, more than 1,000 amendments, an unprecedented pause and reflection and long periods where the issue has dominated debate in Parliament, most voters have remained uncomprehending either of *why* the government was pressing ahead with reform or *what* the reforms were intended to achieve.

He warned that 'for longstanding reasons of political brand association most voters are dubious about whether the Conservative party is as committed as Labour (or the Lib Dems) to the concept of a free NHS'. The majority of voters expected the reforms to 'make the NHS worse, not better', he added. 'Lack of public trust in our motives and lack of understanding about the reforms remain huge weaknesses.'[27] He also said that without a team in the Department of Health that was capable of rebuilding

---

[25] Chris Ham, 'The rise and decline of the NHS in England, 2000–20', report for the King's Fund, 12 April 2023, p. 9.

[26] Private note from Andrew Cooper to David Cameron, shared with the author.

[27] Memo to the prime minister, by Andrew Cooper, shared with the author.

the damaged relationships with the professionals and putting the case effectively to the public, 'the burden for restoring our political position on the NHS will fall overwhelmingly (to an unrealistic degree) on you, as Prime Minister.' In September 2012, Lansley was demoted to the position of Leader of the House of Commons.

Lasting damage had been done, however, and ministers were determined to avoid going anywhere near any further NHS reform. Jeremy Hunt, health secretary from 2012 to 2018, arrived at the department with an instruction to lower the temperature. 'I had a pretty strong signal from Number 10, generally, that they wanted a calm life as far as health was concerned,' he says.

> Our fingers were burned by the very hostile reaction to the 2012 Health and Social Care Act. The result was that we didn't want to do any further legislation, and the opportunity to put in place a structure for the NHS that allowed local decision-making and a focus on prevention not cure, was delayed. During my entire time as health secretary, whoever the occupant of Number 10 was, the signal was, 'We don't want to have a big health bill.' It was always incremental.[28]

OFSTED-STYLE RATINGS FOR THE NHS

Instead, patient safety quickly became Hunt's top priority. In February 2013, the report of the Francis Inquiry into the failings in care at Mid Staffordshire NHS Foundation Trust was published. The barrister Sir Robert Francis identified serious systemic flaws and cultural problems on a huge scale that had led to hundreds of unnecessary and often cruel deaths. He made 290 recommendations including a statutory duty of candour in the NHS and stronger health care leadership. It did not take Hunt long to realise that the Mid Staffs scandal was not an isolated incident but part of a horrifying pattern. Soon after becoming health secretary he had asked his officials to give him one letter from a patient every day to which he

[28] Interview with the author.

would personally reply. To start with they offered up missives from the grateful recipients of excellent care, but this was not what he had in mind at all. He asked to see the complaints so that he could understand what was going wrong. In August 2013, he met James Titcombe, a former project manager in the nuclear industry whose baby son Joshua had tragically died just nine days after he had been born at Furness General Hospital, part of the Morecambe Bay NHS Trust. Again, an inquiry had found 'significant or major failures of care' associated with the deaths of three mothers and sixteen babies. Hunt was shocked to discover that there were around 150 avoidable deaths in NHS hospitals every single week, many of which were being covered up.

He made it his mission to challenge the culture that allowed this to happen. He reformed the Care Quality Commission (CQC), the regulator for the NHS, to make it give an Ofsted-style rating for each hospital. All organisations were graded 'outstanding', 'good', 'requires improvement' or 'inadequate'. Underneath the overall rating were subratings on safety, outcomes, responsiveness, compassion and leadership. Titcombe was appointed as the CQC's national adviser on safety. In the first three years of the new regime, twenty-eight hospitals were put into special measures. Hunt says:

> You tend to arrive running a department of state saying, 'I'm not going to do cultural change, because that's too nebulous and it's too difficult.' But actually, the only permanent changes are cultural. I do believe the NHS has a safety culture now that it didn't have before. My approach was to say – I believe in the values of the NHS very passionately, but it has to be high quality healthcare for all. It can't be mediocre healthcare for all. So if you want the NHS to work, you have to have a focus on standards. By the time I left, there were four million more patients every year using good or outstanding hospitals. When I arrived, we didn't know which the good or outstanding hospitals were.[29]

---

[29] Interview with the author.

As the longest serving health secretary in the history of the NHS, Hunt can with some justification claim the advances he made on patient safety as a high point. He also, however, got embroiled in a damaging row with junior doctors over a proposed new contract that again set the Conservative government against the medical profession. Hunt's plan was to change the classification of normal working hours from 7 am to 7 pm Monday to Friday to 7 am to 10 pm Monday to Saturday. He argued that this was fair for doctors, and necessary for safety in the NHS. Patients admitted to hospital at the weekend were around 15 per cent more likely to die. The British Medical Association was furious and in November 2015 members of the doctors' union voted to go on strike. After several bruising walk-outs, the industrial action was eventually called off after the *Health Service Journal* published an explosive cache of WhatsApp messages between members of the BMA junior doctors' committee revealing a 'strategy that tied the DH up in knots for the next 16–18 months' and conceding that pay rather than patient safety was 'the only real red line'. But the bitter negotiations caused lasting damage to the relationship between politicians and clinicians.

Appointed chancellor in October 2022 by Liz Truss, Hunt defends his party's record on health since 2010. 'I think it's quite easy to be unfair on the Conservative period of running the NHS, because it happened that we had a once-in-a-century pandemic after a decade. Any judgement you make inevitably will look at the pandemic shock,' he says. 'That doesn't mean to say that there aren't things that we should have done better over that period.'[30] One example is a long-term strategy for the work force. Although Hunt increased the number of medical school training places as health secretary, it was not until 2023 when he was in the Treasury that the government announced a proper work force plan for the NHS that doubled the training of doctors and nurses.

---

[30] Interview with the author.

AN OPPORTUNITY MISSED ON SOCIAL CARE

Hunt's 'biggest regret' is 'not getting a long term plan for the social care system like I got for the NHS'. Although he rejects the idea that austerity went too far in terms of health service funding, he does admit that: 'in social care, it did and that had a knock-on back to the NHS'. With the benefit of hindsight, he says, 'you can see that, in some areas, the cuts had unintended consequences. The squeeze on local government finances meant that access into the social care system was reduced, and that pressure transferred to the NHS and that showed itself in people not being able to get out of hospital.'[31] Hunt used his first Autumn Statement as chancellor in 2022 to announce a £5.7 billion annual increase in funding for social care, but many thought that this was another inadequate, short-term fix. By 2023 there were around 13,000 patients who were medically fit to leave hospital but could not be discharged often because of a lack of social care.

Not putting social care on a sustainable footing was a clear failure of the Conservative years. Demand for social care is rising as a result of the ageing population but the supply has not kept up. Over 11 million people in England and Wales were 65 or older when the last census was taken in 2021. This included over half a million people who were at least 90. The proportion of over-65s rose from 16.4 per cent in 2011 to 18.6 per cent in 2021. According to Age UK, 1.6 million older people do not receive the support they need with activities essential for living, 2.6 million over-50s have some kind of unmet need for care and 28 per cent of people who have asked for a social care assessment had been waiting six months or more. In 2023 there were 165,000 staff vacancies in social care in England, a 52 per cent increase on the previous year.[32] Services are in a fragile state, with many care homes struggling to afford the rising cost of food, heating and wages.

---

[31] Interview with the author.

[32] Tom Gentry, Kate Jopling and Chloe Reeves, *Fixing the Foundations* (London: Age UK, 2023).

Social care became a political football that successive ministers repeatedly kicked down the road. In 2010, Lansley had been discussing a cross-party approach with the then Labour health secretary Andy Burnham. But as soon as Labour hinted that its social care plans could be funded by an inheritance levy, the Conservative Party denounced this as a 'death tax' and launched a poster campaign illustrated by a photograph of New Labour's red rose on a tomb stone.

There was a momentary outbreak of common sense when the Dilnot Commission, which was set up by Cameron and reported in 2011, proposed a lifetime cap on care costs. Under the plans, once someone reached the limit the state would pick up the costs, meaning that people would not have to sell their home to pay for care. The reform would also have driven up standards by creating a market in provision. Those who could afford to do so would be willing to spend more at the start of their time in care knowing that their total costs would be capped, so they would not run out of money if they ended up needing long-term support. The proposals had cross-party support and legislation was passed in 2013, with implementation due in 2017, but reform was shelved.

Then in the heat of the 2017 general election campaign Theresa May sprung her own proposals for social care reform on an unsuspecting public. The plans had been drawn up by her adviser Nick Timothy, without input from the civil servants at the Department of Health or policy experts who would have been able to warn him about the flaws. Even Hunt, who was then health secretary, had not been properly consulted in advance. The problem was that May's plan – which involved people paying for their own care using the value of their home, until the last £100,000 worth of assets – created many potential losers without spreading the risk of catastrophic costs. Some people would end up paying nothing for their care, but others could find themselves spending hundreds of thousands of pounds on care home fees. The policy did not solve one of the fundamental problems and simply highlighted the inequity between cancer treatment, which is free on the NHS, and Alzheimer's care, which must be paid for by individuals. It was quickly dubbed the 'Dementia Tax' by Labour. Even though May dumped the policy, while insisting unconvincingly that 'nothing had changed', she still lost her parliamentary majority. The reputation of social care as the dangerous 'third rail' of politics was confirmed.

Boris Johnson arrived in Downing Street in 2019 promising in his first speech as prime minister to 'fix the crisis in social care once and for all with a clear plan we have prepared to give every older person the dignity and security they deserve'. The Conservative Party's 2019 general election manifesto stated that a future Tory government would seek a cross-party consensus to bring forward proposals for reform of how people pay for adult social care. The principle would be that 'no one needing care has to sell their home to pay for it'. Legislation based on the Dilnot plan was agreed by both Houses of Parliament, with an implementation date of October 2023. A new £86,000 cap on the amount anyone would have to spend would be introduced and the means test for accessing financial support would be made more generous.

The policy had in fact been the subject of ferocious internal wrangling around the Cabinet table. Sajid Javid, who was chancellor between 2019 and 2020 and health secretary from 2021 to 2022, had resisted the cap when he was at the Treasury on the grounds that it was unaffordable. Johnson, always keen to have his cake and eat it, had wanted to announce the plan and leave a future prime minister to work out how to pay for it, but Javid had refused to agree to this. He had also killed a proposal by Matt Hancock, health secretary from 2018 to 2021, to introduce a much more generous system of free personal care for all, similar to the arrangement which had been introduced in Scotland.

Then Hancock quit, having been caught on camera canoodling with an aide in the Department of Health in breach of lockdown rules. Javid returned to the Cabinet as health secretary in June 2021 and found the discussions about social care were still live. Now, though, the balance of power in the Cabinet subcommittee discussing it had changed. Rishi Sunak, then chancellor, was holding the Treasury line that any reform had to be paid for. However, instead of being outnumbered by the prime minister and the health secretary, Johnson was outnumbered by Sunak and Javid, who were both sceptical about an expensive social care reform. 'I didn't agree with the cap, I never did,' says Javid.

> My view was that if there was some more cash I'd rather put it into the NHS. There was an economic reason for that – I didn't think it was right to increase the size of the state to pay for social care. But also I had a moral reason. I thought it was OK for people to sell their homes to pay for their social care and Boris didn't. I thought if you have got the money then you should pay for your own social care. If you haven't got the money, then the state should step in. But why should you cap it for rich people? That was a constant argument that we had.[33]

In the end Sunak would only sign off on the policy if Johnson agreed to raise taxes to fund it. 'Boris tried to have the spending without the tax and Rishi made it clear that it had to be paid for and Boris then accepted that trade-off,' Javid recalls.[34]

In September 2021, Johnson announced to parliament that National Insurance contributions would rise by 1.25 per cent, to pay for an increased investment in health and social care. The prime minister told MPs that the tax rise would fund 'the biggest catch-up programme in the NHS's history'. The plan – which broke a Tory manifesto pledge – infuriated Conservative right-wingers and a rebellion started to brew. But Johnson soon had bigger political problems on his plate. Within weeks the 'partygate' story broke and a chaotic Downing Street started to unravel. Liz Truss became prime minister and Kwasi Kwarteng, her chancellor, scrapped the National Insurance rise as part of his career-ending mini-budget. Social care reform was yet again on the rocks along with Truss's premiership. In November 2022, her successor Rishi Sunak announced that the £86,000 cap on care costs – which had already been approved by parliament – would not be implemented until at least 2025 – after the next general election. Reflecting on this decision and the catalogue

---

[33] Interview with the author.   [34] Interview with the author.

of dither and delay, Sir Andrew Dilnot, the author of the land-mark government review, is damning about the Conservative record. Many people had been left approaching old age 'as though they're standing in the middle of the road with a lorry driving towards them and the best they can hope for is that they die before the lorry hits them', he said. It was 'very distressing to see social care at the bottom of the priority list again,' he added. 'We have at the moment in this country people who need care who wish they would die to help their families. We have people who need care whose family members sometimes can't help themselves thinking "gosh I wish X would die". This is not a civilised way to behave.'[35]

THE BURNING INJUSTICE OF MENTAL HEALTH

The failure on social care was part of wider weakness that saw politically salient hospitals prioritised over wider community provision. While the number of hospital consultants has grown by 26 per cent since 2015, the number of GPs has fallen by almost 7 per cent. There were repeated promises by ministers to create 'parity of esteem' between physical and mental health, but the rhetoric was never really matched by reality.

Theresa May gave the cause of mental health a decisive push as prime minister. She had been struck as home secretary by the large number of people being detained in police cells with some form of mental health condition. When she got to Number 10 she wanted to do something about it. In January 2017, she delivered a speech at the Charity Commission entitled 'The Shared Society'. 'The burning injustice of mental health and inadequate treatment . . . demands a new approach from govern-ment and society as a whole,' she said. She announced that the distinguished psychiatrist Simon Wessely would conduct a review of the Mental Health Act to improve existing legislation. It was a noble ambition but May quickly became bogged down in the

---

[35] Rachel Sylvester, 'The false economy of UK's social care failings', *The Times*, 16 January 2023.

Brexit negotiations, battling her party at every turn. She had no time or political energy left to embed change in the support for those with mental health problems. Wessely's widely supported recommendations were eventually kicked into the long grass by Rishi Sunak, who failed to find time for the necessary bill in his 2023 King's Speech. A 'disappointed' Wessely saw his proposals as the victim of partisan self-interest rather than intellectual or ideological disagreement. 'I don't think it's because they're against anything in it, I think it's purely political that they need the time to try and avoid losing the election,' he said when the Sunak government shelved his recommendations. 'Obviously I'm cross. In the end it's their choice about what they spend parliamentary time on but a huge amount of effort has gone into this, it's gone through all the right stages, it's not opposed by any political party. We got scuppered first by the EU chaos, then by Covid now by the political chaos they're in. It's disappointing.'[36]

There were some positive steps made on mental health during the Conservative years – including the introduction of mental health leads in schools and specialised mental health ambulances. But provision remained patchy and the supply of support failed to keep up with the rapid rise in demand during and after the pandemic, particularly among the young. In July 2021, one in six children and young people aged 6–16 were identified as having a probable mental health disorder, up from one in nine in 2017. There was a 47 per cent increase in the number of new emergency referrals to crisis care teams in under-18s between December 2019 and April 2021. At the end of April 2022, 388,887 young people were in contact with children's and young people's mental health services. Yet less than a quarter of children referred to services started treatment within the four-week waiting target.[37] When Anne Longfield was appointed children's commissioner in 2015 she was shocked to hear from young people that they could only get help if they had attempted suicide. By 2023 the situation had deteriorated

---

[36] Evidence to The Times Health Commission, 3 October 2023.

[37] Evidence to The Times Health Commission from Anne Longfield, Chair Commission on Young Lives, 31 October 2023.

still further. 'Now young people are saying that not only do they have to try and take their own life, they have to try to take their own life several times and there'll be an assessment of levels of intent within that,'[38] she said. After thirteen years of Conservative-led government, the mental health injustice continued to burn.

RUNNING AWAY FROM THE NANNY STATE

Equally shortsighted has been the failure to tackle a growing obesity crisis. According to the Organisation for Economic Cooperation and Development (OECD) obesity rates in the UK are the highest in Western Europe and rates in England have increased faster than in most developed countries.[39] Two-thirds of adults in England are overweight or obese. Ten per cent of children are obese before they even start school and an additional 12 per cent are overweight. Since 1993 the proportion of people who are obese (with a body mass index of 30 or above) has doubled. There is a strong correlation between poverty and obesity. Children living in the most deprived parts of England are more than twice as likely to be obese as those living in the wealthiest areas. The costs to the NHS are set to rise from £6 billion a year to almost £10 billion by 2050, with obesity linked to an increased risk of diabetes, cancer, heart disease and strokes.

The Conservative government that came to power in 2015 set out to take action with some success. In his March 2016 Budget, Osborne announced a sugar tax which came into force in April 2018. The soft drinks industry levy had a significant effect on the content of drinks, driving reformulation even before it was introduced because companies knew it was coming. The total sugar sold in soft drinks by retailers and manufacturers decreased by 35.4 per cent between 2015 and 2019, from 135,500 tonnes to 87,600 tonnes. Over the

---

[38] Ibid.

[39] OECD, *Obesity and the Economics of Prevention: Fit not Fat* (Paris: OECD, 2010).

same period the sales-weighted average sugar content of soft drinks declined by 43.7 per cent from 5.7 g/100 ml to 2.2g/ 100 ml.[40] Far from harming profits, while sugar consumption from soft drinks fell, total soft drink sales increased by 14.9 per cent from 2015 to 2019.[41] The levy worked well but it was limited in its scope and does not apply to milkshakes or sugary fruit juice.

After that attempts to tackle obesity stalled. Public health interventions to encourage people to have a better lifestyle repeatedly fell foul of Conservative free marketeers who criticise interventionist policies as examples of the 'nanny state'. In 2020 Boris Johnson announced a crackdown on obesity after coming out of hospital where he was treated for Covid-19. Admitting he had been 'way overweight', he pledged to ban junk food advertising on television before the 9 pm watershed and end 'buy one get one free' promotions on unhealthy products. But the measures were shelved by Rishi Sunak. He blamed the cost of living crisis, but he had also come under pressure from Tory right-wingers to abandon the 'illiberal' anti-obesity plans. Sunak did, however, announce in his 2023 party conference speech a plan to completely phase out smoking in England.

Henry Dimbleby – who quit as a government adviser on food policy in frustration at the failure to act – says the health service has paid the price for these political decisions:

> The crisis in social care and the crisis in the NHS are predominantly being brought about because the underlying health of our population is so poor. We need to be spending more on prevention to reduce the cost of treatment, but politically that shift is difficult not only because of the money but because of attitudes to the nanny state – a phrase created by the people who ran the country at the time who had nannies and had ambivalent feelings about those nannies. That kind of mentality is causing all kinds of problems.[42]

---

[40] Institute for Government, 'Sugar tax', 14 November 2022.   [41] Ibid.
[42] 'NHS "forced to clear up dirt" as obesity soars', *The Times*, 17 January 2023.

When Covid-19 hit, a clear link between obesity and vulnerability to the virus emerged. Deaths from the virus were nearly four times higher in the most deprived areas of the UK than in the least deprived areas for the working-age population.

A FLAWED COVID RESPONSE

No government could have been fully prepared for a global pandemic like Covid-19, but it is clear that opportunities to build resilience were missed and risks were exacerbated. In 2016, a simulation exercise called Exercise Cygnus was held which involved 1,000 officials, medics and ministers practising their response to a flu pandemic. The scenario they were working on involved between 200,000 and 400,000 deaths and it did not go well. The report on the simulation concluded: 'The UK's preparedness and response in terms of its plans, policies and capability, is currently not sufficient to cope with the extreme demands of a severe pandemic that will have a nationwide impact across all sectors.' In particular, it warned of concerns about 'the expectation that the social care system would be able to provided the level of support needed if the NHS implemented its proposed reverse triage plans, which would entail the movement of patients from hospitals into social care facilities'.[43] The assessment proved to be remarkably prescient. Between early March and early June 2020, nearly 20,000 care home residents in England and Wales died with Covid-19. That followed a government decision to rapidly discharge hospital patients into care homes without testing or a requirement for them to isolate. A 2022 high court judgment ruled that this decision was unlawful as it failed to take into account the risk to vulnerable residents of asymptomatic transmission of the virus.[44]

The Vaccine Task Force, chaired by Kate Bingham, was a triumph and helped to save thousands of lives by ensuring the country had enough coronavirus vaccines to get jabs into

[43] Hardman, *Fighting for Life*, p. 285.
[44] 'Families sue government for failing to protect care homes from Covid', BBC, 25 August 2023.

arms at speed. But afterwards Bingham said that if she had ever been asked what was the biggest threat to the success of the vaccine task force, 'the honest answer would have been "Large parts of the rest of Whitehall"'.[45] Despite working unpaid seven days a week, from 7 am to 10 pm, she believed that she was 'thrown under a bus' by Johnson's Downing Street, who thought she was 'getting too big for [her] boots'. On one occasion she was the victim of 'an extraordinary ambush' by Matt Hancock, then the health secretary, who accused her of incompetence in front of other ministers. Everything, she said, 'was seen through a political lens'.[46]

WhatsApp messages released to the Covid Inquiry in October 2023 revealed the chaos and dysfunctionality at the heart of Number 10 during the pandemic. Simon Case, the head of the civil service, wrote to colleagues that the government looked like a 'terrible tragic joke' over its handling of the virus. He said Johnson 'cannot lead' and made good government 'impossible' by changing direction every day. Patrick Vallance, the former chief scientific adviser, raged in his contemporaneous diary about the 'ridiculous flip-flopping' by the prime minister who judged at the end of February 2020 that the biggest risk was 'overreaction' to Covid.[47]

But in truth the instability was there before the crisis broke. The Health Foundation think tank concluded in 2021 that the UK entered the pandemic 'in a vulnerable position both in terms of systemic weaknesses in the health care system and poor underlying population health'. Jennifer Dixon, the chief executive, said: 'Underinvestment in the NHS over many years has resulted in fewer doctors, nurses, beds and scanners relative to our European neighbours. These weaknesses reduced the health

---

[45] Kate Bingham and Tim Hames, *The Long Shot: The Inside Story of the Race to Vaccinate Britain* (London: Oneworld, 2022).

[46] Interview with the author, 'Kate Bingham: No. 10 felt I was getting too big for my boots', *The Times*, 15 October 2022.

[47] Chris Smyth, 'Who is to blame for wasted month spent flip-flopping over virus?', *The Times*, 31 October 2023.

and social care system's resilience to a shock like the pandemic. They will also affect how quickly services can recover.'[48]

In a report for the Institute of Government, published in 2023, Rachel Wolf and Sam Freedman argued that there has been underinvestment in capital, including a lack of hospital beds and too many beds filled by people who should not be in them. England has two hospital beds per 1,000 residents compared to three in France and six in Germany, and the UK has the fifth lowest number of CT and PET scanners and MRI units per capita in the OECD. Productivity has also been harmed, they suggested, by an exodus of senior staff, with inexperienced replacements recruited. 'The trigger for the problems the NHS now faces may have been Covid, but the bullet had been loaded,' they wrote.[49]

No country's health care system was able to avoid disruption from Covid-19, but the lack of spare capacity in the NHS meant that elective surgery was more disrupted in the UK than in other countries during the pandemic. The decision was taken to slash the number of planned operations, which inevitably drove up waiting lists. Between 2019 and 2020 there was a 46 per cent fall in hip replacements and a 68 per cent drop in knee replacements in the UK. The EU average was 14 per cent and 24 per cent respectively.[50] The Nuffield Trust found that in Italy, Portugal and Spain, waiting lists appeared to be stabilising or even decreasing by 2023. Some hospitals in other countries barely halted planned surgery at all even at the height of the Covid-19 crisis.

CONCLUSION

The NHS must bear some of the blame for such operational decisions. Craig Oliver, who was Number 10 director of

[48] Health Foundation response to OECD 'Health at a Glance 2021 report', 9 November 2021.

[49] Sam Freedman and Rachel Wolf, 'The NHS productivity puzzle', report for the Institute for Government, 13 June 2023.

[50] The King's Fund, 'What caused the UK's elective care backlog and how do we tackle it?', 24 February 2023.

communications under Cameron, says ministers feel strangely powerless over the NHS:

> We live in a country where we have the Royal College of Physicians, the Royal College of GPs, the Royal College of X, Y and Z and they are presented as professional bodies full of saintly people who will understand what's going on. But they are essentially unions. We need much more clarity about who is really responsible and that actually the power of the secretary of state is not as great as we say it is. The Health Secretary became a weird sort of figurehead who basically had to go to NHS England and try to influence them.[51]

But politicians set the parameters and priorities for the NHS. Successive Conservative health secretaries have failed to bring the professionals with them – a critical error in a public service that relies so heavily on its work force. Politically motivated targets drove too much activity and money into hospitals, the most expensive part of the system, and away from the community.

The NHS has always had enormous political power because of its hold over the public imagination. During the Brexit referendum in 2016, Vote Leave promised to transfer resources from the EU to the NHS. The slogan on the side of its campaign bus read: 'We send the EU £350 million a week, let's fund our NHS instead.' Since 2010, spending on the health service increased much faster than on other parts of the public sector. According to the Institute for Fiscal Studies, health funding has gone up 42 per cent while that on education has risen by only 3 per cent. The NHS is sucking up an ever greater share of taxpayers' money and now accounts for almost 40 per cent of day-to-day public spending, excluding welfare supports and pensions. Yet outcomes have gone backwards.

There has been a shocking lack of political stability at the top of the Department of Health and Social Care, with seven secretaries of state appointed in seven years (including one of them,

[51] Interview with the author.

Steve Barclay, who was given the role twice). Such merry-go-round government has made it almost impossible for decisions to be taken with the long-term health of the nation in mind. There have been too many short-term emergency handouts and an underinvestment in long-term capital expenditure on critical infrastructure, beds, scanners and technology. Spending on the core functions of the health service may have been ring-fenced, but social care and public health budgets were slashed as part of the deep cuts to local government.

The fiasco over Lansley's legislation and the controversy over May's social care plans have left ministers nervous of contemplating necessary reform.

While other countries around the world seized on technology to transform their health systems, large parts of the NHS remained paper-based, with letters to patients all too often arriving after appointments. Despite some advances with the introduction of virtual wards and the roll out of the NHS app during the pandemic, the health service is still in many ways an analogue system in a digital age. The chance to personalise health care, reduce bureaucracy for clinicians and create efficiency gains through technology has been missed. There have been improvements to patient safety and accountability, but the wider health of the nation has been neglected. Ministers have backed away from tackling the obesity crisis and taking action to reduce health inequalities. After the Conservative years, the NHS is still a sickness service rather than a system that promotes health. Sunak's key pledge to cut waiting lists looks increasingly impossible to meet. The British public started to lose faith in the national religion and their belief in the Tory party began to waver too.

6

Education

Alan Smithers

THE CONSERVATIVES CAME TO POWER IN 2010 with ready-made education ministers, Michael Gove as secretary of state, Nick Gibb as minister for schools and David Willetts as minister for universities. All had shadowed their posts for at least three years and were clear about what they wanted to achieve. The Conservatives' partners in coalition, the Liberal Democrats, came to office determined to provide more support for the underprivileged. It proved to be a potent combination.

A binding Coalition Agreement[1] set out their joint commitments in detail. In the sections devoted to schools and higher education, it was stated that schools would be reformed, the curriculum reviewed and accountability strengthened. It was agreed to create a new type of school, the free school, state-funded but opened subject to approval, by anyone with the capacity and capability. The Liberal Democrats' priority of a funding premium to enable schools to provide extra support to children from low-income homes was also enshrined but, significantly in view of the difficulties which arose later, that of providing free schools meals for all primary school children, was not. In higher education, it was agreed to wait for the report from a review of university funding commissioned by the outgoing government from Lord Browne, the former CEO of BP, before reaching a decision on student fees, with an opt out for the Liberal Democrats if necessary.

---

[1] David Cameron and Nick Clegg, *The Coalition: Our Programme for Government* (London: HM Government, 20 May 2010).

Gove immediately got on to freeing schools from local authorities. He had inherited 203 academies from Blair, and envisaged a time when every school – special, primary and secondary – would be one. An Academies Act[2] was passed within weeks and Gove wrote to all head teachers inviting them to apply for academy status. An Education Act [3] with further provisions for academies followed a year later. In parallel, he initiated fundamental revisions of the curriculum and examinations. Meanwhile Nick Clegg, the Liberal Democrat leader and deputy prime minister, secured within the austerity context a relatively good settlement for education in the 2010 Spending Review. The 5–16 schools budget, including £2.5 billion for the pupil premium, was set to rise for the next four years, but only by 0.1 per cent per year. Overall, the Department for Education (DfE) was asked to make savings of 3.4 per cent by 2014–15.

Complying almost led to Gove's departure before he had really started. The DfE had identified Labour's £55 billion Building Schools for the Future programme (BSF) as one that could be scrapped, and it was Gove's responsibility to inform the House in person. But when asked by MPs which schools would be affected he could not provide an accurate list on two occasions in the House. He apologised profusely, but such was the outcry that he went to David Cameron to ask whether he should resign. 'Of course I wouldn't let him go.'[4] But faced with a third session in the Commons that week, he secretly sought out the advice of Dominic Cummings, who had been blocked from becoming his chief of staff by Number 10 over suspected leaks. Cummings advised him to go on the attack. While preparing, it emerged that there had not been a list when Gove had asked for it, but without him being told, one had been quickly cobbled together. Called to account by the Commons, he successfully put the blame on the body that ran BSF and his officials.

Had he had to resign he would almost certainly have been replaced by the senior Liberal Democrat, David Laws, who had

[2] Academies Act 2010 – Explanatory Notes (legislation.gov.uk).

[3] Education Act 2011 (legislation.gov.uk).

[4] David Cameron, *For the Record* (London: William Collins, 2019), p. 222.

been shadow education secretary for his party, and it is highly likely that the Coalition's education agenda would have been very different. Instead it became the first step on Dominic Cummings' way back – which was to have baleful consequences for Gove. Moreover, the binning of BSF came back to haunt the Conservatives when, in 2023, the deterioration in the fabric of some schools required that they be wholly or partly shut just before the start of the academic year, provoking a barrage of complaints from head teachers and parents about thoughtlessness and inconvenience.

Nick Gibb, the schools minister who had already made his mark by putting phonics at the heart of the literacy strategy, was asked to stand down in September 2012, to make way for David Laws, which he did loyally and uncomplainingly. Laws had originally been appointed chief secretary to the Treasury but felt he had had to resign. Two years later his party wanted to appoint him to another post commensurate with his seniority and skills. The Department for Education was an obvious choice, and he was made schools minister, as well as minister for the Cabinet Office. He was thus more powerful than other schools ministers in that he was able to attend Cabinet.

Fortunately, at first Gove and Laws got on well, having got to know each other as shadow education secretaries and, on occasions, jointly opposing Labour's policies. Laws turned out to be an important moderating influence. He talked Gove out of returning to O-levels and CSEs, an idea which infuriated the Liberal Democrat leader, by persuading him that he could achieve the same end by fundamentally reforming GCSEs. Laws was supportive of Gove's enthusiasm for giving schools more autonomy since it accorded with his party's principles, but he could not see how 24,000 schools could be overseen from Whitehall. He advised that there should be an intermediate layer, but he was ignored. Ultimately he was proved correct, but he did not make an issue of it.

The passion of the Liberal Democrats was for reducing educational inequality. A 'catch-up premium' had been agreed at the outset, but free school meals for all primary children was left for negotiation. Initially, discussions went well, with Gove already having commissioned a School Food Plan. The Treasury said that free school meals could not be afforded for all primary school children and the Liberal Democrats accepted this, agreeing that the scheme should only apply to infants' classes. But not all the schools had the necessary kitchens and finding the money for them meant less for the extra places needed to accommodate the rising school population. There was already simmering resentment among Liberal Democrats that Gove was continually raiding the capital budget to fund his free schools and the kitchen row brought it to the boil, with leaks to newspapers from both sides, culminating in an attack on Clegg's wife.[5] The irritation between Gove and Clegg boiled over and they stopped speaking to each other. Laws was affected too and he checked every day to make sure there had been no reneging on the school meals agreement.

Gove was moved from his education role in the 2014 reshuffle, ostensibly because he was needed elsewhere to mastermind the 2015 election, but in fact because he and Dominic Cummings had upset so many people both in education and beyond. In his four years as education secretary, Gove had initiated major reforms in partnership with Nick Gibb and David Laws which were the high point in education policy in the fourteen years of Conservative rule. David Willetts resigned as universities minister at the same time. With their departures much of the drive for education reform evaporated. Cameron's post-referendum resignation was also destabilising, but it was the crises of Covid, Ukraine, Hamas and strikes that dropped education right down the agenda.

There were four more prime ministers after Cameron, one only surviving for fifty days, and nine education secretaries after Gove. Only Gibb brought any continuity in Education, serving for ten of the fourteen years, although with two interruptions. There was considerable churn in the DfE civil servants too. The wonder, in the face of this continual upheaval, is that the policy

---

[5] Nick Clegg, *Politics: Between the Extremes* (London: Bodley Head, 2016), p. 104.

directions established by Gove and Willetts continued for the next decade. Some policies, such as the changes to the curriculum and exams, the pupil premium, free school meals for all infant school children and the raising of the participation age to 18, were fully implemented. While others, such as the academisation of the school system and the switch to school-led teacher training, were taken as far as feasible.

Nicky Morgan, Gove's immediate successor who served for two years, passed the Education and Adoption Act 2016, which paved the way for even more academies.[6] But she really wanted schools to focus more on character development. Before she could make it happen, however, Theresa May had become prime minister, and much to Morgan's annoyance, did not reappoint her.[7] The post went to Justine Greening, who also lasted two years, but she was continually at odds with May over grammar schools and was eventually moved on.[8] It fell to Damian Hinds, her replacement, to introduce a new attempt by the DfE to put technical and occupational education on par with the academic, this time through qualifications called T-levels, designed to be equivalent to three A-levels. He did not hold on to the post when Boris Johnson became prime minister, but returned to the DfE in 2023 to replace Gibb.

Next up was Gavin Williamson, who was rewarded for his part in Johnson's election campaign. But he had a very uncomfortable time, it being completely dominated by how schools and universities (reunited once more in the DfE) responded to the Covid crisis. He did introduce the Higher Education (Freedom of Speech Bill) in May 2021, but he was ousted four months later before it was enacted. Williamson was replaced by Nadhim Zahawi, who used his ten months in office to launch a Schools Bill which, among other things, forced all England's state schools to join multi-academy trusts, and gave the DfE powers

[6] Education and Adoption Act 2016 (legislation.gov.uk).

[7] Anthony Seldon with Raymond Newell, *May at 10* (London: Biteback, 2019), pp. 78–9.

[8] Ibid., p. 93.

to control the trusts. So keen was he to get this done he did not take the necessary soundings, and the bill was put on ice.

Four education secretaries later in December 2022, Gillian Keegan announced the bill would be dropped and that she hoped that those parts which did not require new laws – which the academy proposals did – could be introduced in other ways. Before Keegan, herself apprenticeship educated, could settle to the task of overseeing the new T-level-apprenticeship ladder, she was hit by a school-buildings' crisis, with the Public Accounts Committee pointing the finger at the scrapping of Building Schools for the Future. The extent to which the Conservative Party had lost it way on education became starkly apparent when Rishi Sunak in his speech to the party conference in 2023, and reiterated in the King's Speech that year, abandoned Gove's carefully crafted A-levels for a baccalaureate-type award.[9]

David Willetts' immediate task on becoming universities minister was to raise the money to fund an expanding university system. Blair had done some of the heavy lifting by getting parliamentary approval for the principle of student tuition fees, but in order to do so had had to agree a cap of only £3,000. Something like three times that figure was needed, but to charge that amount posed a huge problem for the Coalition. During the election campaign Nick Clegg had been photographed displaying a NUS card pledging not to vote for any increase at all, a commitment which all Liberal Democrat candidates had made.[10] In fact, some senior Liberal Democrats were ambivalent about the pledge, with Clegg telling Cameron that he was prepared to support an increase.[11] Others were persuaded by the financial logic and in the end about half the party voted in favour. But there was a severe reckoning. In 2015 all but eight of the fifty-seven Liberal Democrat MPs lost their seats, including

---

[9] 'Advanced British Standard: Sunak qualification will replace A-levels and T-levels', *BBC News*, 4 October 2023, www.bbc.co.uk/news/education-67008206

[10] Nick Clegg, *Politics: Between the Extremes* (London: Bodley Head, 2016), p. 29; David Laws, *Coalition* (London: Biteback, 2016) p. 56.

[11] David Cameron, *For The Record*, (London, William Collins, 2019), p. 225.

David Laws and Vince Cable, Willetts' boss. Nick Clegg got over the line in Sheffield Hallam in 2015, but resigned as leader the next day, and lost his seat in 2017.

Tuition fees dominated Willetts' time in office, and it is what he is likely to be remembered for, but he achieved much else in Education, such as making it easier for institutions to become universities. In Science for which he was also responsible, he managed to get the science budget ring-fenced at a time of austerity, one of the achievements which led Sir Paul Nurse, president of the Royal Society, to say he had been 'an outstanding science minister, respected not only in the UK but throughout the world'.[12] But elsewhere Willetts' ambitions were thwarted. His hope that student fees would create a market in which their choices would drive up standards came to nothing when fees were capped and almost all universities charged the maximum they were allowed. His wish to bring together in one framework the different ways in which universities were regulated was blocked by Cameron's Number 10 with no reason given.[13] His arguments for taking overseas students out of immigration figures were dismissed by Theresa May's Home Office.[14]

He left the government after four years in the same 2014 reshuffle that saw Gove moved from education. He has never made public the reasons, though it is likely that his frustration will have played a part. He did not stand in the 2015 election and was elevated to the House of Lords. His departure, like Gove's, was followed by frequent changes of minister. In the following ten years there were seven, with two serving on two separate occasions, and two others given a new title, which signified changes to the role. There was also a change of department.

Willetts' idea of a common regulatory framework was taken up after his departure and an Act rushed through before the 2017

---

[12] 'David Willetts quits as universities minister', *Times Higher Education*, 14 July 2014.

[13] David Willetts, *A University Education* (Oxford: Oxford University Press, 2017), p. 288.

[14] Ibid., p. 307.

election.[15] It established the Office for Students as a very powerful regulatory body, replacing both the Higher Education Funding Council and the Office of Fair Access. In 2023, in response to numerous instances of visiting speakers and staff with heterodox views being shouted down, harassed, or even banned, the OfS was given the additional task of promoting free speech and funded to appoint a Director of Free Speech and Academic Freedom.[16]

It was not only the Liberal Democrats who ran into problems from the imposition of realistic tuition fees. May suffered continual criticism whipped up by the then opposition leader Jeremy Corbyn. In February 2018 she set up an independent panel to review post-18 education and funding, chaired by Philip Augar, a banker turned author. It reported in May 2019, with fifty-three recommendations covering the whole of post-18 education.[17] But it was not until January 2021, by which time Boris Johnson had succeeded May, that there was any acknowledgement, and then it took another year for proposals to emerge. It seems that the Augar Report contained so many ideas that the government did not really know what to do with them. Some were not to its taste, such as lowering tuition fees and stopping universities from offering foundation years, but there were others that were taken up, such as a Lifelong Learning entitlement, which is due to be rolled out from 2025.[18] As a package, what Augar recommended is dead, but there are elements in it, including more support for the disadvantaged and developing technical education, that the Conservatives will act upon if re-elected.

REFORMING SCHOOLS

Michael Gove came to office, according to David Laws, determined to make 'as many schools as possible academies, as quickly as possible'.[19] Conservatives had long been keen on self-government

---

[15] Higher Education and Research Act 2017 (legislation.gov.uk).

[16] Higher Education (Freedom of Speech) Act 2023 (legislation.gov.uk).

[17] Independent Panel, *Review of Post-18 Education and Funding* (London: DfE, 30 May 2019).

[18] Lifelong Learning Entitlement overview – GOV.UK (www.gov.uk).

[19] Laws, *Coalition*, p. 213.

for schools and Kenneth Baker in his seminal 1988 Education Reform Act had made it possible by creating two new types of school: 'grant-maintained' and 'city technology college' (CTC). Blair abolished the former, but allowed the fifteen CTCs to continue. Their potential was spotted by his chief education adviser, Andrew Adonis, who adapted the model to become a very successful means of resuscitating intractably failing comprehensives.[20] Mossbourne Community Academy in Hackney is the prime example. Opened on the site of the troubled Hackney Downs comprehensive, it became best-performing non-selective school in London.[21]

Not only did the model offer the prospect of improving performance through autonomy, but also a uniform school system under the direct control of the government. Historically, while central government legislated, it was local authorities that implemented. This has led to an untidy mix of school types, when, as with comprehensive schools, not all authorities adopted the policy. There are so many different school types haphazardly spread that England hardly has what could be properly called a schools system.

Gove got on with turning schools into academies. He enabled schools rated 'outstanding' by Ofsted to be fast-tracked to academy status. Grammar schools could apply and retain the power to select. Local authorities would only be allowed new schools in their areas if they were academies. There were also to be academies called 'free schools' to be set up by anyone who received approval and they would be backed with government funding. Independent schools could become academies, but only by becoming state schools. A very attractive offer was put to the schools, not only would they have control, but also more money since they would receive what had previously gone on their behalf to the local authority. The numbers converting, especially

---

[20] Andrew Adonis, *Education, Education, Education: Reforming England's Schools* (London: Biteback, 2012), p. 11.

[21] Parent Power, 'Best state secondary schools in the UK 2023', *Sunday Times*, 9 December 2022.

secondary schools, grew rapidly. The 203 established by the Blair government had become, by 2023, 10,176. Altogether approaching half (43 per cent) of all state-funded schools – 80 per cent of secondary, 40 per cent of primary and 44 per cent of special – had become academies.[22] But it is still not job done, in spite of all the effort that has gone into it.

Gove also tweaked the model by removing the need to have a subject specialism, a hangover from the city-technology-college days. He also enabled schools for 16–19-year-olds and pupil referral units to become academies. His successors tried to complete the process by moving from voluntarism to compulsion. Nicky Morgan in the 2016 Act compelled schools failed by Ofsted to become academies.[23] Nadhim Zahawi attempted to force all schools to become academies by edict, but this was rejected by parliament as a step too far.[24] It remains, however, a Conservative aspiration for all schools to become academies.

But has the switch to academies had the desired outcome? Disconcertingly, it is not possible to say. Labour's academies are undoubtedly a success in terms of Ofsted ratings and exam results not only in absolute terms, but also in comparison with schools that had approval but had not yet made the change.[25] But these results cannot be extrapolated to Gove's academies, because Adonis's were failing schools starting afresh in many cases, in some cases from the ground upwards, whereas Gove's were the same schools, with the same staff and the same intake but having received academy status. Attempts at comparisons have been made, but are hardly meaningful. Adonis's academies show more improvement, but they have a lower starting point; Gove's have better results because outstanding schools were fast-

---

[22] 'Schools, pupils and their characteristics, Academic year 2022/23', Explore Education Statistics (explore-education-statistics.service.gov.uk).

[23] Education and Adoption Act 2016 (legislation.gov.uk).

[24] Tom Belger, 'The schools bill is dead, so where next for academies?', *Schools Week*, 9 December 2022.

[25] Stephen Machin, 'Academies: old research is being wrongly used to validate them', *Guardian*, 9 April 2012.

tracked into the academy fold. In terms of Ofsted rating there is little difference on average, but with a wider spread among the more recent academies because they now include not only the fast-tracked 'outstanding', but also the compulsorily converted 'inadequate'.[26] There has been an attempt by the Local Government Association to demonstrate that, in fact, it is its schools that do better, but an independent analysis has questioned that interpretation.[27] The government has claimed success for the academies policy pointing to the way England has been climbing the international league tables. But leaving the details till the final section when we reach a verdict, we can say now that if there has been an improvement it is not necessarily academisation that is responsible. A good case can be made for changes to the content of the curriculum and the way that it is taught.

Whitehall eventually accepted that to oversee an academised school system, there would have to be an intermediate layer as Laws had advocated. The vehicle by which academies are created is a special trust. Some of these trusts developed into chains of schools, which came to be known as multi-academy trusts or MATs. It is MATs from which the intermediate layer is to be formed. In a White Paper in March 2022 the government said it intended to create a fully trust-led school system with a single regulatory approach.[28] Trusts would be expected to manage at least ten schools. At the time there were over 2,500 trusts of which 45 per cent looked after ten or more schools, the average was seven, with the largest trust responsible for seventy-five schools. But there are also many single-school trusts that will have to join with others. This raises the question of whether academies will end up any more

26 Jon Andrews and Natalie Perera, *The Impact of Academies on Educational Outcome* (London: Education Policy Institute, July 2017).

27 Freddie Whittaker, 'Fact check: do council schools really outperform academies?', *Schools Week*, 3 August 2023.

28 March 2022 schools White Paper (England), House of Commons Library (parliament.uk).

autonomous than local authority schools. The MATs have executive head teachers and governing bodies to whom the leaders and governors of the individual schools defer; schools cannot opt out of trusts, though the trust can transfer them and, unlike local authorities, the trusts themselves are not inspected by Ofsted, only the schools in them. There is no doubt that some trusts, the Harris Trust for example, are expert at turning round underperforming schools, but that is different from autonomy being the source of improvement. If it is the trusts rather than autonomy, then it is the competence and motives of those setting them up that are crucial. As long as the Conservatives are in power, expect them to look for ways of academising the whole school system.

Among the many types of school in England's jumbled system is the grammar, 163 of which survived Labour's cull sixty years ago as it attempted to make all schools comprehensive. They tend to dominate any state-school league tables and rival the top independents. In their day they were the means of social mobility for children from low-income families who got in (Disclosure: I was one). But, of course, the majority of children did not, and from the age of 11 their life chances were different. From time to time Conservatives have returned to the idea of opening more grammar schools because parental demand greatly exceeds supply. Of the five Conservative prime ministers between 2010 and 2024, two were in favour and three against. The most enthusiastic was Theresa May, who went to one herself and wanted others to have the same opportunity. But she chose the wrong person to be her education secretary, not realising their ideas of social mobility were so very different. Liz Truss, the other prime minster who wanted more grammar schools, was not in office long enough to do anything about it. The excellence of grammar schools continues to be extolled in the Conservative Party, but it is unlikely there will ever be the political traction for them to make a comeback.

ACCOUNTABILITY

It was Kenneth Clarke, as secretary of state in the Major government, who in 1992 laid the foundations of holding schools to account. In the face of the concerted opposition of his civil servants, the teaching profession, teachers' unions and teacher trainers, who were all steeped in 1960s progressive education, he established Ofsted as an independent inspectorate, and also published national test and examination results.[29]

Ofsted

Between 1992 and 2010 when Michael Gove took office, there had already been changes, but Gove was determined that Ofsted should become tougher and more efficient. He first asked it to drop the school self-evaluation form, brought in by the Blair government, that head teachers had to submit before inspections, which they found extremely burdensome. He also announced, more controversially, that schools rated 'outstanding' would no longer be inspected, but that resources would be concentrated on those whose grades were falling below 'good'. This exemption was removed in 2020 and of the 930 schools reinspected by the end of the 2022–3 school year, only 19 per cent retained the grade and 17 per cent were classed as 'requires improvement' or lower.[30] Clearly, regular inspections are necessary to avoid complacency and make sure that schools are keeping up with changing requirements.

Importantly, Gove was able to secure Sir Michael Wilshaw, who had made such a success of the Mossbourne Academy, as the new chief inspector of schools. At first, they were of one mind and initiated a number of major changes to the way Ofsted operated. The inspection framework was greatly simplified with reporting focusing on just four areas, of which

[29] Ken Clarke, *Kind of Blue: A Political Memoir* (London: Macmillan, 2016), pp. 263–79.

[30] HM Government, *Main Findings: State-Funded Schools Inspections and Outcomes as at 31 August 2023* (Ofsted, 14 November 2023).

teaching quality was the key criterion since only if it were rated 'outstanding' could the school receive this as its overall grade. Assessments previously rated 'satisfactory' were now to be reported as 'requires improvement', to underline that schools should not be content with coasting. Cracks in the relationship, however, soon appeared.[31] Gove became disgruntled at the poor grades being given to his free schools, with a third being rated as substandard. Wilshaw became upset when Gove, in the cause of freedom, would not allow Ofsted to inspect academy trusts in the way it did local authorities. The crunch came when Gove did not reappoint Sally Morgan, who was Wilshaw's choice, as chair of Ofsted, and announced the decision without informing him. Wilshaw then heard that two think tanks were about to release critical reports of Ofsted with the backing of Gove's advisers. Wilshaw lost his cool and went public saying he was 'displeased, shocked and outraged',[32] and this ultimately played a part in Gove being moved on, while Wilshaw kept his job.

Although Wilshaw stoutly defended Ofsted, he was aware that much could be improved. He responded to mounting criticism of the quality and consistency of Ofsted inspections by dispensing with additional inspectors employed by three private firms, and appointing more in-house where he would have greater quality control. Of the 2,800 additional inspectors applying to move in-house only 1,600 were accepted. The rest were deemed not good enough, thereby tacitly admitting that the complaints were justified.[33]

In the thirty years of its existence, Ofsted has continually adapted. Following Gove's 2012 Inspection Framework, there have been two others, in 2015 and 2019, in which the relative importance of the criteria and the way they are to be assessed has changed. Since the 'Baby P' scandal in which Ofsted gave a good rating to an authority only weeks before a child that it should

---

[31] Owen Bennett, *Michael Gove: A Man in a Hurry* (London: Biteback, 2019), pp. 284–5.

[32] Laws, *Coalition*, p. 427.

[33] Hannah Richardson, 'Ofsted purges 1,200 "not good enough" inspectors', *BBC Online*, 19 June 2015.

have known about was murdered, safeguarding has moved up the agenda.[34] In the latest framework, a rating of 'inadequate' for safeguarding trumps all others, with that as the school's overall grade no matter how well it performed on other criteria. This, too, can have tragic consequences. In 2023, Ruth Perry, head of Caversham Primary School, took her own life when this happened to her school. Although there was no substantial evidence of any child being at risk, the inspector determined that the safeguarding policy had not been followed sufficiently closely to merit anything other than 'inadequate'.[35] On all other criteria the school was rated 'good'. Ofsted quickly changed its procedures in response to the death so that any school downgraded in this way would be reinspected within a few months. On reinspection, Caversham was indeed found to be 'good'.

The fallout from Ruth Perry's death has led to Ofsted coming under intense scrutiny. The Commons Education Committee had launched an inquiry in June 2023, not specifically about the suicide, but which became an important part of it. Sir Michael Wilshaw told it that it was 'complete nonsense' that 88 per cent of state schools are now 'good or better'. Two former Education Secretaries contacted by the media were similarly critical. Lord Blunkett maintained that one- or two-word ratings are too simplistic, and Lord Baker regretted that the shortening of the inspection process had removed the depth of information once obtained.[36] The Committee also received evidence from a parallel inquiry 'Beyond Ofsted', chaired by Lord Knight, a former minister of state for schools and learning. In its evidence to the Select Committee, the National Educational Union (NEU), the largest teachers' union, cited evidence from the report that 92 per cent of teachers agreed that Ofsted was not 'a reliable and trusted arbiter of standards'. But then it emerged that

---

[34] Polly Curtis, Rachel Williams, and Allegra Stratton, 'Ofsted accused of manipulating Haringey report after Baby P', *Guardian*, 9 October 2009.

[35] Sian Griffiths, 'Head's suicide prompts sister to join campaign to reform "punitive" Ofsted', *Sunday Times*, 19 March 2023.

[36] Richard Adams, 'Ofsted's "simplistic judgments" no longer fit for purpose, schools experts warn', *Guardian*, 4 November 2023.

the inquiry had been funded by the NEU, and the respondents were a self-selected sample mainly of its own members.[37] Much weightier was the report of the inquest into Ruth Perry's death published in December 2023. The coroner recorded a verdict of 'suicide: contributed to by an Ofsted inspection carried out in November 2022'. She determined that the inspection 'lacked fairness, respect and sensitivity' and at times was 'rude and intimidating'.[38]

In presenting her final Annual Report, Amanda Spielman, the longest serving chief inspector, drew attention in her letter to the secretary of state to the very wide range of Ofsted's responsibilities, which includes not only the inspection of all education and training except that in universities apart from apprenticeships, but also children's services. It is expected to do all of this when its funding has been severely cut. She pointed out that in real terms its funding had fallen by three-quarters in the past twenty years, and now the organisation can only afford to do two-day school inspections with a limited number of inspectors.[39] This claim was backed by a report from the National Audit Office, which showed that Ofsted's income had dropped by 40 per cent in the decade to 2015–16 and was expected to fall further to 2019/20.[40]

Ms Spielman's successor, Sir Martyn Oliver, announced his arrival in January 2024 by committing himself to a 'Big Listen' and also delaying the start of routine inspections to allow inspectors to undertake mental awareness training.[41] The Education

[37] Samantha Booth, '"Independent" inquiry's critical Ofsted poll mostly NEU members: leaders slam self-selecting sample of union-funded group that is "dressed up as independent"', *Schools Week*, 2 November 2023.

[38] Vanessa Clarke and Marthe de Ferrer, 'Ruth Perry: Ofsted inspection "contributed" to head teacher's death', *BBC Online*, 7 December 2023.

[39] Amanda Spielman, *Annual Report of His Majesty's Chief Inspector of Education, Children's Services and Skills 2022/23* (Ofsted, HC 40, 23 November 2023), penultimate paragraph of letter presenting report to secretary of state printed inside the report.

[40] National Audit Office, *Ofsted's Inspection of Schools* (NAO, HC 1004, Session 2017–19, 24 May 2018).

[41] Gov.uk, 'Sir Martyn Oliver begins term at Ofsted with mental health awareness training for inspectors', press release, 2 January 2024.

Committee greatly added to his agenda when it reported on January 2024[42] with a number of concerns, prominent among which were: the use of single-word grades; academisation following two consecutive ratings of 'requires improvement'; safeguarding judgement surmounting all others; inspectors' behaviour and expertise; and non-inspection of multi-academy trusts. It notified the chief inspector that it expected him to report to them every six months on progress made.[43]

The Committee did state that 'there is broad agreement on the importance and value of an independent inspectorate in holding schools accountable and assessing their strengths and weaknesses'.[44] This is reassuring because it must be borne in mind that there are those who would like to do away with Ofsted and leap at any chance to criticise it. The NEU, through a sponsored report, for example, advocates 'every school (conducting) its own self-evaluation' and 'working with an external school improvement partner (SIP)'.[45] A report from the left-leaning think tank, Institute for Public Policy Research (IPPR), at the same time, called upon the government to abolish 'overarching judgements'.[46]

But education got into a sorry state before with independent inspections, because neither politicians nor the public really knew what was happening in schools and classrooms. Self-evaluation is not adequate because, as we shall see with the exam grades during the pandemic, it tends to be too generous. Whatever its imperfections – which must be addressed – Ofsted fulfils an essential role.

---

[42] House of Commons Education Committee, *Ofsted's Work with Schools* (HC 117, First Report of Session 2023–24, 29 January 2024).

[43] Ibid., pp. 4–5 [44] Ibid., p. 3.

[45] Jane Perryman, Alice Bradbury, Graham Calvert and Katie Kilian, *Beyond Ofsted: An Inquiry into the Future of School Inspection* (London: National Education Union, 20 November 2023), p. 10.

[46] Loic Menzies, *Improvement Through Empowerment* (London: IPPR, 20 November 2023), p. 7.

Test and Examination Results

Publishing the national test and examination results might be expected to be more straightforward, but here there is the issue of how to organise them so as to be meaningful for the general public. While it was Kenneth Clarke who put the results in the public domain, it was Blair's government which turned them into an accountability measure.[47] His benchmark was any five GCSEs or equivalent at Grade C and above, which he saw rise from 44.5 per cent in 1996 to 58.1 per cent ten years later. But the existence of the accountability measure influenced behaviour. Some schools, for example, responded by steering pupils away from English and maths towards dead-end vocational qualifications which were low-hanging fruit.[48]

The Conservatives tried to turn this signalling effect to advantage by creating an English baccalaureate (Ebacc) specifying what they regarded as the five core areas. Originally, it was intended to issue a certificate on successful completion, but eventually Gove settled on it being a performance measure.[49] Targets were set for 75 per cent to be taking an EBacc combination by 2022 and 90 per cent by 2025, but although there were increases at first, the level became stuck at below 40 per cent, mainly due to a disinclination of young people in England to study a foreign language. Many reasons have been suggested for this, such as, the rest of the world speaks English, it is rarely a job requirement, and the teacher's no good, but I suspect it is more to do with not starting them at a young enough age. The Ebacc has also been criticised for narrowing education by encouraging schools to focus on just the five areas neglecting the arts and technologies. Its limitations mean that it has not become an

---

[47] Alan Smithers, 'The Coalition and society: education', in Anthony Seldon and Mike Finn (eds.), *The Coalition Effect 2010–15* (Cambridge: University Press, 2015), p. 267.

[48] Anastasia de Waal and Nicholas Cowen, *Artificial Achievement* (civitas.org.uk, June 2007).

[49] Robert Long and Shadi Danechi, *English Baccalaureate*, HC Library, Briefing Paper 06045, 4 September 2019, pp. 3, 25–6.

accountability measure but is part of the array of six sets of performance data that is made available to parents and the general public. Although this is intended to be helpful, it can be overkill for parents trying to make sense of the numbers to help decide on a good school. All the measures are also there, however, to discourage schools from concentrating on just one.

The measure by which secondary schools are held to account is a combination called Progress 8, which is an attempt to quantify progress from Sat scores to GCSE results in eight subjects.[50] These are English and maths double-counted, the top three scores in other EBacc subjects and top three scores in other GCSEs or equivalent. Progress 8 focuses on the difference the school has made, removing the advantage that schools with high-ability intakes have in end-point attainment measures. But the difference scores do come out as very small decimals, which are not as memorable as percentages. Nevertheless, falling below a minimum of -0.5, which is half a grade under the national average, triggers an inspection that could result in an 'inadequate' rating; in terms of current legislation, this would entail conversion to an academy. But following the tragedy of the head of Caversham school, 'inadequate' is now being treated more as a basis for discussions with the inspectors on how to improve.

There was a similar progress measure for primary schools in which the change from Key Stage 1 to Key Stage 2 was calculated, but this has been replaced.[51] Most of the assessments were, however, internal, so the reliability has to be open to question. Nevertheless, analysis by the Fisher Family Trust has shown a strong correlation between the progress scores and Ofsted inspections, but it is not

[50] Department for Education, *Secondary Accountability Measures: Guide for Maintained Secondary Schools, Academies and Free Schools*, February 2024 (publishing.service.gov.uk).

[51] New measure from 2023/24 in which a reception baseline assessment (RBA) replaces the KS1 scores. *Standards and Testing Agency Statutory Guidance 2024: Assessment and Reporting Arrangements (Phonics Screening Check)*, updated 1 November 2023.

perfect.[52] More than a third of the schools rated 'outstanding' did not record 'well above average' progress in any of the domains and 6 per cent were 'below average' in at least one, but this could reflect the inspectors reporting on what they had observed, not what the data they had seen indicated. It is also reassuring that given the limitations of the measure the consequences for falling below -0.5 are not set in stone.

CURRICULUM, COURSES AND QUALIFICATIONS

In a speech to the Royal Society of Arts in 2009, when Michael Gove was reasonably sure he would be the secretary of state for education if the Conservatives won the 2010 election, he gave some important clues as to where he wanted to take education.[53] He said, 'I know from my own experience that the opportunities I have enjoyed are entirely the consequences of the education I have been given.' He went on to say that it had empowered him to choose his own path in life and not have it imposed upon him by others as was the case for 'generations of my family before me'. Echoing the nineteenth-century poet Matthew Arnold, he added that his ambition was for all children 'to be introduced to the best that has been thought, and written', because it would enable them to shape their own destinies. Later in the same year at the Conservative Party conference he gave a more red-blooded version attacking both Labour and the teaching profession. He said he needed to rescue schools from the damage done to them by the Brown government, which had made them 'less places of teaching and learning and more community hubs from which a host of children's services can be delivered'. The teaching establishment, he said, had done more than 'squander talent', it had 'squandered money' and facilitated the 'entrenched culture of

---

[52] Steve Rollett and Philip Nye, 'How do Ofsted ratings relate to Key Stage 2 progress scores?', FFT Education Datalab, blogpost, 30 October 2018 (https://ffteducationdatalab.org.uk/).

[53] Owen Bennett, *Michael Gove: A Man in a Hurry* (London: Biteback, 2019), pp. 217–18.

dumbing down'.[54] He had never been much liked by the teaching profession, but his outspoken dismissal of much that was dear to it developed into a series of battles which contributed to the premature end of his time as education secretary.

In his three years shadowing the post Gove had concluded that the existing national curriculum was rigid and unwieldy and did not focus sufficiently on the core subjects; the fragmentation of courses into modules had turned education into an assessment treadmill; and teacher assessment as the dominant form of examination was leading to rampant grade inflation. His focus was on the subjects, not the peripherals as he saw them. According to David Laws, Gove was no fan of careers education and his favourite way of explaining this was that he had met Andreas Schleicher, head of education at the OECD, many times and he 'has never told me that the real problem of English education is that we have too few careers' advisers'. Neither was he interested in taking forward sex and relationships education as Theresa May, then home secretary, was pressing him to do.[55] Gove's preoccupation was unambiguously on how best to support the development of academic excellence.

He was ably supported by his schools minister, Nick Gibb, whose approach was more down to earth. Gibb's ambition was to create a world-class education system, and he thought learning from the current top-performing countries would be one way to do it. In his ten years in office, though not without interruptions, he systematically improved the English school system, particularly primary education, and was rewarded by England climbing the league tables.

Curriculum

In January 2011, just seven months into his tenure, Gove launched a major review of the national curriculum because: 'We have sunk in international league tables and the national curriculum is sub-standard.' He said that the review led by the

---

[54] Ibid., p. 219.   [55] Laws, *Coalition*, p. 214.

DfE with the support of an advisory committee and an expert panel would: 'examine the best school systems in the world and give us a world class curriculum that will help teachers, parents and children know what children should learn at what age.' The press release was clear that the new national curriculum would have a greater focus on subject content and made the important point that it was essential to distinguish between the statutory national curriculum and the wider broad and balanced curriculum over which schools have discretion but they did have to include religious education and RSHE (relationships, sex, and health education).[56]

There followed a tortuous four-year process of reports, publications, announcements and consultations,[57] with some passionate disagreements along the way.[58] A new framework for the primary school curriculum was published in September 2013[59] and for both primary and secondary schools in December 2014.[60] The new curriculum was knowledge-based with tightly specified content for English, maths and science at its core and much shorter programmes of study for the other nine subjects, which allowed teachers to decide what to teach and when. It indicated that history should have at its heart Britain's story, computer science should replace information and communications technology, and the teaching of foreign languages should start in primary schools. In subjects that were optional at Key Stage 4 there was a statutory requirement to provide access to at least one course for those who wished to take it. The new curriculum was eventually rolled out over the period 2014–16, after Gove had moved on.

---

[56] Department for Education and the Rt Hon Michael Gove MP, press release, 'National Curriculum Review launched', 20 January 2011.

[57] Nerys Roberts, *The School Curriculum in England*, HC Library Briefing Paper 06798, 26 March 2021, pp. 10–13.

[58] Daniel Boffey, 'Michael Gove's own experts revolt over "punitive" model for the curriculum', *Observer*, 17 June 2012.

[59] Department for Education, *The National Curriculum in England: Key Stages 1 and 2 Framework Document*, September 2013.

[60] Department for Education, *The National Curriculum in England: Framework Document*, December 2014.

National Examinations

The modularisation of GCSEs and A-levels was an anathema to Gove, and he was determined to return to whole courses with exams at the end.[61] He also wanted exams in which students were stretched and could demonstrate excellence. At one stage, he toyed with the idea of scrapping GCSEs and returning to O-levels for the brighter pupils and CSEs for the rest. A dispute erupted between the Conservatives and Liberal Democrats over this suggestion and after several attempts at resolution, which involved O-levels and CSEs under different names, it was eventually agreed that GCSEs would be retained but made much more demanding.[62] The content would be overhauled, modularisation scrapped and assessment would be by exams at the end.

Gove was insistent on independently set and marked exams because he was deeply concerned at the runaway inflation of GCSE grades shown in Figure 6.1. At the outset, the proportion of top awards was intended to be a maximum of 10 per cent, but from the initial 8.6 per cent in 1988 it had almost trebled to 23.2 per cent by 2011. Gove asked the newly formed regulator, Ofqual, set up by Labour in 2010, to put a stop to it; and they came up with a statistical method of keeping the percentage at the 2010 level adjusted to take account of differences in the cohort's performance in the primary school Sats. The percentages actually dropped and declined even further in 2017 when the first of Gove's reformed GCSEs, English and maths, came on stream. But when Covid struck in 2020, the exams had to be cancelled and grades were left to teachers. If any proof were needed of the generosity of teacher assessment, we can see it in Figure 6.1, where the percentages of top grades in 2020 and 2021 shot up to levels never seen before. With the restoration of full examinations in 2023 there was an attempt to limit the grade percentages to what they had been in 2019, which was not quite

---

[61] Patrick Wintour and Rachel Williams, 'Michael Gove to swap modules for single-exam GCSEs', *Guardian*, 22 November 2010.

[62] Laws, *Coalition,* pp. 162–3 and 218–22.

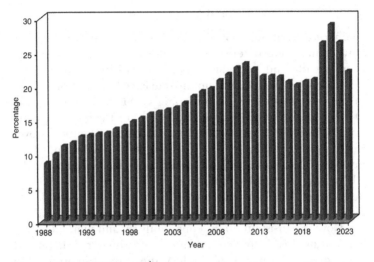

Figure 6.1 Top[a] GCSE grades[b] by year
[a] Top awards defined as at least an 'A' on a literal scale or '7' on a numerical scale.
[b] Includes Wales and Northern Ireland, but England makes up 92 per cent of entries.
Source: Alan Smithers, *Prospects for GCSE Results 2023*, CEER: University of Buckingham (updated).

managed, but was nevertheless criticised as being unfair to that cohort of candidates.

The jump in grades resulting from teacher assessment during the Covid years was even more striking at A-level, with A*/A grades, which had been stabilised in the previous decade at about a quarter of the entries, leaping to almost half. It caused chaos for the universities, who found that so many more applicants had met their conditional offers that they could not all be accommodated. On the flip side, some of the students who were admitted found they could not cope. The pass rate at this level was brought down to 27 per cent in 2023 on the return to full exams. This was similarly met with protestations that more allowance should have been made for the candidates' disrupted education.

A substantially reformed primary school curriculum was introduced in 2016. It included the teaching of a foreign language in Key Stage 2. But the emphasis was on English and maths with children expected to make faster progress. In maths 5-year-olds were expected to be able to count to one hundred, while 9-year-olds should have learned the times-tables up to twelve. The Sats tests were also beefed up and the marks rather than just a category were communicated to parents along with an average score so they could see how their child was doing relative to others. In 2012 a new compulsory phonics screening test was rolled out, to be taken at the end in Year 1 to check on how well children learned to decode words using this method.[63] Any child not reaching a score of 32 out of 40 was expected to receive extra support in Year 2 and be retested. Twelve years later a Multiplication Tables Check was introduced, having been delayed by the pandemic, essentially to identify children who needed more help.[64] These checks were not conceived of as tests, but rather as diagnostic tools. Nevertheless, they gave clear direction to schools on where they should be putting their efforts. The idea of baseline tests across the core subjects, so that primary school progress scores could be calculated as the difference scores between beginning and end, was abandoned because they were found to be unreliable.

CHARACTER

Nicky Morgan, who replaced Michael Gove as secretary of state for education in 2014, held the view that the curriculum changes that Gove and Gibb had been focused on 'were doing only half the job (that) needs to be done to prepare our children for the 21st century'.[65] The missing ingredient was character.

---

[63] Catherine Darnell, Jonathan Solity and Helen Wall, 'Decoding the phonics screen check', *British Educational Research Journal*, 43 (2017), 505–27.

[64] Department for Education, *Multiplication Tables Check* (Standards and Testing Agency, 3 March 2020, regularly updated) (https://explore-education-statistics.service.gov.uk/).

[65] Nicky Morgan, *Taught Not Caught: Educating for 21st Century Character* (Woodbridge: John Catt Education, 2017), p. 14.

Morgan did not subscribe to the prevailing view that character is developed through the whole school experience, but
held that it must be 'taught not caught', which she used as
the title of the book she has written setting out her ideas.[66]
She asked her DfE officials to help her pin down the concept, but after trawling through dictionaries and books,
visiting schools, and university centres specialising in character, all that emerged was long lists of words (such as
resilience, perseverance, confidence) and analytic categories
(such as traits, values and virtues). Morgan initiated
a Character Award for the best approaches to character
development in schools and she visited the winners. There
she found booklets, discussion groups and motivational
speakers, but little of substance. As Morgan was forced to
acknowledge: 'Character clearly means different things to
many different people.' And as a practical person her solution, to paraphrase, was let's not bother with what it is, let us
just get on with it.[67]

But there is a potential exemplar, only everyone has been
looking in the wrong direction. One of Gove's free schools,
Michaela School, which places the emphasis on academic
achievement, also coincidentally looks to have found the
path to character development. In its first years, it was
a school that children went to when they could not get in
anywhere else. It had an intake that ticked every box on disadvantage and the pupils who arrived were disinclined to learn.
Michaela's passionate founder and head teacher, Katharine
Birbalsingh, could see that this called for strong action and
each new intake has a two-week 'bootcamp' laying down the
rules of good behaviour and how they will be enforced. These
have been consistently applied, leading to Ms Birbalsingh
being dubbed the strictest head teacher in the country.
Any parents who objected to the regime were politely told
that they should consider whether their child would be
happier elsewhere. But it has worked. The school has achieved

[66] Ibid.   [67] Ibid., p. 37.

excellent GCSE results, exemplary behaviour and an 'outstanding' rating from the school inspectors. It is much celebrated and has become a place of pilgrimage for educationists. What the school has also arrived at, but which has not been sufficiently acknowledged, is that the key to character development is embedding good habits through clear rules consistently applied. Michaela's way would appear to have the potential to tackle three major current problems in education, which the governments from 2010 to 2024 have struggled to solve: poor discipline; persistent absence; and fragile mental health.

Discipline

Discipline in many schools leaves a lot to be desired and there have been some shocking instances, fortunately very few, of teachers being attacked with knives or in other distressing ways. This has been countered by giving schools the power to search pupils and since 2015 they have been required to report pupils suspected of radicalisation or extremism to the Local Safeguarding Board or the police. But the major manifestation of bad behaviour in schools is the low-level hassling of teachers which they find so wearing. For over twenty years bad behaviour has been the second most frequently given reason by teachers for quitting the profession, behind only 'workload'.[68] Developing good habits the Michaela way would appear to offer hope of tackling it. There has been push back however. The school found itself in the high court in January 2024 facing a claim brought by a Muslim pupil to overturn its ban on prayer rituals, which the headteacher said was necessary because of 'violence, intimidation, and appalling racial harassment of some of our teachers'.[69]

---

[68] Alan Smithers and Pamela Robinson, *Factors Affecting Teachers' Decisions to Leave the Profession*, Department for Education and Skills Research Report 430, June 2003.

[69] Sally Weale, 'Katharine Birbalsingh defends ban on school prayers in high court', *Guardian*, 17 January 2024.

Persistent Absence

Another major problem is persistent absence. During the Covid lockdowns children seem to have got used to not going to school and a not insignificant number have continued to treat it as optional. If persistent absence is defined as missing at least 10 per cent of school sessions, it has doubled since 2018–19 and in the latest figures reached 18 per cent of primary pupils and 28 per cent of those at secondary schools.[70] If the bar is raised to missing half of lessons, the absentee rate is nine times what it was before the pandemic. Absences are concentrated in the top three years of secondary school, with Year 11 the highest. Disadvantaged and special needs children are over-represented and unauthorised absences are the biggest group. Fining parents seemed to be effective before the pandemic, but this is no longer consistently being applied and parents are cheerfully taking advantage of cheaper holiday rates outside school holidays. Alongside its health impacts, Covid has had catastrophic social effects, including losing the habit of regular school attendance. It could be that the way to restore it is through character development the Michaela way, in particularly by underlining the rules and consistently enforcing them through appropriate sanctions.

Mental Health

One of the strongest arguments for paying more attention to the development of character in schools is the epidemic of mental health issues among children that is currently being reported.[71] The research cited covers a period up to July 2020 so the pandemic will have been a factor, and there are undoubtedly several conditions that have a structural basis such as incipient schizophrenia or psychosis. But there could be questions asked over the 34 recently listed mental illnesses,[72] such as general anxiety

---

[70] Persistent absence by pupil group – FFT Education Datalab, 8 November 2023.

[71] NHS Digital, *Mental Health of Children and Young People in England 2020* (digital.nhs.uk, Key Findings, p. 1).

[72] NHS, *Mental Health Conditions* (www.nhs/uk/conditions).

disorder, personality disorder and various phobias, which are leading anxious and unhappy children to see themselves as actually unwell. Receiving a particular label may sometimes prompt them to live out the script of their diagnosis and avoid situations which are said to be triggers – even missing school – which could be making matters worse. Taking a more nuanced view that the mental discomfort can sometimes be temporary unless there is strong evidence to the contrary would be helpful. Nicky Morgan is surely right that if reliable ways can be found of raising levels of resilience, perseverance and moral strength, then they should be prominent in the curriculum. But so far the campaign has been stronger on analysis than performance. Michaela School seems to have found an approach that works, but is quite controversial. Nevertheless, it is important to flag up that the answer to mental health crisis may not just be more medication or therapy, but improved support for character development in the curriculum.

SOCIAL MOBILITY

Social mobility has been high on the government's agenda since 2010, and there have been many pressure groups urging that more be done. The Liberal Democrats did much to ensure that it was high on the agenda of the Coalition. A commitment to a pupil premium to fund schools to provide extra support for children from low-income homes was made in the binding Coalition Agreement at their behest. The Coalition immediately set up a Child Poverty Commission to whose title was added Social Mobility in 2012, which in turn became the Social Mobility Commission in 2016, as an advisory body to the DfE. In their 2019 election manifesto the Conservatives pledged to level up all parts of the UK and this was honoured by establishing a Department for Levelling Up, Housing and Communities, with the nice symmetry of the secretary of state for education in the first government, Michael Gove, completing the circle by becoming levelling up secretary in what looks to be the last. True to form, Gove quickly published a White Paper, which listed twelve missions to be achieved by 2030.[73] They included increasing pay, employment and productivity, 40 per cent more investment in R&D outside the southeast, fixing the education gap, increasing and improving skills training, and decreasing inequalities.

In spite of the commitment to promote social mobility, the narrative of falling behind other countries and failing to make a difference continued to dominate the headlines. It has been reported that: 'poorer pupils do worse at school';[74] 'UK social mobility at its worst in over 50 years';[75] and 'working class people in the UK paid £6,000 less (per annum) for the same professional roles'.[76] The Global Social Mobility Index has the UK languishing in twenty-first place behind our European neighbours. A charity devoted to social mobility in education, the Sutton Trust, and a body focused on employment, the Social Mobility Foundation, have continued to unearth further shortcomings.

But there is evidence that the government's policies are having some effect. It is only a correlation without a direct link being established, but at the very least it is encouraging. The Social Mobility Commission in its State of the Nation Reports for 2022 and 2023 is also more sanguine.[77]

In the first, the Commission outlines its new measurement framework comparing the starting point and the outcome for five types of social mobility – occupational class, income, wealth, education and housing – at three stages in life. Not all the required data is available at present, but what there is shows that the absolute occupational mobility rate has remained stable for many decades, and that relative occupational mobility is not

---

[73] White Paper, *Levelling Up the United Kingdom*, CP 604, 2 February 2020.

[74] Stephen Gorrard, 'Poorer pupils do worse at school – here's how to reduce the attainment gap', *The Conversation*, 30 May 2023.

[75] Faiza Shaheen, 'Now it's clear: hard work doesn't make you rich. Surely that's the death knell for the myth of social mobility', *Guardian*, 19 September 2023.

[76] Jem Bartholomew, 'Working-class people in UK paid £6,000 less for same professional roles', *Guardian*, 17 November 2023.

[77] Social Mobility Commission, *State of the Nation 2022: A Fresh Approach to Social Mobility*, 23 June 2022; Social Mobility Commission, *State of the Nation 2023: People and Places*, 12 September 2023.

in decline but may have improved. The comparisons also reveal that gaps between higher and lower socio-economic groups have been narrowing, as have the gaps between those from professional and working-class backgrounds when it comes to university participation and degree attainment. In measures at the early career stage, the gap between social-class backgrounds has for most occupational and economic outcomes lessened. This is attributed to improvements in the conditions that enable social mobility.

The 2023 report presents new findings which show that social mobility outcomes depend on where you grew up, with regional differences and differences within regions. There are also marked differences between people from the same socioeconomic background but different ethnic groups. Fewer White British people, for example, go to university than many of the other groups, but they tend to go to the more selective universities and are less likely to end up unemployed. Chinese children eligible for free school meals (FSM) perform remarkably in the primary school Sats tests, not only outscoring FSM children in all other ethnic groups, but also exceeding the national average for those children who do not require that support. This suggests that being poor does not necessarily mean that high attainment is beyond reach. Interestingly, the data also show differences with sex. Girls tend to do better at school and university, but are less likely to enter higher professional occupations and to have high earnings later in life. Only about half the women achieved the upward mobility of men and many fewer went on to own their own homes.

The picture which is emerging is that social mobility may be less of a problem than the current narrative would have it and that it is not one dimensional. Remedies will, therefore, need to be specific rather than general. Some of the present policies may have been misdirected. Would it not be better, for example, to aim at reducing the gap between high and low attainers per se rather that between those who are or are not entitled to free school meals? The elephant in the room is ability, which may not be evenly distributed across social groups, so interpreting gaps as biases is itself biased thinking. Thus reducing gaps to counteract biases, as the government has been trying to do through the Office for Students, which is requiring more representative intakes from universities, could well be creating its own kind of unfairness. If there are intrinsic differences, you cannot logically have both equality of opportunity and equality of outcome. Although there has been progress on social mobility between 2010 and 2024, there is still much to do. The new Social Mobility Framework does, however, offer hope of a better basis for policymaking.

TEACHER TRAINING, RECRUITMENT AND RETENTION

Teacher recruitment and retention has long been a problem in England.[78] In its 2010 manifesto the Conservative Party stressed the importance of good teachers and said it would raise the status of the profession and toughen school discipline. In just weeks after taking office the Coalition published a White Paper, 'The Importance of Teaching', setting out how it was going to fulfil these ambitious aims.[79] The main thrusts were to raise the quality of new entrants; provide more training on the job; create a network of Teaching Schools along the lines of Teaching Hospitals; increase the number of head teachers who provided support to other schools; give schools more freedom to reward good performance; and bear down on bureaucracy.

In pursuit of these aims it has introduced a wide range of initiatives: new school-led training routes, some salaried, have been developed; mature entrants (NowTeach) and ex-service personnel (Troops to Teach) have been targeted; an apprenticeship scheme has been brought in; bonuses to attract teachers into shortage subjects such as physics, maths and computing have been created; Teaching Schools have been established; the National Leaders scheme has been expanded; and the salary scale has been made more flexible to enable head teachers to offer incentives. If this were not enough, in 2019 a major reset

[78] Alpesh Maisuria, Nerys Roberts, Robert Long and Shadi Danechi, *Teacher Recruitment and Retention in England*, HC Library, Briefing Paper 07222, 12 December 2023.

[79] Department for Education, *The Importance of Teaching*, policy paper, 24 November 2010.

was announced with a new 'Teacher Recruitment and Retention Strategy', the cornerstone of which is an Early Career Framework with structured support for the first two career years underpinned by phased training bursaries and retention payments.[80]

It has also attempted to reduce workload by giving Ofsted inspectors the task of holding head teachers to account for the scale of it in their schools. A third strand in the new strategy is to create non-leadership career pathways through specialist qualifications. Some schemes, such as Troops to Teach, flopped and were ditched. Others have been replaced: in 2021 the 750 Teaching Schools gave way to 87 Teaching School Hubs each serving 200–300 schools. The Hubs are intended to be centres of excellence for teacher training, to provide support for teachers especially in their first two years and on the new specialist career pathways, and to have a role in school improvement. In 2022 it further increased financial incentives with tax-free scholarships worth £29,000 and bursaries worth £27,000 to train in physics, maths, chemistry and computing, and also a levelling-up premium worth £3,000 tax-free to teach for the first five years in disadvantaged schools.

In short, the Conservatives have tried everything they could think of to boost the availability of high-quality teachers. And it is important to say this given that the record shows that teacher supply has been declining rather than improving. The policies have brought about the desired major shift from university-led to school-led training with the split now about half and half. But overall recruitment is down by a quarter. In the school year ended 2023, recruitment to postgraduate ITT only reached 59 per cent of the target, with some subjects particularly badly hit.[81] In physics only 17 per cent of the target was achieved and in computing only 30 per cent. Even primary education is falling, reaching only 93 per cent compared with 131 per cent when there was a Covid bounce. Yet full-time teacher equivalent numbers were up by 27,000 on 2010–11, with the apparent paradox

---

[80] Department for Education, *Teacher Recruitment and Retention Strategy*, policy paper, 28 January 2019.

[81] Department for Education, *Initial Teacher Training Census 2022/23*, 7 December 2022.

explained by there being more returners to the profession. The increase, however, has not kept pace with a wave of baby-boomers so that the overall pupil to qualified teacher ratio has gone up from 17.6 to 18. There are more entrants to the profession than leavers, but while in 2023, 48,000 took up posts, 44,000 left, most prematurely. The latest figures show that the number of new teacher training entrants declined even further in 2023/24. While recruitment to primary climbed back to 96 per cent of target, that to secondary fell from 59 per cent to just 50 per cent, reducing the overall target met from 70 to 62 per cent.[82]

Difficulties in staffing schools were used by the teacher unions to demand more money, leading to strikes in 2022 and 2023 which further disrupted the education of young people already badly hit by Covid lockdowns.[83] It was argued that poor salaries were the root cause and a substantial increase would make the profession more attractive. The teachers' claims of *de facto* salary cuts were borne out by the Institute for Fiscal Studies which showed a real-terms drop of between 5 per cent and 13 per cent depending on pay grade.[84] A deal was eventually struck, but it is doubtful whether it will make much difference since salary is not the main reason for wanting to be a teacher.[85]

Securing teacher supply is a long-standing and seemingly intractable problem. Papers written long ago could just as easily have been written today.[86] Back then the main reasons for leaving were workload and pupil behaviour, there was a huge

[82] Department for Education, *Initial Teacher Training Census 2023/24*, 7 December 2023.

[83] Nerys Roberts, *School Strike Action in the UK*, HC Library, Research Briefing, 28 December 2023.

[84] Christine Farquharson, Damian Phelan, Luke Sibieta and Imran Tahir, *Teacher Recruitment, Training and Retention: Evidence to Education Committee* (London: Institute for Fiscal Studies, June 2023).

[85] Alan Smithers and Pamela Robinson, *Attracting Teachers*, Archive of Reports by Professor Alan Smithers | CEER, December 2000, pp. 58–62.

[86] Alan Smithers and Sheila Carlisle, 'Reluctant teachers', *New Society*, 15 (1970), 391–2; Alan Smithers and Susan Hill. 'Recruitment to mathematics and physics teaching: a personality problem?' *Research Papers in Education*, 4 (1989), 3–21.

shortage of maths and physics teachers, and recruitment went up and down with the fall and rise of opportunities elsewhere. The government deserves credit for trying so hard to make a difference, and there have been successes, but rather than continually struggling to meet targets which are out of reach, it would be worth its while to consider how the school system could be adapted to the numbers of teachers available. The reorganisation into multi-academy trusts already increases the opportunities for sharing the like of scarce highly qualified physics teachers, and developments in technology enable lessons given by excellent teachers to be transmitted across the country. A new perspective could open the door to ensuring that all children have access to high-quality teaching.

FURTHER EDUCATION AND APPRENTICESHIPS

Thirty years ago, the further education colleges had a bright future. Kenneth Clarke, as the Conservative education secretary, in 1992, transformed them from being an anonymous resource in local authorities to a national education sector with its own Further Education Funding Council (FEFC) led by the dynamic Sir William Stubbs.[87] The 465 newly independent colleges (including 116 sixth-form colleges) now were autonomous and had a distinct collective identity. They catered for more people than did the universities, offering a wide range of provision from catch-up courses to higher education, taking in on the way vocational, academic and adult education, and also leisure activities. But this happy state lasted only nine years, before the Blair government replaced the FEFC with the Learning and Skills Council, which had a wider brief. Then the Brown government split oversight in two with academic provision remaining with the Education Department but their vocational activities now looked after by the Business Department.

---

[87] Alan Smithers and Pamela Robinson, *Changing Colleges in the Market Place* (London: Council for Industry and Higher Education, 1993).

The Coalition took office in 2010 without a clear plan for the colleges. They left Brown's division in place, and it was only with Theresa May's premiership that further education and skills were reintegrated with schools and universities in the DfE. The Coalition did, however, immediately abolish the Learning and Skills Council, replacing it with two Agencies, one for Skills and the other for Young People's Learning. The latter was itself replaced two years later by a newly created Education Funding Agency. In 2017, the Skills and Education Funding Agencies were reunited as the Education and Skills Funding Agency (ESFA). In all this reorganisation the colleges' collective identity was dissipated and, in 2022, all thoughts of independence were lost when the Office for National Statistics ruled that the colleges were in the public sector.[88] In fact, they had been all along, so autonomy had been an illusion. The EFSA, on Treasury orders, had acted immediately to impose a new set of controls on borrowing and investment. The colleges now have the same relationship with the government as the MATs.

Even worse for the colleges than these structural changes has been the drop in funding. Osborne's austerity measures have hit them harder than any other aspect of education. A report by the Institute for Fiscal Studies in 2019 found that further education funding per student was lower in real terms than in 2010 and even a promised increase would still leave them with 7 per cent less spending power than they had had then.[89] When the colleges were incorporated in 1993 there were 465, that had reduced to 356 by 2010 and now there are only 225. This reduction has mainly arisen through mergers of which there have been 199 since 1993, including 96 since 2010. Merging may have occurred because of proximity or mutual advantages, but the financial situation is likely to have been a major factor. Besides mergers, a few colleges have escaped to become universities,

---

[88] Richard Adams, 'Further education colleges in England face losing financial independence', *Guardian*, 29 November 2022.

[89] Jack Britton, Christine Farquharson and Luke Sibieta, *2019 Annual Report on Education Spending in England* (London: Institute for Fiscal Studies, 19 September 2019).

some have closed and others have converted to academies.[90] But altogether it is now a sorry picture compared with the high hopes of thirty years ago; the capricious treatment of colleges is strange, given that the Coalition had seen them as leading its apprenticeship revolution.

Modern apprenticeships[91] were also first announced by Kenneth Clarke, then chancellor of the exchequer. In 1994, he appropriated the highly valued apprenticeship name for a scheme to get young people into work. It was essentially a framework for putting together qualifications said to be equivalent to GCSEs and A-levels in a further education college or work setting. It was slow to take off and had a very high dropout, with only a quarter completing the programme. It was rebranded in 2004 by the Blair government, which removed the upper age limit of 25 and added pre-apprenticeships, young apprenticeships and advanced apprenticeships. By the end of the Brown government, annual starts had risen to 279,700, of whom only about two-fifths were 16–18-year-olds.

The Coalition made important changes in 2012 when it required that for a programme to be recognised as an apprenticeship it should consist of at least 12 months' work-based learning. It also stipulated that an employer should be involved from the outset to put a stop to the practice of setting young people off on an apprenticeship in the hope that an employer would be found later. This toughening up led to a 15 per cent drop in starts from the high point of 520,600 in 2011–12. But Cameron was confident that apprenticeships had the potential to become a highly valued route into employment, a genuine rival to the well-established and prestigious academic route through universities. In the run-up to the 2015 election he pledged that, if a Conservative government were returned, it would create three million more apprenticeships

---

[90] College Mergers | Association of Colleges (aoc.co.uk).

[91] Alan Smithers, 'The philosopher's stone? The case for national apprenticeship qualifications', in Tess Lanning (ed.), *Where Next for Apprenticeships?* (London: The Chartered Institute of Personnel Development, August 2016), pp. 18–24.

by 2020.[92] Having been re-elected, he repeated the commitment in a speech in August that year in which he also announced measures to enable industry to set the standards and introduced a range of nudges to get employers to offer places. At the same time, he began a consultation on introducing a levy in 2017 to fund training and apprenticeships.

Even with two changes of prime minister, the growth of apprenticeships has been impressive. From May 2015 to January 2024 there were 3,349,820 apprenticeship starts.[93] But it has not been smooth progress. The number of starts per year has fallen by 31 per cent since 2015 and only just over half successfully completed the apprenticeship.[94] The main reason given for non-completion has been the poor quality of what was on offer.[95] While there are highly attractive gold-standard apprenticeships, it has emerged that some employers have been using them as cheap sources of labour and providing little or no training. The introduction of the apprenticeship levy in 2017 was accompanied by a fall in starts, seemingly because non-levy paying employers would now have to contribute 10 per cent of the costs of any apprentice that they took on.[96] One of the major contracted providers, Learndirect, was rated 'inadequate' by Ofsted in 2017.[97] Analysis also shows that the pattern of apprenticeship take-up is not what might have been expected for a ladder into employment.[98] Only a fifth of the starts in the latest

[92] Nicholas Watt, 'David Cameron vows to create 3m apprenticeships', *Guardian*, 20 October 2014.

[93] Apprenticeships, Academic year 2023/24 – Explore education statistics – GOV.UK (explore-education-statistics.service.gov.uk).

[94] Andy Powell, *Apprenticeship Statistics for England*, HC Library, Research Briefing, 21 February 2023.

[95] Faarea Masud, 'Warning apprentices quitting over quality of schemes', *BBC Online*, 28 November 2022.

[96] Andy Powell, *Apprenticeship Starts: Has there Been a Big Fall?*, HC Library, Insight, 15 December 2017.

[97] Family and Education, 'Learndirect rated "inadequate" in Ofsted report', *BBC Online*, 17 August 2017.

[98] Andy Powell, *Apprenticeship Statistics for England*, HC Library, Research Briefing, 21 February 2023.

figures are aged 19 or under, while nearly half are 25 plus. While higher apprenticeships including degree studies have increased more than fivefold since 2014–15, the first rung on the ladder, the intermediate apprenticeship, has fallen to a third. This suggests that apprenticeships are being adapted to purposes that were not originally intended, such as a route with costs paid into higher education courses where most students would be paying fees. The Treasury has reportedly become very concerned about this and is considering excluding or restricting the use of levy funds for this purpose, which would pose a threat to teacher training apprenticeships, among others.[99]

There is much still to be ironed out in the development of the T-level-apprenticeship ladder as a vocational equivalent to that provided by A-levels into the universities, but there has been considerable growth and interest in the past thirty years. Much has been got right including putting apprenticeship standards into the hands of employers and getting them to accept a levy. Having them inspected by Ofsted so that we know how they are working out in practice is also reassuring. But the ingenuity that goes into profiting from unintended usage cannot be ignored. The present government has taken the interesting step of appointing Gillian Keegan, who herself has successfully completed an apprenticeship, as its secretary of state for education presumably with one eye on what she can do to make the dream of a prestigious vocational ladder a reality.

THE STATE OF THE UNIVERSITIES

The period 2010 to 2024 has been a difficult time for the universities. It began well enough with them securing extra revenue through the introduction of realistic tuition fees, but the gains were soon eroded by inflation. In order to balance the books, they found themselves having to admit less well-qualified foreign

---

[99] Billy Camden, 'Treasury plans apprenticeship levy restrictions', *Schools Week*, 16 November 2023.

students, who paid much higher fees. Then, almost unthinkable under a Conservative government, especially one intent on giving schools more autonomy, they found themselves to be so tightly regulated as to have, in effect, been nationalised.

Tuition fees were an existential threat to the Coalition.[100] The Conservative and Liberal Democrat partners faced a huge dilemma because they fundamentally and publicly disagreed. In their 2010 manifestos they had taken diametrically opposing positions. While the Conservatives wanted to charge realistic fees, the Liberal Democrats had committed themselves to not increasing them. This was got round in the Coalition agreement by putting off a decision until a report on student fees from Lord Browne, former chief executive of BP, commissioned by Gordon Brown, had been delivered. As anticipated, its findings were music to the ears of the Conservatives. It recommended that the cap on fees should go; universities should be free to set their own and expand provision; government loans to students, repayable from future income, should be made to cover the fees and living costs; and there should be grants for those from low-income families.

Nick Clegg could see the logic of Lord Browne's recommendations, but given the unambiguous position of his party, it was for him a lose–lose situation. If all were to vote against, almost certainly the government would fall. Bravely, for the greater good, he agreed to support a measure based on the Browne report, but with changes including a continuing cap on home-domiciled fees. He urged his colleagues to vote in favour too, and about half did, including Vince Cable and David Laws. The Bill narrowly got through the Commons in December 2010 and more comfortably through the Lords five days later where Lord Browne, himself, spoke in favour.

Agreement had been reached without destroying the Coalition, but the compromises that had had to be made had dire consequences. At the insistence of the Liberal Democrats, the tuition fee for domestic students was capped. This has been

---

[100] See above, pp. 162–4.

raised by only £250, although what cost £10 in 2012, in 2023 cost £13.76.[101] Not surprisingly, this has left universities struggling to make ends meet. They have been increasingly led to recruiting foreign students whose fees are not capped and are willing to pay much more. Because they are so lucrative the requirements on entry qualifications and familiarity with the language tend to be eased, which impacts adversely on the quality of the courses and degrees.[102] Nevertheless, the universities have been left strapped for cash, so salaries have not kept pace with inflation. Lecturers at many universities have reacted by going on strike and staging a marking boycott.[103]

The Liberal Democrats also required that loans to pay the tuition fees and living costs should be made on very generous terms. The scheme that was devised allowed for only half the total of loans ever being repaid. But the figures show the return is even lower. Of full-time undergraduates starting in the academic year 2022–3 only 27 per cent were expected to repay their loan in full.[104] Overall, the Office for Budget Responsibility has recently calculated that only 38 per cent of the total money and interest will ever be repaid.[105] It is highly likely that what was intended to save taxpayers money will end up costing them more.

Not only did the compromise on tuition fees have detrimental effects on the universities and leave the taxpayer unprotected, it was disastrous for the Liberal Democrats. The 57 seats won in the 2010 election were reduced to just eight five years later. Many of those who served in the Coalition government were voted out and Clegg himself only narrowly survived, but felt obliged to

[101] www.bankofengland.co.uk/monetary-policy/inflation/inflation-calculator

[102] Insight, 'Exposed: foreign students get secret route into top universities', *Sunday Times*, 28 January 2024.

[103] Joe Lewis, *University Strike Action in the UK*, HC Library, Research Briefing, 30 January 2024.

[104] Student loan forecasts for England, Financial year 2022–23 – Explore education statistics – GOV.UK (explore-education-statistics.service.gov.uk).

[105] Accounting for student loans – Office for Budget Responsibility (obr.uk).

resign as leader immediately. The party has been little more than a bystander in the years since, although as we approach the 2024 election it has been triumphing in some by-elections.

Theresa May, on becoming prime minister in 2016, reunited the universities (and the further education colleges) with schools in the Department for Education, but left research in the Business Department thereby separating universities from their research funding. An Act reforming university regulation in the way Willetts had envisaged, but was blocked from doing by Cameron's Office, was passed in 2017 and rushed through before the 2017 election, unwisely called by May.[106] It provided for an Office for Students (OfS) to replace both the Higher Education Funding Council and the Office of Fair Access. In creating such a powerful body, the government has taken away much of the autonomy of universities, ironic in view of its stress on the independence of schools. Universities are no longer protected by a Royal Charter and in order to access funding, student support and visas for students from overseas, they must meet the requirements of a number of public bodies, present audited annual reports on their finances, have appropriate management and governance structures, and allow quality assessments. In order to be able to charge the maximum allowable controlled fees, an Access and Participation Plan must be agreed with the OfS setting out how the university is going to increase the proportions of students from underrepresented groups.

The Act thus constrains in crucial ways the freedoms that universities have traditionally enjoyed. They are no longer secure in their charters, but have to comply with OfS requirements whatever they may be. They have to put in place its preferred management and governance structures supported by numerous and detailed policy documents. This has led universities to greatly expand their own bureaucracies and acquiesce in administrators seeing themselves as in charge of academics rather than supporting them. And most pernicious of all, universities can no longer recruit on merit alone but have to take into account social

---

[106] Higher Education and Research Act 2017 (legislation.gov.uk).

factors. They have tacitly accepted that imbalances in entry rates between social groups are due to biases, but this fails to allow for ability differences.

University autonomy is also under threat from attacks on academic freedom which seek to 'cancel' those whose research, publications or presentations are considered offensive, even if they are within the law. Speakers who have been invited to talk about such issues as gender, ethnicity and colonialism have been 'de-platformed', and members of staff addressing sensitive topics risk being driven out of their posts by baying mobs of activists and students.[107]

The government has passed a Freedom of Speech Act[108] which tasks the OfS with promoting free speech, a manifesto commitment in the 2019 election. It fell to Gavin Williamson, as secretary of state for education close to the end of his time in office, to introduce the Higher Education (Freedom of Speech) Bill in May 2021. It would extend the obligation to protect free speech to the student unions, something which had been omitted from an earlier Act. It would also enable the OfS to go beyond promoting free speech to monitoring it by appointing a Director of Free Speech and Academic Freedom with the power to fine culpable institutions. In addition, it was proposed to enable individuals to be able to sue. The Bill did not pass all its stages in the 2021–2 session and was carried over to the next, where, after some amendments to the section covering the right to sue, it became law in May 2023. The intentions are clear; it remains to be seen how effective it will be.

Universities have also come under scrutiny for the huge increases in the proportion of first-class degrees they have been awarding, particularly during the pandemic. The percentage rose from 15.5 in 2010–11 to 37.4 in 2020–1, though it was

---

[107] Richard Adams, 'Sussex professor resigns after transgender rights row', *Guardian*, 28 October 2021; Chris Havergal, 'Open University failed to protect gender-critical scholar–judge', *Times Higher Education*, 22 January 2024.

[108] Higher Education (Freedom of Speech) Act 2023 (legislation.gov.uk).

bought down to 32.8 in 2021–2.[109] Not even the most shameless of publicists would claim that this was an improvement arising from Conservative policies. Neither can it be convincingly accounted for by improved teaching and more effort on the part of students. The OfS has calculated that half of the increase cannot be explained, with rises in nearly all universities that cannot be traced to improved performance.[110] It has warned that it will take regulatory action against culprits, and there are suggestions that it has been doing so already.

A large part of the increases during the Covid years was due to sympathetic marking taking account of the conditions under which the candidates had studied and sat exams. The underlying inflation is, however, most likely driven mainly by universities' attempts increase their standing in the league tables as part of their marketing. It is also true that students like receiving top degrees and are more likely to apply to awarding universities. But the ploy is self-defeating. Degrees have declined in value since they became less accurate in distinguishing levels of performance The universities should have come together a long time ago to end the nonsense, but now they have ceded even more independence to the regulator who will almost certainly impose further requirements on them.

VERDICT ON SCHOOL REFORMS

The first four years of the Conservative-led governments from 2010 to 2024, when they were in coalition with the Liberal Democrats, can be seen as the time when the transformation of education in England begun by Kenneth Baker in 1988 was brought to fruition. Baker set out to create a structure for schools and the classroom. He instituted a national curriculum, testing of all pupils, and self-governing schools, but was slowed by the wiles of his civil servants who briefed his successors that these were

[109] Louisa Clarence-Smith and Ben Butcher, 'Graduates inexplicably outperform their A-level results with first-class degrees', *Telegraph*, 20 July 2023.

[110] Office for Students, 'University grade inflation starts to drop, but half of top grades still unexplained', OfS Press Release, 20 July 2023.

merely trials and could be ignored.[111] John McGregor bought the story, but Kenneth Clarke would have none of it and made the curriculum more knowledge based as Baker had intended, and also created an independent schools inspectorate.[112] Even at the very end of those eighteen years of Conservative rule, Baker's plan was still being elaborated, with Gillian Shepherd, the last Conservative education secretary of that era, announcing literacy and numeracy strategies.[113] The momentum continued through the Blair governments, which produced fully fledged literacy and numeracy strategies,[114] and although abolishing the self-governing 'grant maintained' status for schools, adapted the city-technology-college concept to set up self-governing academies as the solution to chronically failing comprehensives.[115]

Michael Gove came to office wanting to free all schools from local authority control, to bring back rigour to the exams, to make the curriculum less prescriptive, to make teacher training school-led and concentrate inspections on under-performing schools. He was able to set all of these in train in the four years he was education secretary, and they were carried forward by succeeding Conservative administrations under the watchful eye of Nick Gibb, who remained in post, not without interruptions, for ten of those years. Gibb focused on establishing in primary schools a firm foundation in English and maths. The curriculum was made more knowledge-based, phonics was emphasised as the way to master reading, and learning multiplication tables up to 12x12 became compulsory as an invaluable tool in arithmetic. Checks were put in place to ensure that progress was being made and the Sats were made more searching. The Liberal Democrats made the important contributions of the pupil premium, early years provision and free school meals for infants.

---

[111] Ken Clarke, *Kind of Blue: A Political Memoir* (London: Macmillan, 2016), p. 265.

[112] Ibid., p. 273.

[113] LGC Contributor, '£25 million blitz on basics to improve literacy and numeracy', *Local Government Chronicle*, 5 January 1996.

[114] Tony Blair, *A Journey* (London: Hutchinson, 2010), p. 25.

[115] Ibid., p. 285.

The ambition was to make England's school education system world class. The countries at the top of the international league tables were visited and their methods closely studied. Teachers from Singapore and China were invited to this country to show us how they teach maths, and their countries have been visited to see their teachers in action. But have the aspirations and reforms made a difference? What do the international tables say? The indications are positive. In the latest Progress in International Reading Literacy Study (PIRLS) published in 2023 which tests 9–10-year-olds in their reading capability England came fourth out of 43 countries compared with eleventh in the 2011 report.[116] But direct comparison of the actual scores is complicated by Covid, which led to them falling in most countries and some countries not being included. The improvement in England's relative performance stems from advances made by less able children, so better performance overall is accompanied by a narrowing of the gap. The difference between boys and girls is also reduced. These results can be interpreted as consistent with the aims of the phonics screening check and the Hubs for developing expertise in teaching reading.

It is a similar story for the OECD's Programme for International Student Assessment (PISA) results published in December 2023.[117] Like all other countries, except Taiwan, England's actual score went down from 2018 probably due to the interruptions of the pandemic, but by less than other countries, so the relative position improved. The published results show England rising from seventeenth to eleventh out of 81 countries. We cannot be sure whether this relative success is an education or Covid effect, but the apparent improvement continues an upward trend from 2009, following a decline from 2000.[118] England's 2023 PISA maths scores also

---

[116] Department for Education, 'England moves to fourth in international rankings for reading', press release, 16 May 2023 (www.gov.uk).

[117] 'England among highest performing western countries in education', press release, 5 December 2023 (www.gov.uk).

[118] John Jerrim, 'England's "plummeting" PISA test scores between 2000 and 2009: is the performance of our secondary school pupils really in relative

showed a narrowing of the gaps between boys and girls, and high and low performers.

There are other signs of improvement too. The attainment gap between those eligible for free school meals and the rest in England's primary schools has been reducing year-by-year since 2011 when the pupil premium came in.[119] The inspectors are impressed too. Nearly ninety per cent of schools are now graded 'outstanding' or 'good' by Ofsted, but not everyone is convinced by these ratings.[120]

Can then the Conservatives' school education policies be counted a success? My view is that the reform of the curriculum and examinations is one of the best things that the Conservatives achieved during their fourteen years in office. But it is evident that Rishi Sunak does not agree with me since he proposes replacing the new rigorous A-levels by a diploma called the Advanced British Standard (ABS), effectively a return to something that was scrapped because of its weaknesses in 1950.[121] Not only that, but Nick Gibb who held it all together after Gove's departure, following several reprieves, looks to have finally lost his post as schools minister.

How will the education record of the Coalition and Conservatives since 2010 be viewed in hindsight? It depends on what happens next. If the reforms become an established part of the structure of education in England, they will be counted a success. Gove, Gibb, and not to forget Laws, will be celebrated for successfully completing the transformation begun by the Conservatives in the 1980s. But will the changes survive? There is little to go on. Sunak has said he will replace Gove's A-levels with

decline?' Department of Quantitative Social Science Working Paper no. 11–09. December 2011.

[119] Stephen Gorrard, 'Poorer pupils do worse at school – here's how to reduce the attainment gap', *The Conversation,* 30 May 2023.

[120] 88% of schools now rated good or outstanding – and how we're making sure Ofsted ratings are up to date – The Education Hub (blog.gov.uk).

[121] Higher School Certificate for which you had to pass all the elements. If you failed one, you got no credit for the others. To recognise all that has been achieved, single-subject qualifications – O-level and A-level – were brought in 1951.

a diploma-type award, but this would be in ten years' time and could be merely kite-flying.[122] Even if it is not, there has to be considerable doubt as to whether he will ever be in a position to do anything about it. The Labour Party has been notably cagey about its education plans, except for withdrawing the VAT exemption from private schools. Since the reforms are soundly based, I would expect them to endure, because apart from the Brown government, there has been cumulative improvement since the mid 1980s in many areas of school education including autonomy, accountability, literacy, numeracy, the curriculum and national examinations. But given the wavering since 2014, a future government could be forgiven for choosing a different path.

---

[122] Julia Bryson and Branwen Jeffreys, 'Advanced British Standard: Sunak qualification will replace A-levels and T-levels', *BBC Online*, 4 October 2023.

7

Environment

Dieter Helm

THE CONSERVATIVE PARTY has always had a complex
approach to the environment. There are three broad factions. The first sees itself as the friend of business, the private
sector and economic growth. A second (older) faction is rooted
in the land, and in particular in land ownership and the interests
of farmers. A third faction takes the notion of stewardship seriously and sees itself as the leaseholders of the land and puts
small 'c' conservatism and Conservative interests together to
protect the environment.[1]

It is the conflicting interests of these three strands of
Conservative thinking that have played out over the period in
office since 2010. Sometimes it is housebuilding and economic
growth that trumps the natural environment. Sometimes it is the
defence of farmers and their 'rights' to control the land as they
see fit that wins out. And just sometimes, as during Michael
Gove's terms of office at the Department for Environment,
Food and Rural Affairs (Defra), it is the natural environment
and natural capital that dominate.

These three strands have been reflected in different ways by
a succession of secretaries of state at Defra, never a priority
department for the Conservative governments. There have
been ten of them: Spelman, Paterson, Truss, Truss again,
Leadsom, Gove, Villiers, Eustice, Jayawardena, Coffey and
Barclay. Only Spelman and Gove were firmly on the side of the

---

With thanks to Lucy Ritter for research assistance.

[1] The Green Conservative tradition is set out in Roger Scruton, *Green Philosophy:
How to Think Seriously About the Planet* (New York: Atlantic Books, 2014).

natural environment, and in both cases with strong support from the prime minister (PM) of the time.[2]

Like their Labour predecessors, Conservatives have treated climate change, and in particular net zero, as a distinct and separate silo from the natural environment (which of course it is not), and here the climate arguments have played out against the more immediate concerns about affordability and voter sensitivities to the costs of energy. The natural environment has often been seen as something to be sacrificed to the wider net zero good. Only at moments of politically salient tangency – like onshore wind farms and transmission lines and planning – have the two collided. Unlike the natural environment, the succession of secretaries of state covering climate change have largely argued about the speed and costs of decarbonisation, and about pro- and anti-nuclear positions. Since 2010 there have been ten of them, the first two of whom were Liberal Democrats (Lib Dems) in the Coalition government: Huhne, Davey, Rudd (all Department of Energy and Climate Change, DECC), then Clark, Leadsom, Sharma, Kwarteng, Rees-Mogg and Shapps (all Department for Business, Energy and Industrial Strategy, BEIS), then Shapps (Department for Energy Security and Net Zero, DESNZ) and now Coutinho.[3]

---

[2] Caroline Spelman (12 May 2010 – 4 September 2012), Owen Paterson (4 September 2012 – 14 July 2024), Liz Truss (15 July 2014 –14 July 2016), Andrea Leadsom (14 July 2016 – 11 June 2017), Michael Gove (11 June 2017 – 24 July 2019), Theresa Villiers (24 July 2019 – 13 February 2020), George Eustice (13 February 2020 – 6 September 2022), Ranil Jayawardena (6 September – 25 October 2022), Thérèse Coffey (25 October 2022 – 13 November 2023), Steve Barclay (13 November –).

[3] Chris Huhne (12 May 2010 – 3 February 2012), Edward Davey (3 February 2012 – 8 May 2015), Amber Rudd (11 May 2015 – 14 July 2016), Greg Clark (14 July 2016 – 24 July 2019), Andrea Leadsom (24 July 2019 – 13 February 2020), Alok Sharma (13 February 2020 – 8 January 2021), Kwasi Kwarteng (8 January 2021 – 6 September 2022), Jacob Rees-Mogg (6 September 2022 – 25 October 2022), Grant Shapps (25 October 2022 – 31 August 2023), Claire Coutinho (31 August 2023 –).

There are two broad ways to approach the environmental record of the Conservative governments: chronological and by theme. Given the very different complexions of the successive governments – the Coalition, the Cameron majority from 2015 through to the Brexit referendum, the May government and the 2017 election and its aftermath, the Johnson government from 2019, then Truss, and finally Sunak – it makes sense to look at each in turn, before broadly assessing the overall performance on the natural environment and climate change in the latter part of the chapter.

THE COALITION GOVERNMENT

An incoming government can only build on what it inherits, and in 2010 Labour left behind a legacy which was largely the product of David Miliband at Defra and Ed Miliband at DECC. In the case of the Defra agenda, this amounted to not much more than speeches and intent; at DECC, created in 2008 (and closed in 2016), it was nothing short of an inversion of the liberalisation and competition model for the energy sector to one based upon state contracting. The Climate Change Act 2008 was a milestone which determined the subsequent climate change policy, with its 80 per cent decarbonisation target, its Climate Change Committee and carbon budgets. Once passed, there could be no retreat – indeed, Theresa May tightened the 80 per cent to 100 per cent by 2050. Almost all Conservative MPs in opposition voted for the 2008 Act.[4]

The emergence of climate change as a major political force and a priority for the young had not escaped the Conservatives as David Cameron faced up to Gordon Brown in the run-up to the 2010 election. Keen to gain the green vote, Cameron famously got himself photographed in the Arctic in what became known as 'hug a huskie'. The Conservatives tried to position themselves as a 'green' party, echoing much earlier moves by Michael Heseltine, who presented himself as the greenest of the green

---

[4] See the Climate Change Act 2008 (2050 Target Amendment) Order 2019.

and passed the Wildlife and Countryside Act 1981 as secretary of state, and by Chris Patten in his 1990 White Paper *This Common Inheritance*.[5] Oliver Letwin, the key policy coordinator and go-between for Cameron and George Osborne, and to a lesser extent Steve Hilton, Cameron's key adviser, grasped the political opportunities of being green. On the environment, the election slogan for 2010 was 'Vote blue, go green'.[6]

As the Coalition was put together in 2010, the Lib Dems got DECC and the Conservatives got Defra. For the Lib Dems, energy and climate were a big deal, and, after Nick Clegg, Chris Huhne was the leading figure in their party. As secretary of state, he took Ed Miliband's Labour policies and tried to build on them, with notable continuity. The Cameron team could do little about this new fiefdom of their junior partners, and indeed there is little evidence to suggest they thought otherwise.[7] Of the issues in the Coalition Agreement, the most fractious was nuclear power, and it produced a compromise in which the Lib Dem opposition was finessed as acceptance of a role for nuclear if it was cost-effective – which Huhne assumed it would not be.[8]

Under Huhne, Miliband's policies were implemented, notably the Electricity Market Reform (EMR), part of the Energy Act 2013. This made the state the contractor for new electricity generation, breaking the link between suppliers that had been set up to shop around amongst the generators for the best deals for their customers. Huhne also persisted with Miliband's major mistake in locating the smart meters obligation with suppliers and not distributors.[9] Both were 'technical' issues, but both would have profound consequences. Making the state the

---

[5] Department of the Environment, 1990.

[6] See Conservative Party, *Invitation to Join the Government of Britain: The Conservative Manifesto 2010* (2010).

[7] The Conservatives issued a green paper on energy in 2009, prepared by Greg Clark, *The Low Carbon Economy, Security, Stability and Green Growth*.

[8] HM Government, *The Coalition: Our Programme for Government* (2010). See also Chris Huhne, Hansard, HC, vol. 512, col. 979, 1 July 2010.

[9] DECC, *Smart Metering Implementation Programme*, Programme Update April 2012.

contractor for generation sucked the Conservatives into ever-greater interventions, culminating in 2023 in the 1,000-page document *Powering up Britain*.[10] Putting smart meters in supply not distribution would not only be costly, but also leave the UK seriously adrift in its attempts to decarbonise household energy. We return to both below.

Undeterred, Huhne moved on to energy efficiency, and promised 250,000 jobs as households would be insulated on a street-by-street basis.[11] As with subsequent great efficiency drives, all measures were erroneously assumed to reduce the demand for electricity and gas. Huhne wanted to play a central part at the ill-fated Durban Conference of the Parties (COP) in 2012 and, undeterred by its failure to agree a legally binding set of targets, came back to tell the House of Commons what a triumph it had been:

> This is a significant step forward in curbing emissions to tackle global climate change. For the first time we've seen major economies, normally cautious, commit to take the action demanded by the science.[12]

As Huhne was getting into his stride, developing Miliband's policies, what should have been a minor matter of a speeding ticket led to his downfall, as he and his then wife committed perjury about who was driving the car. Ed Davey stepped into Huhne's place, and his term of office was increasingly dogged by the issue of affordability and the conduct of the energy companies, rather than the decarbonisation agenda. 'Hugging the huskies' had been fine whilst gas prices were falling and, with them, electricity prices, but the market turned ugly in the run-up to the fossil-fuel price spikes in 2014. Whilst the voters had been happy with green policies when it cost them nothing, and they were

[10] HM Government, *Powering up Britain*, March 2023.

[11] Chris Huhne, speech to the Economist UK Energy Summit, 24 June, www.gov.uk/government/speeches/the-rt-hon-chris-huhne-mps-speech-to-the-economist-uk-energy-summit

[12] DECC and Chris Huhne, 'Road open to new global legal climate treaty', news story, 11 December 2011.

promised it would lead to lower bills, when the reverse happened, the politics turned altogether more difficult.

Once consumers' bills started on an upward path, there was an attempt by Number 10 to reach for all the levers. Issues which were to dominate the rest of the Conservatives' time in office came to the fore: removing environmental costs from customers' bills and regulating prices. Cameron cut the £50 energy efficiency levy[13] and as the Competition and Markets Authority (CMA) got its teeth into the market abuse by the big six suppliers,[14] he faced off against Ed Miliband, now opposition leader, over imposing a price cap. No one at this stage imagined that by 2021 the government would be subsidising all household energy bills. By 2013 hug the huskies had been replaced with 'cut the green crap'.[15]

Whilst all this was going on under the Lib Dems at DECC, the Conservatives at Defra played a much more muted game. Spelman was at least 'green' and wanted to pursue an environmentally progressive agenda, but lacked political backing in the Conservative Party and was overshadowed by Osborne and the Treasury. Her successor, Paterson, wanted to fight the climate change policies of Ed Davey at DECC, whilst his successor, Truss, had no obvious interest in the environment, and regarded her appointment as but a first step on a political ladder she wanted to climb up – and out of Defra – asap.[16]

The Spelman period was nevertheless notable for two main developments: *The Natural Choice* White Paper and the debacle over privatising forests.[17] *The Natural Choice* was the first White

---

[13] Hansard, HC, vol. 569, col. 294, 23 October 2013.

[14] Competition and Markets Authority, 'Energy market investigation', 9 February 2016.

[15] This phrase was attributed to Cameron in the *Sun* newspaper by a senior Tory source in autumn 2013, www.thesun.co.uk/news/1434895/david-camerons-good-jekyll-won-votes-his-cynical-hyde-lost-him-power/

[16] See Harry Cole, and James Heale, *Out of the Blue: The Inside Story of the Unexpected Rise and Rapid Fall of Liz Truss* (London: HarperCollins, 2022).

[17] HM Government, *The Natural Choice: Securing the Value of Nature*, CM 8082, June 2011.

Paper on biodiversity for a decade, and it was largely without content. Its main pillars were to advance the economic approach to the environment (for which read the Treasury's preferred way of thinking) and, in the absence of any concrete policy proposals, to set up a committee to take forward the key ideas. The former played out when the Treasury moved towards more privatisation, and the latter in the setting-up of the Natural Capital Committee. As with low-priority and ill-thought-out measures, the former came to grief as the public protested against the privatisation of forests and the Bishop of Liverpool was called in to review the policy,[18] enabling it to be quietly buried. The latter turned out to set the path towards the '25 Year Environment Plan',[19] now embedded in the Environment Act 2021, and the revolution in agricultural policy enshrined in the Agriculture Act 2020.

Paterson owed his appointment at Defra more to the need to balance up the Eurosceptic wing in the Cabinet, and in a department without extra funding he was always going to struggle to make a mark. That he chose to use the post as a platform to seek to undermine the DECC agenda under Davey did not help, creating tensions in the Coalition without any obvious benefits. He was also embroiled in the controversies over culling badgers in aid of limiting the spread of tuberculosis (TB). This led to the remark by Ed Miliband that the prime minister had gone from 'hug a huskie' to 'gas a badger'.[20]

Truss was to find Defra every bit as limiting, except that she was ambitious and wanted to be seen to make her mark on the wider political stage and especially with the Conservative Party. She was the farmers' friend, given her (intensive) agricultural

---

[18] The Independent Panel on Forestry advised the government on the future direction of forestry and woodland policy in England, and on the role of the Forestry Commission in implementing it. The Panel published its Final Report on 4 July 2012. See www.gov.uk/government/groups/independ ent-panel-on-forestry

[19] Defra and Michael Gove, 'A green future: our 25 year plan to improve the environment', policy paper, 2018.

[20] Prime Minister's Questions, 16 October 2013.

constituency in Norfolk and her distain for environmentalist NGOs. She already preened as a future Margaret Thatcher, and excelled in offering up further cuts to the Defra budget. Having previously had a stint at the Treasury, she took a Treasury view of Defra. Her ambition at Defra was that nothing should go wrong, so that she should survive Defra on the path to greater things.

Truss showed very little interest in natural capital, and even less in the Natural Capital Committee, and instead sharpened her knife at the expense of the Environment Agency (EA) and Natural England (NE), part of the sprawling Defra empire. Neither she nor the Treasury thought that these bodies were being managed well, and she decided to take a central command-and-control approach. Her remedy was to move their leaders into offices in Defra, sandwiched by the permanent secretary in between them. Apart from cutting their budgets further, it made little difference.

By the time of the election in 2015, the Coalition government had very little to show on the environment side. Most major opportunities to be 'green' had been killed off by the Treasury as part of the wider austerity programme, and followed Osborne's scepticism about how far decarbonisation and the natural environment should be prioritised. The economic inheritance from the Brown government and the great financial crash in 2007/2008 meant that there was little money to spend. Where cuts did need to be applied, it was much easier to take out Defra spending and to push the costs of decarbonisation onto customers than it was to cut health and other core spending.

THE CAMERON MAJORITY GOVERNMENT

The Conservative manifesto in 2015 endorsed the 25-year plan proposed by the Natural Capital Committee (as did the Labour and LibDem manifestos):

> We set up the Natural Capital Committee to put hard economic numbers on the value of our environment, and we will extend its life to at least the end of the next Parliament. We

will work with it to develop a 25 Year Plan to restore the UK's biodiversity, and to ensure that both public and private investment in the environment is directed where we need it most.

The reality was that from the 2015 election onwards, Brexit overshadowed all other policy issues, and the environment was largely to be seen through the prism of Brexit. Surprisingly, this gave the environment a starring role, one that echoes through to 2024. The reason is perhaps surprising to the Brexiteers: the main impacts of the EU directives are to be found in climate change, agriculture and the natural environment. The bulk of the legislative changes relate to the EU's 20–20–20 climate and energy targets, the Renewable Energy Directive, the Common Agricultural Policy (CAP), and water, chemicals and air quality Directives.[21] The Directives cover gene editing and genetically modified organisms (GMOs)[22] and the EU Emissions Trading Scheme (EU ETS),[23] and the UK found itself repeatedly being admonished and taken to the European Court of Justice on environmental matters.[24]

[21] European Commission, 2020 climate & energy package, climate.ec.eur opa.eu/eu-action/climate-strategies-targets/2020-climate-energy-pack age_en; Renewable Energy Directive (Directive (EU) 2018/2001); Common Agricultural Policy, agriculture.ec.europa.eu/common-agri cultural-policy/cap-overview/cap-glance_en; the REACH Regulation (Regulation (EC) no. 1907/2006 of the European Parliament and of the Council of 18 December 2006), the Water Framework Directive (Directive 2000/60/EC), Air quality (Directive 2008/50/EC).

[22] Directive 2001/18/EC of the European Parliament and of the Council of 12 March 2001 on the deliberate release into the environment of genetic- ally modified organisms and repealing Council Directive 90/220/EEC – Commission Declaration, OJ L 106, 17.4.2001, pp. 1–39.

[23] Directive (EU) 2018/410 amending Directive 2003/87/EC to enhance cost-effective emission reductions and low-carbon investments, OJ L 76, 19.3.2018, pp. 3–27.

[24] See, for example, Judgment of the Court (Seventh Chamber) of 4 March 2021. European Commission v United Kingdom of Great Britain and Northern Ireland. Failure of a Member State to fulfil obligations –

This is to jump ahead. The commitment to hold a referendum was fulfilled in 2016, ending the Cameron-led government and bringing in May. Before the referendum, the Conservatives were taken up with international climate negotiations, and notably the 2015 Paris COP, whilst continuing a benign neglect of the natural environment. The reappointment of Truss at Defra saw little change and after Cameron's departure, her successor at Defra, Leadsom, made even Truss look like an activist. Do as little as possible was the political objective, which both Truss and especially Leadsom met in full.

The 2015 Paris COP followed on from the failures at the Durban COP in 2012. The holy grail of a legally binding treaty was the backdrop and with Barack Obama on board, all the major world leaders were heavily into the rhetoric of 'saving the planet'. The Paris COP has been presented ever since as a watershed moment, but the facts speak otherwise. There would be no legally binding targets, something the United States would never sign up to, and which few people had any expectation that China could be held to. The actual pledges made did not even add up to the 2^0C target, but this did not stop the COP signing up to 1.5^0C as a new even more unlikely target.[25] For the UK, things looked good. Emissions had fallen fast and the UK could claim to be the world leader in cutting carbon emissions, something that May and especially Boris Johnson were subsequently keen to boast about. Johnson claimed that not only was the UK a world leader, but that China and Russia were looking to emulate the UK: 'the likes of China and Russia are following our lead with their own net zero

Environment – Directive 2008/50/EC – Ambient air quality – Article 13(1) and Annex XI – Systematic and persistent exceedance of the limit values for nitrogen dioxide (NO2) in certain areas of the United Kingdom – Article 23(1) – Annex XV – Exceedance period to be 'as short as possible' – Appropriate measures. Case C-664/18.

[25] See Dieter Helm, 'The environmental impacts of the coronavirus', *Environmental and Resource Economics*, 76 (2020), 21–38.

targets'.[26] But the complacency about the costs of climate change remained, even as the cost of energy was still a priority. The Cameron government went on to impose a price cap that Cameron had opposed in the election, when it was made a central plank by Miliband. There was to be a *Cost of Energy Review* to try to meet the ambition of having the lowest prices in Europe.[27]

At Defra almost nothing happened under Truss's second term. There was much activity in the background – notably with the development of the 25-year plan that had been in the 2015 manifesto – but it was development without active decisions. The squeeze on the EA and NE intensified, and there was no appetite or bandwidth for any serious institutional reform.

MAY'S GOVERNMENTS

The defeat in the referendum on Brexit was unexpected, and as a result it rapidly became apparent that almost nothing had been done to prepare for this eventuality. It would be a massive undertaking for the civil service to rewrite legislation on agriculture and the environment, and to sort out the trading issues around food, biosecurity, while also finding the resources to engage in the wider environmental diplomacy.

May was obviously preoccupied with trying to get through a Brexit deal with the EU and a withdrawal agreement, in the face of hostility from the core European Research Group (ERG) and Johnson, who was bent on replacing her. Her Cabinet was constructed with this in mind, plus the obvious political necessity of creating a Cabinet of all the factions. It cannot have been in her mind that, in appointing Gove as secretary of state for Environment, Food and Rural Affairs, she would usher in some of the most far-reaching and profound changes in UK environmental policy, including a wholly new agricultural policy around

---

[26] Boris Johnson, 'Foreword from the Prime Minister', in HM Government, *Net Zero Strategy: Build Back Greener*, October 2021, p. 8.

[27] Dieter Helm, *Cost of Energy Review*, independent review for the Department of Business, Energy and Industrial Strategy, October 2017.

the principle of public money for public goods, sweeping away payments under the Common Agricultural Policy's (CAP), Basic Farm Payment (BFP) for the ownership of land, implementing the 25-year plan, setting up the Office for Environmental Protection (OEP) and legislating for statutory environmental targets.

Gove's arrival at Defra is probably the single most important event in the history of the environmental policy under the Conservatives. His brief, as he reported to the BBC *Today* programme on 13 June 2017, was to 'enhance the environment', 'exercise humility' and 'listen and to learn'. He found himself at the sharp end of Brexit, in a department that had done little to prepare for a new Agriculture Act and a new Environment Act. The Agriculture Act 2020 and the Environment Act 2021, passed after Gove had moved on, are the standout achievements of the Conservative period in office, and along with the 2019 amendment to the Climate Change Act setting the 100 per cent net zero target, together they are the three pillars of policy towards the natural environment which are likely to last for a decade or more.[28]

Gove's achievements stem from two distinct characteristics of his approach: his instinctive resistance to vested interests and lobbyists, and a genuine desire to start from first principles that Brexit provided him with. His speech: 'The Unfrozen Moment' summarises the way he saw opportunities to reshape environmental and agricultural policy that Brexit had created.[29] To this is added his belief that the Conservatives needed to be 'green' as a political strategy to regain the youth vote.

The majority of farmers voted for Brexit, presumably in the belief that they would be better protected by the UK Treasury than by the European Commission, and that British politicians would be more mindful of the farmers' interests than those of environmentalists. They could not have been more wrong.

---

[28] In addition to the Fisheries Act 2000, replacing the Common Fisheries Policy (CFP).

[29] Michael Gove, 'The unfrozen moment – delivering a green Brexit', speech at the WWF Living Planet Centre, Woking, 21 July 2017.

Whilst the CAP applied to the whole of the UK, the devolution of agricultural and environmental policies within the UK meant that there would now be separate Northern Irish, Scottish, Welsh and English policies.

In the English case, Gove grasped the concept of 'public goods for public money', something the Treasury had advanced back in 2005 in its reform proposals for the CAP.[30] This stands in sharp contrast to the previous history of agricultural policy before the UK joined the EU, and the EU CAP, which had been based first on production subsidies and then on subsidies to farmers as owners of land. In the CAP, farmers are paid the BFP, which is a sum per hectare, subject only to some minimal environmental 'cross-compliance', but in practice with almost no chance of suffering penalties for environmental failures. Now farmers would gradually lose this land ownership subsidy, and instead have to produce stuff that they would not otherwise do, and which provided public rather than private goods. Though Defra's team proved hopelessly inadequate in developing the new subsidy model – called the Environmental Land Management Scheme (ELMS)[31] – and intensive lobbying by the National Farmers Union (NFU) repeatedly tried to undermine it, the Gove principle has stuck.

A second feature of the new subsidy regime was that the Conservative government set out a gradual profile for eliminating the BFP, and committed to retaining the overall nominal spend on subsidies through to 2027. But if farmers thought this meant that the new policy was the shuffling of monies from one bucket to another, they failed to recognise the risk that the bucket might spring a leak. The commitment was to the nominal value, not the real one, and by 2024 inflation has already seriously reduced the real total. As public expenditure constraints bite over the rest of this decade, farmers may wonder whether

---

[30] HM Treasury and Defra, 'A vision for the Common Agricultural Policy', December 2005.

[31] On ELMS, see www.gov.uk/government/publications/environmental-land-management-schemes-overview/environmental-land-management-scheme-overview

the European Commission, backed by the powerful EU farmers' unions, might have been a better financial bet.[32] The intense lobbying by the NFU (and supported by the Defra Select Committee, chaired by the farmers' advocate, Neil Parish, and with a farmer, George Eustice, as the minister within Defra) could not overcome the Gove policy revolution.

The Environment Act followed in 2021, and, as with the Agriculture Act, Gove started from first principles, and then addressed the practicalities of replacing the EU directives, notably on clean air, water and waste. The principles were set out way back in the 2011 White Paper on *The Natural Choice: Securing the Value of Nature.* The NCC had interpreted that through the lens of natural capital, and it is this lens that Gove embraced. There was much debate about how to turn this concept (and the subsidiary principles) into legislation, but the focus of the legislation is the identification of ten core targets, and then the gradual placing of these onto a statutory basis, to which we return below.

The Environment Act embedded the 25-year plan into five-year Environmental Improvement Plans (EIPs).

There was one further challenge for Gove. He had committed to Brexit leading to higher environmental standards in the UK relative to those in the EU, something which green NGOs had been concerned about during and after the referendum. To make this commitment credible, Gove proposed an Office for Environmental Protection (OEP), which would be an independent body to hold government bodies to account in respect of both the EIPs, which operationalised the 25-year plan, and the statutory targets. After he moved on, the Treasury emaciated the OEP, and 'guidance' from the secretary of state on investigations plus budget squeezes weakened this bit of the new institutional architecture. Added to this was Gove's failure to reform the EA and NE, and in particular to carve out a proper Environment Protection Agency from the EA. He accepted the logic of this,

---

but sought the more expedient route of grafting on yet another body.[33] The 'unfrozen moment' gradually began to ice over again.

Gove pushed his agenda along by commissioning two further reviews – the Glover review on national parks,[34] and the Dimbleby review on food: the 'National Food Strategy'.[35] The former reported in late 2019, just before the December 2019 election and in the maelstrom of the battles over the Brexit deal during Johnson governments. The latter was published in July 2021. In response to the former, actions followed glacially, with a process of creating a new national park not started until late in 2023. On the latter, a White Paper appeared in 2022.[36]

While Gove was driving these major reforms forward at Defra, May played to the net zero agenda with one last throw of the dice as her term of office came to an end. This was the 2019 Climate Change Amendment to raise the 2050 net zero target to 100 per cent rather than 80 per cent. The CCC was asked to opine, and recommended this step on the grounds that it would not be costly, and that when the UK got to net zero it would no longer be causing climate change.[37]

Both claims are false. Despite repeated claims that the costs of net zero would be small, as we will see, and despite the Conservative MPs lining up to vote for the 2019 amendment, the costs would gradually emerge and create the political backlash in 2023. The claim to 'no longer be causing climate change' neglects the fact that the target is set as territorial carbon emissions in the UK, taking no account of carbon embedded in imports, and remarkably also excludes the emissions from the

---

[33] Gove did move to put an environmental activist, Tony Juniper, in charge of NE.

[34] *Landscapes Review: Final Report*, 2019.

[35] See www.nationalfoodstrategy.org. There had been an earlier White Paper on food in 2018 (Defra, 'Health and harmony: the future for food, farming and the environment in a Green Brexit', Cm 9577, 2018).

[36] Defra, 'Government food strategy', policy paper, 2022.

[37] CCC, *Net Zero – The UK's Contribution to Stopping Global Warming*, technical report, May 2019.

large-scale burning of wood pellets at the Drax power station. For an economy that is 80 per cent services, a great deal of carbon is imported, and, as the North Sea runs down, oil and gas exports are falling away.

JOHNSON'S PRIORITIES AND BREXIT

As these great changes in environmental policies were being pushed through, the Conservative government was consumed with the Herculean task of negotiating the Withdrawal Agreement with the EU 'to get Brexit done'. This task was compounded by the political manoeuvres of the ERG, and Johnson in particular. Detailed matters like the retained EU legislation, the recognition that it would take decades to extricate the UK from the EU, and that in the meantime customs and border issues would continue to throw up problems of queues and perishing foodstuff, were all seen through the prism of Johnson's personal ambition to become PM.

Once he achieved this goal in July 2019, there were six months of high drama in the House of Commons, with the illegal proroguing of parliament and the general election. The deal Johnson agreed with the EU cut Northern Ireland adrift from the rest of the UK, put the customs border in the Irish Sea and created multiple problems which Johnson treated as, at best, temporary inconveniences. From the Withdrawal Agreement onwards, there were no longer much by way of UK-wide environment policies.

The detail of the Withdrawal Agreement and the renegotiation of the Northern Ireland Protocol had major impacts on the practice of environmental regulation, standards and administration. Much of it is so complex as to escape the understanding of all but specialists and goes largely unnoticed. It was all the more unnoticed as the coronavirus gained a grip, lockdowns were imposed and much of the day-to-day environmental business of government went into cold storage.

It did not, however, go away. Johnson appointed Villiers to Defra, who turned out to be practically invisible, and replaced Clark with Rees-Mogg at BEIS to oversee climate change policies. Unlike Clark, Rees-Mogg was a known sceptic of the climate change policies then in place. Gove was sent to address the even more intractable levelling-up agenda, and the pursuit of housebuilding targets that rubbed against his environmental policies at Defra, and especially when it came to nutrients and planning permission and the rules that NE upheld.[38] Environmental regulations were seen as reasons why the government failed to meet its target of building 300,000 houses per annum. The green belt, flood plain considerations and pressures to incorporate net zero features in new houses were all listed as constraining new housebuilding. The real culprits lay elsewhere in the behaviour of the housebuilders' oligopoly, the collapse of public sector housebuilding, and the private sector preference for greenfield sites over urban green spaces and affordable social housing.[39] These policy issues came to a head under Sunak, to which we return below.

As with so much of the Johnson government's approach to policy, the natural environment and climate change became much more political and personal, concentrated amongst his inner circle. On climate change, Zac Goldsmith and Johnson's partner Carrie Symonds wanted a more radically green approach, as did both Zac and Ben Goldsmith and Symonds on the natural environment. On climate change, Johnson saw the opportunity to grandstand on the world climate stage at the Glasgow COP in 2021, and he embraced a full 'cake-ism' approach. On the natural environment, Johnson got excited about rewilding and beavers (including his reported attempt to give some beavers to his father to introduce on Exmoor), but

---

[38] In August 2023, the government announced that it would amend the Habitats Regulations, which underpin 'nutrient neutrality', through the Levelling Up and Regeneration Bill 2022–3. The proposed amendments were rejected by the House of Lords in September 2023.

[39] In February 2023, the CMA launched an investigation into the housebuilding market, publishing two working papers: CMA, 'Housebuilding market study: local concentration and land banks', working paper, and 'Housebuilding market study: planning', working paper, 15 November 2023.

that was the limit of his interests, and the detail escaped him. Johnson had no obvious personal interest in Defra and its multiple activities.

The Glasgow COP was for Johnson a bit like the Olympics – he could play the global leader and shine across the media. His hubris knew few bounds. This was Johnson of the *Ten Point Plan* and, as noted earlier, his claim that so great were the UK's achievements that China and Russia would be trying to copy the UK.[40] It was almost as if Vladimir Putin and Xi Jinping would join him at the climate change equivalent of Yalta. Even better, Johnson did not need to do anything – just be the hero on the world stage.

Despite all this rhetoric, the Glasgow COP achieved very little. As with Paris there would be no *legally binding* commitments (nationally determined contributions, NDCs), and the transfer of monies from the Northern Hemisphere to the Southern Hemisphere and the protection of rainforests would not make much impact on the ground. Johnson would not revert to the 0.7 per cent gross domestic product (GDP) as the international aid budget, and the Treasury ensured there was no more money. It was almost all hot air, and as if to signal his own lack of interest in the implications of mitigating climate change, he was keen to emphasise that there would be no need to change lifestyles and stop flying, for example. To prove the point, he took a private plane back from Glasgow to go to a dinner with his journalist friends at the Garrick Club in London. Job done. Lots of publicity. The World Stage. And no need to do anything much. Perfect Johnson.

Behind all this lay the net zero review by the Treasury, interim and final reports,[41] and the tidal wave of documents, consultations, strategies and technology supports that poured out of BEIS, and which has got ever bigger since then. In the desire to be seen to be 'doing something', and in the name of

---

[40] HM Government, *The Ten Point Plan for a Green Industrial Revolution*, November 2020.

[41] HM Treasury, *Net Zero Review: Analysis Exploring the Key Issues*, October 2021.

each of the ten points in the *Ten Point Plan*, there emerged the seeds of the Conservative climate change splits that were to come into the open under the Sunak government. By claiming that it was all upside – all gain and no pain – a set of policies were put in place that would seriously backfire after Johnson was forced from office.

None of this was to be a major priority for Johnson. Having been defined by Brexit, he now faced two black swans: the coronavirus and the Russian invasion of Ukraine with its associated energy crisis. Though there was lots of excitement at the time that the lockdowns would be a turning point towards 'green' as the British public experienced their local urban green spaces and 'countryside', and that nature and mental health and clean air would be winners, there turned out to be no 'green new deal'. Whilst the lockdown gave nature a temporary reprieve from human pressures, what the coronavirus actually did for the environment was make everyone poorer and do great damage to the government's finances.[42] Affordability combined with the damage done to the fabric of the economy through furlough, quantitative easing (QE) and working from home, in a context in which productivity and economic growth had been feeble since the 2007/2008 financial crash, meant that the 'luxury' that the natural environment was treated as was now something that could no longer be so easily afforded. It was fine to be green if it costs very little – as claimed by many of the net zero proponents – and it was fine to cut away at agricultural subsidies that supported the ownership of land in favour of greener public goods. Now the economic outlook was much darker, and the UK would struggle to get people back to work.

The Ukrainian crisis added a further twist. It revealed two things: that energy prices could go up as well as down, and that security of supply mattered. As the gas price rose in advance of the Russian invasion in February 2022, and as the threat of power cuts loomed, the environment went into retreat. Across Europe,

---

[42] See Dieter Helm, *Net Zero: How We Stop Causing Climate Change* (London: William Collins, 2020).

countries reverted to burning coal, and governments across Europe intervened to subsidise customers who could not afford the very large and sudden fuel price increases. The costs of these interventions added to the costs of the pandemic and left the public finances in an even bigger mess. Add in the inflation that was underpinned by the successive rounds of QE plus the energy price shock, and affordability went from a problem to a crisis. Energy, other utility bills and mortgage costs added up to a structural break with economic experience since the turn of the century back in 2000.

The affordability crisis had a political consequence for the Conservative commitment to net zero. Voters could no longer easily afford the electric cars and heat pumps they would be expected to pay for. At a by-election held in the parliamentary constituency of Uxbridge and South Ruislip in southeast England, they revolted against paying the Ultra Low Emission Zone (ULEZ) charges too.[43] The policy's impacts would play out under Sunak, but their origins were under Johnson when he was mayor of London. His *Ten Point Plan* was in tatters when Johnson left office under the cloud of his lying about lockdown parties.

THE TRUSS FORTY-NINE DAYS

Though the Truss government was short, and there was no time to pass any environmental legislation, it did bring to prominence the 'economic growth priority' strand of Conservative thinking. Truss had modelled herself on Thatcher, and a particularly distorted interpretation. Having campaigned and voted for Remain, she had a Keynesian disregard for government deficits, and promoted unfunded tax cuts. Had she had time, she would possibly have pursued the 'Singapore-on-Thames' model of Brexit. Housebuilding, onshore wind farms and a focus on

---

[43] This by-election was the result of Johnson resigning his seat in June 2023. Despite expectations by some that the Labour Party might win it, Steve Tuckwell, the Conservative representative, held it, with a reduced majority of 495 votes. He put his success down to the unpopularity of the proposed expansion of the ULEZ scheme into his constituency.

food production would have crushed the older Conservative tradition of conserving the British countryside.

Her legacy is not only to have reminded the Conservative Party of the merits of fiscal prudence, but also to have provided an approach which is close to that of Keir Starmer. Truss would have shared a desire to put a 'bulldozer through planning' and set ambitious housing targets.[44] She would have undermined the green belt and she can claim to have invented the sentiment behind Starmer's yimby ('yes in my backyard') with her trumpeting of housebuilding in her constituency. Add in her desire to build onshore wind farms (which she advanced later on in 2023), and a preference for more debt to pay for this, all in the service of maximising economic growth, and the Truss–Starmer commonality is very striking.

Truss combined this growth approach with an almost casual dislike of Defra and all it stood for. With this in mind she appointed Jayawardena to be secretary of state, and in the brief forty-five days he gave a glimpse of what an alternative Conservative strategy towards the natural environment would have been.[45] Ironically, it would have been very anti-Thatcher. Truss conveniently ignored Thatcher's early alarm raised at the UN over climate change,[46] the appointment of Michael Heseltine and the passing of the Countryside and Rights of Way Act 2000, and the appointment of Chris Patten and support for his major White Paper. Thatcher preferred an economic approach to the environment, but that was more what David Pearce added to Patten's White Paper, including the economic costs of the environment in the broader economic calculus.[47] Truss would have always subsidised the farmers, though she had been less keen on protecting them from the trade deals she tried

---

[44] See Keir Starmer, speech at the Labour Party Conference, 10 October 2023.

[45] Ranil Jayawardena, speech to Conservative Party Conference, 3 October 2022.

[46] Margaret Thatcher, speech to United Nations General Assembly (Global Environment), 8 November 1989.

[47] Department of the Environment, *This Common Inheritance: A Summary of the White Paper on the Environment.* (1990), appendix F.

to negotiate under the Johnson government. Many of the regulatory controls over pesticides, genetic engineering and other 'obstacles' to maximising food production would probably have been removed too.

SUNAK'S GOVERNMENT

Truss lasted just forty-nine days and was seamlessly replaced by Sunak. The days of high drama of Johnson and Truss were further exacerbated in the economic crisis that Kwasi Kwarteng's mini-budget of 23 September 2022 delivered, and Sunak's government has been more characterised by moderation in the tradition of the Conservative Party. The key feature of his government is a return to fiscal prudence and monetary stability. Deficits and inflation are the twin devils Sunak is set upon slaying, all much more Thatcherite than Truss.

At the time of writing this chapter in January 2024, Sunak did not retreat from the main planks of post-Brexit policy put in place under May; rather, he tried to accommodate the various strands of Conservative thinking. On agriculture, ELMS remained in place, albeit with a considerable steering away, under Treasury guidance, from the more radical Gove overtones. Sunak did not retreat from net zero, but rather took a more pragmatic line on the timetable.[48] He had a hand on the tiller tilting it towards pragmatism and party management of the different strands of Conservative environmental thinking.

The most notable environmental policy development under Sunak has been as much the result of external circumstances as deliberate ambition. The energy crisis that started under Johnson became much more severe under Sunak and, as with the underpinning of wages by furlough when he was chancellor, the Sunak government implemented the energy price support. A new prioritisation was given to security of supply to be further enhanced as concerns about Russia and defence spilled over into

[48] Rishi Sunak, speech on Net Zero, 20 September 2023.

energy policy.[49] As chancellor, he had introduced the windfall taxes, in line with most other European countries.

The most notable steer on the tiller has been the *Powering up Britain* White Paper published in March 2023.[50] It is, like so many energy White Papers published in before it, focused on proving the impossible: that affordability, security of supply and decarbonisation are all mutually compatible. In the Shapps version, it is all going to work out in the lowest prices in Europe by 2035, by investing in wind and solar, with some nuclear added in. Net zero in the power sector is going to be achieved in 2035, just twelve years after the White Paper. There may be costs to powering up Britain, the costs of solar and wind might rise as the supply chains are stretched, the cost of capital has gone up, there may need to be major new transmission lines across the British countryside, new petrol and diesel cars may be banned in 2030 and new gas boilers outlawed as well, batteries are going to solve the intermittency that the planned 50 gigawatt (GW) of offshore wind will bring – but all of this is not going to cost much more, according to the Shapps White Paper. If only, but then the calculations assume that oil and especially gas prices will be high and volatile, hence making people better-off than they would have been.

Shapps ignored too the fact that the UK economy is over 70 per cent dependent on fossil fuels, and the world at 80 per cent. Ignored too were the haemorrhaging of the energy-intensive industries, attracted by cheap oil and especially gas in the United States, and the competition for the key minerals and their refining for the net zero technologies from the US Inflation Reduction Act 2022 and the EU's Green Deal.[51] Lithium, zinc, copper and nickel are all refined and imported from outside the UK, adding to the hole in the balance of payments, exacerbated by the decline of the North Sea oil and gas industries. None of

---

[49] The Energy Bills Discount Scheme was established in regulations made under the Energy Prices Act 2022 (www.legislation.gov.uk/ukpga/2022/44/enacted).

[50] HM Government, DESNZ, 'Powering up Britain', policy paper, March 2023.

[51] See https://commission.europa.eu/strategy-and-policy/priorities-2019-2024/european-green-deal_en

this seemed to bother Shapps. It all passed him and the White Paper by. Shapps was more struck with the headlines and the spin, about the UK becoming the Saudi Arabia of carbon capture and storage (CCS), for example.[52]

Sunak came to question the Shapps agenda and think again about the targets and timetable, and focus on the detail – the need for a step change in grid and network investment as the prior requirements. Coutinho replaced Shapps and brought more rigour to the recently created Department of Energy Security and Net Zero that Shapps had managed.

She would see the Energy Act 2023 onto the statute books, and begin the process of a more radical rethink. Sunak wanted to carry the public with him, adopt a flexible approach, and avoid the hard issues like flying, meat, dairy and agricultural emissions, and also avoid relying on Treasury funding. Successive Conservative governments have sheltered customers whenever they have affordability problems, back to the £50 off fuel bills under Cameron, and the massive subsidies of bills under Sunak as chancellor.

The granting of new North Sea licences for oil and gas is an example of that pragmatism. The UK's reliance on fossil fuels is not going to go away anytime soon, and not before 2050. Not producing in the North Sea does not make any difference to the oil and gas burnt domestically. It might even lead to buying more LNG imported gas, environmentally much worse than domestic pipeline gas supplies. Refusing licences and fast-tracking the closure of the North Sea would both lead to job losses and worsen an already serious balance of payments current-account deficit. Labour's opposition was opportunistic: it is only opposed to new licences, and hence it suits Labour for Sunak to grant the licences before the general election, and hence hold up production, whilst claiming the moral high ground. The Rosebank announcement followed.[53]

In taking a pragmatic line on net zero, Sunak tried to head off the growth of the scepticism on the Conservative right about

[52] Grant Shapps, speech at the Spectator Energy Summit, 'UK opportunities in carbon capture', 26 April 2023.
[53] DESNZ, Claire Coutinho and Jeremy Hunt, 'Government backs new oil and gas to safeguard UK and grow the economy', news release, 27 September 2023.

the net zero target. Across Europe there is a reaction against fast action, on the grounds that the main sources of new emissions are coming from countries elsewhere (e.g. China, India, the Middle East, Indonesia and Nigeria), and a resistance to being told to install heat pumps and ditch petrol and diesel cars. Farmers' protests erupted all over Europe, with tractor demonstrations first in Berlin, then Paris and then Brussels. Farmers variously demanded that livestock numbers be maintained, nutrients should not be penalised, pesticides should not be restricted and subsidies to diesel should be maintained.

This more sceptical approach to policy seeped across mainstream European Conservative parties, as they sought to head off voters haemorrhaging towards far-right parties. Germany and the Netherlands have seen a direct hit in electoral results. From the perspective of January 2024, it looks as though the European elections in June 2024 are likely to reinforce this resistance to the acceleration of green policies. If the UK Conservative Party goes into opposition, this split may become much more serious. Sunak's approach has been pragmatism against dogma.

As ever, events have played their part too. A legacy of the experience of lockdown and wider affordability spills over to criticism of the privatised utilities. The emergence of the issues of sewage discharges by water companies into rivers and onto beaches has shot up the public and media agenda. This is perhaps the first time a major environmental issue has not been actioned in Brussels. All the focus has been on the UK and the British companies and their regulators.

The natural environment has not been a priority of the Sunak government. The appointment of Coffey as secretary of state at Defra was a sop to the Truss faction (Coffey was Truss's deputy PM), a downgrade on the path to the backbenches which she would take in autumn 2023, when she was replaced by Steve Barclay. Sunak left in place the more junior ministers, but as a former chancellor and with an eye to fiscal discipline, Defra has become even more the creature of the Treasury.

This created a big practical question about how to respond to the outcry over sewage discharges. Water investment collapsed in the 1980s, and although it picked up afterwards, it has not kept pace with the growth of population. The priorities under both Conservative and past Labour governments have been to keep a lid on customers' bills, and the capital expenditure has been what can be afforded rather than what environmental considerations dictate. With the exception of the London interceptor sewer when it comes on stream, the practice of spilling sewage into rivers and onto beaches has grown in frequency and intensity.

Water privatisation has never been popular. As with the privatisation of the railways, the public never bought into the concept of water as a private rather than a public good. The fact that the industry has become the playground for private equity under both Conservative and Labour governments, that balance sheets have been used for financial engineering rather than for investment, and that in some cases – notably Thames Water – the necessary capital maintenance, investment in sewers and fixing the leaks have not been what they should have been, have all excited public anger.[54] The problem is that to put all this right requires very major investment, and with the new fiscal prudence, this will have to come from customers. There is a demand that the companies should pay, but this neglects the fact that the horses have bolted with the money.

Given the UK's very low savings, future investment across net zero and the natural environment will have to come from savings from outside the UK. Imposing ex post draconian penalties will not only probably be illegal, but it will do great damage to the kindness of the strangers who finance it. The great privatisation experiment launched by the Conservatives in the late 1980s has run out of money and requires serious increases in customers' bills to fix the natural environment. The fact that customers cannot afford this, and that foreign investors are less willing to come forward with the finance, and at higher interest rates, encourages those on the left to advocate nationalisation. Whatever the merits of public over private ownership, the fact remains that the investment needs are very large and someone has to pay. Nationalisation does not resolve this.

[54] See Dieter Helm, 'Thirty years after water privatization – is the English model the envy of the world?', *Oxford Review of Economic Policy*, 36:1 (2020), 69–85.

Sunak's government came to share with Starmer (and ironically Truss) an obsession with economic growth, hardly surprisingly given the poor record on productivity. Trying to make the UK attractive to overseas investors has meant pushing for a reduction in regulation (including environmental regulation), and making regulators like Ofwat and Ofgem have duties to focus on economic growth. The environmental problem with this is not the growth itself, but the GDP measure of that growth. Increasingly in the second half of 2023, Sunak looked to push back what have come to be regarded as environmental barriers, including on planning for homes, onshore wind and pylons. Rules with good rationale, like nutrient neutrality and planning requirements to take account of biodiversity and natural capital, have come under fire, to become a bigger part of the agenda for 2024. In doing so, he ends up with an agenda that is not dissimilar to the one that Truss had promoted. It is therefore not surprising that when the OEP reported on progress on the EIP and the statutory targets, the delay of the framework that government set up has been found wanting.[55]

AN INTERIM ASSESSMENT

One problem with any assessment of the environmental record of the Conservative governments since 2010 is the counterfactual. What would have happened had Brown won in 2010, Ed Miliband in 2015 or Jeremy Corbyn in 2019? Although this is not the place to critique their environmental policies, we can look back at Brown in power and an almost complete absence of concern for the natural environment (but not climate change, with the 2008 Climate Change Act), and find continuity with that neglect in Corbyn's 2019 manifesto. For Miliband, it is different: the Labour manifesto in 2015 did sign up to the 25-year plan, and pushed the net zero agenda further towards more intervention and planning. In opposition, Starmer proposed that more of the green belt should be built upon, the planning system 'bulldozed',

---

[55] Office for Environmental Protection, 'Progress in improving the natural environment in England 2022/2023', 18 January 2024.

and big infrastructure policies should be pursued even where they are at the expense of the environment. Hence, his very Truss-like focus on 'yimbies'.

Would Labour have been very different over the period since 2010 had it remained in power? The lines of thinking and emphasis on the Conservative side are mostly mirrored in Labour. Opening up the countryside for the wider public is more a Labour policy, but national parks and the green belt are as much Labour as Conservative traditions. Both parties have converged on the central priority of economic growth to restore public finances, increase standards of living and pay for the public services. Labour is more an urban party, and it is not surprising that the rural countryside counts for even less for it than for the Conservatives.

Labour acquiesced and often gave full support for the big legislative initiatives since 2010 on the environment and climate change. It had little to object to in the 2011 White Paper *The Natural Choice* and did not oppose the setting-up of the NCC. In time it became a key supporter. Labour supported a price cap (not surprisingly, since it had first proposed this intervention in energy). Labour supported the 2019 amendment to the Climate Change Act and the 100 per cent net zero target, and it broadly fell into line over the Agriculture Act 2020 and the Environment Act 2021. Even on the great water debate and the sewage issues, it has been remarkably quiet in opposition, giving up on the nationalisation of water, and proposing only a very technical reform by merging OFWAT, the Drinking Water Inspectorate and the EA. In opposition, its net zero policies were presented as more radical than those of the Conservatives, and it (implausibly) proposed to hit net zero for the power sector by 2030 rather than the Conservatives' 2035. Neither target looks achievable.[56] Labour did propose to spend £28 billion per annum on net zero, but has since backtracked, and in any event, once nuclear is included, it is not clear that it is widely more profligate than the Conservatives. Notably, it acquiesced on the requirements for

---

[56] See Dieter Helm, 'Net zero electricity: the UK 2035 target', *Oxford Review of Economic Policy*, 39:4 (2023), 779–95.

the banning of gas-fired boilers that Sunak relaxed, and its commitment to reinstating the ban on diesel and petrol cars was less than it seems.

With these observations in mind, it is fair and reasonable to conclude that Labour would not have led the UK towards very different outcomes, save in one respect. It is very unlikely that Labour would have held a referendum on EU membership, and if it had (and it had lost), it is reasonable to assume under Brexit that it would have stayed closer to the EU's standards and regulations. This means that instead of the Agriculture Act 2020, the UK would probably have stayed in or very close to the CAP (and possibly the CFP too). It would also probably have remained under the coverage of the main EU directives, notably on Air Quality and the Water Framework directives, and also the chemicals directive and on gene editing and GMOs. As the Conservatives had before the Brexit referendum, the UK under Labour would have fallen foul of some or all of these directives and the air quality performance would have continued to be in the European Commission's cross hairs.

Brexit was not moved by the CAP or even the CFP. It was not motivated by the main environmental directives. These were the accidental opportunities (or casualties depending on perspectives) of Brexit. The unintended consequences of Brexit are many, but the chance to reform the CAP, the CFP and the environmental targets and standards was a result. Though it is true that there was nothing to stop the UK exceeding the requirements of the EU's directives – and in particular the 25-year plan was entirely compatible – and though Gove promised that the UK would outperform the EU on environmental outcomes, nevertheless the replacement of the CAP and its central BFP for the ownership of land by the public money for public goods principle has to be a major positive step forward, and one that would not have happened without Brexit or at least not until the EU itself radically reformed the CAP.

The Conservatives can take credit for the 25-year plan, for the creation of the NCC and the implementation of its main proposals, for the EIPs and the statutory targets, for the reform of the CAP, and for the 100 per cent net zero target. It remains to be seen whether the promise materialises over the coming decade. It

is not the Conservatives' fault that they inherited the consequences of a flat economy after the 2007/2008 financial crisis,
nor is the coronavirus and the consequent economic destruction
the Conservatives' fault, but these did conspire to close down
some of the obvious opportunities and lead to a slowdown in
translating the legislation into action on the ground.

That leaves the other question in making an interim assessment, as at January 2024. Could the Conservatives have achieved
more, with better results, and a better record on the natural
environment and climate change? On the natural environment
the answer is obviously yes, and the meagre progress towards
leaving the natural environment in a better state for the next
generation must be a disappointment, and not just for environmentalists and the conservationist side of the Conservative Party. It
is also a litter heap of missed economic opportunities. On climate
change, progress has been as much a result of the deindustrialisa-
tion, except for one thing. The Conservatives killed off the coal
industry, and faster than Germany, the main comparative and now
tarnished claimant to the title of climate change leadership.

ACTS/DIRECTIVES

Agriculture Act 2020.

Air quality (Directive 2008/50/EC).

Climate Change Act 2008 (2050 Target Amendment) Order
2019.

Countryside and Rights of Way Act 2000.

Climate Change Act 2008.

Directive (EU) 2018/410 amending Directive 2003/87/EC to
enhance cost-effective emission reductions and low-carbon
investments, OJ L 76, 19.3.2018.

Directive 2001/18/EC of the European Parliament and of the
Council of 12 March 2001 on the deliberate release into the
environment of genetically modified organisms and repealing
Council Directive 90/220/EEC – Commission Declaration,
OJ L 106, 17.4.2001.

Energy Act 2023.

Energy Prices Act 2022.

Environment Act 2021.

Fisheries Act 2000.

REACH Regulation (Regulation (EC) No. 1907/2006 of the European Parliament and of the Council of 18 December 2006).

Renewable Energy Directive (Directive (EU) 2018/2001).

The Energy Act 2013.

Water Framework Directive (Directive 2000/60/EC).

Wildlife and Countryside Act 1981.

8

Parting the Unions

Brendan O'Leary

IN MAY 2010 THE CONSERVATIVE AND Unionist Party returned to power at Westminster as the senior partners in an unexpected fast-friends coalition with the Liberal Democrats. The Tories owed their electoral recovery under the leadership of David Cameron to both the global recession of 2008 and the exhaustion of New Labour under Gordon Brown. On returning to government the Tories were stewards of three Unions. They were partners in the European Union, and the self-conscious custodians of the Union of Great Britain and the Union of Great Britain and Northern Ireland. In 2010 the EU was in the peak of the Euro crisis, among the polycrises it has weathered since its failure to ratify its constitutional treaty of 2004.[1] The Union of Great Britain, however, seemed stable. Devolution for Scotland and Wales, which the Tories had opposed, was bedding down.[2]

The author would like to thank David McCrone of Edinburgh for improving his knowledge of Scotland, Richard Wyn Jones of Cardiff for the same on Wales, and John Garry and Jamie Pow of Queen's Belfast, Joanne McEvoy of Aberdeen, and Jennifer Todd and Dawn Walsh of UCD for ARINS collaborations across Ireland.

[1] See Manuel Castells (ed.), *Europe's Crises* (Basingstoke: Palgrave Macmillan, 2018). For a contrasting neoliberal appraisal see Giandomenico Majone, *Rethinking the Union of Europe Post-Crisis: Has Integration Gone Too Far?* (Cambridge: Cambridge University Press, 2014).

[2] Edward Heath opened the door to devolution in "The Declaration of Perth" in 1968. James Mitchell, *Conservatives and the Union: A Study of Conservative Party Attitudes to Scotland* (Edinburgh: Edinburgh University Press, 1990). See also Gordon Pentland, "Edward Heath, the Declaration of Perth and the Scottish Conservative and Unionist Party, 1966–70," *Twentieth Century British History* 26: 2 (2015), 249–73. Margaret Thatcher canceled the commitment in 1976.

In the Westminster elections of 2010, the Scottish National Party (SNP) and the Scottish Greens won just over 20 percent of the vote in Scotland, not far ahead of the Tories and the UK Independence Party (UKIP), who won just over 17 percent. In October 2011 a YouGov poll for *The Scotsman* estimated support for independence at 34 percent.[3] In the same Westminster elections in Wales in 2010 Plaid Cymru won just over 11 percent of the vote, and a mere three seats. In March 2011 the Welsh electorate would affirmatively answer the inelegant question, "Do you want the Assembly now to be able to make laws on all matters in the 20 subject areas it has powers for?" The margin of victory to upgrade the Assembly to a full legislature was 27 percent. In February 2010, meanwhile, the Democratic Unionist Party and Sinn Féin had negotiated the Hillsborough Agreement[4] that would devolve the most locally controversial powers, policing and the administration of justice, to Northern Ireland – taken by all as a sign that the implementation of the Good Friday Agreement was making sustained if belated progress.[5] All seemed calm within Her Majesty's realm as the Tories and Liberal Democrats embarked on a program of unparalleled peacetime austerity.

Fast forward nearly a decade. By January 2020 some of the same Tory stewards, governing alone after 2015, had driven a chaotic secession from the European confederation, trampling over multiple constitutional conventions in their rush to exit. It had become hard to recall that in 2006 in Cameron's first address to his party after being elected its leader he had remonstrated against his members "banging on about Europe."[6] Ten

---

[3] YouGov/*Scotsman* Survey Results, October 2011, cdn.yougov.com/cumulus_uploads/document/mkn31luozg/YG-Archives-Pol-Scotsman-results-111028.pdf

[4] Available at dfa.ie/media/dfa/alldfawebsitemedia/ourrolesandpolicies/northernireland/hillsborough-agreement.pdf

[5] Brendan O'Leary, *A Treatise on Northern Ireland, vol. 3: Consociation and Confederation* (Oxford: Oxford University Press, 2020), p. 263.

[6] Bournemouth, Leader's Speech, 2006, britishpoliticalspeech.org/speech-archive.htm?speech=314

years later, however, he had lost a UK-wide referendum that he had called on "in or out" membership of the EU. This unintended exit is a tale of sound and fury and the feeding of angry English lions, and fully covered elsewhere in this volume.[7] However, its impact on the two domestic unions is inescapably part of our subject. Under Cameron and his successors – Theresa May, Boris Johnson, Liz Truss, and Rishi Sunak – the Tories have stress-tested the two domestic unions to the point of shipwreck. Especially after 2016, and intensively after 2019 they have acted as if they were the English National Party while stealing the clothes of the United Kingdom Independence Party. "Muscular unionism," a largely English pose, has ended in multiple policy follies. A policy folly is helpfully defined as having been perceived as counterproductive when initiated, in circumstances where feasible alternative courses were available, and as being the policy of a group, not an individual.[8]

By late 2023 Tory decision-making had seemingly acceler-ated the twilight setting on both domestic unions.[9] These must

[7] A German economist solemnly assessed that Brexit was accidental because the UK system did not take Treasury forecasts seriously; see Paul J. J. Welfens, *An Accidental Brexit: New EU and Transatlantic Perspectives* (Cham: Palgrave Macmillan, 2017). For a highly amusing if not fully convin-cing account of Brexit as driven by English masochism see Fintan O'Toole, *Heroic Failure: Brexit and the Politics of Pain* (London: Apollo, 2018). For a data-driven account by eminent scholars that nevertheless neglects Northern Ireland, Scotland, and Wales see Geoffrey Evans and Anand Menon, *Brexit and British Politics* (Cambridge: Polity, 2017).

[8] Barbara W. Tuchman, *The March of Folly from Troy to Vietnam* (London: Abacus, 1985), p. 4. Tuchman would have insisted that the folly persists beyond one political lifetime. Five prime ministers between 2016 and 2023 meet the criterion.

[9] Brendan O'Leary, "The twilight of the United Kingdom & Tiocfaidh ár lá: twenty years after the Good Friday Agreement," *Ethnopolitics*, 17: 3 (2018), 223–42. A Welshman and a Scot were previous in their expectations, Norman Davies, "Britain is breaking up faster than you think," *The Sunday Times*, May 31, 1998; Tom Nairn, *The Break-Up of Britain: Crisis and Neo-Nationalism*, 2nd ed. (London: New Left Books, 1981). See also the turn of the millennium titles by Andrew Marr, *The Day Britain Died* (London: Profile,

be treated as two different unions, and historical preliminaries recorded because of the English Conservative disposition to talk of "the Union"[10] as if it were a singularity.[11] The Union of Great Britain was formed through the voluntary union of the London and Edinburgh parliaments in 1707, following the previous union of crowns. Scottish debt and English bribes – accompanied by threats – tempered the voluntary component. The Union of Great Britain and Northern Ireland, by contrast, is the legacy of the colonially enforced union with Ireland, the union of Great Britain and Ireland that began life as a union of Protestants in two sectarian parliaments.[12] It too was achieved partly through corruption in 1800–1.[13] That union was amended by the Government of Ireland Act of 1920, and then by the treaty between Great Britain and Ireland signed in 1921 and ratified in 1922. The Act partitioned Ireland without any formal Irish consent: no Westminster MP from Ireland voted for it. Imposed on Irish negotiators under Lloyd George's threat of the renewal of terrible war, the treaty gave Northern Ireland's recently created parliament the right to secede from the Irish Free State, which it exercised upon the ratification of the latter's

---

2000) and Tom Nairn, *After Britain: New Labour and the Return of Scotland* (London: Granta, 2000).

[10] My kind invitation to this book requested a chapter on "The Union." For some historical accounting see Alvin Jackson, *The Two Unions: Ireland, Scotland, and the Survival of the United Kingdom, 1707–2007* (Oxford: Oxford University Press, 2012) and Iain McLean and Alistair McMillan, *State of the Union: Unionism and the Alternatives in the United Kingdom Since 1707* (Oxford: Oxford University Press, 2005).

[11] Theresa May, perhaps influenced by *Lord of the Rings*, tried to rename it the "precious union." bbc.com/news/uk-scotland-scotland-politics-39151250 (Gollum also known as Sméagol, bore "the One Ring.")

[12] Brendan O'Leary, *A Treatise on Northern Ireland, vol. 1: Colonialism* (Oxford: Oxford University Press, 2020), pp. 217–37.

[13] David Wilkinson, " 'How did they pass the Union?' Secret service expenditure in Ireland, 1799–1804," *History*, 87 (1997), 223–51. This article revises the assumptions in G. C. Bolton, *The Passing of the Irish Act of Union: A Study of Parliamentary Politics* (Oxford: Oxford University Press, 1966).

constitution in 1922.[14] Northern Ireland is therefore the outcome of an imposed partition, at least one secession, a war, and a truce, and would be formally de-recognized by sovereign Ireland between 1937 and 1999. The referendums that ratified the Good Friday Agreement in 1998, and which brought over thirty years of armed conflict largely to an end, included modifications to Ireland's constitution. Northern Ireland now had restored devolution but with institutionalized power-sharing. Between 1922 and 1972 Northern Ireland had been the sole part of the UK with a devolved parliament. The Ulster Unionist Party (UUP) had won all elections running a majoritarian system of control on behalf of the descendants of British Protestant settlers at the expense of the descendants of Irish Catholics and natives.[15]

Wales has been within both of these unions, but not as a formal partner. To an outsider it may seem strange. After all, a partly Welsh warlord and usurper formed the modern English state (the older Henry Tudor). Wales is not, however, in the official name of the UK state, nor in its official Union flag. Great Britain, legally, is just the union of England and Scotland because Wales was annexed and submerged within England for nearly five centuries – until 2011. *An Acte for Laws & Justice to be ministred in Wales in like fourme as it is in this Realme* received the royal assent from the younger Henry Tudor in 1536.[16] An *Act for Certain Ordinances in the King's Dominion and Principality of Wales* followed in 1543.[17] Jointly these would be called the Acts of Union in the twentieth century, but misleadingly so. The

---

[14] Brendan O'Leary, *A Treatise on Northern Ireland*, vol. 2: *Control* (Oxford: Oxford University Press, 2020), pp. 17–125.

[15] Ibid.

[16] 27 Hen. 8. c. 26. Thomas Glyn Watkin, "The Tudors and the Union with England," in *The Legal History of Wales* (Cardiff: University of Wales Press, 2007), pp. 124–44.

[17] John Davies, *A History of Wales* (Harmondsworth: Penguin, 1994), p. 236, presents the latter Act as a correction to the first, while recording the subsequent continuing distinctiveness of Wales. Coercive linguistic assimilation in the courts and administration was built into the 1536 Act, but under Elizabeth I and after religious services were permitted in Welsh.

concept of union implies some partnership and mutual consent. The English parliament emphatically annexed Wales.[18] No negotiations with a Welsh parliament took place. Through these acts Wales was shired and Welsh MPs brought into being. Wales had the symbolic consolations of becoming a "principality" and having the heir to the throne of England and Great Britain as its prince (or princess). Not the least of the remarkable features of the last thirteen years of Tory government has been an increase in Welsh "indy-curiosity."[19]

DEMOGRAPHY, DE-BRITIFICATION, AND VARIETIES OF BRITISHNESS

The *longue durée* does not simply mean "the long run." Fernand Braudel's concept encouraged historians and social scientists to chart the effects of processes that occur almost imperceptibly to those going through them.[20] The point here is that not everything that has destabilized the two domestic unions can or should be attributed to the recent machinations of the Conservatives. They are guilty as charged, but not entirely responsible. Slow distinct long-run changes have been reshaping the two unions – namely, demographic restructuring, especially in Scotland and Northern Ireland; a weakening of the British national identity (both as a civic and as a pan-national identity); and, arguably, longer-rooted shifts in the varieties of Britishness.[21] These changes could not have been reversed by

---

[18] Brendan O'Leary, "Annexation," in Neophytos G. Loizides (ed.), *Oxford Research Encyclopedia in International Studies* (Oxford: Oxford University Press, 2023).

[19] Mary C. Murphy and Jonathan Evershed, *A Troubled Constitutional Future: Northern Ireland After Brexit* (Newcastle upon Tyne: Agenda, 2022), p. 145.

[20] Fernand Braudel, "History and the social sciences: the longue durée," in *On History* (Chicago: University of Chicago Press, 1980 [1958]).

[21] Equivocation reflects the absence of very good long-run attitudinal data on national identifications in the Isles, and stable long-run open questions – even those inspired by the five-point Moreno scale, which seeks to evaluate the degree of distribution but not intensity of dual identities. See

more prudent Tory policies toward the two unions, but their conduct in office has weakened identifications with both unions.

Demographic Restructuring. The population of the UK was 67.3 million in 2021, having grown by over 14.4 million between 1961 and 2021, a cumulative increase of over a quarter – interrupted by a decade of stagnation (1971–81). England's population increased by 6.5 percent between 2011 and 2021 to reach 56.5 million, the highest growth-rate among the four territorial components of the UK. Northern Ireland's population increased by 5 percent in that decade to 1.9 million; that of Scotland by 3.4 percent to 5.5 million; and that of Wales by 1.4 percent to 3.1 million. A significant proportion of the overall increase has been driven by immigration, which has particularly reshaped England, especially urban England,[22] now strikingly multiethnic, multiracial, multireligious, multinational – and secular. Scotland, Wales, and Northern Ireland, while also increasingly diverse, are much less diverse than England.[23] That may help explain why recent English nationalism has been xenophobic whereas Scottish, Welsh, and Irish nationalisms are officially left-liberal and pro-European.

Demography speaks: England has not only been the "predominant partner" in the two unions but will increasingly have that standing.[24] England's share of the UK's population was 82 percent in 1961; it is now 84 percent and on current trajectories must increase further. Westminster's composition will reflect these changes, so a steady rise in the significance of English MPs is

David McCrone and Frank Bechhofer, *National Identity* (Cambridge: Cambridge University Press, 2015), pp. 164–87. Likewise, there are "very few survey datasets . . . that might . . . bring English nationalism into sharper focus," Ailsa Henderson and Richard Wyn Jones, *Englishness* (Oxford: Oxford University Press, 2022), p. 4.

[22] London has the largest estimated proportion of non-UK-born of any region (37 percent).

[23] All the above numbers round data found online at the UK's Office for National Statistics.

[24] The expression was first used by Archibald Philip Primrose (Lord Rosebery) in his first speech as prime minister in 1894.

forecast. England's pivotality has never been absent from Conservative and Labour strategic behavior but it will matter even more. Historically Scotland was overrepresented at Westminster until devolution suggested the norm of proportional representation (by population). Scotland had 72 MPs in 1997; that number fell to 59 in 2005; and will come down to 57 in 2024–5. Wales too will experience a fall in its number of MPs at the next general election, from 40 to 32, a fall of one fifth. Northern Ireland, however, will retain 18 MPs, but seven and as many as nine of these are likely to be Sinn Féin representatives and unlikely to take their seats in parliament.

Significant slow, steady, and cumulative demographic change among Scotland's electorate has also been evident. The youngest cohorts firmly favor independence, seemingly and significantly independent of the performance of SNP governments in Edinburgh or Tory governments in London. This evaluation rests on Lindsay Paterson's persuasive analysis of the sociological basis of support for independence in Scotland since 1979.[25] He demonstrates pronounced growth in support for independence among those born since the 1970s, the significant expansion of tertiary educational attainment in the same cohorts, and a shift in a left and socially liberal direction among those who campaign for independence. So, whereas English supporters of secession from the EU are reasonably judged as concentrated among the old, the under-educated, and the disengaged, Scots who favor independence are concentrated among the younger cohorts (at a slightly increasing rate), the graduate-educated, and the engaged. True, Scottish support for independence appeared to stabilize at around the 30 percent mark after Labour's 1997's devolution settlement and was just above that level as late as 2013.

Such data persuaded Cameron he could comfortably gamble on winning the independence referendum demanded by Alex Salmond after the landslide victory of the Scottish National Party in the election to the Scottish Parliament in 2011. Having just

---

[25] Lindsay Paterson, "Independence is not going away: the importance of education and birth cohorts," *Political Quarterly*, 94:4 (2023), 526–34.

won the referendum to keep the winner-takes-all system of elections for Westminster in 2011, Cameron had become super-confident of his ability to win referendums to preserve the status quo.[26] During the campaigning in 2014, however, support for independence rose sharply to 45 percent, briefly reaching 50 percent, before subsiding back to 45 percent on the day of the vote. "Better Together" eventually won, not because of Cameron's cunning, but arguably because of the late campaigning of Gordon Brown and Alistair Darling of Labour. Cameron's gamble had nearly not paid off. Since the referendum, support for Scotland's independence in over 200 polls has largely hovered between 45 and 50 percent. It stood at 54 percent in the last Ipsos poll held in November 2023, before this chapter went to press.[27] During 2020–1 support for independence was consistently above 50 percent when the Scottish public certainly preferred Nicola Sturgeon's management of the Covid pandemic to that of Boris Johnson. And remarkably it persists at a high level despite the unresolved scandals that have enveloped Sturgeon's husband shortly after her unexpected resignation as First Minister. Lindsay Paterson's scholarly contribution emphasizes a ratchet-effect among younger cohorts and suggests that the cause of independence is not directly tied to the performance of the SNP. Each new cohort favors independence at a slightly greater rate than its predecessors.

Differently put, firm Scottish unionists increasingly look like hardline English Brexiteers, that is, older, left-behind, and

---

[26] John Curtice, "Politicians, voters and democracy: the 2011 UK referendum on the alternative vote," *Electoral Studies*, 32:2 (2013), 215–23. Cameron cunningly accepted Labour's established preference for the alternative vote as the alternative to the status quo (as opposed to proportional representation, which may well have won). The Liberal Democrat leadership was not cunning.

[27] "How would you vote in a Scottish independence referendum if held now? (asked after the EU referendum)," *What Scotland Thinks* (accessed at www .whatscotlandthinks.org/questions/how-would-you-vote-in-the-in-a-scottish-independence-referendum-if-held-now-ask/?removed, December 1, 2023).

socially conservative. Paterson's analysis converges with that of Alex Scholes and John Curtice.[28] When this chapter went to press the SNP remained the leading party in polling for the constituency vote in elections for the next Scottish Parliament,[29] and, despite evidence of Labour's recovery, the SNP remained the leading party in polls for the next Westminster elections.[30] So Scottish politics, despite Salmond's and subsequently Sturgeon's implosions, still seems likely to remain poised on the cusp of a second referendum on independence, especially because the terms on which the 2014 referendum was conducted by "Better Together" were not delivered, namely a UK within the EU, and because both Labour and the Conservatives are refusing to consider "a return to Europe." A second referendum will be refused by the pro-union parties as long as possible, but even they recognize that there must be some time-limit on "once in a generation." Demographically speaking, a Scottish state-in-waiting is hibernating just off-stage. The union of Great Britain therefore sleeps uneasy, and not entirely because of Tory incompetence.

Northern Ireland has also been undergoing slow, cumulative demographic change that may end in the termination of the other union. According to the Northern Ireland census of 2021, published in 2022, cultural Catholics – those who identify as Catholics or who were brought up in Catholic households – outnumbered

---

[28] Alex Scholes and John Curtice, "The changing role of identity and values in Scotland's politics," *What Scotland Thinks* (2020) (www.whatscotlandthinks .org/wp-content/uploads/2021/04/WST_The-Changing-Role-of-Identity-and-Values-in-Scotlands-Politics_v2.pdf).

[29] "How would you use your constituency vote in a Scottish Parliament election? (asked since 2021 Scottish Parliament election)," *What Scotland Thinks* (accessed at www.whatscotlandthinks.org/questions/how-would-you-use-y our-constituency-vote-in-a-scottish-parliament-election-asked-since-2021-sc ottish-parliament-election/ December 1, 2023).

[30] "How would you be likely to vote in a UK General Election? (asked since 2019 General Election)," What *Scotland Thinks* (accessed at www.whatsco tlandthinks.org/questions/how-would-you-be-likely-to-vote-in-a-uk-gen eral-election-asked-since-2019-general-election/ accessed December 1, 2023).

cultural Protestants for the first time since a census was counted in the six counties that became Northern Ireland – see Figure 8.1. No one denies the strongly established link between demography and electoral behavior in Northern Ireland: most unionists have been cultural Protestants, and most nationalists have been cultural Catholics. The scope of the effects is what is disputed, and the degree to which they are changing. Recent ARINS–*Irish Times* survey data confirm that the proportion of Catholics who favor the maintenance of the union is still higher than the proportion of Protestants who favor Irish reunification.[31] The absolute numbers of those identifying explicitly with a religion in 2021 are shown in Figure 8.2. Among explicitly religious adherents, a Catholic demographic majority has arrived. Other non-census indicators, not reported here, suggest that all major Christian denominations are experiencing fast-paced secularization. Less clear is whether a cultural Catholic electoral majority will exist before the next census in 2031. Figure 8.3 charts the *cumulative* cultural Catholic demographic lead over cultural Protestants and other Christians according to the broad age cohorts published by the census authorities. The curve rises strongly among the young before fading among the over-65s. By the end of 2031 all those aged between 8 and 17 in 2021 will have joined the electorate provided they are eligible to vote (unless they have died prematurely or emigrated). The maturation of this cohort during the rest of this decade will be decisive.

In 2021, in the entire age-range from 15 upward, cultural Protestants retained a net demographic advantage over cultural Catholics of roughly 17,000 people. But over the 2020s, that lead will be eroded by the steady arrival in the electorate of the cultural Catholics aged 8–17 in 2021. That may complete the demographic reversal in the electorate. Barring major off-trend immigration or a major shift in differential outbound migration at the expense of cultural Catholics, by 2030 the electoral fate of Northern Ireland's future will no longer be in Protestant hands.

---

[31] *Irish Times*, December 2, 2023.

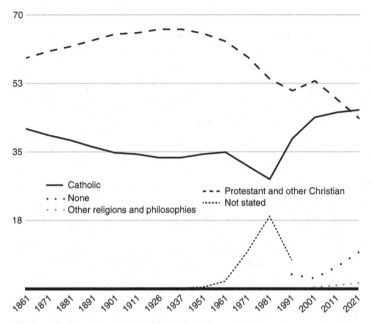

Figure 8.1 Northern Ireland's religious demography: proportions, 1861–2021
Source: © Brendan O'Leary and Jamie Pow, 2023. "The turning point? The Northern Ireland local government elections of 18 May 2023," Royal Irish Academy/ ARINS blog, June 19, 2023, www.ria.ie/news/arins-analysis-and-research-ireland-north-and-south/turning-point-northern-ireland-local.
Data sources: Census of Ireland 1861–1911, Northern Ireland Census 1926–2021.
Notes
(i) The census reports since 2001 assign many of the "none" and "not stated" to "community background" or "religion brought up in" (based on respondents' answers) and they are then classified as "Catholic" or "Protestant" as appropriate, along with those who identify as such. So, from 2001 the Protestant and Catholic lines exaggerate formal religious identification and cannot be taken as a guide to the proportions of believing or practicing Catholics or Protestants. (ii) The 1981 census was subject to a partial boycott by Catholics. (iii) The "Not stated" response was discontinued in 2001. (iv) The "Nones" were 9.3% in 2021.

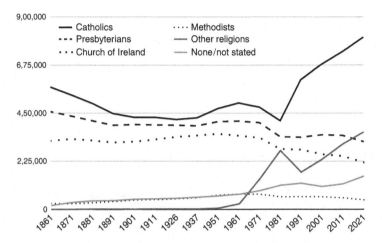

Figure 8.2 Northern Ireland's religious demography: adherents 1861–2021
Source: © Brendan O'Leary and Jamie Pow, 2023. See Figure 8.1.
Data sources: as for Figure 8.1.
Notes

(i) There are now absolutely more Catholics than all Protestants and other Christians (805, 151 > 736, 515), and the Catholic population looks set to grow further. (ii) During 1891–1937 Presbyterians were poised to exceed Catholics in the six counties, but their numbers peaked in 1961. Presbyterians are now 39.3 percent of Catholic numbers, 77,000 less than at the formation of Northern Ireland, and on a downward trajectory. (iii) Church of Ireland (Anglican) numbers peaked in 1951, and are now 27.3 percent of Catholic numbers, and on a downward trajectory. (iv) Over 203,000 Presbyterians and Church of Ireland net losses (1971–2021) are mostly explained by the rise of other Christians (*c.* 194,000 in this period, e.g. evangelicals).

These demographic shifts have manifested in the last three region-wide elections. In the Westminster elections of 2019 for the first time Northern Ireland's delegation had a non-unionist majority. Nationalists returned 9 MPs to Westminster, unionists 8, and the Alliance party, formally neutral on the status of the union, returned 1.[32] For the first time also Belfast returned

[32] Brendan O'Leary, *Making Sense of a United Ireland* (Dublin: Penguin Random House, 2022), plate, figure 1.7.

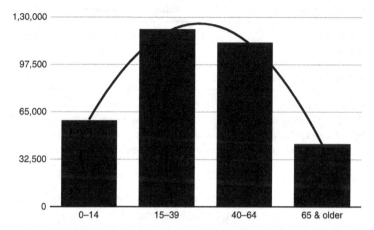

Figure 8.3 Cumulative cultural Catholic demographic lead over cultural Protestants and other Christians

Data source: Northern Ireland Census 2021.

a nationalist majority of MPs: two Sinn Féin and one Social Democratic and Labour Party (SDLP) compared to one DUP MP from East Belfast. In the subsequent Northern Ireland Assembly elections of May 2022 Sinn Féin topped the poll in first-preference votes, but, as Table 8.1 shows, total first-preference votes for Irish nationalists were just behind those of unionist candidates (when independent unionists, independent nationalists, and independent others are coded). By the following year, however, as Table 8.2 shows, nationalists would top the polls in overall first-preference votes in local government elections for the first time, and, again for the first time, the unionist bloc fell below 40 percent of first preference votes.

The demographic *longue durée* of the union of Great Britain with Northern Ireland has therefore evolved delivering a slow erosion of the unionist position that would likely have occurred even without Conservative incompetence.

Table 8.1 Northern Ireland Assembly elections May 2022: first-preference by bloc

Candidates stood as	Unionist	Nationalist	Other
Party nominees	329,227	353, 069	135, 079
Independents	14,546	4,288	6,494
Total first preference vote by bloc	363,773	357,357	141, 573
First preference vote by bloc (percentage)	42.2	41.4	16.4

Source: John Garry, Brendan O'Leary, and James Pow, "Much more than meh: the 2022 Northern Ireland Assembly Elections," Royal Irish Academy/ARINS blog, May 11, 2022, www.ria.ie/news/publications-arins-analysis-and-research-ireland-north-and-south/much-more-meh-northern-ireland

Table 8.2 Northern Ireland local government elections May 2023: first-preference by bloc

Candidates stood as	Unionist	Nationalist	Other
Party nominees	286,058	311,444	113,617
Independents	11,382	15,322	7,692
Total first preference vote by bloc	297,440	326,766	121,309
First preference vote by bloc (percentage)	39.9	43.8	16.3

Source: O'Leary and Pow, "The turning point?," table 1.

A key difference, however, is that in Northern Ireland support for Irish unification in polls and surveys, so far, is not as strong as support for independence in Scotland.[33]

Debate in and over Northern Ireland's future has two camps. One maintains there will be a demographic and electoral stabilization, a stand-off in which the union survives because cultural Catholics will not become a full electoral majority,

---

[33] John Garry, Brendan O'Leary, Jamie Pow, and Pat Leahy, "North and South: what we know now, and what we want to investigate in future," *Irish Times,* January 27, 2024).

because of falling birth-rates, and because cultural Catholics will remain less nationalist than Protestants remain unionists. This school tends to believe that Northern Ireland's future consists not of two polarized camps but of three blocs heading toward equality – nationalist, unionist, and others – and that the others will break toward the pro-union position in any referendum and prevent Irish nationalists from becoming a majority. The second school, to which the author belongs, tends to believe that cultural Catholics will become an electoral majority, that the others may be persuaded to break toward unification with Ireland – as left-liberals and pro-Europeans – and that the others will struggle to get to and past 20 percent of the electorate. This school also believes that the Conservative decision to pursue a hard exit from the European Union has destabilized the union, just when the remarkable performance of the Republic of Ireland – in its economic development within the EU, and in its decisive secularization – is becoming more comparatively evident in contrast with the UK. Joining the Republic will become increasingly attractive to the same type of people in Northern Ireland who favor Scottish independence within the EU. This debate will continue.

De-Britification? Attitudinal shifts in the Isles seem to comport with the nearly imperceptible demographic changes just discussed. Summarizing the relevant work of political scientists, sociologists, and political psychologists over the last three decades is not easy, however, nor is its interpretation. And it is methodologically difficult to link these shifts causally to the conduct of Tories in office since 2010 – and no such direct attempt will be made here.

Scholars remind us that national identity may have cultural, social, and political dimensions that may not move together, may be inadequately measured by survey instruments, and may be variously interpreted – by individuals, by individuals in different regions, and by activists and analysts.[34] Accepting these important

---

[34] David McCrone, "The rise and rise of English nationalism?," *The Political Quarterly*, 94:4 (2023), 604–12; see also the last two chapters of McCrone

qualifications, the consensus seems to be that various instruments suggest a decline among those answering as "British" (or "British and x" in Moreno-scale questions) within both unions, notably in Scotland, Northern Ireland – and England. More people than previously identify as English-only or as more English than British. A sustained increase has occurred in those who identify as Scottish, or as more Scottish than British, and they are significantly disposed toward independence.[35] Since choices have been multiplied beyond "Irish or British?" in Northern Ireland a fall has been registered in British-only identification – including in the 2021 census. A debate rumbles over whether "Northern Irish" is a novel identity (an identification rarely posed in surveys or polls before this century) and what its significance might be.[36] Recent ARINS survey evidence suggests that those selecting this identification among both cultural Catholics and Protestants are political moderates and that "Northern Irish" may act as a bridging identity, now and in the future.[37] If this summary of partial de-Britification in both Great Britain and Northern Ireland is

---

and Bechhofer, *National Identity*; Jennifer Todd, "Partitioned identities? Everday national distinctions in Northern Ireland and the Irish State," *Nations and Nationalism*, 21:1 (2015), 21–42; Jennifer Todd, "From identity politics to identity change: exogenous shocks, constitutional moments and the impact of Brexit on the island of Ireland," *Irish Studies in International Affairs*, 28 (2017), 57–72; and Henderson and Wyn Jones, *Englishness*.

[35] Scholes and Curtice, "The changing role of identity and values."

[36] John Garry and Kevin McNicholl are leading lights in this discussion: John Garry, "Consociationalism and its critics: evidence from the historic Northern Ireland Assembly election 2007," *Electoral Studies*, 28 (2009), 458–66; John Garry, *Consociation and Voting in Northern Ireland: Party Competition and Electoral Behavior* (Philadelphia: University of Pennsylvania Press, 2016); KISS Exchange: Northern Ireland Assembly, *Policy Briefing: The Northern Ireland Identity*, by John Garry and Kevin McNicholl (Belfast, 2014–15); Kevin McNicholl, "The Northern Irish identity: attitudes towards moderate political parties and outgroup leaders," *Irish Political Studies* 34: 1 (2019), 25–47.

[37] John Garry, Brendan O'Leary, and Jamie Pow, "Northern Ireland identity may serve as less adversarial for politically moderate Catholics and Protestants," *Irish Times*, December 11, 2023.

accepted as accurate it is hard to see how more prudent or better Tory government would have inhibited these identity-shifts. Tory conduct may have accentuated them, however, by driving a loss of pride in being British. The decline of Britishness in Great Britain may parallel the decline of "Greater Britain" that accompanied retreat from empire.[38]

Increasing Varieties of Fractious Britishness. In Theresa May's reference to the "precious union" in the speech cited in note 11 she nodded toward multi-national pluralism, but unfortunately displayed sincere though widely common ignorance. She referred to the union as made up of "four nations" that are "at heart one people." Not so, and nor has it ever been so, especially if the one heart is assumed to be "British." Northern Ireland for one is not a nation, and never has been. It has always contained two, and today we know it contains British, Irish, and Northern Irish identifiers. Northern Ireland is just one place where the "British" identification has historically had both strongly ethnic (the fusion of British (English and Scottish) Protestants of settler stock) and civic components (identification with the state of the UK, Britannia, or "Britain"), which have varied in salience.[39] To that established record we now have evidence of variation in "Britishness" across the Union, which may suggest that its chances of playing a bridging role may be diminishing. To identify as British, in surveys at least, means very different things in the four components of the UK. In England "Britishness" is a pro-EU and outward-looking disposition; it is often embraced by people without any long-established English roots; and by self-styled cosmopolitans. By contrast, those who identify with "Britishness" in Northern Ireland are increasingly concentrated among hardline loyalists. And in both Scotland and Wales those

---

[38] Brendan O'Leary, "Toward the final curtain: glimpses of an end foretold," *Transactions of the Royal Historical Society* (2023), https://doi.org/10.1017/S0080440123000130; Stuart Ward, *Untied Kingdom: A Global History of the End of Britain* (Cambridge: Cambridge University Press, 2023).

[39] Jennifer Todd, "Two traditions in unionist political culture," *Irish Political Studies*, 2:1 (1987), 1–26.

who identify as "British" most resemble in their attitudes the ethnocentric and Eurosceptics among the English-only of England.[40] Politically, however, that resemblance creates no stable pan-union alliance. In 2019, when the chips were down, a YouGov survey of Conservative Party members found a clear majority, 63 percent, would be prepared to have Brexit completed even if it meant Scotland leaving the UK, while 59 percent would have preferred to let Northern Ireland go rather than jeopardize their precious "hard Brexit."[41] Did the Brexit imbroglio superheat this variation in Britishness or allow scholars to see it properly for the first time? It is certainly now easier to see how this variation allowed "the party of the union" to act as an English nationalist party, take each union to the verge of shipwreck, and to disaggregate one of them through ratifying "the Protocol" and the Windsor Framework.

THE PARTY OF "THE UNION" UNTIES THE UNION WITH NORTHERN IRELAND

The Tory party owes its official name, the Conservative and Unionist Party, to the merger of the Conservatives with the Liberal Unionists in 1912. These parties had jointly and ferociously opposed Gladstone's decision on behalf of the Liberals to accept the demand for home rule for Ireland. In 1912 this newly merged party mobilized with anti-democratic rhetoric, and practice, to prevent Asquith's Liberals from legislating home rule.[42] So the party's historic status as an overt champion of "the

---

[40] Henderson and Wyn Jones, *Englishness, passim.*

[41] "Most Conservative members would see party destroyed to achieve Brexit", YouGov, June 18, 2019 (yougov.co.uk/politics/articles/23849-most-conservative-members-would-see-party-destroye?).

[42] Some Irish unionists and nationalists welcomed the prospects of support from authoritarian Germany – and invasion – before 1914, Jérôme Aan de Wiel, "German invasion and spy scares in Ireland, 1890s–1914: between fiction and fact," *Études irlandaises*, 37:1 (2012), 25–40. Starting with the Ulster unionists (supported by their British allies), both sides imported arms from Germany before 1914.

Union" can scarcely be gainsaid. Rhetoric was sometimes matched by practice. Unlike the Labour Party, which has always been a British of Great Britain party, the Conservative and Unionist Party organized and stood for elections in Ireland. After enforcing the creation of Northern Ireland, the UUP became its local affiliate, and its Westminster MPs took the Conservative whip until 1972. In 2008, proudly declaring that he had never been a Little Englander, Cameron announced the revival of the Conservative and UUP alliance.[43] The two parties fought the Westminster elections of 2010 together as "Ulster Conservatives and Unionists – New Force." They won no seats, the first time the UUP had done so badly, and the formation of the alliance had led Sylvia Hermon, the solitary UUP MP, to become an independent. Cameron was therefore not obliged to make good on his pledge to put UUP MPs in his Cabinet. Since then, the Conservatives in Northern Ireland have been utterly ineffective.

Cameron's policy toward Northern Ireland was two-faced. Publicly it began with a benign face. The *Report of the Bloody Sunday Inquiry*, known as the Saville Inquiry after its principal presiding judge, was published in June 2010, over a decade after it had been established by Tony Blair.[44] The subject was the killings of unarmed civilians in Derry on January 30, 1972, by British paratroopers. Saville overturned the "findings" of Lord Widgery – in reality the cover-up published in April 1972 at the behest of Edward Heath. Whereas Widgery had exonerated the paratroopers, Saville found they had fired first on a banned civil rights march called in protest against internment without trial. They had lost control, and their killings were without any justification. None of those killed had posed a threat. Among the killed were those in flight. An already wounded man was finished off. On the day of publication Cameron rose to the occasion and eloquently apologized in the Commons on behalf of the British government.[45]

[43] "I want Ulster Unionists in cabinet," *Guardian*, December 7, 2008.

[44] HM Government, *Report of the Bloody Sunday Inquiry* (London: The Stationery Office, 2010).

[45] "Saville: Bloody Sunday killings unjustifiable," RTÉ, June 15, 2010, rte.ie/news/2010/0615/132183-bloodysunday/

This good grace, however, did not make up for his malign face. His first appointment as secretary of state for Northern Ireland (SOSNI) was Owen Paterson, who was later found to have brought the House of Commons into disrepute because he had improperly lobbied for two companies based in Northern Ireland – in one case the relationship went back to when he was shadow secretary. Worse than Paterson's corruption, which would be established later, was the severe damage he did to police reform. In 2011, ten years after the reforms that Christopher Patten had inspired,[46] the proportion of cultural Catholics in the Police Service of Northern Ireland, which had replaced the Royal Ulster Constabulary, had risen dramatically. That was because Patten's recommended quota had been followed: hiring an equal number of Catholics and Protestants, until a balanced service was established. Paterson, a fervent unionist, deferred to a local unionist campaign and did not renew the quota, deliberately letting it lapse. The consequences are now clear. Catholic recruitment stalled. Nominally Catholics make up just 32 percent of police officers (though they are at least 50 percent of all those aged under 40). There's a further catch: Catholic officers born in Northern Ireland are just over 26 percent of the total;[47] Catholic officers are nearly three times more likely than their Protestant counterparts to be born outside of Northern Ireland.

Cameron's next appointment as SOSNI was Theresa Villiers (2012–16). A barrister, she was one of three MPs suspended from the Commons in 2021 because the Standards Committee found they had improperly sought to influence judicial proceedings involving Charles Elphicke, a Conservative MP found guilty of

---

[46] Christopher Patten, *A New Beginning: The Report of the Independent Commission on Policing for Northern Ireland* (Belfast: Independent Commission on Policing for Northern Ireland, 1999); for my contemporaneous review see Brendan O'Leary, "A bright future and less orange (review of *A New Beginning* by the Independent Commission on Policing for Northern Ireland)," *Times Higher Education Supplement,* November 19, 1999.

[47] Freedom of Information request, reported at the website of Slugger O'Toole, https://sluggerotoole.com/2023/05/31/ni-born-catholics-account-for-just-26-of-psni-officers/

three charges of sexual assault.[48] Later she admitted that while serving as environment secretary she had failed to declare ownership of shares in Shell of over £70,000 (the threshold which obliges declarations).[49] At appointment, however, this sleaze lay in the future. At Hillsborough Castle, where SOSNIs reside, Villiers proved a vigorous and uncritical champion of the historical reputations of the security and intelligence services. In a formal speech she declared that "a pernicious counternarrative" was emerging in which responsibility for conflict was being shifted to the security forces "through allegations of collusion, misuse of agents and informers or other forms of unlawful activity."[50] The real problem, however, was that the counternarrative had significant and increasing evidence, especially from the work of authorized UK officials and investigations. Minimally, the security and intelligence forces had colluded with many loyalist murderers.[51] The honest historical question is the scale and seniority of the authorization of collusion and mutual collaboration. For example, Dr. Michael Maguire, the police ombudsman who examined "the Loughinisland massacre," declared he had "no hesitation in unambiguously determining that collusion" had featured in these loyalist murders.[52]

[48] "Theresa Villiers among three Tory MPs to receive Commons suspension," *Times Series*, September 9, 2021.

[49] "Theresa Villiers: ex-environment secretary failed to declare Shell shares," BBC News, August 11, 2023, first reported at mirror.co.uk/news/politics/top-tory-theresa-villiers-70k-30675878

[50] Theresa Villiers, "A way forward for legacy of the past in Northern Ireland," speech, 11 February 2016 (gov.uk/government/speeches/villiers-a-way-forward-for-legacy-of-the-past-in-northern-ireland).

[51] Anne Cadwallader, *Lethal Allies: British Collusion in Ireland* (Cork: Mercer Press, 2013) uses evidence from the local police's Historical Enquiries Team. Margaret Urwin, *A State in Denial: British Collaboration with Loyalist Paramilitaries* (Cork: The Pat Finucane Centre/Justice for the Forgotten/Mercier Press, 2016) also relies on official UK sources. See her latest update at patfinucanecentre.org/relationships-between-british-authorities-and-loyalist-paramilitary-organisations

[52] Loughinisland Report available at www.relativesforjustice.com/wp-content/uploads/2016/06/Loughinisland-Report.pdf. A judge later found

Villiers' disposition represented leading Tory opinion, however,[53] and that would eventually drive fresh Westminster legislation, The Northern Ireland Troubles (Legacy and Reconciliation) Act 2023, which intends to close off criminal investigations and judicial proceedings on "troubles-related" killings.[54] Remarkably, this Act achieved almost total local opposition: from the North's five major political parties, relatives of the bereaved, victims and survivors, and human rights organisations. The Irish Government, and other political parties in Ireland and in Great Britain rejected it. Hilary Benn, the current shadow secretary, has declared Labour will repeal it if they form the next government.[55] The Ad Hoc Committee to Protect the Good Friday Agreement, a bipartisan committee of US experts, of which the author is a member, argued the Act breached the Good Friday Agreement. It also broke the Stormont House Agreement, brokered by the two sovereign governments, the UK and Ireland, in 2015, and was widely condemned in Europe and in the United Nations because it will prevent both truth and justice, and breaches the UK's international human rights obligations. The amnesty provisions are intended to protect army veterans and intelligence operatives. Supporters of the Act, which began life under Johnson and reached the statute book under Sunak, were confined to the Conservative government,

that Maguire had "overstepped" in his report but emphasized that it was appropriate for Maguire to acknowledge what he had uncovered on corrupt relationships between security force personnel and loyalist paramilitary killers: belfasttelegraph.co.uk/news/northern-ireland/police-om budsman-michael-maguire-overstepped-mark-in-loughinisland-report-cri minal-findings-court-rules/39296069.html

[53] James Brokenshire, "We must not allow the past to be rewritten in Northern Ireland," *Daily Telegraph*, January 29, 2017. This article by Villiers' successor on the same theme was insensitively placed the day before the anniversary of Bloody Sunday. At least Brokenshire learned something. On resignation on health grounds in 2018 he recommended reading a history book to any successors. Just one?

[54] See https://bills.parliament.uk/bills/3160

[55] www.breakingnews.ie/world/legacy-act-must-have-a-replacement-to-help-ni-overcome-collective-trauma-1534473.html

veterans' groups, and the right-wing tabloid press. It was steered to completion by Jonathan Caine, ennobled in 2016, a special advisor to six Conservative Northern Ireland Secretaries. Born 40, an old-fashioned gentleman with impeccable manners, Caine is a thoroughly partisan unionist.[56]

Since Cameron became prime minister there have been eight SOSNIs, three in 2022, the year of the Tory meltdown under Johnson and Truss. Namely, Owen Paterson (2010–12), Theresa Villiers (2012–16), James Brokenshire (2016–18), Karen Bradley (2018–19), Julian Smith (July 2019 – February 2020), Brandon Lewis (2020–2), Shailesh Vara (2022), and Christopher Heaton-Harris (2022–). With the notable exception of Julian Smith, they were mediocrities in office, unsuited to the requirements of historical knowledge and "rigorous impartiality" in administration between nationalists and unionists which is demanded by the Good Friday Agreement. Fifty-six years after the reformation of the Ulster Volunteer Force (UVF), a loyalist militia which went on to kill Catholic civilians in large numbers, and twenty-five years after the Good Friday Agreement, the UVF still exists, and still recruits.[57] The governing representatives of the UK's self-defined party of law and order rarely mention these facts. Indeed, their pursuit of Brexit has unintentionally given a new, albeit limited, jolt of life to loyalist organizations – extensively involved in drug-running and protection rackets. Many younger loyalist militants are not just opposed to the compromise reached over Brexit – "the Protocol" – but to both devolution and the Good Friday Agreement – which their parties had endorsed, and under which many of their prisoners were released on license. Rather than seeking the dissolution of loyalist organizations, or at least distancing themselves from them, leading Conservatives, like former home secretary Priti Patel, have recklessly consorted with the loyalist apologist Jamie Bryson, meeting him in the Commons,

---

[56] The knowledge is personal. He took my Ireland course at the LSE many decades ago.

[57] Its best analyst remains Aaron Edwards, *UVF: Behind the Mask* (Newbridge: Merrion Press, 2017).

and writing for his website, *Unionist Voice*.[58] Bryson was among the leaders of the loyalist flag protests in 2012. Outraged that, by local majority resolution, the Union Jack would no longer fly 7/12/365 over Belfast City Hall, loyalists had organized riotous attacks focused on the Alliance Party.

In the 2016 referendum on the UK's membership of the EU, Northern Ireland voted to remain by a margin of 56 to 44 percent.[59] Scotland voted to remain by an even wider margin, 62 to 38 percent. In the UK as a whole, however, the margin was 52 to 48 percent for leave. Shamelessly, Villiers had publicly campaigned for months for a UK exit,[60] an outcome that would inevitably destabilize the Good Friday Agreement, which presumed Irish and UK joint membership of the EU.[61] Leaving the EU would raise questions of how to police the European single market and customs union if the UK left both. Leavers, including Villiers, displayed complete insouciance about the UK's treaty and domestic obligations under the Good Friday Agreement.[62]

Initially Theresa May, Cameron's accidental successor, declared that Brexit would mean Brexit, a delaying tautology,

---

[58] unionistvoice.com/news/exclusive-priti-patel-writes-for-unionist-voice-windsor-framework-poses-a-risk-to-the-integrity-of-our-united-kingdom/. Bryson's CV includes being convicted of possession of a baton with the status of a weapon, being arrested and put on remand for public order offences, and choosing, for his own safety, to be held in the loyalist section of prison. He is in transition from street politics to lawfare – presenting as an expert on constitutional law.

[59] Brendan O'Leary, "The Dalriada document: towards a multinational compromise that respects democratic diversity in the United Kingdom," *Political Quarterly*, 87: 4 (2016), 5618–33.

[60] Nicholas Wright, "Theresa Villiers wants Northern Ireland out of the EU," LSE Blogs, March 4, 2016 (accessed at https://blogs.lse.ac.uk/brexit/201 6/03/04/theresa-villiers-wants-northern-ireland-out-of-the-eu-that-stance-may-be-untenable/ November 2023).

[61] The relevant textual provisions are in O'Leary, *A Treatise on Northern Ireland*, vol. 3: *Consocation and Confederation*, pp. 318-19.

[62] Northern Ireland is not in the index of the revised and updated edition of Tim Shipman, *All Out War: The Full Story of Brexit*, revised and updated ed. (London: William Collins, 2017).

which she would soon define by four red lines: being out of the EU's institutions, being out of the single market, being out of the customs union, and being outside the jurisdiction of the Court of Justice of the EU. That certainly presaged a hard border across the island of Ireland. This possibility was received with strong hostility among border populations across the partition line, and research showed that people feared a return to violence.[63] May promised there would be no return to the hard borders of the past. In the next two years, and after a chastening electoral setback, May learned international economics and international treaties on the job, partly educated by negotiations with the EU, having first tried unsuccessfully to bypass its chief negotiator, Michel Barnier.[64] The Government of Ireland successfully put a commitment to the Good Friday Agreement in all its parts, no hard border, and no diminution of rights in Northern Ireland (under the European Convention and under EU anti-discrimination law) into the EU's negotiating red lines. These Irish provisions proved the hardest obstacles for May to address, and they became harder still when she felt obliged to make a supply and confidence agreement with the DUP after her electoral meltdown in June 2017.

May and her party were on the horns of a trilemma, expertly diagnosed by Professor Daniel Kelemen – see Figure 8.4. She had made three promises but could only keep two of them. She could pursue Option A. That would mean the UK could leave the European single market and the customs union and agree

[63] John Garry, Brendan O'Leary, Kevin McNicholl, and James Pow, "The future of Northern Ireland: border anxieties and support for Irish reunification under varieties of UKEXIT," *Regional Studies*, 55:9 (2020), 1517–27; John Garry, Kevin McNicholl, Brendan O'Leary, and James Pow, *Northern Ireland and the UK's Exit from the EU: What Do People Think? Evidence from Two Investigations: A Survey and a Deliberative Forum* (Belfast: ESRC/The UK in a Changing Europe, 2018).

[64] For accounts by the principal and one of his principal advisors see Michel Barnier, *My Secret Brexit Diary* (Cambridge: Polity Press, 2021); Stefaan De Rynck, *Inside the Deal: How the EU Got Brexit Done* (Newcastle: Agenda, 2023).

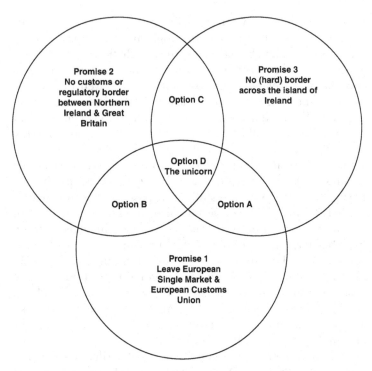

Figure 8.4 Theresa May's Brexit trilemma
Source: Adapted from the work of Professor R. Daniel Kelemen.

there would be no border across the island of Ireland. That, however, would mean EU regulatory and customs would be administered at ports and airports across the North channel (an Irish Sea border), and break her promises to the DUP. Option B would mean the UK could leave the single market and customs union, and have no border in the Irish Sea, but then the UK would violate its pledges to the Government of Ireland and the EU and violate the Good Friday Agreement. Ireland and the EU would sign no treaty based on option B. That would leave the UK with a cliff-edge exit from the EU. Option C, by contrast, would mean not leaving the single market or the customs union, remaining under EU regulatory alignment, while obliged to implement customs and trade agreements it had no future role in making. This "soft Brexit" would likely lead to a Cabinet and parliamentary party revolt, and her loss of office. She eventually tried a version of this option – in which Great Britain would fully leave the EU when amazing border technologies were invented, while Northern Ireland would remain in a soft exit. Pursing this option, honestly arrived at, cost May her job. Kelemen had observed there was in theory an option D, in which all three promises could be kept, but that required magical thinking – unicorn technologies that would render borders redundant, an option fantasized about by many Brexiteers and members of the DUP, to this day.

THE LIAR'S SOLUTION: PERFIDY IN MAKING THE PROTOCOL

We know what happened. When he succeeded May, Boris Johnson pursued Option A to get Brexit done, while assuring the DUP the final solution would be Option B. The DUP's parliamentary party believed him, in a still shocking display of poor judgment.[65] Johnson's version of Option A left Northern Ireland in the single market for goods and agriculture, while leaving the UK to administer the EU's customs code at ports and airports between Northern Ireland and Great Britain. This is now known as "the Protocol," slightly tweaked in the Windsor Framework negotiated by Sunak. Johnson then won a large parliamentary majority in the elections of December 2019. He no longer needed the DUP and left his lieutenants to tidy up the messes of a fast exit.

Insincerity in signing and ratifying a treaty is public lying. Like Cameron, Johnson was willing to gamble to win power and to stay in power, and his first gambles paid off electorally. But did

---

[65] Ian Paisley Jr. DUP MP told the BBC that in October 2019 Boris Johnson promised him that the Protocol would be torn up after the withdrawal agreement was made, bbc.com/news/uk-northern-ireland-58910220. As the first MP to experience a recall attempt over serious misconduct he is not the best witness.

Johnson know what he was doing? In October 2021, his former advisor Dominic Cummings responded to a journalist who had queried Lord Frost's statement that the government had intended to implement the Protocol, but for the EU's conduct. Cummings riposted: "He has to say that! It was never my intention, I always intended an IM [internal market] Bill after we won a majority to tidy things up. The trolley [the expression for Boris Johnson] never understood WTF [no clarification needed] was going on at any stage. He didn't even understand what the CU [customs union] was until Nov 2020."[66] A former official governmental source confirmed that Cummings' statement accurately described then thinking in government circles.[67]

In response to another question, however, Cummings defended Johnson: "No what I've said does NOT mean 'the PM was lying in GE2019,' he never had a scoobydoo what the deal he signed meant. He never understood what leaving the Customs Union meant until 11/20. In 1/20 he was babbling 'I'd never have signed it if I'd understood it' (but that WAS a lie)."[68] This curious defense is that Johnson was ignorant, and therefore not lying, *but* that he would have lied if he had not been ignorant. The consigliere no longer respects his former don – or *omertà*.[69]

The official lie was that HMG would implement the Protocol and would have done so but for the EU's "legal purism." But,

[66] Cummings, replying to Adam Payne, twitter.com/Dominic2306/status/1 448028824143384591?s=20

[67] politicshome.com/news/article/cummings-northern-ireland-protocol

[68] Grammar corrected: twitter.com/Dominic2306/status/144805919580744 0902?ref_src=twsrc%5Etfw%7Ctwcamp%5Etweetembed%7Ctwterm%5E1 448059195807440902%7Ctwgr%5E%7Ctwcon%5Es1_&ref_url=https%3A %2F%2Fjoe.ie%2Fpolitics%2Fboris-johnson-dominic-cummings-north ern-ireland-protocol-733254

[69] Some simply argue that Johnson was lying during the general election, Daniel Finn, "Cloddish insensitivity," LRB blog, 14 April, 2021, www.lrb.co .uk/blog/2021/april/cloddish-insensitivity. Johnson's standing as a liar is discussed in Tom McTague, "Is Boris Johnson a liar?," *The Atlantic*, October 4, 2021.

even earlier, in May 2020, Steve Baker MP, a so-called Spartan in the so-called European Research Group, later sent to a junior ministerial position in Northern Ireland, wrote that Conservative backbenchers had been told by Cummings, "[We] should vote for the original Withdrawal Agreement without reading it, on the basis Michael Gove articulated: we could change it later."[70] Baker revealed this story when calling for Cummings' dismissal. Since Baker and Cummings are partisan and hostile witnesses, perhaps we should draw on someone habituated to objective analysis. Philip Rycroft was the permanent secretary at the Department for Exiting the EU (2017–19). In October 2020 he told the BBC that, "The government knew absolutely what it was signing up to when it signed up to the Protocol."[71] That means the Cabinet, its ministers, and its senior civil service advisors, and would usually be taken to include the prime minister, usually *primus inter pares*.

THE TORIES WERE NOT THE ONLY LIARS

Johnson was not alone in lying. The discourses of leaders of the DUP on the principle of consent related to the Protocol have included multiple untruths. What they cannot admit, and so they lie about it, is that they wanted to exploit their pivotality to achieve a hard border across Ireland.

In exchanges at Westminster on September 8, 2020, Sammy Wilson, the DUP's Brexit spokesman, welcomed potential law-breaking by secretary of state Brandon Lewis, and argued that the Withdrawal Agreement, "which damages the whole of the United Kingdom – this Union splitting, economy destroying and border creating agreement – has to be changed and replaced. It can be replaced and should be replaced."[72] Wilson's

---

[70] "Boris: take back control," *The Critic*, May 24, 2020.

[71] BBC, *World at One*, October 13, 2020 (available at reddit.com/r/ukpolitics/comments/q7ae3g/lewis_goodall_bbc_philip_rycroft_former_perma nent/).

[72] "Northern Ireland Protocol UK legal obligations," Commons Hansard, September 8, 2020, col. 502.

exaggerations – rather than lies – are instructive. The Protocol does not formally split the Union, certainly not asunder. Northern Ireland remains in the UK, though with different trading arrangements than those of Great Britain – to protect the Good Friday Agreement of 1998. Nothing in a political union per se prohibits separate organization of its different components in international relations, provided these arrangements materialize constitutionally.[73] This is where unionists are hoist by their own petard. After the UK's exit from the EU, the Westminster parliament is sovereign, and may do what it wills, provided it follows its own laws.

Ulster unionists believed the Protocol broke the Act of Union. They did not lie on this matter. They just displayed wishful thinking on constitutional norms and the history of the Union. They received salutary instruction before the courts. The leaders of the unionist parties pled the case in Belfast[74] that Article VI of the Act of Union obliges people living in Ireland and Great Britain to be "on the same footing"[75] regarding trade. Mr. Justice Colton who heard the case agreed that Article VI of the Act of Union was not compatible with the Withdrawal Act and its key Protocol. However, he also agreed with the government's lawyers that the Protocol repealed this provision of the Act of Union,[76] and not just because UK courts defer to more recent legislation when assessing conflicting legislation (implied repeal). The Act of Union was indeed a constitutional statute, but the European Union Withdrawal Act was also a major and

---

[73] See my subversive argument to this effect in O'Leary, "The Dalriada Document."

[74] *Allister (James Hugh) et al.'s Application and In the matter of the Protocol NI, Justice Colton* (High Court of Justice in Northern Ireland NIQB 64, 2021), High Court of Justice in Northern Ireland NIQB 64, June 30, 2021.

[75] legislation.gov.uk/aip/Geo3/40/38/contents

[76] For the outraged reaction of one of the litigants on hearing the government's arguments see former Brexit MEP Ben Habib, "In a new low, Boris Johnson is claiming the Act of Union no longer exists," *News Letter*, May 20, 2021, www.newsletter.co.uk/news/opinion/columnists/ben-habib-in-a-ne w-low-boris-johnson-is-claiming-the-act-of-union-no-longer-exists-3243791

later constitutional statute, and so took precedence over conflicting provisions in the Act of Union. Colton rejected all other arguments brought by the unionist litigants – including claims regarding the violation of the cross-community consent provisions in the Good Friday Agreement that apply in the Northern Assembly (these claims were lies). Colton's verdict was largely upheld in the Court of Appeal and in the UK Supreme Court – though the latter did not make much of constitutional statutes.

It is too early to determine whether the Protocol will be "economy destroying" as Sammy Wilson, sometime teacher in economics, asserts, or whether it creates an economic united Ireland in advance of a political united Ireland. Some will gain and some will lose from the Protocol as always happens when trading arrangements are modified – that is what Americans would call "The Economics of International Trade, 101." Wilson is correct about one matter, however. The Protocol creates a regulatory and customs border between Great Britain and Northern Ireland. It is not, however, pedantically speaking a sovereign border, or a formal sea border, just a set of places where customs and regulatory administration take place. Moreover, Wilson cannot admit its causation. Brexit, rather than UKexit, has occurred,[77] because of the DUP's inept tactics and misalliances at Westminster.

Standing back from the misconduct of the Tories and the DUP, May's soft exit, the Protocol, and the Windsor Framework, were negotiated for democratic reasons. Great Britain, one unit of the relevant Union had voted to leave the EU (with Scotland, part of the Union of Great Britain dissenting), whereas another, Northern Ireland, did not. Security reasons mattered, especially to the police and May. Implementing a full UKexit would have undermined the foreseen consequences of the Good Friday Agreement – a borderless Ireland within the EU along with the UK. The successful peace process had led to the demilitarization of the border, and rational fears existed that recreating a hard

---

[77] For the distinction see O'Leary, "The Dalriada Document," where I sought, with little hope, to argue for distinct treatment for Northern Ireland *and* Scotland, based on their separate mandates in the 2016 referendum.

border would create vulnerable fixed targets.[78] Legal reasons mattered too: the UK was bound by treaty to the Good Friday Agreement, endorsed by two referendums in 1998. Lastly, geographic reasons mattered. Northern Ireland *is* part of the island of Ireland, making it the sole place in the UK to have a land border with the EU after the UK's secession. The Protocol enables existing regulatory and customs functions to be repurposed to protect the single market much more easily than would be possible across the porous partition line.

Jeffrey Donaldson, the third DUP leader in 2021, threatened to bring down Northern Ireland's Assembly and Executive in protest at the Protocol, and duly did so in early 2022. His language was polite, "The Protocol harms east–west relationships, it creates barriers between Northern Ireland, that in our opinion represents a change to our constitutional status" and upsets "the very delicate constitutional balance that is at the heart of the agreements that formed the basis of the peace process here."[79] Aside from the questionable syntax, which may not be accurate reporting, was there truth in Donaldson's plea? Not much. The key institutional east–west relationships of the Good Friday Agreement, encoded in the BIC (British–Irish Council), favored by unionists and the BIIGC (the British–Irish Intergovernmental Conference), disfavored by unionists, are not affected by the Protocol, and under the Conservatives the UK has disrespected the BIIGC. Northern Ireland has MPs at Westminster where legislation is made on non-devolved matters. The delicate constitutional balance between nationalists and unionists would be more endangered by scrapping the Protocol, or by precipitating a trade war between the UK and the EU, than by maintaining the Protocol and making it work better. Johnson conceded, in signing the Protocol, that the UK must protect the Good Friday Agreement "in all its parts." He abandoned his claim that "the particular problems around the

---

[78] Garry *et al.*, *Northern Ireland and the UK's Exit from the EU.*

[79] Freya McClements, "Jeffrey Donaldson: talk of a united Ireland is 'premature' when the North is not united," *Irish Times*, September 25, 2021.

Irish border are being used, politically, to frustrate Brexit."[80] Some did use these problems to frustrate Brexit, but the problems were real. No one doubts that Johnson made concessions, and multiple about-faces, to secure the UK's exit from the EU, though there is good cause to suspect the good faith in each of his maneuvers.

In the summer of 2017, the DUP's MPs fortuitously found themselves pivotal to the survival of May's government. They extracted pork-barrel concessions but then deliberately assisted the sustained defeat of all May's proposals put before Westminster that would have led to a softer exit of the UK from the EU. They did so deliberately. That interpretation is stated unequivocally to respect the political rationality of the DUP's MPs. They sought to make the EU's future border with the UK coincident with the historic partition line in Ireland – and to see customs and regulatory barriers re-emerge on the island. They had a cover story: tall and ever-changing tales of "alternative technologies" with near-miraculous regulatory, customs, and VAT-assignment and collection capacities that mysteriously were never found elsewhere. The truth, however, was that they wanted a hard land border restored to render Irish reunification more difficult. No other explanation makes sense of their conduct. They pursued a hard exit against the known preferences of a majority of the electorate in Northern Ireland, as expressed in the referendum of June 2016, and subsequently. They were willing partners to the idea of imposing a solution – a hard Brexit – as far from the consent of a majority in Northern Ireland as would have been imaginable in late June 2016. That is why the DUP's subsequent concerns for consent ring hollow. But during events that made truth stranger than fiction, and tragedy resemble farce, the DUP would support May's chief rival for the leadership of the Conservative Party, who would go on to use and abuse their switch of allegiance by agreeing the Protocol with the Irish Taoiseach, Leo Varadkar, and with the

---

[80] RTÉ Radio 1, Brexit Republic, podcast, www.rte.ie/radio1/podcast/pod cast_brexitrepublic.xml

EU. Johnson did so as the fastest route to accomplishing his allegedly "oven-ready" Brexit.[81]

Someone said that Arlene Foster, the formal leader of the DUP between 2015 and 2021, was the first woman to have believed Johnson's lies but I cannot trace the source. I disbelieve this acidic assessment. As First Minister, Foster was principally the Assembly leader. Within the DUP the Westminster party was empowered by the collapse of Northern Ireland's institutions – in no small part because of Foster's refusal to step aside while corruption allegations in the "cash-for-ash" scandal were investigated.[82] The parliamentary party was unmoored from its local responsibilities and could act in accordance with its ideological preferences. The biggest lie, however, would become the claim that the Protocol violates the principle of consent embedded in the Good Friday Agreement of 1998. As if the EU's negotiators, with the government of Ireland alongside them, and with organized Irish-America overlooking their shoulders, had deliberately broken the Good Friday Agreement to save it.[83] On October 19, 2019, the DUP's parliamentary leader remonstrated with Johnson in the Commons:

[81] At one juncture the DUP accepted the idea of two hard borders – a regulatory border between Great Britain and Northern Ireland, and a customs border across Ireland. A compromise, but against any objective assessment of the interests of Northern Ireland. Having seen the DUP move on the location of one border, Johnson and his advisors knew that it was more flexible than it had suggested, and effectively agreed with Ireland and the EU to put all the bordering in one locus, at ports and airports.

[82] Sam McBride, *Burned: The Inside Story of the 'Cash-for-Ash' Scandal and Northern Ireland's Secretive New Elite* (Dublin: Merrion Press, 2019). For the dissection of Johnson's, Frost's and Lewis's dishonesty by the same unionist author see newsletter.co.uk/news/politics/sam-mcbride-boris-johnsons-past-dishonesty-on-the-irish-sea-border-has-present-consequences-how-do-we-know-if-hes-now-being-truthful-3303383

[83] Colin Murray, "Vichy France and vassalage: hyperbole versus the Northern Ireland Protocol," UK Constitutional Law Association blog, July 1, 2021, available at https://ukconstitutionallaw.org/

Nigel Dodds: This deal puts Northern Ireland, yes, in the UK customs union, but applies, de facto, all the European customs union code.

The Prime Minister: *indicated dissent.*

Nigel Dodds: Yes, it does. Read the detail. It also puts us in the VAT regime. It also puts us in the single market regime for a large part of goods and agrifood, without any consent up front, contrary to the agreement made in December 2017, which said that regulatory difference could happen only with the consent of the Executive and the Assembly. It drives a coach and horses through the Belfast agreement by altering the cross-community consent mechanism. It was once said that no British Prime Minister could ever agree to such terms. Indeed, those who sought the leadership of the Tory party said that at the Democratic Unionist party conference. Will the Prime Minister now abide by that and please reconsider the fact that we must leave as one nation together?

Johnson mumbled that the deal did not violate the Good Friday Agreement but appeared not to know why. The cross-community consent provisions do not apply to non-devolved matters, like trade, and the principle of consent applies only to whether Northern Ireland is to remain part of the UK or become part of a united Ireland. UK legislation provides that the majority will is to be expressed in a future referendum, to be held under specific conditions.[84] That is the consent-to-sovereignty principle.

If the Protocol modified Northern Ireland's constitutional status as part of the United Kingdom, then unionists would have a point – though the correct resolution, if their point was conceded, would be to have a referendum in Northern Ireland on whether to accept the Protocol. Unionists are not correct, however. The Protocol does not put Northern Ireland politically outside the UK. It has not been annexed to the EU. Rather the UK's sovereign Westminster parliament has decided to take Great Britain, not Northern Ireland, out of the EU's single market, and out of its customs union, while leaving Northern

---

[84] Northern Ireland Act 1998, c. 47, section 1.

Ireland within the single market's regulations for goods, and subject to the EU's customs code for imports from Great Britain. The legislation that enacts these arrangements comes from Westminster. Special trading arrangements have certainly been made but these do not modify Northern Ireland's status as part of the UK. Northern Ireland has not become part of sovereign Ireland, and it has not become an independent EU member state. The sovereign UK decided on a differentiated exit of its parts from European arrangements, though Scotland, part of the Union of Great Britain, was not ceded any of its requests for differential treatment.

The cross-community consent arrangements (the concurrent or parallel consent rule, and the weighted majority or qualified majority consent rule) were not applicable.[85] These rules apply solely to the existing powers of the Assembly and its Executive, as defined in the Northern Ireland Act (1998), or in subsequent amendments to that Act. No constitutional, legal, or even conventional requirement of cross-community consent is required by the Good Friday Agreement for the matters related to the Protocol. The functions addressed in the Protocol – mostly customs, EU single market regulation, and VAT – are not Northern Ireland Assembly or Executive functions, under the GFA, or the Northern Ireland Act (1998), or the treaty between the UK and Ireland annexed to the GFA, or in subsequent legislation. Many unionist leaders persistently ignore the reply made to Donaldson by Julian Smith, an honest and law-abiding secretary of state for Northern Ireland:

> Julian Smith: I say again to my colleagues and friends in the
> DUP and to Unionists across this House and in Northern

---

[85] For discussion of these arrangements just after they had been made see Brendan O'Leary, "The nature of the agreement," *Fordham Journal of International Law*, 22:4 (1999), 1628–67, and for their subsequent evolution see Christopher McCrudden, John McGarry, Brendan O'Leary, and Alex Schwartz, "Why Northern Ireland's institutions need stability," *Government and Opposition*, 51:1 (2016), 30–58, http://dx.doi.org/doi:10.1017/gov.2014.28, and O'Leary, *A Treatise on Northern Ireland*, vol. 3: *Consociation and Confederation*.

Ireland that this protocol is for a reserved matter; it is not for the Assembly. The Belfast agreement is extremely clear that there will be matters that are not subject to the consent mechanisms in the Assembly. The Government will continue to work to ensure that this protocol, as the Bill goes through Parliament, is executed in a way that is reassuring to all Members and all parts of the Northern Ireland community. But remember that the issue with the backstop was a lack of consent. This consent mechanism is intended to deal with that, but it has no effect on the Northern Ireland Assembly.[86]

In the lie about consent unionist leaders assert that the 1998 arrangements give unionists a veto on *any* change in Northern Ireland's political arrangements.[87] The more gullible of their supporters appear to believe this falsehood, judging by posters and wall-slogans visible in loyalist-dominated parts of Northern Ireland.

So, curiously, Northern Ireland has ended up as a federacy, in which UK and EU treaties have entrenched the Good Friday Agreement, internationally entrenching it, even though the devolved institutions have not been working for most of the time since 2017. Julian Smith had made a sincere effort along with his Irish opposite number to stabilize matters in *New Decade, New Approach* (January, 2020), largely by returning to previous pledges. He was briefly able to restore the local institutions. His reward was to be sacked by Johnson, who would replace him with Brandon Lewis, a barrister too willing to break international law. It is not clear whether Smith was sacked because he was too outspoken in Cabinet, or because he had made commitments to forward legislation to implement the legacy bodies pledged in the Stormont House agreement.

---

[86] "Northern Ireland: Restoring Devolution," Commons Hansard, October 21, 2019, vol. 666.

[87] See, e.g., David Trimble, "Tear up the Northern Ireland Protocol to save the Belfast Agreement: the withdrawal agreement protocol ignores the fundamental principle of consent," *Irish Times*, February 20, 2021, where *any* constitutional change requires consent, but constitutional is not clarified.

Rishi Sunak has partly tidied up the mess left by Johnson, and which Truss would have made worse. The Windsor Framework reclothes the Protocol, in an act of smoke and mirrors. It does not fool unionists, who regard it as putting lipstick on a pig, but it contains sensible administrative easements, fully agreed with the EU. But in early December 2023 the Northern Ireland Assembly and Executive were not functioning. A three-year Sinn Féin boycott has been followed by what may become a three-year DUP boycott, neither of which can be explained without reference to the repercussions of "Brexit." The Tories, the party of the Union, will likely leave office in 2024/25 with Sinn Féin as the largest party in the North and with a strong chance that Sinn Féin will be the leading party in the South, and perhaps in government. Before it will consider going back to Stormont, the DUP, in the dying days of the Conservatives long tenure of office, is demanding guarantees that it is hard to see Sunak can provide without endangering his hard-won negotiations with the EU. The DUP's members and voters are split, torn between crawling back defeated to work Stormont as the second party, or collapsing the Good Friday Agreement. They fear the Traditional Unionist Voice (TUV) and the loyalists to their right more than they fear the UUP or Alliance. They own their mess. The Tories created it, but the DUP made it exponentially worse.

UNTYING THE UNION WITH SCOTLAND

Cameron gambled with the union of Great Britain before gambling on the EU. He had nearly lost in Scotland only to be saved by Gordon Brown. He drew the wrong lessons. He thought he knew how to win referendums. His maladroit handling of the EU referendum, compounded by his failure to make a real attempt to build an alliance with Labour and the Liberal Democrats, cannot be explained without reference to his overconfidence from winning two previous referendums for the status quo. In the immediate wake of the Scottish result Cameron responded by raising the need for immediate legislation for EVEL – English votes for English Laws – in order to resolve the

"West Lothian question." It was scarcely a demonstration of deep concern for Scotland.

In the 2015 Westminster elections, Saatchi and Saatchi, the Conservatives' advertisers, would target Labour's leader, Ed Miliband. The theme was "Vote Miliband and get Salmond." The poster shown in Figure 8.5 asserted that Labour would be in the pocket of the SNP leader, especially if a hung parliament materialized, as was widely expected. The Tories have started to exploit English resentment against Scotland much as their great-grandfathers had mobilized against the Irish demand for home rule. That did not end well. Their wiser great-great-grandfathers had sought to kill home rule with kindness – a sentiment currently in scarce supply.

Under May, and her successors, the Conservatives did not deeply try to create a pan-UK strategic response to the advisory referendum, which had not defined leave. No structured development of a statewide exit strategy and plan, that would have incorporated the devolved administrations, got under way. Instead, policy was developed as a partisan Brexit, and rushed. There was no thought of a coalition, or even properly structured consultations to address the most serious foreign policy

Figure 8.5 Saatchi and Saatchi poster
Source: Mark Severn/Alamy Stock Photo

decisions since World War II. The contrast with Irish behavior over the same question is striking.

The question of the devolved administrations would arise, however, and not just because of the Good Friday Agreement. If the EU Withdrawal Bill, and other legislation implementing the Withdrawal Agreement, were to change the powers of the Northern Ireland Assembly and Executive, the Welsh Assembly, and the Scottish Parliament, through the repatriation of powers from the EU, the question became how decisions over that repatriation should be organized.

The courts facilitated the May government and its successors in keeping decision-making over repatriated powers to the government at Westminster. In the Miller case the UK Supreme Court unanimously insisted in 2017 that "the Sewel convention," namely, that Westminster should consult the devolved legislatures before changing their powers, is just that, a convention.[88] No veto rights are held by the devolved legislatures over Westminster legislation, even if their existing devolved powers are to be modified against their will. That is now the judicial status quo, even though the convention was written into law. Differently put, when it matters the convention may be set aside. The relevant legislation from Westminster was refused when such consent was eventually sought. Michael Gove, the chancellor of the Duchy of Lancaster, issued a statement to parliament that it was "disappointing" that the three devolved legislatures refused to agree a legislative consent motion (LCM) for the European Union (Withdrawal Agreement) Bill. He went on:

> The Sewel Convention – to which the Government remains committed – states that the UK Parliament "will not normally legislate with regard to devolved matters without the consent"

---

[88] For the Miller case see www.supremecourt.uk/cases/uksc-2016-0196.html, for commentary see Christopher McCrudden and Daniel Halberstam, "*Miller* and Northern Ireland: a critical constitutional response," *Michigan Law: Public Law and Legal Theory Research Paper Series,* no. 575 (October 2017) (also to be published in the *UK Supreme Court Yearbook,* vol. 8).

of the relevant devolved legislatures. The circumstances of our departure from the EU, following the 2016 referendum, are not normal – they are unique.

At every stage of the European Union (Withdrawal Agreement) Bill, the UK Government has demonstrated its enduring commitment and respect for the Sewel Convention and the principles that underpin our constitutional arrangements.[89]

These sentences, especially the last, were constitutional crocodile tears. They are an object lesson for the devolved legislatures: their powers are devolved; they are not their powers; they make the case for federation or independence better than any abstract argument in political science or constitutional law.

The complacent believe that Labour will save the union of Great Britain aided by scandals and crises of leadership within the SNP. It is possible, but other vistas are as likely within the next decade, let alone the *longue durée*. They include a second referendum extracted when the next hung parliament occurs. Conservative leaders have learned from Johnson's conduct that downsizing the Union might be fully acceptable to their English base. Their competitors are the Reform party, the Brexit party, and UKIP, and other Farage-phenomena. Scottish Labour is a charisma-free zone and Keir Starmer seems to have tied his likely future government to austerity.

AWAKENING WALES?

Wales is different, the most British and most English of the three devolved units, which partly explains its pro-Brexit vote in 2016 of 52 percent against 48. It was a vote of maximum feasible ingratitude. No other region of the UK had benefitted as much from EU programs, but the result was driven by the British in Wales as well as the left behind. Nevertheless, under the

---

[89] Update on the EU (Withdrawal Agreement) Bill, January 23, 2020, ques tions-statements.parliament.uk/written-statements/detail/2020-01-23/ HCWS60

Conservative hegemony in London, Welsh autonomous institutions have strengthened. The assembly has become a real parliament. Devolution has become entrenched, despite its initial paucity of support. Labour has kept its dominance in Wales, unlike Scotland, perhaps partly because it has moved closer to Plaid Cymru and the Greens, a strategy which Scottish Labour failed to try. Nevertheless, independence has become a question in Wales. All the polls I can find since the UK left the EU suggest support for Wales becoming an independent country running at above 20 percent, and sometimes such support rises to 30 percent. This is in a country that decisively rejected the most insipid form of devolution in 1978, barely endorsed devolution in 1997, and in which support for independence, if asked before 2016, ran in the teens of percentages, at most. The Conservatives have presided over aversion therapy for the Union, but perhaps that should be the UK because Wales is not in any union.

TOWARD THE FINAL CURTAIN?

The UK is an old state, if dated to 1603 or 1707, a much younger one if dated to 1921. In its most recent custody of office the Conservative and Unionist Party has not conserved. It has put English interests and preferences ahead of accommodations that might have stabilized the two unions – and even appears to have set Wales in motion toward a more nationalist direction. Most of its leaders care less about Northern Ireland when the chips are down, and many of them have recklessly played with anti-Scottish sentiment in England much as their nineteenth-century precursors played with anti-Irish sentiment. Cameron as prime minister was a talented but indolent gambler. Johnson was less talented, even more indolent, and a liar as well as a gambler. May was a sincere but slow learner, undone by the ambitious and the enraged, and could not solve an insoluble trilemma she set for herself. Liz Truss, a fanatic, and a parody of an ideological and instrumental politician, had little time to cause political damage to the two unions: what she did economically in less than fifty days was quite enough. Sunak, a prematurely overpromoted MBA, strikingly resembles a head boy asked to run a school chock full of truants, bullies, and the unlettered. The school, however, is HMS Britannia, and it is steadily moving toward icebergs, not as fast as Irish and Scottish nationalists would like, but it is difficult to see how the ship's course can be corrected.

POSTSCRIPT: THE RESURRECTION OF STORMONT

At a special Saturday sitting on February 3, 2024, the Northern Ireland Assembly elected Edwin Poots MLA, former leader of the DUP, as its speaker, along with three deputy speakers from Sinn Féin, the Alliance Party, and the Ulster Unionist Party (UUP). Then in the main business of the day Michelle O'Neill of Sinn Féin was elected first minister of the Northern Ireland executive while Emma Little-Pengelly of the DUP was elected deputy first minster. Both women made exceptionally gracious speeches. Following their election, a third woman, Naomi Long of Alliance, was elected as justice minister by cross-community consent, with just one MLA opposed, Jim Allister of Traditional Unionist Voice (TUV). The rest of the executive was then filled according to the d'Hondt rule of proportionality, with three ministries taken by Sinn Féin (Economy, Finance, and Infrastructure), and four others taken by the DUP (two), one by the Alliance, and one by the UUP. Sinn Féin's symbolic success was broadcast throughout the world: an Irish nationalist was now the first minister of Northern Ireland, a place that had been deliberately constructed to create a permanent unionist majority. Not the least of ironies of the day was that the role of leader of the opposition is now in the hands of Matthew O'Toole, the Assembly leader of the moderate Irish nationalist party, the SDLP.

The sourest notes during the proceedings were struck by Jim Allister, but that was because he correctly pointed out that the DUP had surrendered: no casual insult to a party famous for saying "No!" or "Never!" or "No surrender!" Allister, a lawyer, and a former MEP for the DUP, took aim:

> This is a day of glee and gloating for republicanism as the DUP leadership returns, after its seismic climbdown, to implement the Union-dismantling protocol. Despite all the fake news and

attempts to spin defeat as victory, this is a climbdown of monumental proportions. It is quite clear that not one word of the protocol has changed – not one word. Northern Ireland remains under the EU's customs code, which decrees GB to be a foreign country. That is of momentous constitutional significance in itself. We continue to be ruled, in significant part, by foreign laws. In annex 2 of the protocol, all 287 of those EU laws remain in place in perpetuity, beyond the reach of the Stormont brake, and therefore under the supervision of the European Court of Justice.

We still have an Irish Sea border. If the Irish Sea border was gone, we would be dismantling, not continuing to build, border posts, yet millions of pounds are being spent in that pursuit. Under EU legislation, Northern Ireland is still determined as EU territory. None of that has changed.

On article 6 [of the Act of Union], despite the weasel attempts in the Donaldson deal to diminish its importance, it is still in suspension and, with it, so is one of the twin pillars of this Union. Northern Ireland's place within the United Kingdom is not restored. We are still constitutionally a condominium, ruled in part by UK laws and in part by foreign laws that we do not make, and all of that with a partitioning border down the Irish Sea.

It is little wonder that this morning, in *The Belfast Telegraph*, Sam McBride described the deal as "the Windsor Framework in drag". That is exactly what it is. The Windsor framework was not good enough to bring the DUP back to vote in a Speaker, nor is this deal, and to roll over now and become protocol implementers is beyond comprehension. I accept that there are many in the DUP – some of them are on the benches today – who are very unhappy with this course of action and agree with many of the things that I am saying, and I urge them to continue to stand strong. I suggest that the moment that we vote to elect a Speaker, that is a vote to proceed to implement the protocol... a step that should not be taken.

Of course, as it turns out, there were many for whom opposition to the protocol was just bluff and bluster, and none more than Mr Poots. This is the man who told us that there had to be seismic changes to the protocol. ... So, from Mr Seismic to Mr Speaker: oh, the irresistible lure of office for those whose principles are expendable. For Mr Poots, the speakership is the fruit of the poison tree, and no good can come of it.[90]

Subsequent to the drafting of this chapter for the press, Jeffrey Donaldson had, with severe difficulty, persuaded his party colleagues to return to the Assembly and bank the concessions that Sunak had previously offered, with some additional crumbs. Sunak's government delivered a command paper, with a red, white, and blue cover, with the title of *Safeguarding the Union*, the first occasion I recall seeing a union jack signaled on a command paper. The text of the paper sought to ease the DUP's surrender, but the legislative text that mattered, though hardly transparent, was broadly as Allister suggested. If one stands back from Sunak's latest act of smoke and mirrors, the unions remain parted in their trading arrangements. The Act of Union has been partially amended – or "suspended" or "subjugated" according to lawyerly linguistic taste. The Protocol has not been unilaterally amended, and the Windsor Framework and the accompanying legislative mice of statutory instruments in Safeguarding the Union mean that all significant changes to the Protocol's administration still require the consent of the EU and UK joint body set up under that Protocol.

Contra Allister, however, Northern Ireland is not precisely a condominium because the UK and the EU do not jointly govern Northern Ireland. Instead, Northern Ireland is a federacy, in which the UK has bound itself, by its own laws, and in an international treaty, to maintain Northern Ireland's compliance with the European Union's single market in goods and its customs code – through UK law, passed at Westminster. It has linked this international arrangement to

<hr />

[90] Northern Ireland Assembly, Official Report, February 3, 2024, https://ai ms.niassembly.gov.uk/officialreport/report.aspx?&eveDate=2024/02/03&docID=386860

the maintenance of the Good Friday Agreement "in all its parts," already an international treaty. It is the UK that maintains EU law in Northern Ireland. Westminster, of course, still reserves its sovereign right to do anything it wants, but in this case, at the known cost, very unlikely to be taken anytime soon, of unraveling the better relations with the EU that Sunak has sought as a domestic priority in the political economy of Great Britain. If the Northern Ireland Assembly serves its full term, it may be expected, in due course, to endorse the Protocol – along with such emendations as the EU approves. One of the most curious and perhaps the feeblest outcomes of Brexit will be a new quango, Intertrade UK, with the mission to promote trade within the UK, a Brexit freedom that no one was promised in 2016.

The DUP's Westminster parliamentary party remains the site of the strongest formal opposition to the latest deal. Sammy Wilson MP has protested the "spineless" and "Brexit-betraying" Conservative government.[91] Whether the informal opposition of armed loyalist militia will go beyond such bluster remains to be seen. Remarkably, Donaldson had briefed the Loyalist Communities Council (set up by Jonathan Powell to provide a political front for (unretired?) loyalist militia) about the details of "Safeguarding the Union," not any business organization or labor union. We shall see whether that briefing restrains their rage. Unionists remain split into three parties, the DUP, the UUP, and the TUV, but the split over living with the Protocol or the Windsor Framework in drag runs through the largest of them, the DUP. It is hard not to believe that they will pay an electoral price in the next Westminster elections for their Brexit adventures. Leaving the major economic ministries to Sinn Féin may seem a cunning wheeze to transfer the difficulties of managing Northern Ireland's distressed public services, but it seems unlikely to succeed in staunching the short-run losses of the unionist bloc.

[91] "DUP MP Sammy Wilson calls British government 'spineless' and 'Brexit-betraying' as deal announced," *Irish News*, January 31, 2024.

In the audit of this book, should this latest restoration of Stormont be counted as a success for Sunak and the Conservatives? Perhaps, but in the same way that we tend to recognize the efforts of a polite and sane person to apologize indirectly on behalf of the reckless damage done by his insane relations.

9

Social and Health Inequalities

Michael Marmot and Clare Bambra

INTRODUCTION[1]

The UK is not a good place to be poor. That has become even more true over the last fourteen years. Our justification for that statement is that, in the UK, the health of the poorest people, always lower than that of the average person, declined since 2010. Regional inequalities in health also increased with the 'Red Wall' North falling further behind. There has also been stagnation in the UK's average life expectancy – and we have dropped down the international rankings. Please let the implications sink in: the health of the poorest people and places got worse; life expectancy went down; living with illness went up; and thousands of families lost loved ones before their time. It is an unprecedented calamity.

---

[1] This chapter is based on the Marmot Reviews 2010 and 2020 as well as the 2023 evidence report that Clare Bambra and Michael Marmot prepared for Module 1 of the UK Public Inquiry into Covid-19: Michael Marmot, *The Marmot Review: Fair Society Healthy Lives* (London: Institute of Health Equity, 1010) (www.instituteof healthequity.org/resources-reports/fair-society-healthy-lives-the-marmot-revie w); Michael Marmot, *Health Equity in England: The Marmot Review 10 Years On* (London: Institute of Health Equity, 2020) (www.health.org.uk/publications/ reports/the-marmot-review-10-years-on); Clare Bambra and Michael Marmot, *Expert Report for the UK COVID-19 Public Inquiry Module 1: Health Inequalities* (2023), https://covid19.public-inquiry.uk/wp-content/uploads/2023/06/16183457/ INQ000195843.pdf. Full details and references for all the points raised in this chapter are available in these reports. Michael Marmot has been commissioned by the Greater London Authority to conduct a comprehensive review of racism and health inequalities – to be published mid 2024.

This chapter will focus on two implications of that statement that are linked. First, people's expectations have been that health will continue to improve year on year. It is an entirely reasonable expectation based on historical fact – outside the two world wars, average life expectancy increased year-on-year in the UK over the twentieth century. The implied, and sometimes explicit, social promise was that things would only get better. Something happened in 2010 that interrupted that historical trend. An obvious question that must be addressed is the extent to which successive Conservative-led governments since 2010 are responsible.

The second implication links to this question. Decades of research evidence has led us to the position that health is a good measure of how a society is doing in meeting the needs of its members. The World Health Organization (WHO) 2008 Global Commission on the Social Determinants of Health (chaired by MM) concluded that the conditions in which *people are born, grow, live, work and age, and inequities in power, money, and resources'*, are the main determinants of the health of individuals and countries.[2] These 'social determinants of health' are responsible for much of the health inequalities that we see in the UK today. Following what we said above, the implication is that, after 2010 in the UK, society stopped improving not just for the poor but for almost everyone, and inequalities increased.

As further illustration of society's impact on health, we need only look at what happened to health in Europe from the 1960s onwards. Life expectancy in the 'west' improved year on year; in the communist countries of central and eastern Europe, life expectancy stagnated. It was a reasonable supposition that the governments of those countries were not meeting the needs of their citizens nor creating the conditions for them to lead flourishing lives.

The UK is not a good place to be poor because, as we will show, many of the social determinants of health got worse over

[2] World Health Organization, *Closing the Gap in a Generation: Health Equity through Action on the Social Determinants of Health* (Geneva: WHO, 2008), www.who.int/publications/i/item/WHO-IER-CSDH-08.1

the last fourteen years – often because of the government's own policies. It is this deterioration which is the most likely cause of the worsening of health amongst the poor. Surely, a minimum requirement for a democratic government is to create the conditions in which all its citizens can live well and avoid early death. Governments are often assessed on economic performance such as economic growth, the national debt, or the annual deficit. We suggest that a better accounting system for assessing the impacts of the last fourteen years is what was the impact of the government on the health and well-being of the population and, more specifically, on inequalities in health and well-being. The picture is bleak.

We look at three threats to health and health inequalities: fourteen + years of austerity; the poor handling of the pandemic; and the inadequate response to the cost-of-living crisis. Before that, two pieces of scene-setting are in order: what are health inequalities and what happened to health inequalities in the period up to 2010, under the Labour government?

NOT 'JUST' POVERTY: SOCIAL INEQUALITIES IN HEALTH

Health inequalities are the differences in health outcomes between different social groups. The usual term in the UK has been 'health inequalities'. A related term is 'inequities' – to describe those health inequalities that are judged to be avoidable by reasonable means. If they are not avoided, they are inequitable. It is injustice. Commonly when people refer to health, or health inequalities, they mean health care. When international agencies speak of health spending, they do not mean spending on reducing child poverty, or improving education – measures that would improve health – but spending on health care. We will address health care in this chapter but there is a reasonable consensus that health inequalities in the UK are not primarily the result of inequalities in health care.

Inequalities in health by socioeconomic position (income, education, occupation or deprivation) are not restricted to differences between the most privileged groups and the most disadvantaged: health inequalities exist across the entire social gradient.[3] Consistently, the finding has been that the lower the socioeconomic position the worse the health, the higher the mortality rates and the shorter the life expectancy.[4] The social gradient in health runs from the top to the bottom of society and '*even comfortably off people somewhere in the middle tend to have poorer health than those above them*'.[5] We first demonstrated the social gradient in health in the Whitehall Studies of British Civil Servants: the higher the grade of employment the longer the life expectancy.[6]

There are also stark geographical inequalities in health in the UK. The most deprived areas – deprivation measured in terms of the social and economic characteristics of areas – have worse health than the least deprived areas. Again, there is a gradient – with the most deprived 20 per cent of local authorities, such as County Durham or Tower Hamlets, experiencing worse health and lower life expectancy than the next fifth and so on up the scale. The least deprived areas, such as Rutland or Kensington and Chelsea, are faring the best. For example, even before the pandemic in 2017–19, both male and female life expectancy was highest in the London borough of Westminster (84.88 years for men, 87.22 years for women), and lowest in Glasgow City (73.60, 78.50).[7] This is a difference in life expectancy of 11.3 years. Westminster is the least deprived local authority in England, whilst Glasgow is the most deprived area in

[3] Michael Marmot, 'Introduction', in Michael Marmot and Richard G. Wilkinson (eds.), *The Social Determinants of Health* (Oxford: Oxford University Press, 2006), pp. 1–5.

[4] Marmot, *The Marmot Review 10 Years On.*

[5] Marmot, 'Introduction', in Marmot and Wilkinson (eds.), *The Social Determinants of Health.*

[6] Michael Marmot, *Status Syndrome* (London: Bloomsbury, 2004).

[7] Office for National Statistics, 'Life expectancy for local areas of the UK: between 2001 to 2003 and 2017 to 2019' (2020), www.ons.gov.uk/people populationandcommunity/healthandsocialcare/healthandlifeexpectan cies/bulletins/lifeexpectancyforlocalareasoftheuk/between2001 to2003and2017to2019#life-expectancy-at-a-local-level-in-the-uk

Scotland. And there are even larger inequalities in life expectancy between neighbourhoods within local authorities – for example, the life expectancy gap between the least and most deprived areas of Glasgow is 11.6 years for women and 15.4 years for men.[8] Life expectancy is also regionally patterned in England with a clear 'north–south health divide': around two years lower on average between the three northern regions (North East, North West, Yorkshire and the Humber) than the rest of England.[9]

There is also an intersection of socioeconomic position and geography as shown in Figure 9.1. This shows that whilst there is a social gradient in life expectancy in both London and the North East regions – the greater the deprivation, the shorter the life expectancy – the gradient is steeper in the North East. This means that the health disadvantage of deprivation is greater in the North East than it is in London. The differences in life expectancy for men and women living in the North East region and in London are small for those in the least deprived decile 10, but the regional gap in life expectancy gets progressively bigger the greater the deprivation. As Figure 9.1 shows, men and women living in the most deprived areas in the North East have a much lower life expectancy than people living in the most deprived areas of London. Or, to put it another way, the health disadvantage of living in the North East increases with greater deprivation. Indeed, the health effects associated with deprivation appear to be 'amplified' in the North East.[10]

Anticipating what we will discuss in more detail below, the time trends in Figure 9.1 also show that regional health inequalities have increased since 2010. In London, life expectancy increased for both men and women across the whole gradient: male and

[8] Glasgow Centre for Population Health, 'Health in a changing city: Glasgow' (2021), www.gcph.co.uk/publications/996_health_in_a_changing_city_glasgow_2021

[9] Clare Bambra, Luke Munford, Sam Khavandi and Natalie Bennett, *Northern Exposure: COVID-19 and Regional Inequalities in Health and Wealth* (Bristol: Policy Press, 2023).

[10] Ibid.

(a) Males

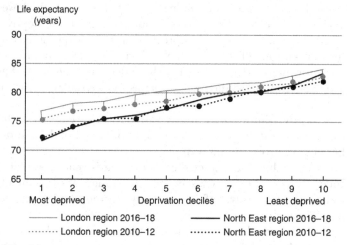

(b) Females

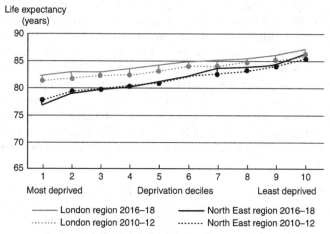

Figure 9.1 Life expectancy at birth by sex and deprivation deciles in London and the North East regions, 2010–12 and 2016–18

Source: Michael Marmot, *Health Equity in England: The Marmot Review 10 Years On* (London: Institute of Health Equity, 2020).

female life expectancy increased in every decile. In contrast, in the North East, life expectancy did not increase for men in the lowest deciles and it actually fell for women in the most deprived 10 per cent. There was no improvement in life expectancy over the period from 2010 for women in deciles 1–6, and no improvement for men in deciles 1–3. For those deciles in the North East where life expectancy did increase, it was a smaller increase than in London.

To put it simply, in the decade after 2010, life expectancy fell for the poorest 10 per cent of people outside London, and it failed to improve for many more.

We use life expectancy data because it is readily available. Inequalities in health are seen across a range of other health indicators: mortality, infant mortality, cardiovascular disease, liver disease, diabetes, obesity.

There are also health inequalities between other social groups. Most notably, there is increasing recognition that membership of a minority ethnic group may also be associated with a health disadvantage. This is particularly stark in relation to maternal mortality rates – women from Black African or Black Caribbean backgrounds over four times are more likely to die in childbirth than women from white ethnic backgrounds;[11] and infant mortality rates – Black and Asian ethnic groups have the highest rates and white groups the lowest.[12] This is in part because ethnic minority groups are much more likely to live in deprivation: people from Pakistani and Bangladeshi and Black African and Black Caribbean backgrounds are twice as likely to

---

[11] Maternal, Newborn and Infant Clinical Outcome Review Programme, *Saving Lives, Improving Mothers' Care* (2020), www.npeu.ox.ac.uk/assets/do wnloads/mbrrace-uk/reports/maternal-report-2020/MBRRACE-UK_Mat ernal_Report_Dec_2020_v10_ONLINE_VERSION_1404.pdf

[12] Commission on Race and Ethnic Disparities, 'Ethnic disparities in the major causes of mortality and their risk factors – a rapid review', 28 April 2021, www.gov.uk/government/publications/the-report-of-the-c ommission-on-race-and-ethnic-disparities-supporting-research/ethnic-dis parities-in-the-major-causes-of-mortality-and-their-risk-factors-by-dr-raghib-ali-et-al#fnref:16

live in the most deprived areas as people from White British backgrounds.[13] The health effects of deprivation that we outline in this chapter are disproportionately experienced by people from minority ethnic backgrounds. There is also growing evidence of the health inequalities experienced by other social minorities, such as LGBTQ+ groups, and people with disabilities.[14]

These different social inequalities in health are experienced intersectionally. People simultaneously belong to multiple social groups, for example, they experience their socioeconomic status, ethnicity, locality and sexuality simultaneously. This leads to complex experiences of social inequalities, which influence health in different ways. Social groups therefore experience different amounts of disadvantage and privilege associated with their different characteristics.[15]

HEALTH INEQUALITIES 2000–2010

Tackling health inequalities was, by and large, not on the agenda of the 1979–97 Conservative governments of Margaret Thatcher and John Major. There is a history, of course. In 1978, the Wilson–Callaghan Labour government commissioned Sir Douglas Black and colleagues to investigate how to reduce the UK's health inequalities.[16] By the time the Black Report was published in 1980, Margaret Thatcher was prime minister and her secretary of state for health made clear that there was no intention of implementing any of its recommendations.

When Labour was elected again in 1997, as a clear statement of difference from the previous governments, they announced

---

[13] Ibid.

[14] Bambra and Marmot, *Expert Report for the UK COVID-19 Public Inquiry*.

[15] Clare Bambra, '*Placing intersectional inequalities in health*', *Health & Place*, 75 (2022), 102761.

[16] Douglas Black *Report of the Working Group on Inequalities in Health* (Department of Health and Social Security, 1980), https://sochealth.co.u k/national-health-service/public-health-and-wellbeing/poverty-and-inequ ality/the-black-report-1980/

that they would set up a new Inquiry into Health Inequalities under former chief medical officer, Sir Donald Acheson (MM was a member of that inquiry).[17] The Inquiry reported in 1998 and shaped the subsequent health inequalities policy of the Labour government. Most notably, it led to the implementation of a national health inequalities strategy in England. This was multifaceted and included a wide range of nationally delivered activities – an increase in NHS budgets, particularly in more deprived areas; establishment of Sure Start Children's Centres; implementation of New Deal for Communities. These were complemented by local activities, including Health Improvement Programmes, Health Action Zones, Healthy Living Centres. Accompanying these activities was an increase in social security, particularly for the poorest families, for example, the Child Tax Credit. In this period, child and pensioner poverty decreased considerably.

The Labour government also set targets for tackling health inequalities: to reduce the life expectancy and infant mortality gaps between the 20 per cent most deprived local authorities and the English average by 10 per cent.[18] These targets – whilst considered ambitious at the time – were largely met with inequalities in life expectancy and infant mortality rates reduced by 2010.[19, 20] For example, in the years before the strategy, the gap in life

[17] Donald Acheson, *Independent Inquiry into Inequalities in Health Report* (London: Stationery Office, 1998), https://assets.publishing.service.gov.uk/government/uploads/system/uploads/attachment_data/file/265503/ih.pdf

[18] Clare Bambra, Katherine E. Smith, Chioma Nwaru et al., *Targeting Health Inequalities: Realising the Potential of Targets in Reducing Health Inequalities* (Newcastle upon Tyne: Health Equity North and The Health Foundation, 2023), www.health.org.uk/publications/reports/targeting-health-inequalities-realising-the-potential-of-targets-in-addressing-health-inequalities

[19] Ben Barr, James Higgerson and Margaret Whitehead, 'Investigating the impact of the English health inequalities strategy: time trend analysis', *BMJ*, 358 (2017), j3310.

[20] Tomos Robinson, Heather Brown, Paul D. Norman, Lorna K. Fraser, Ben Barr and Clare Bambra, 'The impact of New Labour's English health inequalities strategy on geographical inequalities in infant mortality:

expectancy between the most deprived 10 per cent of local authorities and the rest grew.[21] From 2000 to 2010, the gap narrowed: health inequalities diminished.[22] Likewise, the gap in infant mortality rates between the 20 per cent most deprived and the national average – which had been increasing in the 1980s and 1990s – also fell between 2000 and 2010.[23] This is demonstrated in Figure 9.2.

As we examine further in the section below, from 2011, the gaps increased again: health inequalities grew bigger.

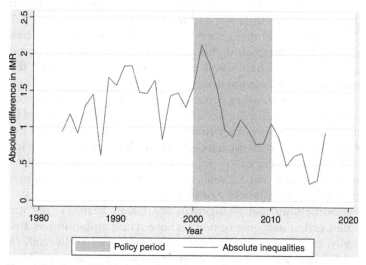

Figure 9.2 Inequalities in infant mortality rates by local authority, 1983–2017
Source: Reproduced from Tomos Robinson, Heather Brown, Paul D. Norman, Lorna K. Fraser, Ben Barr and Clare Bambra, 'The impact of New Labour's English health inequalities strategy on geographical inequalities in infant mortality: a time-trend analysis', *Journal of Epidemiology and Community Health*, 73 (2019), 564–68, with permission from BMJ Publishing Group Ltd.

 a time-trend analysis', *Journal of Epidemiology and Community Health*, 73 (2019), 564–8.

[21] Marmot, *The Marmot Review.*
[22] Marmot, *The Marmot Review 10 Years On.*
[23] Robinson et al., 'Impact of New Labour's English health inequalities strategy'.

TRENDS IN HEALTH AND HEALTH INEQUALITIES
SINCE 2010

Slowdown in Health Improvement

The *Marmot Review 10 Years On* was for England, but what we described was similar in Scotland, Northern Ireland and Wales. Until 2010, life expectancy in England had been increasing at about one year every four years.[24] This trend had continued for all of the twentieth century, with small deviations. In 2010, there was a break in the curve. The rate of improvement slowed dramatically and then stopped improving, shown in Figure 9.3. The trend in the other countries of the UK was similar.[25] When we first drew attention to this slowdown, the question was posed as to whether we have simply reached peak life expectancy; the rate of improvement has to slow some time. Rebuttal comes from comparisons with other countries. The slowdown in life expectancy growth during the decade after 2010 was more marked in the UK than in any other rich country, except Iceland and the USA.[26] In Figure 9.3, we have added an additional data point for 2020, the first year of the pandemic. Life expectancy fell by 0.9 years in women and 1.2 years in men. We lost four years of pre-2010 improvement in just one year.

Something had changed in the UK in 2010/11. It coincided with a new government, whose stated ambition was austerity, cutting public expenditure in response to the 2007/8 Global Financial Crisis. We consider below the extent to which this change in policy could have played a role in the changing health picture.

Increase in Health Inequalities

As noted earlier, life expectancy follows a social gradient. When people are classified by where they live in terms of deprivation, we observe a stepwise association: the greater the deprivation the

---

[24] Marmot, *The Marmot Review 10 Years On.*
[25] Bambra and Marmot, *Expert Report for the UK COVID-19 Public Inquiry.*
[26] Ibid.

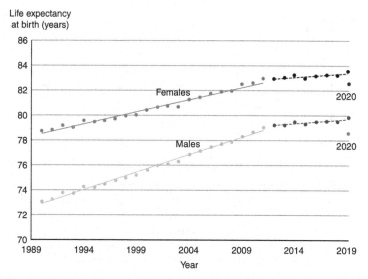

Figure 9.3 Life expectancy at birth by sex, England, 1989 to 2020
Source: Michael Marmot, *Health Equity in England: The Marmot Review 10 Years On* (London: Institute of Health Equity, 2020).

shorter the life expectancy. We lay out below current understanding of the causes of this social gradient in health. Over the decade since 2010, the gradient became steeper, the inequalities greater. These trends are shown in Figure 9.4. These graphs show that inequalities in life expectancy at birth are smaller for women than for men, but that for both men and women, the gap in life expectancy between the least and most deprived quintiles (20 per cent of areas) of deprivation has increased since 2010. Further, life expectancy for both men and women living in the most deprived quintiles flattened out and stopped improving.

These increases in health inequalities are also evident in the other nations of the UK.[27] For example, Figure 9.5 shows that in Scotland, inequalities in life expectancy were also

[27] Ibid.

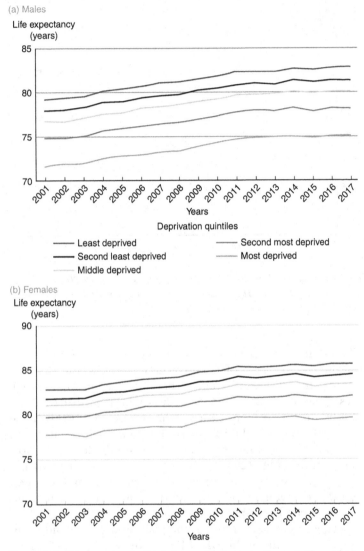

(a) Males

Life expectancy (years)

Years

Deprivation quintiles

— Least deprived
— Second least deprived
— Middle deprived
— Second most deprived
— Most deprived

(b) Females

Life expectancy (years)

Years

Figure 9.4 Life expectancy at birth by area-level deprivation quintiles and sex, England, 2001–17

Source: Michael Marmot, *Health Equity in England: The Marmot Review 10 Years On* (London: Institute of Health Equity, 2020).

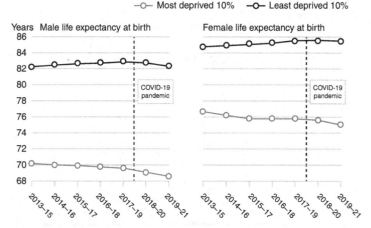

Figure 9.5 Life expectancy at birth by area-level deprivation deciles and sex, Scotland, 2013–15 and 2019–21

Source: David Finch, Heather Wilson and Jo Bibby, *Leave No One Behind: The State of Health and Health Inequalities in Scotland* (London: The Health Foundation, 2023).

widening in the years before the pandemic.[28] Between 2013–15 and 2017–19 the gap in period life expectancy at birth between people living in the least and most deprived 10 per cent of local areas widened by 1 year to 13.3 years for men, and by 1.7 years to 9.8 years for women.

In Figure 9.1, we laid out the contrast between trends in life expectancy in the North East and London. More generally, regional inequalities in health increased in this period. Figure 9.6 compares trends in life expectancy for men and women for the least and most deprived deciles in each region of England for 2010–12 and 2016–18. For both men and women living in the least deprived decile (10 per cent) the regional

[28] David Finch, Heather Wilson and Jo Bibby, *Leave No One Behind: The State of Health and Health Inequalities in Scotland* (London: The Health Foundation, 2023), www.health.org.uk/publications/leave-no-one-behind

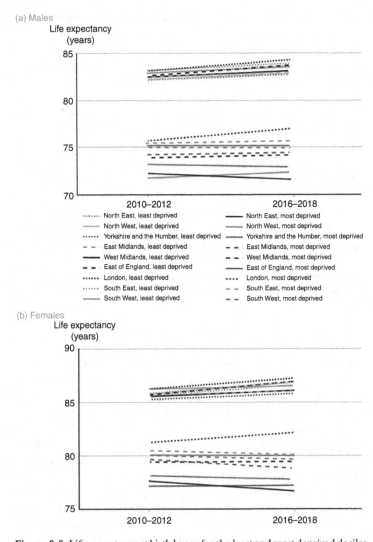

Figure 9.6 Life expectancy at birth by sex for the least and most deprived deciles in each region, England, 2010–12 and 2016–18
Source: Michael Marmot, *Health Equity in England: The Marmot Review 10 Years On* (London: Institute of Health Equity, 2020).

differences are small. For men and women living in the most deprived decile, the regional differences are much bigger. Over the decade, life expectancy for both men and women rose in London but fell in most regions outside London.

The health picture, then, coming into the pandemic was stalling life expectancy, increased regional and deprivation-based health inequalities, and worsening health for the poorest in society.

CAUSES OF HEALTH INEQUALITIES

The causes of such socioeconomic inequalities in health are multifaceted. The scientific consensus is that they are a result of inequalities in the social determinants of health: the conditions in which we are born, grow, live, work and age.[29]

In 2005, the World Health Organisation (WHO) set up the WHO Global Commission on the Social Determinants of Health. The Commission (chaired by MM) was tasked to collect, collate and synthesise global evidence on the social determinants of health and their impact on health inequalities, and to make recommendations for action to address them. It concluded in its 2008 report that health inequalities are driven by socioeconomic inequalities in *growing, living and working conditions; the social and economic policies that shape growing, living, and working; the relative roles of state and market in providing for good and equitable health; and the wide international and global conditions that can help or hinder national and local action for health equity*.[30] These conditions are 'the causes of the causes' and are collectively referred to as the social determinants of health.

Put simply, the social determinants of health are the conditions in which we grow, live, work and age; these, in turn, are driven by inequities in power, money and resources.[31] They are the everyday conditions which influence access to health-enhancing goods and which limit exposure to health-damaging

---

[29] WHO, *Closing the Gap in a Generation.* [30] Ibid., p. vii. [31] Ibid.

risk factors. They include economic resources as they can determine ability to afford, or access, good-quality services, hospitals, schools, transport infrastructure and social care; but they also allow avoidance of harmful circumstances, poor housing, inadequate diet, physical hazards at work and environmental exposures such as air pollution. The social determinants of health also include working conditions, housing and neighbourhood influences, labour market activity including unemployment and welfare receipt, and access to goods and services including health and social care. The social determinants of health are themselves shaped by local, national and international government policies.[32]

Different socioeconomic and ethnic groups are unequally exposed to these health-damaging or health-enhancing factors – resulting in health inequalities. To put it another way, people are not poor because they make poor choices, and the poor health of the poor does not result from poor choices.[33] Rather, it is poverty that leads to unhealthy choices and the poor health of those lower down the social hierarchy results from the restricted range of options available to those on low incomes, as well as the direct health impacts associated with the stresses and poor conditions which result from poverty. As an illustration, the poor diet of people in poverty is, very largely, the result of poverty, not poor choices.[34] So, tackling health inequalities involves tackling social inequalities.[35]

The WHO Commission made recommendations for global application but said that these need to be 'translated' into national contexts. In 2008, the UK Government commissioned MM to conduct a review to consider how the findings and recommendations of the 2008 WHO Global Commission applied to England. The result was the *Marmot Review: Fair Society Healthy Lives*, published in 2010.

Based on the evidence from nine scientific working groups, comprising over eighty experts (including MM and CB), it

---

[32] Ibid.   [33] Marmot, *The Marmot Review 10 Years On*.   [34] Ibid.
[35] Marmot, *The Marmot Review*.

summarised the evidence on the causes of health inequalities – and how to reduce them – in terms of six key social determinants of health:

- *Early child development*: The foundations for virtually every aspect of human development – physical, intellectual and emotional – are laid in early childhood. What happens during these early years, starting in the womb, has lifelong effects on education and economic position and on many aspects of health and well-being – including obesity, heart disease and mental health. There are stark socioeconomic inequalities in childhood with children from lower socioeconomic backgrounds having worse early experiences.
- *Education and lifelong learning*: Inequalities in educational outcomes affect physical and mental health, as well as income, employment and quality of life. There is a strong association between socioeconomic background and educational outcomes: children from deprived areas faring less well than those in the least deprived areas. There are profound implications for subsequent employment, income, living standards, behaviours, and mental and physical health.
- *Employment and working conditions*: Being in good employment is protective of health. Conversely, unemployment contributes to poor health. Patterns of employment both reflect and reinforce the social gradient and there are serious inequalities of access to labour market opportunities. Rates of unemployment are highest among those with no or few qualifications and skills and unemployment is associated with higher mortality rates. Insecure and poor-quality employment is also associated with increased risks of poor physical and mental health.
- *Income and cost of living*: Having insufficient money to lead a healthy life is a highly significant cause of health inequalities. Many households in the UK are below the minimum income needed for adequate nutrition, physical activity, housing, social

interactions, transport, medical care and hygiene. In England there are large gaps between what is needed to afford healthy living and the level of state benefit and work-income that many groups receive.

- *Healthy and sustainable places in which to live and work*: Housing is vital for health, both the characteristics of dwellings and their affordability. Communities are important for physical and mental health and well-being. The physical, economic and social characteristics of communities, and the degree to which they enable and promote healthy behaviours, all make a contribution to social inequalities in health. There is a clear social gradient in 'healthy' community characteristics with more deprived areas faring worse, for example, higher rates of air pollution and lower levels of social cohesion.

- *The social determinants and prevention*: Many of the key health behaviours significant to the development of chronic disease follow the social gradient: smoking, obesity, lack of physical activity and unhealthy nutrition are all higher in more deprived areas. These health behaviours are influenced by the social determinants of health. Smoking, for example, is a social practice which reflects gender roles, social class structures, cultures and income inequalities. The accumulation of experiences a child receives shapes the outcomes and choices they will make when they become adults.

CAUSES OF THE TRENDS IN HEALTH AND HEALTH INEQUALITIES SINCE 2010

Drawing on what we know from the WHO Global Commission and the Marmot Review, in this section we examine how changes in the social determinants of health in the UK since 2010 may have resulted in the worsening health and health inequalities position. We focus on three key areas: austerity; COVID-19; and the cost-of-living crisis. We also consider the impacts of Brexit and the government's levelling-up strategy.

Fourteen Years of Austerity

The Global Financial Crisis of 2007/8 was a result of a downturn in the USA housing market, largely driven by subprime investments, which led to a massive collapse in financial markets across the world. Banks increasingly required state bailouts. For example, in the UK the retail bank Northern Rock was nationalised whilst in the USA Lehman Brothers investment bank filed for bankruptcy and the mortgage companies Freddie Mac and Fannie Mae were given major government bailouts. Stock markets posted massive falls, which continued as the effects in the 'real' economy began to be felt with peak unemployment rates of over 8 per cent in the UK, and over 10 per cent in the USA and the Eurozone. In 2009, the International Monetary Fund (IMF) announced that the global economy was experiencing its worst period for sixty years.[36] The global economic recession continued throughout 2009 and 2010, leading to the moniker the 'Global Financial Crisis'. The Global Financial Crisis was accompanied in the UK, as well as Greece, Portugal and Spain, by escalating public expenditure cuts: austerity. Austerity – reducing budget deficits in economic downturns by decreasing public expenditure and/or increasing taxes – in the UK was characterised by local authority, NHS and welfare expenditure reductions – we discuss these below.

Health Equity in England: The Marmot Review 10 Years On, published in February 2020, looked back on health and health inequalities in the decade after 2010.[37] This report concluded that changes in the social determinants of health, many associated with austerity and other policy changes since 2010, were likely to be the causes of the adverse changes in health and health inequalities in the UK. A study of mortality trends in thirty-seven high-income countries between 2000 and 2019 found that there were slower improvements, or deteriorations,

---

[36] Andrew Gamble, *The Spectre at the Feast: Capitalist Crisis and the Politics of Recession* (London: Bloomsbury, 2009).

[37] See note 22 above.

in life expectancy and mortality trends in most countries after the financial crisis of 2007/8, with the worst trends in England and Wales, Estonia, Iceland, Scotland, Slovenia and the USA.[38] Trends were generally worse for women than men. The study also found that these adverse effects were associated with their measures of austerity, which included public social spending as a percentage of Gross Domestic Product (GDP). The study authors concluded that 'austerity is likely to be a cause of stalled mortality trends'.[39]

All that said, changes in health over time in no way resemble a controlled experiment. It is always challenging to demonstrate causation in these circumstances. We do though have a clear causal model of the social determinants of health, outlined above, and extensive international evidence supporting each piece of the model.[40, 41, 42]

Figure 9.7 shows what happened to public sector expenditure over the period from the global financial crisis, 2008/9, to the first year of the pandemic. The chancellor, George Osborne, said, and still says today, the country had to live within its means. Public sector expenditure was reduced year on year from 42 per cent of GDP to 35 per cent by 2019/20. In the first year of the pandemic, 2020/21, the chancellor, Rishi Sunak, said something quite different: whatever it takes. It is true that the pandemic posed a larger threat to GDP than did the global financial crisis, so perhaps the action taken needed to be stronger. But, in 2010 the threat to the economy was seen as a reason for reducing public sector spending; in 2020 the threat was seen as a reason to increase it. Was austerity a political choice after all, not an economic necessity?

---

[38] Gerry McCartney, Robert McMaster, Frank Popham, Ruth Dundas and David Walsh, 'Is austerity a cause of slower improvements in mortality in high-income countries? A panel analysis', *Social Science and Medicine*, 313 (2022), 115397.

[39] Ibid.   [40] WHO, *Closing the Gap in a Generation*.

[41] Marmot, *The Marmot Review*.

[42] Marmot, *The Marmot Review 10 Years On*.

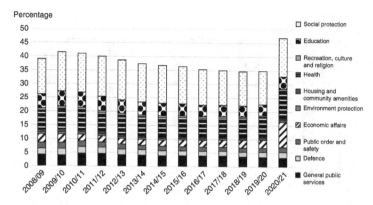

Figure 9.7 Public sector expenditure on services by function as a percentage of GDP 2008/9 to 2020/21
Source: Michael Marmot, *Health Equity in England: The Marmot Review 10 Years On* (London: Institute of Health Equity, 2020).

In the 2010 Marmot Review, we introduced the concept of proportionate universalism. The aim was to combine the typical UK social policy approach of targeting those most in need – means-tested benefits – with a more Nordic approach of universalist policies. The aim was, to coin a phrase, to level up the social gradient: to reduce inequalities by bringing the health of all social groups up towards the high level of the least deprived. Proportionate universalism called for universalist policies with effort proportionate to need.

Figure 9.8 shows spending by local authority by level of deprivation of the area.[43] Total spending per person was reduced by 17 per cent in the least deprived quintile of areas; but by almost twice this – 32 per cent – in the most deprived. What we have here is effort inversely proportionate to need. The greater the deprivation the greater the need, the greater the need the greater the reduction in spending. It is plausible that this could have contributed to the slowdown in improvement in life expectancy, the increase in health inequalities and the decline in life expectancy in the most

---

[43] Marmot, *The Marmot Review 10 Years On.*

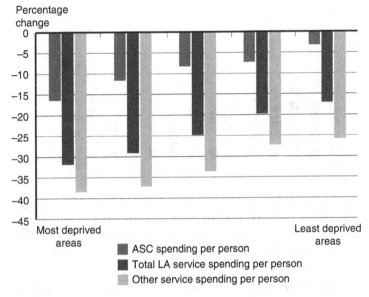

Figure 9.8 Average change in council service spending per person by quintile of Index of Multiple Deprivation average score, 2009/10 to 2017/18
Source: Michael Marmot, *Health Equity in England: The Marmot Review 10 Years On* (London: Institute of Health Equity, 2020).

deprived areas. Indeed, there is evidence for a correlation at local level – the greater the cuts in local government expenditure the greater the adverse effect on life expectancy.[44]

We have stated that the key issues to understanding health inequalities are what happens outside the health service. That said, what happens to the NHS is also important. To understand the funding position, it is best not to listen to what the government is saying: the problems with the NHS are not just about the pandemic, the war in Ukraine, or greedy doctors and nurses. The problems began in 2010. Total amounts spent on the NHS should be adjusted for the growing population and ageing. Health

[44] Alexandros Alexiou, Katie Fahy, Kate Mason et al., 'Local government funding and life expectancies in England: a longitudinal ecological study', *The Lancet Public Health*, 6:9 (2021), e641–e647.

spending per person, adjusted for demographic change grew at 2 per cent a year, under the Conservatives, 1979–97; at 5.7 per cent a year under Labour, 1997–2010; at -0.07 per cent, 2010–15; and at -0.03 per cent, 2015–21.[45] It is notable that Margaret Thatcher declared there's no such thing as society, and increased NHS funding per person by 2 per cent a year. David Cameron declared he wanted to create the Big Society, and he and George Osborne reduced NHS funding per person. Cameron also declared: no more top-down reorganisation of the NHS and, with his health secretary Andrew Lansley, did the opposite. It marked what Chris Ham, former head of the King's Fund, described as the political failure that led to the decline of the NHS.[46]

Other European countries have taken a different approach. If the UK had increased its health care expenditure, 2010–19, as much as France did, we would have increased our current spend by 21 per cent, and by 39 per cent if we had matched Germany.[47] The NHS needs more money. It would help in filling the 150,000 vacant full-time posts and help to reduce the current waiting list of over 7 million patients. Paying doctors and nurses appropriately would help too.

There were substantial changes to the way the benefit system was operated under austerity, reviewed in other chapters. A summary was provided in the IFS Deaton Review of Inequality, Figure 9.9.[48] For working-age households with children, the changes were sharply regressive. Changes to taxes and benefits since 2010 reduced the incomes of the poorest such households by 20 per cent. For the bottom 70 per cent of

---

[45] Chris Ham, *The Rise and Decline of the NHS in England 2000–20* (London: The King's Fund, 2023), www.kingsfund.org.uk/publications/rise-and-decline-nhs-in-england-2000-20

[46] Ibid.

[47] Icaro Rebolledo and Anita Charlesworth, *How Does UK Health Spending Compare across Europe over the Past Decade?* (London: Health Foundation, 2022), www.health.org.uk/news-and-comment/charts-and-infographics/how-does-uk-health-spending-compare-across-europe-over-the-past-decade

[48] Institute for Fiscal Studies (IFS), *Deaton Inequality Review* (London: Institute for Fiscal Studies, 2023), https://ifs.org.uk/inequality/

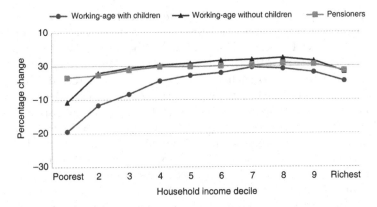

Figure 9.9 Change in net household incomes due to tax and benefit reforms by income, 2010–19

Source: IFS, *Deaton Inequality Review* (London: Institute for Fiscal Studies, 2023).

households, the poorer the household the greater the reduction in income. As many have noted, pensioners were protected – although poverty rates increased amongst pensioners from 2012 and many have been impacted by the cost-of-living crisis.[49] It is difficult to think of any social or economic theory that would justify such a settlement. The default position is that it was driven by political considerations.

Changes to the welfare system, as with cuts to local government spending, had differential impact depending on geography. Research based on Treasury data has suggested that the financial impacts of post-2015 welfare reforms to tax credits, housing benefits and child benefit varied greatly across the country.[50] The UK's older industrial areas (e.g. Middlesbrough) and less prosperous coastal areas (e.g. Blackpool and Great Yarmouth) experienced the largest reductions, whilst more

[49] Helen Barnard, *How Do We Defuse the Pensioner Poverty Time Bomb?* (York: Joseph Rowntree Foundation, 2023), www.jrf.org.uk/blog/how-do-we-def use-pensioner-poverty-time-bomb

[50] Christina Beatty and Stephen Fothergill, *The Uneven Impact of Welfare Reform: The Financial Losses to Places and People* (Sheffield Hallam University Centre

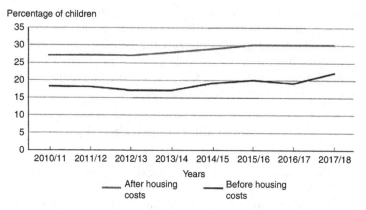

Percentage of children

Figure 9.10 Children living in poverty before and after housing costs in England
Source: Michael Marmot, *Health Equity in England: The Marmot Review 10 Years On* (London: Institute of Health Equity, 2020).

prosperous areas experienced the smallest (e.g. Guildford, Richmond upon Thames and Hart District). This also had a regional impact with the North of England, Scotland, Wales and Northern Ireland faring worse. The higher receipt of benefits and tax credits amongst people living in more deprived areas is why the reforms had a greater financial impact in these places. Likewise, the welfare and local authority cuts also disproportionately impacted on women and people from minority ethnic backgrounds as the former are more likely to be reliant on public services and latter are more likely to live in deprived areas.[51]

One clear effect of changes in the economy and tax and benefits has been the rise in child poverty. The measure most used in international comparisons is one of relative poverty: the

for Regional Economic and Social Research, 2016), https://policy-prac tice.oxfam.org/resources/the-uneven-impact-of-welfare-reform-the-finan cial-losses-to-places-and-people-604630/

[51] Sarah-Marie Hall, Kimberly McIntosh, Eva Neitzert et al., *Intersecting Inequalities: the Impact of Austerity on Black And Ethnic Minority Women in the UK* (London: Runnymede Trust, 2017), www.runnymedetrust.org/publica tions/intersecting-inequalities-the-impact-of-austerity-on-bme-women-in-t he-uk

percentage of children living in households at less than 60 per cent median income. Figure 9.10 shows that, in 2010, it was 18 per cent before housing costs. But housing is a contributor to poverty. After housing costs, 27 per cent of children were in poverty-afflicted households. Over the decade that figure rose to 30 per cent. It is predicted to rise further.

Brexit and Levelling Up

Amid the gloom of these effects of government policy on living conditions came the promises of Brexit, 'taking back control' and the levelling-up strategy.

In a referendum held on 23 June 2016, the majority of those who voted chose to leave the European Union (52 versus 48 per cent). Brexit was promoted by its supporters – which included Boris Johnson and other prominent Conservative politicians – as a way of 'taking back control' with promises of large increases in NHS funding because of a 'Brexit dividend' and a revitalisation of our economy as 'Global Britain'. The process of exiting the EU was protracted and accompanied by deep political discord and uncertainty, the proroguing of parliament and the resignations of two prime ministers – David Cameron and Theresa May. 'Getting Brexit Done' was the central tenet of Boris Johnson's landslide 2019 election win, in which many former Labour strongholds in the North and the Midlands (the 'Red Wall') voted Conservative for the first time. Eventually, on 31 January 2020, the UK left the EU and entered a transition period until 31 December 2020 when the UK eventually left the EU single market and customs union.[52]

The eight-year period after the 'Brexit vote' of June 2016 has been characterised by considerable political instability within the UK government. For example, between June 2016 and November 2023 there were seven secretaries of state for health and social care (Hunt, Hancock, Javid, Barclay, Coffey, Barclay,

[52] Nigel Walker, 'Brexit timeline: events leading to the UK's exit from the European Union', Commons Library Briefing, 6 January 2021, https://commonsli brary.parliament.uk/research-briefings/cbp-7960/

Atkins), seven chancellors of the exchequer (Osborne, Hammond, Javid, Sunak, Zahawi, Kwarteng, Hunt) and five different prime ministers (Cameron, May, Johnson, Truss, Sunak), and we had two general elections within just three years (2017 and 2019). As has been heard multiple times in evidence to the UK Public Inquiry into Covid-19, this political volatility – and the policy focus in Westminster given to 'Brexit' – may have impeded the development of medium to long-term health and social care planning, especially in England, including addressing inequalities in health and care. For example, reform of social care in England had been a feature in both the 2017 and 2019 party-election manifestos but no substantial policies have been enacted.

A further relevant issue is how the UK's impending and actual departure from the European Union may have impacted on immigration into the UK of health and social care workers – exacerbating the workforce crisis and lengthening waiting lists. Data compiled by the House of Commons Library demonstrates that between 2016 and 2020, the proportion of all NHS staff in England from the EU remained stable, at about 5.5 per cent of all staff.[53] This has declined slightly since Brexit in 2020 to 5.3 per cent in 2022. The proportion of EU nurses and health visitors employed in NHS trusts in England has declined more noticeably from 7.4 per cent of staff in 2016 to 5.1 per cent in 2022. Likewise, for hospital doctors there has been a decline from 9.7 per cent in 2016 to 8.1 per cent in 2022. As we noted earlier – there was no post-Brexit increase in the NHS budget.

The third issue is how Brexit may have affected the UK's GDP, economic growth and inequalities within these. Since 2016, the government's Office for Budget Responsibility (OBR) has been regularly analysing the potential effects of Brexit on the economy and public finances. In their March 2020 report, they estimated that in the long term *'the additional trade barriers associated with leaving the EU would reduce the long run [15 years] productivity of the UK by around 4 per cent'* in comparison to what would have happened if we had not

---

[53] Carl Baker, *'NHS staff from overseas: statistics'*, Commons Library Briefing, 20 November 2023, https://researchbriefings.files.parliament.uk/documents/CBP-7783/CBP-7783.pdf

left the EU. They estimated that between 1.0 and 1.4 per cent of this reduction in productivity had already occurred between 2016 and 2020.[54] These declines in the UK economy are likely to be unequally experienced. Analysis conducted in 2019 by economists from the CAGE Research Centre, University of Warwick, found that '*the economic costs of the Brexit-vote are both sizable and far from evenly distributed*'.[55] Areas of the country that had a larger manufacturing sector and a larger number of low-skilled workers in the labour force (North East of England, London, Scotland and the South East) were most likely to experience reductions in growth. A 2018 Treasury report also acknowledges that '*the UK's exit from the EU will affect the regions and nations of the UK differently*'.[56] Some – but not all – of the areas and regions of the country estimated to be most negatively economically impacted by Brexit already had some of the worst economic and health outcomes in the country (e.g. the North East of England has the lowest life expectancy of all English regions and Scotland has the lowest life expectancy of the four UK nations), so it is possible that Brexit – in the long run – *may* exacerbate health inequalities by increasing economic inequalities.

The levelling-up commitment was a central tenet of the 2019 election. It was eventually fleshed out in the Levelling-Up White Paper published in February 2022.[57] It includes a commitment

[54] Office for Budget Responsibility, 'The effect of productivity on leaving the EU', March 2020, https://obr.uk/box/the-effect-on-productivity-of-leaving-the-eu/

[55] Thiemo Fetzer and Shizhuo Wang, *Measuring the Regional Economic Cost of Brexit: Evidence up to 2019* (Warwick: CAGE Research Centre, 2020), https://warwick.ac.uk/fac/soc/economics/research/centres/cage/manage/publications/wp486.2020.pdf

[56] HM Government, 'EU Exit: Long-term economic analysis', November 2018, p. 26, https://assets.publishing.service.gov.uk/government/uploads/system/uploads/attachment_data/file/760484/28_November_EU_Exit_-_Long-term_economic_analysis__1_.pdf

[57] Department for Levelling Up, Housing and Communities, *Levelling Up the United Kingdom* (2022), www.gov.uk/government/publications/levelling-up-the-united-kingdom

to narrow the gap between areas with highest and lowest life expectancy by 2030 and increase healthy life expectancy overall by five years by 2035. The strategy encompasses a series of new funding streams (e.g. regional investment funds, the Levelling-Up Fund, Towns Fund, Community Renewal Fund and Shared Prosperity Fund) alongside changes to existing funding to focus resources on areas outside London and the Southeast. The levelling-up budget in the White Paper was £4.8 billion over four years. By contrast, as the White Paper points out, when Germany 'levelled up' – incorporating the former Communist German Democratic Republic into the Federal Republic – they spent the equivalent of £70 billion a year for twenty-five years. The large health gap between the East and the West was closed in a generation.[58] But the UK levelling-up budget is an order of magnitude too small to make a difference.

Another flagship Conservative policy push – and integrated into levelling up – has been to raise educational standards across the country. However, as we show in the *Marmot Review 10 Years On*, there is still a clear and persistent social gradient in educational attainment: the higher the level of deprivation, the lower the proportion of children with five or more GCSEs at grades A–C*.[59] Figure 9.11 shows that nearly 17 per cent more children from the least deprived decile had an educational achievement of five or more GCSEs than those from the most deprived decile in 2016.

Another assessment of attainment at age 16 is the Attainment 8 score, which measures pupils' performance in eight GCSE-level qualifications. Figure 9.12 shows significant inequalities related to eligibility for free school meals and ethnicity. For each ethnic group described, those eligible for free school meals do worse but there are different levels of attainment related to ethnicity with Chinese, Asian and mixed ethnic background children scoring higher than average.

[58] Clare Bambra, *Health Divides: Where You Live Can Kill You* (Bristol: Policy Press, 2016).

[59] Marmot, *The Marmot Review 10 Years On*.

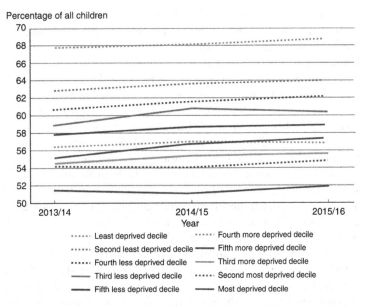

Percentage of all children

······ Least deprived decile	······ Fourth more deprived decile	
······ Second least deprived decile	■■■■ Fifth more deprived decile	
······ Fourth less deprived decile	■■■■ Third more deprived decile	
■■■■ Third less deprived decile	······ Second most deprived decile	
■■■■ Fifth less deprived decile	■■■■ Most deprived decile	

Figure 9.11 Percentage of all children aged 15–16 achieving five or more GCSEs at grades A*–C, by local authority deprivation deciles, England, 2013–16
Source: Michael Marmot, *Health Equity in England: The Marmot Review 10 Years On* (London: Institute of Health Equity, 2020).

These inequalities in educational outcomes are closely related to a range of socioeconomic inequalities that children and their families experience. As noted earlier, key indicators of children's well-being such as poverty have worsened over the last fourteen years.

Then Came the Pandemic . . .

At the onset of the pandemic, we quoted Albert Camus's *La Peste*: 'the pestilence is at once blight and revelation. It brings the hidden truth of a corrupt world to the surface.'[60] Corrupt

---

[60] Michael Marmot and Jessica Allen, '*COVID-19: exposing and amplifying inequalities*', *Journal of Epidemiology and Community Health*, 74 (2020), 681–2.

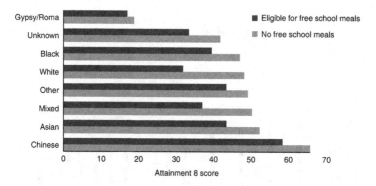

Figure 9.12 Average Attainment 8 score, by ethnicity and free school meal eligibility, England 2017/18
Source: Michael Marmot, *Health Equity in England: The Marmot Review 10 Years On* (London: Institute of Health Equity, 2020).

world is perhaps a bit strong, but we did say that the pandemic would reveal the underlying inequalities in health in society and amplify them. And so it proved.

The social gradient in all-cause mortality is clear in Figure 9.13, the greater the level of deprivation of the area of residence, the higher the mortality rate. There is a similar social gradient in mortality from Covid-19. The gradient is slightly steeper for Covid: higher mortality rates in the most deprived groups because of exposure in overcrowded households and working in front-line occupations as well as from having higher rates of underlying poor health such as diabetes. Indeed, we have called the Covid-19 pandemic a 'syndemic' because of the synergistic way in which the disease interacted with and exacerbated existing social, economic and health inequalities.[61, 62] The implications, though, are clear. Important as specific

[61] Clare Bambra, Ryan Riordan, John Ford and Fiona Matthews 'The COVID-19 pandemic and health inequalities', *Journal of Epidemiology and Community Health*, 174(2020), 964–8.

[62] Marmot and Allen, 'COVID-19: exposing and amplifying inequalities'.

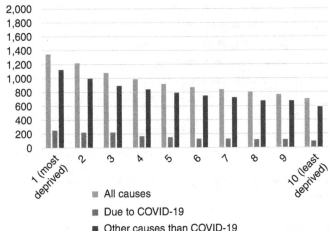

(a) Female
Age-standardised mortality rate (per 100,000)

■ All causes
■ Due to COVID-19
■ Other causes than COVID-19

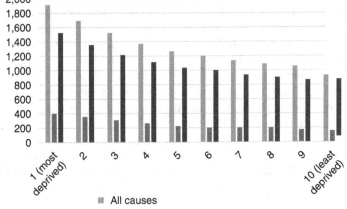

(b) Male
Age-standardised mortality rate (per 100,000)

■ All causes
■ Due to COVID-19
■ Other causes than COVID-19

Figure 9.13 Age-standardised mortality rates from all causes, COVID-19 and other causes per 100,000 by sex and deprivation deciles, England from March 2020 to April 2021

Source: Michael Marmot, *Build Back Fairer: The COVID-19 Marmot Review* (2020), www.health.org.uk/publications/build-back-fairer-the-covid-19-marmot-review

control of the virus is – vaccination, social distancing, test and trace – it is also urgent to deal with inequalities.[63]

A striking effect of the pandemic was its revelation of ethnic inequalities in health. Covid mortality was particularly high in people classified as Black Caribbean, Black African, Bangladeshi, Pakistani and, to a lesser extent, Indian. Official data examining Covid-19 deaths from wave 1 (March 2020 to July 2020), published by the Office for National Statistics, found that the age-adjusted mortality rate per 100,000 for people from a white ethnic background was around 107 per 100,000; for Indian 175; for Pakistani 200; for Black Caribbean it was 270; for Bangladeshi 271; and for Black African it was 288.[64] So, Covid-19 deaths were more than 60 per cent higher amongst our minority ethnic communities during the first wave. The virus fed off pre-existing inequalities.

As with austerity, there were also geographical inequalities in deaths from Covid-19. This is shown by English region in Figure 9.14. The death rates were higher in the urban areas of London and the West Midlands and in the North of England – 17 per cent higher in the three northern regions compared to the rest of England.[65]

A pandemic is a large external shock to society. That it should amplify inequalities is consistent with the effects of other external shocks.

Hurricane Maria was a deadly Category 5 hurricane that devastated the northeastern Caribbean in September 2017, particularly Dominica, Saint Croix and Puerto Rico. It is regarded as the worst natural disaster in recorded history to affect those

---

[63] Bambra and Marmot, *Expert Report for the UK COVID-19 Public Inquiry.*

[64] Office for National Statistics, 'Updating ethnic contrasts in deaths involving the coronavirus (COVID-19), England and Wales: deaths occurring 2 March to 28 July 2020', www.ons.gov.uk/peoplepopulationandcommu nity/birthsdeathsandmarriages/deaths/articles/updatingethniccontrast sindeathsinvolvingthecoronaviruscovid19englandandwales/deathsoccur ring2marchto28july2020#age-standardised-rates-of-death-involving-covid-1 9-by-ethnic-group

[65] Bambra et al., *Northern Exposure.*

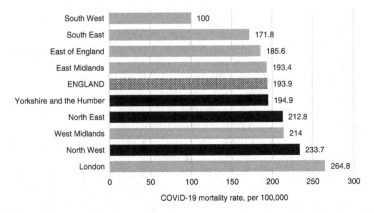

Figure 9.14 Deaths from Covid-19 by English region, March 2020 – March 2021*

*The three regions in the north are coloured black. The remaining six regions in the rest of England are coloured grey. The English average in shown as a hashed bar.

Source: Clare Bambra, Luke Munford, Sam Khavandi and Natalie Bennett, *Northern Exposure: COVID-19 and Regional Inequalities in Health and Wealth* (Bristol: Policy Press, 2023).

islands. Maria brought catastrophic devastation to the impacted areas, destroying housing stock and infrastructure beyond repair. Total monetary losses are estimated at upwards of $90 billion (2017 USD), mostly in Puerto Rico. Maria's total death toll is 3,059. The George Washington University Milken Institute School of Public Health assessed Maria's impact in Puerto Rico. Excess mortality due to Hurricane Maria is estimated at 2,975 excess deaths.[66] The impact differed by age and socioeconomic conditions: risk of death was around 45 per cent higher for populations living in low socioeconomic municipalities than those in more developed areas.

---

[66] The George Washington University Milken Institute School of Public Health, *Ascertainment of the Estimated Excess Mortality from Hurricane María in Puerto Rico* (2018), https://prstudy.publichealth.gwu.edu/

Past pandemics have also been deeply unequal. In 1918, the world experienced a global pandemic comparable in scale to Covid-19. The 'Spanish flu' pandemic swept across the globe in three waves, infecting 500 million people – a third of the world's population – leading to an estimated 50–100 million deaths with rates particularly high in war-ravaged Europe.[67] Historians have demonstrated that there were clear socioeconomic and geographical inequalities in the impact of the Spanish flu pandemic. Infection and death rates were substantially higher in less affluent neighbourhoods; amongst the working classes and lower-paid workers; and in urban areas.[68] The most affluent London borough, Kensington, had the lowest death rate from the Spanish flu (340 per 100,000 people) whilst St Pancras, the poorest borough, had the highest (620 per 100,000 people).[69] USA research also found that Black Americans were more likely to die if infected (case-fatality rate).[70] In England and Wales, there were notable geographical inequalities with Wales, the North of England and the Midlands having higher death rates than the South of England.[71] At the extremes, the highest death rate in Hebburn near Newcastle in the North East of England (1,194 per 100,000) was six times that of the lowest in Sutton in Surrey in the southeast of England (188 per 100,000). These regional inequalities were noted at the time, with the Registrar

---

[67] Niall P. A. S. Johnson and Juergen Mueller, 'Updating the accounts: global mortality of the 1918–1920 "Spanish" influenza pandemic', *Bulletin of the History of Medicine*, 76:1 (2002), 105–15.

[68] Svenn-Erik Mamelund, Clare Shelley-Egan and Ole Rogeberg, 'The association between socioeconomic status and pandemic influenza: systematic review and meta-analysis', *PLOS One*, 16:9 (2021), e0244346.

[69] Niall Johnson, *Britain and the 1918-19 Influenza Pandemic: A Dark Epilogue* (London: Routledge, 2006).

[70] Helene Økland and Svenn-Erik Mamelund 'Race and 1918 influenza pandemic in the United States: a review of the literature', *International Journal of Environmental Research and Public Health*, 16:14 (2019), 2487.

[71] Clare Bambra, Paul Norman and Niall Johnson, 'Visualising regional inequalities in the 1918 Spanish flu pandemic in England and Wales', *Environment and Planning A: Economy and Space*, 53:4 (2021), 607–11.

General (the top government official for medical statistics) commenting in 1920 that 'the northern parts of the country suffered decidedly more, on the whole, than the southern'.[72]

The Covid-19 Public Inquiry will keep many of us occupied during its years-long duration (MM and CB are expert witnesses).[73] So far, its hearings have thrown up ample evidence of chaos at the heart of government. It suggests that the pandemic was poorly managed in the UK. Evidence bears this out. American colleagues have looked not just at Covid, but at life expectancy in 2019, 2020 and 2021 in the US and nineteen other countries; see Figure 9.15.

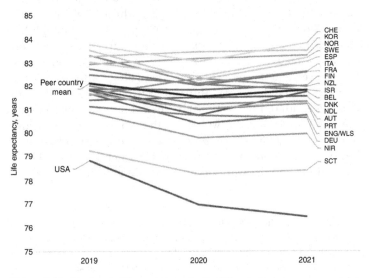

Figure 9.15 Changes in life expectancy in the US and nineteen peer countries, 2019 to 2021
Source: Steven H. Woolf, Ryab K. Masters and Laudan Y. Aron, 'Changes in life expectancy between 2019 and 2020 in the US and 21 peer countries', *JAMA Network Open*, 5:4 (2022), e227067.

---

[72] 'Registrar-General's eighty-first annual report', *The Lancet*, 196:5055 (1920), 148–9.

[73] Bambra and Marmot, *Expert Report for the UK COVID-19 Public Inquiry*.

In the US, life expectancy declined in 2020 and 2021, the first two years of the pandemic. The 'peer countries' that did worst during these two years of the pandemic, after the US, were Scotland, Northern Ireland, Germany and England and Wales.

It will be noted from earlier in the chapter that in the decade prior to the pandemic the two big countries with the slowest improvement in life expectancy were the US and the UK. Now we see that these countries had among the worst health performance during the pandemic. Why?

We speculate that the link, between ill-health pre-pandemic and management of the pandemic, could happen at four levels. First is poor governance and political culture – a decade of austerity with its damaging effects on health and health inequalities; and since the Brexit referendum in 2016, five prime ministers, seven chancellors … Second, increased social and economic inequalities, documented above. Third, disinvestment from public services, done in a regressive way. Fourth, we were not a very healthy – or happy – country coming into the pandemic.

The Cost-of-Living Crisis

The fourth recommendation in the Marmot Reviews was that everyone should have at least the minimum income necessary for a healthy life. The post-pandemic cost-of-living crisis will, of course, have greater effects on those at or below the poverty threshold. It is likely this will have adverse effects on health, and it is readily predictable that health inequalities will be increased.

The cost-of-living crisis – characterised by a volatile economy, high inflation including rising food and energy prices, and interest rate increases which threaten a housing crisis – is putting considerable pressure on household budgets across the country. As a result, child poverty rates – which had already been increasing in more deprived parts of the country since 2010 – have increased further.[74] The high cost of energy – even with the government's Energy Price

---

[74] Loughborough University, *Child Poverty Data* (2022) https://endchildpov erty.org.uk/child-poverty/

Guarantee – has pulled more households into fuel poverty. The government's own figures show that 13.4 per cent of households were experiencing fuel poverty in 2022 – up from 13.1 per cent in 2021.[75] There are also concerns that increased housing costs could lead to a wave of home repossessions, evictions and more homelessness. Falling consumer spending and rising business costs have contributed to record business closures.[76]

A recent report from the Joseph Rowntree Foundation (JRF) on destitution showed that in the UK, in 2022, 2.8 million adults were in a state of destitution and 1 million children. That number of destitute children was a nearly threefold increase from 2017.[77] They also found that destitution was highest in London, the North East and the North West of England. Destitution was defined as, in the last month, going without at least two of: adequate shelter, heat, light, food, appropriate clothing for the conditions, and toiletries for personal hygiene. In addition to the physical effects on health of these basics, the stress of such destitution will further damage the mental and physical health of children and adults.

Destitution and poverty restrict people's ability to cover their basic needs and support their children. As shown in the Marmot Reviews, children in poverty, on average, live for almost ten years less than those who grow up in affluence, and spend twenty years less in good health. They are also much less likely to do well at school and are, in turn, less likely to be employed.[78] Poverty is

---

[75] Department for Energy Security and Net Zero, 'Annual fuel poverty statistics' (2023). https://assets.publishing.service.gov.uk/government/uploads/system/uploads/attachment_data/file/1139133/annual-fuel-poverty-statistics-lilee-report-2023-2022-data.pdf

[76] Katharine Swindells, 'Business closures outnumber business creations in the UK by record levels', City Monitor, 11 May 2023, https://citymonitor.ai/economy/business-closures-outnumber-business-creations-by-record-levels

[77] Peter Matejic, *The Geography of Destitution 2023* (York: Joseph Rowntree Foundation, 2023), www.jrf.org.uk/report/geography-destitution-2023

[78] Kate Pickett and David Taylor-Robinson, *Child of the North: Building a Fairer Future after COVID-19* (Northern Health Sciences Alliance and N8, 2021), www.thenhsa.co.uk/app/uploads/2022/01/Child-of-the-North-Report-FINAL-1.pdf

associated with lower-quality diets leading to higher rates of obesity and other forms of malnutrition, worse mental health and in the longer-term hypertension, diabetes and cardiovascular disease.[79] As increasing numbers of people experience fuel poverty, the resulting damp and cold may increase respiratory and circulatory conditions, cardiovascular disease, mental ill health and excess winter deaths.[80] People with chronic conditions – who are already more likely to live in poverty – may well see their health problems exacerbated. This could increase pressure on overstretched NHS services. Rising rates of debt may well increase the incidence of poor mental health, as people experiencing debt are twice as likely to experience anxiety or depression.[81] Even the threat of eviction or home repossession can increase the risk of depression, anxiety, psychological distress and suicide, and people experiencing homelessness have an average age of death of just 52 years.[82, 83]

With many more people unable to meet their basic needs of food, shelter and heat, the prevalence of these public health risks will increase. The crisis is also deeply unequal as it will especially impact on low-income families, more deprived and

[79] Zoe Bell, Steph Scott, Shelina Visram et al., 'Experiences and perceptions of nutritional health and wellbeing amongst food insecure women in Europe: a qualitative meta-ethnography', *Social Science & Medicine*, 311 (2022), 15313.

[80] Alice Lee, Ian Sinha, Tammy Boyce, Jessica Allen and Peter Goldblatt, *Fuel Poverty, Cold Homes and Health Inequalities in the UK* (London: Institute of Health Equity, 2022), www.instituteofhealthequity.org/resources-reports/fuel-poverty-cold-homes-and-health-inequalities-in-the-uk/read-the-report.pdf

[81] Petros Skapinakis, Scott Weich, Glyn Lewis, Nicola Singleton and Ricardo Araya, 'Socio-economic position and common mental disorders: Longitudinal study in the general population in the UK', *The British Journal of Psychiatry*, 189:2 (2006), 109–17.

[82] Hugo Vásquez-Vera, Laia Palència, Ingrid Magna, Carlos Mena, Jaime Neira and Carme Borrell, 'The threat of home eviction and its effects on health through the equity lens: a systematic review', *Social Science & Medicine*, 175 (2017), 199–208.

[83] Robert W. Aldridge, Dee Menezes, Dan Lewer et al., 'Causes of death among homeless people: a population-based cross-sectional study of linked hospitalisation and mortality data in England', *Wellcome Open Research*, 4:49 (2019), https://doi.org/10.12688/wellcomeopenres.15151.1

minoritised communities, and those parts of the country – disproportionately located in London and the North of England – already experiencing above average levels of poverty, unemployment and poor health.[84]

A *Guardian* report revealed the differential impact of the cost of living on the conditions of life, depending on income.[85] In the UK, as in France, the richest 10 per cent of households spend around 6 per cent of their household budgets on energy. In France, the poorest 10 per cent spend about 10 per cent of their budgets on energy. In the UK, the figure is nearly 18 per cent. This gap, between rich and poor, in the amount spent on energy is larger in the UK than in any of the other European countries listed. The UK is not a good place to be poor.

The majority of people in a state of destitution are in receipt of welfare benefits. The Trussell Trust and JRF produced a report on essentials: food, utilities, vital household goods, but excluding rent and council tax. They calculated that Universal Credit covers about 70 per cent of these essentials.[86] The implication is that individuals and families who rely on Universal Credit are at high risk of preventable illness.

It means that government policy could improve the situation at a stroke, provided calls for tax cuts were not heeded. In addition to the dire situation of people on benefits, most people below the poverty line are in households where at least one adult is working. We have a low-wage economy. That situation, too, could be improved by a government policy of increasing the level and spread of a real living wage. Improving Universal Credit and pension rates, expanding housing benefit, providing targeted energy cost support for vulnerable households and taking stronger action on child poverty could mitigate the extent to which the cost-of-living crisis does become a health and health inequalities crisis.

[84] Bambra et al., *Northern Exposure.*

[85] 'Percentage of household budget spent on energy, 2022, top 10 countries', *Guardian* (based on IMF data), 1 September 2022.

[86] Joseph Rowntree Foundation and Trussell Trust, *Guarantee our Essentials: Reforming Universal Credit to Ensure We Can All Afford the Essentials in Hard Times,* 27 February 2023. www.jrf.org.uk/social-security/guarantee-our-essentials

AN ACCOUNTING OF THE LAST FOURTEEN YEARS:
UNHEALTHY AND UNEQUAL

Whenever he was asked in parliament about the NHS being starved of funding, David Cameron as prime minister had three stock responses: we have protected NHS funding; look at Wales; and a strong economy enables us to fund the health service. As shown above, the first is wrong. The second is irrelevant. What about the third?

There are numerous ways to look at how well the British economy did, after the global financial crisis, compared to other countries. A report in the *Financial Times* gives the lie to the boast that whatever pain was caused, it was worth it to get economic recovery. [87] Real wages in the UK showed a steeper decline post 2010 than in all other peer countries. They are lower today than eighteen years ago.

If the supposed justification for austerity was to get the economy in good shape, after the global financial crisis, so that society could begin to function again, it didn't work. We had a slow economic recovery; crumbling public services – with funding reduced in a regressive way; slowed health improvement; increased health inequalities; and declining health for the poorest people. The current cost of living crisis and levels of destitution suggest that these adverse effects are continuing.

If, as we propose in this chapter, we measure the last fourteen years in terms of the government's performance in terms of the health of the population then it has been fourteen years of failure. Austerity, poor performance in the pandemic, and an inadequate response to the suffering being caused by the cost-of-living crisis means that the UK's stalling life expectancy, declining health of the poorest and increasing health inequalities, is this government's legacy.

---

[87] 'Record wage drop signals more cost of living pain for UK households', *Financial Times*, 16 August 2022, www.ft.com/content/28f2b344-e2a6-4e10-bf4a-c924660eded0

10

Science

Jon Agar

INTRODUCTION

Science and central, national political structures are the two greatest modern institutional forms of authority. They can sometimes align and sometimes clash. Science and technology policy has, in the UK, been seen since the twentieth century as an important lever to encourage innovation and ultimately economic growth. Some of the most challenging issues facing politicians depend, partly, on scientific understanding and advice. This chapter reviews and assesses the experience of policy-for-science and science-for-policy under the Coalition and Conservative administrations. It is a pattern of modified continuity and the articulation of the possibility of radical change. While there were instances of effective political leadership, especially in the more settled early 2010s, ultimately both, in ways that will be described, were undermined by the tumultuous events of Brexit and Covid.

WHAT WAS UK SCIENCE BEFORE 2010?

During the Cold War the UK had spent about half of its R&D budget on defence. This proportion had declined since 1990 and just before the 2010 election expenditure on research and development stood at over a £25 billion, less than 2 per cent of GDP, with defence research forming only

Background interviews with George Freeman, Greg Clark, David Willetts and Mark Walport assisted the author in writing this chapter.

a tenth of the effort.[1] The spending on science had gently increased under New Labour, although not at the same pace as the rest of the economy. In relative terms the UK spent much less on research than the United States, Japan and Israel, and just shy of the Organisation for Economic Co-operation and Development (OECD) average. In proportional terms other industrialised nations, therefore, spent more of their GDP on science, but not by much, and some – such as Italy and Canada – spent less. The UK science budget was weak but unexceptional for an economy of its type.

The other major shift from the late twentieth century was the proportion carried out by private rather than public funds. Two-thirds of research in Britain by the first decade of the twenty-first century was funded and performed by business enterprises.[2] Only three UK companies spent over a billion pounds on research – GlaxoSmithKline, AstraZeneca and BT – and only the first two would be found on a global list of the top twenty-five business enterprises by research spending, reflecting the distinctive prominence of the pharmaceutical sector.[3] There was a very long tail of smaller companies. Of the remainder of UK research, only a quarter was performed in universities. Again there was an uneven concentration, with high investment in the so-called 'golden triangle' of Cambridge, Oxford and London. In general then, when we think of 'typical' scientific research in early twenty-first-century Britain we should think of private-funded research

[1] Gross domestic expenditure on R&D (2008). Office of National Statistics, SET statistics (accessed at www.statistics.gov.uk/pdfdir/gerd0310.pdf, 10 October 2023).

[2] Gross domestic expenditure on R&D (Total GERD) 2008, according to the sector carrying out the work, Office of National Statistics, SET statistics (accessed at www.statistics.gov.uk/pdfdir/gerd0310.pdf, 10 October 2023).

[3] Department for Business, Innovation & Skills (BIS), *2009 R&D Scoreboard* (London: Department of Business, Innovation and Skills, 2009), 'Top 25 UK companies by R&D expenditure' and 'Top 25 global companies by R&D expenditure'. GlaxoSmithKline and AstraZeneca were ranked twenty-first and twenty-fourth respectively.

performed in a medium or even small enterprise.[4] In contrast, what we tend to think of when picturing UK science, misleadingly, are the prestigious research universities and the biggest research-intensive corporations.

Furthermore, the linkage between private and public science had been decisively reshaped, almost severed, late in the Thatcher administration. Whereas previously an informal industrial strategy pumped money into promising areas of research, from around 1986 a crucial shift disfavoured such 'near market' research.[5] The argument, which stemmed from the Number 10 Policy Unit, was a Thatcherite one: public money disincentivised private companies from making their own, market-led investments in science. There should be no more picking winners. Only by government stepping aside would the private innovators and entrepreneurs step up. The ending of near-market research was accompanied, deliberately, by a celebration of pure science, now branded as 'curiosity-driven' research.[6] The Royal Society and research-intensive universities had applauded. The end of the Cold War, which had justified pump-priming science through funding military R&D, pushed in the same direction. The result was an impoverished role for the state as a supporter of innovation. It would be two decades before talk of a science-based 'industrial strategy' returned, as we shall see.

But 'science' is more than 'research'. Around 2010 the total science workforce was calculated to be over 6 million employees, around a fifth of the UK total.[7] As broadly defined, this workforce included roles such as health professionals, science teachers, environmental health officers, civil and mechanical

---

[4] Twenty-seven per cent of the scientific workforce worked in firms of 500 or more; the majority therefore worked in smaller firms. Royal Society, *A Picture of the UK Scientific Workforce. Diversity Data Analysis for the Royal Society. Summary Report* (London: Royal Society, 2014), p. 21.

[5] Jon Agar, *Science Policy under Thatcher* (London: UCL Press, 2019), pp. 88-99.

[6] Jon Agar, '2016 Wilkins-Bernal-Medawar lecture: The curious history of curiosity-driven research', *Notes and Records of the Royal Society*, 71:4 (2017), 409–29.

[7] Royal Society, *A Picture of the UK Scientific Workforce*, p. 19.

engineers or in nature conservation. A core of just over one million people worked in occupations defined as 'primary science workers', in which the consistent application of scientific knowledge and skills was central.[8] Members of this core group were relatively more likely to be male than female, and possess higher levels of formal qualifications as well as socioeconomic status than the non-science workforce.[9] Despite its size and distinct character, the 'science workforce' has not been regarded or targeted as a significant political demographic. Politicians have not made it a priority to secure the science 'vote'.

The politics of science, therefore, was not so much a matter of public debate and elections as of decision-making and govern-ance internal to the state. Within Whitehall, departmentally, sci-ence has moved back and forth between being placed with education or with industry. Ministers responsible for science have mostly, in our period, but not always, had Cabinet rank. A useful distinction can be made between 'science-for-policy', the many ways that scientific understanding and advice underpins policy on a wide range of areas and issues, and 'policy-for science', the decisions and choices made by government that guide science funding and shape the science sector. The Coalition and Conservative governments from 2010, like their predecessors, faced many science-for-policy issues. The scientific advice for the policies during the Covid pandemic was perhaps the outstanding example, in which despite the claims to be 'following the science', scientific advice was one input among many that had to be con-sidered as choices were made.[10] In terms of policy-for-science, the

---

[8] Ibid., p. 12.   [9] Ibid., pp. 22, 24.

[10] The sheer scale of the Covid challenge nearly overwhelmed the science-for-policy processes, as discussed below. This situation was despite the fact that the systems for provision of scientific advice around emergent diseases had been significantly strengthened prior to 2020, and tested against the threats of ebola, influenza and MERS, especially in the 2010s under the GCSA Mark Walport. Walport told the Covid inquiry it was his 'opinion that in the area of natural hazards, health was amongst the best prepared areas in relation to access to strong scientific evidence and an exceptional array of scientific advisory groups' ('UK Covid-19 Inquiry. Witness statement of Sir

Conservative administrations after 2010 inherited and largely continued the approach that had been decisively shaped under Thatcher and had continued under Major, Blair and Brown.[11]

The relationships between policy advisers and politicians were nevertheless important. Internal advice was channelled through the system of scientific advisers, headed by a government chief scientific adviser (GCSA). In our period there were four GCSAs: the population biologist John Beddington (2008–13), the medical scientist Mark Walport (2013–17), both academics who had come from Imperial College, the previous head of research at GSK Patrick Vallance (2018–23), and the Oxford mathematical biologist Angela McLean (2023 onwards).[12] The GCSA worked from a unit – the Government Office of Science, or GO-Science – supported by staff. External advice came from many sources, including academics, think tanks, business, campaigning organisations and learned societies. One major, traditional conduit was the Royal Society, led by its president, always an accomplished scientist. In our period the three presidents of the Royal Society were Paul Nurse, who was also head of the new, flagship London biomedical Crick Institute (2010–15), the Cambridge molecular biologist Venki Ramakrishnan (2015–20), and the statistician and head of another new London science flagship, the Alan Turing Institute, Adrian Smith (2020–5).

SCIENCE UNDER CAMERON (AND CLEGG)

Even before the 2010 general election, the financial crisis of 2008 left many countries, including the UK, with a hole in public

Mark Walport FRS', 8 April 2023, p. 25). In 'smaller' emergencies, such as the response to the disruption caused by the Eyjafjallajökull volcano in Iceland to UK air travel in 2010 and the UK decision-making following the Fukushima nuclear accident in Japan in 2011, scientific advice and the response of politicians seems to have been fast and effective.

[11] Kieron Flanagan, David Edgerton, Claire Craig, Sabine Clarke and Jon Agar, *Lessons from the History of UK Science Policy* (London: British Academy, 2019).

[12] Chris Whitty served as interim GSCA between 2017 and 2018.

finances. In 2009 Brown's government had signalled the likelihood of cuts in public expenditure, including research and £950 million from university budgets.[13] With the economy failing to improve, the next decade and a half would witness cycles of threatened cuts, the mobilisation of opposition, limited reprieves and a resumption of the cycle. In the election campaign of 2010, Labour made a few minimal offerings to scientists (postponing, perhaps, the onerous evaluation of academic research), while the Liberal Democrats possessed more appeal, not least via their Oxford West and Abingdon MP Evan Harris, regarded by the scientific community as one of its own.[14] The Conservatives offered no reassurances. In 2010 the new coalition government under Cameron and Clegg, perhaps partly because Harris lost his seat, indicated, like Brown's Labour, that cuts would have to be found.

The ministry responsible for science, the Department of Innovation, Business and Skills, asked research councils to model three scenarios, in which science funding was either kept flat (still, with albeit minimal inflation, a real-terms reduction), or cut by 10 or 20 per cent. Word soon leaked out.[15] The Royal Society and the Campaign for Science and Engineering (CaSE), a lobbying group that had been born out of the fierce opposition to Thatcher's public sector cuts of the mid 1980s, led the fight. The Royal Society's argument, evidenced in its earlier report *The Scientific Century*, for example, was that UK science was not only international, but internationally outstanding, with the UK producing proportionately more, higher-cited research papers than its peers, while such excellence in pure science was the eventual, if unpredictable, spring of innovation.[16] According

---

[13] Geoff Brumfiel, 'Debt crisis threatens UK science', *Nature*, 463 (28 January 2010), pp. 410–11.

[14] Geoff Brumfiel, 'High stakes for science in UK election', *Nature*, 464 (29 April 2010), pp. 1254–5.

[15] Richard Van Noorden, 'UK government warned over "catastrophic" cuts', *Nature*, 466 (22 July 2010), pp. 420–1.

[16] Royal Society, *The Scientific Century: Securing our Future Prosperity* (London: Royal Society, March 2010).

to the Royal Society, a special case for protection, therefore, existed for (pure) science. At a press conference hastily convened alongside university heads and other science organisations, Martin Rees, the astronomer and outgoing president of the Royal Society, summarised a submission to the Treasury and spoke in apocalyptic terms:

> 'Constant cash' – a reduction in real terms – 'could be accommodated', a ten per cent cut termed 'slash and burn' would have 'serious consequences', and a 20 per cent cut which they say would mean 'game over' for British science.[17]

As was the case during the cuts under Thatcher, a grassroots campaign emerged to oppose reductions in the science budget. Founded by cell biologist Jennifer Rohn, the Science is Vital campaign organised a petition that gathered 20,000 signatures and held a rally outside the Treasury in October 2010. Protestors, many in white coats, heard speeches from Dr Evan Harris, author Simon Singh and activist-medic Ben Goldacre, among others, and waved placards with slogans such as 'Science – it beats living in a cave' and 'No more Dr Nice Guy'.[18]

In George Osborne's austerity budget of October 2010, scientists were relieved to hear that science funding would be 'ring-fenced'. It seemed to be a victory for UK scientists and their supporters. David Willetts, science minister, was even presented with a bouquet of white roses, sent by William Cullerne Bown, the founding editor of *Research Fortnight*, the leading science policy newsletter.[19] John Beddington, the GCSA, said that the

---

[17] Anon, 'Game over for British science?', *Nature* blogpost, 24 September 2010 (accessed at blogs.nature.com/page/888/?action=report&comment=687, 12 October 2023). See also Van Noorden, 'UK government warned over "catastrophic" cuts'.

[18] https://scienceisvital.org.uk/2010/10/19/rally-report/ (accessed 15 October 2023) has links to news coverage (BBC, CBC), as well as blog reports from scientists attending the rally.

[19] Geoff Brumfiel, 'UK science saved from deepest cuts', *Nature* (20 October 2010).

chancellor of the exchequer had been 'won over by arguments from high-profile scientists and industrialists that cuts could hinder the long-term growth of the British economy'.[20] Funds were also finally released for building the massive Crick institute in London. Enthusiasm was tempered when it was realised that, while grants for researchers and universities were to be protected, the small print in the budget cut capital expenditure on the facilities of big science by 44 per cent.

The episode can therefore be seen as part of a larger pattern of failure to invest, through capital spending, in the long term into the facilities and infrastructure of Britain. Canny observers also noted that the underpinning argument, that funding UK basic research was the direct route to improved UK economic performance, was persuasive, again, this time to Osborne, despite plenty of evidence that this 'linear model' was flawed.[21]

If the government remained reluctant to fund near-market research, the presumption was still that the central problem of innovation in the UK was failure to move ideas from universities to industry where they would create wealth. When the Cambridge computing entrepreneur Hermann Hauser had been asked by Peter Mandelson, in the last days of New Labour, to report on the matter he stated what was a commonplace: 'The UK has a science capability second only to the US: an undoubted source of competitive advantage. However, it falls short on translating scientific leads into leading positions in new industries.'[22] Hauser called for

[20] Geoff Brumfiel, 'UK scientists celebrate budget reprieve', *Nature*, 467 (27 October 2010), p. 1017.

[21] Kieron Flanagan, 'Science is vital, just not in the way you think', *The Conversation*, 24 May 2013 (accessed at theconversation.com/science-is-vital-j ust-not-in-the-way-you-think-14461, 15 October 2023). See David Edgerton, '"The linear model" did not exist: reflections on the history and historiography of science and research in industry in the twentieth century', in Karl Grandin and Nina Wormbs (eds.), *The Science–Industry Nexus: History, Policy, Implications* (New York: Watson, 2004), pp. 37-51, for a typically sceptical view.

[22] Hermann Hauser, *The Current and Future Role of Technology and Innovation Centres in the UK* (London: Department of Business, Innovation and Skills, March 2010), p. 1. The Conservatives had commissioned a parallel report,

a much strengthened 'translational infrastructure', a national mode of coordination that would 'close the gap between universities and industry'. He proposed calling them Clerk Maxwell Centres, commemorating the great Scottish mathematical physicist. Hauser's report lay in the Cameron government's inbox.

When implemented, Hauser's recommendation became the Catapult network – note the directionality of the metaphor. The Catapults – the first was in 2011 and the ninth opened in 2019 – are private bodies that identified the areas where, in early twenty-first-century Britain, it was hoped that research, business and investment interests most strongly overlapped: biomedical and pharmaceutical science (Cell and Gene Therapy, Medicines Discovery); electronics and digital technology (Compound Semiconductor Applications, Connected Places, Digital, Satellite Applications); decarbonisation (Offshore Renewable Systems, Energy Systems); and manufacturing (High Value Manufacturing). The language was of 'catalysing', 'accelerating' and 'leveraging' (and rarely, simply, 'funding'). The initial reaction from scientists and science policy commentators was lukewarm, regarding the measures as inadequate recompense for cuts or as old measures recycled, for example, when the cell therapy Catapult was unveiled by Cameron and Willetts in 2011 as part of a billed new 'Strategy for UK Life Sciences'.[23] Meanwhile, overall business investment in research and development continued to decline.

Nevertheless, the Catapult initiative was one case, amongst others, of a reawakening of a willingness in government to talk 'strategy'. Here we can see the Coalition effect. For example, it

from the inventor-entrepreneur James Dyson, that made remarkably similar suggestions. James Dyson, *Ingenious Britain: Making the UK the Leading High Tech Exporter in Europe*, March 2010 (accessed at media.dyson.com/i mages_resize_sites/inside_dyson/assets/UK/downloads/IngeniousBritai n.PDF, 30 November 2023).

[23] Ewen Callaway, 'Lukewarm reception for UK life-sciences investment', *Nature*, 12 December 2011. Cameron, for tragic family reasons, had a strong interest in genomic science.

was Vince Cable, the Liberal Democrat who sat in the Cabinet as business secretary, who, in a speech at Imperial College on 11 September 2012, resurrected the term 'industrial strategy' while speaking of long-term support for business and science.[24] No doubt this framing was deliberate, and awkwardly counter-balanced the deregulation announced at the same time and favoured by the Conservative right. There was a strong sense of policy being pulled in two contradictory directions. (Another tension relevant to science concerned immigration: Cable favoured easing restrictions on movement of students and skilled workers, for example from China, to the UK, while Theresa May, then home secretary, wanted controls tightened.[25])

The tension was not simply a matter of different parties in the Coalition. The Conservative science minister David Willetts, closely aligned to Cable, led the way. On 24 January 2013, in a speech given at the Policy Exchange think tank, Willetts not only set out what he called 'Industrial Strategy 101' but also identified eight technological areas that would be targeted with support.[26] The speech is perhaps the most significant one concerning science policy during our period and merits detailed attention. Starting by crediting Cable, Willetts noted the distinctively broad and deep science base of the UK while acknowledging the retreat from strategy and economic interventionism since the 1980s. The result, in combination, had been 'classic British policy on science and technology'. But what was missing, argued Willetts, was the 'crucial stuff in the middle – real decisions on backing key technologies on their journey from the lab to the marketplace ... We are living now with the long-term consequences of the failure to have a policy backing these key

[24] Ananyo Bhattacharya, 'UK technology-boost plan disappoints', *Nature*, 489 (19 September 2012), p. 347.

[25] Patrick Wintour, 'Vince Cable rebuffs Conservative right on deregulation', *Guardian*, 9 September 2012.

[26] David Willetts, 'Eight great technologies', speech delivered at Policy Exchange, 24 January 2013 (accessed at www.gov.uk/government/spee ches/eight-great-technologies, 20 October 2023).

technologies.' He held up US practice as better, and after considering and dismantling objections, set out his Industrial Strategy 101 – a rather top-down process of gatherings of ministers, researchers, regulators and business interests that set out road maps prior to public funding – and announced (without acknowledging the rather jarring contradiction with the aim to consult first) £600 million of funding, additional to that already 'ring-fenced', to support big data, space, robotics, synthetic biology, regenerative medicine, agricultural science, advanced materials and energy technologies.

Overall, then, science fared relatively well under the early years of austerity: ring-fenced funding for research (if not facilities), and vocal, informed support from a talented minister. When Willetts resigned, as Cameron prepared a major reshuffle in July 2014, the tributes were unusually positive, even glowing. Paul Nurse, president of the Royal Society, called him 'an outstanding science minister'; Sarah Main, of CaSE, said he was 'liked and respected throughout the [science] sector for "getting it"'; Jeremy Farrar, of the Wellcome, called his efforts 'tireless'; the leading neuroscientist Colin Blakemore said science owed Willetts a 'huge debt' and observed that his 'personal affection and enthusiasm for science have been crucially important in sustaining the government's commitment to science in challenging times'.[27] Willetts was replaced by Greg Clark, the MP for Tunbridge Wells who, critics soon noted, had previously spoken in favour of homeopathy. (Clark, nevertheless, was a supporter of the 'strategy' approach; he was well regarded by senior science advisers in government and would later prove to be an effective chair of the science select committee.)

Having fared well, scientists in the UK have been asked to demonstrate the effectiveness and accessibility of their research. Two trends were clearly established in the 2010s. First, while universities were already measured and partly paid by performance via a mechanism called the Research Assessment Exercise

---

[27] 'David Willetts quits as universities minister', *Times Higher Education*, 14 July 2014.

(RAE, the first of which took place in 1986), in the 2014 iteration, rebranded as the Research Excellence Framework (REF), university researchers had to report on the measurable 'impact' of their work. Public money had to be shown to have public – economic, social, cultural – benefits.[28] For critics the REF was a restriction on freedom to choose research directions, a disincentive to the conduct of 'blue sky' research, or an onerous bureaucratic burden. Second, the movement for 'open access' publication gathered momentum. The scientific publication system, as it had massively expanded from the 1960s onwards, was largely in the ownership of a handful of companies and was extremely profitable, charging considerable sums to university libraries for licences and hiding research papers from non-academic users behind lofty paywalls. The public, critics said, paid twice, once for the research and again to see the results. In 2014, the Wellcome, a private philanthropic foundation that had become a top-rank funder of biomedical research, having encouraged open access publication by its grant-holders from 2006, began to sanction them if they didn't comply.[29] European funders, and eventually, in the early 2020s, UK research councils, followed suit.[30]

BREXIT/COVID/BREXIT

In the general election of May 2015, the Conservatives were returned with a majority and the Liberal Democrat vote collapsed, ending the Coalition government. Scientists again lost a visible friend of science, the Liberal Democrat MP for Cambridge and former biochemist, Julian Huppert. Greg Clark ended his short stint as science minister and was replaced by Jo Johnson, brother of Boris. Johnson, unlike Clark and Willetts

---

[28] Natasha Gilbert, 'UK science will be judged on impact', *Nature*, 468 (17 November 2010), p. 357.

[29] Richard Van Noorden, 'UK funder explains clamp-down on open access', *Nature*, 9 April 2014.

[30] Richard Van Noorden, 'Major UK science funder unveils strict open-access policy', *Nature*, 6 August 2021.

before him, did not sit in the Cabinet, suggesting science was not to be a political priority. While another initial concern for scientists was funding – neither the Conservatives nor Labour had promised to protect the science budget – the new worry was Europe. UK scientists had always been well supported under European research funding schemes, notably Horizon, receiving back more money than was put in and benefiting immensely from the scale and ease of European networks. But Cameron had promised a vote on Britain leaving the EU. In retrospect, it was apparent that informed commentators on science policy, as was the case more broadly, underestimated the danger, anticipating either a win for Remain, or a continuation of access to European science funding in the unlikely event of Brexit.[31]

In the year before the 2016 Brexit vote, science policy continued in normal mode, although three significant longer-term trends saw significant movement. First, the organisations that lobbied government for the support of science – the Campaign for Science and Engineering and the Royal Society – increasingly focused on a simple percentage target – 2.4 per cent, or 3 per cent of GDP for the ambitious – of research and development intensity as a proportion of the economy. The pressure was relayed via the select committees which listened sympathetically to the call.[32] As a rallying cry, the percentage target had the advantage of clarity. As science policy it was simplistic, a crude measure of input, that hid the important questions of what, where, how and why the science might be done. Jo Johnson, the science minister, was notably unimpressed, telling the Science and Technology select committee that spending 3 per cent of GDP was 'a nice round number, more than anything else', and counselled against 'focusing on such targets,

---

[31] Elizabeth Gibney, 'What the UK election results mean for science', *Nature*, 521 (8 May 2015), p. 134.

[32] Business, Innovation and Skills Committee, *Seventh Report of Session 2014–15, Business-University Collaboration*, HC 249, recommended 3 per cent. The House of Commons Science and Technology Committee, in *The Science Budget, First Report of Session 2015–16*, HC 340 (London: The Stationery Office, 9 November 2015), p. 3, called for the government to produce a 'road map' to 3 per cent.

338

arguing that research outputs were a more reasonable consideration than spending "inputs"'.[33] Nevertheless, 2.4 per cent (or 3 per cent) became embedded and increasingly equated with the UK's ambition to be a 'science superpower'.[34] This curious phrase had begun to be used in the 2000s almost exclusively in policy framings of the rise of China;[35] in the 2010s it became the framing for the UK, in a manner that would only be made stronger as the UK struggled with the fallout of Brexit. (George Freeman, who, until late 2023, had been an ever-present politician within Conservative science policymaking, claims credit for using the label.) The quotidian reality of austerity contrasted sharply. In the November 2015 budget, science spending was allowed to increase with inflation, while other public funding was slashed; the mood among scientists was that it could have 'been much worse'.[36]

Second, the research council system was consolidated into a single structure. The research councils were already loosely coordinated when Paul Nurse, president of the Royal Society, began his inquiry. While some feared that a full-blown merger would result, the Nurse Review stopped short in its recommendations.[37] However, Jo Johnson did accept the advice to set up what would become, by 2018, UK Research and Innovation (UKRI), with an individual at its head, in principle a new powerful role in UK science. The first chief executive was the outgoing GCSA, Mark Walport. A central argument made by Nurse was that a centralised UKRI would be a stronger voice for

---

[33] Johnson, quoted in House of Commons Science and Technology Committee, *The Science Budget, First Report of Session 2015–16*, p. 17.

[34] The first line of the 2015 select committee report, cited above, was: 'The United Kingdom is a science superpower'.

[35] James Wilsdon and James Keeley, *China: the Next Science Superpower* (London: Demos, 2007).

[36] Jennifer Rohn, of the campaigning group Science is Vital, quoted alongside other similar voices, in Elizabeth Gibney, 'UK scientists celebrate slight rise in research budget', *Nature*, 528 (3 December 2015), p. 20.

[37] Paul Nurse, *Ensuring a Successful UK Research Endeavour: a Review of the UK Research Councils* (London: Department of Business, Innovation and Skills, November 2015).

science in the face of arguments with government: 'The present system has not been strong enough,' Nurse had said. 'Properly set up, UKRI can deliver that.'[38]

The third trend was towards the setting of 'grand challenges'. The term 'grand challenge' does a lot of interesting rhetorical work. A challenge is a mission, ambitious and noble. But a challenge does not direct how it should be met. A grand challenge therefore has the advantage of signalling lofty public benefit without the worrying, socialistic implications associated with planning. The new wave of grand challenge discourse began in the United States (home of the Manhattan Project and the Apollo programme) in the late 1980s and 1990s, around high-performance computing (a response to Japanese innovation) and in such initiatives as the Bill and Melinda Gates Grand Challenges on Global Health announced at Davos in 2003. In the 2010s the language of grand challenges was embraced by the European Union and by universities (such as University College London). In November 2015, George Osborne, in the same UK budget that barely maintained science funding, rebranded a portion of it as a new Global Challenges research fund, £1.5 billion over five years. Greg Clark deserves credit for arguing the case for uplift here.

Challenges could sometimes seem superficial, even gimmicky. In 2013 David Cameron announced a Longitude Prize, commemorating and loosely inspired by the eighteenth-century encouragement to search for an accurate means of determining the position of ships at sea.[39] In Dava Sobel's bestselling version of the story the plucky independent clockmaker John Harrison had overcome bureaucratic hostility to win the original prize.[40] In 2014 the audience of BBC's *Horizon* TV programme was asked to vote on six challenges, shortlisted by a committee. The

[38] Daniel Cressey, 'Leading scientists clash over sweeping UK research reforms', *Nature*, 13 October 2016.

[39] Katia Moskvitch, 'UK prize lets public decide on world's biggest science problem', *Nature*, 19 May 2014.

[40] Dava Sobel, *Longitude: the True Story of a Lone Genius Who Solved the Greatest Scientific Problem of His Time* (London: Fourth Estate, 1995).

winner, a challenge to make a new means of testing for infection as part of a fight against antimicrobial resistance, would receive the lion's share of a £10 million pot. It was nostalgic, gave the public what it wanted by a simple vote, discounted the complexities of the real world, looked backwards to the supposed glory days of the nation's history, and, while acknowledging a problem, was woefully short of matching adequate means to ends.

In June 2016 the UK voted, by a very narrow margin, for Brexit. It was not the result scientists wanted: a poll of researchers held in March had suggested more than 4 out of 5 scientists preferred Remain.[41] Some fears concerned funding. A sixth of UK university research funding came from the European Union, much of which came through its Horizon programme. Other anxieties concerned freedom of movement to travel. Scientists are often internationalists, and UK laboratories are cosmopolitan places. Would the 'hostile environment' extend to science?

While it may well be said that the voters were not told what Brexit they had voted for, it is also apparent that there were different views about policy-for-science in a post-Brexit Britain. One approach was to double down on industrial strategy. Theresa May, now prime minister, in a speech to the Confederation of British Industry (CBI) in November 2016, spoke of how the opportunity presented by Brexit to 'do things differently' meant that the 'forces of capitalism' could be harnessed to benefit the 'let down, left behind and marginalised'.[42] The harness was a 'modern Industrial Strategy ... that will back Britain's strategic strengths and tackle our underlying weaknesses'. She placed science at the centre of these strengths. 'We're ambitious for Britain to become the global go-to place for scientists, innovators and tech investors', she said, promising

---

[41] Daniel Cressey, 'Scientists say "no" to UK exit from Europe in Nature poll', *Nature*, 531 (2016), p. 559.

[42] Theresa May, CBI annual conference 2016: prime minister's speech, 21 November 2016 (www.gov.uk/government/speeches/cbi-annual-con ference-2016-prime-ministers-speech).

action on freer movement for 'the brightest and the best', although adding the significant qualification that the UK could 'only do so by bringing immigration down to sustainable levels overall so we maintain public faith in the system'. She promised government investment in R&D, 'an extra £2 billion a year by the end of this parliament to help put post-Brexit Britain at the cutting edge of science and tech'. (Again science was doing relatively well in terms of funding.) She kept the challenge frame, announcing a new Industrial Strategy Challenge Fund (ISCF) that would 'direct some of that investment to scientific research and the development of a number of priority technologies in particular, helping to address Britain's historic weakness on commercialisation and turning our world-leading research into long-term success'. She claimed it amounted to 'a new way of thinking', and a break from 'business-as-usual', neither of which was correct.

Yet in the reporting[43] that the ISCF might model itself after the US Advanced Projects Agency (ARPA, subsequently DARPA) we can spy another vision of science and government. ARPA was the organisation that had been created in 1958 after the shock of Sputnik and that had backed, with light bureaucratic oversight, risky and innovative ideas with generous funds in return for technologies that might leapfrog those of Cold War enemies. ARPA had claimed the ARPANET (the origins of the internet) as one of its successes. ARPA was a lodestar for Dominic Cummings.

Assessing Cummings' influence is difficult, not least because he was the figure, and already often falsely mythologised figure, at the centre of the Brexit and Covid stories. He also offered a distinct vision for science and government. An Oxford history graduate, he spent time in Russia in the mid 1990s 'starting businesses ... experience [that he later reflected] was very useful

---

[43] 'Some of the money will go directly to applied R&D through a new Industrial Strategy Challenge Fund, modelled on the US Defense Advanced Research Projects Agency (DARPA), the Pentagon's high-risk research arm', see Elizabeth Gibney, 'UK scientists excited by surprise £2-billion government windfall', *Nature*, 540 (23 November 2016), pp. 16-17.

in politics as I had an understanding of how large complex organisations work, both badly and well'.[44] He also read narrowly and deeply into a few subjects, notably Bismarck's disruptive diplomacy, predictive data science, US Cold War technological successes, and the computer libertarianism of Silicon Valley. After cutting his political teeth in campaigns (for example, against the Euro) and a brief, awkward stint advising Iain Duncan Smith, by the time of the Coalition government Cummings was, more compatibly, a special adviser to the Education secretary Michael Gove. He commissioned Ben Goldacre to write a report that recommended the application of randomised-controlled trials to policymaking, and made the department take out subscriptions to *Nature* and *Science*. The message was that politics could learn from science. Specifically, he had an analysis and a prescription. The analysis was that Whitehall was too slow, a bureaucracy ingrained against challenge and change; its politicians, educated at Oxford in PPE (Politics, Philosophy and Economics), trained in 'superficial bluffing, misplaced confidence ... [with] little or no idea about fundamental issues concerning mathematical models of the economy ... [untrained to] make decisions in complex organisations'.[45] The prescription was to 'move from Whitehall control to distributed systems',[46] to strip out the bureaucracy

[44] Dominic Cummings, 'A few responses to comments, misconceptions etc. about my Times interview', 20 June 2014 (accessed at dominiccummings .com/2014/06/20/a-few-responses-to-comments-misconceptions-etc-abo ut-my-times-interview/, 30 October 2023).

[45] Dominic Cummings, 'My essay on an "Odyssean" education', March 2014 referring to an earlier version from 2013 (accessed at dominiccummings .com/the-odyssean-project-2/, 25 October 2023).

[46] Dominic Cummings, '"Standin' by the window, where the light is strong": de-extinction, machine intelligence, the search for extra-solar life, autonomous drone swarms bombing Parliament, genetics & IQ, science & politics, and much more @ SciFoo 2014', 19 August 2014 (accessed at dominiccum mings.com/2014/08/19/standin-by-the-window-where-the-light-is-strong-de-extinction-machine-intelligence-the-search-for-extra-solar-life-neural-n etworks-autonomous-drone-swarms-bombing-parliament-genetics-amp/, 30 October 2023).

and replace it, at the centre of government, with 'high-performance teams', educated in maths and physics, housed in modern 'seeing rooms', who would integrate data science into decision-making.[47] In turn this would allow the creation of a UK 'civilian version of DARPA aimed at high-risk/high-impact breakthroughs ... For it to work, it would have to operate outside all existing Whitehall HR rules, EU procurement rules and so on – otherwise it would be as dysfunctional as the rest of the system.'[48] It has to be stressed that this whole was a package for Cummings – destruction of traditional Whitehall, replacement by cybernetic (i.e. feedback-driven) data science, a new political class educated in science, encouragement of inward migration of scientists, and leaving the EU. The ultimate outcome would be an answer to Dean Acheson's quip that Britain had lost an empire but not yet found a role: this role, repeated Cummings, often, should be 'making ourselves the leading country for education and science'.[49] 'We could make Britain the best place in the world', stated Cummings, referencing one of his favourite Silicon Valley heroes, 'for those who can invent the future'.[50]

---

[47] For 'high-performance teams' see dominiccummings.com/2018/09/11/29-on-the-referendum-4c-on-expertise-on-the-arpa-parc-dream-machine-science-funding-high-performance-and-uk-national-strategy/; for 'integrate physicist-dominated data science in decision-making', see dominiccummings.com/2016/10/29/on-the-referendum-20-the-campaign-physics-and-data-science-vote-leaves-voter-intention-collection-system-vics-now-available-for-all/; for 'seeing rooms', see dominiccummings.com/2019/06/26/on-the-referendum-33-high-performance-government-cognitive-technologies-michael-nielsen-bret-victor-seeing-rooms/ (all accessed 30 October 2023).

[48] Dominic Cummings, *Times* op-ed: 'What is to be done? An answer to Dean Acheson's famous quip', 4 December 2014 (accessed at dominiccummings.com/2014/12/04/times-op-ed-what-is-to-be-done-an-answer-to-dean-achesons-famous-quip/, 30 October 2023).

[49] Cummings, 'My essay on an "Odyssean" education'.

[50] The reference is to Alan Kay, computer scientist at Xerox PARC, where much of the interface of modern consumer information technology was first imagined, who may have said 'The best way to predict the future is to invent it.' Dominic Cummings, 'On the referendum #23, a year after

Cummings, tragically, was successful in implementing some, but not all, of this package. He directed the Vote Leave campaign, guided by an impressive data science. Brexit happened. Back at Number 10, as the political adviser to prime minister Boris Johnson he attempted to recruit a new political class – advertising on his blog in January 2020 for an 'unusual set of people', 'Data scientists and software developers, Economists, Policy experts, Project managers, Communication experts ... [and] Weirdos and misfits with odd skills'.[51] (Some of these misfits turned out to be too weird and soon had to leave.[52]) A new civilian British science funding body, modelled on DARPA, the Advanced Research and Invention Agency (ARIA) was formally announced in 2021 and launched in 2023. But if Cummings' revolution failed then overly ambitious aims were only part of the explanation.

In December 2019 news arrived from Wuhan, China, of cases of human infection by a novel coronavirus. The first UK cases were confirmed in January 2020. The Covid pandemic would prove to be the most extraordinary test of the UK science-government system; a test, it seems, it largely failed. In March 2020, with the first UK deaths, and with modelling predicting many more, the risk to the UK was officially categorised as 'high'. On the 12th the prime minister, Boris Johnson, addressed the nation via television from 10 Downing Street. He was flanked, to his right by Chris Whitty, the chief medical

victory: "a change of perspective is worth 80 IQ points" & "how to capture the heavens"', 23 June 2017 (accessed at dominiccummings.com/2017/0 6/23/on-the-referendum-23-a-year-after-victory-a-change-of-perspective-is-worth-80-iq-points-how-to-capture-the-heavens/, 30 October 2023).

[51] Dominic Cummings, '"Two hands are a lot" – we're hiring data scientists, project managers, policy experts, assorted weirdos...', 2 January 2020 (accessed at dominiccummings.com/2020/01/02/two-hands-are-a-lot-we re-hiring-data-scientists-project-managers-policy-experts-assorted-weirdos/ , 30 October 2023).

[52] 'Andrew Sabisky: No. 10 adviser resigns over alleged race comments', BBC News, 18 February 2020 (accessed at www.bbc.co.uk/news/uk-politics-515 38493, 30 October 2023).

officer, to his left by Patrick Vallance, the government chief scientific adviser. Johnson called the pandemic 'the worst public health crisis for a generation' and warned that 'many more families are going to lose loved ones before their time'. 'At all stages,' Johnson said, 'we have been guided by the science, and we will do the right thing at the right time.'[53] 'Guided by science', sometimes 'led by science',[54] became a mantra; and the repeated spectacle of politicians flanked by scientific and medical advisers at the peak-time televised briefings was the visual reinforcement of this framing.

But the frame was misleading. Vallance and Whitty were the individual pinnacles of advice in the system, but behind them was a complex, and initially to the public eye obscure, structure of committees. The principal set was the Scientific Advisory Group for Emergencies (SAGE), which in turn was informed by the work of specialist bodies, notably the New and Emerging Respiratory Virus Threats Advisory Group (NERVTAG), the Scientific Pandemic Insights Group on Behaviours (SPI-B), a similar one on Modelling (SPI-M), amongst others I will not name in full (JCVI, COG-UK, and so on). During the Brexit debate, Michael Gove, in an interview with Faisal Islam on *Sky News*, had flippantly observed that the British public had 'had enough of experts [shocked laughter from audience] ... from acronyms'. Four years later, under Covid, acronymic bodies staffed by experts were indispensable. The serious point is that a populist and unserious Conservative government had serial dysfunctions working with organised expertise.

The full extent of the dysfunction will only be clear after the completion of the Covid Inquiry, underway in 2023. But we can

---

[53] Boris Johnson, 'Prime Minister's statement on coronavirus (COVID-19)', 12 March 2020 (www.gov.uk/government/speeches/pm-statement-on-cor onavirus-12-march-2020).

[54] Even 'We are just being entirely science-led' (Grant Shapps, on *Sky News*, March 2020), quoted in Peter Walker, 'UK government response to coronavirus "led by science" – Grant Shapps', *Guardian*, 16 March 2023 (www .theguardian.com/world/2020/mar/16/government-response-to-corona virus-led-by-science-grant-shapps).

say the following. First, in the early months, in addition to multiple distractions to the prime minister's attention, there were also deficiencies: in the collection and timeliness of data, and in that the response was being patterned after preparations for influenza. Big sporting events went ahead partly because the chief medical officer was working from data that was already out of date. The Coronavirus Action Plan – 'Contain, Delay, Mitigate, Research' – was based on an existing strategy for an influenza pandemic.[55] Borders were kept open, even as other countries chose different, robuster responses, such as vigorous testing and quarantine (South Korea) or closing borders (New Zealand).

Second, in the tumultuous, fearful month of March 2020, the realisation that the NHS would be overwhelmed under the existing strategy and the shift to major restrictions happened because politicians were being confronted with the stark results of scientific modelling. SPI-M-O reported on 2 March that modelling showed that it was 'highly likely' that there was sustained transmission of Covid in the United Kingdom; on the 9th, Professor Steven Riley, epidemiologist at Imperial College, informed via SPI-M that care services would be 'overrun'; on the 10th, Professor Neil Ferguson emailed a Number 10 adviser, pleading that the prime minister be given sight of a graph showing the overrun of NHS bed capacity and a likelihood of peak daily death rates of between 4,000 and 6,000 per day.[56] Even then there was confused talk of 'herd immunity', of 'taking it on the chin' (Johnson) and 'allowing the disease, as it were, to move through the population' (Johnson); while Vallance stated at the press conference of 12 March that 'It's not possible to stop everyone getting it and it's also not desirable because you want some immunity in the population. We need to have immunity to protect ourselves.'[57] The new advice, 'Stay home, Protect the NHS, Save Lives', was accompanied by much talk of following

---

[55] Hugo Keith, recorded in 'Transcript of Module 2 Public Hearing on 3 October 2023', 3 October 2023 (covid19.public-inquiry.uk/documents/transcript-of-module-2-public-hearing-on-3-october-2023/).
[56] Ibid.   [57] Ibid.

the science. Or was it hiding behind the science? 'The diaries of Sir Professor Vallance', summarised the lead counsel to the Covid inquiry, who had access to the documents, 'speak of SAGE and the CMO [chief medical officer] and the CSA [chief scientific adviser] being positioned as human shields.'[58]

Third, Covid hit the centre of government directly: Johnson tested positive on 27 March, the same day as health secretary Matt Hancock. Johnson was in intensive care by April. Whitty and Cummings also succumbed. Cummings, with Covid but feeling unsafe in London, drove his family to Durham; on 12 April he drove them to Barnard Castle, a breach of lockdown that became a scandal in May 2020 and hung over him until leaving Number 10 in November. The epidemiologist Neil Ferguson resigned from SAGE, also in May 2020, after his lockdown breach was revealed. By then SAGE was fraying. In the words of the Inquiry lead counsel: 'SAGE was never designed to be run at such speed, with such heat or for so long. It sat for over 100 meetings. In past crises it's met generally on no more than five occasions. Its members worked around the clock unceasingly in the public interest and pro bono. ... they were placed under sustained and also unfair media scrutiny and, increasingly, attacked.'[59] But SAGE also had weaknesses in its design: it drew on an overly narrow range of scientific expertise (only behavioural scientists rather than a broader but relevant set of social scientists, for example), and, until May 2020, refused to publish its minutes, an unnecessary level of secrecy that limited accountability and encouraged conspiracy theories. (A confusingly named 'Independent SAGE', under David King, a chief scientific adviser during New Labour, was launched in May 2020 precisely because SAGE was too secretive.)

Fourth, politics could cherry-pick, or even ignore the science. By May 2020, even with a vastly expensive Test and Trace system launched and the cumulative number of deaths from Covid in the UK passing Italy's to become the highest in Europe, the first wave was easing. 'Stay at home' became 'Stay alert'. In August, Rishi

[58] Ibid.   [59] Ibid.

Sunak announced 'Eat out to help out'. Vallance and Whitty, in their evidence to the Inquiry, have stated that '*had they* been consulted they would have advised it was highly likely to increase transmission'.[60] Likewise, when guidance was changed on allowing 1- or 2-metre distancing, the chief scientific adviser recorded in his diary it was 'abundantly clear that no one in [Number 10] or [the Cabinet Office] had really read or taken time to understand the science advice on [2 metres]. Quite extraordinary'; while on the same issue, commenting on how SAGE advice had been integrated: 'Some person has completely rewritten the science advice as though it is the definitive version. They have just cherry picked.'[61] Other examples of Covid science being 'led by politics' have been identified.[62] Yet at the same time the scientific advisers were being asked to go beyond advice and therefore beyond their role: Vallance noted in May 2020 'Ministers try to make the science give the answers rather than them making decisions.'[63] SAGE is meant to be advisory only; decisions have to be taken by the executive, by elected, responsible and accountable politicians.

Finally, the products of science, or rather the science-based biomedical industries, would change the narrative. The second wave of Covid hit the UK in autumn 2020, and a second national lockdown began in November. But on 2 December 2020 the Medicines and Healthcare products Regulatory Agency (MHRA) approved the Pfizer-BioNTech vaccine after innovative trials. It was relatively expensive, required refrigeration, but came out of genuinely novel discoveries in mRNA techniques (ones that have immense promise for other infectious diseases). It was the first Covid vaccine approval in the world. Immunisation began six days later. By the end of the month the Oxford AstraZeneca vaccine, which was cheap, developed

---

[60] Ibid. Emphasis added. [61] Ibid.

[62] Susan Michie, Philip Ball, James Wilsdon and Robert West, 'Lessons from the UK's handling of Covid-19 for the future of scientific advice to government: a contribution to the UK Covid-19 Public Inquiry', *Contemporary Social Science*, 17:5 (2022), 418–33, p. 422.

[63] Keith, recorded in 'Transcript of Module 2 Public Hearing on 3 October 2023'.

with largely traditional methods, had no need for refrigeration, but also benefited from accelerated trials, was also approved. Mass vaccination, dependent on an army of volunteers (and indeed at times, the Army) began in earnest. 'A successful Covid-19 vaccine rollout in 2021', note the authors of a paper on lessons to be learned, retrospectively 'created a generalised positive impression or "halo effect" ... about the way the pandemic had been handled'.[64]

Politicians were not shy of taking credit for the success of the vaccine programme. A similar simplification had been found in the campaign messaging ('Get Brexit done') that led to Boris Johnson's election victory of December 2019. But political fortunes would unravel thereafter. The halo around science and government would also fade. Re-entry into the EU's Horizon funding scheme, a symbol or renormalisation of UK–Europe relations, stalled for many months, much to scientists' concern, while the Covid inquiry began to document in detail the dysfunction in the operation of science advice.

CONCLUSION

No doubt the historians' interpretation of science and government between 2010 and 2024 will change as the full range of primary source evidence becomes available. The thirteen years of Conservative science policy from 1951 to 1964 had been judged as 'thirteen wasted years' in 1969, but have since been revised (along with the Wilson years) as a period of significant national investment and effort.[65] The thirteen years of New Labour science policy have been described as largely a continuation of that of Thatcher and Major, but a reassessment, enabled by access to

---

[64] Michie et al., 'Lessons from the UK's handling of Covid-19'.

[65] For 'thirteen wasted years' see, for example, Hilary Rose and Steven Rose, *Science and Society* (Harmondsworth: Penguin, 1969), p. 78. For 'techno-nationalism' in the period, see amongst his other output, David Edgerton in Kieron Flanagan, David Edgerton, Claire Craig, Sabine Clarke and Jon Agar, *Lessons from the History of UK Science Policy* (London: British Academy, 2019), p. 55.

sources, is only just beginning.[66] We may have been misled by hot takes and obscured views.

Under the Coalition and Conservative governments there was also continuity and change in science policy. More precisely there was modified continuity and the articulation of the possibility of radical change. Modified continuity is best represented by the figure of David Willetts. As science minister he promoted a re-emergence of science-based industrial strategy, gradually reshaping a reluctance to intervene in 'near market' research that had its roots in the late years of the Thatcher administration and had continued under Major, Blair and Brown. The possibility of radical change, on the other hand, is best represented by the provocations of Dominic Cummings, who had in mind a revolution in ways of governing that would serve the purpose of giving the UK, finally, a post-Imperial role as the best place in the world for science and education. Willetts' vision faltered and Cummings' vision failed because of events, internally and externally generated.

When Willetts set out his 'Industrial Strategy 101' in 2013, he ended his speech with six possible versions of where the UK would be in 2023 if his advice was followed. Pessimistically, the brand-new wealth-creating science-based industries would wither or move abroad. Optimistically, the UK would now have its home-grown and home-owned equivalents of the giant innovative companies such as Google, and the UK would be 'purveyors of R&D to the world':

> Britain is increasingly recognised as the world's best R&D lab. We have achieved our ambition of being the best place in the world to do science. Multinationals base their R&D facilities here. Smart people from around the world want to come and research here. We have also earned a reputation as the best managers of big international scientific projects.[67]

---

[66] See Jon Agar, *Science Policy from Major to Blair* (London: UCL Press, forthcoming).

[67] Willetts, 'Eight great technologies'.

In reality, by 2022, the potential great companies had been bought (AI science pioneers Deepmind was snapped up by Google in 2014) and R&D levels remained in effect static.[68] What happened was political turmoil and especially Brexit.

The rapid turnover of administrations meant that while Willetts had been science minister for four years, enough to build strong relationships and build policy, in the years since 2014 there have been eight science ministers (one serving twice). The churn above also affected policy: Sajid Javid, as a free market chancellor, disliked and discontinued the strategic approach, until he too soon left and policies flipped back again. Cummings was both an agent and victim of this turmoil. He was an agent of Brexit. But he wanted Brexit as part of an overall vision of revolution in government in the name of science. When granted power, as Johnson's adviser, implementing that vision was impossible, first because of the political instability of Brexit (and therefore partly his own doing) and factional infighting within the court of Johnson, and second because of the extraordinary pressure of Covid.

What is remarkable is that science continued to do well. It had been relatively protected in austerity budgets, and science-based industry delivered vaccines when challenged. The significant failings on issues where science-for-policy was critical – climate change is the outstanding long-term example, while AI represents a more sudden emergence – are due to the complexities of committing to necessary action globally rather than nationally

---

[68] Ironically, one of the measures of being a 'science superpower', R&D spending at a level between 2.4% and 3% of GDP, was achieved overnight in 2022 when the Office of National Statistics changed its methods of calculating GERD (Gross Expenditure on R&D). GERD in 2020 was now said to have been 2.9%. At a stroke a central message of the science lobby's campaigning strategy was nullified – a lesson in the dangers of oversimplifying science policy. For the reasons of the recalculation, see Abbas Panjani, *Research and Development Spending* (London: House of Commons Library, 2023), pp. 8-9.

(although there was always more that could and should have been done within the UK). Public trust in scientific expertise, as polling shows[69] and in stark contradiction to the populist line that the British people had had enough of experts, remained high, and considerably higher than trust in Britain's politicians.

[69] Wellcome/Gallup polling for Wellcome Global Monitor 2020, cited in Michie et al., 'Lessons from the UK's handling of Covid-19', p. 427. Contrary evidence can be found in cases where UK citizens have resisted involvement in scientists' projects, in other words where trust is a direct and immediate issue rather than a general polling question. An example might be found in Helen Pearson, 'Massive UK baby study cancelled', *Nature*, 526 (27 October 2015), pp. 620–1.

11

Culture

John Kampfner

INTRODUCTION

The fishing industry contributes barely £1 billion to the British economy. That is 0.03 per cent of GDP. Put it another way: it is roughly equivalent in size to visual effects, a sub-category of a category of the creative industries.

Yet for several years, during and after the 2016 Brexit referendum, government ministers made repeated visits to the nation's ports to extol the virtues of an almost moribund trade. By contrast, a sector that has been the fastest growing for two decades, that contributes more than £120 billion of gross added value, that in other countries would be considered an essential component of the good society, is largely seen as an afterthought.

The fourteen years of Tory rule constitute a stunning missed opportunity to seize on one of Britain's few internationally renowned assets – its creativity.

The sector contains three components: the commercial creative industries (architecture to fashion, design to video games, television to film, advertising to software); the not-for-profit arts (museums and galleries, orchestras, dance and theatre); and an education system that is supposed to nurture the next generation of talent. One of the many reasons why the cultural world has struggled to be heard is its disparateness.

Another is its 'otherness'. As Grayson Perry once pointed out,[1] part mockingly, part seriously, to an embarrassed audience of arts

---

[1] 'Grayson Perry argues Donald Trump and Brexit are "fantastic" for the arts', *Standard*, 28 November 2016 (www.standard.co.uk/culture/grayson-perry-trump-and-brexit-are-fantastic-for-the-arts-a3404636.html).

leaders, very few of them have ever leant towards the Conservatives. Even fewer saw any positives in Brexit, leading some ministers to wonder: where are the votes in this? Why should they care?

The government did step in to save organisations from disaster during the pandemic; it did, early on, extend its successful system of tax credits from film and TV to other cultural forms. It did beat the drum for extending demographic opportunities, even if in its actions it did not follow through.

Set against that, however, was a series of failures, made in Whitehall. Twelve culture secretaries in fourteen years invites ridicule. But this statistic was no different to elsewhere. Seven foreign secretaries in seven years, six home secretaries in six years or the most astonishing of all – sixteen housing ministers during the entire Tory term. That is no way to run a country, no way to ensure any level of continuity.

The Department of Culture, Media and Sport (DCMS) is rarely seen as a destination of choice. It is usually an early rung on the ladder towards 'higher' office; occasionally it is a resting home on the way down, or onto *I'm a Celebrity* . . . . It has been mocked as the ministry of fun and the ministry of free tickets. Apart from Chris Smith in the early Blair years, few previous incumbents saw it as more than a transit point.

This tendency has been even more pronounced in this Tory era. Jeremy Hunt, the first, talked a good talk, but offered up even greater cuts to the arts budget than the chancellor George Osborne could stomach. (The total agreed was already radical.) He was followed by Maria Miller, who could not name anything she had seen at the British Museum beyond the mummies. Sajid Javid had little time for the 'luvvies'. Karen Bradley? Nobody remembers her. John Whittingdale hit the headlines for his colourful sex life, but his main professional passion was his assault on the BBC. Matt Hancock will also be most remembered for his private life and for his steerage of the pandemic response, but paradoxically, he was one of the most effective culture secretaries, advocating for the digital and music briefs particularly strongly.

It was hard for civil servants at the DCMS to produce a consistent plan when Peter was robbed to pay Paul. Swingeing cuts to Arts Council England (ACE) budgets were offset, inexactly, by tax credits. Even larger reductions in funding to local authorities, which decimated the amount of money they could give to cultural institutions, were replaced by competitions for funding under the 'levelling-up' agenda.[2] Initiatives such as these were usually small in scale and seen as one-offs designed to capture headlines rather than produce sustainable outcomes.

While the creative industries side fared less badly, it could also have achieved so much more in this period if supported by a more holistic approach. It still receives considerably less research and development funding than other parts of the knowledge economy such as life sciences. Emerging technologies like generative AI, 3D printing and visual effects have out-sized impacts on the creative industries and yet investment is, at best, trickling in from government. Sometimes ministers had an industrial policy, at other times they didn't.

By the end, progress of sorts had been made. Whereas the creative industries had not been deemed worthy of a place as one of eleven priority sectors in 2010, by 2023 they were listed as one of the government's top five.

Yet two areas of policy consistently undermined what good work was being done: the almost complete removal of creative education from the classroom, and the UK's departure from the European Union. The damage they have already caused in accessing talent at home and abroad will take a generation or more to redress.

ARTS FUNDING

In January 2010, four months before the election, Hunt promised a 'golden age for the arts'.[3] A 'US-style culture of philanthropy' would take the strain from the public purse, releasing new cash and a new era of entrepreneurialism. Amid the

---

[2] Eliza Easton and Salvatore Di Novo, 'A new deal for arts funding in England?' Creative Industries Policy and Evidence Centre, 12 January 2023 (https://pec .ac.uk/blog/a-new-deal-for-arts-funding-in-england).

[3] 'Arts funding cuts proposed by UK Conservatives', Artforum, 15 January 2010 (www.artforum.com/news/arts-funding-cuts-proposed-by-uk-conservatives-193 315/).

warnings of a 'credit crunch', Hunt talked of Treasury civil servants 'getting their teeth' into ministerial budgets. Arts Council and other non-governmental funding bodies would slash their costs, becoming 'leaner, though not meaner'.

In one fell swoop, the arts sector suffered a 21 per cent cut in real terms, while 30 per cent was removed from local authority budgets. ACE was reduced in size and told not to make political interventions. Its grant, which has been reduced to just over £450 million, constitutes less than 0.05 per cent of total government spending. Or rather, a rounding-up exercise on the average overspend on a single aircraft carrier.[4] Or a decimal point of other departments' spending. Sir Peter Bazalgette, chair of ACE from 2012–16 and later chair of the Creative Industries Council (a government-industry body), laments the cuts, but insists: 'The cuts in 2010 were not specifically aimed at the arts. They were not punitive. They were across the board.'[5]

The UK is a hybrid, embracing in part European-style state funding, part American private and corporate giving. The Conservatives have not provided the tax advantage, as enjoyed in the US, however, for philanthropy. Other routes to finance have been equally difficult. Austerity made art and other 'discretionary' spend all the harder to entice audiences.

In January 2007, the Labour government introduced tax credits for the film industry.[6] With governments around the world offering incentives for film and TV companies to shoot and base post-production in their countries, Britain could not lose out, particularly with its history of the small and big screen.

---

[4] Matthew Powell, 'Big defence projects are usually late and over budget', *The Conversation*, 7 February 2023 (https://theconversation.com/big-defence-projects-are-usually-late-and-over-budget-heres-what-we-can-learn-from-the-build-up-to-ww2-198608).

[5] Interview with the author.

[6] HM Customs & Revenue, 'Film tax relief: summary of tax credit claims 2006 to 2014' (https://assets.publishing.service.gov.uk/government/uploads/system/uploads/attachment_data/file/405783/FTR_Monitoring_Summary_July_2014.pdf).

As soon as the UK offered to refund 25 of 80 per cent of each production, it became an attractive destination again.

Others in the arts started lobbying for similar tax credits and were pleasantly surprised by their success. In 2013, the credits were extended to high-end television, video games and animation, a year later to theatre, and in 2016 to orchestras, opera, and museums. 'Tax relief was Osborne's way of showing mitigation,' Bazalgette comments. 'It was putting money back in that they had taken out. But we stayed quiet about that in case anyone had second thoughts.'[7] Alex Beard, director of the Royal Opera House, describes the scheme as 'a brilliantly designed intervention as it incentivises performance'.[8] Others are less sanguine, pointing out that many organisations were not similarly recompensed because of differences in their work and business models.

From the mid 1990s, the first steps were taken to professionalise the sector's political activities. But they remained haphazard. In 2014 the Creative Industries Federation was formed, bringing together the creative industries, arts and education institutions. Sir John Sorrell, one of the UK's foremost designers, was its brainchild and first chair. The other key figure was Marcus Davey, who runs London's Roundhouse, which is at the forefront of helping young people from diverse backgrounds find their way into the creative sector.

Even in the early to mid 2010s, when cuts were biting, there was considerable enthusiasm for harnessing the sector. Sorrell was joined on the founding board by other senior figures such as Lord Hall, then director general of the BBC, Sir Nicholas Serota, who would go onto chair ACE after running Tate, Amanda Nevill of the British Film Institute, Caroline Rush of the British Fashion Council, Bazalgette and others. I was asked to be its chief executive.

Our aim was to present a different, more forthright face to government.[9] Osborne was guest of honour at the launch of CIF. In the years that followed, data were presented, arguments

---

[7] Interview with the author.   [8] Interview with the author.

[9] 'Head of Creative Industries Federation fears "dangerous" cost of austerity', *Guardian*, 1 January 2015 (www.theguardian.com/culture/2015/jan/01/john-kampfner-creative-industries-federation-austerity-fears-arts).

made, over and again. The message was direct: the creative industries are growing at twice the rate of the overall economy, producing more in gross value added than aerospace, automotive and life sciences combined. They are essential, not nice to have. So why, despite all these efforts, has the sector struggled so much?

It has not always been the government's fault. Arts leaders have had a tendency to come across to ministers as both shrill and unctuous – an unfortunate combination. Their lobbying strategies were far less effective than those of the motor industry over Brexit and hospitality during Covid. Also their arguments have a certain circularity. Osborne complained that too much emphasis was being laid on instrumental rather than intrinsic value. That was, however, the only language his officials understood. It has remained difficult to present an economics-based justification for culture. Certain matrices can be used, but pure financial return on investment is hard to enumerate.

Only in the UK perhaps would a sector which delivers so much to so many constantly be required to justify its existence. Over the years, reports have come and gone. The most recent was published in November 2023 and authored by the consultancy giant, McKinsey.[10] The document is a mapping exercise, linking the disparate art forms, funding models and scales of organisations. Instead of trying to minimise differences, it makes a virtue of them. 'The complexity, in and of itself, is what delivers value,' says Beard,[11] who helped to commission the report. The new buzzword is 'extrinsic', demonstrating a link between art, mental health, individual horizons, community benefit and soft power. In other word: public goods.

Will this convince the current government or a future Labour one? Arts leaders are keenly anticipating a return of Labour. The hopes they are vesting in Sir Keir Starmer as

---

[10] Jonathan Deakin, Tom Meakin, Tunde Olanrewaju and Van Nguyen, 'Introduction: seeing the big picture', McKinsey Report, 20 November 2023 (www.mckinsey.com/uk/our-insights/introduction-seeing-the-big-picture).

[11] Interview with the author.

prime minister are equally strong, but this time tempered with caution.

Britain has more pronounced regional disparities than equivalent countries. Through the Northern Powerhouse, Birmingham Engine and 'levelling-up' agenda, successive Conservative administrations have been ardent advocates of regional redistribution. The problem, as the debacle of HS2 demonstrated, has been follow-through and long-term focus on infrastructure. Arts investment in the regions has been given in very public flurries rather than as part of a wider strategy. For example, the Cultural Investment Fund,[12] designed to assist seventy deprived areas from Bradford to Basildon, totals a mere £50 million overall. Historic England's Heritage Action Zones is similarly worthy but small.[13]

I remember being invited into DCMS for an early discussion on a festival that would be a 'showcase on the best of Britain'. The series of events and projects that took place in dozens of venues over eight months in 2022, widely mocked as 'the festival of Brexit', cost £120 million – money that could have been spent to greater effect elsewhere, and without the overt political messaging.

Of the many difficult moments of the past fourteen years for the arts, the nadir may have been Nadine Dorries's 'letter of instruction' in February 2022.[14] In this first formal directive from a culture secretary in living memory, she ordered ACE to redirect £24 million from London organisations to the regions. ACE decided it could not carry out Dorries's instruction through salami slicing and had to take dramatic decisions.

---

[12] DCMS, 'Over 70 cultural venues, museums and libraries supported with £60 million boost', press release, 20 March 2023 (www.gov.uk/govern ment/news/over-70-cultural-venues-museums-and-libraries-supported-wit h-60-million-boost).

[13] 'Historic England celebrates success of its first 10 Heritage Action Zones', Museums and Heritage Advisor, 8 June 2022 (advisor.museumsandheri tage.com/news/historic-england-celebrates-success-first-10-heritage-actio n-zones).

[14] Nadine Dorries, letter to Sir Nicholas Serota, 18 February 2022.

Alongside news of 300 organisations being funded for the first time was the withdrawal of support for several successful London organisations such as the Donmar Warehouse. It was the defenestration of English National Opera (ENO) that grabbed the headlines. It was told that if it did not move out of the capital, it would lose its £17 million of funding. What followed was chaos and acrimony. In the end, a compromise was reached in which ENO was tided over, with money found from elsewhere, and agreed that it would eventually move to Manchester.[15] The saga symbolised a mutual distrust that had steadily increased over the fourteen years. It was not so much the principle, but the manner of the peremptory approach of government to what is supposed to be an arms-length body. Dorries had delivered her 'instruction' to please a political base often dismissive of the value of the arts. She had done so with no consultation or idea about implementation.

BREXIT

In January 2017, Sadiq Khan tried some gallows humour. Speaking at the CIF's annual gala, the Mayor of London noted that 96 per cent of its members had voted in its survey to remain in the EU.[16] 'What I would like to know,' Khan said, scouring the vast atrium of the newly opened Design Museum, 'is where are the other four per cent?'[17]

The cultural sector was still reeling from the referendum. It quickly concluded, however, that the only way to minimise damage was to engage positively with government, assuming that some form of arrangement would be found to keep the UK

---

[15] 'ENO and Greater Manchester announce plans for new home in city region', ENO, 5 December 2023 (www.eno.org/news/eno-and-greater-manchester-announce-plans-for-new-home-in-city-region/).

[16] 'Creative Industries Federation members survey shows 96% want to stay in EU', Design Week, 27 May 2016 (www.designweek.co.uk/issues/23-29-may-2016/creative-industries-federation-members-survey-shows-96-want-stay-eu/).

[17] Speech at Creative industries Federation, second anniversary celebration 2017 (https://the-dots.com/projects/creative-industries-federation-second-anniversary-celebration-2017-150208).

linked to the customs union and single market. Yet, as the May and then Johnson governments pursued the hardest possible form of Brexit deal, the scale of the damage on a sector that relies on the free movement of talent became apparent.

This should not have come as a surprise. As creative industries researcher Eliza Easton says: 'In 2018, with freedom of movement still in effect, almost half of creative businesses were struggling to find the skills they needed. With no proper visa system for freelancers in place, a sector reliant on self-employment was always going to be screwed without a major shake-up of the migration system.'[18]

More than 70 per cent of UK creative firms employed EU nationals.[19] With half of all creative workers freelance, most earning below the £35,000 salary initially needed to qualify for a non-EU visa,[20] a hard immigration policy would prove deeply problematic, particularly for the self-employed. Thanks to the flaws in the UK education system, it was a struggle to find enough British workers with the right skills. Or to put it more positively: Britain had for some time benefited from being able to attract some of the best in the world.

The government listened intently to the sectors deemed politically beneficial (such as fishing), while largely ignoring the needs of the creative industries and others in the service sector as it prepared its position for negotiations with Brussels.

A report by the DCMS Select Committee in January 2018 set out the potential pitfalls.[21] Most of them came to pass. Another detrimental decision was the withdrawal from the Creative Europe funding scheme, depriving the cultural sector of

---

[18] Interview with the author.

[19] Creative Industries Federation, *Brexit Report*, October 2016 (www.creativein dustriesfederation.com/sites/default/files/2017-05/BrexitReport%20web .pdf).

[20] 'The non-EU workers who'll be deported for earning less than £35,000', *Guardian*, 12 March 2016.

[21] DCMS Select Committee, 'The potential impact of Brexit on the creative industries, tourism and the digital single market', 25 January 2018 (https://publica tions.parliament.uk/pa/cm201719/cmselect/cmcumeds/365/365.pdf).

£160 million of EU funding.[22] Withdrawal from the Erasmus+ education scheme had repercussions for creative organisations.

Artistic exchanges became mired in bureaucracy, with museum curators, touring rock bands and orchestras confronted with copious bureaucracy. Performers took to social media to complain. In April 2023 a punk band from Stuttgart called Trigger Cut that was booked to play gigs at seven British venues was turned back by UK authorities at Calais because they had not filled out the paperwork properly.[23] Mutual recognition of professional qualifications, such as for architects, also became a thing of the past.

The most comprehensive assessments of the damage that Brexit has caused the creative sector have focused on workforce problems. Some of these could be solved relatively easily, with goodwill. After all, the ejection of the UK from the EU's respected science research programme, Horizon, was eventually solved during Rishi Sunak's term. At least as important were the direct and indirect trade consequences. The creative industries were ostentatiously deprioritised in negotiations on goods and services.

The more societal consequences are harder to enumerate. The near impossibility in planning school trips to the UK has made cultural exchanges more difficult. It forms part of a widening trend of Britain's artistic scene, possibly British life in general, becoming far less European. The demise of language teaching in schools is another example.

As I argued when appearing before the House of Commons Brexit Select Committee in January 2018, it is not just the practicalities but the atmospherics, too. 'It's one thing to permit people to come and work in Britain, another to welcome them.' The well-remunerated museum director or television executive would continue to come, as do Premier League soccer managers, as HR departments would be on hand to deal with visa applications. But

---

[22] 'Brexit caused UK creative industries to lose £160m in funding, analysis reveals', *Independent*, 25 January 2023.

[23] 'German punk band "humiliated" after being refused UK entry due to post-Brexit rules', *Guardian*, 10 April 2023.

small organisations would miss out. As would the young graphic artist, the musician who before would come to Manchester or London just to hang out. Previously, they could have ended up making a major contribution to UK creative life.

The failure, or refusal, to listen seriously to the creative sector was not purely an issue of funding or Brexit or other policy priorities. It was deeply ingrained. Unlike in France, Germany and other countries where culture is openly embraced by politicians, in the UK, it has a tendency to embarrass politicians.

One story is particularly apposite. In April 2013, David Cameron visited Angela Merkel. The prime minister was only the third European leader to be invited to the chancellor's residence at Schloss Meseberg, north of Berlin. The main aim was to discuss the forthcoming British referendum. On the Saturday evening, Merkel invited a small group of cultural and political figures with links to both countries. To break the ice, she talked about recent operas at Bayreuth and theatres and museums she had visited. Even as chancellor, she sometimes would personally phone gallery directors to request if she might sneak into a particular exhibition at the end of the day. She asked Cameron what he would recommend in London. The prime minister stuttered and said he liked watching TV. He added that he would have loved to go to concerts but feared being hounded by the press as elitist.[24]

Given the political discomfort that art seemingly brings, given Britain's monolingualism, it might seem incongruous that successive governments trumpet 'soft power' as one of the country's most important assets.

The 2021 Integrated Review of Security, Defence, Development and Foreign Policy namechecks 'soft power' no less than fifteen times. Deploying his signature bombast in the foreword, Johnson declared: 'Our country overflows with creativity in the arts and sciences: the wellsprings of unique soft power that spans the globe.' Britain, the review declares airily, is a 'soft

[24] John Kampfner, 'Why does Germany value the arts so much more than Britain?', *Telegraph*, 16 August 2020.

power superpower'. By way of evidence, it falls back on a poll conducted for the British Council in which the UK is found to be 'the most attractive country' for young people across the G20. The British Council's own report was also upbeat, even if its language was more circumspect. It referred to the UK's 'soft power advantage', while issuing the cryptic caveat: 'for all the buccaneering spirit evident in the thinking around Global Britain, there remain real challenges closer to home. The UK needs its European neighbours, and they need an engaged and collaborative UK.' [25]

That is about as far as a quasi-government agency can go in daring to criticise. The British Council has been emasculated, with a series of budget cuts, reducing it in many countries to little more than a language provider. Its semi-independence has been undermined. It was reported that in late 2020 Johnson had put forward a close associate, who had provided him with a loan guarantee, onto the shortlist to run the Council.[26]

That Appointment Came to Nothing

The government's GREAT campaign (its name speaks volumes) has been one of the main vehicles for 'selling' Britain around the world. As it and the Integrated Review were happy to proclaim, one of the UK's unique selling points to the world is the BBC. And yet throughout this period, relations were toxic. Funding was successively cut in real terms, through either freezes or below-inflation increases for the Licence Fee, and the decriminalisation of non-payment, which further denuded the corporation of revenues. The organisation's political independence was consistently challenged. Frequently, the BBC was its own worst enemy, finding itself engulfed in a series of scandals around sex and safeguarding involving TV presenters and

---

[25] Alistair MacDonald, 'Global Britain: the UK's soft power advantage', British Council report, July 2021 (www.britishcouncil.org/research-insight/global-britain-uk-soft-power-advantage).

[26] 'How was Boris Johnson's loan guarantor put forward to run the British Council?', *Financial Times*, 24 August 2023.

radio disc jockeys, journalistic deception (such as Martin Bashir and the Princess Diana interview) and others. The BBC's own chairman was forced to resign after it was revealed that he had provided credit guarantees to his friend, Boris Johnson, before his appointment.

With record low morale and significant job losses in the news and current affairs division, the damage went beyond Britain's shores. Just when Russia and China were boosting their output around the world, the BBC was cutting its output and presence in key markets across the Global South. The trend was consistent throughout this period, though the intensity varied according to the personal animus felt towards the corporation by specific prime ministers and culture secretaries. Whittingdale and Dorries were the most pugilistic, spurred on by pro-Conservative newspapers, who saw political and business advantage in a fearful and emasculated BBC.

If 'soft power' means anything, it is surely about what a country does – such as adhering to international law – rather than what it proclaims. 'We seemed to stop wanting to be magnetic,' says Tom Fletcher, former adviser to three prime ministers and one of the UK's most serious thinkers on cultural diplomacy. 'The UK has serious work to do to restore its national brand based on agility, openness, liberty and competence. We must hope that our future leaders are tougher in defence of our soft power.'[27]

CREATIVE INDUSTRIES

Given everything ministers have thrown in the way of the sector, it is even more remarkable that the creative industries continue to be as successful as they are.

At various times, the government appeared to have settled on a coherent industrial strategy. One of those moments took place in November 2017 when Greg Clark, a distinctively sensible business secretary, announced before a gathering at the Francis

---

[27] Interview with the author.

Crick Institute a new industrial strategy. Shortly after that, a 'sector deal' for the creative industries was unveiled. Its flagship announcement was research funding to develop immersive technologies such as virtual and augmented reality. Nine 'creative clusters' were identified, from Northern Ireland to Yorkshire to Dundee, bringing together digital technologies and creative talent. The £80 million was not to be scoffed at, but it felt more like a pin prick than a sustained attempt to tackle the UK's deep-rooted productivity problems (one of the main reasons cited by ministers for the industrial strategy) and to boost Britain's chronically low levels of R&D investment. In 2021, while still chancellor, Sunak binned Clark's industrial strategy. Those who had been there before were not pleased.[28]

In June 2023, yet another 'Sector Vision' was produced for the creative industries. Alongside the ubiquitous nod in the prime ministerial foreword (this time from Sunak) to Adele, Ed Sheeran and 'world-class cultural institutions like the National Theatre', another round of money was allocated for clusters and R&D hubs, alongside an extra £5 million for ACE to nurture young music talent and a similar amount for early-stage investment in video games. Three new societal 'objectives' were identified – wellbeing, environment and soft power. The wheel continued to grind.

Fashion houses, design studios, architects' practices and TV companies take what support comes their way but carry on regardless. Most of the strengths of British creators are endogenous, and impossible to measure, such as irreverence and ingenuity. Their biggest single market advantage – the English language – is not, whatever politicians (and the odd practitioner) might say, a reflection of British greatness, rather a holdover from American post-war dominance. That said, Britain has in its cultural sector inordinate strengths. Think of what it could achieve with a government that really understood it.

---

[28] 'Rishi Sunak's lack of industrial strategy attacked by former business secretaries', *Financial Times*, 17 May 2023.

COVID

It could easily have come tumbling down. 'I can't think of a project so well executed', says Lord Neil Mendoza.[29] Two months after the start of the pandemic, he was appointed Commissioner for Cultural Recovery and Renewal.

A quintessential establishment figure, he chaired the DCMS's review into museums in 2017, he has also worked in film and publishing, while serving on the boards of the Soho and Almeida theatres. He is now provost of Oriel College, Oxford, chair of Historic England, and a member of the House of Lords. Mendoza has managed to secure the trust of the arts world and the government. He is one of a microscopic number of cultural leaders who is an avowed Conservative.

When the pandemic struck, the arts sector was particularly vulnerable. A third of the creative workforce is self-employed, double the proportion of the rest of the economy. Even in relatively good times, theirs is a precarious existence, relying on artistic commissions and cross-subsidised often by jobs in hospitality. These were among the two most effective sectors. All forms of performing arts were staring down a barrel, as was anyone whose business model relied on audiences. Worthy efforts were made to perform online, or to gain revenues from streaming previous shows.

Rather than relying on established organisations, several arts leaders constructed their own Zoom meeting rooms. CEOs gathered on Fridays. On Tuesdays, a group of public and commercial theatre leaders met. 'What's Next', a long-established loose collective, continued to meet, albeit digitally, on Wednesdays.

What mattered was access to ministers, and fast, and that required a return to the old school tie. Anyone who knew anyone was urged to send a WhatsApp or, better still, to go for a walk or, once it was allowed from mid May 2020, on the socially distanced golf course. Apart from Sunak's controversial 'eat out to help out' scheme in summer of that year, culture was the only sector to have a specific support mechanism put in place. The Treasury,

---

[29] Interview with the author.

institutionally unconvinced by the principle of investment in the arts, was reluctant to intervene. One proposal doing the rounds was to spend £750 million on mothballing the whole sector, to see which pieces were worth picking up afterwards.

The various virtual breakfast and lunch groups agreed on a small group to lobby Sunak. Ahead of a meeting, they were schooled in what to say by Osborne. During their one-hour Teams session, the former chancellor was 'brutal'. One participant recalls: 'he told us we were being fluffy. His arguments were: "if you let this go, it will take decades to build it back up again, our international reputation will be damaged. It's not worth the hassle. Just pay them off."' Sunak was said to be courteous but gave little away. Several Treasury civil servants were on the call, on mute and off video.

These ad hoc groups worked on a plan. Mendoza's role as fixer and go-between was crucial. 'Nobody in government knew who needed what, so they left it largely to us,' says one involved. They came up with a number: £1.5 billion. The first of three tranches of the Culture Recovery Fund was announced in July 2020, a mix of grants, loans and capital awards. Applicants were required to demonstrate that they were 'culturally significant' and had been financially viable prior to Covid. In three rounds, just under 8,000 awards were made and just over 5,000 organisations were supported. A further £500 million was given to film and TV, which after a couple of months were allowed to start shooting again but faced huge hikes in insurance premiums. A large proportion of companies also benefited from furlough schemes and from the reduction in VAT.

By all accounts, there were few mistakes and – unlike furlough and emergency assistance for the wider economy – little fraud. A government-commissioned, but independently conducted, evaluation of the Culture Recovery Fund was broadly positive.[30] The one area of criticism was help for freelancers, only around half of whom received support. They had been

---

[30] *Evaluation of the Culture Recovery Fund: Final Report*, 4 July 2022 (https://assets.publishing.service.gov.uk/media/6424078960a35e000c0cb056/GOV.UK_17.3_CRF_Final_Report_accessible_v3.pdf).

encouraged to apply through the generic Self-Employment Income Support Scheme. The assessment concluded, however, that some of the detailed eligibility rules were not well suited to the cultural sector, and many people were deemed ineligible.

Other countries like France and Germany, even the United States (for some parts of the sector) provided more. But by British, and Treasury, standards it was widely seen as a success. It turned out that Tory ministers were open to persuasion – as long as the message was conveyed by Mendoza, by one of their own.

EDUCATION

In October 2020, as the first 1,300 recipients of the Cultural Recovery Fund were being announced, a government advertisement appeared, depicting a ballet dancer tying up her shoes, alongside the caption: 'Fatima's next job could be in cyber.'[31] The culture secretary at the time, Oliver Dowden, described it as 'crass' and it was immediately withdrawn. It might have been insensitive, in the context of the time, but it reflected deep-rooted prejudices. Arts education had been dismissed throughout the Tory years as effete and inessential. The government became obsessed with STEM – science, technology, engineering and maths. It was driven by two goals: to deliver an education system to serve the jobs market and to meet global competition.

The flaws in the argument were clear for all to see. Competitive states such as Singapore and China were queuing up to send their next generation to British art schools; meanwhile expensive independent schools in the UK trumpeted their swanky theatre and music facilities on their prospectuses.

The STEM agenda succeeded in its own terms; levels of literacy and particularly numeracy in state schools did increase. The UK rose in international league tables on English and maths, leading ministers to feel vindicated. Yet they did not

---

[31] 'Government scraps ballet dancer reskilling ad criticised as "crass"', *Guardian*, 12 October 2020.

need to see it as zero sum. Creative subjects were not the enemy of academic rigour.

The two key drivers of this agenda were Michael Gove, as education secretary, and Nick Gibb, a long-serving minister of state. Gove announced plans in late 2012 to replace GCSEs with an English Baccalaureate, in which creative subjects would barely get a look in. After opposition inside and outside parliament, the proposals were watered down. Even some Conservative-supporting newspapers pointed out the damage they would wreak on social mobility, listing the cultural icons from the late twentieth century – from Michael Caine to Twiggy and David Bailey – who had working-class backgrounds.[32]

The Ebacc was brought in alongside the GSCE, to be guided by a performance measure called Progress 8. It did not include a single creative subject. Hence why should schools bother teaching any? According to figures published by the Cultural Learning Alliance, the number of students taking arts GCSEs has fallen by 47 per cent since 2010.[33] The largest declines have been in design and technology (73 per cent) and performing arts (72 per cent). One in seven music teachers and one in eight art and design teachers have left the profession. The training of new teachers in these subjects dropped commensurately, meaning that even if the policy were to be amended or reversed, it would take many further years for the decline to be reversed.

A similar approach was taken to higher education. After a joint consultation with the Office for Students, the government announced it was cutting funding for arts courses by 50 per cent. This is despite the UK housing the two best art and design schools in the world, according to the annual QS ranking. The Treasury was increasingly concerned that a disproportionate amount of tuition fee debt was not being paid by students who had gone on to the creative sector. This followed a report in 2019

---

[32] 'Rishi needs to realise that the point of a degree is not to give you a job', *Telegraph*, 18 July 2023.

[33] 'Huge decline in arts subjects worsens at GCSE and A-level', Campaign for the Arts, 24 August 2023 (www.campaignforthearts.org/huge-decline-in-arts-subjects-worsens-at-gcse-and-a-level/).

called the Augur Review, which cited creative and certain humanities subjects at universities as providing the worst value for money – based on absolute measures of graduate salaries, a set of crude criteria seldom used in other countries.[34]

This is one area where the Conservatives at least could not be accused of inconsistency. From the start of Gove's tenure under the Cameron-led coalition until Sunak himself, they have dismissed the wider societal benefits of a rounded education, something that is afforded the wealthy in the independent sector. As recently as July 2023, Sunak announced a fresh offensive against 'rip-off' degree courses.[35] 'Too many young people are being sold a false dream and end up doing a poor-quality course at the taxpayers' expense that doesn't offer the prospect of a decent job at the end of it,' he declared. On the specifics, Sunak may not be wrong, in the sense that certain creative degrees do churn out young people who struggle in the workplace. The issue at stake is a wider one, though: the denigration of cultural learning across the piece, from primary to tertiary education and beyond.

In pure employment terms, the approach is backfiring. Ministers proclaim the economic success of the creative industries, while choking off much of the talent stream (through short-sighted education policies) and, thanks to Brexit, ending free movement for Europeans, who were extremely active in the sector. Perhaps in a belated acknowledgement that all is not well, the government announced at the same time the establishment of an advisory panel to discuss wider questions around creative education. The group, led by Deborah Bull, former ballet dancer, now a member of the Lords, may end up producing proposals better suited to an incoming Labour government.

The mood music so far suggests that Labour is closer to the sector's position on arts in schools. The shadow culture secretary, Thangam Debbonaire, a former professional cellist, has been working with her education counterpart, Bridget

---

[34] *Review of Post-18 Education and Funding*, CP 117, May 2019.

[35] Department for Education, 'Crackdown on rip-off university degrees', press release, 17 July 2023 (www.gov.uk/government/news/crackdown-on-rip-off-university-degrees).

Phillipson, on draft plans to reinstate creative subjects into the curriculum.[36] They appear to have the backing of Starmer.

In a broadside against the government, Debbonaire's predecessor, Lucy Powell, accused Conservative ministers of squeezing creative subjects out of the curriculum, 'with philistine ministers devaluing their importance,' adding that the government was 'more comfortable stoking the culture wars than championing culture'.[37] Amid an intensification of what the Tories like to call 'the war on woke', this was an eye-catching intervention, but perhaps one aimed more at the sector itself than the wider population. The arts community, or at least most of it, is happy to see itself as on the opposite side of the barricades of this identity battle. The government, while promoting formal diversity requirements – in ethnicity, gender, sexual orientation and regional representation – has increasingly also stressed the need for diversity of thought. In other words, an arts scene that is not instinctively left-liberal. Starmer is instinctively cautious and will try hard not to be trapped into 'woke' battles during the election campaign.

CONCLUSION

The sector may not be thriving, but it is good at surviving. That, politically, can be a problem. Artistic directors point to more risk-averse commissioning and higher ticket prices. Deterioration in quality is hard to measure, however. Very few theatres or museums have shut, which makes damage harder to demonstrate.

These fourteen Conservative years have presided over consistent cuts to arts funding, ameliorated only very slightly by specific interventions. Money matters. Nicholas Hytner, former

---

[36] 'The Labour Party's new education strategy and what it means for the cultural learning sector', Cultural Learning Alliance, 24 July 2023 (www.culturallearningalliance.org.uk/the-labour-partys-new-education-strategy-and-what-it-means-for-the-cultural-learning-sector/).

[37] *The Art Newspaper*, 13 September 2023 (www.theartnewspaper.com/2023/09/13/culture-wars-new-labour-culture-secretary-thangam-debbonaire-addresses-the-art-world).

director of the National Theatre, suggests the end of the second Blair term may have marked the peak of investment in the arts. Between 1997 and 2007 spending doubled; dance, opera and classical music flourished.[38] 'Seats had never been cheaper, audiences never been bigger,' he says.[39]

Culture-led regeneration of the regions spawned highly successful organisations such as Turner Contemporary (of which I was founder-chair) in Margate, Wakefield's Hepworth Gallery, and Nottingham Contemporary, alongside the arrival or revival of regional theatres. Investments such as these were more sustained than the haphazard levelling-up schemes that followed. 'Today, I don't know a single subsidised arts organisation in the country that feels financially secure,' Hytner says. 'Many freelance artists have given up, battered by the pandemic and removal of their right to work freely in the EU.'[40]

The halcyon era – if it really was that – will not come back any time soon. The fiftieth anniversary of the 1965 White Paper on the Arts (the only one to have been published by a post-war government) gave cause for much soul-searching. While intrinsically better disposed towards Labour, cultural leaders recall with affection John Major's establishment of the lottery in 1993 – deemed highly controversial at the time – that is now a lifeline for the arts. What mattered at least as much as specific decisions in this latest Tory era, particularly the latter part under May, Johnson, Truss and Sunak, was the manner of government engagement. Many in the sector are demoralised, having to raise private funds while being disparaged by ministers.

They know that under Labour, public finances will remain desperately tight for years to come. Britain is not about to rejoin the EU. They know that, unlike in other countries, the arts sector in the UK will have to prove its worth, again and again. It will knuckle down and try to do so. 'Thanks to the work we had to scramble to do to salvage something from the pandemic, the sector has a greater spirit of togetherness now,' says Davey of

---

[38] 'Blair pledges to protect arts funding', *Guardian*, 6 March 2007.
[39] Interview with the author.   [40] Ibid.

the Roundhouse. 'But it does feel underrepresented, especially the performing arts, in terms of political muscle.'[41]

The probable advent of a different kind of government will not lead to exultation, but a sense of relief. Just a few steps in the right direction would go a long way to helping this weary sector rediscover its mojo.

[41] Interview with the author.

12

Government, Parliament
and the Constitution

Meg Russell

A SUSTAINED PERIOD OF CONSERVATIVE government would
normally be expected to usher in constitutional stability.
But the reverse applied to most of the period 2010–24. During
these years constitutional controversies were rarely far from the
news, thanks at times to deliberately planned changes, but more
often to radically shifting conventions and political behaviour.
The direction of change was also very far from consistent across
these fourteen years. The initial coalition period was marked
primarily by pressures towards greater constitutional pluralism,
though Liberal Democrat reform ambitions were often held
back by Cameron's Conservatives. Later, any prospect of calm
when single-party government returned was soon punctured by
the pressures of Brexit. This eventually brought into question
almost every aspect of the UK's constitutional arrangements,
and inflicted painful splits within the Conservative Party over
questions of governance. Boris Johnson's populist approach, in
particular, was characterised by wholesale disregard for constitutional norms – which highlighted vulnerabilities in the UK's key
democratic arrangements that few would previously have anticipated. If one commonality can be discerned across this period of
constitutional extremes, it is its largely unconservative nature.

This chapter reviews the large-c Conservative effect on the
constitution, and is structured in seven main sections. It starts with
context, including the inheritance from Labour in 2010, the
nature of the various Conservative-led governments and their
leaders, the major shocks to the system over the period which
helped shape its constitutional trajectory, and what Conservative
traditions might have led us to expect. The next three sections

review three central aspects of the constitution: the management of government in Whitehall, of parliament in Westminster and of constitutional standards. The remaining sections are then more strongly analytical. The first reviews the central conflicts over the role of the executive in the constitution that emerged over this period, taking in all of the previous dimensions, as well as touching briefly on the role of the courts, the monarch and devolution. The next shorter section provides some international context, locating UK developments within the worldwide rise of populism and 'democratic backsliding', and associated pressures on parties of the centre-right. The final section of the chapter then draws all this together, asking how we should assess the Conservative effect on the constitution during the turbulent period 2010–24.

CONTEXT

Two aspects of the Conservative Party's 2010 inheritance are important in contextualising and framing what happened during the subsequent years. The most obvious is that the preceding governments of Labour's Tony Blair and Gordon Brown (particularly the former) had presided over a deliberate and wide-ranging programme of constitutional reform. These changes have been reviewed elsewhere, but included most obviously the establishment of devolved legislatures in Northern Ireland, Scotland and Wales; the partial reform of the House of Lords (to remove most hereditary peers); the passage of the Human Rights Act 1998 and establishment of the Supreme Court; and other matters such as the passage of the Freedom of Information Act. The effects of these changes were much debated, with common criticisms being that they were too timid, too piecemeal and lacked an overall plan.[1] But scholars have generally agreed that their collective effect was to disperse power away from the executive at Westminster. Robert

---

[1] Philip Norton, 'The constitution', in Anthony Seldon (ed.), *Blair's Britain, 1997–2007* (Cambridge: Cambridge University Press, 2007), pp. 104–22; Meg Russell, 'Constitutional politics', in Richard Heffernan, Philip Cowley and Colin Hay (eds.), *Developments in British Politics 9* (Basingstoke: Palgrave Macmillan, 2011), pp. 7-28.

Hazell portrayed this as a two-dimensional shift – from a traditionally 'political' to a more 'legal' or rule-based constitution, and (in the classic schema of Arend Lijphart), from a 'majoritarian' or centralised democracy, to a more 'consensual' one incorporating greater checks and balances.[2]

The second important inheritance in 2010, though more immediate, was the MPs' expenses crisis which had rocked Westminster the previous year.[3] This resulted in an unusually high turnover of members, and – alongside the concurrent financial crisis – a major blow to public confidence in the political class. The stream of headlines related to the crisis fed common perceptions that MPs were 'in it for themselves', creating additional fragility in the system.

The first Conservative-led government of 2010 could itself be seen as something of a shock to the system, being – very unusually at Westminster – a coalition. Conservative prime minister David Cameron was supported by deputy prime minister Nick Clegg, the leader of the Liberal Democrats, and each department included at least one Liberal Democrat minister.[4] Clegg himself took responsibility for constitutional reform. Coalition required various adjustments, and had some clear knock-on effects for government and parliament, as further discussed below. It ended following the election of 2015, when the Conservatives won a narrow Commons majority. But the shock of the unexpected

---

[2] Robert Hazell, 'Conclusion: where will the Westminster model end up?', in Robert Hazell (ed.), *Constitutional Futures Revisited: Britain's Constitution to 2020* (Basingstoke: Palgrave Macmillan, 2008), pp. 285–300; Arend Lijphart, *Patterns of Democracy: Government Forms and Performance in Thirty-Six Countries* (New Haven, CT: Yale University Press, 2009).

[3] Jennifer van Heerde-Hudson (ed.), *The Political Costs of the 2009 British MPs' Expenses Scandal* (Basingstoke: Palgrave Macmillan, 2014).

[4] For a wide-ranging assessment of the coalition, see Anthony Seldon and Mike Finn (eds.), *The Coalition Effect, 2010–2015* (Cambridge: Cambridge University Press, 2015). For a more detailed assessment of some of its more constitutional aspects, see Robert Hazell and Ben Yong (eds.), *The Politics of Coalition: How the Conservative-Liberal Democrat Government Works* (London: Bloomsbury, 2012).

Leave vote in the Brexit referendum of 2016 was a major turning point. Its far-reaching consequences began immediately, with Cameron's resignation. He was replaced by Theresa May, whose small majority vanished in 2017, after she gambled on an early general election in the hopes instead of boosting it. She ended up heading a minority government, propped up by the increasingly unreliable support of the Northern Ireland Democratic Unionist Party (DUP). The dual shocks of Brexit and minority government on Whitehall and Westminster are in practice hard to disentangle in their effects, as the problems generated by both coexisted for a matter of years.

This creates essentially three periods for analysis, of the coalition years, a brief interregnum of calm Conservative majority rule, followed by the increasingly chaotic post-referendum period, much of it under minority government. In summer 2019, Theresa May was toppled and replaced by Boris Johnson, whose premiership was marked by much division, particularly before the December 2019 general election – but even afterwards, despite his initial eighty-seat Commons majority. The Brexit and Johnson years are also difficult to disentangle, so – notwithstanding the radical change in numbers at Westminster – are most easily seen as a continuation of this third, chaotic period. The additional external shock of the Covid pandemic also occurred during this time.

Johnson's fall was initially followed by the unprecedentedly short Liz Truss premiership, July–October 2022. Despite its spectacular implosion, this made little independent impact constitutionally (although remarkably it was Truss who spoke as prime minister at Queen Elizabeth II's funeral, marking the end of her seventy-year reign). A fourth discernible period, of renewed relative constitutional tranquillity under Conservative majority government, began only with her replacement by Rishi Sunak. Even here, following what had gone before, the qualifier 'relative' is important.

The remainder of this chapter analyses developments more thematically, with reference to these four periods. The longest and most eventful were clearly the coalition period 2010–15 and the Brexit and Johnson period 2016–22. This simplifies matters, perhaps somewhat unfairly rolling Theresa May's premiership together with Boris Johnson's (as should be clear below, the two were quite different characters); but the constitutional chaos that hit UK politics after June 2016 really did not abate until after Johnson's departure.

The constitutional significance of the Brexit referendum deserves some context of its own given its centrality to events in the chapter. Prior to Cameron's premiership, there had been only one UK-wide referendum, on the country's continued membership of the European bloc (then formally the EEC) in 1975. At that point, many saw referendums as anathema to the UK's traditions of parliamentary politics – the then opposition leader Margaret Thatcher memorably referring to them that year as 'a device of dictators and demagogues'.[5] It was Labour's Harold Wilson who promised and staged the 1975 vote, primarily to resolve splits in his own party. By 2010 the device had become more commonplace, at least at subnational level, having been used by Blair's government to secure support for devolution in Northern Ireland, Scotland, Wales, London and (unsuccessfully) the northeast of England. Cameron himself then presided over three major referendums. The first two were under coalition: on the voting system for the House of Commons in 2011 and Scottish independence in 2014. As Martin Loughlin and Cal Viney noted in their chapter on the constitution in *The Coalition Effect*, 'the most distinctive feature of the coalition government's constitutional programme has been their promotion of referendums', leading the authors to ask whether this marked 'a shift from parliamentary to popular government'.[6] Of course, both of those first referendums were won by Cameron and resulted in no change to the status quo. This no doubt boosted his confidence to have a third try with Brexit. He therefore instigated two of the UK's three nationwide referendums, the third with seismic effect.

[5] Robert Saunders, *Yes to Europe! The 1975 Referendum and Seventies Britain* (Cambridge: Cambridge University Press, 2018) p. 7.

[6] Martin Loughlin and Cal Viney, 'The coalition and the constitution', in Seldon and Finn (eds.), *The Coalition Effect*, pp. 59–86, p. 85.

This is far from the only way in which constitutional developments 2010–24 could be seen to depart from Conservative traditions. As Loughlin and Viney emphasised, Conservatives had been habitual defenders of the UK's long-standing institutions and ways of doing politics. Norton notes that Conservative traditions value constitutional conventions, parliament, and a strong government tempered by checks and balances, are 'wary of … the transient will of the majority determining the affairs of the nation', and may contemplate change that would 'maintain, not destroy, the system'.[7] The Conservatives had resisted many of Labour's constitutional reforms in the preceding period, so did not necessarily want to defend the status quo that they had inherited. But while viewing various elements of Blair's changes as a mistake, most seemed largely to have accepted them – and the party did not enter power proposing to reverse such changes. Radical constitutional reforms, in any direction, were therefore hardly to be expected.

THE MANAGEMENT OF THE GOVERNMENT MACHINE

A first area in which significant change took place over the period, in directions which were strongly mutually contradictory, concerned the role of Whitehall and the civil service.

The Conservatives fought the 2010 general election on a manifesto committed to 'cutting the scope of Whitehall, and cutting the cost of politics'.[8] The shrinking of the civil service had been a hallmark of the Thatcher government, and the context of 'austerity' which marked the coalition years brought this goal back onto the political agenda. As charted in greater detail by Peter Riddell for the coalition period, and over a longer timeframe by the Institute for Government, civil service numbers reduced by almost 20 per cent – from around 470,000 to

---

[7] Philip Norton, 'Speaking for the people: a conservative narrative of democracy', *Policy Studies*, 33:2 (2012), 121–32, pp. 121, 127.

[8] *The Conservative Manifesto 2010*, The Conservative Party, 2010.

390,000 – in the five years after 2010.[9] By the time of the Brexit referendum they had fallen to 384,230 full-time equivalent (FTE) positions – lower than in any period since World War II. But the policy challenges of implementing Brexit, including the need to negotiate an agreement with the EU, seek bilateral trade deals throughout the wider world, and plan policy in numerous areas that had been subject to EU decision-making for up to forty years, saw a rapid reversal in this situation. Civil service numbers rose to around 430,000 by 2020 and, aided by the impact of the Covid pandemic, had effectively returned to pre-coalition levels by 2022.

Despite its novelty and challenges, the advent of coalition government in many ways resulted in high levels of government stability. The passage of the Fixed-term Parliaments Act 2011 (discussed below) guaranteed a timescale for the government, and therefore Whitehall policy-making. The need for delicate balancing between representation of the two parties in Cabinet, and within departmental ministerial teams, prompted a refreshing reduction in ministerial turnover. Such political 'churn' is often seen as damaging to sensible decision-making, as new ministers both have to learn their brief and often want to make a mark by departing from the decisions of their predecessors.[10] But the need for cross-party agreement on ministerial appointments, and to maintain balance in personnel between the parties, acted as a greater constraint than usual on the prime minister's temptation to reshuffle his team.

Equally importantly, the arrangements put in place to secure cross-party coordination and (at least as far as possible) agreement inside the coalition saw decision-making become more formalised and regularised. This contrasted with the informal so-called 'sofa government' sometimes lamented in the

---

[9] Peter Riddell, 'The coalition and the executive', in Seldon and Finn (eds.), *The Coalition Effect*, pp. 113–35; *Whitehall Monitor 2023*, Institute for Government, January 2023.

[10] Tom Sasse, Tim Durrant, Emma Norris and Ketaki Zodgekar, *Government Reshuffles: The Case for Keeping Ministers in Post Longer*, Institute for Government, January 2020.

Labour years. Chroniclers of the coalition noted a distinct 'return to Cabinet government' during this period.[11] Meanwhile new structures including the 'Quad', comprising Cameron and Clegg, plus Conservative chancellor of the exchequer George Osborne and Liberal Democrat chief secretary to the Treasury Danny Alexander, had to sign off major policy decisions. Detailed arrangements such as these for government decision-making were outlined in a formal agreement published at the start of the coalition period, alongside a longer document laying out the coalition's agreed policy programme.[12] All of this created an environment of considerable certainty for civil servants.

After the coalition period ended, though only in the short period prior to the Brexit referendum, Cameron clearly had greater freedom to set the tone and direction of government. One such decision was that to hold the Brexit referendum itself. Some have suggested that Cameron hoped to avoid this – despite the commitment appearing in the 2015 Conservative manifesto – through continued constraints applied by his Liberal Democrat partners; but this is much disputed.[13] He had been under pressure on this question for years from the Eurosceptic wing of his parliamentary party, and the Conservatives faced electoral pressures from the UK Independence Party (UKIP).

Post-referendum, the reversal in terms of stability and rule-based government was rapid and stark – becoming extreme in its extent under Boris Johnson. Theresa May constantly struggled to keep her ministerial team together, and lost an (at that time) unprecedented number of ministers through resignation. Her approach was always to try and keep her deeply divided party united, including around the Cabinet table. Her first secretary of state in the newly established Department for Exiting the

---

[11] Robert Hazell, 'How the coalition works at the centre', in Hazell and Yong, *The Politics of Coalition*, pp. 49–70, p. 50.

[12] *Coalition Agreement for Stability and Reform* (London: Cabinet Office, 2010); *The Coalition: Our Programme for Government* (London: Cabinet Office, 2010).

[13] Meg Russell and Lisa James, *The Parliamentary Battle Over Brexit* (Oxford: Oxford University Press, 2023).

European Union (DExEU) was Brexiteer David Davis, but he resigned from Cabinet in July 2018 (as did Boris Johnson) over her approach to Brexit. His successor, Dominic Raab, did the same just four months later. Several of those resigning ministerial office were Brexiteers, but others – such as Sam Gyimah and Phillip Lee – were Brexit sceptics. Those with experience of coalition noted the irony that the cross-party government under Cameron had been far more united. Ultimately Gyimah and Lee, plus various other former Conservative MPs, ended their parliamentary careers as Liberal Democrats; others quit the party to sit as independents.

Whitehall life after the referendum was highly pressured and full of uncertainties – including those created by Cameron having refused to allow civil servants to prepare for a Leave result. Brexit supporters in parliament expressed some suspicions about 'Remainer' civil servants. But under Theresa May there were few internal spats with officials or allegations of ministerial misconduct, and those that emerged were dealt with efficiently. All of this changed under Boris Johnson.

Johnson's senior adviser Dominic Cummings (who had been the campaign director for Vote Leave in the referendum) had firm views about the inadequacies of Whitehall. Arguments, and concerns about propriety, emerged almost immediately – not least over Johnson's plans to prorogue parliament (discussed below), which had emerged obliquely during the Conservative leadership contest of summer 2019. Very soon, civil servants were facing dilemmas regarding what behaviour from their political masters they were prepared to withstand. The diplomat whose job it was to explain Brexit to US audiences resigned, on the basis that the government's briefing materials on the topic were 'nakedly dishonest'. [14] After the 2019 general election, when Johnson's Brexit deal had been approved by parliament, sights shifted more directly to Whitehall. Cummings threatened a 'hard rain' on the civil service, and several permanent secretaries (i.e. departmental heads) were effectively forced out. By September 2020

---

[14] Alexandra Hall Hall, 'Should I stay or should I go? The dilemma of a conflicted civil servant', *Texas National Security Review*, 4:4 (2021), 91–114, p. 109.

Whitehall's most senior official, the Cabinet secretary Mark Sedwill, had himself resigned. Extraordinary accounts have been told of Cummings' role not only in this departure, but also the departure of Sajid Javid as chancellor of the exchequer (all of whose special advisers Cummings planned to sack), and likewise in attempts to select a governor of the Bank of England.[15] During this period the ability of impartial officials to 'speak truth to power', as well as to maintain constitutional standards (further discussed below), was substantially weakened. The official Covid inquiry exposed an astonishing picture of life at the centre of government, including a 'toxic' and highly masculine culture which spawned rule-breaking Downing Street parties and, more fundamentally, numerous questionable policy decisions.

The dramatic end of the Johnson period soon eclipsed Theresa May's record for presiding over ministerial departures. There were over fifty resignations from his government between 5 and 7 July 2022 (including ministers, parliamentary private secretaries and others), in increasingly desperate attempts by parliamentarians to force the prime minister himself to go. This – followed by the brief premiership of Liz Truss – moved the turbulence of previous years on to absurd proportions. The year 2022 alone saw for example four chancellors of the exchequer and five education secretaries, as well as three prime ministers. Overall during 2010–24 the education brief was held by a total of ten secretaries of state, while the role of secretary of state for culture was held by twelve different people.

The final Sunak period brought somewhat more calm, but the effects of the preceding turbulence were going to take time to repair. The new prime minister did not always jump to the defence of the civil service – most notably, when his secretary of state for justice Dominic Raab issued fierce criticisms after being forced out in spring 2023 over allegations of bullying. Like various other problems over standards, and the rule of law, Sunak often appeared to feel trapped by the desire to placate his party's rightwingers.

---

[15] Anthony Seldon and Raymond Newell, *Johnson at 10: The Inside Story* (London: Atlantic Books, 2023).

THE MANAGEMENT OF PARLIAMENT

Parliament is central to the UK system of government, even more than is the case in most other states. Like many, the UK is a 'parliamentary democracy', in that the government is responsible to parliament, and must maintain the confidence of the House of Commons. If it loses that, it can be forced from office. Beyond this, the UK has a more unusual tradition of 'parliamentary sovereignty'. Both the meaning and appropriateness of this are disputed, and became increasingly so during the Brexit years – but it indicates that parliament is the highest legal authority. In contrast, in countries with formal written constitutions, the courts may enforce limits on what parliament can do. UK constitutional arrangements instead remain flexible, and potentially able to adapt to changing political circumstances. Parliament is a scrutineer of government, a national assembly for debate, a representative institution, and a maker of the law – but it is, more than in most states, also a guardian of the constitution. All of these functions came under significant pressure when the Conservatives were in government during 2010–24, and particularly after 2016.

This section briefly discusses parliament's functioning, and its relations with government, first focusing largely on the House of Commons, and then on the House of Lords. Relations with both chambers became increasingly strained during this period, though did stabilise somewhat under Sunak.

Other dimensions of parliamentary management were also significant in this period, but cannot properly be done justice here. In their *Coalition Effect* chapters, both Loughlin and Viney and Philip Cowley describe key reforms that failed: the initiative by the Conservatives to reduce the number of MPs, and the referendum forced by the Liberal Democrats to change the House of Commons voting system from 'first past the post' to the Alternative Vote.[16] These questions caused significant frictions inside the coalition, and became subject to something of

---

[16] Loughlin and Viney, 'The coalition and the constitution'; Philip Cowley, 'The coalition and Parliament', in Seldon and Finn (eds.), *The Coalition Effect*, pp. 136–56.

a 'tit-for-tat' destruction by the coalition partners (also involving the Conservatives' scuppering of Nick Clegg's proposals for House of Lords reform – touched on below). In addition, the period saw significant controversies over bullying and harassment inside parliament, and the 'restoration and renewal' of the parliamentary estate. The first of these issues made progress, and the second very little.[17]

The Commons: The Decline of Scrutiny?

As indicated earlier, the 2010 general election had been preceded by a difficult period in parliamentary politics, thanks to the MPs' expenses crisis. This had not only triggered the departure of many members of the House of Commons, but debates about its reform. These debates, coupled with the dynamics of coalition, shaped parliament in the early years under Cameron.

The Select Committee on the Reform of the House of Commons (generally referred to as the 'Wright Committee', after its chair, the Labour MP Tony Wright) was established as a direct result of the expenses crisis. It considered largely unconnected matters, but was designed to put forward reform proposals that would help to restore the Commons' reputation. The committee's key recommendations were threefold: to change the way in which select committee chairs and members were chosen; to establish a Backbench Business Committee which would schedule a new category of backbench business; and to create a new system for scheduling all time in the House of Commons, comprising a cross-party House Business Committee and a weekly vote on its recommendations by MPs.[18] The first two of these changes were put into effect, but the third never was.

---

[17] For discussion see Hannah White, *Held in Contempt: What's Wrong with the House of Commons?* (Manchester: Manchester University Press, 2022); Christ Bryant, *Code of Conduct: Why We Need to Fix Parliament – and How to Do It* (London: Bloomsbury, 2023).

[18] Meg Russell, '"Never allow a crisis to go to waste": the Wright Committee reforms to strengthen the House of Commons', *Parliamentary Affairs*, 64:4 (2011), 612–33.

The reforms to select committees were first written into standing orders just before the 2010 election, and implemented at the start of the new parliament. These changes significantly reduced the power of party whips over who chaired and sat on the committees, introducing a system of cross-party chamber-wide elections for committee chairs, followed by elections inside the parties for remaining committee members. This encouraged more independent-minded members to put themselves forward as chairs, in particular. It was widely seen as having strengthened the select committees, and thereby the Commons' capacity for scrutiny.

The coalition agreement committed the partners to establishing a Backbench Business Committee immediately, and a House Business Committee within three years. The Liberal Democrats, largely shut out of the 'usual channels' discussions between whips which decide the programme in the House of Commons, strongly supported the latter. But this reform was quietly dropped. The Backbench Business Committee was formed in 2010, and went on to schedule regular debates with cross-party support – including one in October 2011 which saw eighty-one Conservative backbenchers rebelling on a proposal for a referendum on EU membership. This played some part in nudging David Cameron to commit to such a referendum, in a speech at Bloomberg in January 2013.[19]

Generally, despite these developments facilitating more effective scrutiny, such scrutiny became more difficult in this initial period. Coalition government policies generated much disquiet at times on the backbenches of both governing parties, and levels of backbench rebellion were high.[20] But the need to draw up cross-party deals carefully inside the executive left less flexibility than usual for ministers to respond to parliament through offering concessions to their backbenchers. Hence while this period was more fractious than usual, it was not necessarily one in which parliament exercised more influence over government.

[19] Russell and James, *The Parliamentary Battle Over Brexit.*
[20] Cowley, 'The coalition and Parliament'.

Another product of the expenses crisis had been the election of John Bercow as speaker of the House of Commons in 2009. Bercow was a former Conservative right-winger, whose views had softened, and whose stance on issues such as gay rights had won him respect on the Labour benches. He had fought the cross-party speakership election on a manifesto of empowering backbenchers. Bercow also played an early part in facilitating Conservative backbenchers arguing for an EU referendum, but later on increasingly became a hate figure for Brexiteers.

The Brexit referendum, and arrival of Theresa May as prime minister, fundamentally changed relations between government and the House of Commons.[21] It was well known that the majority of MPs (including most Conservatives) had backed Remain, but the government now needed to deliver Brexit. This made both the prime minister and Brexit voters doubtful regarding parliamentarians' motives. Theresa May was by nature wary of parliamentary scrutiny, which was reinforced by her slender majority – a situation that worsened after the 2017 election, under minority government. In fact, May's strength in the Commons was far worse even than the party balance might have implied. Large numbers of Conservative MPs, from both the Remain and Leave wings of the party, were deeply suspicious of the government's plans on Brexit – and while most of the former group ultimately fell in behind her deal with the EU, large numbers of the latter did not. Her Brexit deal was voted on in the Commons three times, and initially was subject to defeats of record-breaking proportions. The first defeat, in January 2019, was by 432 votes to 202, with 118 Conservative MPs rebelling. By the third occasion, on 29 March 2019, the number of rebels was down to 34, of whom 28 were hardline Brexiteers (the so-called 'Spartans'). Their votes, along with those of the DUP, were enough to kill the deal.

In this environment it was unsurprising that Theresa May was inclined to bypass parliament when she could. Given the enormity of Brexit, it was also unsurprising that many

---

[21] Russell and James, *The Parliamentary Battle Over Brexit.*

parliamentarians – including on her own benches – pushed hard for there to be careful scrutiny of decision-making. Ultimately, back-benchers sought to break the parliamentary deadlock by taking matters into their own hands – including many loyal Conservatives who had voted for May's deal. Former Cabinet minister Oliver Letwin was one of those who worked alongside opposition members to 'take control' of the House of Commons agenda and stage 'indicative votes' on alternative Brexit options. Others supported bills (proposed by Labour select committee chairs Yvette Cooper and Hilary Benn) to force the prime minister to request a longer negotiating period from the EU. These exceptional tensions resulted from a minority government seeking to pursue an unavoid-able but deeply divisive policy; but also from that minority govern-ment controlling – and manipulating – the Commons agenda. The Wright Committee's third proposal had been to end the gov-ernment's monopoly control over the Commons' main business, and – if implemented – might perhaps have somewhat eased these difficulties. Speaker Bercow frequently expressed his frustrations at the government, and was criticised for facilitating the rebels.

Although Theresa May faced, and survived, one formal no-confidence vote in the House of Commons, her party finally brought her down. Her successor Boris Johnson was in a parliamentary situation even more perilous than hers, since some anti-Brexit rebels had by then departed the party, and his pugnacious style alienated opposition members. Even more than May, his response was to shut parliament out, or even (as discussed below) to shut it down. Having rebelled himself twice against May's Brexit deal, he also took the extraordinary step of stripping twenty-one Conservative MPs (including Letwin and several former members of May's Cabinet) of the whip in September 2019 for supporting moves to prevent a no-deal exit. This was well beyond the normal conventions of party management, and left several of his senior internal opponents unable to stand for re-election in 2019 as Conservative candi-dates. His victory with an eighty-seat majority brought a considerably more pliant House of Commons.

The Covid pandemic, hitting shortly after that election, had further deleterious effects on parliament. Johnson's initial deal with the EU had been rushed through the House of Commons in three days. This was trumped by the Coronavirus Act, which was passed in a single day. The Brexit process had seen a huge rise in the use of delegated legislation, which receives little to no parliamentary scrutiny, in order to rapidly amend arrangements in multiple policy areas in preparation for the UK's departure from the EU. Covid again accelerated this, with radical measures to manage the pandemic being implemented in such a way. Announcements were routinely made in Downing Street press conferences rather than in parliament; indeed for much of the period parliament did not actually sit in its usual form. Clearly both crises justified some legislative haste; but the lack of scrutiny and parliamentary engagement also suited Johnson's political style. Senior Conservative backbenchers, including the pro-Brexit 1922 Committee chair Graham Brady, publicly spoke out about how parliament was being sidelined. House of Commons speaker Lindsay Hoyle, seen on his election in 2019 as a less combative replacement for Bercow, frequently admonished the government.

Johnson's unsympathetic management of his parliamentary party, and unwillingness to listen to its concerns, was one factor (among others discussed below) that ultimately contributed to his downfall. This was forced not by a no-confidence vote among his MPs – though he narrowly survived one in June 2022 – but by the aforementioned mass ministerial resignations a month later. Parliamentary mismanagement also played a part in the collapse of the Truss premiership, which ended on the day after a chaotic Commons vote on fracking, where the whipping arrangements seemingly changed midway through the proceedings.[22]

Rishi Sunak had always been Conservative MPs' preferred choice for the leadership (Truss having been imposed on them by a vote of party members). His subsequent relationship with

---

[22] Thomas Caygill, 'Liz Truss: what happened in the night of Westminster chaos that triggered the PM's resignation?', *The Conversation*, 20 October 2022 (accessed at https://theconversation.com/liz-truss-what-happened-in-the-night-of-westminster-chaos-that-triggered-the-pms-resignation-192968, 6 December 2023).

the Commons was thus rather less troubled. But he inherited a weakened culture of scrutiny and parliamentary accountability, and made little attempt to change this. He too was regularly criticised by Speaker Hoyle for key announcements being made outside parliament, and he maintained bad habits from the Brexit and Covid years in terms of seeking to rush legislation through with minimal opportunity for oversight. This most obviously applied to his immigration measures designed to 'stop the boats', through deporting asylum seekers to Rwanda. Like Johnson, he also faced significant criticism for the rule of law implications of this and other policies, as further discussed below.

The House of Lords: A Distinctly Unconservative Approach

The 2010–24 period, overall, demonstrated some really fundamental changes in the relationship between the Conservatives and the House of Lords. In this area there was some continuity across the entire period, but also some clear distinctions between the coalition government and the others that followed.

Historically, the Conservatives have been natural defenders of the House of Lords. It served traditionally as a powerbase for the party, and it was Liberal and Labour governments that faced challenge by the chamber, though – as the twentieth century went on – its peculiar composition made this increasingly muted.[23] Conservative governments could occasionally face tough scrutiny in the chamber (this was noted particularly during the Thatcher years), but nonetheless suffered only limited head-on challenge and few legislative defeats.[24] The Liberals (and successor parties) and Labour traditionally favoured radical reform of the Lords, while Conservatives preferred largely to preserve it, including through occasional incremental change.

---

[23] Meg Russell, *The Contemporary House of Lords: Westminster Bicameralism Revived* (Oxford: Oxford University Press, 2013).

[24] Donald Shell, *The House of Lords* (Hemel Hempstead: Harvester Wheatsheaf, 1992).

Most notably the Life Peerages Act 1958, which introduced the system of life (rather than hereditary) peerages, revived and helped maintain the unelected chamber – and was introduced by a Conservative government.

Labour acted in 1999 to remove most remaining hereditary peers, but failed repeatedly to implement a promised second stage of Lords reform. The Conservatives enjoyed highlighting this failure, and entered the 2010 election on a promise to 'work to build a consensus for a mainly-elected second chamber to replace the current House of Lords'.[25] Past experience suggested that any such agreement would be very hard to achieve, so this statement could appeal to reformers while almost certainly being a recipe for inaction. But the Liberal Democrats were more sincerely dedicated to reform. The coalition agreement therefore committed the government to 'bring forward proposals for a wholly or mainly elected upper chamber on the basis of proportional representation'.[26] Nick Clegg was personally in charge of this policy, and published a draft bill and white paper in 2011. But when a bill was formally introduced the following year, ninety-one Conservative MPs voted against its second reading. Realising that its Commons passage was doomed, the government withdrew the bill, and no further progress on reform was made.

The 1999 reform had radically altered the chamber's party balance, as hundreds of departing hereditary peers had been Conservatives. This, plus appointments by Labour in government, left a chamber in which the two main parties were fairly equally matched, with the balance of power held by Liberal Democrats and Crossbench independents. Labour suffered hundreds of defeats on its legislation in the Lords, where members now felt more confident to challenge the government. But this changed under coalition, due to Liberal Democrat peers voting with the government. It was hence only with the return of single-party government in 2015 that the Conservatives really felt the full force of the 1999 reform, and experienced what governments of

[25] *The Conservative Manifesto 2010*, p. 67.
[26] *The Coalition: Our Programme for Government*, p. 27.

the left had always done – in terms of serious challenge from the second chamber.

A major showdown occurred soon afterwards, in October 2015, when chancellor George Osborne attempted to make significant changes to the regime of tax credits using delegated legislation.[27] The Lords retains a veto on such legislation, though had rarely used it. Peers felt that the introduction of such significant changes through a mechanism requiring little parliamentary scrutiny was inappropriate, and effectively blocked the move. They did so knowing that many Conservative MPs disliked the policy. Osborne could in theory have reintroduced the measure via a bill or a replacement statutory instrument, but he chose not to do so. Nonetheless, his exasperation with the Lords sparked a government-sponsored review into the chamber's powers, conducted by former Conservative leader of the chamber, Lord Strathclyde – which proposed a weakening of its powers over delegated legislation.[28] To act upon this would have required a controversial bill – and no such measure was introduced. Indeed, the House of Commons Public Administration and Constitutional Affairs Committee (PACAC), chaired by senior Conservative Bernard Jenkin, concluded that the Strathclyde review was misplaced, and that the worst problem with the Lords was the prime minister's unregulated and excessive appointments.[29]

The Brexit situation, including increasing battles in the House of Commons, saw any difficulties that the government had with the House of Lords' role in policy largely disappear from focus. The chamber tends to defer to its elected counterpart, and did so even more in the wake of a referendum whose

---

[27] Meg Russell, 'The Lords and tax credits: fact and myth', Constitution Unit blog, 22 October 2015 (accessed at https://constitution-unit.com/2015/10/22/the-lords-and-tax-credits-fact-and-myth/, 6 December 2023).

[28] *Strathclyde Review: Secondary Legislation and The Primacy of the House of Commons* (London: Cabinet Office, 2015).

[29] Public Administration and Constitutional Affairs Committee, *The Strathclyde Review: Statutory Instruments and the Power of the House of Lords* (*Eighth Report of Session 2015–16*), HC 752 (London: House of Commons).

result MPs were struggling to implement. Peers pointed out technical problems with the government's Brexit implementation, and increasingly raised the alarm about the overuse of delegated legislation, but the biggest arguments were left to the Commons. Serious showdowns with the Lords recurred only later, over the Johnson government's attitude to international law (touched on below), though the overall level of defeats inflicted by the chamber far exceeded that under previous Conservative governments.

The problems highlighted by PACAC about government overappointment to the Lords were a major feature of this period. Tony Blair had appointed 374 peers during his more than ten years as prime minister; Cameron appointed 245 in six years (i.e. roughly 40 per year to Blair's 37 – Thatcher's rate had been 17). During Cameron's tenure the size of the chamber increased by around 100 – from approximately 750 to 850. Political and media attention therefore increasingly shifted to its bloated state – which weakened its reputation and therefore its ability to exert influence over the government. Among those expressing strongest concern was well-respected former Conservative Cabinet minister Lord (Norman) Fowler, who was elected as Lord Speaker in 2016. With the overwhelming endorsement of the House of Lords itself, he established a Lord Speaker's Committee on the Size of the House, which reported in 2017. It recommended a principle of 'two out, one in', to gradually reduce numbers in the chamber, and the strict application of a formula to share appointments fairly between the parties.[30]

These were typically small-c, incremental proposals, designed to rebuild the House of Lords' reputation and preserve the chamber. Theresa May as prime minister was inclined to comply, and during her three-year tenure appointed just 43 peers, allowing the size of the House of Lords gradually to fall. But this progress was abruptly reversed by Boris Johnson. During his three years in office he appointed 87 peers, and then left Rishi Sunak a resignation honours

---

[30] Lord Speaker's Committee, *Report of the Lord Speaker's Committee on the Size of the House* (London: House of Lords, 2017).

list resulting in appointment of seven more. And it was not just the volume of Johnson's appointments that caused concern. Like Cameron's they were disproportionately Conservative, in clear breach of the Lord Speaker's Committee recommendation on proportionality. They also attracted criticisms over quality and propriety. Johnson became the first prime minister to overrule a propriety recommendation of the House of Lords Appointments Commission (HOLAC) since its establishment in 2000. Other controversial appointees included *Evening Standard* proprietor Evgeny Lebedev and 30-year-old former Johnson aide Charlotte Owen, who became the youngest life peer ever appointed. Rishi Sunak failed to block Johnson's dubious resignation honours, and raised eyebrows by appointing David Cameron to the chamber in late 2023 to serve as foreign secretary, leading to concerns about how MPs could hold him to account.

By the end of the Conservatives' period in office, the status of the House of Lords had been severely damaged. This weakened the chamber significantly, thereby damaging the power of parliament as a whole. Some commentators even speculated that the reputational harm was deliberate, to strengthen the government against the Lords.[31] Serious challenge by the second chamber was certainly both unfamiliar and uncomfortable for the Conservatives. The period ended with reform strongly back on the agenda, and the ironic prospect that the next incremental reform would fall to Labour.

THE MANAGEMENT OF CONSTITUTIONAL STANDARDS

As already indicated by the preceding sections, some grave concerns developed about constitutional standards over this period of Conservative government, largely during the Johnson premiership.

---

[31] Rosie Kinchen, 'Is Boris Johnson trying to push the House of Lords into extinction?', *The Sunday Times*, 3 January 2021; Meg Russell 'Is David Cameron actually seeking to destroy the Lords?', Constitution Unit blog, 28 August 2015 (accessed at https://constitution-unit.com/2015/08/28/is-david-cameron-actually-seeking-to-destroy-the-lords/, 6 December 2023).

Reference has already been made to the standards issues that surrounded the handover of power in 2010, in terms of the MPs' expenses crisis. Prior to this, a similar focus on standards had been notable during John Major's premiership, with allegations of 'sleaze' also playing a part in the handover to Labour in 1997. Major took important actions to deal with perceptions of impropriety and poor standards, through the establishment of the Committee on Standards in Public Life (CSPL), originally chaired by Lord Nolan. The so-called 'Nolan principles' of public life (selflessness, integrity, objectivity, accountability, openness, honesty and leadership) subsequently became accepted benchmarks, while CSPL continued to exist and recommend improvements. These resulted in the creation of other constitutional regulators, such as the Commissioner for Public Appointments (1995). It was Major's government that first published the Ministerial Code (under a different name), which has been overseen by an Independent Adviser on Ministers' Interests (also proposed by CSPL) since 2006. The MPs' expenses crisis later resulted in the formation of the Independent Parliamentary Standards Authority (IPSA) in 2009, and standards systems inside both the Commons and the Lords also gradually strengthened. The Labour government added to this growing landscape of independent regulators through the creation of the Electoral Commission and HOLAC in 2000, and putting the Civil Service Commission on a statutory footing in 2010.

The initial years post-2010 were relatively quiet on the standards front, with these regulators occasionally identifying problem cases, but no signs of systematic decline or challenge to the system. Regulation began to become more politicised post-2016, notably following Electoral Commission rulings against Vote Leave, which created anger among Brexit supporters. Suspicions grew among some – particularly on the right of politics – about the role of unelected regulators.

Numerous problems then arose during the premiership of Boris Johnson. As indicated above, tensions emerged between the Johnson government and the civil service, with a series of departmental heads (and ultimately the Cabinet secretary himself) forced out. One of these departures in particular demonstrated the vulnerabilities in the standards system, when the permanent secretary of the Home Office, Philip Rutnam, resigned in early 2020. He lodged a constructive dismissal claim, accusing home secretary Priti Patel of briefing against him and of bullying Home Office staff. The legal case was settled for a six-figure sum, and an inquiry by the Independent Adviser, Sir Alex Allan, concluded that Patel had broken the Ministerial Code. But the prime minister had the power to overrule the adviser, and Johnson refused to act against his home secretary. Consequently Allan resigned. His successor in the role, Lord Geidt, lasted barely more than a year, before also resigning in protest at Johnson's behaviour. The post then remained vacant for six months. Liz Truss suggested that it was unnecessary. Rishi Sunak then resurrected it, but chose not to implement recommendations from the CSPL and others to strengthen the role.

Similar problems emerged in the ambit of numerous other constitutional regulators. There were concerns about public appointments, when for example Johnson sought to install former *Daily Mail* editor Paul Dacre as chair of Ofcom against the wishes of the recruitment panel. Johnson ally Richard Sharp was appointed chair of the BBC, but subsequently resigned after it emerged that he had helped the prime minister to secure an £800,000 loan.[32] Johnson appointed Peter Cruddas, a major Conservative donor, to the House of Lords in breach of HOLAC's advice on propriety. There was very widespread anxiety that provisions in Johnson's Elections Bill to make the Electoral Commission subject to a 'strategy and policy statement' would compromise the body's independence. Notwithstanding concerns being expressed by the Commission itself and the Conservative-chaired Commons PACAC, the provisions passed into law.

In November 2021, one of several standards arguments occurred which ultimately contributed to Johnson's downfall.

---

[32] Digital, Culture, Media and Sport Committee, *Appointment of Richard Sharp as Chair of the BBC (Eighth Report of Session 2022–23)*, HC 1157 (London: House of Commons, 2023).

The House of Commons Standards Committee had published a report concluding that Conservative MP Owen Paterson – a Johnson ally – had broken lobbying rules.[33] It concluded that his actions were 'egregious', and that he should be suspended from the chamber for thirty days. As the result of the Recall of MPs Act 2015 – a propriety reform introduced by the coalition government – this would make him subject to a potential recall petition in his constituency if MPs approved the suspension. But rather than following standard practice, allowing them to vote freely on the committee's recommendation, the government supported an amendment to set aside its conclusions, and to revise the standards system. This was initially approved, despite many Conservative MPs' discomfort at the whips' recommendation. But it quickly became clear that the outcome was untenable; Paterson resigned from the Commons, and the proposed changes to the system were dropped.

The single most high-profile standards problem, which dominated the final months of Johnson's premiership, related to 'partygate': the revelations about numerous social events held inside 10 Downing Street in breach of Covid rules. The initial story appeared four weeks after the Paterson vote, in the *Daily Mirror*. This sparked a gradual drip-drip of further media revelations about different events. An internal government investigation was set up under Simon Case, the Cabinet secretary appointed by Johnson, which was handed on to senior civil servant Sue Gray when it materialised that Case had attended one of the parties. The Metropolitan Police also launched an investigation. Johnson strenuously denied throughout, including repeatedly in parliament, that rules had been broken or that parties had taken place; but the emerging evidence made this appear increasingly less credible. The police investigation resulted in him, alongside various others including then-chancellor of the exchequer Rishi Sunak, being issued fines. Public and parliamentary concern grew about Johnson

---

[33] House of Commons Committee on Standards, *Mr Owen Paterson (Third Report of Session 2021–22)*, HC 797 (London: House of Commons, 2021).

misleading the House of Commons, which is both a serious breach of the Ministerial Code and a contempt of parliament.

Throughout this whole period, mounting voices had expressed concern about the general decline of standards, and the need to respect established conventions. In February 2022 Sir John Major himself intervened with an anguished speech lamenting many aspects of recent decline and endorsing recommendations from the CSPL to strengthen the standards system. Major pointedly stated that 'lies are just not acceptable. To imply otherwise is to cheapen public life and slander the vast majority of elected politicians.'[34] This was clearly a rallying cry, including for increasingly troubled Conservative MPs. Two months later, against the odds given the government's majority, the House of Commons voted to refer Johnson to its Privileges Committee to investigate claims that he had misled parliament. He was forced out as prime minister before the committee reported, but its conclusions were damning. Not only was Johnson condemned for deliberately misleading parliament, but also for his behaviour towards the committee (which his parliamentary supporters dismissively dubbed a 'kangaroo court').[35] Despite rubbishing the committee, Johnson chose to resign as an MP rather than face a House of Commons vote on its conclusions. If accepted, the committee's proposed lengthy suspension could have triggered a recall petition and by-election in his constituency. While Johnson sought to gain some control of his Commons departure, this was an extraordinary and ignominious end to a prime ministerial career.

Rishi Sunak's speech on the steps of Downing Street upon becoming prime minister included a commitment to lead a government of 'integrity, professionalism and accountability'. While signalling a desire to distance himself from the Johnson

---

[34] John Major, speech to the Institute for Government, 10 February 2022 (accessed at www.instituteforgovernment.org.uk/event/online-event/democracy-we-trust-keynote-speech-rt-hon-sir-john-major, 6 December 2023).

[35] Committee of Privileges, *Matter referred on 21 April 2022: Conduct of Rt Hon Boris Johnson MP: Final Report (Fifth Report of Session* 2022-23), HC 564 (London: House of Commons).

years, he in practice struggled to do so. Most notably, Sunak stayed away from a House of Commons vote on the Privileges Committee report, and chose not to block Johnson's resignation honours. This appeared, at least in part, to be driven by his need to hold his fractious party together.

THE PLACE OF THE EXECUTIVE IN THE CONSTITUTION

As well as provoking serious questions about constitutional standards, the period of Conservative-led government 2010–24 raised even more fundamental ones about the place of the political executive in the constitution. These two issues became strongly intertwined after the Brexit referendum, with allegations on all sides about established conventions being broken. Such controversies reached their high point with Boris Johnson's attempted prorogation of parliament in the autumn of 2019.

As already indicated, the UK constitution is traditionally one which is seen as having parliament at its heart. But despite the tradition of 'parliamentary sovereignty', the executive is often assumed really to be the dominant partner. While parliament formally holds government to account, and can *in extremis* remove it from office, the executive's House of Commons majority means parliament has often been portrayed as little more than a rubber stamp. Nowhere was this more evident than in Lord Hailsham's memorable phrase claiming that the UK was an 'elective dictatorship'. Hailsham went on to become Margaret Thatcher's lord chancellor, having made this allegation in 1976 – notably when Labour was in government.

There were always good reasons to question some of these assumptions. Parliament exercises its control over the executive in numerous and subtle ways.[36] Ministers are also carefully watched by the media and pressure groups, and remain sensitive

[36] Meg Russell and Daniel Gover, *Legislation at Westminster: Parliamentary Actors and Influence in the Making of British Law* (Oxford: Oxford University Press, 2017).

to public opinion. In the Blair/Brown years, reforms sought deliberately to disperse political power. But these years also ushered in the more frequent use of referendums, which had the potential to bring the UK's tradition of 'representative' democracy (through parliament) into conflict with the alternative of 'direct' democracy (by the people).

The coalition years were marked by attempts, particularly supported by the Liberal Democrats, to further weaken central executive power in favour of parliament. The Wright Committee reforms, discussed above, were consistent with that. Already in this period tensions were visible between what David Howarth, himself a Liberal Democrat MP 2005–10 and a member of the Wright Committee, later described as the competing 'Westminster' and 'Whitehall' interpretations of parliamentary sovereignty.[37] The first of these sees power resting in parliament itself, but the second privileges the government (or 'Crown') in parliament.

While various coalition initiatives failed, partly due to resistance on the Conservative side, one notable achievement was the introduction of the Fixed-term Parliaments Act 2011. This brought to an end the prime minister's exercise of a prerogative power to dissolve parliament, instead requiring a vote in the House of Commons to support any such move. While often seen as a sop to the Liberal Democrats (to avoid Cameron bouncing his coalition partners into an election at the time of his choosing), such a reform had been on the agenda for years, and was in line with other moves to rein in the prerogative.[38] The Labour manifesto in 2010 proposed such a change, and the Conservative manifesto of 2015 celebrated it, noting that the government had 'passed the Fixed Term Parliament Act [sic], an unprecedented transfer of Executive power'.[39]

[37] David Howarth, 'Westminster versus Whitehall: what the Brexit debate revealed about an unresolved conflict at the heart of the British constitution' in Oran Doyle, Aileen McHarg and Jo Murkens (eds.), *The Brexit Challenge for Ireland and the United Kingdom: Constitutions Under Pressure* (Cambridge: Cambridge University Press, 2021).

[38] Robert Hazell and Timothy Foot, *Executive Power: The Prerogative, Past, Present and Future* (Oxford: Hart, 2022).

[39] *The Conservative Manifesto 2015*, The Conservative Party, 2015, p. 49.

The Brexit referendum, followed by minority government, created great tensions over the executive's role in the constitution. Supporters of the UK's exit from the EU had long lamented the decline of 'parliamentary sovereignty', but their use of this term was to a large extent interchangeable with the idea of national sovereignty. Their prime concern was a loss of power to EU institutions, rather than any rebalancing of the domestic relationship. The referendum, meanwhile, could be seen as an instrument of popular rather than parliamentary sovereignty. But its result sent only a very blunt signal to the politicians – specifying that the UK should leave the EU, but not how or with what future relationship – leaving the detail to them. Theresa May, with her narrow to non-existent parliamentary majority, sought to take the referendum result as a mandate for government action and a reason to resist parliamentary involvement in the next steps. Boris Johnson, while fundamentally disagreeing with her about how that mandate should be interpreted, nonetheless subsequently sought to do the same. Hence rather than placing limits on prerogative powers, as the coalition had done, May and Johnson sought to use such powers to the full.

This was played out in the parliamentary battles over Brexit, touched on above.[40] Parliamentarians complained that they were being excluded from decision-making, while the prime minister complained that parliamentarians were overstepping the mark by taking control of the House of Commons' agenda and passing legislation against the executive's wishes. There were also major flashpoints with the courts. In early 2017, the Supreme Court ruled on the first of two cases brought against the government by the businesswoman Gina Miller. It concluded that legislation was needed to trigger the start of the formal Article 50 process whereby the UK would negotiate its exit from the EU. The ruling placed parliament back at the centre of proceedings. But the case had earlier prompted the *Daily Mail* to brand judges 'enemies of the people', which the government (including then-lord chancellor,

---

[40] Russell and James, *The Parliamentary Battle Over Brexit.*

Liz Truss) failed to condemn.[41] In autumn 2019, Boris Johnson then made an extraordinary attempt to prorogue parliament for five weeks at the height of the Brexit crisis. This sparked a second Miller case and a second defeat for the government in the Supreme Court. Again, Johnson's actions were judged to be an unlawful attempt to overextend prerogative power, causing the courts to step in in defence of parliament. John Major notably intervened in the prorogation case in support of Gina Miller and against the government.

Johnson pushed constitutional boundaries in numerous other ways during the second half of 2019. He hinted strongly that he would not obey a statute (the 'Benn-Burt Act', to extend the Article 50 period), and supporters briefed that he might even refuse to surrender office if subject to a parliamentary no-confidence vote.[42] Like the prorogation dispute, such actions risked drawing the role of the monarchy into controversy. Theresa May had sometimes engaged in anti-parliamentary rhetoric, but Johnson took this far further. His 2019 Conservative Party manifesto suggested that the UK had been 'paralysed by a broken parliament' and criticised 'the way so many MPs have devoted themselves to thwarting the democratic decision of the British people in the 2016 referendum' (though, as already noted, Johnson himself had been among those voting against May's Brexit deal).[43] The manifesto also, somewhat ominously, promised a constitutional review, including examination of the relationship between 'Government, Parliament and the courts'. The clear intention seemed to be to strengthen the former institution against the latter two.

The unexpected Covid crisis contributed to this pledge never being implemented; but the tone of wishing to strengthen executive control nonetheless continued. This was seen in an alleged 'muscular Unionism', whereby central government sought increasingly to take decisions for the devolved areas (a pattern

---

[41] James Slack, 'Enemies of the people', *Daily Mail,* 4 November 2016.

[42] Tim Shipman and Caroline Wheeler, '"Sack me if you dare," Boris Johnson will tell the Queen', *Sunday Times,* 6 October 2019.

[43] *The Conservative Manifesto 2019,* The Conservative Party, 2019, pp. 47–8.

which had begun with Theresa May over Brexit), as detailed in Chapter 8. It was also seen in repeated resistance to the constraints of international law. The permanent secretary to the Government Legal Department resigned in September 2020 over Johnson's Internal Market Bill, which sought to override parts of the EU withdrawal deal that he had recently signed, regarding Northern Ireland. This triggered protests from former Conservative leaders Theresa May, John Major and Michael Howard, and resistance from the House of Lords. It was dropped, as eventually was Johnson's Northern Ireland Protocol Bill, which included similar provisions. The most direct reversal from the earlier period (presaged in the 2019 manifesto) was Johnson's repeal of the Fixed-term Parliaments Act 2011. Although Theresa May had successfully gained MPs' approval for her early election in 2017, Johnson was frustrated by his inability unilaterally to call an election in 2019 (which was ultimately achieved through one-off legislation to circumvent the Act). MPs subsequently approved the Act's repeal in 2022. But the wisdom of this was brought immediately into question, when rumours began that Johnson would – against the wishes of his own MPs – request a parliamentary dissolution in order to avoid being removed as prime minister. This is something that he seems to have at least contemplated during his final days in office.[44]

The Brexit and Johnson period was a deeply troubled one, which brought into doubt central constitutional tenets that most Conservatives had long held dear: the UK's traditional institutions, the value of conventions and respect for the rule of law. Rishi Sunak's premiership initially steadied matters to a significant degree, but bore clear scars and shadows of these conflicts – many of which had played out in the Conservative Party itself. In particular, controversies about international law continued, with arguments over the European Convention on Human Rights (ECHR), most notably in relation to immigration policy and Sunak's pledge to 'stop the boats' used to smuggle

---

[44] Sebastian Payne, *The Fall of Boris Johnson: The Full Story* (London: Macmillan, 2022).

immigrants across the Channel. Rights concerns were also raised over determined attempts by Sunak's government to restrict the right to protest. The sacking of Sunak's home secretary Suella Braverman, a Brexit 'Spartan', immediately before the government was defeated in the Supreme Court over its policy to transport migrants to Rwanda, began a new period of fierce arguments inside the party. Braverman's proposal that Sunak should legislate to disapply the Human Rights Act, ECHR and international Refugee Convention, and to block the courts from intervening, was described by Damian Green, a senior member of Theresa May's Cabinet as 'the most unconservative statement I have ever heard from a Conservative politician'. Sunak's subsequent Safety of Rwanda Bill attracted rebel amendments from two sides – members of Green's 'one nation' caucus and hardline allies of Braverman – pulling in opposing directions. This bore a striking resemblance to the party's internal Brexit wars, with the prime minister preferring to stoke arguments with the House of Lords and the courts, rather than face down his own rightwingers.

THE EXTERNAL CONTEXT

In evaluating this period, specific UK context is clearly vital – the unusual circumstances of a coalition government, followed by minority government; the unique circumstances around the Brexit referendum; plus long-standing Conservative beliefs and traditions. But the troubled events described above cannot fully be understood without a wider, international, context. The UK was far from alone in suffering democratic instability over this period, or challenges to traditional political institutions and discourse.

The journalist Anne Applebaum has written persuasively about the *Twilight of Democracy*, and its relationship to dilemmas on the political right.[45] Many others have written of the interconnected challenges of the rise of populism on the one hand, and

---

[45] Anne Applebaum, *Twilight of Democracy: The Failure of Politics and the Parting of Friends* (London: Allen Lane, 2020).

'democratic backsliding' on the other.[46] Populist politicians make a mass appeal by claiming to be on the side of 'the people' against 'elites'. These alleged elites are likely to include traditional power holders, such as mainstream politicians, parties, judges and parliaments, which are presented as getting in the way of delivering for 'the people'. Consequently, populist leaders will often move to sideline or disempower such institutions. These patterns are now familiar from the US under Donald Trump, and from many other countries as diverse as Hungary, Poland, Turkey, Brazil and India. Parties of the right, as Applebaum explores, face particular dilemmas in such countries – between following a populist strategy, or defending the core institutions of democracy that have previously served them well, and seeking to hold back the populist tide.[47] Developments in the UK Conservative Party over the period described in this chapter clearly fit that mould.

Former Conservative Cabinet minister Rory Stewart, who stood for the leadership against Boris Johnson in 2019, and was subsequently stripped of the whip for joining attempts to block a no-deal Brexit, has written of a 'populist turn', fuelled by the effects of the 2007–8 global financial crisis.[48] A key product of this was the growth of anti-establishment movements, of which the movement against membership of the EU (spearheaded in the UK by UKIP) was one. Referendums themselves can be polarising devices, necessarily boiling down complex choices into binary alternatives, and potentially encouraging populist 'us' versus 'them' rhetoric. The Brexit referendum can be seen as both a symptom and cause of such division, much of which was played out inside the Conservative Party itself.

---

[46] E.g. Stephan Haggard and Robert Kaufman, *Backsliding: Democratic Regress in the Contemporary World* (Cambridge: Cambridge University Press, 2021); Moisés Naím, *The Revenge of Power* (New York: St Martin's Press, 2022).

[47] See also Tim Bale and Cristóbal Rovira Kaltwasser (eds.), *Riding the Populist Wave: Europe's Mainstream Right in Crisis* (Cambridge: Cambridge University Press, 2021).

[48] Rory Stewart, 'Populism's price', in David Gauke (ed.), *The Case for the Centre Right* (Cambridge: Polity, 2023), pp. 50-64, p. 56.

Some argue that the UK, with its uncodified constitution, is particularly vulnerable to such problems – but the presence of written constitutions in other states which have fared much worse in the battle against populism and backsliding does not bear this out. Others argue that the UK constitution has succeeded by re-stabilising itself – but this risks complacency. Populism and polarisation remain rife around the world, and the UK is far from immune. The Conservative Party continues to be riven by the kinds of splits that Applebaum describes, with some influential figures in the party tempted by 'culture wars', while others view these with horror.

GOVERNMENT, PARLIAMENT AND CONSTITUTION: AN ASSESSMENT

Despite natural expectations of constitutional calm, probably in no other area of policy during 2010–24 has the Conservative Party been more divided than over matters of governance itself. Certainly if Brexit is classed as a question of governance, this area wins hands down. There may also be no other area of policy in which reversals across this fourteen-year period were so stark, not just thanks to differences between the Conservatives and their initial governing partners the Liberal Democrats, but because of those same splits inside the party.

The Conservative Party has (like the Labour Party) always by necessity been a broad church, and therefore subject to tensions between competing factions. Control of the leadership has during this most recent period, as explored further in Chapter 13 of this book, veered between different groups, and also was influenced by circumstances. Cameron was by instinct a moderniser, and comfortable to enter government with the Liberal Democrats – indeed he realised that this would partially shield him from the party's Eurosceptic right. Cameron's attitude to questions of government and parliament could be seen as consistent with those of earlier centrist Conservatives – resistant to radical change, for example of the voting system, control of the House of Commons, or Lords reform, but supportive of moderate change and a smaller civil service. But particularly after 2015, his government faced unfamiliar challenges for Conservatives from the House of Lords, and his excessive appointments left a difficult, and rather unconservative, legacy.

It was only after Cameron's departure, however, that developments swerved increasingly wildly away from what could be considered the party's traditions. Theresa May was also a centrist, and a respecter of propriety and convention. But she was more tribal than Cameron, and proved unable to build relationships with others outside her party in order to freeze out her increasingly dominant internal Eurosceptic opponents – which arguably she should have done. May was dealt an extraordinarily difficult hand, but did not play it well in terms of her relations with parliament, and the wider public, over Brexit. Frustrated by the inability to garner agreement over her Brexit deal, she instinctively lashed out against parliament, and did not defend the judges when they sought to protect it. This helped to lay the ground for the populist, anti-pluralist, Johnson premiership. He sought to exploit public frustration (particularly among Brexit supporters) with traditional institutions such as parliament and the courts that Conservatives could have been expected conventionally to defend, and bent almost every possible constitutional convention. Rishi Sunak initially sought to steady matters in the years after Johnson, but inherited a fractious party and a legacy of years of bad behaviour. In particular, he did little to calm the deep divisions within the party over respect for the rule of law .

In terms of actual reform, beyond the delivery of Brexit itself (which clearly dominated), there is very little on the scorecard. Writing in the predecessor volume to this one, Cowley noted that the 'coalition effect in Parliament was . . . a pale imitation of what had been promised', and Loughlin and Viney list various promises undelivered on the constitution, judging this lack of delivery to be 'stark'.[49] Ironically, almost all that these latter authors could point to as succeeding was the passage of the Fixed-term Parliaments Act, which went on to be repealed by Boris

---

[49] Cowley, 'The coalition and Parliament', p. 137; Loughlin and Viney, 'The coalition and the constitution', p. 85.

Johnson. Some other clear reversals were also evident from the sections above. The coalition arrived wishing to cut civil service numbers, which was achieved, but Brexit, followed by Covid, saw these shoot up again. It arrived following high-profile allegations of impropriety, on promises to clean up politics (notably, the published coalition programme stated that 'The Government believes that our political system is broken').[50] Although regulation of standards in parliament generally improved, in other areas they increasingly came under attack. Even after the attempted prorogation, arguments with the courts, expulsion of long-standing Conservatives from the parliamentary party, and controversies over management of the civil service and public appointments, the 'partygate' revelations were shocking, and played a central role in forcing Boris Johnson out of power. Having quit the premiership, the findings of the Privileges Committee over his misleading of parliament saw him resign as an MP as well. This catalogue of misbehaviour makes the 'sleaze' of the John Major era, and even the MPs' expenses 'crisis', seem relatively small beer. It seems hard to conclude that the system is any less 'broken' than it was in 2010.

Some of the difficulties of this period – not just in the UK, but also overseas – can be seen as facilitated by public disillusionment with politics. When the public lose faith in their politicians, and political institutions are perceived to be illegitimate or corrupt, that creates great dangers for democracy. There were various alarming polls about the public's attitudes to politics over this period – the single most alarming of which was probably a 2018 Hansard Society poll which suggested that a majority of the public would support 'a strong leader willing to break the rules'.[51] Boris Johnson tapped into this frustration, and to a significant extent delivered what the public said they desired. But having seen the consequences, they appeared to recoil, and a large-scale survey in 2022 found 78 per cent agreeing that 'healthy democracy' requires politicians who 'always act within

[50] *The Coalition: Our Programme for Government*, p. 26.
[51] Hansard Society, *Audit of Political Engagement 16: The 2019 Report* (London: Hansard Society, 2019).

the rules', against just 6 per cent believing that it was acceptable for politicians sometimes to break the rules in order to 'get things done'. The same poll found that the most highly valued attribute of politicians (above, for example, working hard, getting things done or being clever) was honesty.[52] In the run-up to a general election, these results appeared problematic for the Conservatives, and offered clear opportunities for their opponents.

At the opening of this chapter, the circumstances inherited by the Conservatives were indicated to include not only the legacy of the expenses crisis, but also the effects of the Blair and Brown governments' constitutional reforms. While criticised often for being piecemeal and without a clear narrative, these reforms were widely seen as having dispersed power, in an attempt to get away from the UK's perceived 'elective dictatorship' (which Labour itself had railed against under Thatcher and Major). While few formal reforms were achieved in the subsequent Conservative years, the direction of travel, in terms of culture and behaviour, was often the reverse of this – particularly after 2016. Parliament and regulators were weakened, the courts and aspects of the devolution settlement were threatened, and conventions that constrain executive power were quite frequently set aside. In some regards this could be seen as reflecting instincts to return to the 'old' pre-1997 constitution. Had moves in this direction been planned and articulated, and pursued in a transparent way, they might even have been seen as a form of 'conservatism'. But much of what happened between 2010 and 2024 had an effect on government, parliament and the constitution that was very unconservative indeed.

---

[52] Alan Renwick, Ben Lauderdale and Meg Russell, *The Future of Democracy in the UK: Public Attitudes and Policy Responses: Final Report of the Democracy in the UK after Brexit Project* (London: Constitution Unit, November 2023).

13

The Conservative Party

Tim Bale

THE TORY PARTY'S LONGEVITY IS ROUTINELY put down to its ability to move and morph with the times – often in fairly short order. It should come as no surprise, then, that the decade and a half that followed David Cameron's appointment as prime minister saw a good deal of change at all levels of the party, whether we're talking about its leadership, its MPs, its grassroots members, CCHQ, or what deserves to be called 'the party in the media' – the Conservative-supporting print and broadcast outlets which are an integral and influential force. By taking each of its component parts in turn, but at the same time recognising, of course, that they overlap and interconnect, this chapter tries to provide a 360-degree portrait of an organisation (and, indeed, a milieu) that anyone hoping to make sense of the Conservative effect post-2010 needs to understand.

THE LEADERSHIP

If the four changes of leader that took place between 2016 and 2022 proved anything, they proved the wisdom of late John Ramsden's assertion that the party is best characterised as 'an autocracy tempered by assassination'.[1]

This is not the place for a detailed account of the (occasionally tragic, often farcical) twists and turns that led to such rapid turnover. Nor is it the place to explore the motives and man-oeuvring of those most heavily implicated – not least because the

---

[1] See Peter Hennessy, 'Churchill and the premiership', *Transactions of the Royal Historical Society*, 11:6 (2001), 295–306, p. 295.

combustible combination of high politics and genuinely held beliefs involved can hardly be said to represent a break from previous periods of Tory rule. What did change, however, were the rules under which the resulting leadership contests were held, the degree of public and broadcast scrutiny involved, and the increased availability and sophistication of polling data about candidates' likely chances. All this effectively narrowed the range of realistic options available, undermined the authority of the winner, and, eventually, created a situation in which, for the first time, there was a mismatch between the choice of leader made by MPs on the one hand, and the choice made by the grassroots on the other.

When it came to the rules, 'flex' might actually be a more accurate term to use than 'change' since, superficially, the basics established by William Hague's reforms of the late 1990s remained in place: Tory MPs, via a series of exhaustive secret ballots, continued to be tasked with whittling down a bunch of hopefuls until just two are left for the wider membership to choose between in a mail-in ballot. In reality, however, there were subtle, but important, variations in how each of the four contests were conducted, largely as a result of consultations between the representatives of the rank and file (traditionally referred to as the 'voluntary membership') via the Party Board and the body to which the party has, since the leadership first became an elected position in 1965, charged with running the process – the Executive of the 1922 Committee of Conservative backbenchers.[2]

One of the first tweaks was to the nomination process, the aim being to cut the number of MPs eligible to go into the first (parliamentary) stage of the contest, primarily in order to reduce the time it would take to conduct it. In 2016, all any of

---

[2] The role and composition of the Party Board is laid out in the party's constitution, available at https://public.conservatives.com/organisation-d epartment/202101/Conservative%20Party%20Constitution%20%20as%2 0amended%20January%202021.pdf. For everything you need to know about the '22, see Philip Norton, *The 1922 Committee: Power Behind the Scenes* (Manchester: Manchester University Press, 2023).

the hopefuls needed was one proposer and one seconder. In 2019, they needed eight of their colleagues. Moreover, in order to proceed further, those who crossed that initial threshold would need to win at least 5 per cent support in the first ballot and 10 per cent support in the second ballot, ensuring (in that contest at least) that only half of an initial ten candidates were left in the race after round two. The requirements were tightened still further for the first of the two contests in 2022, with contenders needing nominations from twenty colleagues (equivalent to 5.6 per cent of the parliamentary party; up from 2.6 per cent in 2019). They would then have to win the support of at least thirty colleagues in the first round to make it into subsequent rounds (i.e. 8.4 per cent of the parliamentary party compared to 5.4 per cent three years previously) – a hurdle that eventually saw two of the eight hopefuls fall at the first fence. The requirements for the second leadership contest of 2022 were more stringent still. Those wanting to run were given less than four days to collect one hundred nominations – a high bar that many suspected was set in the hope that Boris Johnson would be unable to surmount it. Given the number of Conservative MPs sitting at Westminster, this guaranteed that no more than three people would be able enter the race – a race that ended early anyway after only two people (Rishi Sunak and, to the amazement of many, Johnson) could boast sufficient support, one of whom (Johnson) promptly dropped out after calculating he would lose.

That he did so was an enormous relief to most Tory MPs, who were desperate to see Liz Truss replaced as soon as possible and who had little or no desire to see the voluntary party foist another unpopular leader on them, let alone to watch yet another episode of the Johnson psychodrama play out. Just as importantly, it also avoided what could well have been a car-crash attempt to conduct a ballot of grassroots members online over just three days – a process that would have been fraught with cybersecurity concerns, which would almost certainly have disenfranchised thousands (if not tens of thousands) of the rank and file, and which would anyway have denied them the opportunity to put the final two through their paces at hustings.[3]

Those hustings had become an integral part of the second stage of Tory leadership contests in 2019 (having been rendered unnecessary in 2016 by the decision of one of the final two, Andrea Leadsom, to drop out of the contest). Some sixteen events were staged over three-and-a-half weeks, while twelve were held over four-and-a-half weeks when Liz Truss beat Rishi Sunak in the summer of 2022. The 2019 contest was also the first to see broadcast debates between the candidates (two during the parliamentary stage of the contest and two following it) – a process repeated in 2022 (with, once again, two taking place during the parliamentary stage and two after it had finished).

All of this has arguably contributed to what political scientists have labelled the presidentialisation of politics, as well as making the leadership of the Conservative Party even less of a collective enterprise than it traditionally had been.[4] Ironically, this has happened at the same time as the rules governing the party's leadership contests (and, some argue, the poor quality of the candidates standing in them) have effectively ensured that the winners have been unable to boast that they have been elected with the overwhelming support of their fellow MPs. Theresa May could at least claim in 2016 that her 60.5 per cent in the final MPs ballot represented an impressive margin of victory over her nearest rival (Leadsom on just 25.5 per cent) – a result far more impressive, incidentally, than the one achieved in 2005 by David Cameron, whom only 45.5 per cent of his colleagues supported. In 2019, for all that second-placed Jeremy Hunt only managed to garner the support of a meagre 24.6 per cent of Tory MPs, the winner, Boris

---

[3] Matthew Sparkes, 'Tory leadership contest's online vote is still vulnerable to hackers', *New Scientist*, 25 August 2022. Worryingly, these concerns were voiced again when Truss's resignation initially looked as if it might trigger another grassroots ballot: see Richard Holmes, 'Tory leadership election: vote open to cyber attacks from hostile states like Russia, security sources warn', *i-paper*, 21 October 2022.

[4] See Paul Webb and Thomas Poguntke, 'The presidentialisation of politics thesis defended', *Parliamentary Affairs*, 66:3 (2013), 646–54.

Johnson, still only managed to scrape the barest of bare majorities (51.1 per cent) at the parliamentary stage. Things got even worse in the summer of 2022, when the eventual runner-up Rishi Sunak actually outscored Liz Truss in that stage, yet could hardly claim to be the MPs' favourite, winning over a mere 38.3 per cent of them to Truss's even more paltry 31.6 per cent. And as the years rolled on, the increasing availability and sophistication of membership polling, especially by YouGov, made a nonsense of the notion that Tory MPs play a gatekeeping function, at least in the strictest sense of that term. Since those MPs now have a fair idea of who is likely to do well in the second stage of the contest, every parliamentary ballot is cast (and indeed every public endorsement is given) with even more focus than ever on the likely outcome (and what it might mean for their promotion prospects as well as for the ideological direction of the party) rather than on who might be best qualified to do the job. While it would be an exaggeration, then, to say that the way the party selected its leaders was responsible in and of itself for the fact that it burned through four prime ministers in six years, one would have to say that the process – and the tweaks made to that process, as well as the second-guessing that polling has encouraged – may have helped to radically destabilise it.

THE PARLIAMENTARY PARTY

The parliamentary Conservative Party changed considerably between 2010 and 2024, both demographically and (possibly even more so) ideologically. By far the most obvious change on the Tory benches in the Commons was the increase in the number of women. This was achieved mainly as a result of the party enjoying greater electoral success following more than a decade in opposition. But it also owed something to efforts by David Cameron, supported by organisations like Anne Jenkin's *Women2Win*, to boost the number of female candidates standing in winnable constituencies. In 2010, some 49 Tory women were elected to parliament – a total that, admittedly, meant they constituted just 16 per cent of the party's MPs but which nevertheless represented a threefold increase on the 17 who won seats in 2005.[5] Even more women made it into the Commons in 2015 on the back of Cameron's unexpected win that year. However, although the party could boast 68 female MPs, they still constituted just 21 per cent of the party's strength at Westminster, while the loss of the party's majority under Theresa May in 2017 actually reduced their number to 67. Boris Johnson's big win in 2019 brought the total up to 87, but once again the absolute number was rather more impressive than the relative strength of female representation: men still made up three-quarters of all Conservative MPs.

The same caveats apply to any discussion of the party's contingent of ethnic minority MPs. Their number also increased very visibly over the years in government – all the more so, perhaps, because many of them found themselves rapidly promoted into the Cabinet and eventually, in Rishi Sunak's case, into Number 10. Standing in virtually all cases in seats so safe that the party could afford to take a risk on a candidate of Afro-Caribbean or Asian descent, the number of ethnic minority MPs increased from just two in 2005 to 11 in 2010 and 17 and 19 in 2015 and 2017 respectively.[6] In 2019 that number rose to 22 – impressive progress, perhaps, until one remembers that it constitutes just 6 per cent of all Tories representing the party in a House of Commons chosen by an electorate containing more than twice that many ethnic minority voters.

Other, less visible changes, may therefore be more significant. One example would be in the employment background of Conservative MPs. The proportion of them with business backgrounds dropped from nearly half in 2010 to just a quarter in 2019, while at the same time, lawyers went from 20 per cent to

[5] Figures on the composition of the parliamentary Conservative Party are taken from the 'Nuffield' *British General Election* of ... series published a year or so after each contest, each of which contains a chapter on candidates and MPs.

[6] On the 'ethnic penalty' that still exists in the UK, see Nicole Martin and Scott Blinder, 'Biases at the ballot box: how multiple forms of voter discrimination impede the descriptive and substantive representation of ethnic minority groups', *Political Behavior*, 43 (2021), 1487–1510.

just 8 per cent of the parliamentary party. The biggest growth was in the number of MPs with so-called 'instrumental' backgrounds (essentially jobs in politics like local councillor and political/policy research, as well a smattering of journalists). However, what the party did not manage to do (and, to be frank, showed zero interest in doing) was to increase its stock of representatives employed in vital public services like health and education, with neither sector accounting for more than ten Tory MPs (and often accounting for far fewer than that). Nor, in spite of the fact that the party won over more working-class voters than ever in 2019, could it boast many MPs from a working-class background.

Partly as a result of its increasing success in winning over working-class voters in England, as well as unionist voters in Scotland, the Conservatives were able, however, to claim that they now sent MPs to Westminster from parts of the country that had not traditionally proven particularly fertile electoral territory. In 2010, for instance, the parliamentary party contained fewer than fifty MPs representing constituencies in the north of England and only one MP representing a Scottish seat. The 2017 general election saw a marked change, however, and in Scotland, the Tories' marked increase in vote share translated into thirteen seats. In 2019 seven of those seats were lost but those losses were more than compensated for by successes south of the border, with the party able to boast – primarily as a result of its 'Get Brexit Done' pitch to culturally conservative voters in former Labour seats – around seventy MPs from the north of England. That said, two or three caveats are in order. First, the party found it more and more difficult to persuade people living in the country's large urban conurbations to support it. Second, the increase in MPs representing northern constituencies was far less impressive in relative than absolute terms: they made up 15 per cent of the parliamentary party in 2010 and still only 20 per cent after 2019.[7] Third, once things began to turn sour

---

[7] Thanks go to David Jeffery for providing the regional breakdown of constituencies represented by Tory MPs.

for the Tories in the wake of partygate and the disastrous Truss interregnum, an awful lot of them looked set to lose their seats, turning the party back into one confined to rural and small-town southern (and eastern) England.

Another shift that occurred was in the educational background of MPs, although there was arguably less to that shift than met the eye. In 2010, some 54 per cent of Tory members had been privately educated, a proportion that fell to 48 per cent in 2015 and 44 per cent in both 2017 and 2019 – still around six times higher, of course, than the population as a whole. True, the numbers of Conservative MPs who attended state comprehensives has increased; but that is almost certainly a result of the abandonment in most English counties of highly selective state grammar schools rather than any deliberate attempt on the part of the party to make its parliamentary ranks look and sound more like the country it competes to govern, educationally speaking at least. Meanwhile, any relative decline in the proportion of Tory MPs who attended either Oxford or Cambridge has more to do with the expansion of higher education than it does with some sort of affirmative action. Moreover, research by the Sutton Trust reveals again and again that those Conservative parliamentarians educated privately and at Oxbridge were more likely than their less privileged colleagues to make it into the Cabinets of all the prime ministers who served between 2010 and 2024.[8]

What David Cameron, despite his best efforts to get so-called 'A-listers' into winnable seats, was clearly unable to do between taking over the Tory leadership in 2005 and becoming prime minister five years later was to create a parliamentary party in his own image. Painstaking research to map the ideological composition of the MPs elected in 2010 suggests that a mere 13 per cent of them could be called 'Cameroons' in the sense of them being both social liberals and soft Eurosceptics (i.e. critical of the EU but not bent, like hard Eurosceptics, on root and branch

---

[8] The Trust has taken to analysing the educational background of the Cabinets of each new prime minister. They can be found on its website at www.suttontrust.com/our-research/

renegotiation or even departure).[9] That did not, of course, imply that the vast majority of those on the Tory benches were necessarily hostile towards Cameron; after all, half of all Conservative MPs in 2010 could be classified as socially liberal or not particularly socially conservative, while some 73 per cent (most of whom were soft Eurosceptics) were by no means implacably opposed to 'Europe'. Nevertheless, it did mean that what one might loosely term the 'hard right' of the party (those who were both social conservatives and hard Eurosceptics) constituted, at fifty individuals, some 16 per cent of the total – more than enough (especially because a fair few of them were new MPs looking to make their mark) to cause trouble. And that is what they duly did – along with some of the older hands upset that they had been passed over by a prime minister forced by coalition to cede government jobs to Lib Dem MPs.

Interestingly, while some of that embittered minority held that Cameron added insult to injury by appointing only Conservative colleagues in his own image to the frontbench, meticulous examination of his ministerial selections found 'no evidence of bias or disproportionate representation ... with regard to age, schooling, regional base, [social liberalism] and gender', even if it did find MPs with an Oxbridge education and/ or with safer seats were more likely to find favour. It did not, though, find 'any significant association between prior support for Cameron in the 2005 Conservative Party leadership election and subsequent ministerial advancement'[10] – something which differentiates Cameron from most of those who followed him as prime minister.

Theresa May, it is true, 'claimed her place among the butchers of Downing Street by demoting six former Cabinet colleagues to non-Cabinet posts and dispensing entirely with the

---

[9] See Timothy Heppell, 'Cameron and Liberal Conservatism: attitudes within the Parliamentary Conservative Party and conservative ministers', *British Journal of Politics and International Relations*, 15:3 (2013), 340–61.

[10] Tim Heppell and Andrew Crines, 'Conservative ministers in the Coalition government of 2010–15: evidence of bias in the ministerial selections of David Cameron?', *The Journal of Legislative Studies*, 22:3 (2016), 385–403.

services of seven others' in order to signal a big break from the Cameron years.[11] Nevertheless she went out of her way (possibly sensibly given how Brexit had split the party; possibly recklessly given it meant welcoming a number of vipers into the proverbial nest) to avoid creating a Cabinet full of Remainers (even if, strictly speaking, they were disproportionately included in its ranks) and/or those who had backed her in the aborted 2016 leadership contest. Boris Johnson and Liz Truss had no such qualms. In the summer of 2019, when Johnson helped take out May in order to succeed her, fewer than a third of those in or attending her Cabinet made the cut. Equally glaring was Johnson's determination to reward only those MPs who eventually endorsed him in the leadership contest. Only one member of his first Cabinet (Amber Rudd) had supported his rival, Jeremy Hunt (who was himself left on the backbenches) and she soon resigned. Four had chosen not to lend either man their support but the other fifteen had backed Johnson. As for the eleven (yes, eleven) MPs permitted to 'attend' rather than to join Cabinet, ten of them had done likewise.

Of the 22 MPs Truss appointed to Cabinet when she took over, 16 had eventually endorsed her for the leadership, while none had endorsed her rival, Rishi Sunak. That Truss did at least include early leadership contenders, Penny Mordaunt, Kemi Badenoch and Suella Braverman, and included 13 colleagues who had served in Johnson's outgoing 'caretaker' Cabinet, should not detract from the fact that, like Johnson, she rewarded loyalty rather than reaching out across the party. Nor was Sunak very different in that respect. True, he brought back a few old faces from the Johnson years who Truss had left out (such as Dominic Raab, Oliver Dowden, Michael Gove and Steve Barclay). But, like virtually all of his Cabinet picks, they had all eventually endorsed him in the autumn 2022 leadership-contest-that-never-was. The only one of his Cabinet choices who had stayed loyal to Johnson until the bitter end was Ben Wallace;

---

[11] Nicholas Allen, 'Brexit, butchery and Boris: Theresa May and her first Cabinet', *Parliamentary Affairs*, 70:3 (2017), 633–44.

but, as the incumbent defence secretary in the middle of the Ukraine conflict, he was all but unsackable anyway. Whether this trend toward appointing mainly on the basis of personal loyalty (rather than, say, perceived competence or the desire to achieve a degree of ideological and regional balance) is entirely healthy, of course, is a moot point.

By 2022, whether an MP had voted Leave or Remain had become far less of a factor in their promotion prospects than had been the case just after the 2016 referendum, not least because (in a shift which gained far less attention than perhaps it should have done) the vast majority of those who had opposed Brexit not only accepted the result but positively embraced it. Indeed, some of the conversions that occurred were so damascene that they can only have been driven by ambition: some Remainers simply rushed to adjust to the new dispensation (particularly if their own constituency looked likely to have voted Leave), while others finally felt able to come out of the closet as Leavers having previously demurred for fear of damaging their chances of preferment under David Cameron and his presumed successor, George Osborne. Meanwhile, the 135-plus Tory MPs (making up over 40 per cent of the parliamentary party) who had openly declared for Leave (many of them socially conservative backbenchers from Leave-voting areas who had been passed over for preferment or else already discarded by Cameron and Osborne) prepared to hold Theresa May's feet to the fire in order to achieve the 'hard Brexit' they so evidently wanted.[12]

May's gamble on an early general election, of course, failed to pay off in fairly spectacular fashion, resulting not just in a minority government but in Remain-voting Tories suffering a net loss of 17 seats compared to a net loss of just 2 seats for their Leave-voting counterparts. As a result, the leverage that these 'Brexit ultras' could exert over the leadership increased massively. Former Remainers may still have constituted a majority of the parliamentary party; but, at 170 versus 138, that majority was

---

[12] Luke Moore, 'Policy, office and votes: Conservative MPs and the Brexit referendum', *Parliamentary Affairs*, 71:1 (2018), 1–27.

now a little tighter[13] – and arguably increasingly meaningless now that some previously ardent Remainers had become enthusiastic backers of Brexit. The ultras were also far more organised. Indeed, the transmogrification of the sceptical European Research Group (ERG) into something resembling a guerrilla army is a reminder of another significant change during the party's decade and a half in office – namely, the further erosion (shading on occasion into complete collapse) of parliamentary discipline.

Anybody familiar with the post-war history of the Conservative Party will be aware that the near total voting cohesion that had long characterised it in the Commons began to break down in the early 1970s – most obviously (although not solely) over Europe. Indeed, even Margaret Thatcher in her pomp faced the odd rebellion. In the 1990s, however, the decline of deference and discipline became especially acute, triggered (but not confined) to the ratification of the Maastricht Treaty by John Major's government. It did not, then, come as any great surprise when David Cameron began to run into trouble with his own backbenchers, a number of whom were in any case (i) upset by the way he had thrown some colleagues under the proverbial bus during the parliamentary expenses scandal prior to the election, (ii) unimpressed by his failure to win an outright victory at the general election and (iii) frustrated (as we have seen) by the limitations that this (as well as his well-publicised desire to promote female MPs) imposed on his ability to give them frontbench jobs. Moreover, the passing of the Fixed Term Parliaments Act meant that Whips could no longer threaten potential rebels with the prospect of a parliamentary vote of confidence should they vote to defeat the government.

The sheer scale and scope of the rebellions that Cameron (who also, lest we forget, had to contend with a couple of his MPs defecting to the UK Independence Party (UKIP)) had to cope

---

[13] Philip Lynch and Richard Whitaker, 'All Brexiteers now? Brexit, the Conservatives and party change', *British Politics*, 13 (2018), 31–47.

with, however, was nevertheless shocking. Predictably enough, the worst and surely the most significant challenge came on Europe. Indeed by the time some 81 of his own MPs (49 of whom were from the 2010 intake) in October 2011 spectacularly defied a three-line whip in order to support an in–out referendum, the government had already faced twenty-two rebellions on the EU – all of which (along with the electoral threat posed by UKIP, which was beginning to spook so many Tories at Westminster) helped convince him to call for just such a referendum in January 2013.[14]

Yet Europe wasn't Cameron's only problem. House of Lords reform was never a particularly popular issue for Conservative MPs, but it was an important measure when it came to keeping their coalition partners happy. That didn't, however, prevent around a hundred of them effectively obliging the Liberal Democratic deputy prime minister Nick Clegg to pull his bill in the summer of 2012, scuppering Tory plans to reduce the size of the Commons in return. And, although Cameron would go on to list the introduction of 'same-sex' or 'gay' (i.e. equal) marriage as one of his proudest achievements, the Act only passed in early 2013 on the back of opposition votes after 136 Tories voted against, outnumbering the 127 colleagues who backed it. A few months later, Cameron failed to obtain parliamentary sanction for punitive missile strikes on Syria in order to punish Bashar-al-Assad for the use of chemical weapons against his own people. This was principally due to Labour controversially deciding at the eleventh hour not to offer its support. That should not be allowed to disguise the fact that some sixty Tory MPs (concerned that the UK might get dragged into another American-led debacle in the Middle East) also refused to back their government's motion, with thirty of them going so far as to vote against it.

Ultimately, however, it was Europe where Cameron's and, of course, May's lack of authority was most cruelly exposed. Both found that making concessions to their most troublesome troops

[14] Tim Bale, *Brexit: An Accident Waiting to Happen?* (London: KDP, 2022).

failed to satisfy them, Cameron gifting them a referendum and allowing Cabinet ministers to campaign for Leave, May opting immediately for a hard Brexit and even suggesting that 'No Deal is better than a bad deal'. Indeed May's failure was so complete that (in marked contrast to Cameron) she had to endure multiple hostile resignations from her Cabinet, a no-confidence vote (albeit one that she won in late 2018), and, in the winter of 2019 when the Commons voted on the Withdrawal Agreement she had negotiated with the EU, one of the worst parliamentary defeats ever inflicted on a Conservative prime minister by their own side. And like Cameron, she had to cope with defections, although this time not to a party on the populist radical right but to the short-lived Change UK (and from there to the Lib Dems).

Whether Tory MPs would have demonstrated rather more loyalty had May not taken the fateful (and in the end probably fatal) decision in 2017 to call an early election and so lose her Commons majority is debatable. After all, one of the reasons for calling the election in the first place was because the comfortable victory she and her closest advisers were hoping for would supposedly provide her (a 'reluctant Remainer' rather than an out-and-out Leaver) with a cushion against widely expected rebellions by the party's Brexit ultras. On the other hand, it is difficult to believe that the bulk of Tory MPs (who were never part of his sometimes hysterically dedicated fandom) would have put up with Boris Johnson's evident inability to do the job of prime minister as long as they did had it not been for his having pulled the party out of the nosedive it appeared to be in by the summer of 2019 before leading them to an eighty-seat majority less than half a year later.

That majority was only achieved, of course, after Johnson took the unprecedented step, in September 2019, of effectively expelling twenty-one MPs, including several former Cabinet ministers, after they voted against a three-line whip in order to head off a no-deal Brexit. True, ten of them were later readmitted (and several later became Tory peers). But the expulsions, which, in both scale and scope, went way beyond John Major's temporary withdrawal of the whip from a hard-core of Eurosceptic ultras in the 1990s, represented a break with the party's long tradition of tolerance, as well as reducing its already fairly shallow talent pool. Johnson, unlike his immediate predecessors, however, only had to cope with one defection, albeit to Labour – something that hadn't happened to a Tory prime minister since John Major's time in Number 10. On the other hand, no Conservative prime minister in modern times has had to cope with anything like the jaw-dropping mass resignations from the frontbench that finally finished Johnson off in July 2022.[15]

The draining away of Cameron's, May's and Johnson's authority was as evident (and to some extent driven) outside the Commons as it was inside – sometimes literally, given the propensity of some of their most troublesome colleagues to pop across the road to College Green in order to openly criticise them to journalists working for the proliferation of 24/7 broadcast news channels that occurred after 2010. Social media apps like Twitter/X also provided disaffected Tories with a platform that, under previous prime ministers, literally didn't exist and which created an alternative route to public prominence for MPs who might well have languished much longer (if not permanently) on the backbenches in days gone by. Some were very much individuals, happy to criticise whichever leader they'd decided to take on in the most colourful terms, Nadine Dorries being perhaps the best example: long before she became Boris Johnson's biggest fan, she was laying into David Cameron and George Osborne, memorably labelling them in the spring of 2012 as 'two arrogant posh boys who don't know the price of milk'.

Other so-called 'rent-a-quotes' owed their profile, at least in part, to their association with the proliferation of backbench groups advocating for a particular cause, most obviously the ERG, which helped provide a launch pad for ambitious publicity-seekers like Mark Francois, Jacob Rees-Mogg and Suella Braverman, as well as MPs who felt unfairly passed over or discarded. Not surprisingly, MPs who hoped to grab some

---

[15] Some 62 out of 179 government ministers, parliamentary private secretaries, trade envoys and party vice-chairmen are said to have resigned in the course of the crisis.

attention themselves were soon setting up other groups, partly in the hope that journalists, now able to bill them not simply as an individual backbencher but (supposedly far more impressively) as the representative of a whole bunch of colleagues concerned about a particular issue, would up their profile – hence the Northern Research Group, the China Research Group, the Covid Recovery Group, the Common Sense Group, the Net Zero Scrutiny Group, the Conservative Growth Group and the self-styled New Conservatives.[16] None of those groups, however, managed to attain anything like the leverage exercised by the ERG. Nor (this time in common with the ERG) did any of them constitute a faction in the strict sense of that term since, although some of their memberships overlapped, none of them developed a systematic, encompassing critique of the leadership that went much beyond the single issue (or set of issues) that they were set up to campaign on.[17] This reflects something that is all-too-easily forgotten – namely that the vast bulk of Tory MPs are basically bog-standard Thatcherites, positioned on a narrow spectrum at one end of which is the kind of fiscal conservatism favoured by Rishi Sunak and, at the other, the commitment to tax-cuts-at-all-costs associated with Liz Truss. This, along with Europe, climate change, the emphasis or otherwise on anti-woke rhetoric, and the scope, legality and feasibility of the government's attempts to tackle immigration, provided (and will continue to provide) plenty of room for argument. They nevertheless remain united in their belief that the market delivers better outcomes than an active welfare state, which therefore must be kept as small as possible, within the constraints imposed by the electorate's continued support for key pubic services. Inasmuch as any Tory MPs

---

[16] For more detail, see Tim Bale, *The Conservative Party after Brexit: Turmoil and Transformation* (Cambridge: Polity, 2023), pp. 171–3.

[17] See Tim Bale, 'Northern Research Group: faction or tendency', UK in a Changing Europe, 28 October 2020, https://ukandeu.ac.uk/northern-r esearch-group-faction-or-tendency/ and 'Rebels with a cause: backbench groups in the parliamentary Conservative Party', Hansard Society, 30 March 2023, www.hansardsociety.org.uk/blog/rebels-with-a-cause-back bench-groups-in-the-parliamentary-conservative-party

ever genuinely believed in levelling up – and, given how rapidly the phrase fell out of fashion as soon as Johnson departed the scene, there seem to have been very few of them – it was only in the sense of getting more spent on their constituency rather than a genuinely strategic attempt to reduce regional inequality.

None of this is to argue that the leadership was perfectly relaxed about the formation and the activities of such groups. While (arguably at least) they provided a pressure valve for discontent, they also provided a focus for it – and one, rightly or wrongly, taken seriously by lobby journalists always keen to write about dissent and disunity at Westminster. The other forum, of course, that could often be relied on to provide those same journalists with grist for their mills was the 1922 Committee, whose weekly meetings allowed backbenchers the chance to vent their frustration both with each other and with ministers. Moreover, elections to it were often factional affairs – not just because the results could be used to make claims about the balance of power within the parliamentary party but also because of its role in setting (and, as we have seen, varying) the rules for leadership contests. Little wonder that David Cameron and one or two of his successors toyed on occasion with trying to influence the selection of the 22's executive and its chairman, the resolutely independent and generally pretty popular Graham Brady. Little wonder, either, however, that such moves invariably failed to make much difference and, since they created no little resentment on the part of its backbenchers, may well have proved counterproductive. Whether well-publicised attempts by all five prime ministers to curry favour with backbenchers (by, for instance, inviting small groups of them to Downing Street or Chequers for getting-to-know-you or catch-up meetings, or else away-days in country-house hotels, or BBQs in the back garden of Number 10) were any more successful is difficult to tell. They certainly didn't stop each and every one of those leaders being routinely accused (often in anonymous briefings by their parliamentary colleagues) of being 'inaccessible', 'out of touch' and cocooned by a bunch of staffers supposedly giving them all the wrong advice (always defined, of course, as being the exact opposite of whatever advice the MP in question would themselves have given). Indeed, the fact that calls for Rishi Sunak to be replaced came barely a year after he took over, only to get louder as a general election approached, suggests that regicide risks becoming a habit among Tory MPs rather than a wholly rational response to electoral difficulties.

THE MEMBERSHIP

A complaint about the leadership only rarely heard (or at least voiced) in public from Tory MPs is that it views them with contempt. Ordinary party members, however, sometimes wonder whether that might be true in their case – and not, some allege, completely without cause.[18] Whether that suspicion contributed to the party losing members during its time in office is impossible to tell. But lose members it did. Since the Conservatives rarely reveal the numbers unless they absolutely have to (for example, during leadership contests when ballots have to be issued), we cannot be sure of the size of the Tory rank and file, when they entered government in 2010. We do know, however, that, some 254,000 people were eligible to vote in 2005 when David Cameron took over as leader from Michael Howard, the latter having narrowly failed to remove the final say ordinary members had been given in leadership contests and return it to MPs. When Boris Johnson was chosen to lead the party in 2019, that quarter of a million figure had dropped to 159,000, although – perhaps as a result of some kind of 'Boris bounce' as he became prime minister – that figure had risen to 172,000 when he was replaced by Liz Truss in the summer of 2022.

We also know from survey research that the Conservative Party's membership has become relatively inactive compared to the memberships of its main rivals, although that isn't saying much given that members of all parties seem to be doing less and less for them than they used to, whether it be during election

---

[18] See Paul Goodman, 'Party Chairman Lord Feldman denies calling Party members "mad, swivel-eyed loons"', ConservativeHome, 18 May 2013, https://con servativehome.com/2013/05/18/party-chairman-lord-feldman-denies-call ing-party-members-mad-swivel-eyed-loons/

campaigns or between them.[19] Some 29 per cent of Tory members confessed to the ESRC-funded Party Members Project that they had done absolutely nothing for the party during the 2015 election campaign – a figure that rose to 44 per cent in 2017 and an astonishing 57 per cent in 2019 (suggesting, incidentally, that a big election win doesn't really require a party to have that many 'boots on the ground'). Meanwhile, what one might conceive of as the hardest of the hard-core grassroots activists – those who claimed they had put in over forty hours of work for the party in the election campaign – also declined in number, accounting for 17 per cent of members in 2015, 10 per cent in 2017 and just 6 per cent in 2019. As for specific activities, the proportion of members claiming to have done some leafletting in the three elections in question dropped precipitately from 43 to 30 to 21 per cent; and when it came to canvassing, the proportion fell from 36 to 21 to 15 per cent. Activity between elections also fell: in 2015, nearly a third of members said they'd attended at least one party meeting; nowadays a local association would be lucky to see one in ten of them turn up.

There were also some significant shifts in ideology and policy preferences at the grassroots. Surveys picked up a noticeable increase between 2015 and 2019 in the proportion of members willing to criticise big business, management, and the fact that ordinary people and the poor were getting a raw deal, even if that increase failed to translate into a significant rise in support among members for redistribution. It did seem, however, to be associated with a noticeable decline in support for government cost-cutting: between 2015 and 2017 the proportion of Tory members thinking austerity hadn't gone far enough halved from 56 to 28 per cent, while the proportion thinking it had

[19] All the figures on members' activity, attitudes and demographics come from the work of the ESRC-funded Party Members Project, most obviously Tim Bale, Paul Webb and Monica Poletti, *Footsoldiers: Political Party Membership in the 21st Century* (Abingdon: Routledge, 2019). See also the project's website (https://esrcpartymembersproject.org/) and Sarah Childs and Paul Webb, *Sex, Gender and the Conservative Party: From Iron Lady to Kitten Heels* (Basingstoke: Palgrave, 2011).

gone too far went up from just 3 to 20 per cent (the rest thinking it was 'about right').

This reflects the fact that, after a decade in power, some fairly significant differences between the party's grassroots and its parliamentary representatives had begun to emerge – and not just on the economy but also social and cultural stances. For instance, offered the chance in early 2020 to agree or disagree on a number of statements routinely used by researchers to tap into people's underlying values, Tory MPs turned out to be significantly further to the market-oriented, small-state right than Tory members, even if the latter weren't quite as centrist as Tory voters. On the other hand, those MPs were (at least on average and in private if not in public) significantly more socially liberal than both their local association rank and file and their voters, the majority of whom would be classified by political scientists as 'authoritarian' or, in more common parlance, 'culturally conservative'.[20]

Moreover, we can see from a survey of party members conducted after the 2017 election that this was likely to result not only in Tory MPs and would-be MPs being pressed to show they were on the same page in that respect, but also in the party being less diverse than it might aspire to be. True, this was not necessarily the case when it came to gender: although 48 per cent of grassroots members said they'd like the number of female MPs to stay about the same, nearly as many (42 per cent) wanted to see more women in parliament. But the corresponding figures for ethnic minorities were 49 and 31 per cent respectively, while when it came to Muslim MPs in particular they were 44 and 17 per cent, with 26 per cent of members confessing they'd actually like to see *fewer* of them. As for MPs from working-class backgrounds, 53 per cent of Tory members were happy with the way things were (which, of course, means very, very few across parliament as a whole, let alone on the Conservative benches), even if 32 per cent said they'd like to see more.[21]

---

[20] Alan Wager, Tim Bale, Philip Cowley and Anand Menon, 'The death of May's Law: intra- and inter-party value differences in Britain's Labour and Conservative Parties', *Political Studies*, 70:4 (2022), 939–61.

[21] Bale et al., *Footsoldiers*, pp. 134–9.

The biggest change over time, as far as the membership was concerned, however, was on Brexit. When asked, just after the 2015 election, how they thought they would vote in the EU referendum, a mere 16 per cent said they were definitely going to vote Leave, compared to 19 per cent who said they would vote Remain and a whopping 65 per cent who said it would depend on the deal David Cameron brought back.[22] By the time the Party Members Project conducted a special survey about Brexit at the very end of 2018, getting on for eight out of ten Tory members said they had voted Leave – and nearly two-thirds said they would be happy to see the UK depart without a deal.[23] Six months later, 54 per cent were telling YouGov that they were even prepared to see the destruction of the Conservative Party if that was what it would take to ensure the country left the European Union, while 63 per cent were prepared to see the end of the union with Scotland and 61 per cent were prepared to put up with significant damage to the economy in order to achieve that outcome. Some 46 per cent also said they'd be happy to see Nigel Farage lead the Tories.[24] Hardly surprising, then, that when his fellow populist politician, Boris Johnson, was forced out of Number 10 by his parliamentary colleagues, some 53 per cent of the Conservative rank and file thought they had been wrong to oust him.[25] How much they were influenced in all this by their favourite newspaper (in 2017 some 33 per cent said

---

[22] See Tim Bale, Paul Webb and Monica Poletti, 'Cameron and Tebbit are both wrong', 5 February 2016, https://esrcpartymembersproject.org/2016/02/05/cameron-and-tebbit-are-both-wrong/

[23] See Party Members Project, 'No deal is better than May's deal', 4 January 2019, https://esrcpartymembersproject.org/2019/01/04/no-deal-is-better-than-mays-deal/

[24] Matthew Smith, 'Most Conservative members would see party destroyed to achieve Brexit', YouGov, 18 June 2019, https://yougov.co.uk/topics/politics/articles-reports/2019/06/18/most-conservative-members-would-see-party-destroye

[25] Matthew Smith, 'More from our Conservative members poll', YouGov, 3 August 2022, https://yougov.co.uk/topics/politics/articles-reports/2022/08/03/more-our-conservative-members-poll

they were readers of the *Telegraph* and 17 per cent said they were readers of the *Mail*) is hard to tell.[26] It is worth noting, however, that their charity did not extend to Johnson's successor, Liz Truss, who they had only very recently chosen as their leader by 57 per cent to Rishi Sunak's 43 per cent. Asked about her performance by YouGov in the wake of the disastrous 'mini-budget', 83 per cent said she was doing badly.[27]

What didn't change much, though, was the demographic composition of the party's rank and file. Throughout, around eight out of ten Tory members were middle class, with seven out of ten of them working in (or, if they were retired, having worked in) the private sector and, in many cases, on higher incomes (and sometimes much higher incomes) than the members of other parties. Women continued to make up only around a third of the total, while the proportion of grassroots Conservatives who were white British remained well over 95 per cent. At least a third (and probably more) of the membership were (and still are) of pensionable age, and around the same proportion lived (and still live) in southern England (excluding London) – many of them, presumably in the so-called 'Blue Wall' seats in the home counties. Given this, the low turnout at the inaugural conference in true-blue Bournemouth of the self-appointed Conservative Democratic Organisation, set up after the ouster of Boris Johnson prompted some of his biggest backers to argue that ordinary members needed more say in the party's affairs, suggests (for good or ill) that it found precious little support among them.[28]

---

[26] Bale et al., *Footsoldiers*, p. 49.

[27] Patrick English, 'Conservative members have buyer's remorse', YouGov, 18 October 2022, https://yougov.co.uk/topics/politics/articles-reports/2022/10/18/conservative-members-have-buyers-remorse

[28] On the CDO, see its website: www.conservativedems.co.uk. See also William Atkinson, 'Party Chairman Lord Feldman denies calling Party members "mad, swivel-eyed loons"', ConservativeHome, 16 May 2023, https://conservativehome.com/2023/05/16/the-conservative-democratic-organisation-conference-a-campaign-rally-for-a-man-who-didnt-bother-to-turn-up/

CCHQ, STAFFERS AND ADVISERS

So much for what political scientists like to call 'the party in public office' (the MPs) and 'the party on the ground' (the membership). What about 'the party in central office' – the operation (located mainly in Conservative Campaign Headquarters (CCHQ) in Westminster's Matthew Parker Street) charged with keeping the whole thing well resourced, well informed and electorally competitive?

Money, it has to be said, was rarely a problem throughout the period in question – in marked contrast to when Labour was led by Tony Blair and regularly outperformed the Conservatives on the financial front.[29] Not long after Blair's departure as prime minister, however, the tables began to turn – so much so that at the 2010 election, the Conservatives (unlike Labour, which by then had slipped back badly) had no difficulty whatsoever in spending the £18.9 million permitted by the formula introduced by the 2001 Political Parties, Elections and Referendums Act. Although there was much talk of campaigning entering the digital age, the vast bulk of the Tories' outlay actually went on fairly traditional media, including billboards and (especially) direct mail to key voters (identified by centrally organised tele-phone canvassing) in target constituencies. After the election, Labour began to do better, only for the Conservatives to overtake it once again from late 2013 onwards; indeed between the last quarter of that year and the dissolution of parliament for the 2015 election, the party raised £40.5 million (more than twice as much as Labour and well over five times as much as the Lib

---

[29] All the cash sums cited in this and subsequent paragraphs are taken from Justin Fisher's authoritative chapters on party finance in the following volumes: Andrew Geddes and Jonathan Tonge (eds.), *Britain Votes 2010* (Oxford: Oxford University Press, 2010); Andrew Geddes and Jonathan Tonge (eds.), *Britain Votes 2015* (Oxford: : Oxford University Press, 2015); Jonathan Tonge, Cristina Leston-Bandeira and Stuart Wilks-Heeg (eds.), *Britain Votes 2017* (Oxford: Oxford University Press, 2018); and Jonathan Tonge, Stuart Wilks-Heeg and Louise Thompson (eds.), *Britain Votes: The 2019 General Election* (Oxford: Oxford University Press, 2020).

Dems) and during the six-week election period it received a further £6.1 million. All that allowed the Conservatives both to plan and execute an effective campaign which was even more closely directed towards particular voters in target seats, with activists being bussed from safer seats in order to boost capacity – a practice that, although it was to lead to problems further down the line when questions were raised about bullying and about the blurring of expenditure between the national and local campaigns, may well have been worth a few votes.[30] Direct mail was once again very important (and still more important than digital), but this time backed up not with billboards but extensive advertising in local newspapers – often via 'wraparounds' covering their back and front pages. The party also made use of its superior resources to get campaign organisers in place well in advance of the election itself.

The same was not true in 2017, with an election called at short notice cruelly exposing the party's decision to let go many of the staff who had helped it win two years before as well as the inadequacies of both its IT and its canvassing, especially in Labour seats it expected (at the outset anyway) to be able to win. The problem, however, was organisational (and indeed strategic) rather than financial.[31] For sure, Labour benefited from the huge rise in membership income generated by the excitement around Jeremy Corbyn. But the elevation to the leadership of a radical left-winger ensured that the Conservatives, while they had far fewer members, continued to have little difficulty in soliciting donations. Between the second quarters of 2015 and 2017, the party's central income hit £48.8 million – nearly twice as much as Labour's. The election period in particular proved very fruitful, with the party taking in £12.7 million compared to Labour's £4.5 million and the Lib Dems' £1.2 million. Sadly, although the increasing importance of digital campaigning (particularly on Facebook) meant that some of that money could usefully be spent (online ads being much quicker to produce and space quicker to procure than is

---

[30] See Ed Howker and Guy Basnett, 'The inside story of the Tory election scandal', *Guardian*, 23 March 2017.

[31] For more detail, see Bale, *The Conservative Party after Brexit*, pp. 35–46.

the case with print), much of the canvassing data that might have allowed it to be well targeted was of relatively poor quality.

The 2019 election, although seemingly called at similarly short notice, was in fact much better planned, better researched and better executed, as well as (once again) much better resourced.[32] Unlike 2017 (and to a lesser extent 2010), it was clear who was in charge of the party's campaign (the Australian strategist Isaac Levido), and the party was able to make full use of the considerable resources at its command, not least because CCHQ, its fundraising operations, its research capacity and its campaign capacity in the constituencies had been significantly retooled under Sir Mick Davis, who became the party's first proper CEO in the aftermath of the 2017 disaster.[33] Partly as a result of his efforts and partly from the fear of the wealthy that the country might elect an out-and-out socialist, although the party's income fell away as usual after the election of that year, it did so less than in previous years. And that same fear ensured that the campaign period itself was even more of a bonanza than usual, with the Tories raising £19.4 million compared to Labour's £5.4 million and the Lib Dems' £1.2 million. Corporate donations as a proportion of centrally collected campaign income were particularly significant, rising from 24 per cent in 2010, 19 per cent in 2015, and 23 per cent in 2017 to 31 per cent. Once again, the increase in digital campaigning (which moved away from preponderant reliance on Facebook towards YouTube, Google and other platforms) meant that some of that money could actually be used even though, as always, direct mail played an important part too.

In the aftermath of the election and the chaos brought about by first Covid, then Partygate, and finally Liz Truss's and Kwasi Kwarteng's 'mini-budget', the party's finances took a hit. However, once Rishi Sunak took over, donations began to flow back in, with the party's coffers swelled (to the tune of £12.3 million in the first three months of 2023) by a handful of

---

[32] See Robert Ford, Tim Bale, Will Jennings and Paula Surridge, *The British General Election of 2019* (London: Palgrave, 2021), pp. 97–1, 193–275.

[33] See Bale, *Conservative Party after Brexit*, pp. 58–61.

spectacularly large gifts from a handful of spectacularly well-off individuals, one of the largest being a record-equalling £5 million from Mohamed Mansour, a billionaire businessman who served as a minister under the former dictator of Egypt, Hosni Mubarak. This only added to an ongoing controversy over the sometimes questionable sources of the party's funding, as well as over the access to ministers, including the prime minister, that it seems to grant its benefactors.[34] The party, however, refused (as usual) to engage with such criticism, sticking to the line that, as long as donations complied with the letter of the law, then everything was above board, ignoring the fact, critics observed, that the law was full of loopholes, particularly when it comes to 'foreign donations' and anonymous donations made through 'unincorporated associations' – loopholes which the Conservatives showed no signs of wanting to close[35] – especially after the Sunak government, in the autumn of 2023, raised the maximum amount that could be spent by parties at election by 80 per cent to around £35 million.

Not everyone who works for the Conservatives is based in CCHQ, of course. Out in the country, the party continues to employ organisers and agents, whether funded centrally or by local associations or a combination of the two, albeit often on temporary contracts that come to an end after general elections. Meanwhile, back in London there are a raft of advisers (including taxpayer-funded 'SpAds') who work for ministers and, indeed, prime ministers.[36] Many of them have political ambitions of their own and have a background either in journalism and lobbying/public affairs and/or in centre-right think tanks that help constitute what one might call the wider Conservative

---

[34] See, for example, Peter Geoghegan, *Democracy for Sale: Dark Money and Dirty Politics* (London: Head of Zeus, 2021) and for ongoing coverage, check the following investigative news websites: www.opendemocracy.net; https://bylinetimes.com/; and www.tortoisemedia.com

[35] See Ben Quinn, 'Government defeats move to tighten UK foreign donations law', *Guardian*, 3 May 2023.

[36] See Peter Cardwell, *The Secret Life of Special Advisers* (London: Biteback, 2020).

milieu and claim (some more persuasively than others) to influence party policy – in pursuit of which influence they have attempted (perhaps increasingly so) to occupy particular niches: the oldest, the Institute for Economic Affairs (IEA), the Adam Smith Institute (ASI) and the Centre for Policy Studies (CPS), continue to major on market solutions for economic problems; the Centre for Social Justice (CSJ) founded by former leader Iain Duncan Smith focuses on welfare and poverty (the growth in which since 2010 had given it plenty to talk about); slightly more eclectic newer entrants like the liberal Conservative Bright Blue and the more communitarian Onward cover issues like environment, education, energy and housing, often backed up by polling; meanwhile Policy Exchange, which was originally founded by Cameroon modernisers, while also covering foreign policy and Europe, has become preoccupied with the 'war on woke'.

Irrespective of which think tank or media outlet they came from, some of the advisers employed by Conservative politicians from 2010 onward have garnered a degree of influence and notoriety that relatively few of their forerunners managed to achieve. Under David Cameron, Steve Hilton and Andy Coulson wielded considerable (and by the end of their time in Downing Street highly controversial) sway.[37] Likewise, under Theresa May, Nick Timothy and Fiona Hill.[38] Ditto (in spades) Dominic Cummings and Lee Cain under Boris Johnson.[39] Other media and policy advisers and chiefs of staff (among them Andrew Cooper, Craig Oliver, Gavin Barwell, Munira Mirza and Guto Harri) have also played important roles, although arguably not as important as the parts played by Australian 'election gurus' Lynton Crosby (who also played a significant role in Boris Johnson's several leadership bids) and, more recently, Isaac Levido. None of this, of course, is entirely new: Ted Heath set

---

[37] See Tim Bale, *The Conservative Party from Thatcher to Cameron*, 2nd ed. (Cambridge: Polity, 2016), pp. 370–1 and 376–7.

[38] See Anthony Seldon with Raymond Newell, *May at 10* (London: Biteback, 2020), pp. 102–46.

[39] Anthony Seldon and Raymond Newell, *Johnson at 10: the Inside Story* (London: HarperCollins, 2023), pp. 243–312.

up the original government think tank, the Central Policy Review Staff, initially under Shell's Nathaniel Rothschild, while Margaret Thatcher sought counsel and inspiration from several 'outsiders', including (most controversially since it led to the resignation of her chancellor, Nigel Lawson) Alan Walters and the advertising executive (and future *House of Cards* author) Michael Dobbs.

THE PARTY IN THE MEDIA

No analysis of the Conservative Party since 2010 would be complete without mention, however brief, of the Tory-supporting news outlets and websites which pump out its propaganda, help set its agenda, and provide a forum for both the aggrieved and the ambitious. And while it might be tempting (especially for those who remember, for instance, the *Sun* under Kelvin MacKenzie in the 1980s and 1970s or even the *Telegraph* demanding to hear 'the smack of firm government' back in the 1950s) to argue *plus ça change, plus c'est la même chose*, that would be to understate the profound shifts that have occurred over the last decade or so.

While precise figures are hard to obtain, there is little doubt that the drop in circulation suffered by the Tory press (and indeed the press as a whole) has continued apace and, indeed, probably accelerated.[40] The best estimate, dating from the summer of 2023, suggested that the weekday print circulation of the *Mail* was 780,000, followed by the *Sun* on 718,000, then, a long way behind, the *Telegraph* on 188,000 and the *Express* on 173,000.[41] The equivalent figures for May 2010 were 2,090,000 for the *Mail*, 2,940,000 for the *Sun*, 700,000 for the *Telegraph* and 660,000 for

---

[40] Charlotte Tobitt and Aisha Majid, 'National press ABCs', *Press Gazette*, 20 June 2023, https://pressgazette.co.uk/media-audience-and-business-data/media_metrics/most-popular-newspapers-uk-abc-monthly-circulation-figures-2/

[41] Bron Maher, 'DMGT acquisition of Telegraph could give it 50% daily newspaper market share', *Press Gazette*, 12 June 2023, https://pressgazette.co.uk/media_business/dmgt-daily-mail-telegraph-acquisition-market-share/

the *Express*. As a result, one might have expected their influence on Tory MPs to have lessened considerably. Yet this does not seem to have happened. This is partly because the idea that newspapers influence voters, while greeted with scepticism by many political scientists, seems to have retained its hold on politicians.[42] It may also be because those politicians are impressed by their seemingly impressive online reach: taking only visits to their websites from the UK in April 2023, for example, the figure for the *Sun* was 26.1 million, for the *Mail* 24.8 million, the *Telegraph* 15.9 million and the *Express* 14 million.[43]

Whether that reach means they still help to decide the outcomes of general elections (inasmuch as they ever did), who knows? But what is clear to anyone reading them every day is that those titles – particularly in the wake of Brexit but also, presumably, because they are now in the market for 'clicks' in an increasingly competitive 'attention economy' driven by 'social' rather than 'legacy' media – have become more hyperbolic (and even on occasion hysterical) than ever.[44] It would probably be unfair to say the same of the weekly news magazine the *Spectator* (which has a print circulation of over 70,000 and a digital circulation of just over half that figure), although it certainly showed considerable enthusiasm for Brexit and arguably actually led the pack when it came to criticising Covid lockdowns as they were happening – both causes that exercised the dailies, sometimes beyond measure. It would, however, be completely fair to say the

---

[42] For a well-reasoned and well-regarded example of that scepticism, see Kenneth Newton, 'May the weak force be with you: the power of the mass media in modern politics', *European Journal of Political Research*, 45:2 (2006), 209–34.

[43] Source: www.statista.com/statistics/288763/newspaper-websites-ranked-by-monthly-visitors-united-kingdom-uk/ Note that these figures do not equate, of course, to circulation since each webpage viewed will constitute a visit. Note, too, that the vast majority of such visits are unlikely to involve pages with political content!

[44] See Liz Gerard, *TRUSSED UP: How the Daily Mail Tied Itself in Knots over the Tory Leadership* (London: Bite-Sized Books, 2022), or practically any op-ed in the *Telegraph* by figures such as Allister Heath or Brexit negotiator David Frost.

same about GB News – the avowedly populist, 'culture-war'-waging television station which by 2023 could boast getting on for three-quarters of a million YouTube subscribers and which, after giving Nigel Farage his own show, went on to employ several current and former Conservative MPs (among them right-wingers like former Cabinet minister Jacob Rees Mogg, deputy party chairman Lee Anderson, and Boris Johnson über-fan Nadine Dorries) as hosts.[45]

All this, along with what at times verged on their obsessive support for Boris Johnson, even when his actions and continued presence in Number 10 were clearly driving down the Conservatives' poll ratings, has arguably pushed the party in a more radical right-wing populist and determinedly nationalist direction. Johnson himself memorably referred (in conversation with Dominic Cummings) to the *Telegraph* as his 'real boss', and there is plenty of evidence to suggest, for instance, that the anti-lockdown campaigning by that newspaper and other titles influenced not just his stance on Covid but also that of the two politicians who were clearly hoping to replace him, most obviously Liz Truss and Rishi Sunak.[46] And the latter's row-back on policies designed to hasten the country's progress towards net zero announced in September 2023 came after months of campaigning by the same outlets, all of which insisted that the party's unexpected retention of Johnson's Uxbridge seat in a by-election held earlier in the year was proof positive that ditching 'the green crap' (as David Cameron had once insisted during his time in Number 10) was the way to go. That said, the apex of their influence was surely the plan to solve the 'small boats crisis' by sending a few hundred of the tens of thousands of asylum seekers washing up on the Kent coast to landlocked Rwanda in West Africa – a policy that many voters (and, indeed, many Tory MPs and peers) deemed expensive, unworkable and potentially unlawful.

---

[45] For a critical but informative take on the station, see Tim Adams, 'Farage, Fox and rolling outrage: the inside story of GB News', *Observer*, 12 March 2023.

[46] See Bale, *The Conservative Party after Brexit*, chapter 7.

CONCLUSION

After well over a decade in power, the Conservative Party remained, as always, a leadership-driven organisation, albeit one whose leaders often found it difficult to assert their authority over an increasingly 'Brexity' and increasingly restive parliamentary party – especially once they were branded a loser rather than a winner. That parliamentary party came over time to look a little more like the country it was governing – but only a little. The same could not be said of the party's grassroots, although neither that nor their shrinking numbers and much-reduced activism stopped them playing an outsize role in determining the direction of a party in which, paradoxically, they had no formal role in deciding policy. Underneath all the froth, the party organisation, although not always the finely tuned campaign-machine of legend, continued to provide the Tories with a ready supply of cash, while unelected advisers – some employed by the party, some funded by the taxpayer – probably exerted more influence than ever before. The same applied to the party's representatives in the media – in spite of the ongoing decline in circulation since 2010.

All this, along with the need to combat several Farage-led insurgencies on its right flank, has arguably helped push Tories further from the centre and towards what some call national populism.[47] Whether anyone proves willing and able to push it back again, who knows? Some might argue that there will be no need to. After all, Poland and Hungary (and, if Donald Trump were to win the presidency again, the USA) provide proof that transitioning from the mainstream to the populist radical right can be an electorally successful strategy. Then again, the outcomes for other centre-right parties in Europe (whether they be conservatives, market liberals, or Christian democrats) that have, even if they haven't adopted it holus-bolus, flirted with

[47] See Roger Eatwell and Matthew Goodwin, *National Populism: The Revolt against Liberal Democracy* (London: Pelican, 2018).

such a strategy have been decidedly mixed.[48] The fate of Les Républicains in France (the only other European country employing first-past-the-post), for example, should serve as a dire warning to those Tories convinced that aping the rhetoric of more hard-line challengers on their right flank is the way to go. Meanwhile, evidence from the gold-standard British Social Attitudes survey on the UK's growing social liberalism suggests that there is likely to be far less mileage in pursuing some kind of war on woke on this side of the Atlantic than there is in the far more polarised United States. Whether MPs associated with the Common Sense Group and those who like to call themselves 'National Conservatives' will be persuaded by that evidence, however, remains doubtful, opening up the possibility of a debilitating internal conflict with the majority of their colleagues who, reluctantly or otherwise, see little if any long-term gain in the party pursuing some kind of culture war.

There are, of course, other issues that could generate infighting, the most obvious, perhaps, being Brexit. Although many Tories hope that, having left the EU, they can leave the issue behind, the fall-out from the referendum demonstrated its potential to divide the party to an extent not seen (and maybe not even matched) by its disputes over the Corn Laws in the mid nineteenth century and Tariff Reform in the early twentieth – not least because (like those disputes) it places two fundamental Tory tenets (namely, national sovereignty and free markets) in direct competition. If surveys continue to show more and more people thinking Brexit was a mistake and saying they want to see the UK forging closer links with the EU (even to the extent of actually rejoining), some Conservatives may find it difficult to maintain the silence they have observed for the sake of their careers since 2016, particularly if evidence continues to mount that the damage to the UK economy is turning out to be just as serious as many experts predicted back then. However, the likelihood that the party's Brexit ultras will ever concede the whole

[48] For an extended discussion, Tim Bale and Cristóbal Rovira Kaltwasser (eds.), *Riding the Populist Wave: Europe's Mainstream Right in Crisis* (Cambridge: Cambridge University Press, 2021).

thing was a mistake, let alone concede defeat, is vanishingly small, setting the stage for yet another battle royal over 'Europe' – one which could make the 'Tory wars' over the single currency in the 1990s and early 2000s and 'soft' versus 'hard' Brexit in the aftermath of 2016 look tame in comparison.

Certainly, should such a battle take place and should the party pick a leader who, rather than pursuing a more moderate, pragmatic path, chooses to double down on national populism and the 'war on woke' (perhaps by pledging to leave the European Convention on Human Rights), then it could well find itself in a far more parlous state than it did when it lost office in 1964 and 1997. That said, the idea that the Conservatives will – at least if the UK continues to reject the idea of moving toward proportional representation – experience some sort of historic split still seems highly unlikely. The party's will to power tends to reassert itself, even if it takes rather more election defeats than one might consider necessary for it to do so. When it comes to the crunch – just as it did, for instance, in the autumn of 2007 and (most spectacularly of all) in the autumn of 2019 – Tory MPs eventually come to realise that, in words attributed (albeit with no hard evidence) to Benjamin Franklin at the signing of the American Declaration of Independence in 1776, 'We must all hang together or, most assuredly, we will all hang separately.'[49]

More often than not (and not surprisingly, perhaps, in such a top-down and office-driven party) this realisation is forced upon them by a leader – normally one who looks capable of winning the next general election. Sadly, however, as the Ancient Greek historian, Polybius, famously noted, 'Those who know how to win are much more numerous than those who know how to make proper use of their victories.' Arguably, this may not have been true of Churchill after 1951 (or at least those around him who did most of the legwork) and possibly Macmillan (although more so, perhaps, after he became PM in 1957 than after he won the general election two years later). But,

---

[49] On the disappointingly dodgy provenance of this oft-quoted remark, see https://professorbuzzkill.com/ben-franklin-we-must-all-hang-together-or-all-hang-separately-quote-or-no-quote/

unless one believes that austerity was fully justified rather than counterproductive, or else that it was right to leave the EU at any cost, then it applies as much to Cameron and Johnson as it does to Heath, whilst Home, May, Truss and Sunak are only spared because victory (or at least outright victory) eluded them. Indeed, the only post-war Conservative prime minister to whom the dictum most definitely does not apply is Margaret Thatcher. Whether that has something to do with the decline in party loyalty not just among MPs but among voters, thus leading the party to put more of a premium on presumed electability than executive experience and an aura of command, we cannot know for sure. But, if so, then Rishi Sunak looks unlikely to live up to the example set by his icon.

14

The Realigning Party System

Paul Webb

INTRODUCTION

How should we best characterise the UK party system in the wake of nearly a decade and a half of Conservative government? Has it undergone a significant and enduring realignment, or merely experienced passing turbulence, after which things have returned to the seemingly eternal verities of stable two-party competition? The notion of party system realignment was pioneered by American political scientists[1] and essentially refers to the process by which blocs of electoral support which have habitually been associated with particular parties shift towards established rivals or new parties; such a process also generally entails a change in the ideological or programmatic nature of party competition. The closely related concept of a 'critical election' refers to an election in which the process of changing links between social groups and parties is catalysed or rendered especially transparent by the impact of particular issues, candidates or events. These are the moments when a long-term process of realignment becomes manifest. While realignment may be something that only occurs once every few generations, and is therefore likely to be driven by gradual forces of underlying change, it may take one or sometimes two consecutive elections for these forces to achieve a critical mass that will effect the realignment. In the UK, the elections of 1924 (when the Liberals were definitively replaced by Labour as one of the major two parties), 1945 (when Labour first achieved

[1] V. O. Key, 'A theory of critical elections', *Journal of Politics*, 17 (1955), 3–18; Walter Dean Burnham, *Critical Elections and the Mainsprings of American Politics* (New York: W. W. Norton, 1970).

a parliamentary majority as millions of working-class voters previously loyal to the Conservatives flocked to its banner), and perhaps 1979 or 1983 (when Margaret Thatcher's Conservatives wrested back the support of a large chunk of working-class support and changed the terrain of policy debate in an enduring way) feature among the usual candidates for critical election status.

The question for us to consider in this chapter is whether we can regard the period since 2010 in such terms: in particular, does the general election of December 2019 constitute a moment of critical realignment? Or is it more sensible to view this as the mere culmination of a relatively prolonged period of Conservative Party ascendancy based on a regular swing of the electoral pendulum – a swing which will inevitably reverse itself as the centre of electoral gravity shifts in favour of Labour once more? In other words, a simple affirmation of the age-old dynamics of the two-party system.

We will start by reviewing the concepts of realignment and dealignment, and examining the context of long-term change in the party system from 1970 to 2019 (and beyond, in so far as subsequent opinion poll data can inform us), before proceeding to consider the key developments of the past few years, noting in particular the effects of the coalition experience on Conservative and Liberal Democrat support, the strategic travails of Labour, and the surge in popularity enjoyed by the UK Independence Party (UKIP)/the Brexit Party, Reform UK, the Scottish National Party (SNP) and the Greens. How have these things affected the dynamics of the party system? The answer, I would suggest, is that while there undoubtedly have been powerful realigning forces at play during this period, an equally compelling interpretation is one of continuing dealignment. The deracination of the electorate as a whole means that the central story is one of high electoral volatility in which there is an extraordinary amount of individual-level churn as voters switch from one party to another (or to and from abstention). Thus, the realignments that have been observed – for example, of working-class voters from Labour to the Conservatives in England, or of erstwhile Labour loyalists to the SNP in Scotland – seem set to endure for the time being, but the long-term erosion of partisan identification is here to stay, which means that the potential for future volatility will persist.

THE CONCEPTS: REALIGNMENT AND DEALIGNMENT

The terms realignment and dealignment were coined by the American political scientist V. O. Key.[2] In his view, the USA was subject to prolonged periods of stable electoral alignment in which certain social groups offered sustained support to their preferred parties. Realignment refers to the process of transition that party systems periodically undergo when new ties between social groups and political parties are forged. In the wake of a realignment there will exist a clear social group basis of party support, but this will not be the same as that which preceded the transition. This often happens because new cleavages come to structure the party system and patterns of electoral support in a new phase of stable alignment. By contrast, the process of dealignment is one whereby established connections between party and society break down, but are not replaced by new structural links. Instead, the party system floats increasingly free of its social moorings, with a smaller proportion of the electorate maintaining any general partisan loyalty. As a result, factors which are only salient in the short-term context of specific election campaigns (such as candidate and issue assessments) are likely to have a permanently enhanced bearing on the voting decisions that people make. Fewer voters will maintain long-term predispositions to vote for a particular party and, consequently, dealignment means that a greater proportion of the electorate will be susceptible to the effects of party election campaigns. This in turn implies the possibility of greater electoral volatility as voters switch party preferences, or opt to abstain from voting altogether.

So, has Britain's electorate been realigning or dealigning? Long term, it is likely that a mixture of both processes has been taking place, but it is not easy to be more precise since the initial symptoms of both phenomena are similar – for instance, weakening partisan identification, declining party membership, falling electoral turnout and increasing volatility. However, in answering the question we are helped by the fact that half

---

[2] Key, 'A theory of critical elections'.

a century has passed since signs of electoral change first manifested themselves, affording us the opportunity to conduct
a detailed review of the evidence on the causes of electoral
change. In the next section, I will review indications of long-
term change in the party system which are consistent with the
process of dealignment, before focusing on the evidence of
realignment that emerged in the period after 2010.

THE LONG-TERM CONTEXT: DEALIGNMENT
AND THE PARTY SYSTEM AFTER 1970

Since 1970, the party system has become significantly more
fragmented as the major parties have haemorrhaged support
to the smaller parties, and the politics of coalition has become
increasingly normal across the UK's multiple levels of government. In essence, these developments are important features of
the ongoing transformation of the UK from a unitary state with
a simple two-party system into a multilevel state with a complex
multiparty system. While the central focus of this chapter is upon
developments during the period 2010–24, it is important to set
these in the context of the longer-term processes of secular
transformation that characterised the erosion of the simple old
two-party duopoly after 1970.

Explicit in much of the literature on electoral behaviour and
party competition in the UK is the notion that something started
to change from the general election of February 1974. A number
of key features characterised the period up to 1974, including:
the high proportion of votes absorbed by Labour and the
Conservatives; the degree of electoral balance between them;
a centripetal pattern of competition usually targeted on trying to
command the electoral centre-ground; the ability of one or the
other of the major parties to govern alone; and a regular alter-
nation in power of the major parties.

Since 1974, much in this picture of simple two-party competition has changed. First, the average share of the vote absorbed
by the major parties, which stood at 90.3 per cent for the period
1945–70, has generally remained below 75 per cent since 1974,
reaching a nadir of 65 per cent in 2010, before recovering to

75.7 per cent in 2019. Second, the degree of electoral imbalance between the major parties has grown perceptibly, from a mean difference of 3.9 per cent in their levels of national support up to and including 1970, to 8.5 per cent thereafter (and 10.2 per cent in 2019). Third, and as a corollary of major-party decline, we have witnessed the emergence of significant 'minor' parties since 1970; most notably, of course, the Liberal Democrats (and their predecessors) achieved an average vote of around 20 per cent in the elections from 1974 to 2010 (compared to just 7.1 per cent previously), although this dropped to 9 per cent from 2015 to 2019, while the Scottish and Welsh nationalists emerged as significant electoral forces in their respective regions. The advent of devolution has only served to enhance the importance of the nationalist parties to the British political system, as the devolved parts of the UK have continued to gain more powers at the expense of Westminster. Moreover, the fragmentation of the party system has handed the minor parties an increasing significance at Westminster as well, given their potential for coalition-building.

The simplest way of measuring this growing party system fragmentation which threatens the norm of single-party government at Westminster is by referring to the changing 'effective number of parties'.[3] This well-known indicator takes account of both the number of parties in the system and their relative strength and tells us, for instance, that in any system comprised of just two equally strong parties, the effective number will indeed be 2.0, while a system consisting of three equally strong parties will generate an effective number of 3.0, and so on. However, a system consisting of two large parties and one small party would have an effective number far closer to 2.0 than to 3.0. This measure can be calculated either on the basis of party shares of the popular vote (the effective number of electoral parties (ENEP)), or on the basis of shares of seats won in parliament (the effective number of parliamentary parties (ENPP)). There

[3] Markku Laakso and Rein Taagepera, '"Effective" number of parties: a measure with application to West Europe', *Comparative Political Studies*, 12 (1979), 3–27.

has been a clear growth in the effective number of parties since 1970. Given the distorting effect of the 'first-past-the-post' single-member plurality electoral system, this is less pronounced in respect of parliamentary parties than electoral parties, though it is still apparent. Thus, while the average ENPP from 1945 to 1970 was 2.05, it increased to 2.30 for the period from 1974 to 2019; the ENEP average shows a more marked increase, from 2.36 (up to 1970) to 3.30 (post-1970). These trends neatly summarise the emergence of a multiparty system in both electoral and legislative arenas at central government level.

Underpinning the loosening grip of the traditional two-party system has been a general loss of partisan attachment among voters. Although British Election Study (BES) data suggests that the average number of voters claiming habitual partisan identification only dropped moderately, from 92 per cent in the 1960s to 74 per cent by 2019, the number admitting to a 'very strong' partisan identification has fallen more sharply – from 44 per cent in 1964, to just 16 per cent by 2019. Even more notable has been the precipitous decline in the proportion of Britons who join political parties. Although in purely numerical terms the Conservative Party was probably for many a year the closest thing to a mass membership party in Britain, it is evident that it has suffered greatly from membership decline. In 1953, the Conservatives claimed some 2,800,000 members nationally; in 1974, the Royal Commission on party finance (the Houghton Commission) estimated that this had fallen to 1,500,000; by the time of the 1997 general election this had collapsed to 400,000; and by 2022 to 172,000. Labour, too, has suffered a dramatic loss of individual members since 1970, although this derives in part from a change in party rules in 1980,[4] and has occurred notwithstanding moments of resurgence, such as the early years of Tony Blair's leadership in the mid 1990s, and most obviously in the aftermath of the general election of 2015 when a wave of Corbyn-inspired enthusiasts was motivated to join up. From

---

[4] Paul Webb, *The Modern British Party System* (London: Sage Publications, 2000), p. 220.

claiming 830,000 individual members in the 1960s, and even 405,000 members at the height of the 'Blair bounce' in 1997, membership fell back to 177,000 by the time that Ed Miliband was elected leader in the autumn of 2010. This recovered slightly to 190,000 by the end of 2014, and rose to more than half a million during Jeremy Corbyn's leadership before dropping back to 407,44 under Keir Starmer. The Liberals/Liberal Democrats suffered in the same span of time – from 278,690 in 1974 to just 44,576 members at the time of the 2015 election. That said, the party has enjoyed a surge in membership since then; by 2022 their membership stood at 74,000. The minor parties offer something of a counterpoint to this generalised picture of membership decline – a clear corollary of the fragmentation of the party system. In the wake of the Scottish independence referendum of September 2014, there was a surge in SNP popularity which enabled the party to draw in many new members; by 2022 it could claim 104,000, making it the UK's third largest party by this indicator (which was also the case in terms of representation at Westminster). At the same time the Green Party of England and Wales claimed 54,000 members, Plaid Cymru had around 10,000 members, while UKIP's membership fluctuated in line with its electoral surge and decline: by 2015 it claimed 41,500 members, but this collapsed to less than 4,000 as of 2020.[5]

A dealigned electorate lacking deep roots of habitual partisan loyalty is likely to be volatile in its voting behaviour, and we have seen clear evidence of this in recent elections. The Pedersen Index is a standard way of gauging electoral volatility.[6] The index is calculated by summing the percentage point changes in each party's share of the vote from one election to the next, and dividing by two. This is equal to the sum of the cumulative gains of all winning parties

[5] Unless otherwise stated, all membership figures cited in this paragraph are taken from the annual statements of account submitted to the Electoral Commission by parties.

[6] Mogens N. Pedersen, 'The dynamics of European party systems: changing patterns of electoral volatility', *European Journal of Political Research*, 7 (1979), 1–26.

(or obversely, the sum of cumulative losses of all losing parties) at an election. Theoretically, the index has a range running from 0 to 100, although a score above 10 generally signifies a high-volatility election in a European context.[7] In fact, compared to the rest of Europe, the UK has generally been characterised by relatively low levels of net volatility.[8] The moments of greatest volatility in the UK's electoral history were the dramatic elections of 1918 (when women first gained the vote in the wake of the Great War) and 1931, which convulsed the Labour Party in the context of global economic crisis.[9] These each produced Pedersen Index scores over 20. Since 1945, the UK has not followed a neat secular trend, but fluctuated between low- and high-volatility elections. Nevertheless, if we employ the usual periodisation of post-war elections, it becomes clear that average volatility is higher after 1970 (9.5 compared to 4.9). Moreover, it is striking that the two highest-volatility elections since 1945 were those of 2015 and 2017, while the 2019 election ranks as the sixth most volatile election of the twenty that have taken place since 1950. Plainly, electoral instability has become a prominent feature of the past few decades – and especially of the turbulent decade since 2010.

In summary, the changes that have affected the UK party system since 1970 – declining party identification and membership, greater electoral volatility, and party system fragmentation – have mainly been gradual, as if the tectonic plates of the country's politics have been slowly shifting. But when the movement of tectonic plates reaches a certain point, the cumulative pressure of change can become critical and lead to structural realignment. By 2019, there was a clear case to be made that such an inflexion point had been reached.

---

[7] Stefano Bartolini and Peter Mair, *Identity, Competition and Electoral Availability: The Stabilisation of European Electorates 1885–1985* (Cambridge: Cambridge University Press, 1990), appendix 2.

[8] Alessandro Chiaramonte and Vincenzo Emanuele, 'Party system volatility, regeneration and de-institutionalization in Western Europe (1945–2015)', *Party Politics*, 23 (2017), 376–88.

[9] Edward Fieldhouse, Geoffrey Evans, Jane Green et al., *Electoral Shocks: The Volatile Voter in a Turbulent World* (Oxford: Oxford University Press, 2019).

Brexit, Globalisation and the Case
for Realignment

The single most unmissable fact of British politics in recent years has been the prominence of the European issue – specifically, Brexit. The narrow referendum victory for the 'Leave' campaign in June 2016 (51.9 per cent – 48.1 per cent) generated an extraordinary passage of three years in political history, during which the vexed question of exactly how to interpret exactly what 'leaving' the EU meant was debated, often bitterly, both inside and outside parliament. This saw the resignation of two Conservative prime ministers (David Cameron and Theresa May), a record number of government parliamentary defeats per session, a series of massive street demonstrations (mainly against Brexit) and the assassination of one MP (Labour's Jo Cox). The degree of hostility suggested a level of political polarization unprecedented in post-war Britain; the question for us is, to what extent has this represented a realigning cleavage in British politics?

There are grounds for supposing that issues relating to European integration might already have come to cross-cut existing lines of party differentiation by the 1990s. The traditionally low political salience of European issues was replaced after 1987 by their growing prominence on the agenda of British politics, and their capacity to provoke internal tensions within both major parties – but especially the Conservatives – has been plain to see. The European dimension was a leading factor in the Conservative Party leadership contests of 1990, 1995, 1997, 2001, 2016 and 2019, and was central to a number of high-profile parliamentary party rebellions in the 1990s and after 2016. Moreover, it seems clear that the weight of public opinion began to swing against further European integration after the early 1990s.[10] So, did the combination of increasing issue salience, shifting party strategies, intraparty dissent

---

[10] Geoffrey Evans, 'Europe: a new cleavage?', in Geoffrey Evans and Pippa Norris (eds.), *Critical Elections: British Parties and Voters in Long-Term Perspective* (London: Sage Publications, 1999), 207–22.

and changing public opinion foster a degree of electoral realignment?

Prior to the 2016 referendum, the short answer seemed to be that it had done, but only to a limited extent. It was already evident by 1997 that voters' attitudes on Europe cut right across their positions on the main left–right dimension of party competition, which confirmed in principle the realigning potential of the European dimension, as it served to erode patterns of class alignment. In particular, New Labour's appeal to the educated middle classes attracted the most pro-European group of voters.[11] The magnitude of the effect appeared to be minor at the turn of the twenty-first century, but twenty or more years later the impact of Europe on British party and electoral politics has surely been far greater – not least because of the capacity of Brexit to realign significant numbers of working-class voters to the Tories and UKIP.

Notwithstanding evidence of growing public concern about levels of immigration from Eastern Europe after 2004,[12] the salience of the EU as an issue was still relatively low by the time of the 2015 general election,[13] but the electoral progress made by UKIP at local and European parliamentary elections after 2012 posed a threat to the Conservative Party's right flank. David Cameron's decision to offer a referendum on Brexit in the Tories' 2015 general election manifesto was, at least in part, designed to placate his own party's Eurosceptic wing, and to prevent further loss of support to UKIP.[14] Having won the election, he made up his mind to hold the referendum as quickly as possible, believing he would win it and thus finally put the issue to bed. However, his decision to do so and to begin renegotiating the terms of UK membership of the EU only served

[11] Ibid., p. 219.

[12] Robert Ford, Gareth Morrell and Anthony Heath, '"Fewer but better?" Public views about immigration', in Alison Park et al. (eds.), *British Social Attitudes: The 29th Report* (London: NatCen Social Research, 2012), pp. 26–44.

[13] Fieldhouse et al., *Electoral Shocks*, p. 165.

[14] Tim Bale, *The Conservative Party: From Thatcher to Cameron* (Cambridge: Polity Press, 2016), pp. 378–81.

to boost the salience of the European dimension dramatically. Moreover, voters' positions on Brexit did not correlate strongly with left–right attitudes, but they did with a second attitudinal dimension – social liberalism versus social authoritarianism/conservatism. That is, it tends to pit voters who have a strong sense of social tradition, national identity, hostility towards the EU and concerns about immigration against those who are socially liberal, cosmopolitan, pro-European and relaxed about immigration. Moreover, there are notable demographic correlates of these two 'tribes' – age and education; the former, socially authoritarian Eurosceptic group are typically older, and more likely to be white British and less educated, while the latter group of liberal, cosmopolitan pro-Europeans are generally younger, more middle class and better educated.[15]

Although the Tories had been split over Brexit prior to 2016, and Cameron's successor as prime minister, Theresa May, had herself been a Remainer, the conclusion she drew from the referendum result was that the UK would now have to pursue a 'Hard Brexit' strategy – departure from the EU, its customs union and the single market. By and large, Tory MPs, members[16] and voters fell in line behind this position (though not without some friction, especially in parliament), so that it became the party of Brexit. In the 2017 general election, this strategy enabled it to siphon off much of the Eurosceptic support that had flowed to UKIP in 2015. Labour's position was more ambivalent, although its offer came to be widely regarded as constituting a 'softer' version of Brexit, holding out the prospect of closer future cooperation with the EU. By 2019, it was proposing to put any deal on the future relationship between the UK and the EU to voters in a new referendum – in which 'Remain' would be on the ballot paper. Thus, the extraordinary election of December 2019 was almost entirely about resolving the question of Brexit, with the new prime minister Boris Johnson insisting he would 'Get Brexit

[15]   Paul Webb and Tim Bale, *The Modern British Party System* (Oxford: Oxford University Press, 2021), table 3.5.

[16]   Tim Bale, Paul Webb and Monica Poletti, *Footsoldiers: Political Party Members in the 21st Century* (Abingdon: Routledge, 2019), pp. 65–71.

Done', while Jeremy Corbyn's Labour offered the hope to Remainers of further renegotiation and a referendum. The result was a resounding triumph for Johnson in which he was able to use Brexit to lever former Labour Leave voters into his own camp. The Tories, by becoming an unambiguously pro-Brexit party after 2016, managed to absorb the majority of Leave support, its share of the vote among those choosing Brexit in the referendum increasing from 44 per cent (2015) to 75 per cent (2019). Labour's support among Remainers grew less emphatically across the same period, from 44 per cent to 50 per cent.[17]

The realigning impact of this on older patterns of class voting has been extraordinarily powerful. Although the erosion of class alignment is a long-term process which can be traced back to the 1970s, Brexit seems to have given it a sharp added twist. Robert Alford's classic index of class voting is a simple measure normally calculated by subtracting the percentage of middle-class voters supporting parties of the left from the percentage of working-class voters doing so.[18] It is a measure that captures the relative strength of a given party in two different classes; in Britain's case, it is generally used to contrast the levels of support for Labour among manual workers and non-manual employees. There have been several main steps down in the standard Alford index since the 1960s, confirming that this has been a secular process – first in 1970 (from 43 to 33), then again in 1979 (to 27) and in 1997 (to 22), before starting a precipitous slide down from 2005 (18) onwards: in 2010 it was 9, in 2015 it was 3, in 2017 it was 4 and, remarkably, it reached zero in 2019.[19] On the first two occasions, these sudden drops in class voting almost certainly reflected working-class disenchantment with Labour governments,[20] whereas

---

[17] Webb and Bale, *The Modern British Party System*, table 3.6.

[18] Robert Alford, *Party and Society: Anglo-American Democracies* (Chicago: Rand McNally, 1963).

[19] Note that all figures cited here are based on author's own calculations using BES data (see Webb and Bale, *The Modern British Party System*, p. 333).

[20] Paul D. Webb, *Trade Unions and the British Electorate* (Aldershot: Dartmouth, 1992); Geoffrey Evans and James Tilley, *The New Politics of Class: The Political Exclusion of the British Working Class* (Oxford: Oxford University Press, 2017).

1997 seems to have had more to do with the increasingly hetero-geneous social appeal of New Labour across a range of social categories. In 2010 the drop most probably reflected of a loss of working-class support by Labour again in the context of the global financial crisis, but in 2017 and 2019 it almost certainly also owed much to the cross-cutting impact of Brexit.

The realigning impact of Brexit is suggested by the fact that this shifting pattern of support connects people's views on Brexit with a wider set of (probably longstanding) attitudes towards immigration, identity, social liberty and authority. For instance, if we look at attitudinal scales constructed from BES data, each running from 0 (left-wing/socially liberal) to 10 (right-wing/socially authoritarian), we find that while Remain and Leave voters are only separated by 0.6 points on the Left–Right attitudinal scale, they are considerably further apart (2.1 points) on the Liberty–Authority scale. Clearly, the latter dimension distinguished Leavers and Remainers far more strongly than the former in 2019. This finding is corroborated in various ways by other research.[21] For instance, Hobolt and her colleagues have demonstrated that Brexit drove new levels of 'affective polarization' among British voters; that is, as many voters are likely to self-identify as adherents of the 'Leave' or 'Remain' tribes as with any particular political party, and to feel positively towards other members of their 'in-group' but hostile towards the 'out-group'.[22] Furthermore, the findings about Brexit's impact and its connection with questions of identity and social authority resonate strongly with developments in other democracies. As far back as the early 1990s, the Italian political scientist Piero Ignazi noted a socially conservative 'Silent Counter-Revolution' that was emerging in reaction to

[21] Sara B. Hobolt, 'The Brexit vote: a divided nation, a divided continent', *Journal of European Public Policy*, 23 (2016), 1259–77; Maria Sobolewska and Robert Ford, *Brexitland: Diversity, Immigration and the Rise of Identity Conflicts in British Politics* (Cambridge: Cambridge University Press, 2020), chapter 8.

[22] Sara B. Hobolt, Thomas J. Leeper and James Tilley, 'Divided by the vote: affective polarization in the wake of the Brexit referendum', *British Journal of Political Science*, 51 (2021), 1476–93.

the spread of social liberalism, cosmopolitanism and post-materialism.[23] More recently, Hanspeter Kriesi has led the way in arguing that all this revolves around a new cleavage separating the winners and losers of globalisation in advanced industrial societies – the former including 'entrepreneurs and qualified employees in sectors open to international competition as well as all kinds of cosmopolitan citizens. The expected losers, by contrast, include entrepreneurs and qualified employees in traditionally protected sectors, all unqualified employees and citizens who strongly identify themselves with their national community.'[24] This latter group of 'left-behinds' are exactly those most susceptible to the appeals of social conservatism, opposition to immigration and Euroscepticism.[25] In 2019, it seemed that it was especially these left-behind voters in northern and midland 'Red Wall' seats who deserted Labour for the Tories.

In short, it appears the Conservatives' enduring capacity for chameleon-like adaptation to changing historical circumstances – this time by embracing a Hard Brexit and a socially conservative 'anti-woke' agenda – succeeded in prising a large chunk of Labour's traditional support base to its side. But how enduring might this apparent realignment prove to be? Of course, it is impossible to be sure until we have the luxury of one or more future general elections to study, but at the time of writing we can at least consider some post-2019 evidence.

---

[23] Piero Ignazi, 'The silent counter-revolution: hypotheses on the emergence of extreme right-wing parties', *European Journal of Political Research*, 22 (1992), 3–34.

[24] Hanspeter Kriesi, Edgar Grande, Romain Lachat et al., 'Globalization and the transformation of the national political space: six European countries compared', *European Journal of Political Research*, 45 (2006), 921–56; Hanspeter Kriesi, 'Restructuration of partisan politics and the emergence of a new cleavage based on values', *West European Politics*, 33 (2010), 673–85.

[25] Robert Ford and Matthew Goodwin, *Revolt on the Right: Explaining Support for the Radical Right in Britain* (Abingdon: Routledge, 2014); Sobolewska and Ford, *Brexitland*.

CAN THE REALIGNMENT OF 2010-2019 ENDURE?

As we look ahead to the next general election, the Conservatives have been languishing well behind Labour in the opinion polls since late 2021. As the 'Partygate' crisis concerning the conduct of Boris Johnson's administration impacted, Labour's lead stretched into double figures. Across 318 polls conducted between July 2022 and April 2023, the average advantage Keir Starmer's party enjoyed over the Conservatives was 18.7 per cent.[26] Under such circumstances it would certainly be reasonable to suppose that much of the support that Labour had lost to the Tories in the run-up to 2019 was finding its way back 'home'. If so, then the apparent realignment that had been observed could be dismissed as contingent and transient. In short, electoral business would seem to be back to 'normal'. A particular pointer in this direction was the opinion research conducted in the Red Wall constituencies that Labour had dominated prior to 2019. For instance, in forty such seats surveyed by Redfield & Wilton the Conservatives won all but Hartlepool in 2019 (and even this was claimed by the Tories in a subsequent parliamentary by-election), with 46.7 per cent of the vote to Labour's 37.9 per cent. As of October 2023, Redfield & Wilton found Labour leading the Conservatives by 16 points (48 to 32 per cent) in these seats, while the Liberal Democrats polled 7 per cent, with Reform UK close behind on 6 per cent.[27] Given that many of these seats are marginals, most of them can be expected to switch back to Labour at the next election, absent a further major shift in party preferences.

So, no enduring realignment, then? Close analysis of data gives pause for thought. First, the class basis of party support has barely changed, despite the switch in relative popularity of the major parties. Labour is far more popular than it was in 2019, and the Conservatives far less popular – but this pattern has

[26] Mark Pack, *Pollbase: Opinion Polls Database From 1943–Today* (accessed at www.markpack.org.uk/opinion-polls/, 25 November 2023).

[27] Redfield & Wilton Strategies, *Latest Red Wall Voting Intention*, 22 October 2023 (accessed at https://redfieldandwiltonstrategies.com/latest-red-wall-voting-intention-22-october-2023/, 23 November 2023).

occurred across all occupational classes to approximately the same extent, so the level of relative class voting has not changed. Drawing on BES data gathered in April 2023 (wave 24), we find that the Alford index has actually gone into reverse since 2019: while 29.7 per cent of C2DE respondents indicated an indication to vote for Labour at the next general election, some 33.8 per cent of ABC1 respondents did, giving an Alford index of -4.1 (see Table 14.1). Similarly, it does not appear likely that the relationships between age or education and party preference have altered greatly; the young and those with degrees are still preponderantly more Labour-inclined than older and less-educated voters. The BES data shows a marginal advantage (0.9 per cent) for the Tories over Labour among those with no formal educational qualifications, but very considerable Labour leads among those whose highest qualifications are A-levels (12.5 per cent), first degrees (22.6 per cent) and postgraduate degrees (28.8 per cent). Similarly, the Tories enjoy an 8-point

Table 14.1 Voting intention by occupational class, 2023

	ABC1	C2DE
Will not vote	7.0	12.8
Conservative	19.4	17.1
Labour	33.8	29.7
LibDem	6.8	4.0
SNP	3.1	2.9
Plaid Cymru	0.4	0.5
Green	4.3	3.3
Reform UK	5.0	6.5
Other	1.2	1.4
Don't know	19.0	21.9
Total	100.0	100.0
Number	9,184	5,803

Note: All figures are percentages unless otherwise stated.

Source: British Election Study 2019 Panel Wave 24.

lead among voters aged 66 and older, while Labour's lead grows with each younger age group, from 8.2 points among 56–65-year-olds, to 17.9 points among 46–55-year-olds, 25.9 points among 36–45-year-olds, 37.3 points among 26–35-year-olds, and a huge 43.9 points among 18–25-year-olds. Neither does there appear to have been any change since 2019 in terms of the main attitudinal profiles of party support, as Figure 14.1 illustrates. Using the 10-point ideological scales referred to above, we see that Conservative and Reform UK supporters are more right-wing and decidedly more socially conservative than those of other parties. Therefore, we can summarise by saying that Labour continues to be a party of socially liberal middle-class graduates and professionals, while the Tories remain the preferred option of socially conservative voters, many of whom are older non-graduates from lower occupational grades.

In view of all this, it is little surprise that analysis of the flow of support since 2019 does not show much evidence of direct switching between the major parties. Rather, voters are overwhelmingly likely to remain within ideological silos on either the socially conservative right or liberal left of the party system. Of those who voted Conservative in 2019, 46 per cent said in 2023 that they were

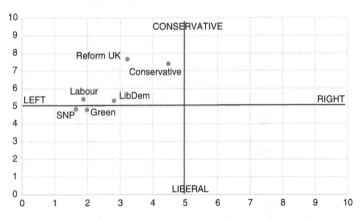

Figure 14.1 A two-dimensional representation of party supporters, 2023
Source: British Election Study 2019 Panel Wave 24.

planning to stick with the party at the next general election, while only 7.8 per cent were expecting to choose Labour. Significantly more – 11.5 per cent – claimed that they would be opting for Reform UK, which suggests that Brexit – or the libertarian/social conservative dimension more generally – continues to shape their party preference. Note, however, that very nearly one quarter (24.5 per cent) remained undecided about what they would do at the time this survey was conducted. If anything, Labour's 2019 voter base seems even more firmly rooted on their 'side' of the party system – the liberal left: only 1.1 per cent of them claimed to be contemplating a switch to the Tories, while 4.8 per cent would switch to the Greens and 3.0 per cent to the Liberal Democrats. Just 12 per cent were undecided. Labour could also expect to benefit from net transfers of support from the SNP, Plaid Cymru and the Greens. Looking forward, we can also say that even though Brexit is likely to be far less obviously salient than in 2019, its influence on partisan choice is set to persist. Only 17.1 per cent of those who claimed they would choose to stay out of the EU in the (for now unlikely) event of a new referendum on the issue envisaged voting for anti-Brexit parties (Labour, Liberal Democrat, SNP, Plaid Cymru or Green) at the next general election, while just 7 per cent of those who say they would vote to rejoin the EU could conceive of supporting either of the two pro-Brexit options of Conservative or Reform UK.

CONCLUSION

In conclusion then, the evidence currently available suggests that the major features of electoral realignment that emerged during the period after 2010 – the final erosion of the occupational class cleavage, the growing demographic influence of age and education, the continuing salience of the libertarian–authoritarian dimension even after Brexit has been 'done' – will persist for the foreseeable future. At the same time, however, this does not necessarily mean that the party system, when understood as the predominant pattern of party competition, will change much. Electoral realignment and dealignment may well both have occurred without altering the fundamental structure of the party system greatly. Although it is a little more fragmented than a generation or more ago – thanks to the greater electoral presence of the SNP, Plaid Cymru, Liberal Democrats and the Greens – the enduring major party duopoly remains at the core of the system. To this extent, the British party system remains an outlier in the European context.[28] Much of the change that we have witnessed since 2010 can reasonably be regarded as having been catalysed by the Conservatives, in so far as they are the major party that has brought Brexit and the libertarian–authoritarian dimension to the centre of the political agenda – the 'Conservative effect', if you will – but when this development threatened to tear them apart they adapted by embracing a clear stance on the socially conservative side of the spectrum, and shedding any adherents who could not accept this strategic shift. Labour under Corbyn, and only slightly less under Starmer, has taken its place near the opposite ideological pole. The economic left–right faultline remains salient to British politics, of course, but the two parties have continued to hold broadly consistent positions on this dimension, with Labour to the left of the Conservatives (albeit less so than in 2019). The political turmoil of the period since 2010 has therefore largely been about the struggle of the major parties to absorb issues that do not fit into the dimension of left–right class politics: Brexit is the major such issue, but the cause of Scottish nationalism, which so strengthened the SNP at Labour's expense, should not be overlooked in this regard. In a way this too may be thought of as a 'Conservative effect', inasmuch as David Cameron's decision to accede to the demand for a referendum on Scottish independence in 2014 served to ratchet-up support for the SNP and its causal *raison d'être*, even though the 'No' side won. 'Overall support for independence was 8% in 1979, rose to 23% in 1992, and then fluctuated around 30% between 1997 and as late as 2013. During the summer leading to the 2014 referendum in September, it sharply rose to 45%, where it has mostly

---

[28]   Paul Webb, *An Advanced Introduction to Party Systems* (Cheltenham: Edward Elgar, 2024), table 1.1.

remained since.'[29] Thus, two referendums on major constitutional questions, both called by David Cameron even though he was in favour of the status quo on both issues, have been major drivers of realignment and shifting partisan strength since 2010. In this sense, the Conservative Party has been the motor of party system change in this period, in much the same way as Blair's New Labour was from 1997 to 2010, and Thatcher's Tories were from 1979 to 1992. Each of these regimes enjoyed prolonged periods of power by mobilising blocks of electoral support that had previously eluded it. However, what is perhaps unique about the period since 2010 compared to these earlier phases of single-party dominance is the strategic deployment of new wedge issues that cut across the usual lines of left–right conflict. Thatcher drew working-class support away from Labour by critiquing the shortcomings of social democratic corporatism in the 1970s and offering an alternative vision of individual aspiration and upward mobility. New Labour attracted swathes of hitherto untapped public sector middle-class support by accepting elements of the Thatcherite revolution while promising investment in declining public services and a spirit of communitarian regeneration. Notwithstanding Blair's programme of constitutional reform, these were both projects that revolved centrally around traditional questions of left–right distributional politics – state versus market, spending versus taxation, equality versus liberty. Such questions have undeniably been central to politics since 2010, of course, but the major drivers of realignment seem to have been questions relating to other dimensions of political conflict: Brexit, immigration, the union. The Conservatives in power have either sought to manage or to exploit these issues to their political advantage. The process has not been comfortable and may prove to be of questionable long-run benefit to them or the UK as a whole.

---

[29] Lindsay Paterson, 'Independence is not going away: the importance of education and birth cohorts', *The Political Quarterly*, 12 August 2023 (accessed at https://onlinelibrary.wiley.com/doi/10.1111/1467-923X.13 306, 23 November 2023).

15

Elections and Voting

John Curtice

S UPERFICIALLY, THE PERIOD OF CONSERVATIVE rule since 2010 has been one of electoral stability. The Conservatives emerged as the largest party in four general elections in a row. As a result, the party has retained the reins of power for fourteen years. This represents the second-longest period of government tenure for any one party in post-war British politics.

Yet, in truth, it has been a period of unprecedented electoral instability and political change. Two of the four elections produced a hung parliament, an outcome that had only occurred once before in the post-war period, while a third only produced a small overall majority. After the first of these hung parliaments, in 2010, Britain was governed by a coalition for the first time since 1945, while in the second such parliament, between 2017 and 2019, a minority government entered into a 'confidence and supply' agreement with the Northern Irish Democratic Unionists. The right of prime ministers to call an election at a time of their own choosing was taken away, only to result in parliamentary tussles that, in the event, failed to stop two prime ministers from eventually holding an election well before the parliamentary term was due to come to an end. Not that prime ministers were secure in office – no less than four changes of prime minister occurred between elections. Meanwhile, two smaller parties, the Scottish National Party (SNP) and the United Kingdom Independence Party (UKIP) posed unprecedented third-party challenges. Above all, referendums played a more important role in the country's democratic life than ever before. First, the coalition held a UK-wide referendum on changing the voting system in elections to the House of Commons. Then, two further referendums, on Scottish independence and the UK's membership of the EU, were to have a profound impact on Britain's electoral politics, with the latter resulting in the Conservative Party doing a volte face on its stance on EU membership.

This chapter assesses the impact that the fourteen years of stability and turbulence since 2010 have had on elections and voter preferences in Britain. It falls into three main parts. In the first we examine the rises and falls in party support between the 2010 and 2019 elections and assess how far these represented departures from the traditional patterns of electoral support. We look, in particular, at how the outcome of the four elections during this period both shaped and were shaped by the referendums that were held during the period and assess the impact of the decision to remove the prime minister's right to call an election at a time of his or her own choosing. In the second part, we analyse how the character of the support for the parties has changed during the years of Conservative rule and show how Brexit – and, in Scotland, the independence referendum – has induced a marked change in how Britain votes. Finally, in the third part, we turn to how party support and the pattern of voter preference has evolved since the 2019 election, when the Conservatives finally secured their first safe overall parliamentary majority for over thirty years.

THE ELECTORAL RECORD

Since 1945, Britain's democracy could be characterised as a two-party system of alternating majoritarian government. The reins of office switched between the Conservatives (on the centre right) and Labour (on the centre left), albeit, typically, a changeover only happened after two or three elections. With just one exception, February 1974, the winning party always enjoyed an overall parliamentary majority, albeit not always a large one. True, there was also a small third party, the Liberal Party (more recently, the Liberal Democrats), but it struggled to secure seats under the country's single-member plurality electoral system. Not least of the reasons was that the Liberal Party's support came relatively evenly from across Britain's class divide, whereas support for the Conservatives was rooted in the middle class and Labour's in the working class, a feature that helped ensure that both parties enjoyed geographical concentrations of support that helped them, unlike the Liberals, turn votes into seats.[1]

None of the last four elections, the results of which are summarised in Table 15.1, has conformed wholly to this picture. In 2010, neither the Conservatives nor Labour came close to winning an overall majority. One key reason was that, in line with a pattern that had first become evident in 1997, the Liberal Democrats were, thanks to a geographically more concentrated pattern of support, able to convert what was the second highest third-party share of the vote since 1945 into a level of representation that, until recently, the party had not enjoyed since the 1920s.[2] This had come on top of a long-term decline in the number of seats that were marginal between the Conservatives and Labour, a decline that made it less likely that a narrow Conservative or Labour lead in votes would be converted into a large majority in seats. Consequently, the Liberal Democrats found themselves, together with the Conservatives, part of Britain's first coalition government since 1945.

THE COALITION YEARS: TWO REFERENDUMS AND THE PROMISE OF A THIRD

The coalition agreement contained provisions that potentially had important implications for future elections to the House of Commons. Hitherto the prime minister had had the almost unfettered right to request a dissolution of parliament – and thus call an election – at a time of his or her choosing. However, the Liberal

---

[1] Andrew Russell and Edward Fieldhouse, *Neither Left nor Right? The Liberal Democrats and the Electorate* (Manchester: Manchester University Press, 2005).

[2] John Curtice, 'So what went wrong with the electoral system? The 2010 election result and the debate about electoral reform', *Parliamentary Affairs*, 63:4 (2010), 623–38.

Table 15.1 Results of UK general elections 2010-19

	2010		2015		2017		2019	
	Votes (%)	Seats	Votes (%)	Seats	Votes (%)	Seats	Votes (%)	Seats
Conservative	37.0	307	37.8	331	43.5	317	44.7	365
Labour	29.7	258	31.2	232	41.0	262	33.0	203
Liberal Democrat	23.6	57	8.1	8	7.6	12	11.8	11
UKIP/Brexit	3.2	0	12.9	1	1.9	0	2.1	0
SNP/PC	2.3	9	5.5	59	3.6	39	4.5	52
Greens	1.0	1	3.8	1	1.7	1	2.8	1
Other	3.4	18	0.8	18	0.7	18	1.1	18

Democrats wished to remove this right and move to a system of fixed-length parliaments, not least because the party did not want to take the risk that a Conservative prime minister could pull the plug on the coalition and call an election at a time when the Liberal Democrats were unpopular and the Conservatives able to win an overall majority. Thus, in 2011, parliament passed the Fixed Terms Parliament Act (FTPA) that stated that an election could only be held every five years (already the maximum length of a parliament) unless either the government lost a formal vote of no confidence, something that had happened only once – to Labour in 1979 – in nearly a hundred years, or if two-thirds of MPs voted in favour of a dissolution, a condition that in practice could only be satisfied if both the government and the principal opposition party wanted a ballot. The Act was potentially a significant change in Britain's electoral arrangements.

Meanwhile, a second feature of the coalition agreement was that there would be a referendum – only the second such UK-wide ballot in the country's history, the previous one being on Britain's membership of the then Common Market in 1975 – on replacing the single-member plurality system in elections to the House of Commons with the alternative vote. Under this system, all MPs would continue to be elected in single-member constituencies, but instead of simply putting an 'X' against the name of their preferred candidate, voters would be invited to rank the candidates in order of preference. Should no candidate secure 50 per cent plus one of all first preferences, the votes cast for lower placed candidates would be redistributed in accordance with their second and subsequent preferences until one candidate did pass the 50 per cent mark.

This was, in truth, a modest proposal that fell far short of a switch to proportional representation, the Liberal Democrats' preference. Nevertheless, it was one from which the party might still reasonably hope to derive some benefit.[3] However, the Liberal Democrats' popularity fell markedly in the wake of their decision to form the coalition, and especially after they backed a hike in university tuition fees even though at the election they had been committed to their removal. Together with a more effective campaign by those opposed to the idea, strong opposition from the Conservatives including the prime minister, David Cameron, and a lack of enthusiasm from Labour, the Liberal Democrats' unpopularity ensured that the alternative vote was rejected (on a turnout of just 42 per cent) by 68 to 32 per cent.

However, on the same day that the Alternative Vote was rejected, the Scottish National Party (SNP), which had had been running a minority Scottish Government administration in Edinburgh since 2007, won an overall majority in an election to the Scottish Parliament, even though for this election a system of proportional representation was in place.[4] The SNP had campaigned to hold a referendum on Scottish independence. Such a referendum could only be held with the permission of the UK Parliament, but David Cameron accepted the result gave the SNP a moral right to hold a referendum. Anticipating it would produce a decisive vote in favour of Scotland remaining part of the UK, he paved the way for a referendum of voters living in Scotland that was eventually held in September 2014.

---

[3] John Curtice, 'Politicians, voters and democracy: the 2011 UK referendum on the alternative vote', *Electoral Studies*, 32:2 (2013), 215–23.

[4] Christopher Carman, Robert Johns and James Mitchell, *More Scottish than British? The 2011 Scottish Parliament Election* (Basingstoke: Palgrave Macmillan, 2014).

That referendum did indeed produce a majority in favour of remaining inside the UK. But, at 55 to 45 per cent, the result was closer than had originally been anticipated.[5] In particular, according to the British Election Study, no less than 42 per cent of those who had voted Labour in the 2010 Westminster election voted Yes to independence. Shortly after the referendum, there was a sharp and sudden swing from Labour to the SNP, a swing that was subsequently reflected in the outcome of the general election in Scotland the following year. The SNP won all but three of Scotland's fifty-nine seats on just under 50 per cent of the vote north of the border, overturning what had hitherto been a Labour dominance of Scotland's representation at Westminster.

In the meantime, the 2010–15 parliament also witnessed a marked increase in support for UKIP. In favour of Britain leaving the European Union (EU) and focusing in particular on a recent marked increase in inward migration from the EU,[6] the party, led by the charismatic Nigel Farage, had already recorded in the 2010 election the highest ever share of the vote across Great Britain for a fourth party. The Liberal Democrats' decision to form a coalition with the Conservatives meant they were unable, as they hitherto had often done, to gain support in the mid-term of a parliament from those unhappy at the performance of a Conservative incumbent government. When the Conservatives' position in the polls weakened in spring 2012 in the wake of an ill-judged Budget, it was UKIP that enjoyed a marked increase in support.[7] Concerned about the threat that UKIP potentially posed to his party's chances at the next general election, David Cameron came out the following January

---

[5] John Curtice, 'The Scottish independence referendum of 2014', in Julie Smith (ed.), *The Palgrave Handbook of European Referendums* (Cham: Palgrave Macmillan, 2021).

[6] Mihnea Cubius, *EU Migration to and from the UK* (Oxford: Migration Observatory, 2023), available at https://migrationobservatory.ox.ac.uk/re sources/briefings/eu-migration-to-and-from-the-uk/

[7] Phillip Cowley and Dennis Kavanagh, *The British General Election of 2015* (Basingstoke: Palgrave Macmillan, 2016), pp. 16-19.

in favour of holding a referendum on the UK's membership of the European Union following a renegotiation of the terms of its membership[8] – though because of the opposition of the Liberal Democrats there was no prospect of this happening during the current parliament. Instead, it became a policy pledge in the Conservatives' 2015 manifesto. In the meantime, Mr Cameron's change of stance did not stop UKIP topping the poll in the European Parliament election in 2014, the first time since 1910 that a party other than Conservative or Labour had won most votes in a UK-wide election.

A REVOLUTION IN THIRD-PARTY POLITICS

In combination, these ups and downs in third-party fortunes resulted in the 2015 election in a transformation of the character of third-party support and representation in the Commons. The Liberal Democrats lost to UKIP their hitherto unrivalled position as Britain's third party in terms of votes, while the position of the third-largest party in the House of Commons, together with the attendant advantages that come with that position in terms of parliamentary procedure, was ceded to the SNP. Although only the fifth-largest party in terms of votes, the SNP's newly secured dominance in Scotland was enough to catapult it into that position – and effectively to create a pattern of party competition in Scotland that was significantly different from that in England and Wales (as, of course, was already the position in Northern Ireland). As a result, it could be argued that no longer was there a Britain-wide party system. The one consolation for the Liberal Democrats was that UKIP, whose vote was geographically particularly evenly spread, struggled even more than the Liberal Party once did to convert votes into seats. The party won just one heavily Eurosceptic constituency where the UKIP candidate had been the former Conservative MP. At least the Liberal Democrats still had eight MPs.

---

[8] David Cameron, 'EU Speech at Bloomberg' (2013), available at www.gov.uk/government/speeches/eu-speech-at-bloomberg

However, in one respect the outcome of the 2015 election was more familiar – it did produce a government with an overall majority, albeit one of only twelve seats. And it was a government that was committed to holding the country's third UK-wide referendum, this time, as David Cameron had promised, on whether the UK should remain in or leave the EU. In a not dissimilar fashion to Harold Wilson forty years earlier, Mr Cameron set about trying to 'improve' the UK's terms of membership in the hope that he could then recommend to voters that the UK should remain inside the EU. However, in contrast to Mr Wilson, Mr Cameron emerged from the conclusion of his talks at a European Council in February 2016 with a deal that failed to move a divided public in favour of membership.[9] Although Mr Cameron advocated a vote for 'Remain', on 23 June 2016, the UK voted narrowly to exit the EU by 52 to 48 per cent. Mr Cameron resigned as prime minister, to be succeeded by Theresa May, who, despite having voted to Remain in the EU now took on the task of negotiating the UK's exit from the institution. It was to prove a challenge that would lead to unprecedented political turmoil that was only resolved three years later after two more general elections had been held.

THE SEARCH FOR A BREXIT MAJORITY

One potential problem with small parliamentary majorities is that they can leave a government exposed to backbench rebellion on any issue on which their parliamentary party is divided. Although a decision in principle had been made to leave the EU, there was still plenty of debate within the Conservative Party about what the UK's exit from the EU, now termed 'Brexit', should mean in practice. Should it be a 'soft' exit under which the UK might still be closely aligned with the EU single market and subject to few non-tariff barriers, or a 'hard' one under which the regulatory framework in the UK might diverge sharply

---

[9]   John Curtice, 'Why Leave won the UK's EU referendum', *Journal of Common Market Studies*, 55:S1 (2017), 1–19.

from the EU at the cost of greater friction in trading across the English Channel? By the spring of 2017, Mrs May had come to the conclusion that, given this disagreement within her party, her government's majority was too small to be sure she could secure parliamentary approval for whatever exit agreement she eventually made with the EU. Well ahead in the polls against a Labour Party that since 2015 had been led by Jeremy Corbyn, a long-standing left-wing member whose leadership had given rise to serious division within his party, she decided she needed another election.

However, in principle the FTPA stood in her way. One possible route – engineering a vote of no confidence in her own government – could be politically damaging. So, Mrs May required Labour's acquiescence to secure the necessary two-thirds majority. Alternatively, the government could introduce new primary legislation that overrode the FTPA and secure its passage through the Commons and the Lords, a process that would not need a two-thirds vote.[10] In the event, Labour, despite being badly behind in the polls, felt it could not afford to appear reluctant to fight an election, and the party's backing ensured that far more than two-thirds of all MPs voted for an early dissolution under the provisions of the FTPA. Here was an early indication that the legislation on a fixed parliament was potentially a weak barrier against the entrenched custom and practice in British politics of a prime minister calling an election at a time of their own choosing.

However, even though there was a marked decline in SNP representation (down from 56 seats to 35), even though too the Liberal Democrats only made minimal progress (in terms of seats), and although support for UKIP collapsed, rather than increasing their majority the Conservatives found themselves after the 2017 election without a majority in a hung parliament. Labour under Jeremy Corbyn had campaigned more effectively than most had anticipated, while Mrs May herself proved to be

---

[10] Phillip Cowley and Dennis Kavanagh, *The British General Election of 2017* (Cham: Palgrave Macmillan, 2018), pp. 11–14.

rather ill at ease with the business of trying to persuade voters. As a result, what had been a double-digit opinion poll lead for the Conservatives when the election had been called became just a two-and-a-half-point lead in the ballot boxes. Given the decline in the number of constituencies that were marginal between Conservative and Labour, together with the still substantial level of third-party representation, this lead was too small to produce an overall majority in terms of seats.[11] As a result, the UK found itself dealing once more with the relative unfamiliarity of a hung parliament.

On this occasion, the Liberal Democrats, opposed as they were to Brexit, were not potential allies for the Conservatives. Instead, Mrs May found herself reaching out to the Eurosceptic Democratic Unionist Party (DUP), whose ten seats in Northern Ireland were just enough to give the government a majority. The 'confidence and supply' agreement between the two parties committed the DUP to vote for the government in all key votes, including on Brexit, while Northern Ireland was to receive an extra £1 billion of government funding. Thus, an election resulted in a minority government for only the second time in post-war British history (the previous occasion was February 1974), although both the parliaments of 1974–9 and 1992–7 became hung during their lifetime. Indeed, the 'pact' between Labour and the Liberal Party that helped to sustain the Labour government between 1977 and 1978 was more elaborate than the agreement that was reached on this occasion between the Conservatives and the DUP.

Nevertheless, Mrs May's original judgement that her party needed a substantial majority if it was going to pursue Brexit successfully proved to be correct. Thanks to rebellions by her own MPs, the House of Commons rejected the deal she reached with the EU on no less than three occasions, and in May 2019 she indicated that she intended to resign, the second PM to be forced out of office by Brexit. By this point, the Conservatives

---

[11] John Curtice, 'How the electoral system failed to deliver – again', *Parliamentary Affairs*, 17:S1 (2018), 29–45.

were deeply unpopular in the polls – but so also were Labour. Indeed, in European Elections held in May 2019 because the UK had not succeeded in exiting the EU at the end of March as originally planned, both Labour (in third place) and the Conservatives (in fifth) found themselves trailing both the Brexit Party, which, led by Nigel Farage, had now displaced UKIP as the principal Eurosceptic party, and the pro-EU Liberal Democrats.[12] Indeed, Britain's two-party system appeared to be under greater threat than at any point since at least the 1980s, when the Liberal–SDP Alliance attempted but eventually failed to 'break the mould of British politics'.

THE ARRIVAL OF BORIS JOHNSON

However, Mrs May was succeeded as prime minister in July by the highly charismatic Boris Johnson, who was prepared to play 'hardball' to secure the UK's exit from the EU by what now was the proposed date of 31 October. One possible pathway out of the impasse that had led to Mrs May's downfall was to hold yet another election in the hope this would generate a substantial Conservative majority – though the polls suggested such an outcome was far from certain. Mr Johnson's government twice put down a motion for an early election, but both times the opposition parties refused to back it, fearing the government would hold the election after the end of October deadline and thereby leave the EU without a deal. As a result, these motions lacked the necessary two-thirds majority and, for the first time, the FTPA deflected the prospect of an early election.

But not for long. In October Mr Johnson negotiated amendments to the provisions on Northern Ireland in Mrs May's exit deal. Designed to avoid the creation of a hard border on the island of Ireland given that the UK was now leaving the EU while the Republic was remaining, it had been these provisions above

---

[12] Elise Uberoi, Stefano Fella and Richard Cracknell, *European Parliament Elections 2019: Results and Analysis*, CBP 8600 (London: House of Commons Library, 2019), available at https://commonslibrary.parlia ment.uk/research-briefings/cbp-8600/

all that had fuelled much of the opposition to Mrs May's deal among Conservative MPs. Later that month, the government had a partial success in securing MPs' approval for the revised deal, though the government still found itself having to seek a further extension of the deadline for the UK's withdrawal from the EU. Although a third attempt by the government to seek a vote for dissolution also failed, the tide was now turning in favour of an election. Fearful that the government would eventually be able to deliver Brexit, albeit perhaps without a deal, both the Liberal Democrats and the SNP switched to being in favour of an election. After all, the polls suggested that both parties might enjoy significant gains in any early contest, gains that might help secure a parliamentary majority for a second EU referendum that could potentially reverse the outcome of the 2016 ballot.

However, the votes of those two parties alone would not be enough to secure the two-thirds vote for dissolution required under the FTPA. But, as Mrs May's government had recognised in 2017, if a majority of MPs were in favour of having an election it would be possible to hold one by passing primary legislation that brought forward the date of the next election to one specified by that legislation. This was the method that the Liberal Democrats were now willing to back. It meant, of course, that they were proposing a parliamentary manoeuvre that would effectively bypass constitutional provisions on which they themselves had insisted after the 2010 election. In any event, the government took up the offer and secured the passage of primary legislation that set 12 December 2019 as the date of the next election (with future elections to be held every five years after that), though by now Labour had reluctantly come to back the idea of an early contest. Once again, the FTPA had proven to be a flimsy barrier to a governmental push for an early election.[13]

With a twelve-point lead over Labour in the ballot boxes, the contest resulted in a Conservative majority of eighty – the largest overall majority for any party since Tony Blair's second electoral

---

[13] Phillip Cowley, 'The calling of the election', in Robert Ford, Tim Bale, William Jennings and Paula Surridge, *The British General Election of 2019* (Cham: Palgrave Macmillan, 2021).

victory in 2001. The charismatic Boris Johnson's call to 'get Brexit done' was more than a match for Jeremy Corbyn's equivocation on Brexit and his reputation as an 'extreme' left-winger. To that extent, the election produced a result more typical of post-war elections, and Mr Johnson used his majority to secure the UK's exit from the EU at the end of January 2020. Meanwhile, the Liberal Democrats' hopes of making significant gains evaporated in the heat of the election campaign, and despite some increase in their share of the vote the party ended up with just eleven seats, one fewer than in 2017. However, the SNP were more fortunate and regained much of the ground the party had lost in 2017. With 52 of Scotland's 59 seats it was firmly ensconced once again as the third largest party in the Commons.

HOW THE SUPPORT BASE OF THE PARTIES CHANGED

It was not just the continued parliamentary strength of the SNP that ensured that, despite the election of a government with a safe overall majority, the outcome of the 2019 election did not simply reflect a return to the familiar patterns of post-war British politics. For underneath the surface of an election result that, despite their joint poor performances in the European elections six months earlier, was primarily a competition between the Conservatives and Labour, the character of the support for those two parties had changed significantly. The source of this transformation lay in the debate about Brexit, the merits of which came in the 2017 and 2019 elections to dominate the choice that people made at the ballot box.

The evolution of the relationship between attitude towards the EU and party choice is shown in Table 15.2. Using data from the British Election Study Internet Panel, it shows, first, how those who backed Remain in 2016 voted at each general election since 2010, and then how those who supported Leave did so. It shows that even before the 2016 referendum, those who eventually backed Leave were more likely than those who supported Remain to vote Conservative. Indeed, this helps explain why many Conservative MPs were concerned about the rise in the popularity of UKIP during the 2010–15 parliament – nearly all

Table 15.2 Vote choice 2010–19 by 2016 EU referendum vote

	2010	2015	2017	2019	Change 2010–19
Remain voters	%	%	%	%	
Conservative	29	32	23	18	−9
Labour	33	44	53	49	+16
Liberal Democrat	31	12	14	21	−10
UKIP/Brexit	1	1	0	0	−1
Other	6	13	10	12	+6
Leave voters	%	%	%	%	
Conservative	50	44	60	75	+25
Labour	20	21	26	15	−5
Liberal Democrat	16	4	5	2	−14
UKIP/Brexit	7	25	5	3	−4
Other	7	6	4	5	−2

Source: British Election Study Internet Panel Waves, 9, 13 and 16.

UKIP's support came from those who backed Leave. In contrast, Labour and the Liberal Democrats were more popular among 'Remainers' than 'Leavers', a pattern that in Labour's case became more marked in 2015 in the wake of the rise of UKIP.

Nevertheless, the relationship between vote choice and attitudes towards Brexit strengthened further in both 2017 and again in 2019. Support for the Conservatives among those who backed Remain fell at both elections, while backing among those who had supported Leave mushroomed. Meanwhile, although the divergence was nothing like as big, by 2019 support for Labour was five points higher among Remainers than it had been in 2015, while the party's tally among Leavers was five points lower. Indeed, analysis of the relationship between people's current attitude towards Brexit in 2019 and how they voted at that election indicated that over 80 per cent of voters supported a party whose policy position on Brexit matched their own.[14] The 2019 election

[14] John Curtice, *Was the 2019 General Election a Success?* (London: National Centre for Social Research, 2020), available at www.whatukthinks.org/eu/wp-content/uploads/2020/12/WUKT_Was-The-2019-General-Election-A-Success_v4.pdf

came remarkably close to a one-issue election at which Brexit divided the country into two polarised camps.

CHANGED DEMOGRAPHICS

This development posed a challenge to the traditional demographics of party support whereby the Conservatives were more popular among middle-class voters and Labour their working-class counterparts. Brexit was less an issue that divided the country by social class than one that polarised it by education and age. According to the British Social Attitudes survey, just 22 per cent of university graduates voted for Leave, while as many as 72 per cent of those without any educational qualifications did so.[15] Meanwhile, just 28 per cent of those aged 18–24 voted to Leave the EU, compared with as many as 63 per cent of those 65 and over. In large part, this age difference is a consequence of the fact that younger people are more likely to be graduates, though there was also some tendency for older people to be more likely to vote Leave irrespective of their educational background.[16] Meanwhile, the relationship with education ensured that those in professional and managerial occupations (36 per cent) were less likely to vote Leave than those in semi-routine and routine (that is, working-class) jobs (60 per cent). So, in increasingly winning over Leave voters, the Conservatives were likely to be gaining ground among working-class voters while losing support among their middle-class counterparts, thereby eroding the traditional relationship between social class and party support.

[15] John Curtice, 'Litmus test or lightening rod? Assessing the vote to leave the EU', in Elizabeth Clery, John Curtice and Roger Harding (eds.), *British Social Attitudes: The 34th Report* (London: National Centre for Social Research), available at https://bsa.natcen.ac.uk/latest-report/british-soci al-attitudes-34/brexit.aspx

[16] For example, just 20 per cent of graduates aged under 35 voted Leave, compared with 30 per cent of graduates aged over 65. However, as many as 55 per cent of under 35s whose highest qualification was the equivalent of a GCSE Grade A–C voted Leave.

Table 15.3 Vote choice among managerial and professional workers, and semi-routine/routine workers, 2001-19

General election vote	2001	2005	2010	2015	2017	2019	Change 2010-19
Managerial & professional occupations	%	%	%	%	%	%	
Conservative	30	36	41	44	41	38	−3
Labour	42	37	26	30	42	35	+9
Liberal Democrat	24	23	28	11	10	18	−10
UKIP/Brexit	n/a	1	1	6	1	1	0
Other	5	3	4	10	7	9	+5
Semi-routine & routine occupations	%	%	%	%	%	%	
Conservative	20	21	32	28	36	44	+12
Labour	59	56	43	45	50	35	−8
Liberal Democrat	15	16	15	4	5	5	−10
UKIP/Brexit	n/a	1	3	12	3	3	0
Other	6	6	7	11	6	13	+6

Source: 2001–17: British Social Attitudes; 2019: National Centre for Social Research Random Probability Panel

Table 15.3, which shows the relationship between social class and party support in all six elections since the turn of the century, demonstrates that this is precisely what happened. Not that the link between social class and party support was that strong before Brexit came along. While at all three elections between 2001 and 2010 support for Labour was 17–19 points higher among semi-routine and routine workers than it was among those in professional and managerial occupations, between 2001 and 2010, the gap in the case of the Conservatives was a more modest 9–15 points. The advent of New Labour, in particular, had already been accompanied by a reduction in the strength of the relationship between class and party support.[17] Nevertheless, the gap narrowed further in 2017 and 2019.

[17] Geoffrey Evans and James Tilley, *The New Politics of Class* (Oxford: Oxford University Press, 2017).

Indeed, by 2019 support for Labour was, unprecedently, no higher among working-class voters than it was among those in managerial and professional jobs, while the Conservatives were actually a little more popular among the former than the latter. The coalition of voters that gave the Conservatives their victory in 2019 was markedly different in character from anything they had secured at any previous election.

But if by 2019 there was no longer much of a link between party support and social class, there was now a clear relationship between vote choice and age. Not that such a relationship was entirely absent beforehand. As Table 15.4 shows, the Conservatives had long been more popular among older voters (aged 65 and over) than their younger counterparts (aged 18 to 34); indeed, the difference was as much as 16–18 points in 2005 and 2010. However, support for Labour had largely been much the same in the two age groups, though an 11-point difference did emerge in 2015. But in 2017 and 2019 a chasm opened up. By 2019 support for the Conservatives was as much as 44 points higher among those 65 and over than it was among those under 35, while backing for Labour was 37 points higher among the younger age group. Age not social class had come to be the biggest demographic division in Britain's voting behaviour.

Table 15.4 Vote choice among those aged 18-34 and 65 and over, 2001-19

General election vote	2001	2005	2010	2015	2017	2019	Change 2010–19
Aged 18–34	%	%	%	%	%	%	
Conservative	25	23	32	32	22	18	−14
Labour	50	43	32	39	62	55	+23
Liberal Democrat	17	25	25	8	8	12	−13
UKIP/Brexit	n/a	1	3	6	1	2	−1
Other	8	8	8	16	8	7	−1
Aged 65+	%	%	%	%	%	%	
Conservative	34	41	48	49	55	62	+14
Labour	49	42	28	28	30	18	−10
Liberal Democrat	13	15	18	6	8	11	−7
UKIP/Brexit	n/a	1	3	11	3	2	−1
Other	4	2	3	5	4	7	+4

Source: 2001–17: British Social Attitudes; 2019: National Centre for Social Research Random Probability Panel.

Table 15.5 Vote choice among graduates and those with no formal educational qualifications, 2001-19

General election vote	2001	2005	2010	2015	2017	2019	Change 2010-19
Graduates	%	%	%	%	%	%	
Conservative	22	29	31	37	32	31	+0
Labour	41	33	27	35	48	40	+13
Liberal Democrat	31	31	36	13	12	18	−18
UKIP/Brexit	n/a	1	1	3	1	1	−2
Other	5	6	4	12	7	11	+7
No qualifications	%	%	%	%	%	%	
Conservative	25	28	38	35	47	54	+16
Labour	58	57	38	43	43	24	−`14
Liberal Democrat	12	12	17	3	4	7	−10
UKIP/Brexit	n/a	1	3	12	4	4	+1
Other	5	3	5	6	3	11	+6

Source: 2001–17: British Social Attitudes; 2019: National Centre for Social Research Random Probability Panel

Equally, Brexit left its imprint on the relationship between party support and educational background (see Table 15.5). For the most part, between 2001 and 2010, support for the Conservatives was much the same among those without any educational qualifications as it was among those with a university degree – as we have seen, while the party was more popular among those in professional and managerial occupations (who were more likely to be graduates), it was also more popular among older voters (more likely not to have any qualifications). Labour, in contrast, was more popular among those without any educational qualifications than it was among graduates, though the gap was somewhat narrower in 2010 and 2015 than it had been previously. However, by 2017 the Conservatives were more popular among those without educational qualifications than they were among graduates, while the opposite was true of Labour. This new pattern then strengthened further in 2019.[18]

---

[18] The relationship between party choice and education is, of course, in part a reflection of the fact that younger people are more likely to be graduates –

A CHANGED GEOGRAPHY

We have already seen that Scotland diverged politically from England and Wales in 2015. Meanwhile, Brexit also left its impression on the geography of party support within England and Wales. As Table 15.6 shows, the average level of support for the Conservatives grew most (by sixteen points) between 2010 and 2019 in those constituencies in England and Wales that are estimated to have voted most heavily for Leave in 2016.[19] In contrast, although already relatively low, the party's vote actually fell back by four points in seats that backed Remain most heavily. All this divergence in the pattern of Conservative support occurred in the two Brexit-dominated elections of 2017 and 2019.

Conversely, although the differences are not quite as stark, Labour's vote increased by nearly fifteen points between 2010 and 2019 in seats in England and Wales that had voted most heavily for Remain, while it fell back slightly (by just under a point) in those that were most supportive of leaving. In Labour's case, however, some of this divergence occurred between 2010 and 2015. Whereas the Conservatives managed to retain their support in 2015 in those constituencies that voted most heavily for Brexit in 2016, even though UKIP performed most strongly in these seats, the same was not true of Labour.[20] In any event, as a result of these movements Labour lost to the Conservatives a number of working-class constituencies located

and vice versa. However, the two relationships are independent of each other, albeit with age being somewhat the stronger correlate. Thus, for example, among those aged under 35 with a degree, 14 per cent voted Conservative in 2019, 57 per cent Labour. In contrast, among those under 35s whose highest qualification is the equivalent of a GCSE A–C, 35 per cent voted Conservative, 42 per cent Labour. Meanwhile, among graduates over 55, 42 per cent backed the Conservatives, 27 per cent Labour.

[19] This analysis uses the estimates of the outcome of the EU referendum in each constituency in Chris Hanretty, 'Areal interpolation and the UK's referendum on EU membership', *Journal of Elections, Public Opinion, and Parties*, 27:4 (2017), 466–83.

[20] John Curtice, Stephen Fisher and Patrick English, 'Appendix 1: Further analysis of the results', in Ford et al., *General Election of 2019*, pp. 590–3.

Table 15.6 Mean Conservative, Labour, and Liberal Democrat share of the vote, 2010–19, in England and Wales by EU referendum vote

2016 EU referendum result	Conservative	Labour	Liberal Democrat
	%	%	%
Remain over 60%			
2010	28.7	35.3	28.8
2015	29.9	43.8	11.2
2017	27.2	55.8	12.4
2019	24.4	50.1	19.3
Change 2010–19	−4.3	+14.8	−9.5
Remain 50–60%			
2010	40.1	27.0	25.7
2015	41.5	32.1	9.3
2017	43.1	43.1	9.3
2019	41.4	36.6	16.1
Change 2010–19	+1.3	+9.6	−9.6
Leave 50–60%			
2010	39.6	27.3	24.5
2015	41.6	29.9	8.4
2017	47.2	40.5	7.4
2019	49.2	32.9	11.5
Change 2010–19	+9.6	+5.6	−13.0
Leave over 60%			
2010	36.8	33.4	18.8
2015	36.8	34.5	4.8
2017	47.0	43.1	3.7
2019	52.9	32.5	6.3
Change 2010–19	+16.1	−0.9	−12.5

north of Birmingham that had traditionally been party strongholds and many of which had been continuously in the party's hands since the 1930s. This loss of this so-called 'Red Wall' came to be regarded as symbolic of the scale and unprecedented character of the Conservatives' success and Labour's defeat in 2019.[21]

[21] James Kanagasooriam and Elizabeth Simon, 'Red Wall: the definitive description', *Political Insight*, 12:3 (2021), 8-11.

VALUES AND PARTY CHOICE

Not only were the demographics and geography of party choice very different in 2019 from what they had been less than a decade earlier, but so also was the ideological basis of party support. Traditionally, how people vote in Britain has reflected whether they were on the 'left' or the 'right', that is, whether they felt Britain was too unequal and government should do more to reduce it (more likely to vote Labour), or whether they believe government should ensure that there are sufficient incentives for entrepreneurs to invest and thereby generate the economic growth from which all might profit (more likely to support the Conservatives).[22] However, Brexit, where much of the debate was about sovereignty and immigration rather than inequality or the role of the state, was not an issue that divided voters on left–right lines. Rather, at 52 per cent, support for Leave among those on the 'left' was, according to the British Social Attitudes survey, little different from that among those on the 'right' (45 per cent).[23]

Attitudes towards Brexit were, however, related to another ideological division. This is between 'liberals' and 'authoritarians'.

---

[22] John Curtice, Victoria Ratti, Ian Montagu and Chris Deeming, 'Age differences: a new generational divide?', in Sarah Frankenburg, Elizabeth Clery and John Curtice (eds.), *British Social Attitudes: The 40th Report* (London: National Centre for Social Research, 2023), available at https://natcen.ac.uk/publications/bsa-40-age-differences

[23] Respondents are classified as 'left' or 'right' wing on the basis of how much they agree or disagree with a series of statements on inequality and the role that government might play in reducing it, the answers to which are turned into a Likert scale score. Those on the left are those with the one-third most left-wing scores and those on the right those with the one-third most right-wing. See 'Technical details', in Elizabeth Clery, John Curtice, and Roger Harding (eds.), *British Social Attitudes: The 34th Report* (London: National Centre for Social Research, 2017), available at https://bsa.natcen.ac.uk/latest-report/british-social-attitudes-34/technical-details.aspx. See also Kirby Swales, *Understanding The Leave Vote* (London: National Centre for Social Research, 2016), available at www.whatukthinks.org/eu/wp-content/uploads/2016/12/NatCen_Brexplanations-report-FINAL-WEB2.pdf

Liberals are inclined to the view that individuals should have freedom to decide for themselves how they live their lives, whereas authoritarians believe the state should enforce society's moral code and cultural values. The former group (21 per cent) were much less likely to vote Leave than the latter (72 per cent). This division was not entirely absent in the pattern of party support in the years before Brexit, but as we shall see it tended to be less important than the difference between left and right.[24]

Table 15.7 charts the relationship between party choice and where people stand on the left–right division since 2001. Between 2001 and 2010 the Conservatives were consistently 30 points more popular among those on the right than they were among those on the left. Labour was between 22 and 29 points more popular among those on the left. In both cases the divide was even bigger in 2015, a reflection perhaps of the fact that Labour had somewhat moved away from the centrist position it had held under New Labour, while the Conservative-led coalition had implemented a programme of financial austerity. But as we might anticipate, the divide narrowed somewhat thereafter. Support for the Conservatives fell between 2015 and 2019 by 10 points among those on the right, while it increased by 14 points among those on the left. Meanwhile, Labour's support fell by 6 points among those on the left while it edged up by 2 points among more right-wing voters. Even so, that still meant that the left–right divide in support of the Conservatives and Labour was only a little less than it had been in 2010. Attitudes towards equality remained an important feature of the pattern of party support at all four elections between 2010 and 2019.

Nevertheless, as Brexit came increasingly to influence how people voted, by 2019 the left–right division was sharing the limelight with the liberal–authoritarian divide to a greater extent

[24] Respondents are classified as 'liberal' or 'authoritarian' on the basis of how much they agree or disagree with a series of statements on law and order, conformity and traditional values, the answers to which are turned into a Likert scale score. Liberals are those with the one-third most liberal scores while authoritarians are those with the one-third most right-wing scores. See 'Technical details', in Clery et al., *British Social Attitudes 34.*

Table 15.7 Vote choice, by left–right position, 2001–19

General election vote	2001	2005	2010	2015	2017	2019	Change 2010–19
Left-wing voters	%	%	%	%	%	%	
Conservative	14	17	21	17	20	31	+10
Labour	62	54	43	51	60	45	+2
Liberal Democrat	17	22	22	7	10	10	−12
UKIP/Brexit	n/a	1	3	10	3	2	−1
Other	8	6	11	15	8	12	−1
Centre voters	%	%	%	%	%	%	
Conservative	24	27	39	36	39	43	+4
Labour	50	45	33	33	45	35	+2
Liberal Democrat	21	23	22	9	7	12	−10
UKIP/Brexit	n/a	1	2	11	2	1	−1
Other	5	5	4	11	6	8	+4
Right-wing voters	%	%	%	%	%	%	
Conservative	44	47	51	66	64	56	+5
Labour	33	29	21	15	23	17	−4
Liberal Democrat	19	19	24	7	8	17	−7
UKIP/Brexit	n/a	1	2	6	1	2	0
Other	4	4	3	5	4	9	+6

Source: 2001–17: British Social Attitudes; 2019: National Centre for Social Research Random Probability Panel.

than in the past. Table 15.8 shows that between 2001 and 2010 where people stood on the liberal–authoritarian divide made little difference at all to their chances of voting Labour. In 2010, for example, the party won 32 per cent support among authoritarians, and 30 per cent among liberals. That said, the Conservatives were more popular among authoritarians than liberals; indeed, the gap was 19 points in both 2005 and 2010, not least because the Liberal Democrats, whose support differed little between left and right, were around 20 points more popular among liberals than authoritarians.

However, thereafter a gap opened in the level of support for Labour among liberals and authoritarians. In 2017 and 2019 support for Labour was 20–22 points higher among liberals than authoritarians. Meanwhile, by 2019 the Conservatives were 41 points more popular among authoritarians than liberals, a bigger

Table 15.8 Vote choice by liberal–authoritarian position, 2001–19

General election vote	2001	2005	2010	2015	2017	2019	Change 2010–19
Liberal voters	%	%	%	%	%	%	
Conservative	20	20	28	33	22	23	−5
Labour	48	44	32	37	55	43	+11
Liberal Democrat	26	30	33	12	14	19	−14
UKIP/Brexit	n/a	*	1	3	1	1	0
Other	7	6	6	16	7	13	+7
Centre voters	%	%	%	%	%	%	
Conservative	31	36	40	45	49	49	+9
Labour	49	42	35	31	37	28	−7
Liberal Democrat	16	17	19	6	5	11	−8
UKIP/Brexit	n/a	1	2	12	1	2	0
Other	4	5	3	7	7	10	+7
Authoritarian voters	%	%	%	%	%	%	
Conservative	34	39	47	48	56	64	+17
Labour	47	40	30	28	33	23	−7
Liberal Democrat	14	15	13	3	3	5	−8
UKIP/Brexit	n/a	2	3	15	4	2	−1
Other	5	4	7	6	4	5	−2

Source: 2001–17: British Social Attitudes; 2019: National Centre for Social Research Random Probability Panel.

difference than the gap in the party's support than there was between those on the left and those on the right. Rather than being focused primarily on the debate between left and right, party choice in Britain had become a two-dimensional battleground.

SCOTLAND

As previously noted, in the wake of the 2014 independence referendum, the pattern of party competition in Scotland – already very different in devolved elections to the Scottish Parliament from that in elections to Westminster – diverged sharply from the rest of Great Britain, with the SNP dominating Scotland's representation north of the border. However, not only did the level of SNP support increase in the wake of the 2014 ballot, but so also did its character. Just as attitudes towards Brexit after the 2016 referendum became more strongly related to how people voted across Britain as a whole, so also within Scotland the pattern of vote choice increasingly reflected their constitutional preference.

This change is illustrated in Table 15.9, which shows the level of support for the SNP at all Westminster and devolved elections since 2010, broken down by people's current attitude towards independence. While there was a link before 2014 between people's constitutional preference and their propensity to vote SNP, it was far from perfect. At the 2010 UK general election, only just over half of those who at that time supported independence voted for the SNP, while in the devolved election of 2011, when the SNP won an overall majority in the Scottish Parliament, nearly two in five of those who opposed independence voted for the party. But in the 2015 election, support for the SNP among supporters of independence increased on the position in 2011, while it fell back among opponents. Meanwhile, in the two most recent elections, the party came close to replicating its 2015 level of popularity among those who back independence, while its support fell to around just one in eight among its

Table 15.9 SNP support by current constitutional preference 2010–21

	Attitude towards independence	
	Support	**Oppose**
	% voted SNP	**% voted SNP**
2010 (Westminster)	55	12
2011 (Holyrood)	79	38
2015 (Westminster)	85	25
2016 (Holyrood)	81	24
2017 (Westminster)	72	15
2019 (Westminster)	81	13
2021 (Holyrood)	84	11

Source: Scottish Social Attitudes. In the case of 2019, respondents' constitutional preference is as obtained in 2021.

opponents. Constitutional preference had come to dominate the pattern of party support in Scotland to a degree that was redolent of the position in Northern Ireland.

POST-BREXIT MAJORITARIAN GOVERNMENT

The Conservatives' success in 2019 in winning their first secure overall majority in four elections meant they were in a position to repeal the FTPA and restore the status quo ante whereby a prime minister can ask the monarch to dissolve parliament at any time within its maximum life of five years. The flexibility this affords on the timing of an election means, of course, that a prime minister can again hope to call an election when his party seems best placed to win. As a result, the next election could take place at any point up to and including January 2025 (that is, a month after the automatic dissolution of the current parliament in December 2024, five years after it first met after the 2019 election), though a decision to leave it that late would mean the election campaign would encompass the Christmas and New Year holiday season. The idea of having fixed-term parliaments, an idea that had been more honoured in the breach than the observance, had finally bitten the dust.

More immediately, the government's eighty-seat majority enabled it to secure speedy parliamentary approval of the withdrawal agreement with the European Union, and the UK formally left the EU at the end of January 2020. During the ensuring eleven months the UK and the EU negotiated a Trade and Cooperation Agreement that set out the rules under which trade between them was to be conducted once the UK left the EU single market and customs union, which it duly did at the end of 2020. Meanwhile, Labour under their new leader, Sir Keir Starmer, accepted that the Brexit decision was not for overturning, and while the Liberal Democrats signalled their hope that the decision would eventually be reversed, their new leader, Sir Ed Davey, stated they were 'not a rejoin party'. Although the Scottish National Party maintained their vocal opposition to Brexit, for the most part it seemed that, for the politicians at least, the debate about Brexit was over.

Yet despite the advent of a government with a safe overall majority and a conclusion to the Brexit debate, normality and stability were not about to return to British politics. The winter of 2020 witnessed the onset of Covid-19, which posed the biggest public health crisis in a century. The UK went into 'lockdown' in March 2020, and measures of varying intensity limiting social interaction were in place for the next two years. The pandemic, together with the Russian invasion of Ukraine in February 2022, was to leave its imprint on the rest of the parliament, not least in the form of an expanded state, a weakened economy, increased taxation, high inflation, rising inflation rates and struggling public services.[25] More immediately, the pandemic and its aftermath were also to play a significant role in the downfall of not just one, but two prime ministers in a matter of months.

Both these prime ministerial downfalls were accompanied by sharp changes in the popularity of the parties in the polls – but for reasons that had nothing to do with Brexit. Figure 15.1 shows how the standing of the parties in the polls has changed from month to month in the opinion polls since January 2020. For the first two years of the current parliament, the government was remarkably successful at retaining the support it secured in the 2019 election. Indeed, the early weeks of the pandemic witnessed a 'rally to the flag' effect, with support for the governing party reaching 50 per cent. However, in a pointer to later developments, that support fell away quite markedly in the wake of the publicity given in May 2020 to the decision of the prime minister's chief adviser, Dominic Cummings, to drive – in apparent breach of the lockdown rules – to his parents' property in Durham after he became concerned that he and his wife had contracted Covid-19. Nevertheless, for two years the Conservatives were never behind the opposition in the polls.

[25] Office for Budget Responsibility, *Economic and Fiscal Outlook March 2024* (London: His Majesty's Stationery Office, 2024), available at https://obr.uk/docs/dlm_uploads/E03057758_OBR_EFO-March-2024_Web-AccessibleFinal.pdf; Carl Baker, *NHS Key Statistics: England*, CBP7281 (London: House of Commons Library, 2023), available at https://researchbriefings.files.parliament.uk/documents/CBP-7281/CBP-7281.pdf

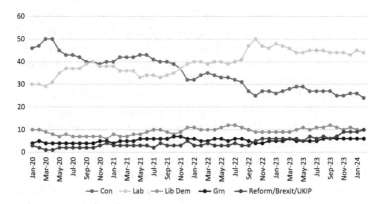

Figure 15.1 The trajectory of UK party support since December 2019
Source: Average of the polls conducted closest to the end of each month by each polling company. Not all companies polled every month.

Indeed, they appeared to benefit from a swift rollout of a Covid-19 vaccine at the end of 2020 and an increase in economic optimism as the country gradually emerged from the restrictions that had been imposed to control the pandemic.[26] The attempts of Labour's centrist new leader, Sir Keir Starmer, to distance himself and his party from the era of his left-wing predecessor, Jeremy Corbyn, appeared to be bearing relatively little electoral fruit.

Nevertheless, during the autumn of 2021 the government's lead began to fall as inflation started to pick up and economic optimism waned. However, support for the Conservatives fell by as much as five points in December 2021, putting them behind Labour for the first time, after it emerged that various 'gatherings' had taken place in 10 Downing Street in 2020 and 2021 in apparent breach of lockdown regulations that had stopped families visiting relatives in care homes or being with their partner when they died. Thereafter, doubts were raised about

---

[26] Ipsos, 'Economic Optimism Index (EOI): State of the economy 1997–present', posted at www.ipsos.com/en-uk/economic-optimism-index-eoi-state-economy-1997-present

the veracity of the prime minister's account to the House of Commons of what he had known about these events, and indeed he was subsequently adjudged by a Commons committee to have misled the House.[27] But long before that determination was reached, in early July 2022 it emerged that Mr Johnson had not been entirely straightforward about his knowledge of allegations of improper behaviour against the deputy chief whip, Chris Pincher. Willingness to trust Mr Johnson began to evaporate. Both the chancellor and the health secretary resigned followed by nearly sixty other ministers and aides. Mr Johnson was forced to admit he could no longer form a government, and the way was paved for a Conservative leadership contest between the foreign secretary, Liz Truss, and the former chancellor, Rishi Sunak.

Ms Truss, who won that contest, articulated in her leadership campaign the concern that had arisen in the Conservative Party about the growth in the size of the state and the increase in taxation that had occurred during the pandemic, together with the fact that the economy had long been stuttering. Meanwhile, by the time that the leadership contest was over at the beginning of September, the inflationary pressure created by the pandemic and the Ukraine War, especially in respect of the cost of energy, was becoming intense. Ms Truss's government decided both to increase spending by subsidising the cost of domestic energy and, in a 'dash for growth', to cut £45 billion worth of taxes, including, most controversially, the abolition of the top rate of income tax. However, the financial markets baulked at these unfunded tax cuts, interest rates on government debt rose dramatically and the value of the pound fell.

As our figure shows, support for the Conservatives fell heavily in the wake of this adverse market reaction. By the end of October, it was Labour that now stood at 50 per cent in the polls, while, at 25 per cent, the Conservatives were six points

[27] House of Commons Committee of Privileges, *Matter referred on 21 April 2022 (conduct of Rt Hon Boris Johnson): Final Report*, HC 564 (London: House of Commons, 2023), available at https://committees.parliament.uk/publications/40412/documents/197897/default/

adrift of where they had been at the end of August. But by the end of October too, Liz Truss was no longer prime minister, forced to resign after just forty-nine days in office after support for her rapidly waned among her parliamentary colleagues. She was replaced – without a contest – by the man she had defeated in the leadership contest, Mr Sunak. However, the damage done to the Conservatives' popularity proved difficult for her predecessor to reverse. Indeed, even as much as sixteen months on from the debacle of Ms Truss's administration, the Conservatives were doing no better than an average of 24 per cent in the polls.

THE SOURCES OF DISCONTENT

After 2019, then, politics had reverted to being dominated by familiar topics such as the economy, taxation, spending and leadership – albeit with unprecedented consequences. Not since the unusually long parliament of 1935–45 had the tenancy of 10 Downing Street changed more than once between elections. Moreover, as our account of the timeline of the changing popularity of the parties has already implied, the marked changes in the popularity of the government reflected voters' perceptions on these domestic issues rather than the politics of Brexit.

For example, the crisis in the bond and sterling markets under Liz Truss severely damaged the government's reputation for economic competence, much as 'Black Wednesday' in September 1992 and the financial crisis of 2007–8 adversely impacted on the perceived capability of the governments of John Major and Gordon Brown that had presided over those crises. According to Ipsos, at the time of the 2019 election, as many as 44 per cent thought that the Conservatives were best able to run the economy, while only 20 per cent said that Labour were. Although the gap had narrowed by April 2022, at 32 per cent the Conservatives were still ahead of Labour on 26 per cent – despite the substantial lead Labour had in the polls by then. But by October, after the wobble in the markets, just 21 per cent felt the Conservatives were best at running the economy – little better than the position of Labour in 2019 – while 34 per cent now nominated Labour.[28]

Meanwhile, perceptions of the state of the economy were clearly linked to the willingness or otherwise of those who had voted Conservative in 2019 to back the party again. According to the British Election Study, by May 2023 only 25 per cent of those 2019 Conservative voters who thought the economy was getting 'a lot worse' were inclined to vote for the party again, as were just 44 per cent of those who thought that the economy was getting 'a little worse'. In contrast, as many as 74 per cent of those who thought the economy was getting better were willing to vote Conservative again. Unfortunately for the government, only 12 per cent of 2019 Conservative voters believed that the economy was getting better, while 39 per cent believed it was getting a little worse, and 29 per cent a lot worse.

Perceptions of the state of the public services, and especially of the health service where waiting lists had reached a record high in the wake of the pandemic,[29] also ate away at Conservative support. According to the same study, only 34 per cent of those who voted Conservative in 2019 and who felt the NHS was getting a lot worse were willing to vote Conservative again, compared with an equivalent figure of 62 per cent of those who felt the NHS was the same or getting better. Again, these figures matter because as many as 46 per cent of 2019 Conservative voters felt that the NHS was getting a lot worse, while just 18 per cent felt that it was either the same or better.

There was, though, one aspect of the Brexit debate that did come back to the forefront of the political agenda. A central claim of those who campaigned for a Leave vote was that it would enable Britain 'to take back control' of its borders by ending freedom of movement between the United Kingdom and the European Union. Yet although net migration between the UK and the EU did decline, it was accompanied by a substantial increase in migration from outside the EU, such that overall

---

[28] Ipsos, 'Best party on key issues: managing the economy', posted at www.ipsos.com/en-uk/best-party-key-issues-managing-economy

[29] Baker, *NHS Key Statistics*.

net migration reached a record high of 745,000 in 2022.[30] Meanwhile, increasing numbers of refugees were crossing the English Channel in small, and often fragile boats, with a view to claiming asylum in the UK, a development that seemingly contradicted the aim of taking back control of the border.

Voters – including those who had voted Leave in 2016 and Conservative in 2019 – certainly noticed the increase in immigration. By May 2023 no less than 58 per cent of Conservative Leavers said that immigration was getting a lot higher, while another 20 per cent said that it was becoming a little higher. Yet, at 41 per cent, the proportion of those saying a lot higher who said they would vote Conservative again was only marginally below the equivalent proportion of 46 per cent among those who felt that immigration was either the same or falling.[31] In short, while many Conservative voters were unhappy about the level of immigration, on its own it was not a perception that appeared to influence people's willingness to vote Conservative again.[32] Even here, then, Brexit and its consequences have played little role in shaping the parties' fortunes during the current parliament.

[30] Office for National Statistics, *Long-Term International Migration, provisional: year ending June 2023* (Newport: Office for National Statistics, 2023), available at www.ons.gov.uk/peoplepopulationandcommunity/po pulationandmigration/internationalmigration/bulletins/longterminter nationalmigrationprovisional/yearendingjune2023; Madeleine Sumption, Peter Walsh and Ben Brindle, *Net Migration to the UK* (Oxford: Migration Observatory, 2023), available at migrationobservatory.ox.ac.uk/resources/ briefings/long-term-international-migration-flows-to-and-from-the-uk/

[31] The figures for all those who voted Conservative in 2019 are 42 per cent and 46 per cent respectively.

[32] This remark is confirmed by the results of a logistic regression analysis that takes into account the apparent impact of perceptions of the economy, the NHS and immigration on the likelihood of 2019 Conservative voters saying that they would vote Conservative again. In contrast to both perceptions of the economy and of the NHS, perceptions of immigration are overall only weakly related to willingness to vote Conservative again, and in particular those who felt that immigration is getting a lot higher were not significantly different from those who thought that it was the same in their reported willingness to vote Conservative again.

IS THERE STILL A BREXIT LEGACY?

So, whereas the elections of 2017 and 2019 were primarily registering voters' reactions to Brexit, the ups and downs of party fortunes in the 2019–24 parliament have primarily reflected perceptions of leadership, economics and public services. But this does not necessarily mean that the restructuring of party support that was occasioned by Brexit in the years before the 2019 election has disappeared. Perhaps support for the parties has risen and fallen among 'Remainers' and 'Leavers' in more or less equal measure, leaving the difference in their popularity in the two groups much the same? Or has the fact that neither Labour nor the Liberal Democrats have been articulating an anti-Brexit stance since 2019 meant that those parties have been particularly successful at securing the support of those who support Britain's decision to leave the EU, thereby facilitating a depolarisation of the Brexit divide?

Table 15.10 addresses this question by examining the relationship between people's current attitude towards Brexit and party support. We use current preference rather than how people voted in 2016 because of the now not inconsiderable number of people who have reached their eighteenth birthday since June 2016 and thus could not vote in the EU referendum but will be able to do so at the next election, and because there has been a decline in the popularity of Brexit. According to the polls, support for being outside the EU had already dipped from the 52 per cent registered in the June 2016 referendum to 48 per cent by the time of the 2019 election, while since the autumn of 2022 it has typically been around 43 per cent.[33] Moreover, those who have changed their mind about Brexit have often also changed their party preference – for example, in May 2023 just 22 per cent of those 2016 Leave voters who voted Conservative in 2019 and who would now vote to rejoin were saying they would vote Conservative again. As a result, simply

---

[33] John Curtice, 'Seven years on: why has Brexit become less popular?', posted at www.whatukthinks.org/eu/2023/06/23/seven-years-on-why-has-brexit-become-less-popular/

Table 15.10 Vote choice/intention by current attitude towards Brexit, 2019-23

	December 2019 %	May 2021 %	May 2022 %	December 2022 %	May 2023 %	Change 2019-23
Remain/Rejoin supporters						
Conservative	11	12	8	7	9	−2
Brexit/Reform	*	*	*	1	1	+1
Labour	55	51	58	65	59	+4
Liberal Democrat	22	13	15	11	14	−8
Green	4	14	10	8	10	+6
SNP/PC	7	10	7	7	5	−2
Leave/Stay Out supporters						
Conservative	80	78	63	51	53	−27
Brexit/Reform	5	4	9	20	17	+12
Labour	9	10	16	20	19	+10
Liberal Democrat	2	2	5	3	5	+3
Green	1	3	3	2	3	+2
SNP/PC	1	2	1	2	1	n/c

Source: British Election Study Internet Panel waves 19, 21, 23, 24 and 25.

analysing people's vote preferences by how they voted in 2016 is at risk of painting a less than accurate picture of how far vote choice is now related to people's attitudes towards the EU.[34]

Table 15.10 shows that when Conservative support initially fell in the wake of 'Partygate' (see the figures for May 2022) and

---

[34] This point is confirmed if we analyse the relationship in May 2023 between how people voted in 2016 and their current vote preference. This shows a weaker relationship between attitude towards Brexit and party support than shown in Table 15.9. In May 2023 Conservative support stood at 16 per cent among those who voted Remain (7 points higher than among current supporters of Rejoin) while it was 43 per cent among those who voted Leave (10 points lower). The equivalent figures for Labour are 53 per cent (6 points lower) and 28 per cent (9 points higher).

when it did so further following the Liz Truss crisis on the financial markets (December 2022), the party's standing fell most heavily among those who were in favour of staying out of the EU. This was an arithmetical inevitability given that so few current supporters of Brexit had voted for the Conservatives in 2019. Even so, it was still the case in May 2023 that as much as 78 per cent of the party's support came from those who currently wanted to be outside the EU, only somewhat down on the equivalent figure of 87 per cent at the 2019 election.

As a result, it is not surprising that, at ten points, the increase in Labour support between 2019 and May 2023 among those who wish to be outside the EU was somewhat higher than the increase (of four points) among those who would prefer to be part of the European organisation. Even so, Labour's support evidently increased on both sides of the Brexit divide. Meanwhile, once we take into account the fact that support for being inside the EU had increased since the 2019 election, we find that as much as 84 per cent of Labour's support in May 2023 came from those who wish to be part of the EU, only marginally down on the 87 per cent figure in 2019.[35]

In short, while the changes in the popularity of the parties since 2019 have had relatively little to do with Brexit, there is still a substantial link between people's attitude towards Brexit and party preference.[36] Domestic developments since 2021 have served to change the vote intentions of both 'Remainers' and

---

[35] For an alternative analysis of the change in the relationship between attitudes towards Brexit and party support based on opinion polls conducted in autumn 2023, see John Curtice, 'A return to normality? The next UK general election', *Political Insight*, 14:4 (2023), 7–9. Although the figures are somewhat different, the implications are similar to those drawn here.

[36] Note that if we use 2016 vote as our metric of the relationship (see fn. 34), we find that the drop in Conservative support as compared with 2010 and 2015 is greater among Remain voters than Leave supporters, while the increase in Labour support is higher among Remainers than Leavers. In other words, even by this measure the link between attitude towards Brexit and party support is still stronger than before the 2016 referendum.

'Leavers'. That said, the sharp decline in the Conservatives' popularity has severely undermined the key foundation of the party's electoral success in 2019 – its grip on the loyalties of pro-Brexit supporters, some of whom have now switched to Labour but others of whom have moved to the equally pro-Brexit Reform UK Party.

Moreover, much of the change in the demographics of party support that we have seen occurred between 2010 and 2019 is still in place. Support for Conservative and Labour still varies little by social class – both parties are more or less equally popular among middle-class and working-class voters. There continues to be a marked divide by age – among those aged 18–34 Labour, with 60 per cent, were 48 points ahead of the Conservatives in May 2023, while the Conservatives, with 44 per cent, were still as much as 18 points ahead of Labour among those aged 65 and over. Equally, in contrast to the position before 2017, the Conservatives are still more popular among those with few, if any, educational qualifications than they are among graduates, while the opposite is true of Labour.

Meanwhile, the difference in the party preferences of liberals and authoritarians, while not so big as in 2019, is still notable. According to the British Election Study, although in May 2023 the figure is 19 points down on 2019, the Conservatives were still 33 points more popular among authoritarians than among liberals. Meanwhile, Labour are still 25 points more popular among liberals than authoritarians, a narrowing of just 9 points compared with 2019.[37] At the same time there is no sign of the left–right divide in party support having strengthened since 2019 – if anything, the opposite appears to be the case. Consequently, the value divide in the pattern of Conservative and Labour support still looks more like a two-dimensional battle than the primarily one-dimensional affair that was in evidence in 2010.

---

[37] Note that people's positions on the liberal–authoritarian and left–right scales are measured a little differently in the British Election Study than in British Social Attitudes. The figures quoted in this paragraph therefore cannot be compared directly with those in Table 15.8.

Indeed, the liberal–authoritarian divide seemed to be one that some in the Conservative Party wished to keep alive, perhaps in the hope that it would enable the party to reforge the coalition of (predominantly authoritarian) Leave voters that had delivered the party victory. They took up an 'anti-woke' stance on so-called 'culture wars' issues such as pride in Britain and its imperial past, equal opportunities for minority groups, immigration, and the recognition of transgender people, on all of which 'authoritarians' tend to take a more conservative stance. However, attitudes towards most of these issues have become more liberal over the years, such that the socially conservative or anti-woke stance is now the minority view.[38] Meanwhile, as we have already seen, immigration in particular has played little role in accounting for the decline in Conservative fortunes since 2021, and thus seems unlikely to be an issue where a policy success would help bring voters back into the Tory fold.

A CHANGED GEOGRAPHY?

For the most part then, our analysis suggests that much of the legacy of Brexit is still apparent in the structure of party choice even though the issue has not played a significant role in accounting for the dynamics of party support. Even so, the particularly sharp decline in support for the Conservatives since 2019 does potentially have implications for the geography of party support at the next election. As Table 15.11 shows, while support for the Conservatives was still somewhat higher in May 2023 in constituencies that voted most heavily for Leave, the party's support has fallen more heavily in such seats. As a result, the relative strength of the Conservative Party in the most pro-Leave seats was now only marginally greater than in 2015, before the Brexit referendum (see Table 15.6).

---

[38] John Curtice and Victoria Ratti, 'Culture wars: keeping the Brexit divide alive?', in Sarah Butt, Elizabeth Clery and John Curtice (eds.), *British Social Attitudes: The 39th Report* (London: National Centre for Social Research, 2022), available at https://bsa.natcen.ac.uk/media/39478/bsa39_culture-wars.pdf

Table 15.11 Vote intention May 2023 (and change since 2019) by percentage of Leave vote in constituency in 2019

	% Leave 2016			
	Less than 40%	40–50%	50–60%	60% or more
	%	%	%	%
Conservative	16 (−10)	25 (−15)	28 (−21)	29 (−24)
Labour	53 (+7)	44 (+8)	44 (+12)	46 (+15)
Liberal Democrat	13 (−7)	14 (−3)	11 (−1)	7 (n/c)

Source: British Election Study Internet Panel wave 25. Respondents in England and Wales only. Figures in brackets represent change on 2019 vote as measured in that wave.

Meanwhile, Labour have advanced rather more strongly in the most pro-Leave constituencies, though the difference in the change in Labour support between pro-Leave and pro-Remain seats is rather less than in the case of the Conservatives. Moreover, Labour's support is still relatively stronger in the most pro-Remain seats than it was in 2010. Even so, it is possible that much of the reshaping of the geography of party support that occurred in 2017 and 2019 will be reversed at the next election despite the fact that much of the imprint of Brexit on the voting behaviour of individual voters will still be in place. The geography of party support could change significantly even though much of the change since 2010 in the pattern of individual voting behaviour remains in place. In particular, it appears that the Conservatives are at risk of losing support most heavily in places where they were previously strongest, a pattern that could have a significant adverse impact on the party's tally of seats.

Recent developments north of the border also potentially have implications for the geography of the next election. As might be anticipated, the Labour Party in Scotland enjoyed a revival in its fortunes from December 2021 onwards, in tandem with the increase in the party's popularity across the UK as a whole. By the end of 2022 the party was averaging 29 per cent in polls of Westminster vote intentions, up ten points on its tally in 2019, while the Conservatives, on 16 per cent, were down nine points. However, the SNP, on 45 per cent, were still as popular as they had been in 2019. But the announcement of her resignation by the party leader, Nicola Sturgeon, in February 2023, marked the beginning of a decline in the party's standing following a divisive leadership contest, the election as her successor of the less popular Humza Yousaf, and a police investigation into the party's finances.[39] By the beginning of 2024 support for the SNP had fallen to 36 per cent, only two points ahead of Labour on 34 per cent. That development has opened up the prospect that the Labour Party might make significant gains north of the border. Such an outcome would end the dominance of Scotland's representation at Westminster that the SNP has enjoyed since 2015, might threaten the status the party has enjoyed since then as the third party at Westminster, and would make it more likely that the Labour Party would be able to win an overall majority at the next election.

This decline in SNP support has occurred even though support for independence has remained at just below 50 per cent. However, the strong relationship between support for independence and willingness to vote SNP that emerged after the 2014 referendum on independence has weakened. Whereas, according to the British Election Study, in May 2022, 80 per cent of those currently in favour of independence said they would vote SNP, by May 2023, that figure had dropped to 67 per cent. Meanwhile, further analysis also suggests that whereas perceptions of the state of the health service in Scotland were unrelated to the willingness of 2019 SNP voters to vote for the party again, a year later only 54 per cent of those who felt that the NHS was getting worse were now supporting the SNP, compared with 71 per cent of those who felt the NHS was the same or getting better. It appeared that voters in Scotland were no longer simply focused on the country's constitutional question.

---

[39] John Curtice, 'Mr Yousaf's conference challenge', posted at www.whatsco tlandthinks.org/2023/10/mr-yousafs-conference-challenge/

CONCLUSION

Post-war British electoral politics has long been characterised as a system of stable, alternating single-party majoritarian government in which the battle for power is contested between two parties, one positioned on the right that is relatively popular among those in middle-class occupations, and one on the left that is relatively successful among working-class voters. The fourteen years of Conservative rule have witnessed a significant challenge to that portrayal. The Conservatives only managed to win a safe overall parliamentary majority at the fourth attempt – two earlier elections resulted in a hung parliament, while a third only produced a small overall majority. Moreover, the party only secured a firm grip on power after the link between occupational class and party support had more or less disappeared – to be replaced by divisions between young and old, between graduates and non-graduates – and only after a largely new ideological division between 'liberals' and 'authoritarians' had come to accompany the existing one between 'left' and 'right'. Although Britain's two-party system eventually survived the disruptive impact of a referendum decision to leave the European Union that neither the Conservatives nor Labour had originally wanted, it only did so because the Conservatives and Labour forged new coalitions of support that were markedly different from anything they had previously assembled. However, that adaptation has ensured that the British party system has proven resilient against potential electoral earthquakes, in sharp contrast to the significant changes that have occurred in the face of not dissimilar pressures in the party systems of many of Britain's European neighbours.[40]

Meanwhile, third parties have been more important, more numerous and more influential than ever before. The hung

---

[40] Swen Hutter and Hanspeter Kriesi (eds.), *European Party Politics in Times of Crisis* (Cambridge: Cambridge University Press, 2019); Robert Ford and William Jennings, 'The changing cleavage politics of Western Europe', *Annual Review of Politics*, 23 (2020), 295–314.

parliament produced by the 2010 election enabled the Liberal Democrats to enjoy their first taste of governmental office since 1945, though the party was then to pay a heavy electoral price for its involvement. UKIP posed the biggest independent fourth-party challenge to the existing party structure in England and Wales and in so doing played a key role in persuading David Cameron to promise the referendum on Brexit that was to prove so disruptive. Another referendum – on Scottish independence – helped the SNP displace the Liberal Democrats as the third party at Westminster and ensured the pattern of party politics and electoral support north of the border became markedly different from that in England and Wales, albeit that more recent developments suggest that the SNP's Scottish hegemony may now be under challenge. Meanwhile, the hung parliament of 2017–19 gave the Democratic Unionist Party the opportunity to exercise influence over the then minority Conservative administration.

Yet the eventual arrival of majority government since 2019 has not been accompanied by the stability that such an arrangement is supposed to provide. Rather it has witnessed further remarkable instability. In addition to the two prime ministers who had already been brought down by their party before 2019, the parliament of 2019–24 has witnessed the downfall of another two. Never before in the post-war era have there been as many as four changes in a row to the tenancy of 10 Downing Street without any intervention from the ballot box. The connection between who holds the reins of office and the outcome of elections has proven to be remarkably fragile since 2010.

Although elected with the task of getting Brexit done, the parliament elected in 2019 soon found itself dealing instead with the worst public health crisis in a century. Together with the most significant military conflict in Europe since 1945, this took its toll on the economy and occasioned the biggest expansion in the size of the state since 1945. With the debate about Brexit largely resolved, this helped ensure that the political agenda returned to the more familiar themes of the economy, public services and governmental competence. Indeed, much of the slump in Conservative support and the restoration of Labour's popularity can be accounted for by how the public have reacted to the Conservatives' performance on these issues. Yet the legacy of Brexit has not disappeared. Party support is still more strongly related to attitudes to Brexit than it was before the 2016 referendum. Social class still plays little role in shaping how people vote, while the division between 'liberals' and 'authoritarians' is still more marked than in the past. Fourteen years of Conservative rule have, it seems, left a long-term legacy, albeit perhaps one that neither David Cameron nor the then Liberal Democrat leader, Nick Clegg, could have anticipated – or wanted – when they made their historic decision in May 2010 to form Britain's first post-war coalition.

Conclusion: Fourteen Wasted Years? The Verdict

Anthony Seldon and Tom Egerton

In this final chapter, we consider how history might judge these years of Conservative governments. Our focus, as laid out in the Introduction, is: what were the achievements of these years? Were there mitigating factors? What is the overall verdict?

WHAT WAS THE CONSERVATIVE EFFECT IN 2010–2024?

The Conservatives were in power for over fourteen years after 2010, which makes it the longest period of one-party dominance since 1945 bar one, the Conservatives from 1979 to 1997, in power for eighteen years. There was thus time aplenty to embed enduring and much-needed change and improvement. They had longer than the three other periods of one-party dominance: the Conservatives from 1951 to 1964, Labour from 1997 to 2010, and again from 1964 to 1979, which saw Labour in power for eleven years (with a Conservative interlude from 1970 to 1974).

Time in office is vital if governments want to make a difference. The fourteen and a half years the Conservatives were in power far outstripped the length of the two great reforming administrations of the last century, the Liberals from 1905 to 1915 and Labour from 1945 to 1951, the benchmarks against which all other governments can be judged on delivering lasting change.

How, then, did this most recent batch of Conservatives fare compared to these highly regarded governments of the last century? The party from 1951 to 1964 saw four prime ministers, Winston Churchill, Anthony Eden, Harold Macmillan and

Alec Douglas-Home. Peter Kellner considers their record in the first chapter. They continued Labour's policy on the welfare state and of decolonisation, spread homeownership and improved standards of living, though they failed to modernise the economy or significantly increase productivity. Labour after 1964 under Harold Wilson and James Callaghan after 1976 largely completed the process of post-imperial adjustment, introduced a series of liberalising reforms, but became embroiled in economic and industrial relations woes which, to differing extents, bedevilled the end of all these five post-war periods of single-party dominance.

None of the periods after 1951 was more dynamic than the governments under Margaret Thatcher and John Major, despite starting from a low point in 1979. The British state and economy were remodelled during these years, and Britain's standing in the world transformed as a global force. Labour after 1997 started from a much more positive base, with a strong economy and a united Labour movement achieved by years of hard work. Tony Blair and Gordon Brown oversaw a new constitutional settlement and some significant and enduring public service reforms, but fell well short of remodelling the country commensurate with the unique advantages they had, and in line with the expectations they themselves aroused. The achievements of 1997–2010 pale against those of the Labour governments of 1945–51: the inheritance will be much less rosy for the incoming government after 2024.

Drawing on the contributors' chapters above, what record of achievement across the board do they suggest?

The economic record has been a significant point of weakness for the 2010–24 governments, not least in comparison to the immediate predecessor 1997–2010 period. Inconsistent economic policy under seven chancellors of the exchequer (compared to two under Labour) didn't help. Nor did fractious relations between prime minister and chancellor from 2016 to 2022. Nor did the unprecedented dismissal of the Treasury permanent secretary, Tom Scholar, in September 2022. The five prime ministers were markedly diverse in outlook, and faced very different challenges: minority governments in 2010–15 and 2017–19, and notionally large majorities for the three final PMs, when more might have been expected. Earnings growth remained stagnant since 2008. True, other developed countries experienced similar problems, but the Cameron–Osborne policy of austerity after 2010 with the biggest and longest-lasting cuts in public spending since World War II was a supressant. Many countries struck a happier balance between tax rises and spending cuts. The inflation rate in the UK was higher than that of the US or the Eurozone. As the self-inflicted shock of Brexit and uneven response to Covid hit home, the economy suffered further. Britain became plagued by astronomic levels of debt, the highest taxes since the war, and steeply rising interest rates on top of the inflation. All the while growth remained almost non-existent. The final chancellor, Jeremy Hunt, steadied the ship, but couldn't overcome the fundamentally weak position. As Paul Johnson put it, the famous pronouncement from Labour in 2010 that 'there is no money' remained true fourteen years on.

In defence and foreign policy the record is patchy. The transformation of geopolitics left Britain behind after the 2008 financial crash, with its economy and military constrained. Cameron's forays into the Middle East as prime minister proved to be precipitous. Rather than focusing steadfastly on the opportunities that have arisen from the last decade in Eastern Europe, the Middle East, Asia and South America, the Conservatives were primarily preoccupied with their own internal politics and national questions, whether the breakup of the Union in 2014 or the 2016 Brexit referendum and its ensuing disasters. After formally leaving the EU, its ally and trading partner for nearly fifty years, the shift to a 'global' Britain barely translated from rhetoric into substance, for all the quality of the Integrated Reviews of 2021 and 2023. Having made Brexit happen, the Conservatives conspicuously failed to demonstrate the economic and diplomatic benefits of standing alone in the world. Britain's staple ally, the United States, edged away from Britain after Brexit, while new trading arrangements failed to materialise. The main stand in the post-Brexit years was Britain's pugilistic response to the Russo-Ukrainian War from February 2022, a demonstration that when Britain engaged with its allies it could still play a role in geopolitics, successfully aligning its economic, military and political aims. But Britain emerged as only a minor player in the war, as it did in the war in Gaza from October 2023, for all the lustre that David Cameron brought to the job of foreign secretary from November 2023. By early 2024, questions were increasingly being asked about Britain's ability to defend itself in the event of war, with rising concerns that economic downturn had made the armed services ineffective. Overall, the record of the 2010–24 foreign and defence policy, as Michael Clarke noted, is 'more depressing than uplifting'.

In health and social care policy, not many lasting or positive advances were made. The 2010–24 period began with the bold if flawed 'Lansley reforms' that created more problems than they solved. Opportunities for using technology to modernise the NHS were missed, not least in comparison to other countries. Rachel Sylvester identifies that the NHS remains a 'sickness' rather than a health and prevention service. In the period of pandemic in 2020–22, it was repeatedly overwhelmed. Waiting lists remained high, with Sunak as prime minister making little progress in the years after Covid, despite setting very clear targets. The Conservatives leave the NHS in a perilous state, amidst strikes, loss of confidence among patients and low morale amongst staff, a stark comparison to the much more robust NHS they inherited in 2010. Neither Theresa May's proposals from 2017 nor Boris Johnson's after 2019 solved the chronic social care problem. It is hard to be anything other than critical of the overall record on both health and social care.

Education reforms were, for Alan Smithers, 'one of the best things that the Conservatives achieved during their fourteen years in office' – the Gove reforms (2010–14) notable for improving results and refining the curriculum. However, years of education spending cuts, the unprecedented churn of ten education secretaries and the narrow focus on formulaic exam results compromised the objective of a 'world-class' system. Minister of state Nick Gibb, present for nearly eleven years, provided what little stability there was, and was responsible for one of the achievements of these years with his advocacy of synthetic phonics. By the end of the fourteen years, nevertheless, one-third of young people (the most vulnerable) were still being failed by the exam system, teacher shortages became acute, mental health problems were rising, employers' dissatisfaction with the quality and lack of skills among school leavers was rising, and the accountability system with an overloaded Ofsted losing the support of teachers and parents. The focus remained fixated on twentieth-century paradigms rather than a more holistic system, including the skills the young would need to negotiate and succeed in the vastly different new century. After years of denial about AI the government only began to reckon with it in the final two years. Successes came with the 2022 results of the respected Programme for International Student Assessment (PISA). Although it showed a fall in pupils' mathematics and reading scores in 2022 compared to 2018, with science steady, in many other countries they fell by more, and a significant improvement since 2009 was seen in maths and reading. Primary and secondary curricula were reformed, and academies and free schools accelerated. The Conservatives' neglectful stance on further education and universities and their reluctance to champion universities as drivers of economic and social change in favour of vexing about culture wars contributed to some wasted opportunities for higher education.

On the environment, the 2010–24 government built well on Labour's early reforms. The 2008 Climate Change Act has continued to support the structures, through the Climate Change Committee, for further progress. While the UK's progress has been far from revolutionary, the continued evolution in climate policy saw some notable successes, including the net zero target, near eradication of the coal industry, decline in emissions, and investment in renewable energy and climate technology. COP26 in Glasgow in 2021 was a global golden opportunity to show leadership, but because of his inability to work hard and take the subject seriously, it was a missed opportunity for Boris Johnson. Gaps in energy infrastructure contributed to the severe inflation experienced in 2022–3, while the planning system still remains a block on necessary energy transition. Overall, the UK's aims still fall short of action promised and investment available, especially in comparison to the US's Inflation Reduction Act or the EU's expanding green subsidies. Sunak's watering down of targets in September 2023 damaged Britain's credibility internationally on the environment. Dieter Helm, though, is right to conclude on a positive note that 'the Conservatives can take credit' for the progress made.

Housing is also covered by Dieter Helm in his chapter on the environment, but we highlight the topic separately in this conclusion because of the great need after 2010 for housing to be addressed by serious government policy. A report in late 2018 suggested a backlog of approximately 4.75 million households across the United Kingdom. The need was particularly severe in England, where, according to the homeless charity Crisis: 'The total level of new house building required is around 340,000 a year.'[1] The Conservatives could dismiss this critique as coming from a charity associated with the left. But they found it harder to contest the conclusions of a report from the right-of-centre Centre for Policy Studies in 2023.[2] The report was searing: in the 1960s decade, some 3.6 million houses were built, but in the 2010s, just 1.5 million. 'Britain has a housing shortage', it said starkly in its opening. The various attempts by politicians to address it have not worked. Conservative MPs may understand the desperate need to build new houses, but don't want to see them put up if it means upsetting their own constituents. Central government has been washing its hands of the problem, looking to local councils to solve it, or relying on monetary policy to stimulate building, which hasn't worked either. The shortages meant prices, notably in London and the southeast, have continued to rise much faster than elsewhere, including in France and the Netherlands. Prime ministers were unable or unwilling to find a way through planning restrictions and the green belt, which had grown larger than when Thatcher fell in 1990. When Major fell seven years later, the average house price in England was 3.5 times average earnings; by 2024, it was a

---

[1] 'Housing supply requirements: low-income households & homeless people', Crisis, 6 December 2018 (accessed at www.crisis.org.uk/ending-homeless ness/homelessness-knowledge-hub/housing-models-and-access/housing-s upply-requirements-across-great-britain-2018/, 17 December 2023).

[2] 'The case for housebuilding', CPS, January 2023 (accessed at https://cps .org.uk/wp-content/uploads/2023/01/CPS_THE_CASE_FOR_HOUSEB UILDING2.pdf, 16 December 2023).

fearsome 9.1. Attempts to address the problem from Cameron with his 'Help to Buy' scheme to Sunak with the revised 'National Planning Policy Framework' failed to cut through, even worsening the situation at times. We conclude housing was an unsatisfactory area of strategic leadership, adding to the list of unfinished tasks for any new government after 2024 to resolve.

In transport we see inconsistency and some poor policy outcomes. Stephen Glaister, who has written on transport in an earlier volume in the series, says the overall record in these years has been 'disappointing'. He points to the Infrastructure Act of 2015, which set up the strategic highways company, as a rare policy success: it improved efficiency and transparency. The National Infrastructure Commission, set up in 2015, was typical though of the lost opportunities. Its effectiveness was constrained because, rather than being a truly independent body, it became established as an executive agency of the Treasury in 2017. Few of the seven Transport secretaries in the fourteen and a half years were around long enough to make much impact. Philip Hammond (2010–11) was one of the best, but his term in office was cut short. An ambitious attempt to reform the railways, which ground to a halt, was one of many disappointments, with strikes prevalent in the final years of the government. The summary scrapping of the northern branches of HS2 by Rishi Sunak in October 2023 after thirteen years of enabling legislation and development, leaving an unnecessarily expensive and largely pointless stump, was, Glaister believes, glaring evidence of the fundamental flaws in strategic planning.

On the Union, the record again is far from convincing. For a party that prided itself on its commitment to unionism, its approach could be seen as reckless. The 2014 Scottish referendum did anything but secure the Union in perpetuity, with the late interventions of Gordon Brown and the late Queen helping get the Unionist cause over the line, sparing the government's blushes. The Brexit referendum was called despite real risks to the stability of the Union. Brexit further divided the Union, with Northern Ireland and Scotland voting 'remain' in contrast to Wales and England. The Brexit deal and negotiations threw Northern Ireland into its most vulnerable position since the Good Friday Agreement, and threatens to further divide the Union with lasting threats of economic divergence and the border in the Irish Sea. Serious policy thinking often gave away to 'gesture politics' as when Johnson appointed himself the Minister for the Union. Sunak's 'Windsor Framework' of February 2023, as well as the return to power sharing at Stormont in 2024, went some way to repair the damage that had been caused by Johnson's insensitive handling of Northern Ireland. But lack of cohesive policy, and lack of success overall, characterise the Conservatives' record on the Union over the years. As Brendan O'Leary's final words in his chapter declare: 'HMS Britannia … is steadily moving toward icebergs, not as fast as Irish and Scottish nationalists would like, but it is difficult to see how the ship's course can be corrected.'

On science policy the 2010–24 period was more positive, if more despite than because of government policy. Science was relatively well protected in the period of austerity. The vaccine science-based industry performed well in the pandemic. However, opportunities for the UK's science industry to stimulate meaningful industrial strategy and climate policy were missed. The sudden emergence of generative AI towards the end of the period highlighted the lack of capital investment and prioritisation by government, with the UK science industry lagging behind, despite Sunak's efforts to talk up science. The promises of Cummings' science revolution at the heart of government in 2019–20 were only very partially realised. Overall, the Conservatives' impact has been one of some progress not helped by ministerial churn and Brexit (especially impacting R&D), rather than regression. Jon Agar's conclusion is more nuanced, contending '[it] is remarkable is that science continued to do well'.

In culture, the government squandered opportunities to support and celebrate Britain's powerful creative industries sector. The BBC, the media at large and the arts needed a steady hand: they received the opposite. Brexit hurt the industry, limiting talent, training and investment, as well as the industry's profile and capacity. Covid then posed a cataclysmic threat to parts of the industry, but the government's Culture Recovery Fund announced in July 2020, after the industry's intensive lobbying, mitigated long-term harm and will be the Conservatives' enduring legacy. Policy thereafter, as in so many other areas, was damaged by constant ministerial change, incoherent ideas and a myriad relaunches failing to optimise the pots of funding. The culture wars, fanned by the government and whipped up by the right-wing press, posed a threat to the freedom and independence of the industry. The record of the Conservatives on culture is indifferent – a missed opportunity for an industry, as John Kampfner notes, which makes up £120 billion of the economy. The cultural industry, an economic bright spot in 2010–24, managed to survive mostly despite not because of government.

We can assess the 'effect' of government policy in part on how well the most vulnerable fared during the time in power. So it is significant that societal and health, if not income, inequality grew under the Conservatives. A combination of austerity, health policy and the Covid pandemic, as well as the cost-of-living crisis, meant health inequalities had dramatically increased by 2024. Public services have become weaker, improvements in life expectancy stalled, and there has been a significant rise in mental health concerns. During these years, the poorest in the country suffered worsening health. The deteriorating economy translated into further inequality and worsened the health of the population – a political choice the chapter above says for the Tory party. As Michael Marmot and Clare Bambra conclude, the UK in these fourteen and a half years became more 'unhealthy and unequal'. The public sphere saw notable declines, for example, in libraries and playing fields, after 2010. Green spaces and their upkeep also suffered. A 2022 report found: 'Between 2013 and 2021, the proportion of parks in "good condition" … slipped from 60% to just over 40%.'[3]

Keeping the country safe from violence is a primary task of any government. The record on criminal justice was not strong, with repeated failures to solve the prison crisis, sentencing and the probation system, and with the courts unable to keep up with rising cases. Severe shortages of judges and lawyers, with the Crown Courts seeing a record

[3] Alex Chapman, 'The collapse of green space provision', New Economics Foundation, 3 May 2022, https://neweconomics.org/2022/05/exposed-th e-collapse-of-green-space-provision-in-england-and-wales

backlog of 65,000 cases, were highlighted in the OBR's analysis of the autumn statement in November 2023.[4] The rapid change of leadership with eleven secretaries of state for justice didn't help continuity of approach. Immigration policy consistently had difficulties meeting its objectives, with figures reaching 672k in the year ending June 2023, despite the promise of Brexit to address the issue, culminating in the fraught and deeply divisive Rwanda policy.[5] However, increases must take into account recent spikes from the intake of refugees from Hong Kong and Ukraine – a commendable government policy. Overall, though, it is hard not to conclude the Conservatives fared worse in keeping the public safe, or in their aims at reducing immigration, than any of the governments in the four earlier periods of one-party domination after 1945.

How well did the state's other apparatus operate from 2010 to 2024? Parliament, the executive and the constitution experienced a whirlwind of instability and controversy under the Conservatives, historically the party of tradition and institutional stability. Meg Russell concluded that 'in no other area of policy during 2010–24 has the Conservative Party probably been more divided than over matters of governance itself'. Surprisingly perhaps, one of the most stable periods of governance was in 2010–15 when the Conservatives did not govern alone. The coalition, with strongly defined legislative programmes and boundaries which the leadership knew it could not cross, provided an element that the Conservatives couldn't on their own. Once they transitioned in 2015 to governing alone, the party became irreconcilably divided by Brexit, resulting in several changes in party leader. The parliamentary party sparked numerous rebellions, with threats it might break itself apart especially in the 2018–19 period. Johnson,

---

[4] Cited in 'Further cuts to compound justice crisis', Law Society, 27 November 2023.

[5] ONS, 'Long-term international migration, provisional: year ending June 2023' (accessed at www.ons.gov.uk/peoplepopulationandcommunity/pop ulationandmigration/internationalmigration/bulletins/longterminterna tionalmigrationprovisional/yearendingjune2023).

pushing the uncodified constitution to its limit, brought further disruption through prorogation and expulsions of his MPs to achieve his objectives. The executive, in both Whitehall and Number 10 has been under constant scrutiny and regular attack. Five prime ministers in fourteen years, including two, Johnson and Truss, not up to the job, did not help. Nor did the historically unprecedented churn of four cabinet secretaries, and eight principal private secretaries to the prime minister. The civil service, in desperate need of reform, was instead pilloried and attacked, resulting in historically low levels of morale and departures of some of the brightest and best. Trust in government, in the executive, legislature, civil service and the judiciary is at its lowest in the post-war period.

The Conservative Party itself saw the most divided and ideologically incoherent period in government since it was created in the 1840s. Cameron opened with a period of fiscal consolidation blended with liberal reforms, as in the Same Sex Marriages Act of 2013. Three distinct strands of Cameron's thinking can be identified: a neoliberal economic strand, a desire to reduce the size of government, and a celebration of the public realm and civil society.[6] May revoked much of this after 2016, when the mantra became 'burning injustices', with a return of industrial strategy and the end of austerity. But her fleeting dreams of a revival of a Joseph Chamberlain-style activist state were crushed by the general election result in 2017 after which mere survival became the only show in town. Johnson, the most ideologically ambiguous of all the five prime ministers, had dynamic ambitions informed by his time as London mayor from 2008 to 2016 with attempts to combat regional inequality by 'levelling up', then spending vast sums to mitigate the worst aspects of Covid, repudiating the cap on spending in the previous years of Tory rule. Truss's hapless 49-day run further divided the party on economic lines with her breathtaking leap to the right in economic policy, the party under her looking more like a student union than a mature

---

[6] M. Lakin, 'Cameron's conservatisms and the problem of ideology', unpublished DPhil thesis, University of Oxford, 2014, pp. 122–90.

governing party. Sunak's attempts to return to stability and 'long-term' pledges came up against intransigent ministers and MPs unwilling to toe his line. While some calm returned, the scars of the previous fights remained, while his agency to legislate and govern meaningfully became steadily narrower. By the end, even with the cliff-edge of a general election suggesting the need for unity, there was little agreement on the vision of the party. Sunak's leadership saw continued challenges to his authority, not least from supporters of Johnson or Truss. Many in the party were left asking what was the point of the last fourteen years? As Tim Bale concludes, if it continues down its ideological path of escalation 'then it could well find itself in a far more parlous state than it did when it lost office in 1964 and 1997'.

The traditional party system has seen significant and perhaps long-lasting erosion over fourteen years. A series of fragmentations in cleavages and partisanship has ushered in an era of unpredictable elections and reignited the fears over the electoral system's ability to deliver clear majorities. For Paul Webb, Cameron's Scottish (2014) and Brexit referendums (2016) have been the 'major drivers of realignment and shifting partisan strength'. Parties that were neither Labour nor the Tories rose and fell, beginning with the Lib Dems who shared power between 2010 and 2015, but were punished for coalition policy. Second, UKIP, who won the 2014 EU elections and helped pressure Cameron into a EU referendum with its massive implications. Third, the SNP, who after the 2014 Scottish referendum achieved a majority of seats in Scotland in the subsequent elections, ensuring the salience of Scottish independence but then suffering from internal division. Fourth, the DUP in Northern Ireland partook indirectly in government via a confidence and supply motion between 2017 and 2019, but became embroiled in the union-damaging implications of the Brexit deal. The Brexit Party, later becoming 'Reform', was the final insurgent party to influence power, winning the 2019 EU elections and prompting the fall of May and the Tories' switch to a harder Brexit strategy. What's clear is that Cameron's referendums – mixing direct democracy with representative democracy – threw up into the air fourteen years of a fragmenting party system. It's difficult to say as the era ends where all the elements will land after 2024.

Elections have inevitably shown considerable volatility, as John Curtice illuminates. Despite the Conservatives failing to win an overall majority in 2010, the governing period that followed was surprisingly stable and resulted in a workable administration. Cameron then won a majority for the Conservatives to rule alone in 2015, but fell on his sword after the Brexit referendum, clearing the way for Theresa May. Her unforced 2017 election was a nadir for the Conservatives electorally after a campaign run incompetently, though she still won 42.3 per cent of the vote (more than in 2010, 1987 or 1992 by percentage) and built the groundwork for the eighty-seat majority in 2019. What the Conservatives were effective at until 2022 was switching leaders and electoral strategy to present their candidates as 'change' after unpopular or unsuccessful periods of government. The post-Brexit election in 2019 saw an effective strategy to target socially traditional voters in so-called 'Red Wall' seats. Though more traditional factors including the economy and NHS reasserted themselves again after 2019, the Brexit realignment continued to be felt. It is important too to note that the Conservatives have benefited from several years of Labour being unable to win a majority, partly due to the loss of Scotland, but primarily because of the ineffectiveness/unpopularity of their leaders, notably, Jeremy Corbyn (2015–20). But the lawlessness of Conservative MPs and instability of the leaders undermined the party at every turn.

Outside the areas of failure significant bright spots stand out, including education policy, the national living wage, the idea (though not implementation) of Universal Credit, the vaccine production and roll-out, and climate policy, all broadly positive aspects of the last fourteen years. Before we reach an overall verdict, we consider the mitigating factors that prevented further achievement.

WHAT WERE THE MITIGATING FACTORS?

External Shocks. All the five periods of single-party dominance since 1945 had external shocks. The Conservatives after 1951 had the Suez crisis of 1956, albeit of their own making, a series of rebellions across the Empire and an intensification of the Cold War, an enormous burden on defence spending. Labour after 1964 had to contend with the worsening position of sterling, resurgence of European industry and the impact of the oil price shocks of 1973 and 1978–9. The Conservatives after 1979 faced the worst industrial turbulence since the 1920s, the end of the Cold War, the Iraqi invasion of Kuwait in 1990 and 'Black Wednesday' in 1992 when Britain departed from the European exchange rate mechanism. Labour after 1997 endured 9/11 and the global financial crisis of 2007–8. So external shocks are not unique: but were they unique in their intensity during these years? Tom Egerton in Chapter 2 explores six – the enduring impact of the global financial and Eurozone crises, the impact of Brexit, of Covid, of the Russian invasion of Ukraine, and the ensuing economic instability and increase in prices. The self-imposed Brexit stands out: it weakened the economy, consumed vast quantities of government time and lost policy focus. We might justly conclude that no other period saw so many crises. But governments abroad, facing similar problems, appeared to have weathered them often more successfully. The most effective governments respond well to crises, taking effective action and avoiding the disproportionate or the reactive.

Institutional Weaknesses. Significant elements among the Conservatives believe that their policies were thwarted by 'the blob', with left-of-centre (and anti-free-enterprise/anti-Brexit) figures and woke culture dominating the civil service and especially the Treasury, the Bank of England, the judiciary, the BBC and the media at large. They believe that the Truss/Kwarteng mini-budget of September 2022 was brought down by the Treasury, the Office of Budget Responsibility (OBR) and the Bank of England. It is certainly true that these institutions were deeply sceptical about the 'mini-budget', as they had been of Brexit, but their sin, if one there was, is not to have raised their reservations for fear of invoking ministerial displeasure. Throughout recent history, ineffective ministers and poor governments have blamed civil servants and the system at large. This is not to say Whitehall does not need modernisation – it undoubtedly does. But the civil service functions better when it can serve ministers who know what they are doing, and with clear and legitimate guidance from Number

10. We believe that the blame for the poor record can be laid more at the ministerial door rather than establishment institutions.

Churn. Sustainable policy change requires stability of ministers. It takes time to learn the job, know the people and the issues, and to make an impact. The five prime ministers served on average less than three years each, insufficient to make much mark: David Cameron was the only figure to serve a length in office sufficient to make lasting change. In the same period stewarding the economic life of the nation, there have been seven chancellors of the exchequer, seven transport and nine business secretaries. Oversight of social policy and the culture has seen even more transition: nine work and pensions, ten education and thirteen media/digital secretaries. None of the earlier four periods saw any comparable rate of change, nor did they see such weak ministerial quality or ignorance from ministers about how to do the job. How could they possibly know when they were often appointed for political and expedient reasons, rather than knowledge or interest in the ministerial portfolio? Very few cabinet ministers from 2010 to 2024 could hold a candle to the team who served under Clement Attlee – which included Ernest Bevin, Nye Bevan, Stafford Cripps, Hugh Gaitskell and Herbert Morrison. Or the teams who served under Wilson, Thatcher or Blair. Michael Gove, Jeremy Hunt, Amber Rudd and Philip Hammond were rare examples of ministers of quality after 2010. Matching the ministerial churn was the rapid movement of top civil servants. There were notable performances from advisers such as Kate Bingham and Emily Lawson in the vaccine rollout. But too many officials served too short periods to command their departments. Until 2010, cabinet secretaries served on average nine years in office: since 2010 the three to be appointed averaged four years and included one appointed at the instigation of a senior aide to the prime minister. The departure through illness and subsequent death in 2018 of the cabinet secretary, Jeremy Heywood, left a vacuum at the centre of government which was never filled. Conclusion: churn, ignorance and arrogance amongst ministers, and churn/denigration of officials, significantly contributed to poor performance.

Quality of the Prime Minister. A strong and capable prime minister is essential to governmental success in the British system. The earlier periods saw three historic and landmark prime ministers, i.e. Churchill, Attlee and Thatcher, with a succession of others who were capable if not agenda-changing PMs, including Macmillan, Wilson, Major, Blair and Brown. Since 2010, only Cameron came close to that level, with Sunak the best of the rest. Policy virtually stopped under May as Brexit consumed almost all the machine's time, while serious policymaking ground to a halt under Johnson's inept leadership, the worst premiership in modern times, and the hapless Truss. Continuity of policy was not helped by each incoming prime minister blanking their predecessor, with Truss's admiration for Johnson the only exception. Thus they took no time to understand what it was their predecessors were trying to do, and how to build on it rather than belittle it.

Lack of Purpose/Consistency. High-achieving governments and periods of single-party domination have a strategic clarity of purpose. All the earlier four periods saw ideological change, from the laissez-faire of Churchill to the paternalism of Macmillan, the state planning of Wilson to the market discipline of Callaghan, the small state of Thatcher to the limited interventionism of Major, and the third way of Blair to the small 's' socialism of Brown. But none of these early periods saw anything approaching the crazy salad of these fourteen years, from Cameron's 'big society', via May's 'burning injustices', Johnson's 'levelling up', to Truss's 'anti-growth coalition' and Rishi Sunak's 'long-term decisions' taking tax levels to the highest since the war. The general election manifestos, which might've provided some continuity and consistency, were often relegated early on. The 2010 'coalition agreement' between Cameron and Clegg overtook many of the Tory manifesto commitments. The 2015 manifesto on which the Conservatives won was shelved when May took over. Her own hopes for the 2017 manifesto were sidelined after the loss of the majority and the arrival of Boris Johnson. The 2019 document was written to avoid anything that could undermine the Conservative cause, so failed to provide any kind of roadmap for the zigzag years ahead.

Chronic Weakness at the Centre of Government. While shortcomings of the different prime ministers all militated, to

differing degrees, against achievements by the successive administrations, institutional weaknesses at the heart of government,
never more keenly felt than during these fourteen years, played a
significant part too. Number 10 and the Cabinet Office were far
too reactive and short-termist and were neither institutionally nor
temperamentally equipped to deal well with the strategic and the
long term. This problem is addressed in the March 2024 report on
the centre of government from the Institute for Government.[7]

The Fissiparous Tory Party. The exact identity of the
Conservative Party being in 2014 more unclear than at any point
since the party was founded 180 years ago did not help. Does it
believe in the free market or interventionism? In a big or small
state? Celebrating or despising immigration? Wanting to champion or trash national institutions? Desiring Britain to play a major
part in the world, with all the expense that goes with it, or retreat
from global obligations? In protecting the environment and
greenbelt, or letting the economy rip and not being overly fussy
about carbon or planning restrictions? In maintaining the welfare
state or dismantling it? The fact that Sunak's premiership became
consumed by immigration battles epitomises the vacuum.

The identity crisis within the Conservative Party, combining
with the rise of right-wing populism and an explosion of splinter
groups, few more menacing for the PM than the European
Research Group (ERG), and the inability of whips to bring them
into line, further distracted the prime minister and militated against
strong coherent action.

THE VERDICT

In comparison to the earlier four periods of one-party dominance post-1945, it is hard to see the years since 2010 as anything
but disappointing. By 2024, Britain's standing in the world was
lower, the Union was less strong, the country in some respects
less equal, the population less well protected, growth more sluggish with the outlook poor, public services underperforming and

---

[7] 'A stronger and smaller centre of government', the Institute for
Government, March 2024.

largely unreformed, while respect for the institutions of the British state, including the civil service, judiciary and the police, was lower, as it was for other bodies, including the universities and the BBC, repeatedly attacked not least by government, ministers and right-wing commentators.

Do the unusually high number of external shocks to some extent let the governments off the hook? One above all – Brexit – was entirely of their own making and will be seen in history as the defining decision of these years. In 2024, the verdict on Brexit is almost entirely negative, with those who are suffering the most from it, as sceptics at the time predicted, the most vulnerable. The nation was certainly difficult to rule in these fourteen years, the Conservative Party still more so. Long-standing problems certainly contributed to the difficulties the prime minister faced in providing clear strategy, including the 24-hour news cycle, the rise of social media and AI, and the frequency of scandals and crises. But it was the decision of the prime minister to choose to be distracted by the short term, rather than focusing on the strategic and the long term. The prime minister has agency: the incumbents often overlooked it.

Overall, it is hard to find a comparable period in history of a Conservative, or other, government which achieved so little, or which left the country at its conclusion in a more troubling state.

Acknowledgements

Anthony Seldon

I would like to thank the contributors for all their hard work and patience. Thanks are due to Cambridge University Press, who have been outstanding as always. I would also like to thank Raymond Newell and Lewis Baston for their helpful comments, Luca Boot for editorial assistance on the proofs, as well as my colleagues at Epsom College, in particular politics staff Andy Bustard, James Dunn and Luke Fisher, and finally, my co-editor Tom Egerton.

Tom Egerton

I would like to thank all the fantastic contributors for their work and dedication. I would also like to thank my co-editor Anthony Seldon, without whom this project (and many, many others) would have never happened, and for his incredible hard work and phenomenal skill. Thanks are due to the brilliant Cambridge editorial team, John Haslam and Carrie Parkinson, who were pivotal in helping us deliver the project. Laura Simmons and the rest of the production team were excellent in bringing everything together, and have our deep gratitude for the work they put into the project. We would like to thank our outstanding copy-editor, Kay McKechnie.

Kit Haukeland deserves huge credit and thanks for his editorial and research work on the book and the overall thesis; if there is an unsung hero in the thoughts behind this book, it is him. Raymond Newell was immensely helpful with his comments and thoughts, and continues to be an inspiration for me and my work. Peter Kellner also deserves my thanks for taking the time to read and amend beyond his chapter, as does Tim Bale.

Lastly, deep thanks go to those who have enabled me to get where I am today: Marc Scruby and George Lear, who initiated and grew my love for the subject, my loving friends who have supported me throughout the years, and finally my parents, Jem and Esther, for without their love and support I would be nowhere.

Index

Printed in the United States
by Baker & Taylor Publisher Services